NEW ZEALAND

THE ESSENTIAL TOURING ATLAS

FIRST EDITION

Published in New Zealand by Gregory's Publishing Company
(A division of Universal Publishers Pty Ltd)
ABN 83 000 087 132

www.gregorys-online.com

The publisher would be please to receive additional or updated material, or suggestions for future editions. Please address these to the Publishing Manager at Universal Publishers Pty Ltd.
If you would like to use any of the maps in this book please contact the Cartographic Manager at Terralink International Limited.

Universal Publishers Pty Ltd
1 Waterloo Road, Macquarie Park NSW 2113 Australia
Ph: + 61 2 9857 3700 or Toll Free (from New Zealand) 0800 558 998
Fax: + 61 2 9888 9850

ISBN: 0 7319 1716 2

1ˢᵗ edition published 2006

Research and writing by Caren Wilton. Editing, indexing, photographic research, DTP project management and cartography by the staff of Terralink International Limited.

Front and Back End Papers: Terralink International Limited

Printed by Sirivatana Interprint Public Co. Ltd

Cover Design: PlanBookTravel (www.planbooktravel.com)

Internal Design: *DiZign*

Front Cover:
Main Photograph (also book spine and title page):
Reflections on tranquil Lake Matheson, South Island

From Left to right:
Scenic Lindis Pass, South Island
Arrowtown, Central Otago, South Island
Punakaiki Blowhole, produced by the erosion of the limestone cliffs, South Island
Limestone formations, Castle Hill, South Island

Back Cover:
From Left to right:
Cape Kidnappers is one of Hawke's Bay most memorable natural attractions, North Island.
Franz Josef Glacier, South Island
Dramatic golden landscape of Central Otago, South Island
Boiling mud pool in Rotorua, North Island

Disclaimer
The publisher disclaims any responsibility to any person for loss or damage suffered from any use of this atlas for any purpose. While considerable care has been taken by the publisher in researching and compiling this atlas, the publisher accepts no responsibility for errors or omissions. No person should rely upon this atlas for the purpose of making any business, investment or real estate decision.

New Zealand native fern

CONTENTS

Lake Wakatipu, Queenstown

New Zealand

South Island 192

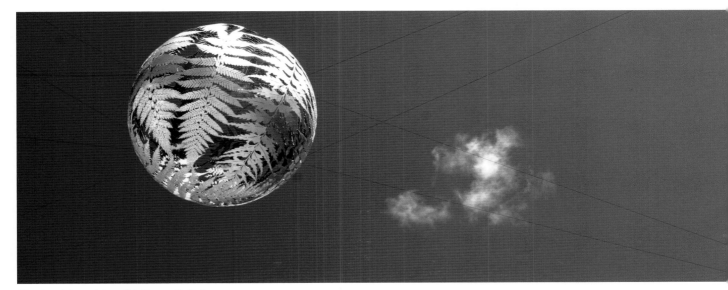

Silver fern globe sculpture, Civic Square, Wellington

MAP SYMBOLS

City

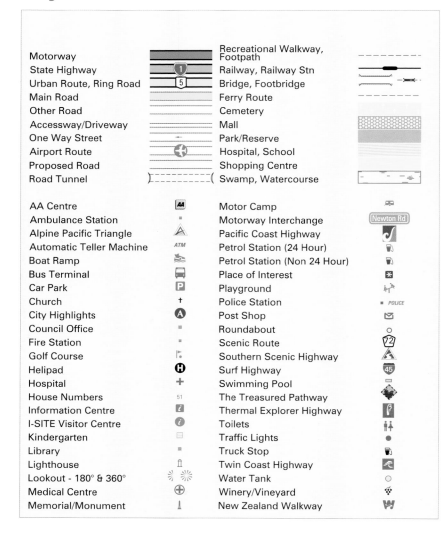

Motorway		Recreational Walkway, Footpath	
State Highway		Railway, Railway Stn	
Urban Route, Ring Road		Bridge, Footbridge	
Main Road		Ferry Route	
Other Road		Cemetery	
Accessway/Driveway		Mall	
One Way Street		Park/Reserve	
Airport Route		Hospital, School	
Proposed Road		Shopping Centre	
Road Tunnel		Swamp, Watercourse	

AA Centre		Motor Camp	
Ambulance Station		Motorway Interchange	Newton Rd
Alpine Pacific Triangle		Pacific Coast Highway	
Automatic Teller Machine	ATM	Petrol Station (24 Hour)	
Boat Ramp		Petrol Station (Non 24 Hour)	
Bus Terminal		Place of Interest	
Car Park	P	Playground	
Church	†	Police Station	POLICE
City Highlights	A	Post Shop	
Council Office		Roundabout	
Fire Station		Scenic Route	72
Golf Course		Southern Scenic Highway	
Helipad	H	Surf Highway	45
Hospital	+	Swimming Pool	
House Numbers	51	The Treasured Pathway	
Information Centre	i	Thermal Explorer Highway	
I-SITE Visitor Centre	i	Toilets	
Kindergarten		Traffic Lights	
Library		Truck Stop	
Lighthouse		Twin Coast Highway	
Lookout - 180° & 360°		Water Tank	
Medical Centre		Winery/Vineyard	
Memorial/Monument		New Zealand Walkway	W

Suburban

Motorway		I-SITE Visitor Centre	
State Highway		Pacific Coast Highway	
Urban Route, Ring Road		Place of Interest	
Main Road		Scenic Route	72
Airport Route		Twin Coast Highway	
Medium Road		Park/Reserve	
Railway Line, Railway Station		Cemetery	
Airport - International		Hospital	
Airport - Domestic		School	+
Golf Course		Shopping Centre	
Information Centre	i	Ferry Route	

Milford Sound/Piopiotahi

Raukawa Falls, Wanganui

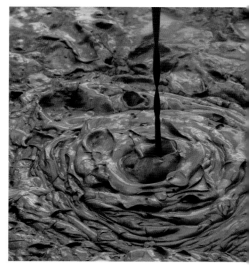

Bubbling mud pool, Rotorua

New Zealand

KEY TO ATLAS

Regional & Tourism Regions

	SEALED	UNSEALED
Motorway		①
State Highway		①
Major Road		
Minor Road		
Railway Line		
Urban Road		
Vehicle Track		
Foot Track		
Ferry Route		
Distance in kilometres	▼ 20 ▼	
National Park		
Forest Park		
Other Parks		
Marine Park		
Built Up Area		
Town/Locality	○ ○	
Alpine Pacific Triangle	△	
Information Centre	𝑖	
I-SITE Visitor Centre	𝑖	
Inland Scenic Route	72	
Mountain, height in metres	+	
Pacific Coast Highway	✓	
Place of Interest	✱	
Southern Scenic Route	▲	
Surf Highway	45	
The Treasured Pathway	◆	
Thermal Explorer Highway	♠	
Twin Coast Discovery Highway	↝	
Winery	⚘	

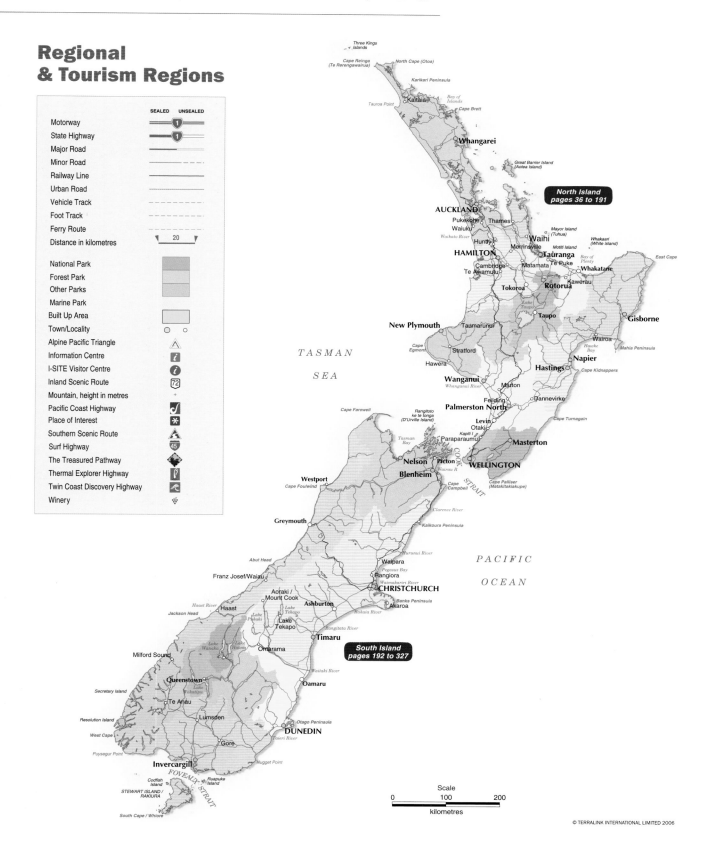

Three Kings Islands
Cape Reinga (Te Rerengawairua)
North Cape (Otoa)
Karikari Peninsula
Tauroa Point
Kaitaia
Bay of Islands
Cape Brett

Whangarei

Great Barrier Island (Aotea Island)

AUCKLAND
Pukekohe Thames
Waiuku
Waikato River Huntly **Waihi**
Morrinsville
HAMILTON Motiti Island Mayor Island (Tuhua)
Cambridge Te Puke **Tauranga**
Te Awamutu Matamata **Whakatane**
Kawerau
Tokoroa **Rotorua**
Lake Taupo
Taupo

Whakaari (White Island)
Bay of Plenty East Cape

New Plymouth Taumarunui
Cape Egmont Stratford
Hawera
Wanganui
Whanganui River Marton
Feilding
Palmerston North

Gisborne
Wairoa
Hawke Bay Mahia Peninsula
Napier
Hastings Cape Kidnappers
Dannevirke
Cape Turnagain

TASMAN
SEA

Cape Farewell
Rangitoto ke te tonga (D'Urville Island)
Tasman Bay
Cape Foulwind Westport
Nelson **Picton**
Blenheim
Wairau R
Cape Campbell

Levin
Otaki
Kapiti I
Paraparaumu
Masterton
WELLINGTON
Cape Palliser (Matakitakiakupe)

COOK STRAIT

Greymouth
Clarence River
Kaikoura Peninsula

Abut Head
Franz Josef/Waiau
Hurunui River
Waipara
Pegasus Bay
Rangiora
Waimakariri River
CHRISTCHURCH
Banks Peninsula
Akaroa

PACIFIC
OCEAN

Haast River Jackson Head
Aoraki / Mount Cook Haast
Lake Pukaki Lake Tekapo **Ashburton**
Rakaia River
Lake Tekapo
Rangitata River
Timaru

Milford Sound
Lake Wanaka Lake Hawea
Omarama
Waitaki River

Secretary Island
Queenstown
Lake Wakatipu
Te Anau
Oamaru
Otago Peninsula
DUNEDIN
Taieri River

Resolution Island
Lumsden
West Cape
Puysegur Point
Gore
Nugget Point
Invercargill
FOVEAUX STRAIT
Codfish Island Ruapuke Island
STEWART ISLAND / RAKIURA
South Cape / Whiore

North Island
pages 36 to 191

South Island
pages 192 to 327

Scale
0   100   200
kilometres

© TERRALINK INTERNATIONAL LIMITED 2006

DISTANCE CHARTS

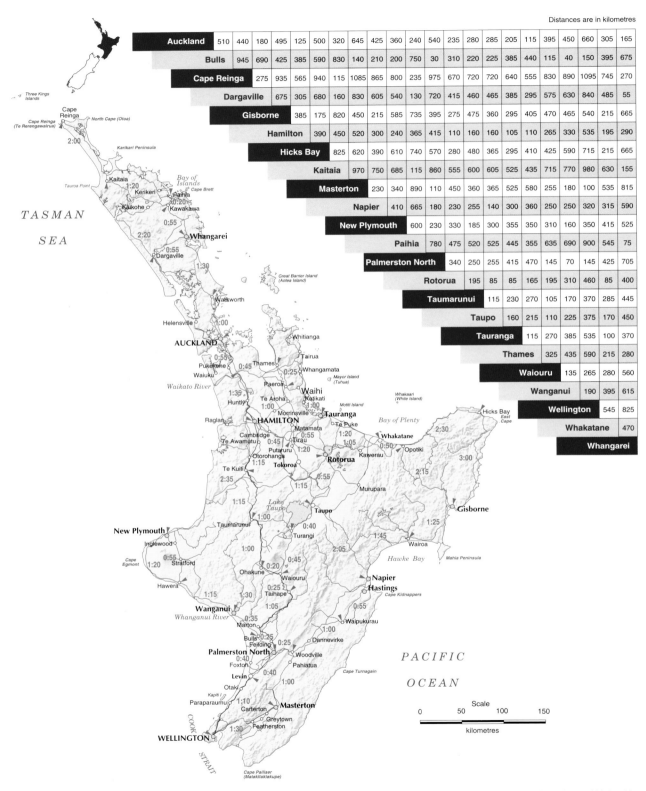

Distances are in kilometres

	Bulls	Cape Reinga	Dargaville	Gisborne	Hamilton	Hicks Bay	Kaitaia	Masterton	Napier	New Plymouth	Paihia	Palmerston North	Rotorua	Taumarunui	Taupo	Tauranga	Thames	Waiouru	Wanganui	Wellington	Whakatane	Whangarei
Auckland	510	440	180	495	125	500	320	645	425	360	240	540	235	280	285	205	115	395	450	660	305	165
Bulls		945	690	425	385	590	830	140	210	200	750	30	310	220	225	385	440	115	40	150	395	675
Cape Reinga			275	935	565	940	115	1085	865	800	235	975	670	720	720	640	555	830	890	1095	745	270
Dargaville				675	305	680	160	830	605	540	130	720	415	460	465	385	295	575	630	840	485	55
Gisborne					385	175	820	450	215	585	735	395	275	475	360	295	405	470	465	540	215	665
Hamilton						390	450	520	300	240	365	415	110	160	160	105	110	265	330	535	195	290
Hicks Bay							825	620	390	610	740	570	280	480	365	295	410	425	590	715	215	665
Kaitaia								970	750	685	115	860	555	600	605	525	435	715	770	980	630	155
Masterton									230	340	890	110	450	360	365	525	580	255	180	100	535	815
Napier										410	665	180	230	255	140	300	360	250	250	320	315	590
New Plymouth											600	230	330	185	300	355	350	310	160	350	415	525
Paihia												780	475	520	525	445	355	635	690	900	545	75
Palmerston North													340	250	255	415	470	145	70	145	425	705
Rotorua														195	85	85	165	195	310	460	85	400
Taumarunui															115	230	270	105	170	370	285	445
Taupo																160	215	110	225	375	170	450
Tauranga																	115	270	385	535	100	370
Thames																		325	435	590	215	280
Waiouru																			135	265	280	560
Wanganui																				190	395	615
Wellington																					545	825
Whakatane																						470
Whangarei																						

© TERRALINK INTERNATIONAL LIMITED 2006

Times shown are based on travel times of experienced drivers who are generally familiar with conditions on the roads over which they drive.

North Island

Distances are in kilometres

650	85	300	280	625	95	790	225	820	400	635	215	230	550	145	370	190	920	450	775	365	235	**Alexandra**
665	205	205	450	585	260	665	210	755	570	510	450	350	530	380	490	325	855	330	640	240	**Aoraki/Mount Cook**	
395	335	75	575	345	390	425	165	515	690	270	490	480	295	430	430	275	615	85	400	**Ashburton**		
260	750	475	970	245	805	30	560	115	1090	130	890	640	325	830	500	675	245	310	**Blenheim**			
335	425	165	660	255	480	340	250	425	775	185	575	530	250	520	390	365	530	**Christchurch**				
330	835	690	1140	320	950	275	780	130	1255	375	1105	690	395	1040	575	890	**Collingwood**					
675	280	200	300	620	285	700	115	790	415	545	215	425	570	155	565	**Dunedin**						
280	285	510	585	255	400	540	515	475	705	570	585	140	180	515	**Franz Josef/Waiau**							
795	230	355	140	770	175	860	270	945	260	700	70	375	695	**Gore**								
100	465	370	765	80	575	360	460	295	880	400	762	320	**Greymouth**									
420	145	420	445	395	260	680	375	590	565	710	445	**Haast**										
860	300	410	160	835	190	915	330	1005	275	760	**Invercargill**											
395	605	345	850	320	660	155	435	245	960	**Kaikoura**												
980	420	615	115	960	305	1115	530	1155	**Milford Sound**													
230	735	590	1035	220	850	145	680	**Nelson**														
560	230	85	415	510	290	590	**Oamaru**															
295	765	505	1000	285	820	**Picton**																
675	115	330	190	655	**Queenstown**																	
80	540	420	845	**Reefton**																		
840	300	495	**Te Anau**																			
470	275	**Timaru**																				
565	**Wanaka**																					
Westport																						

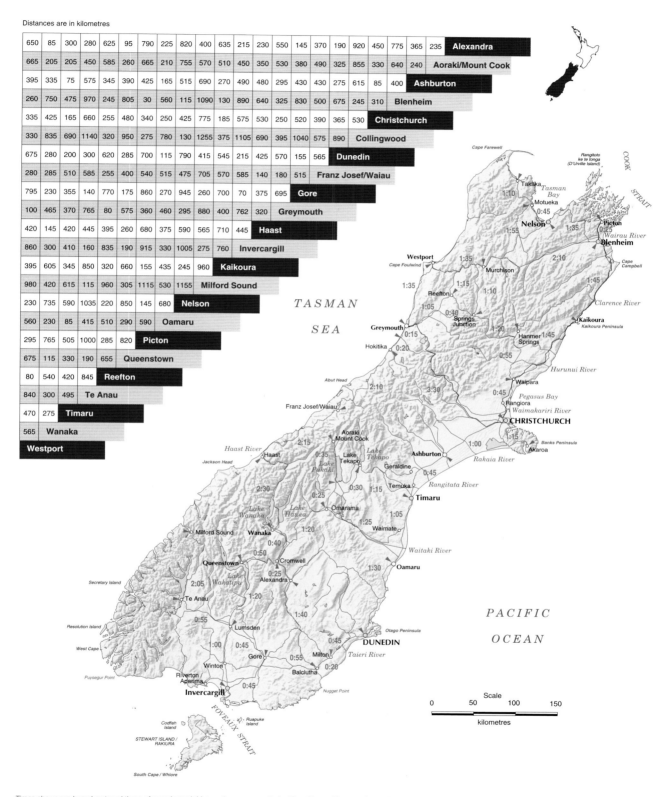

Times shown are based on travel times of experienced drivers who are generally familiar with conditions on the roads over which they drive.

South Island

TOURING NEW ZEALAND

Geography

Known to Maori as **Aotearoa** (Land of the Long White Cloud), New Zealand is located in the south-west Pacific, around 1600km east of Australia; the **Tasman Sea** lies to its west, and the **Pacific Ocean** to the east. The country's two largest islands, the **North** and **South Islands**, are separated by **Cook Strait**, which is 20km wide at its narrowest point. The smaller **Stewart Island** is located just below the southern end of the South Island. New Zealand also includes more than 700 smaller outlying islands, mostly within 50km of the coast, but some as far away as 1000km.

The combined area of all these is 268 021 km², slightly larger than Great Britain. For its size, New Zealand has an extremely long coastline; estimates vary from 15 000 to 18 000km, as the many bays, inlets and peninsulas make it difficult to settle on an accurate figure.

New Zealand's three main islands feature prominently in Maori mythology. The North Island (**Te Ika a Maui**, literally 'the Fish of Maui') is the giant fish the trickster demi-god Maui hauled from the ocean; the South Island is sometimes seen as Maui's canoe, and Stewart Island as its anchor.

Geologically, New Zealand is a small piece of the supercontinent Gondwana. It separated from Australia, another part of Gondwana, some 80 million years ago. New Zealand sits astride the boundary of the Indo-Australian and Pacific tectonic plates, part of the Pacific's 'ring of fire'. New Zealand's mountain ranges were pushed up by pressure on that boundary between one and six million years ago, and the country continues to experience both earthquakes and volcanic activity.

Mountain ranges up to 1700m high form the backbone of the North Island, flanked by rolling farmland. The island's central **Volcanic Plateau** is home to most of the country's active volcanoes as well as much geothermal activity, including hot thermal pools,

Maori carving

bubbling mud and geysers; 616km² **Lake Taupo** is the water-filled caldera of a massive volcano.

The South Island's main feature is the **Southern Alps**, a mountain chain which stretches most of the island's length and rises to over

Mount Ruapehu seen from near Wanganui

New Zealand: Land of the Long White Cloud

- Area, including offshore islands: 268 021km²
- Administrative boundaries: from 33° to 53° south latitude, and 160° east to 173° west longitude
- Highest point: Aoraki/Mount Cook, 3754m
- Largest lake: Lake Taupo, 616km²
- Longest river: Waikato River, 425km
- Largest city: Auckland, pop 1.2 million
- Capital: Wellington
- Maori name: Aotearoa (Land of the Long White Cloud)
- National anthems: God Defend New Zealand, God Save the Queen
- Official languages: English, Maori
- New Zealand flag: features the Union Jack and the four stars of the Southern Cross on a royal blue background

3000m. Around two-thirds of the South Island is mountainous. The slender west coast lowlands are rainforested, and to the east lie the alluvial **Canterbury Plains** and the ranges and basins of **Central Otago**. Glaciers carved the sounds of **Fiordland** and many of the South Island's lakes.

Climate

New Zealand's climate is largely temperate, and is influenced by two main factors: the mountains and the sea. Nowhere in this long, narrow country is further than 130km from the sea, and this moderates temperatures and provides ample rain. Exceptions are the far north's subtropical summer, and icy winter temperatures in the South Island's alpine areas. The average temperature in the far north is around 15°C, and in the far south is 9°C.

Rainfall is generally high around the country, but there's great variation, from a mean annual rainfall of only 300mm in parts of Central Otago to more than 6000mm at **Milford Sound**. The climate is generally wetter in the west and drier in the east, a result of the predominant moisture-laden westerly winds from the Tasman Sea meeting the main mountain chain down the country's centre. This effect is particularly pronounced in the South Island, where the Southern Alps are a major barrier.

The sunniest areas are **Nelson**, **Marlborough**, **Hawke's Bay** and the **Bay of Plenty**, all of which receive more than 2350 hours of sun each year on average. Most of the country gets at least 2000 sunshine hours annually, but the harshness of the sun can be a mixed blessing; skin cancer rates are high in New Zealand, especially in the north. A good sunscreen is recommended.

New Zealand's weather is also highly changeable. Typically there are brief periods of settled or unsettled weather for a few days, but conditions can also change dramatically within a single day.

New Zealand's summer is from December to February, autumn from March to May, winter from June to August and spring from September to November.

Summer is the best time for outdoor pursuits and for enjoying New Zealand's beaches and marine activities. Autumn can bring pleasant temperatures and settled weather, and dramatic displays of coloured leaves, particularly in Central Otago and Hawke's Bay. Winter provides dramatic vistas of snowy mountains, great skiing and snow sports. The countryside is lovely in spring with blossoms, daffodils and gambolling lambs.

History

New Zealand's human history is a relatively short one. While exact migration dates are uncertain, current understanding suggests that the country's earliest human inhabitants arrived from east Polynesia in the later thirteenth century, not much more than seven hundred years ago.

It appears that these first settlers came to New Zealand on planned journeys of exploration, using stars, ocean currents and winds as navigation aids. Some Maori oral traditions refer to the early navigator **Kupe** as the discoverer of the country, followed by a series of voyaging groups who settled in different areas.

The earliest migrants lived in clusters, hunting and eating seals, moa (large flightless birds, hunted to extinction probably within 150 years) and other birds, fish and shellfish. Where climatically feasible they also cultivated kumara (sweet potato) and yams, crops brought from their Polynesian

Fern, koru, a much loved New Zealand symbol

homeland; the emphasis on gardening increased as the big game died out. Before European arrival, the population may have been as high as 100 000, and while life expectancy was short by today's standards, it was probably similar to Europeans of the time.

Maori society was — and in part remains — tribally based; the word 'Maori', which meant 'ordinary', only came into use after the arrival of Europeans to refer to the people as a whole. Maori developed a rich, orally-transmitted culture, with tribal and personal identity based on both whakapapa (genealogy) and geographical place. Tribes exercised authority over distinct areas, and pa (fortified villages) were developed to ward off attacks from other groups.

The first European arrival was the Dutch navigator **Abel Tasman**, who sailed up — and mapped — the west coast in 1642. Some of Tasman's men were killed in an

Beehive, Wellington

altercation with Maori in Golden Bay, but he never set foot on land. Dutch mapmakers subsequently named the country Nieuw Zeeland.

The next European visitor, 127 years later in 1769, was the British **Captain James Cook** in the ship *Endeavour*. Cook was the first European to make landfall in New Zealand; then and on two subsequent voyages he circumnavigated and charted the country.

European sealers and whalers arrived in the late 18th century. The first Christian mission station was established by **Samuel Marsden** in the **Bay of Islands** in 1814, followed by many more such stations in other parts of the country.

Kororareka (later **Russell**), also in the Bay of Islands, was the site of the first European town, with Maori in the area provisioning the visiting whalers. For Maori, the novel opportunity to acquire muskets for use in inter-tribal conflicts had lethal consequences. European diseases also took their toll both on those living and on rates of reproduction.

1840 saw the signing of the **Treaty of Waitangi** between the British Crown and more than 500 Maori chiefs. Under the Treaty, Maori relinquished governing power to the British Queen, in return for the status of British subjects and a guarantee of their lands and their authority. (Over time, however, divergent views of the Treaty — for a start, the Maori and English texts differed significantly — have provoked recurrent disputes between Maori and the Crown.)

In British eyes, New Zealand was now a colony. Organised immigration began, much of it under the auspices of the London-based **New Zealand Company**, which established several planned settlements.

Maori welcomed the opportunities provided by larger numbers of Pakeha (Europeans), but chiefs remained jealous of their authority. Northern chiefs fought the Crown in the mid-1840s. From the 1850s the Maori King movement resisted land alienation and in the 1860s battled government forces in **Taranaki** and **Waikato**. Maori won a number of the battles, but government troops, with far larger resources and numbers (buttressed at times by Maori pursuing inter-tribal

rivalries) prevailed completely by 1872. Much fertile land had been confiscated; with fighting now ended, land sales proceeded without restriction, whilst a rapid increase in the European population saw the Maori proportion fall to less than 10 percent.

Wool was the mainstay of the early colonial economy, but gold rushes in **Otago** in 1861–63, on the South Island's **West Coast** in 1865–66, and at **Thames** in 1868 proved equally lucrative. Intensive pastoral farming became feasible when technological advances made it possible to export frozen meat and refrigerated dairy products to Britain; the first meat shipment was successfully sent in 1882. Family farms became a cornerstone of the economy.

Government

New Zealand's constitutional history dates from the 1840 signing of the Treaty of Waitangi. **Okiato** in the Bay of Islands was New Zealand's first capital, but was replaced soon after by **Auckland**. The seat of government was shifted again in 1865 to the more centrally-located **Wellington**, where it remains today.

In 1879 New Zealand gave all adult men the vote; in 1893 it was the first country in the world to give all adult women the vote. Governments both then and in

Summer picnics, North Shore, Auckland

Children with boogie boards, Whananaki

the 1930s passed progressive social and economic laws but also restricted immigration. Since the 1980s, governments have accorded the market a greater role in shaping economic life. Immigration has been liberalised.

New Zealand fought alongside Britain in both world wars but since the 1980s has kept at arms' length from military alliances. It is a strong supporter of the United Nations.

New Zealand is a parliamentary democracy. The British **Queen Elizabeth II** is the country's Head of State, with her role in New Zealand being performed by a **Governor-General** who is appointed for a five year term. Neither the Queen nor the Governor-General involve themselves in political matters.

The country is governed by a single parliamentary chamber, the **House of Representatives**, which is democratically elected every three years using a system of **mixed member proportional representation (MMP)**. This means that parties are represented in Parliament in exact proportion to the share of the vote they gain in an election. After the election, the government is formed by the party or coalition of parties which commands a majority of votes in the House of Representatives. The leader of the winning party or coalition serves as **Prime Minister**.

People

New Zealand today has just over four million people. Three-quarters of these live in the North Island; more than half are in the northern half of the North Island. The country's population is 86% urban, and around 1.2 million live in Auckland, the nation's largest city (and the world's largest Polynesian city). The population grows from both immigration and natural increase.

About three-quarters of New Zealand's people are of **European** (primarily British) descent. Around 15% consider themselves to be **Maori**. Many people identify with both categories. Other significant ethnic groups are **Pacific Islanders** (about 230 000, largely the result of considerable immigration in the 1970s), and **Asians**, who make up about 7% of the population and many of whom are recent migrants or their children.

Compared to European New Zealanders, Maori experience disadvantage in education, employment, income and life expectancy, although there are big variations within both groups. However, Maori culture and language have enjoyed a considerable renaissance since the 1980s.

In 1975 the **Waitangi Tribunal** was established to investigate breaches of the Treaty of Waitangi. Settlements have been negotiated between a number of Maori tribal groups and the government, and these tribes have been compensated through monetary settlements and the return of some assets.

Economy

New Zealand has a capitalist economy, with a per capita income about the same as Spain's.

For most of the 20th century, the country's export economy was based around the sale of **wool**, **meat**, **butter** and **cheese** to Britain. Today, **farming** remains central to exports but accounts for just 8% of the economy as a whole. **Dairy products** comprise about a sixth of all exports. Newer primary sector exports include **venison**, **fruit**, **flowers**, **olives** and **wine**.

Timber and **coal** are also exported. **Commercial fishing** is an important industry, and New Zealand's exclusive maritime economic zone is one of the world's largest at 3.1 million nautical square kilometres.

New Zealand's **manufacturing sector** accounts for 15% of the economy and is centred on Auckland. It produces **food**, **drink**, **tobacco products**, **machinery**, **equipment** and other goods, for both the domestic and Australian markets.

Most of the urban labour force works in the large **service sector**, often in **commerce**, **health** or **education**. The **film industry** is a highly visible service industry. **Tourism** is also important; numbers of overseas visitors doubled in the 1990s.

Sheep farm, north west of Wanganui

MAORI CULTURE

Maori carving

Maori today make up around 15% of the country's population, and see themselves as the country's **tangata whenua**, literally 'people of the land'. While some Maori still live in traditional tribal areas, their population is increasingly urbanised. **Rotorua**, **Northland** and **Eastland** all have particularly large Maori populations.

Maori culture and language have undergone a considerable renaissance in the last 30 years.

Maori legends

In the Maori mythical account of the world's origins, life began with the emergence from nothingness of **Papatuanuku**, the Earth Mother, and **Ranginui**, the Sky Father, who lay in a close embrace. The pair bore many male children, who eventually became tired of living in darkness, pressed between their parents; as a result, they decided to push their mother and father apart. Their son **Tane-mahuta**, god of the forests, was able to separate his parents, and light came flooding into the world.

Another vital mythical character is **Maui**, a mischievous demigod who makes appearances in stories around the Pacific. Maui is particularly important in New Zealand for the heroic feat of fishing up the **North Island**.

Tribal life

From the early days after their ancestors arrived by canoe from eastern Polynesia, Maori culture has been tribally based. The largest unit of organisation is the **iwi** (tribe); people are also organised by **hapu** (sub-tribe) and **whanau** (extended family). Many iwi are named for an important ancestor, eg **Ngati Kahungunu**, the descendants of Kahungunu. Some iwi are grouped into alliances based on their lines of descent from a common migratory canoe.

Whakapapa (genealogy) and **tupuna** (ancestors) are seen as very important. Tribes identify themselves with (and have traditionally held authority over) a particular geographical area, often including important local landmarks, such as mountains, lakes or rivers.

The **South Island** iwi **Ngai Tahu** has the largest tribal territory of all tribes; its territory covers most of the South Island. **Ngapuhi**, of the far north, is the country's largest tribe in terms of membership. The **Tainui** confederation of tribes, based in the **Waikato** and descended from the Tainui canoe, is also a grouping of political importance, and is the base of the Maori King movement.

For more information on Maori culture, society and practices, see **www.maori.org.nz**

Te reo Maori – the Maori language

Te reo Maori (the Maori language) is an official language of New Zealand. Related to other languages throughout Polynesia, today it is spoken by about one in four Maori, and about 30000 non-Maori.

The Maori language follows consistent rules of pronunciation. Vowels can be either short or long, and are pronounced as follows: A as in c*a*r; E as in p*e*g; I as in mar*i*ne; O as in p*a*w; U as in t*oo*. Vowels are also combined into a number of diphthongs.

Maori has only 10 consonants. Most of these (H, K, M, N, P, T and W) are pronounced similarly to their English equivalents. R is a quick flap of the tongue (and can sound similar to an English D); WH is like the English F. NG is pronounced as in si*ng*, but, unlike in English, may occur at the beginning of a word, eg ngeru (cat).

In most cases, the first syllable of the word is emphasised.

Basic Conversational Maori Phrases

Kia ora	Hi, hello (lit. Be well)
Tena koe	Hello (to one person)
Tena korua	Hello (to two people)
Tena koutou	Hello (to more than two people)
Kei te pehea koe?	How are you? (to one person)
Kei te pai	Well, thanks
Haere mai	Welcome/come here
E noho ra	Goodbye (to person remaining)
Haere ra	Goodbye (to person leaving)
Ka kite ano	See you later

VISITING A MARAE

Challenging visitor on a marae, Rotorua

The base for Maori tribal groups is the **marae**, a complex which usually includes the meeting-house, the whare kai (the building where people are fed), and an open area in front of the meeting-house. The marae is a place for hui (meetings), tangihanga (funerals), weddings and other important occasions. The distinctive meeting-houses of marae, many of them strikingly carved and decorated, can be seen around the country, especially in rural areas with a high Maori population. They're private property; visitors need permission to enter a marae.

When visiting groups go onto a marae, they are often welcomed by a formal ritual called a **powhiri**. This highly structured protocol involves the manuhiri (visitors) being formally challenged (to determine if their intentions are peaceful) and then called onto the marae and welcomed by the marae's tangata whenua (local people). Tributes are paid to ancestors and the dead, and greetings, formal introductions, songs and speeches ensue, usually concluding with a **hongi** (pressing of noses) and followed by a shared meal. On a marae, visitors should remove their shoes before entering any buildings. It's also customary to offer a **koha** (donation) in exchange for hospitality.

Some marae (notably around Rotorua, but also in other areas) open their doors to visitors and tourists, allowing them to experience a powhiri and some traditional Maori hospitality.

Hongi

Interpreting place names

Many New Zealand place names are Maori, and were named for geographical features, or for events which took place there. The following words are commonly used as a basis for place names; however, the best way to find out the real meaning of a name is to talk to a local who knows its origins.

ana	cave
ao	cloud, world, day
ara	road, way
awa	river
hine	woman, daughter
iti	small
kai	food
kare	rippling
kino	bad
koura	crayfish
manga	stream
maunga	mountain
moana	sea, lake
motu	island
nui	large, great
pai	good
puke	hill
puna	spring
rangi	sky
rawhiti	east
roa	long
roto	lake
rua	two
tahi	one
tahuna	beach, sandbank
tai	sea
tonga	south
uru	west
wai	water
whanga	harbour, bay
whenua	land

Woman weaving kits from harakeke (flax)

Haka party, Te Tii Marae, Waitangi

NEW ZEALAND FLORA

Pohutukawa flower

New Zealand was one of the last countries on earth to be settled by humans, but the impact of its 700-odd years of human habitation has been severe on the native flora. In that time, more than 75% of the country's forests have been burnt or cut down, and largely turned into farmland. Some 25 000 species of exotic plants have also been introduced, some of which have become pests. However, 10 to 15 percent of the country is still covered in native flora, and some large areas of native forest still remain, notably within the 14 national parks. More than five million hectares of New Zealand today are in protected parks and reserves, which allow the visitor to experience much of the country's native bush.

New Zealand has some highly distinctive native plant species, and around 80% of the country's native flora is endemic (found only in New Zealand).

Native forests

The North Island's forests are largely **podocarp-broadleaf forests**, found in lowland areas with good soil. These complex forests generally have five layers. At the top is a canopy layer of podocarps (conifers) which may include **kauri** (in the north), **rimu**, **matai** and

Native forest, Oparara Basin, Kahurangi National Park

totara, all trees which have links to the ancient forests of Gondwana. Below this canopy is a layer of smaller trees, then a layer of emerging, younger conifers, a shrub layer, and ground plants including **ferns** and **tree ferns**. Many of these forest areas have been heavily logged for timber, as the mature podocarp trees have massive, tall, straight trunks, ideal for building.

Beech forest dominates in the South Island (and also occurs in some of the North Island's mountain areas). This less complex forest is more open and dominated by beech (*Nothofagus* spp), and is largely found in the high country.

New Zealand's alpine areas, above the tree line, are home to 25% of the country's native plants; 93% of these alpine plants are endemic. The high alpine meadows are beautiful with flowers in spring, including *Celmisia* **mountain daisies** and **giant buttercups** (*Ranunculus* spp).

Iconic plants

In December, the coastal areas of the northern North Island are splashed with the crimson flowers of the **pohutukawa** (*Metrosideros excelsa*). These coastal trees are known as the New Zealand Christmas tree due to the timing and colour of their flowering. The related **tree ratas** are striking forest trees which also have deep red flowers in summer. The **northern rata** (*Metrosideros robusta*) generally starts life as an epiphyte in a host tree, and sends down roots to the ground, finally enclosing and strangling its host, and growing into a massive tree up to 25m in height. The **southern rata** (*Metrosideros umbellata*) usually grows on the ground,

THE MAJESTIC KAURI

New Zealand's mighty **kauri** (*Agathis australis*) are among the world's most majestic trees. They can live for thousands of years, and may grow to heights of more than 50m, with trunk girths as much as 16m.

Adolescent kauri have narrow trunks and narrow, conical crowns; as they mature, the trunk thickens, lower branches are shed and the crown widens. Despite their imposing size and age, kauri are shallow-rooted and are vulnerable to having their roots disturbed by walkers.

The northern third of the North Island was once covered in kauri forest, but these forests were decimated after the arrival of European settlers, who milled the forests for building ships and houses. Maori had already made use of kauri for carving and building, but it was European settlement that really made an impact, reducing kauri forests from 1.2 million hectares to the 80 000ha that remain today. Kauri gum too was sought after and exported for the manufacture of varnish.

Stands of forest containing mature kauri remain in the **Coromandel** and **Northland**. Most impressive is 13 384ha **Waipoua Kauri Forest**, about 50km north of **Dargaville**. This beautiful forest area is home to the largest living kauri tree, 1500-year-old **Tane Mahuta**, which is 51m in height. **Te Matua Ngahere** (Father of the Forest), an estimated 2000 years in age, has a trunk diameter of more than 5m.

Kauri tree grove, Coromandel Peninsula

Giant buttercups

and can reach 20m in height.

Another beautiful genus of native tree the **kowhai** (*Sophora* spp), which have showy clusters of bell-shaped golden flowers in spring. These are a rich food source for native birds, which revel in the kowhai flowers' nectar.

The striking spiky leaves and dramatic flowers of **harakeke** or **flax** (*Phormium* spp) can be seen throughout New Zealand in gardens, on hillsides and in coastal areas. One of the country's oldest plant species, the hardy harakeke is also one of its most useful, and has long been of great importance to Maori. Early Maori villages typically had their own flax plantations, using the fibres for producing mats, baskets, rope and fabric, the flower nectar for sweetening food, and various parts of the plant for medicinal purposes. Today, flax contributes to various cosmetics and to flaxseed oil. It's also popular with tui, bellbirds, geckos and insects, which feed on nectar from the flowers.

Flax (harakeke)

NEW ZEALAND FAUNA

Kea, a cheeky alpine parrot

New Zealand's geographic isolation over some 80 million years has allowed some fascinating and unusual species to evolve, including whole orders and families which are endemic to the country.

New Zealand originally was home to huge numbers of birds. There were around 219 species, about 159 of which were endemic. Many of these were nocturnal, some of them giant, and a number were flightless and ground-nesting. As the only native land mammals were three species of **bat**, these birds had few natural predators, and hence were very vulnerable to hunting when humans and other mammal predators arrived. Although people did not settle in New Zealand until comparatively late, they have wreaked havoc on the country's fauna in just a few hundred years, through hunting, destruction of habitats, and the introduction of predator species.

When Maori settled in the country, they brought with them rats and dogs, and hunted birds for food. They soon hunted to extinction the 10 species of **moa**, which were giant, flightless, wingless birds up to 3m in height.

By the early 20th century, Europeans had introduced more predators: ferrets, stoats, weasels, cats, dogs, pigs, and, devastatingly, the Australian brush-tailed possum. These were deliberately introduced in 1858 to provide a fur trade, and found New Zealand conditions more than favourable; the country today is infested with more than 70 million possums, which have been highly destructive to the country's forests and wildlife.

The destruction by humans of around 75% of the country's forest cover has also had a huge impact on species which made their home in the bush.

Conservation efforts

Today there are some concerted efforts at conservation and species recovery, mostly under the auspices of the Department of Conservation. Of particular importance are initiatives on offshore islands where predators have been wiped out and native bush restored; notable among these are **Kapiti Island**, **Little Barrier Island**, **Tiritiri Matangi Island** and **Codfish Island**. There are also a number of predator-free 'mainland island' reserves, including a privately-run wildlife sanctuary in Wellington city. Some of these reserves are open to visitors, and they provide a wonderful way to experience a rich array of native wildlife. However, around 30 bird species are still considered endangered — including New Zealand's symbol, the **kiwi**.

Birds and other animals

New Zealand's native bird species are a lively, quirky bunch, including the nectar-eating **tui**, a terrific mimic which includes clicks, barks and wheezes in its song; the playful, comical **kaka**; the inquisitive **kea**, a green alpine parrot known for attacking car windscreen wipers and tearing off the rubber with its strong beak; and the musical **bellbird** with its beautiful, liquid-sounding song.

The endangered **kakapo** is the world's only flightless parrot. Kakapo are eccentric, nocturnal

Tuatara, a dinosaur-related reptile

KIWI: A NATIONAL ICON

A national icon of great symbolic importance to New Zealanders (who are also informally known as Kiwis), the unique **kiwi** is a flightless, largely nocturnal native bird with loose, hair-like feathers and long, cat-like whiskers. The kiwi is the only bird in the world to have nostrils at the end of its beak. Kiwi have a well-developed sense of smell and can locate food by sniffing; they also have excellent hearing. Kiwi have a lower blood temperature than most birds, and excavate burrows like a badger. These unusual factors have led scientists to speculate that kiwi may have evolved in mammal-free New Zealand to fill the evolutionary place normally occupied by land mammals.

Related to ostrich, emu and the extinct moa, kiwi live in pairs, mating for life. The kiwi's egg is, on average, 15% of the female's body weight — huge compared with other birds — and is largely incubated by the male.

Sadly, all species of kiwi are threatened, and their populations are continuing to decline, except for key populations protected by intensive predator control. These flightless, ground-nesting, nocturnal birds are highly vulnerable to introduced predator species, which kill a large proportion of young kiwi chicks at unmanaged sites. Kiwi are also threatened by habitat loss. **Brown kiwi** remain widespread in the central and northern North Island, but populations are declining. The **little spotted kiwi** is now found only on offshore islands, and numbers of **Rowi** and **Haast Tokoeka kiwi** are extremely low.

South Island brown Kiwi

Around New Zealand, kiwi can be viewed in a number of artificially darkened 'nocturnal houses'.

birds which can weigh as much as 3.6kg and have a distinctive low booming call; sadly, their numbers are extremely low and they are now confined only to two offshore islands.

Other notable native wildlife includes the **tuatara**, a slow-moving reptile up to 24cm in length. A dinosaur relative, it's the only remaining species of a reptile family which otherwise died out about 60 million years ago. Tuatara today are found only on offshore islands and in zoos.

There are around 70 endemic species of **weta**, a large native insect which resembles a cricket. Giant weta are among the world's largest insects; their fierce appearance is belied by their harmless nature. Giant, carnivorous **land snails** weighing as much as 90g and living up to 20 years also make their home in New Zealand's forests.

New Zealand is rich in marine mammals, including the endemic **Hector's dolphin** (the world's rarest), some rare **whale** species, the **Hooker's sea lion**, and the **New Zealand fur seal**. Commercial whaling and sealing from the 18th century reduced some of these populations to near-extinction, and some species remain threatened. Commercially operated whale watch tours — particularly around **Kaikoura**, where offshore submarine trenches are thousands of metres in depth — allow visitors to see these impressive mammals. There are also plenty of chances to view **dolphins**, seals, sea lions and penguins, including the rare **yellow-eyed penguin** or **hoiho**.

Rare yellow-eyed penguins or hoiho

FROM NEW ZEALAND TO MIDDLE-EARTH

Bilbo Baggins' house, 'Hobbiton', Matamata

When New Zealand film director Peter Jackson made the movie trilogy of JRR Tolkien's classic masterpiece *The Lord of the Rings*, he insisted the films be shot in New Zealand.

Wellington was a base for cast and crew on the three films, including many staff producing special effects at Jackson's **Weta** studios. The third film, *The Return of the King*, had its world premiere at the city's restored **Embassy Theatre** in December 2003, with a red-carpet parade of stars through the streets; Wellington's residents turned out en masse to celebrate. *The Return of the King* went on to win 11 Oscars.

Around the country, the trilogy took full advantage of New Zealand's extraordinary range of landscapes, filming at over 150 sites. Locations included the grassy farmland near **Matamata,** transformed into '**Hobbiton**'; volcanic **Mount Ngauruhoe**, which became menacing '**Mount Doom**'; the beautiful **Southern Alps**, used as the '**Misty Mountains**'; and remote **Poolburn**, which was '**Rohan**'.

A number of the filming locations can be visited independently or on guided tours; some tours are by 4WD or even by helicopter. Local information centres can advise on locations and tours; Ian Brodie's *The Lord of the Rings Location Guidebook* gives detailed information on how to find the sites. See also **www.filmnz.com/middleearth**

Filming Locations

North Island

Auckland
Port Waikato, Map 160 A1:
 "Weathertop Hollow"
Waikato
Matamata, Map 161 G4: *"Hobbiton"*
Ruapehu
Mount Ngauruhoe, Map 168 B5:
 "Mount Doom", "Plains of Gorgorath"
Ohakune, Map 168 B6: *"Ithilien"*
Whakapapa Ski Area, Map 168 B5:
 "Mordor", "Emyn Muil"
Manawatu
Rangitikei River Gorge, Map 174 D3:
 "River Anduin"
Waitarere Forest, Map 176 B4:
 "Trollshaw Forest", "Osgiliath Wood"
Wellington
Harcourt Park, Map 178 C3:
 "Isengard Gardens", "Orc Tree"
Haywards Hill Rd, Map 178 B3:
 "Helm's Deep", "Minas Tirith"
Hutt River, Map 178 C3:
 "River Anduin", "Rohan River"
Kaitoke Regional Park, Map 178 D3:
 "Rivendell", "Fords of Isen"
Paraparaumu, Map 178 C2:
 "Pelennor Fields"
Otaki Gorge, Map 178 D2:
 "Outer Shire"
Wellington city, Map 178 B4:
 "Outer Shire", "Dunharrow", "Bree"
Wairarapa
Fernside, Map 178 E3:
 "Gladden Fields", "Lothlorien"
Putangirua Pinnacles, Map 178 D5:
 "Dimholt Road"

South Island

Nelson
Kahurangi National Park, Map 280 C3:
 "South of Rivendell", "Eregion Hills"
Mount Owen, Map 285 H2:
 "Dimrill Dale"

Takaka Hill, Map 281 F4:
 "Chetwood Forest"
Westland
Franz Josef/Waiau, Map 293 J2:
 "Lighting of the Beacons"
Canterbury
 Mount Potts station, Map 295 F3:
 "Edoras"
Southern Alps: *"Misty Mountains"*
Twizel, Map 301 H2:
 "Eastemnet Gullies",
 "Plains of Rohan",
 "Pelennor Fields"
Central Otago
Poolburn, Map 308 C3:
 "Plains of Rohan", "Rohirrim Village"
Lake Wanaka
Tarras, Map 300 E6:
 "Flight to the Ford",
 "Great East Road"
Wanaka, Map 300 C5:
 "South of Rivendell"
Queenstown
Arrowtown, Map 306 E1:
 "Ford of Bruinen", "Gladden Fields"
Closeburn, Map 306 D2: *"Amon Hen"*
Deer Park Heights, Map 306 D1:
 Middle-earth scenes
Glenorchy, Map 299 F5: *"Isengard",*
 "Lothlorien", "Amon Hen"
Kawarau River, Map 306 E1:
 "Pillars of the Kings", "River Anduin"
Skippers Canyon, Map 300 A6:
 "Ford of Bruinen"
The Remarkables, Map 306 E2:
 "Dimrill Dale"
Twelve Mile Delta, Map 306 D2:
 "Ithilien"
Fiordland
Mavora Lakes, Map 305 J3:
 "Fangorn Forest", "Nen Hithoel",
 "Orc Mound", "Silverlode River"
Norwest Lakes, Map 304 E5:
 "South of Rivendell",
 "Flight to the Ford"
Te Anau, Map 305 H4:
 "Fangorn Forest"
Waiau River, Map 305 F5:
 "River Anduin", "Dead Marshes"

ARTS & CULTURE

New Zealand boasts a thriving arts and cultural scene. Local practitioners of literature, visual arts, dance, classical and contemporary music, film and theatre have all gone from strength to strength, often drawing on Maori, Pacific and European cultural traditions.

A growing number of arts festivals throughout the country showcase everything from comedy to short films to literature to Maori 'kapa haka' performance. Particularly noteworthy are **Wellington**'s biennial three-week **International Festival of the Arts**, the **Auckland Arts Festival** and the **Christchurch Arts Festival**, also held biennially.

The national museum **Te Papa**, on Wellington's waterfront, displays some of the country's treasures of visual art, including wonderful traditional Maori works. The **Auckland Museum** has an excellent collection of Maori and Pacific artworks; **Christchurch** has a dynamic **Arts Centre**, and the country's smaller centres are home to excellent provincial galleries.

New Zealand has three professional symphony orchestras, including the acclaimed **New Zealand Symphony Orchestra**. The **Royal New Zealand Ballet** offers several productions per year; there are also a number of innovative contemporary dance troupes and choreographers. Excellent live music can be seen around the country; again this often draws on Maori and Pacific cultures, sometimes fusing Polynesian musical traditions with reggae, hip-hop or folk styles.

Contemporary theatre too is alive and well in New Zealand, with interesting drama on offer in most cities. Wellington in particular is known for its high number of theatres and ground-breaking productions.

The current crop of New Zealand film makers are increasingly in the international eye; *The Lord of the Rings* director Peter Jackson is perhaps the most obvious of these, but impressive success has also been had by Jane Campion (*The Piano*, *Holy Smoke*), Niki Caro (*Whale Rider*), Christine Jeffs (*Rain*, *Sylvia*) and Lee Tamahori (*Once Were Warriors*).

The early short story writer Katherine Mansfield is known for her rich, exacting portraits of colonial New Zealand. Janet Frame produced novels and autobiography distinguished by startling language and a sharp, unflinching poet's eye; in 1985, Keri Hulme became the only New Zealander to win the Booker Prize with her novel *the bone people*. Other contemporary writers of note include Maori fiction writers Witi Ihimaera and Patricia Grace, and novelist and children's author Maurice Gee.

Maori Arts

Today's Maori cultural renaissance has included a strong resurgence of Maori arts, both traditional and contemporary. Maori artists in all genres are combining their ancestral art forms with modern tools, techniques, materials and concerns to create vibrant and ground-breaking work.

Traditional Maori art forms include intricate carving of wood, bone and greenstone; weaving of kete (bags), cloaks and mats; whaikorero (oratory); and ta moko (tattooing). Maori taonga (treasures) can be seen, and sometimes bought, in museums, galleries and shops around the country. The 'Toi Maori' label is a trademark protecting Maori-made work.

Kapa haka is a traditional Maori group performance form which includes haka (the action dance made famous by the national rugby team, the All Blacks), waiata-a-ringa (action songs) and poi (performance involving the graceful movements of poi, balls on string). Maori performances are on offer for visitors around the country; the biennial **Te Matatini National Festival** is a great chance to see the cream of kapa haka groups.

Outdoor theatre, Christchurch Arts Centre

SPORT & RECREATION

Sport has long been a major focus for New Zealanders, both as participants and spectators. **Rugby union** in particular is a central part of New Zealand culture and identity.

Of all sports, **golf** has the most participants, and New Zealand has almost 400 golf courses — the highest number per capita of any country.

In winter, the women's sport of **netball** enjoys great popularity in terms of participation and spectator interest; the national team, the **Silver Ferns**, were world champions in 2003.

Tennis, **soccer** and **rugby league** also draw many participants, and **cricket** is New Zealand's primary organised summer sport.

Runners **Jack Lovelock**, **Peter Snell**, **Murray Halberg** and **John Walker** all won gold in Olympic track events, from the 1930s to the 1970s. Recent Olympic gold medal success has been for **rowing**, **canoeing**, **windsurfing** and **yachting**. In July 2004 New Zealand was listed in the all-time top ten countries for winning Olympic medals, assessed on a per capita basis.

Golfers on Frankton Golf Course

New Zealand won the **America's Cup** yachting trophy in 1995, and in 2000 was the first non-American team ever to successfully defend the Cup, with the race held on home waters. However, Team New Zealand then lost the Cup in 2003, to Swiss team Alinghi.

The National Game

For many years, rugby union (usually known just as rugby) has been considered New Zealand's national game. The national team, the **All Blacks**, enjoy an enormous following within New Zealand, and rugby is hugely popular with spectators. It became a professional sport in 1996.

In terms of participation, rugby is the fifth most popular sport for males, and high numbers of Maori and Pacific Islanders take part. Just a few women play, but the national women's team, the **Black Ferns**, were victorious in the 1998 **Women's Rugby World Cup**.

The first organised rugby match played in New Zealand was in 1870, in **Nelson**. The first representative team to tour internationally was the largely Maori team of the **Natives** in 1888-89, which played a demanding schedule of games in Australia and Britain.

The 1905–06 team touring Britain — which was known as the **Originals**, and returned home to New Zealand as conquering heroes — was the first to be called the All Blacks. There are varying accounts as to the origins of the name. One suggestion is that it resulted from a typographical error which added an L to 'all backs'; another is that the moniker was due to the team's black uniforms.

The All Blacks are strongly associated with the **haka**, the stirring Maori dance which is performed at the start of each game, and plays a strong part in unsettling opponents and encouraging supporters. It's unclear when this practice started, but the 1905–06 team certainly began some of their games in Britain with a haka. The All Blacks are known in particular for performing the famous haka of Ngati Toa warrior chief Te Rauparaha; in 2005, a new haka was written especially for the All Blacks.

The All Blacks performing the haka

WATER RECREATION

New Zealand has more than 15000km of coastline, and no place in the country is further than 130km from the sea, so it's unsurprising that beaches are an important place for New Zealanders to relax and play. New Zealand also has many rivers and lakes; swimming, fishing, diving, snorkelling, kayaking and boating are all popular recreational activities.

However, drowning is New Zealand's third highest cause of accidental death. Many drownings happen without warning.

When taking part in water-based recreation, keep yourself safe by following these suggestions. See **www.watersafety.org.nz** for more information.

Water Safety

Most importantly, learn to swim. It may save your life, or the life of someone close to you.

Don't mix alcohol with water recreation activities. Alcohol impairs your judgement and co-ordination, and reduces your chances of survival.

At the beach:
- Swim between the flags, where lifeguards are patrolling.

Playing in the surf, Moureeses Bay, Whananaki

- Never swim alone. Always swim under supervision.
- If in doubt stay out. Know your limits.
- Read and obey the safety signs.
- Always use safe equipment.
- Learn to recognise and avoid rips. A rip is a strong current of water running out to sea. Rips are likely to be a darker colour, and have a calm rippled surface, with debris or foam floating out to sea.
- If you get caught in a rip, stay calm. Tread water or float. Once you're out past the breakers, swim parallel to the shore and catch waves in, or signal for help by raising your arm and wait for a lifesaver.

In rivers:
- Over 45% of drownings are in rivers.
- Currents may be stronger than they appear. A cubic metre of water weighs one tonne!
- If you get caught in a river current, float on your back and travel downstream feet first. Angle yourself toward the shore. Don't fight the current; head downstream to a suitable landing beach.
- Take care when standing close to river banks. The current may hollow out the ground under the bank, which may collapse.

In boats:
It's compulsory for all recreational craft to carry Personal Flotation Devices (PFDs, or lifejackets). Wear a PFD at all times of heightened risk.

Take the time to do a Day Skipper or Boatmaster course with Coastguard, ph: 0800 408 090, **www.cbes.org.nz**. Also see **www.boatsafe.org.nz**.

Underwater recreation:
- Learn to dive from a professional instructor. If you haven't dived for a while, take a refresher course.
- Never dive alone. Always dive with a buddy.
- Check and service your equipment regularly.
- Always use a dive flag.

With children:
- Supervise small children near water. ALWAYS! Children can move quickly, so supervise them without distractions.
- Remind children of safety rules.
- Don't let children swim alone.
- Don't let children play unsupervised with inflatable toys. These toys are not lifesaving devices.
- Give children the chance to become confident in the water and learn water safety rules.
- From the age of three, children can begin swimming lessons.

When rock fishing:
- Don't turn your back on the water.
- Wear a buoyancy aid.
- Check the weather, especially swell forecasts. Avoid a rising swell with an incoming tide.
- Don't stand too close to the water's edge.
- Make sure you have an escape route. Don't fish where you can't back away from a rising wave.
- Know how to swim.

Information provided courtesy of Water Safety New Zealand—educating in, on, and under the water.

OUTDOOR NEW ZEALAND

Climbers on final slope to summit, Aoraki/Mount Cook

New Zealanders are active people who love getting out in the great outdoors, and take access to the natural world for granted. The notion — and experience — of 'going bush' plays a considerable part in the national psyche, taking almost a spiritual role for many, who relish the chance to commune with nature while exploring an unspoilt forest or beach. Another iconic experience is that of the great Kiwi beach holiday in a rustic bach. These small holiday homes — often roughly and quirkily built, and offering only basic facilities — hold an important place in the hearts and lives of New Zealanders.

For visitors and locals alike, New Zealand offers a huge range of outdoor pursuits — from the restful (walking, fishing) to the adrenalin-supercharged (jet boating, bungy jumping) to the extraordinary (zorbing, canyon swinging). There are plenty of chances to try out different activities, either independently or with the guidance of tourism operators.

Snow sports

New Zealand is a premier southern hemisphere destination for skiing and snowboarding. The ski season is usually from June to October, but varies depending on the area.

In the **North Island**, the majority of ski areas are on volcanic mountains. They're primarily around active **Mount Ruapehu**, where **Whakapapa** and **Turoa** together make up New Zealand's largest ski area; there's also skiing on **Mount Taranaki**. New Zealand's best known ski areas are in the **South Island**, mostly in the vicinity of **Queenstown** and **Wanaka**; these fields include **Coronet Peak**, **Treble Cone**, **Cardrona** and **Waiorau**. **Mt Hutt**, close to **Methven**, is one of the southern hemisphere's highest ski areas.

See **www.snow.co.nz** for more information.

Tramping (hiking) & walking

New Zealand's 14 national parks and numerous other wilderness areas offer thousands of kilometres of tracks, many of them through remote and beautiful areas. They offer a range of experiences, from short, easy walks to gruelling multi-day hikes only suitable for experienced trampers.

There are many huts and campsites managed by the Department of Conservation (DOC) in New Zealand's wilderness areas. A small fee is charged for accommodation in these.

Nine iconic, popular tracks through national park scenery are designated as 'Great Walks'. These are the **Lake Waikaremoana Track** and **Tongariro Northern Circuit** in the North Island, and in the South Island, the **Abel Tasman Coastal Track**, the **Heaphy Track**, the **Milford Track**, the **Routeburn Track**, the **Kepler Track**, and the **Rakiura Track**; there's also one 'Great Walk' which isn't a walk, the **Whanganui River Journey**. 'Great Walks' feature a higher standard of accommodation; some also require walkers to book ahead.

Wilderness areas can be dangerous: respect them! When going hiking, make sure you choose a trip that's appropriate for the skills, knowledge and experience of your group. Don't go alone.

Before you leave home, tell someone where you're going and when you intend to be back; when you return, let them know you're back. During your trip, fill in hut books, even if you're not staying in the hut.

Be aware that weather can change fast in New Zealand. Check current weather forecasts before leaving; always carry warm and waterproof clothing.

DOC visitor centres can provide the latest information about facilities, local conditions and weather, hut passes and tickets, and conservation.

If you're venturing into the back country, find out about where you're going, any natural hazards and how to deal with them. Equip yourself appropriately, and make sure you have the skills you need. The New Zealand Mountain Safety

Trampers at Mount Holdsworth, Tararua Ranges

Trout fisherman, Lake Rotoaira

Council offers training courses in bushcraft and handling survival situations; see **www.mountainsafety.org.nz** and **www.doc.govt.nz**.

Climbing

With its great array of mountain peaks, New Zealand has long been a mecca for mountaineers. There are some outstanding climbs in the **Southern Alps**, including **Aoraki/Mount Cook**, **Mount Aspiring** and **Mount Earnslaw**.

However, the high mountain peaks should be approached with the greatest of care. Mountaineering can be a dangerous pursuit even for the experienced, and lethal for the inexperienced. Tourism operators around mountain areas offer mountaineering courses, instruction and guiding.

Adventure activities

For lovers of the adrenalin rush, New Zealand offers a plethora of activities; Queenstown and **Taupo** in particular are centres for adventure pursuits.

New Zealand is synonymous with bungy jumping; notable bungy jumps include a 43m leap from a historic bridge over the **Kawarau River** near Queenstown, a 102m bungy in **Skippers Canyon**, a 47m jump over the **Waikato River** at Taupo, and the 40m bungy from the **Auckland Harbour Bridge**.

Many of New Zealand's rivers offer great white water rafting, and there are plenty of operators who run rafting trips. The **Shotover**, Kawarau and **Rangitata Rivers** are particularly good; on the **Kaituna River** near **Rotorua**, the 7m **Okere Falls** are the highest commercially rafted waterfall in the world.

Jet boating was invented in New Zealand; it's popular on many rivers, including the Waikato, **Rangitaiki** and Whanganui Rivers, and the remote wilderness areas of the **Dart** and **Wilkin Rivers**.

Canoeing and kayaking are also popular; the five-day journey down the remote, historic Whanganui River is an unforgettable trip. Sea kayaking is excellent around New Zealand, often allowing close encounters with marine life. Other adventure activities include canyon swinging, cave rafting, zorbing, river sledging, skydiving and more.

Hunting & fishing

It's legal in New Zealand to hunt a number of exotic species, including pigs, deer, wild goats, chamois and some birds. People wanting to hunt on public conservation land need to apply for hunting permits from DOC (see **www.doc.govt.nz**). Permits for hunting game birds are available from the Fish and Game Council, **www.fishandgame.org.nz** A firearms licence is required from the NZ police, and hunters must observe the firearms code; see **www.police.govt.nz**

Many of New Zealand's rivers are rich in trout and salmon. The central North Island is famous for its excellent trout fishing, particularly in **Lake Taupo** and the rivers which feed it. There's also plentiful trout in the South Island's lakes and rivers, particularly **Lake Brunner (Moana)** and **Southland**'s **Mataura River**. Great salmon fishing is available in **Otago** and Southland's rivers.

Fishing permits are needed for fishing in inland waters. You can buy permits (daily, monthly, or for a season) online at **www.fishandgame.org.nz** or from sports shops or Post Shops. To fish at Lake Taupo, you need a Lake Taupo fishing licence, available from retailers near the lake.

New Zealand also offers great salt water fishing. The **Bay of Islands**, **Tutukaka**, **Whitianga** and **Tuhua (Mayor Island)** are known for their excellent big game fishing. Surfcasting is also good from many beaches around the country. See the Ministry of Fisheries website, **www.fish.govt.nz**, for information on rules for marine recreational fishing. Fishing is not permitted in marine reserve protected areas, but they are great places for diving and snorkelling.

Bungy jumping above the Waikato River, Taupo

CAR PREPARATION

New Zealand's roads are suitable for most cars and driving conditions. However, if venturing off the bitumen and into the rough is more your style, it may be worth investigating buying a 4-wheel drive. If you plan to tow a caravan or trailer, it's best to stay on sealed roads or well-maintained unsealed roads, regardless of whether you are travelling in a 4-wheel drive or not.

Before you leave home

Get your car checked by a qualified mechanic and let him/her know that you're going on a long trip. If you are towing a caravan or trailer, get that serviced as well — particularly the tyres, wheel bearings, suspension, brakes, coupling and lights.

Key items for checking are:
- Cooling system — check the radiator, hoses, thermostat and condition of inhibitor/anti-freeze
- Lubricant levels — top up or replace engine and transmission fluids. Replace the oil filter if you replace the engine oil
- Cam belts and fuel filters: check the manufacturer's recommended replacement period, and change if needed

Pre-trip inspection by a qualified mechanic

- Heater and demister work properly
- Battery's condition and security
- Tyre condition and pressure, including the spare, and tyres on the trailer or caravan
- Wheel balance and alignment
- Wheel bearings
- Condition of windscreen wipers — blades and reservoir
- Brake system
- Exhaust system
- All auxiliary drive belts
- Air conditioning
- Lights, including high/low beam
- Air and oil filters
- Suspension
- On-road performance of engine and transmission

During the trip

Check:
- Engine and cooling system levels (check cooling system when engine is cold)
- Oil or fuel leaks under the car (on the ground)
- Tyre pressures. Don't forget the spare, trailer or caravan tyres

- Windscreen washer bottle level
- Temperature gauge — keep an eye on this when driving

Packing the car

Try not to overload your vehicle, as extra loads can cause suspension problems. Pack the heaviest items inside the car or in the boot or trailer, as the weight of heavy items on the roof could easily throw the car off balance. When packing lighter items on a roof rack, make the load lower at the front and higher at the back. This reduces wind resistance when travelling.

If carrying tools and equipment inside the car, make sure they are tightly secured. It's sensible to install a cargo barrier for this purpose. Keep close at hand the things you may want or need during the journey. If you're towing a trailer or caravan, make sure you have the correct size wheel brace to remove the trailer or caravan wheel.

Extras to take

It's sensible to carry a spare set of car keys. Most cars are now equipped with engine immobilisers, which rely on getting a coded

Servicing the air filter

electronic signal from the ignition key or remote unit. Without spare keys, the car may have to be towed a long distance to an authorised dealer, or you may have to wait until spares can be sent from home.

Always carry a spare wheel.

Quick maintenance checks

Petrol
Keep the petrol tank at least half full. This helps keep any sediment out of the fuel system. An empty tank also attracts water vapour. Only use the grade of petrol recommended in your handbook.

Tyres
Once a month, check the tyre pressure. For accuracy, it's best to do this when the tyres are cold. Tyres should have at least 1.5mm tread depth over 75% of the tyre. Replace tyres that have less tread than this.

Fluids
The engine oil level and brake and clutch fluid should be checked once a month, and topped up as needed. So should the radiator coolant, which should always

be checked when the engine is cold. (Seek advice if the coolant level is low.) Always check for fluid leakage stains on your driveway or garage floor.

Battery
Most batteries are maintenance-free. But if you have one that needs regular inspection of the fluid level, do this every three months. Top up the battery as needed with distilled water. Batteries over five years of age should be considered near the end of their useful life.

Modern safety technology
Some cars are a lot safer than others. Check car safety ratings at **www.landtransport.govt.nz/ vehicle-safety/ancap/**

The following features can improve vehicle safety.

ABS
An Anti-lock braking system helps keep you safe when you brake hard in slippery conditions. If your wheels are about to lock, the system automatically varies the brake pressure (like 'pumping' the brakes) so they keep turning, allowing the

Highway north of Murchison

driver to maintain steering control. ABS doesn't stop you losing control on corners from driving too fast.

Airbags
Front airbags inflate from the steering wheel hub or dashboard during a crash and help save many lives. If a vehicle doesn't have airbags, you can't have them fitted. Front airbags are of little benefit in a side, rear or rollover crash, so it's still essential to wear a safety belt. Some vehicles now have side airbags which inflate from the seat, roof, door or a pillar. They offer significant protection to your head, chest, abdomen and pelvis in a side-on crash.

Traction control/4WD
Some new vehicles offer traction control systems to help stop wheel-spin. This makes it easier to accelerate smoothly on slippery surfaces. Four-wheel drive also helps traction by delivering the power of the engine more evenly to all four wheels.

Head restraints
These can help prevent whiplash in a crash. Adjust them so they are at eye level and as close to your head as possible.

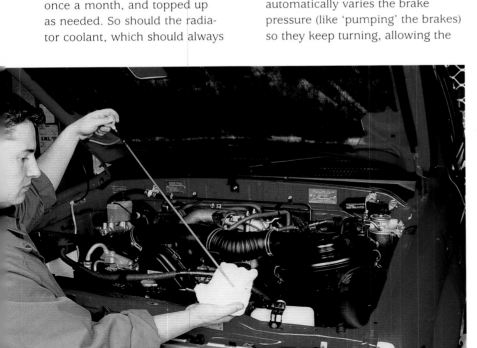

Checking the oil level

MOTORING HINTS & DRIVING SKILLS

Lindis Pass, Otago

Stay focused

Crashes can happen to anyone, not just bad drivers. Driving can become so familiar that we get blasé. A key to staying safe is to avoid distractions. Here are key risks to avoid:

- Juggling driving with other thinking. Research shows drivers can safely drive and listen or give basic replies. But when answering complex questions, they missed red lights, wove across lanes and failed to see pedestrians.
- Using a mobile phone while driving carries the same risk as driving drunk. Australian research shows one in five young drivers text message while driving. This has an even higher crash risk.
- Driving after a heavy meal or taking prescription drugs can make it harder to stay alert.
- Driving with loud, fast music can

lead people to take more risks.
- Eating, drinking and smoking while driving all increase the risk of crashing.
- Anything that takes your eyes from the road. Pull over if you have to read maps, manage fighting kids or admire the scenery. A vehicle, pedestrian or cyclist can come out of nowhere, and on the open road you can travel around 55m in just two seconds.

On the roads at holiday time

The roads will be busy, so plan to leave early.

Before you leave:
- Get your tyres, lights, brakes and cooling systems checked.
- Put heavy items at the bottom of the boot, and don't jam things in too high — you should be able to see out the back window.

- Stow items securely — any loose object can be lethal in a crash.

Plan your trip
- Long journeys aren't easy. Get plenty of sleep first, and try to drive at times you are normally awake.
- Plan rest breaks every couple of hours. If you feel drowsy, take that nap. A driver who falls asleep can be a killer. Share the driving if you can.

Stay fresh on the road
- Let others merge into traffic. If you are travelling slower than the rest, pull over regularly and let them pass.
- Be patient — what's really to gain by being aggressive behind the wheel? If traffic is heavy, overtaking may not be worth it.

Driving in rural areas

Rural roads have unique challenges. Expect:
- Other road users and animals coming out of hidden intersections and driveways
- People working, walking or cycling on the road
- Farm machinery and slow-moving vehicles
- Roadside hazards such as unsealed edges and ditches
- One-lane bridges — follow the signs showing who should give way
- School buses — the speed limit when passing a stationary school bus in either direction is 20km/h.

When driving on gravel roads:
- Turn your lights on and remember vehicles can be hidden in the dust. Drive in the wheel tracks. Keep your speed down and stay well to

the left at bends. Slow right down for oncoming traffic.

When stock is on the road:

- Slow right down or stop. Do not use the horn or rev the engine. Pass as far away from the animals as possible.

At night:

- In the country, it's easy to out-drive your headlights. You should be able to stop within the distance lit by your headlights, or half that distance if there are no lane markings.
- Increase your following distance to at least four seconds.
- A clean windscreen can make a big difference to visibility.

Towing a trailer, caravan or boat

- Spread the load evenly and tie it down or cover it. Don't overload; this affects stability and control. Check the tyres. Attach the safety chain and lights.
- On the open road, the limit is 90km/h. Only drive this fast if it is safe.
- Leave at least a four second gap between you and the vehicle in front — slowing down takes longer when towing. Slow well before corners and avoid sudden braking, or you could risk

jackknifing your trailer.

- Use a lower gear when going downhill — it improves your control of your vehicle.
- All trailers, caravans, boat-trailers and horse floats need a current warrant of fitness and registration to be on the road.

Bad weather driving

- Wet roads increase stopping distances — for other drivers as well as you. Drive at a speed so you can stop well within the distance you can see.
- Keep your headlights on dip, whatever the time of day.
- If rain, hail or snow gets too heavy, pull over and stop off the road for a few minutes.
- Ice can be hard to see, so stay alert for any signs of slipping and look out for road ice warning signs. You can skid and crash on ice easily. Use snow chains if necessary — practise fitting them before you need them.
- If you feel the car start to slide, steer into the direction of the skid. When the vehicle regains traction carefully reapply the brakes.

Driving after dark

- Drive to the conditions.
- Turn your lights on 30 minutes before sunset. Keep your lights

Driving Laws

- Drive on the left side of the road.
- On most main roads, the speed limit is 100 km/h unless a sign says a lower speed limit applies. In urban areas, the speed limit is usually 50 km/h, unless a sign says otherwise.
- Everyone in the vehicle, front and back, must wear a safety belt.
- Don't drink and drive. The laws against this are strictly enforced, and penalties are severe.
- Drivers must carry their driver licence when driving.
- Helmets must be worn when riding cycles and motorbikes.
- Cycling is not permitted on motorways.
- International drivers can legally drive in New Zealand for up to 12 months if they have either a current driver licence from your home country or an International Driving Permit. See p.35 for more information on driving in New Zealand for international visitors.

on until 30 minutes after sunrise.

- Look to the left of oncoming headlights to avoid the glare.
- Dip your lights when approaching or following another vehicle, or in a built up area.
- You should be able to stop within the distance lit by your headlights, or half that distance if there are no lane markings. Think about increasing your following distance to at least four seconds.
- Marker posts have white reflectors on the left side of the road and yellow on the right — helping you see whether the road veers left or right.

Stock being moved on the road, St Bathans

ACCIDENTS & BREAKDOWNS

Car broken down on side of the road

Coming across a crash

You can help out — no matter how big or small the crash.

1. Park in a safe spot, away from the immediate crash area. Leave plenty of space for emergency vehicles and crew. Switch on your hazard lights.
2. Phone **111** immediately for help, particularly if anyone is injured.
3. Put out warning triangles or have people stand on all approaches to the crash site, around 200m away to give approaching drivers time to slow down.
4. Turn off the ignition of the crashed vehicles. Don't move injured people unless there is immediate danger. Write down the names and phone numbers of any witnesses.

Keep a first aid kit and hazard triangle in your boot. They don't take up much space, but they can be lifesavers.

In the event of an accident

Record the following details, which could help with an insurance claim later.

Accident details
- Time and date
- Location
- Did emergency services attend?
- Name of police officer (if applicable)

Witnesses
- Name, address and phone number of witnesses of the accident who were not passengers in your vehicle

Other vehicles involved
- Driver's name, address and phone number
- Vehicle owner's name, address and phone number
- Make, model and registration of vehicle
- Insurance company

Details of what occurred

Breaking down

Get as far off the road as you can and stay there.

1. Don't brake suddenly. Stay calm. Find a safe place to stop and move off the road.
2. Turn your hazard lights on. If you have hazard triangles, put them out. Stay clear of traffic.
3. If your car is a hazard call police on *555. If not, and you are an AA member, call the AA on *222 from your mobile, or 0800 500 222.

Detecting a flat tyre

Your car may begin to wander or become harder to steer. There may be the smell of burning rubber, or a thudding noise. Know how to use your car jack and check the condition and pressure of your spare tyre every few months.

Flat battery

Crash start: If you have a manual car you may be able to 'crash start'. To do this, turn the ignition on, select third gear and push in the clutch. Have someone else push the car. When you're moving, release the clutch, then be ready to push it in again when the engine starts. Caution: power steering will be disabled and brake efficiency will be reduced.

Jump start: Connect 'jumper leads' from another car's battery to your car battery. Make sure the leads are connected red to red (positive) and black to earth (negative).

There are risks associated with this procedure. See **www.aa.co.nz/motoring** for full instructions.
AA members call 0800 500 222 or *222 from your mobile.

The material on pp.26–30, and the information on child restraints on p.32, is from *The Real Kiwi Driver's Guide*, and is used by permission of Land Transport New Zealand and the New Zealand Automobile Association.

Motorway emergency phone

FIRST AID

Professional first aid training can help people gain the knowledge and skills needed to deal with accidents and emergencies. St John offers first aid courses throughout New Zealand and has a comprehensive first aid manual for sale. Visit **www.stjohn.org.nz**, or call 0800 ST JOHN (0800 785 646).

There is no substitute for practical training at an approved course, but the tips below, supplied by St John, give some useful pointers.

Managing a first aid incident
In a major incident:
- Appear calm and take charge. Immediately call **111** and ask for the ambulance.
- Follow the SRABCS plan: see below for more details.
- Get bystanders to help with patients. They can check the patient's level of consciousness, offer reassurance, collect information, treat or position the patient, and cover them to maintain warmth.
- Patients who are wide awake should be allowed to find their own position; patients who are not wide awake should be lying down. Unconscious patients should be put on their side (supported) if reasonably possible, or in the recovery position. Patients in cardiac arrest should be placed on their back.
- When a person is unresponsive with no signs of life, place them on their back and give them cardiopulmonary resuscitation (CPR). If you have to give CPR and find it hard to perform breaths, do perform chest compressions alone. This greatly enhances your patient's chance of survival.
- Gather information to give to the emergency services: the exact location, a description of the accident, number of casualties, initial patient assessment, hazards, other emergency services if required, your name and contact phone number.
- Account for all occupants of all vehicles. Stay with patients and keep them at the scene until the ambulance staff arrive and take over the situation.

The SRABCS plan
This step-by-step strategy for managing a first aid incident allows you to identify and deal with initial life-threatening conditions before starting to treat non-life-threatening injuries.
Safety – Keep yourself, bystanders, patients and the scene safe.
Response – Does the patient respond to a loud voice and a gentle shake or tap on the shoulder? An unconscious person does not respond to voice and touch.
Airway – Open and clear airways.
Breathing – Look, listen and feel for breathing for up to 10 seconds.
Circulation – Look for signs of life: breathing, coughing and movement.
Severe bleeding is a risk following injury. Check the patient, first their head and neck, then lower spine, trunk, arms and legs.

Managing severe bleeding
Follow the SRABCS plan. Wear protective gloves if available. Control bleeding by applying direct pressure to the wound; use the patient's hands, or your hands. Elevate the limb (unless it's fractured). Apply the cleanest pad available and secure with a bandage. Do not remove objects embedded in the wound.

Managing burns
Follow the SRABCS plan. Remove the patient from danger. If burns are larger than a patient's hand, call an ambulance early. Flood the area with cold (not ice cold) water for 20 minutes to reduce pain and damage. Don't remove clothing adhering to the skin. Lightly cover with cling film or a clean dressing to prevent infection. Continue to cool the area with cold compresses on the outside of the cling film.

Managing fractures
Follow the SRABCS plan. Call an ambulance. Control external bleeding, but don't apply pressure over a fracture site, or to the wound associated with an open fracture. Support the fracture in the most comfortable position, ensuring there is no unnecessary movement. *Do not* attempt to straighten a misshapen limb. Do not move the patient unless the fracture is securely immobilised. Splinting of a large bone is not necessary unless help is delayed. If possible, slightly elevate the fracture to minimise bleeding and swelling.

First Aid Kits
Keep a first aid kit in your car. You can buy a mobile first aid kit from St John, ideal for use in vehicles. Visit **www.stjohn.org.nz**, or call 0800 ST JOHN (0800 785 646). Alternatively, make up your own kit in a clean, waterproof container.

INFORMATION FOR
INTERNATIONAL TRAVELLERS

Picnicking at Butchers Dam, Central Otago

Entering New Zealand

All visitors to New Zealand must carry a passport that is valid for at least three months beyond the date they intend to leave the country. You do not need a visa or permit to visit New Zealand if you are:

- a New Zealand citizen or Resident Permit holder,
- an Australian citizen travelling on an Australian passport,
- an Australian resident with a current Australian resident return visa, or
- a citizen of a country which has a visa waiver agreement with New Zealand.

Travellers from more than 50 countries can stay in New Zealand up to three months without a visitor's visa. (For a stay of more than three months, further permits are required.) You must have:

- a passport that is valid for at least three months after your planned departure date, or one month if the government of your country has consular representation in New Zealand and can issue and renew travel documents
- an onward ticket to a country that you have permission to enter, and

- enough money to support yourself during your stay.

Citizens of the UK can enter without a visa and stay in New Zealand for up to six months.

Biosecurity is important to New Zealand, as an island nation with an important agricultural industry. Plant, animal and food products must be declared on arrival in New Zealand. Hiking gear will be checked, and may require cleaning.

New Zealand has no restrictions on the amount of foreign currency that can be brought in or taken out of the country. However amounts over NZ$10 000 (or foreign equivalent) in cash, with you or in your baggage, must be declared.

For more information, see **www.customs.govt.nz** and **www.immigration.govt.nz**

Time

New Zealand time is 12 hours ahead of Coordinated Universal Time (UTC)/GMT. From the first Sunday in October to the third Sunday in March, New Zealand observes one hour of daylight saving, ie is 13 hours ahead of UTC/GMT.

Money

The New Zealand unit of currency is the New Zealand dollar (100 cents).

All major credit cards can be used in New Zealand. Banks are open from 9.30am to 4.30pm, Monday to Friday, and automated teller machines (ATMs) are very common.

Most goods and services attract a Goods and Services Tax (GST) of 12.5%, included in the displayed price.

Tipping is not obligatory.

Emergencies

In an emergency, call **111** and ask for fire, ambulance or police.

Driving in New Zealand

You can legally drive in New Zealand for up to 12 months if you have either a current driver licence from your home country or an International Driving Permit.

Keep left

Always drive on the **left** side of the road. If you drive on the right hand side in your own country, please take a moment to re-familiarise yourself with this rule before pulling out onto the road after a break — it's easy to forget where you are.

Giving way at intersections

Always use your indicators when turning.

In general: If you're turning, give way to all vehicles that are not turning. In all other situations, give way to vehicles crossing or coming from your **right**.

No left turn on red

In New Zealand you're not allowed to turn left at an intersection when the traffic lights are red.

Travelling times

It's easy to underestimate travelling times in New Zealand. Although distances may seem short on paper, New Zealand roads may be narrower than you are used to, cover hilly terrain and vary from motorways to unsealed gravel roads.

Driving speeds

Speed limit signs show the maximum speed you can travel. However, at times you will need to drive at a slower speed due to weather or road conditions. Varying speed limits apply throughout New Zealand — look out for speed limit signs.

On most of New Zealand's main

FOOD & WINE

New Zealand produces some wonderful fresh produce, and has very good cafés and restaurants around the country. Local specialties include pavlova (a meringue dessert with cream and fresh fruit), kiwifruit, and delicious lamb from the country's 40 million sheep. The excellent seafood includes fish, greenshell mussels, Bluff oysters, whitebait and crayfish; paua (abalone) and kina (sea urchins, often eaten raw) may be more of an acquired taste for some.

Hangi are traditional Maori feasts prepared by steaming food in flax baskets over hot stones in an underground oven, which imparts a strong smoky taste to the food. New Zealanders also love to barbecue food, at home and at the beach.

Restaurant food is just as likely to draw on Italian, Middle Eastern, Asian or Pacific cooking styles; artisan food producers offer excellent breads, cheeses, olives and much more. Coffee is also very good, and espresso machines are ubiquitous.

In the last two decades, New Zealand wine has made quite an impression on the international wine scene. Particularly impressive are the sauvignon blancs of Marlborough, the pinot noirs of Central Otago and the Wairarapa, and the chardonnays of Gisborne; excellent wine is also produced in Hawke's Bay, Canterbury, Nelson and around Auckland. Many wineries welcome visitors for tastings; an increasing number provide food as well.

Smoking is prohibited in NZ restaurants, cafés, bars and casinos. Many venues provide an outside area for smokers.

The famous New Zealand dessert, pavlova

roads, the speed limit is 100 km/h unless a sign says a lower speed limit applies.

In urban areas, the speed limit is usually 50 km/h, unless a sign says otherwise.

Safety belts
By law, everyone in the vehicle must wear a safety belt — whether they're in the front or back.

Southern Alps from Franz Josef

Alcohol
Don't drink and drive. The laws against this are strictly enforced in New Zealand, and penalties are severe.

Overtaking
Most roads have a single lane each way, but may provide passing lanes at regular intervals. Use these where possible. You must not cross a solid yellow line on your side of the centre-line, as this indicates it's too dangerous to overtake.

One lane bridges
Many roads in New Zealand have one lane bridges, where vehicles travelling in one direction must give way to vehicles going in the opposite direction. Slow down and check for traffic coming the other way.

Unsealed (gravel) roads
Avoid unsealed roads if possible. If you need to drive on them, remember they can be very narrow. Reduce your speed to below 40–50km/h, and slow down even further when approaching oncoming traffic, as the dust will obscure your vision.

Parallel parking
In New Zealand, you can be fined or towed away for parallel parking on the wrong side of the road. You may only park in the direction of traffic flow on your side of the road (ie the left side, unless it's a one-way street).

Driving information courtesy of Land Transport New Zealand. See www.landtransport.govt.nz/overseasdrivers/ for more information.

TRAVELLING WITH CHILDREN

Keeping children safe

Use an approved child restraint (a seat, harness, capsule or booster) that's right for the child's age and size.
The law says:

- Birth to five years — all children must be in approved child restraints.
- Five, six and seven-year-olds — must be in child restraints, or, if none are available, safety belts. If no belts are available, they must sit in the back.
- Eight to 14 years old — children must wear standard safety belts. If there aren't any belts, they must sit in the back.

What's the right restraint?
This depends on how old and how big your child is. Be guided by the manufacturer's recommendation — usually on a label on the seat. A restraint is probably too small if your child's head is above the back of the restraint.

Rear- facing restraints are recommended for babies under one year old.

- Infant restraints or 'baby capsules':
  Birth to around 9kg, or six months old
- Restraints or 'car seats':
  For children who weigh 8 to 18kg and up to four years old
- Harnesses and booster seats:
  For those who weigh 14 to 26kg, or around three to seven years old
  If buying second hand, don't get a restraint that has been in a crash, or is worn, damaged or repaired. Check for a 'date of manufacture' or a 'do not use after' date. Don't use any restraint over 10 years old.

Check your car

- Check that the restraint will fit your car. Some can only be secured by a normal three-point safety belt. Others can also be secured by a back-seat lap belt.
- Some restraints also have a tether strap that must be clipped to a special anchor point in the car.
- Follow the manufacturer's instructions for fitting details.

Back seat is best

- It is strongly recommended you put all child restraints in rear seats.
- Never put a rear-facing child restraint in the front seat of a car fitted with airbags.

Keeping children happy

Here are some tips for making long car trips more enjoyable for your children — and you!

- Schedule enough time to make frequent stops. Use parks, rest stops and picnic areas to let children run around and play. At lunchtime, have a picnic outside.
- Pack separate bags for your children and place them on top of other luggage.
- If they are old enough, give them a map of the route and a highlighter, and let them follow the road. Entertain younger children with stories — made up or true.
- Play interactive games like 'I spy' and 'Guess what I am'.
- Leave early in the morning. Children may sleep for a couple of hours at the start and wake up for a breakfast stop.
- Make children comfortable. Use car shades and sunglasses to stop the heat and glare, and pillows and blankets for warmth and comfort.

- Pack tissues, face cleaners, a towel and a change of clothes.
- Dress your children in layers so they can be comfortable whatever the temperature is.

Avoiding travel sickness

Motion or travel sickness occurs because of a conflict between what the eyes and ears are taking in. If your children complain of feeling 'yucky' or 'sick', there are a few different things you can do.

- Suggest they look outside the car. Play 'I spy...' or, if necessary, reposition the seats so they can see out.
- Limit reading and hand-held games.
- Give them some fresh air. Avoid strong smelling food, and don't smoke in the car.
- Drive smoothly.
- Stop for frequent rests.
- Inquire about over-the-counter medication and remedies from your chemist or doctor before you leave.

Children feeding lambs at SheepWorld, Warkworth

USEFUL CONTACTS

Visitor information

New Zealand is served by an extensive network of more than 80 i-SITE visitor centres. These official visitor centres offer free, friendly, objective information on local attractions and accommodation. Professionally trained staff can give advice and book holiday requirements.

See **www.i-site.org** for more information about i-SITE centres.

New Zealand i-SITE Visitor Centre
137 Quay St, Princes Wharf
Auckland
Ph: 0800 AUCKLAND
www.aucklandnz.com

Wellington i-SITE Visitor Centre
Cnr Wakefield and Victoria Sts
Wellington
Ph: (04) 802 4860
www.WellingtonNZ.com

Christchurch i-SITE Visitor Centre
Old Chief Post Office,
Cathedral Sq West
Christchurch
Ph: (03) 379 9629
www.christchurchnz.net

Dunedin i-SITE Visitor Centre
48 The Octagon
Dunedin
Ph: (03) 474 3300
www.dunedinnz.com

Excellent visitor information is also available online from Tourism New Zealand at **www.newzealand.com**

Department of Conservation information

The Department of Conservation (DOC) manages New Zealand's 14 national parks and many other areas of conservation land. DOC visitor centres offer information about recreational activities, conservation work and local and regional places of interest. Most visitor centres are located close to significant conservation areas; there are also centres in the major cities.

Auckland Conservation Information Centre
Ferry Bldgs, Quay St
Auckland
Ph: (09) 379 6476

Wellington Conservation Information Centre
Government Bldgs Historic Reserve,
Lambton Quay
Wellington
Ph: (04) 472 7356

Christchurch Conservation Information Centre
133 Victoria St
Christchurch
Ph: (03) 371 3706

Extensive information about national and forest parks, marine reserves, other places of interest, New Zealand flora and fauna, tracks and walks and conservation work is available online at www.doc.govt.nz

Weather information

MetService phone weather reports
Ph: 0900 999 + your area code
www.metservice.co.nz

Information for road users

To report dangerous driving or a road hazard
Ph: *555 from your mobile

Road safety enquiries
Ph: 0800 699 000

Motor vehicle registration
Ph: 0800 108 809

Signpost, Bluff, Southland

Driver licence enquiries
Ph: 0800 822 422

New Zealand Automobile Association (AA)
99 Albert Street
Auckland
Ph: (09) 966 8800
www.aa.co.nz

AA breakdown service (for AA members)
Ph: 0800 500 222, or *222 from your mobile

AA report on current road conditions
Ph: 0900 33 222
www.aaroadwatch.co.nz

For information about highway conditions in the South Island, Wanganui and Taranaki,
ph: 0800 44 44 49

Information on New Zealand's road rules is available online at www.landtransport.govt.nz.

EMERGENCIES
Ph: **111**

New Zealand's North Island offers a myriad of options to satisfy all tastes. Visitors can swim, surf and enjoy water sports on beautiful beaches; walk through unspoilt forests among rich native bird life; marvel at majestic giant kauri trees thousands of years in age; explore extraordinary volcanic landscapes with colourful terraces, bubbling mud pools and dramatic geysers; fish for trout in wild rivers; raise adrenalin levels with a bungy jump or jet boat ride; or ski and snowboard on snowy slopes, surrounded by spectacular mountain scenery.

The main cities of Auckland and Wellington, as well as the provincial cities, offer lively urban and cultural attractions, including excellent theatre, galleries and museums. Several North Island regions produce very good wine, and visitors are welcome at most wineries. Farms, orchards and an increasing number of boutique food producers also mean great food is on offer in most places.

The majority of New Zealand's Maori population live in the North Island, and Maori culture is strongest here, particularly around Rotorua, Northland and Eastland.

Cultural tours, performances and visits to marae (Maori community meeting-places) allow visitors to learn more about this rich cultural tradition. Some wonderful Maori taonga (treasures) can be found in galleries and museums; visitors can also see artisan carvers and weavers demonstrating

North Island:

Population: 3 million
Total area: 113 729km^2
% of New Zealand: 42%
Highest mountain: Mount Ruapehu, 2797m
Maori name: Te Ika a Maui
(The Fish of Maui)

Mounts Ruapehu, Ngauruhoe and Tongariro

their craft. The North Island also has many historic sites, both Maori and European.

From the milder north to the cooler south, the North Island's climate is largely temperate. Hawke's Bay and the Bay of Plenty are known for their long sunshine hours; Wellington is known for its wind.

An excellent network of roads makes it easy to travel by car, although in the most remote areas, some roads are unsealed. There are also good bus services, regular flights between most cities, and a limited number of train services;

however, for those who are keen to get off the beaten track and really explore, their own transport is best. Cycling is also an increasingly popular way to tour the country.

 Visitor information

New Zealand i-SITE Visitor Centre
137 Quay St, Princes Wharf, Auckland
Ph: 0800 AUCKLAND

Wellington i-SITE Visitor Centre
Cnr Wakefield and Victoria Sts, Wellington
Ph: (04) 802 4860

www.newzealand.com
www.i-site.org

Main ATTRACTIONS

◈ **Auckland**

New Zealand's largest city, nestled between two lovely harbours, offers a vibrant urban lifestyle and Pacific culture.

◈ **Bay of Islands**

Known as the birthplace of the nation, the Bay of Islands is renowned for its coastal scenery, unspoilt beaches and historic towns.

◈ **Coromandel Peninsula**

The relaxed Coromandel Peninsula has lovely beaches, rich native bush and historic attractions.

◈ **Egmont National Park**

Beautiful Mount Taranaki is at the centre of this richly forested national park.

◈ **Hawke's Bay**

Hawke's Bay has art deco architecture, wineries, gourmet food producers, and the world's largest mainland gannet colony.

◈ **Lake Taupo**

New Zealand's largest lake is known internationally for its trout fishing; swimming and water sports are also popular.

◈ **Rotorua**

Thermal attractions, volcanically-formed lakes and Maori culture have drawn visitors to Rotorua since the 19th century.

◈ **Te Papa, Wellington**

New Zealand's national museum has a wealth of innovative displays about the country's culture, heritage and natural history.

◈ **Te Urewera National Park**

This remote and lovely park has lush forests, much bird life and beautiful Lake Waikaremoana.

◈ **Tongariro National Park**

A dual World Heritage Area, New Zealand's first national park preserves three active volcanoes, and offers snow sports and extraordinary walks.

◈ **Waitomo Caves**

Formed more than 30 million years ago, these caves have spectacular limestone formations and glow-worms.

◈ **Whanganui National Park**

Centred around the majestic Whanganui River, this park has lush forests, rugged valleys, picturesque settlements and rich history.

NORTH ISLAND

To Maori, the North Island is **Te Ika a Maui**, literally 'the Fish of Maui'; in Maori legend the fish-shaped island (with **Wellington** at the head) was fished up by the trickster demi-god Maui. The island's mountains and valleys resulted from the fish thrashing in pain as Maui's brothers fought to carve it up.

The North Island is largely rolling hill country, much of it in farmland; around 20% of the island is mountainous, with a central spine of major mountain ranges up to 1700m. The central North Island is dominated by the thermally active volcanic plateau; most northern regions have thermal hot springs, and there are a number of active volcanoes. **Lake Taupo**, the country's largest lake at 616km^2, is the result of a massive volcanic explosion. The far north and east coast have attractive sandy beaches, with black-sand beaches on the west coast.

Maori lore tells that the early Polynesian explorer Kupe first made landfall at **Hokianga Harbour** in **Northland**. Canoes of Maori migrants followed, probably in the 13th century; Maori settled largely in the North Island, a situation which continues today, with 90% of

North Island farmland, north of Wanganui

Maori living north of Cook Strait.

The British explorer Captain James Cook landed at **Poverty Bay** in 1769. The first European town grew in the **Bay of Islands** at **Kororareka** (later known as **Russell**), and the first Christian mission was founded nearby in 1814.

The Treaty of Waitangi was signed at **Waitangi** between Maori chiefs and the British Crown in 1840, making the country officially a British colony; by the 1850s, most of the North Island's interior had been explored by Europeans. However progress was limited for a number of years by conflict between Maori and Europeans over land ownership and sovereignty.

Although it's smaller than the South Island, today the North Island is home to three-quarters of the country's population, about three

million people. More than half of all New Zealanders live in the island's northern half; around 1.2 million of these are in **Auckland**, New Zealand's largest city and the world's largest Polynesian city. The smaller city of **Wellington**, at the southern end of the North Island, is the nation's capital.

The early European economy was based on sealing, whaling, gold, native timber and kauri gum. Later a farming economy developed, and much of the island was put into pasture.

Today, wool and dairy production continue in their importance to the economy. Other important industries include forestry, fishing and energy production; tourism is also a significant earner, and new industries such as wine production and film making are increasingly important.

Mount Taranaki seen from Lake Mangamahoe

North Island

TOURISM REGION HIGHLIGHTS

From sub-tropical beaches to sophisticated urban areas, from unspoilt wilderness areas to snow-topped mountains, winery regions, unique thermal attractions and fascinating Maori culture, the North Island has a huge amount to offer visitors.

A Auckland (pp.46–53)
Auckland War Memorial Museum; Clevedon; Goat Island; Great Barrier Island; Karekare; Kelly Tarlton's Antarctic Encounter & Underwater World; Miranda; Piha; Sky Tower; Tiritiri Matangi Island; Waiheke Island; Waitemata Harbour; Wineries

B Bay of Plenty (pp.58–59)
Kaimai-Mamaku Forest Park; Katikati; Mount Maunganui; Nga Tapuwae o Toi Walkway; Paengaroa; Papamoa Beach; Whakaari/White Island

C Coromandel (pp.54–55)
Cathedral Cove; Coromandel Coastal Walkway; Coromandel Forest Park; Driving Creek Railway and Potteries; Hahei; Hot Water Beach; Opoutere Beach; Te Whanganui-A-Hei Marine Reserve

D Eastland (pp.64–65)
East Cape Lighthouse; Lake Waikaremoana; Mahia Peninsula; Mount Hikurangi; St Mary's Church; Tairawhiti Museum; Te Urewera National Park; Tolaga Bay Wharf; Wineries

Island Bay, Wellington

E Hawke's Bay (pp.68–69)
Boundary Stream Mainland Island; Cape Kidnappers gannet colony; Hawke's Bay wineries; Napier art deco; Te Mata Peak; Te Awanga; Waimarama Beach

F Lake Taupo (pp.62–63)
Aratiatia Rapids; Huka Falls; Lake Taupo; Mine Bay rock carvings; Orakei Korako; Wairakei Geothermal Power Project; Volcanic Activity Centre

G Manawatu (pp.72–73)
Manawatu Gorge; Mokai Canyon; Pipiriki; Pukaha Mount Bruce National Wildlife Centre; Rangitikei River; Tararua Forest Park; Whanganui National Park; Whanganui River

H Northland (pp.44–45)
Bay of Islands; Cape Reinga; Doubtless Bay; Hokianga Harbour; Kauri Museum; Kerikeri; Mission House; Ninety Mile Beach; Pompallier; Poor Knights Islands; Russell; Tutukaka; Waipoua Kauri Forest; Waitangi National Reserve

I Rotorua (pp.60–61)
Buried Village; Hell's Gate and Wai Ora Spa; Lake Rotorua; Lake Tarawera; Mount Tarawera; Polynesian Spa; Rotorua Museum of Art and History; Tamaki Maori Village; Wai-o-Tapu Thermal Wonderland; Waimangu Volcanic Valley; Whakarewarewa

J Ruapehu (pp.66–67)
Army Museum Waiouru; Mount Ngauruhoe; Mount Ruapehu; Mount Tongariro; Pureora Forest Park; Raurimu Spiral; Tongariro Crossing; Tongariro National Park; Turoa Ski Area; Whakapapa Ski Area

K Taranaki (pp.70–71)
Dawson Falls; Egmont National Park; Forgotten World Highway; Govett-Brewster Art Gallery; Mount Taranaki; Parihaka; Puke Ariki; Pukeiti Rhododendron Trust; Surf Highway 45

L Waikato (pp.56–57)
'Hobbiton'; Kaimai Mamaku Forest Park; Mangapohue Natural Bridge; Mokau; Otorohanga Kiwi House; Pureora Forest Park; Raglan; Rangiriri Battle Site Heritage Centre; Waikato River; Waitomo Caves

M Wairarapa (pp.74–75)
Cape Palliser; Castlepoint; Greytown; Holdsworth; Lake Ferry; Martinborough; Palliser Bay; Putangirua Pinnacles; Tararua Forest Park; Wineries

N Wellington (pp.76–83)
Botanic Gardens; Cable Car; Kapiti Coast; Kapiti Island; Karori Wildlife Sanctuary; Matiu/Somes Island; Oriental Bay; Parliament Buildings; Red Rocks; Tararua Forest Park; Te Papa

PARKS & RESERVES

Mills Stream, Te Urewera National Park

Four of New Zealand's 14 national parks are found in the North Island. There are also many other protected areas, including some important wildlife sanctuaries and marine reserves. These protect a wide range of landscapes and marine areas, including unique volcanic landscapes, snow-capped mountains, majestic rivers, lakes, unspoilt forests, wetlands and historic sites.

A Egmont National Park
(Map 172, C3)

New Zealand's second oldest national park, Egmont National Park was created in 1900, and is located in **Taranaki**, about 25km south of New Plymouth. The park is centred around impressive **Mount Taranaki**, a 2518m dormant volcanic cone, and two older volcanoes, **Kaitake** and **Pouakai**. There are more than 300km of walking tracks in the 33534ha park, which lead through lush forest to waterfalls, wetlands and lookouts. Summit climbs are also popular, and skiing is available at the **Manganui Skifield**. The North Egmont visitors centre has interpretation about the mountain, activities and conservation work.

B Kapiti Island
(Map 178, B1)

Kapiti Island, about 50km north of Wellington and 5km off the west coast, is a significant site for bird recovery. The 1965ha island is a protected wildlife sanctuary where pests have been eradicated and native birds and animals re-established, including some rare species. Kapiti Island is also rich in Maori and European history. Visitor numbers are limited to 50 people per day; the surrounding marine reserve offers spectacular underwater scenery and excellent diving. Visits are also possible to the island's northern end, where accommodation is available.

C Pukaha Mount Bruce National Wildlife Centre
(Map 176, D6)

Pukaha Mount Bruce National Wildlife Centre, 133km north-east of Wellington in the **Tararua** district, is an important native wildlife sanctuary in a 1000ha remnant of lowland forest. The centre runs captive breeding programmes for threatened species. Wildlife at the centre include kiwi, kokako and tuatara. There are daily feeding sessions for eels and kaka, and some good walks through the ancient forest; guided tours are also available.

D Pureora Forest Park
(Map 167, J4)

This magnificent 78000ha podocarp forest, about 45km west of Taupo, was saved from logging in the 1970s. The park has giant totara trees, rich bird life, a 12m observation tower and uncovered logs from a forest buried in the Taupo eruption 1800 years ago. Long and short walks are available, including to the summits of 1165m **Mount Pureora** and 1042m **Mount Titiraupenga**; hunting is possible in the park's north section, but requires a permit.

E Te Urewera National Park
(Map 170, B3)

Located in the **Eastland** region, about 50km north-west of Wairoa, this remote 212672ha National Park is home to the Tuhoe tribe. Its unspoilt forests are richly populated with bird life, and there are many tracks and huts. The beautiful lakes and rivers are popular for swimming, boating and fishing, and **Lake Waikaremoana** is skirted by a 46km walk, one of New Zealand's nine 'Great Walks'. Bookings are required all year for huts on the track. The township of **Aniwaniwa** has a visitor centre, motor camp and museum, and a beautiful one-hour walk leads to **Lake Waikareiti**.

North Island

F Tiritiri Matangi Island

(Map 157, G5)

This beautiful 210ha wildlife sanctuary, 30km north-east of Auckland and 4km off the coast of the **Whangaparaoa Peninsula**, is one of the world's most successful conservation projects. Volunteers have replanted the island with more than 280 000 native trees; predators have been eliminated, and rare native birds and animals established. There are many archaeological sites of early Maori occupation, and an 1864 lighthouse with associated buildings. The island also has a small visitor centre and shop.

G Tongariro National Park

(Map 168, B5)

A dual World Heritage Area due to its cultural and geological significance, Tongariro National Park protects three active volcanoes, **Mount Tongariro**, **Mount Ngauruhoe** and **Mount Ruapehu**, given to the nation by the Ngati

Tane Mahuta in Waipoua Kauri Forest

Tuwharetoa tribe. The 79 598ha park was created in 1887; it was the country's first national park, and the world's fourth. Located on the North Island's central plateau, about 60km south-west of Taupo, Tongariro National Park offers excellent walking, mountaineering, rock climbing and snow sports. The park's many tracks lead through varied forests and to spectacular waterfalls; the **Tongariro Crossing**, known as one of New Zealand's best one-day walks, leads through an extraordinary volcanic landscape.

H Waipoua Kauri Forest

(Map 154, C4)

This beautiful 13 384ha forest area is a remnant of the grand kauri forests which once covered New Zealand's far north, but were destroyed by logging and fire. Located in **Northland**, about 50km north of Dargaville, Waipoua Kauri Forest is home to the largest living kauri tree, 51m **Tane Mahuta**; the tree **Te Matua Ngahere** (Father of the Forest) has a trunk diameter of more than 5m, and is estimated to be 2000 years old. An 18km section of State Highway 12 leads through the forest, and there are a number of walking tracks.

I Whanganui National Park

(Map 173, H3)

Whanganui National Park, about 35km north of Wanganui, protects the **Whanganui River**, New Zealand's longest navigable waterway, which flows 290km from the mountains to the Tasman Sea. The park's rich forests surround the river, which was once a major thoroughfare for Maori and later also for European settlers. Maori culture is still strong in the area. The river is canoeable for more than 200km, and the five-day 145km canoe trip from **Taumarunui** to **Pipiriki** is classed as a 'Great Walk';

in summer, passes are required to use the huts and campsites beside the river. Bird life is plentiful in the park, and there are many short and long walks.

J Whirinaki Forest Park

(Map 169, H3)

This 55 000ha park adjoins the western side of Te Urewera National Park, and was a conservation battleground in the 1970s as protesters fought to prevent logging of the forest. Whirinaki Forest Park is the site of massive, awe-inspiring trees; the terrain varies from river flats to gorges and waterfalls. A network of trails leads through the park; the **Whirinaki Circuit** is a popular 4–5 day hike, and there are some excellent short walks. Hut tickets are required on the Circuit. Hunting is also possible.

National Park Information

Auckland Information Centre
Ferry Bldgs, Quay St, Auckland
Ph: (09) 379 6476

Wellington Conservation Information Centre
Government Bldgs Historic Reserve,
Lambton Quay, Wellington
Ph: (04) 472 7356

www.doc.govt.nz

WINERIES

Palliser Estate Vineyard, Martinborough

The North Island was the scene of New Zealand's earliest grape growing and wine production; the missionary Samuel Marsden introduced grape vines at **Kerikeri** in 1819, and the first wines were made by British government representative James Busby, who planted a vineyard near **Waitangi** in 1833.

In 1851, **Mission Vineyards** was established in **Hawke's Bay** by French Catholic missionaries, to produce sacramental and table wine; the company still operates today. By the end of the 19th century there were a number of small commercial vineyards in Hawke's Bay, **Auckland** and **Northland**.

Croatian immigrants were some of the country's earliest wine makers, planting small vineyards around west Auckland; among them were the now well-known names of Babich, Brajkovich, Selak, Nobilo and Delegat. By the 1950s, the majority of New Zealand's 80 wineries were Yugoslav-owned.

New Zealand wines first began achieving international success in the 1980s; today, the North Island's important wine regions include Hawke's Bay, **Gisborne** and the **Wairarapa**. Wine production continues to be a growing industry, with new vineyards being planted throughout many of the North Island's wine regions.

Many wineries welcome visitors and offer tastings, and a growing number have restaurants. Informative wine tours are possible in most of the wine production areas, and wine festivals draw huge crowds.

A Auckland
(pp.96-97)
New Zealand's three largest wine producers are based in Auckland, and make wine predominantly from grapes supplied from vineyards in other regions, as well as a small amount grown locally. All three companies are of Croatian origin; north-west Auckland is where Croatian immigrants established New Zealand's commercial wine industry, and some vineyards have been in commercial production for 70 years. Wineries in the area today are based around **Kumeu–Huapai** and **Henderson**, and are known for their pinot gris, chardonnay and Bordeaux-style reds. South of

Auckland, **Clevedon** is a developing wine area, and produces merlot, malbec, cabernet franc and Bordeaux-styled blends, as well as some unusual Verona-style Italian wines. There are also a handful of wineries around **Waiuku** and **Drury**.

B Gisborne
(pp.92-93)
Long hours of hot sunshine and clay loam soils make Gisborne an excellent area for wine production. Vines were first planted there in the 1850s, and wines were first made in the 1920s by German winemaker Friedrich Wohnsiedler. Gisborne is known as the chardonnay capital of New Zealand. Just over half the region's plantings are in chardonnay, but gewürztraminer, semillon, chenin blanc and merlot are also produced, and viognier and pinot gris look likely to have a bright future. Gisborne chardonnay is known for being highly drinkable at a young age; chardonnay only six months old can be delicious, a result of the hot climate ripening grapes to a high level with low acidity. Each year the **International Chardonnay Challenge** attracts hundreds of entries; the annual events of the **Wine and Food Festival** and **Taste Gisborne** are also popular.

C Hawke's Bay
(pp.108-109)
One of New Zealand's major wine regions, Hawke's Bay is blessed with long, hot summers and cool winters. Farmers made some of New Zealand's earliest table wines there in the 1890s; the area is home to the country's oldest surviving wine producer, **Mission Vineyards**, first set up by French missionaries, and now in operation for over 150 years. Many of Hawke's Bay's

North Island

wineries cluster around **Havelock North**, with others west of **Napier**, and north in the **Esk Valley**. There's an excellent wine museum at **Church Road Winery**, and wine festivals and events — including a charity wine auction — draw visitors throughout the year. Hawke's Bay produces excellent chardonnay, sauvignon blanc, merlot, cabernet sauvignon, cabernet franc, pinot noir and syrah; for many years, the region has been a consistent winner of international trophies.

D Matakana

(pp.96-97)

Only an hour's drive from Auckland, this rural coastal area has been planted with grapes since the 19th century. Today it's a burgeoning wine region with a growing reputation for pinot gris, chardonnay, Bordeaux-style red wine blends, and even the famous Tuscan red, sangiovese.

E Northland (pp.152-153)

The Northland region has a long history of wine making; New Zealand's first vine plantings were made at **Kerikeri** in 1819, and the first wine at **Waitangi** in 1833. Northland today is an emerging wine region with strong wine making potential. An impressive new development on the **Karikari Peninsula** has major plantings and a winery restaurant in a dramatic setting with coastal views. Chardonnay, syrah, cabernet franc, pinotage and malbec are all grown in Northland.

F Waiheke Island (p.96-97)

This pretty island in the **Hauraki Gulf**, a 35-minute ferry ride from Auckland, is home to an increasing number of wineries in its lush valleys. Waiheke's first vineyard was established in 1978; over the last 20 years, some very successful Bordeaux-style reds have been

produced. Cabernet sauvignon, cabernet franc, malbec and merlot are all grown on the island.

G Waikato/Bay of Plenty

(p.160)

There are just a few wineries and tiny plantings of grapes in this farming and horticultural area. At **Te Kauwhata**, the government established a Viticultural Research Station in 1902; the picturesque station building is still home to a winery. The region produces chardonnay, pinot noir, sauvignon blanc, gewürztraminer, dessert wines, fortified wines and kiwifruit wine.

H Wairarapa

(p.106)

Relatively new on New Zealand's winemaking scene, the Wairarapa has become an important area for wine production. The area around **Martinborough** produces some of the country's most impressive pinot noirs, which have been winning international awards since the 1980s. The versatile Wairarapa also makes good merlot,

chardonnay, gewürztraminer, sauvignon blanc, riesling and pinot gris. Martinborough's village square is surrounded by vineyards, and the annual **Toast Martinborough** festival draws thousands of wine lovers to the area each November. Recently, the wine production region has expanded to the north, and a handful of wineries now cluster around **Gladstone** and **Masterton**.

Green chardonnay grapes on vine, Hawke's Bay

NORTHLAND

Known for its mild sub-tropical climate, the beautiful area of Northland offers spectacular coastal scenery, lush forests and fascinating Maori and European history. Northland's west coast has secluded, dramatic surf beaches, huge harbours and sand dunes; the east coast offers sandy beaches, rocky islands and world-class diving. Kayaking, snorkelling, sailing, fishing, swimming with dolphins and boat cruises are all popular activities.

The area was settled early by Maori, and many people trace their ancestry back to the Polynesian explorer Kupe, who landed his canoe on the shores of the **Hokianga Harbour**. Europeans first settled in Northland in the late 18th century, and the region is dotted with historic, pretty towns. The many historic sites include New Zealand's oldest stone building and oldest house in **Kerikeri**, and the **Treaty House** in **Waitangi**, where the 1840 treaty, seen as the country's founding document, was signed between Maori and European leaders.

The timber milling industry of the 19th century logged much of the region's majestic kauri forests, but the giant trees can still be seen in a few areas, particularly in impressive **Waipoua Kauri Forest**.

Cape Reinga

The Pacific Ocean meets the Tasman Sea at Cape Reinga, and views from the lighthouse over the windswept sea are spectacular. In Maori legend, Cape Reinga is believed to be the departure place for the spirits of the dead. South of the cape, **Ninety Mile Beach** is one of New Zealand's best surfcasting beaches.

main attractions

◈ **Bay of Islands**

Historic towns and beautiful coastal scenery are a focus in the Bay of Islands, the site of New Zealand's first permanent European settlement.

◈ **Doubtless Bay**

Doubtless Bay has beautiful white-sand beaches, and offers excellent swimming, snorkelling, fishing and sailing.

◈ **Hokianga Harbour**

This unspoilt, peaceful harbour has huge sand dunes and small, picturesque villages.

◈ **Kauri Museum**

Matakohe's wonderful Kauri Museum explores the region's long involvement with its kauri forests through excellent displays.

◈ **Poor Knights Islands**

Warm currents, clear water and plentiful marine life provide excellent diving in this marine reserve, 24km from the east coast.

◈ **Russell**

Now an elegant, historic town in the Bay of Islands, Russell was originally a fortified Maori settlement and later a rugged port.

◈ **Waipoua Kauri Forest**

Giant kauri trees in this forest sanctuary, a remnant of the once extensive northern kauri forests, include the 1400-year-old tree Tane Mahuta.

◈ **Waitangi**

One of New Zealand's most historic places, Waitangi was the site of the 1840 signing of the Treaty of Waitangi between Maori and European leaders.

ⓘ Visitor information

Bay of Islands i-SITE Visitor Centre
The Wharf, Marsden Rd, Paihia
Ph: (09) 402 7345
www.northlandnz.com

Whangarei i-SITE Visitor Centre
92 Otaika Rd, Tarewa Park, Whangarei
Ph: (09) 438 1079
www.whangareinz.org.nz

Coastal farmland, Northland

North Island

Scale 1:1 050 000

0   40
kilometres

A   B   C   D   E

PACIFIC OCEAN

1

Cape Reinga (Te Rerengawairua)
Spirits Bay (Piwhane Bay)
North Cape (Otou)
Cape Maria Van Diemen
+310
Te Hapua
Waitiki Landing
Parengarenga Harbour

Te Kao

Great Exhibition Bay

2

Simmonds Islands
Moturoa Islands
Cape Karikari (Whakapouaka)
Rangaunu Bay
Pukenui
Houhora Heads

Kaimaumau

Tokerau Beach
Doubtless Bay
Cavalli Islands
Coopers Beach
Hihi
Taupo Bay
Whangaroa Bay
Motukawanui Island
Waipapakauri Beach
Taipa
Mangonui
Kaingaroa
377
10
Totara North
Whangaroa
Takou Bay

3

i **Kaitaia**
Ahipara Bay
Rangitihi
Peria
Kaeo
Ahipara
Parapara
Pukepoto
Bay Of Islands
Cape Brett
Tauroa Point (Reef Point)
N.F.P.
Waipapa
Kerikeri
Rawhiti
Manukau
Mangamuka Bridge
+744
N.F.P.
Waitangi
Russell
Parekura Bay
Herekino
Umawera
Okaihau
i Paihia
Okiato
Rotokakahi
Kohukohu
Horeke
Ohaeawai
Oromahoe
Waikare
Whangaruru North
Panguru
Ngawha
Pakaraka
11
Whangaruru
Karetu
Whangaruru South
Motuti
Rawene
Kaikohe
Moerewa
Kawakawa
N.F.P.
Whangaruru Bay
Rangi Point
Ngawha Springs
Tuhipa
Helena Bay
Poor Knights Islands

4

Whirinaki
Waima
12
Oponom
Omapere
+781
Hukerenui
Whananaki
Sandy Bay
Matapouri
Hokianga Harbour
NORTHLAND
Hikurangi
626
FOREST
Pipiwai
Purua
Hikurangi
PARK
697
Ngunguru
12
Aranga
Titoki
Poroti
Ngunguru Bay
Kaihu
Maungatapere
WHANGAREI *i*
Pataua
14
Portland
Parua Bay
Omamari
Tangiteroria
Whangarei Harbour
Oakleigh
Marsden Bay
Maungakaramea
Mangapai
N.F.P.
Ruakaka
Bream Head
Hen & Chickens Islands

5

Dargaville *i*
Mangawhai River
Waiotira
Bream Bay
Waipu
Baylys Beach
Te Kopuru
Mititai
Langs Beach
Taranga Island
Waipu Cove
Mangawhai Heads
Glinks Gully
Paparoa
Maungaturoto
Mangawhai Point
Raupo
12
Matakohe
Hakaru
Ruawai
Pahi
Whakapirau
Kaiwaka

6

TASMAN SEA
Kellys Bay
Tinopai
Port Albert
Pakiri
Kaipara Harbour
Tapora
Wellsford
437
Omaha
16
Matakana
North Head
Pouto Point
South Head
i Warkworth
Buckleton Beach
Kaipara Entrance
Kaipara Flats
Snells Beach
357
Mahurangi
Shelly Beach
Puhoi
Kaukapakapa
Waiwera
i Silverdale
Orewa
Parakai
Waitoki
Stillwater
Dairy Flat

NINETY MILE BEACH

© TERRALINK INTERNATIONAL LIMITED 2006

Joins map 47

NORTH ISLAND   45

AUCKLAND

Combining a cosmopolitan urban environment with stunning outdoor attractions, the Auckland region is more than just New Zealand's biggest population centre.

With outstanding shopping, museums and its own Polynesian cultural flavour, **Auckland city** has all the vibrancy of a modern urban centre, along with scenic harbours teeming with boats — not for nothing is Auckland called the 'City of Sails'.

Nearby, however, is a host of outdoor attractions and recreation opportunities. To the west of the city are forest parks and the stunning **Piha** and **Karekare** beaches, dramatic enough to become iconic movie settings. To the south-east there is the **Pacific Coast Highway** and the **Seabird Coast**, including hot springs and a bird reserve at **Miranda**.

To the north there are wineries at **Matakana**, more beautiful beaches and the **Goat Island** marine reserve, while visitors to the **Hauraki Gulf** islands can see volcanoes, historic villages and native bird sanctuaries. Outstanding wineries can be found all over the Auckland region. Warm weather means that visitors will find something to do all year round.

West Coast Beaches

This is an area of wild natural beauty just 45 minutes west of Auckland. Beaches at **Piha** are popular with surfers — though sometimes dangerous — while **Karekare**'s dramatic beach became iconic in the film *The Piano*. Nature lovers will appreciate the gannet colony at **Muriwai Beach** and forest walks in the nearby **Waitakere Ranges**.

main attractions

◈ **Clevedon**
A burgeoning wine district, Clevedon Valley offers a genuine country experience plus excellent dining and wineries.

◈ **Goat Island**
Located at the north of the region, Goat Island was New Zealand's first marine reserve and is fantastic for snorkelling.

◈ **Great Barrier Island**
This rugged and beautiful island offers beaches, hiking, hot springs, lush forests and ecotourism.

◈ **Matakana**
The Matakana region is home to boutique accommodation, wineries, arts and crafts, and a Saturday morning farmers' market.

◈ **Miranda**
Located on the Seabird Coast south-east of the city, Miranda is renowned for its shorebird colony and its hot springs.

◈ **Sky Tower**
The tallest building in the southern hemisphere, Sky Tower has great views of the city. Casinos, bars and theatres form part of the Sky City complex.

◈ **Tiritiri Matangi Island**
This is a beautiful wildlife sanctuary. Many of New Zealand's rare native birds, including the takahe, kokako and stitchbird, can be found here.

◈ **Waiheke Island**
The popular Hauraki Gulf island includes a historic village, wineries, restaurants, beaches and great nature walks.

◈ **Whangaparaoa Peninsula**
This holiday spot offers parks, beaches, boating and golf courses, with the Waiwera Hot Springs just to the north.

Auckland harbour and city

 Visitor information

New Zealand i-SITE Visitor Centre
137 Quay St, Princes Wharf, Auckland
Ph: 0800 AUCKLAND
www.aucklandnz.com

North Island

Scale 1:1 050 000

0   40 kilometres

PACIFIC OCEAN

TASMAN SEA

WHANGAREI
Hikurangi
Hukerenui
Purua
Maungatapere
Titoki
Poroti
Tangiteroria
Maungakaramea
Portland
Oakleigh
Mangapai
N.F.P.
Dargaville
Mititai
Te Kopuru
Glinks Gully
Raupo
Ruawai
Matakohe
Pahi
Paparoa
Whakapirau
Kellys Bay
Tinopai
Pouto Point
Maungaturoto
Kaiwaka
Hakaru
Mangawhai Point
Mangawhai Heads
Waipu Cove
Langs Beach
Waipu
Bream Bay
Ruakaka
Marsden Bay
Pataua
Parua Bay
Ngunguru
Ngunguru Bay
Matapouri
Sandy Bay
Bream Head

Hen and Chickens Islands
Taranga Island

Parry Channel
Bream Head Channel

Mokohinau Islands
Fanal Island (Motukino)
Aiguilles Island
Rakitu Island (Arid Island)
Port Fitzroy
Kaikoura I (Selwyn I)
Broken Is (Pig Is)
Okiwi
Claris
Great Barrier Island (Aotea Island)
Tryphena

Jellicoe Channel
Craddock Channel
Colville Channel

Cuvier Island (Repanga Island)

Cape Rodney
Leigh
Omaha
Matakana
Warkworth
Kaipara Flats
Snells Beach
Mahurangi
Puhoi
Waiwera
Orewa
Silverdale
Stillwater
Whangaparaoa
Wellsford
Tapora
Port Albert
Pakiri
Kaiwaka

Omaha Bay
Buckleton Beach
Kawau Bay
Kawau Island
Motuora Island
Mahurangi Harbour
Whangaparaoa Bay
Whangaparaoa Peninsula

HAURAKI GULF

Cape Colville
Moehau 892
Colville
Little Bay
Amodeo Bay
Papaaroha
Whangapoua
Kennedy Bay
Kuaotunu West
Matarangi
Opito
Ohinau Island
Coromandel
Te Kouma

Mercury Bay
Mercury Islands (Iles D'Haussez)
Great Mercury Island (Ahuahu)
Red Mercury Island (Whakau)

Shelly Beach
Harbour
North Head
Kaipara Entrance
South Head
Kaukapakapa
Parakai
Helensville
Albany Village
Riverhead
Woodhill
Huapai
Kumeu
North Shore
Waitoki
Dairy Flat

Tiritiri Matangi Island
Whangaparaoa Peninsula
The Noises
Rangitoto Island
Motutapu I
Rakino I
Waiheke Island
Oneroa
Onetangi
Cowes
Orapiu
Rotoroa I
Ponui Island (Chamberlins Island)
Pakihi Island
Whitianga
Manaia
Cooks Beach
Hahei
Hot Water Beach
COROMANDEL PENINSULA

AUCKLAND
Muriwai Beach
Te Henga (Bethells Beach)
Piha
Karekare
Little Huia
Whatipu
Wattle Bay
Manukau Harbour
Kawakawa Bay
Clevedon
Tamaki Strait
Grahams Beach
Orua Bay
Matakawau
Pollok
Glenbrook Beach
Clarks Beach
Karaka
Kingseat
Ramarama
Drury
Manurewa
Papakura
Kohukohunu 688
Orere Point
Te Mata
Tapu
Waiomu
Ruamahunga
Te Puru
FIRTH OF THAMES
Kaiaua
Miranda
Thames
Coroglen
Tairua
Shoe Island
Tairua Harbour
Pauanui
Slipper Island (Whakahau)
Opoutere
FOREST

Waiuku
Waipipi
Patumahoe
Pukekohe
Pokeno
Mercer
Tuakau
Meremere
Bombay
Maramarua
Mangatangi
Mangatawhiri
Waitakaruru
Turua
Matatoki
Puriri
Kopu
Ngatea
Kerepehi
Patetonga
Turua
Tirohia
Mackaytown
Karangahake
Paeroa
Waikino
Waihi
Waihi Beach
Whangamata
Whiritoa
RANGE
KAIMAI RANGE
PARK
Whakamoehau 750

Otaua
Te Kohanga
Onewhero
Pukekawa
Port Waikato
Glen Murray
Rangiriri
Naike
Te Kauwhata
Taniwha
Lake Waikare
Mangatarata
Lake Whangape
Waikokowai
Rotowaro
Pukemiro
Glen Afton
Taupiri
Whitikahu
Orini
Mangateparu
Springdale
Tahuna
Te Aroha
Te Aroha 953
Waihou
Katikati
Omokoroa Beach
Manawaru
Te Aroha West
Waitoa
Hungahunga
Walton
Waharoa
Turangaomoana
McLaren Falls
Okauia
Tauranga Harbour
Opureora

Glen Massey
Waingaro
Horsham Downs
Gordonton
Motumaoho
Ngaruawahia
Morrinsville
Eureka
Tauwhare
Te Miro
Horotiu
Whatawhata
Hamilton
Raglan Harbour (Whaingaroa)
Raglan
Mt Karioi 756
Te Uku
Te Mata
Ngahinapouri
Cambridge
Matamata
Tauhei
Te Poi
Whitehall
Hinuera

Waikato River
Waipa River

© TERRALINK INTERNATIONAL LIMITED 2006

AUCKLAND CITY

main attractions

◈ **Auckland Art Gallery**

This gallery houses an extensive collection of New Zealand art, including the iconic portraits of Maori people by Charles Goldie.

◈ **Auckland War Memorial Museum**

This museum boasts one of the best artefact collections in New Zealand, and has daily Maori cultural shows.

◈ **Devonport**

The relaxed suburb of Devonport has two volcanoes, museums, naval relics, 19th century buildings, cafés and shops.

◈ **Kelly Tarlton's Antarctic Encounter & Underwater World**

Visitors can see sharks, stingrays and fish swim around them, and an Antarctic world with penguins and a replica of Scott's 1911 hut.

◈ **Parnell**

A spot of old Auckland, Parnell contains historic buildings and churches along with some of the best restaurants in the city.

◈ **Ponsonby Road**

One of Auckland's best-known café spots, Ponsonby Road also has a good range of houseware and fashion shops.

◈ **Sky Tower**

The Sky Tower is the tallest building in the southern hemisphere, and offers spectacular views of the city and harbours.

◈ **THE EDGE entertainment precinct**

At the central hub of downtown Auckland, THE EDGE includes the Aotea Centre, Civic Theatre, Auckland Town Hall and a popular weekend market in Aotea Square.

◈ **Waitemata Harbour**

Auckland's 'City of Sails' reputation is most evident here. Boat trips, ferries to Hauraki Gulf islands and dolphin safaris are available.

◈ **Viaduct Basin**

Waterfront cafés, bars, nightclubs and the National Maritime Museum make this a vibrant spot.

New Zealand's most cosmopolitan city, Auckland is the gateway to the country for most visitors. With 1.2 million people calling it home it is New Zealand's largest city, and with about a quarter of them of either Maori or Pacific Island descent, it's also the largest Polynesian city in the world.

Known by Maori as **Tamaki Makau Rau** (Tamaki of 100 lovers), Auckland was first settled by Maori in about 1000AD. Europeans arrived in the 1830s, and it became the first capital of New Zealand in 1840, a status it held until 1865. Since then it has become the commercial hub of the country. Called the 'City of Sails' by locals, most of Auckland is nestled between the **Waitemata** and **Manukau** harbours and the city is surrounded by some 48 extinct volcanic cones. With its harbours, warm climate, urban lifestyle, Pacific culture and a multitude of outdoor attractions in the city or nearby, Auckland is a vibrant city with plenty to offer residents and visitors.

facts

- ◈ Population: 1.2 million
- ◈ Date founded: 1840
- ◈ Tallest building: Sky Tower (328m)
- ◈ Oldest buildings: Hulme Court (1843); worker's cottage, 1 Bankside Street (between 1841 and 1847)
- ◈ Average temperature: 23.1°C (January), 14.3°C (July)

 Visitor information

New Zealand i-SITE Visitor Centre
137 Quay St, Princes Wharf, Auckland
Ph: 0800 AUCKLAND
www.aucklandnz.com

Sky Tower at night

Places of Interest

Albert Park **A** D3
Aotea Square **B** C3
Auckland Art Gallery **C** D3
Auckland Domain **D** D5
Auckland Harbour Bridge **E** A1
Auckland Library **F** C3
Auckland Town Hall **G** C3
Auckland War Memorial Museum **H** E4
Britomart **I** D2
Bruce Wilkinson Collection **J** D3
Civic Theatre **K** C3
Karangahape Road **L** C4
Kinder House **M** E4
Kingsland **N** A6
National Maritime Museum **O** C2
Newmarket **P** E5
Parnell Road **Q** E4
Ponsonby Road **R** A3
Queen Street **S** C4
Sky Tower **T** C3
Viaduct Basin **U** C2
Victoria Market **V** B3
Waitemata Harbour **W** B1

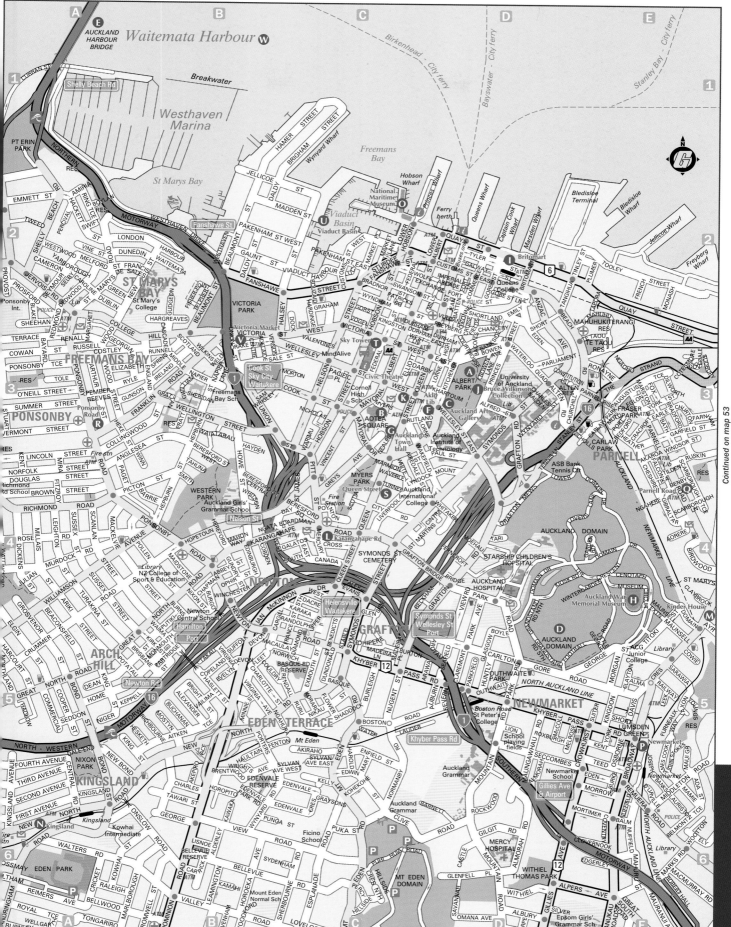

Continued on map 53

Auckland's attractions are well-spread. Public transport may be a good idea to help get around in the central city; traffic is often very heavy and parking is costly. However, much of it can be covered in a walk. A car may be best for visiting attractions in the suburbs.

Walking tour of central Auckland

The best place to start is probably **Britomart**, the central train and bus terminal. **Waitemata Harbour** is just to the north; ferries to the **Hauraki Gulf** or just for a trip on the harbour can be caught from here. From the ferry terminal walk west towards the **National Maritime Museum**, where displays of New Zealand's seafaring past from Maori waka (canoes) to the America's Cup can be found. Close by is **Viaduct Basin**, an area built for the America's Cup regatta in 2000. Though the cup was taken from New Zealand in 2004, Viaduct Basin remains one of Auckland's favourite café and bar spots.

From here head south along Hobson Street to the **Sky Tower**, the syringe-shaped tower which at 328m is the tallest building in the

Mission Bay, Auckland

southern hemisphere. There's a charge to enter the main viewing area and an extra fare to get to the top viewing floor; both provide spectacular views. Once back on firmer ground, the adjoining **Sky City** complex has restaurants, bars, casinos and two hotels.

Walk east along Wellesley Street to **Queen Street**, Auckland's main street and the main haven for shopaholics. On the corner of Queen Street and Wellesley Street is the recently-restored **Civic Theatre**, well worth a look if there's a show on for its 1920s décor and starry ceiling. Just to the south is **Aotea Square**, a great spot to relax. There are theatres at the adjoining **Aotea Centre**, with cinemas to the north, while on the south side is the **Auckland Town Hall**. The square itself hosts a market on Saturdays.

Further east on Wellesley Street is the **Auckland Art Gallery**, which contains a fine collection of New Zealand art, contemporary and historic. It's especially worth looking for the turn of the century Maori portrait paintings by Charles Goldie. Close by is **Albert Park**, the central city's prettiest green space, featuring flower collections, statues and the **Bruce Wilkinson Collection** of antiques.

About 15 minutes' walk to the east is **Auckland Domain**, the largest park in the central city area. On the park's east side is **Auckland War Memorial Museum**. One of the best collections in the country, it has great sections on natural history, art and especially Maori culture. A short walk south-east of the museum is **Kinder House**, an 1857 stone building which houses the art and memorabilia of the Rev Dr John Kinder, and the restored 1860s **Ewelme Cottage**.

Viaduct Basin, Auckland

A walk north from here is **Parnell Road**, which contains more historic buildings and some of Auckland's best cafés and restaurants.

The centre of Auckland's café culture, just west of the central city, is **Ponsonby Road**, accessible by bus from Britomart. Relaxed but hip, the shops are worth checking out as well as the coffee. Ponsonby Road's southern intersection joins onto **Karangahape Road**, or K Road. The stretch of K Road east from here to Queen Street is the centre of the city's night-time youth culture with its ethnic eating spots, cafés and clubs.

Suburban attractions

Many of Auckland's attractions are in the suburbs, and though public transport visits most of them, it is not always frequent and a car is probably the best way to get to these.

East of the central city along the seaside **Tamaki Drive** is **Kelly Tarlton's Antarctic Encounter & Underwater World**. This spectacular aquarium takes people on a conveyor belt past sharks, stingrays and a variety of other marine life. It also has an Antarctic area complete with penguins and a replica of Scott's 1911 Antarctic

FESTIVALS AND EVENTS

Auckland's calendar is crowded with festivals and events, including the biennial **Auckland Arts Festival** and yearly **Waiheke Island Wine Festival**, both held in February.

As befits the largest Polynesian city in the world, the **Pasifika Festival** is an annual highlight. Held in March, this festival attracts more than 200 000 to enjoy food, art, performance, and anything else to do with Pacific culture. For art lovers, May offers the annual **Comedy Festival** and the **Auckland Writers and Readers Festival** (held biennially).

The renowned **All Blacks** national rugby team usually plays in Auckland between June and August. Also popular are **New Zealand Fashion Week** in October, and November's **Ellerslie Flower Show**.

Rarotongan dancers, Pasifika Festival

Auckland War Memorial Museum

base. Further east is **Mission Bay**, which has fine beaches and cafés.

South of the city centre are several of Auckland's **volcanoes**, many of which have parks around them. Among the most interesting are **Mt Eden**, **One Tree Hill** and **Mt Wellington**. A little further south is **Otara Market** (Sunday mornings only), a fabulous slice of Auckland's Maori and Pacific Island community life. A little further south, in **Manukau City**, is **Rainbow's End**, the largest adventure park in New Zealand and a perfect place for restless children. Further south are the **Auckland Regional Botanic Gardens**, in **Manurewa**.

A little north-east of Otara Market is **Howick Historical Village**, an award-winning collection of 30 restored 19th century buildings, where your guides are all in period costume.

One of the main tourist spots west of the central city is **Western Springs**. This is host to the **Auckland Zoo**, an attractively laid out zoo noted for its meerkat and primates enclosures and its nocturnal house, where kiwi can be found. Adjoining it is the **Museum of Transport and Technology**, or **MOTAT**, two parks that have great exhibits of old trains, cars, and planes.

Auckland's **North Shore** is suburban but it has some lovely beaches. One highlight is **Devonport**, which is easily accessible by ferry from the central city. Its retail area retains a Victorian feel, and there are interesting galleries, antique shops and cafés. The suburb includes two volcanoes; **Mt Victoria**, north of the shops, has fabulous views, and **North Head**, to the east, contains many old naval fortifications. The **Navy Museum** is also in Devonport, to the west of the retail area.

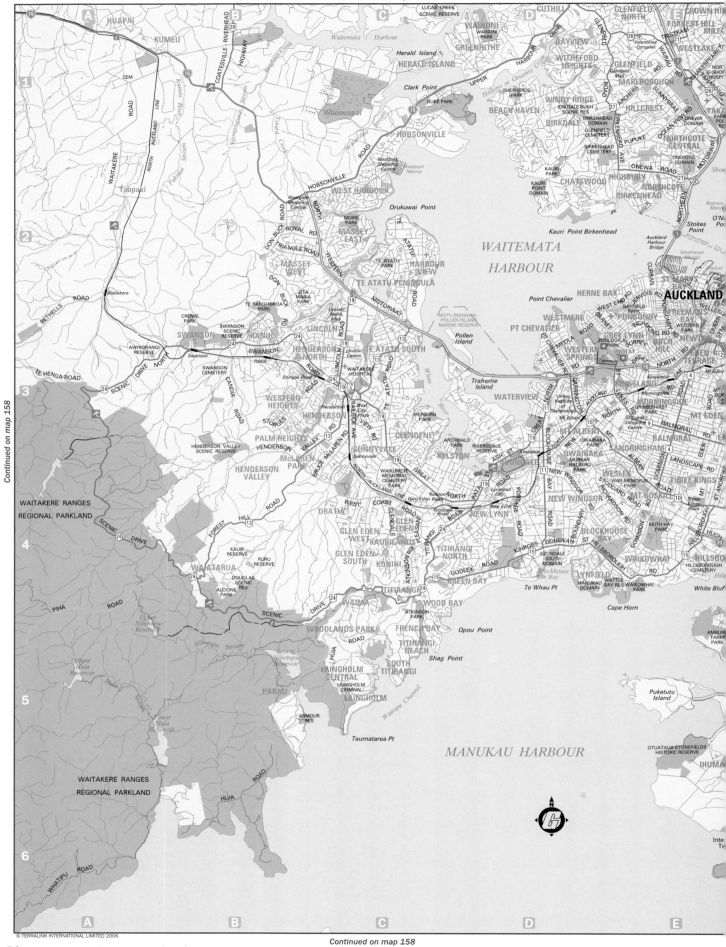

Continued on map 158

Auckland

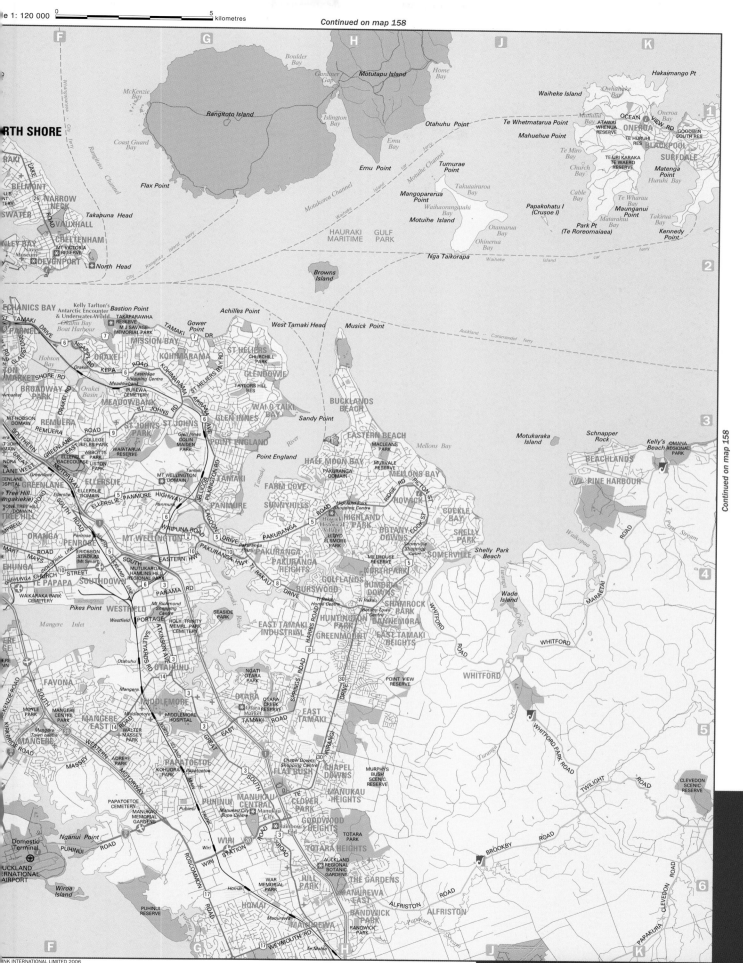

Scale 1 : 120 000

0   5
kilometres

NORTH SHORE

© INK INTERNATIONAL LIMITED 2006

COROMANDEL

Less than an hour's drive from Auckland, the Coromandel Peninsula is justly famous for its magnificent scenery. This narrow, rugged strip of land lies between sheltered **Hauraki Gulf** bays to the west and breathtaking Pacific coast surf beaches to the east.

The region's gold mining and kauri logging past is much in evidence and features in many excellent museums and historic displays, such as the **Goldmine Experience** in **Thames**. Remnants of the original kauri forest can still be seen, most notably from the **309 Road**. The forest-clad interior ranges provide first-rate hiking and nature-watching opportunities. Walkers and cyclists are well catered for, and boating, diving and fishing charters operate in most of the settlements dotted along the coast.

The Coromandel is known for its beautiful beaches, including the unique **Hot Water Beach** on the Pacific coast, where thermally heated spring water bubbles through the sand at low tide. Accommodation, cafés and restaurants can be found to suit most tastes and budgets, and good galleries and craft markets operate in several of the small towns.

Coromandel Forest Park

The mountainous Coromandel Forest Park stretches for almost the whole length of the peninsula. The Coromandel's most rugged terrain lies within its boundaries, including 892m **Mt Moehau**, the peninsula's highest point. A wide range of walking tracks lead through the park, which is home to many species of native flora and fauna.

 Visitor information

Coromandel i-SITE Visitor Centre
355 Kapanga Rd, Coromandel
Ph: (07) 866 8598

Thames i-SITE Visitor Centre
206 Pollen St, Thames
Ph: (07) 868 7284
www.coromandelnz.com

Hot Water Beach, Coromandel

main attractions

❖ **309 Road**
This unsealed road between Coromandel town and Whitianga features great sightseeing, including the Kauri Grove, Waiau Falls and Castle Rock extinct volcano.

❖ **Coromandel Coastal Walkway**
This 7km walkway along the remote and beautiful north coast takes three to four hours.

❖ **Driving Creek Railway and Potteries**
A unique narrow-gauge railway runs through a natural bush setting, and incorporates a pottery and wildlife sanctuary.

❖ **Goldmine Experience**
This Thames-based guided tour explores a gold stamper battery and goldmine. There is an associated museum and colony of cave weta (a large native insect).

❖ **Hot Water Beach**
Thermal springs located at the beach's low tide mark allow visitors to enjoy their own mineral spa dug out of the sands, free of charge.

❖ **Opoutere Beach**
The unspoilt white sand beach of Opoutere provides superb surfing and a safe swimming environment for families.

❖ **Te Whanganui-A-Hei Marine Reserve**
This stunning 900ha marine reserve provides diving, kayaking and sightseeing opportunities through the beautiful Cathedral Cove area.

Cathedral Cove, Hahei, Coromandel Peninsula

North Island

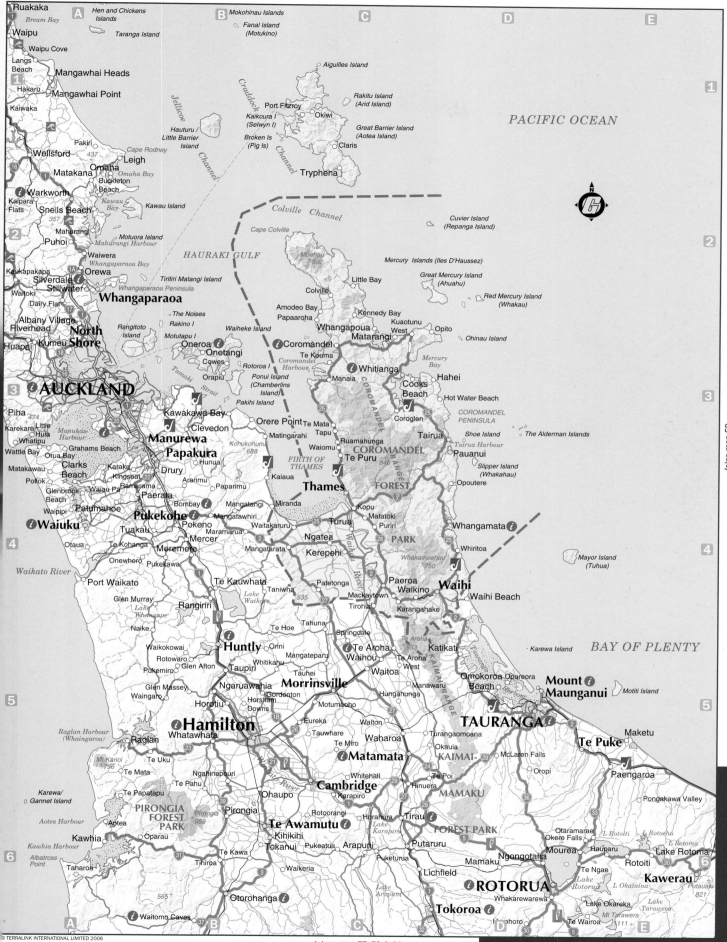

Ruakaka
Bream Bay
Waipu
Waipu Cove
Langs Beach
Hakaru
Mangawhai Heads
Mangawhai Point
Kaiwaka

Hen and Chickens Islands
Taranga Island

Mokohinau Islands
Fanal Island (Motukino)

PACIFIC OCEAN

Aiguilles Island

Pakiri
Wellsford
Leigh
Matakana
Omaha
Warkworth
Buckleton Beach
Snells Beach
Mahurangi
Puhoi
Kaukapakapa
Orewa
Silverdale
Stillwater
Dairy Flat
Albany Village
Riverhead
Whangaparaoa
North Shore
Kumeu
Huapai
Waitoki

Cape Rodney
Omaha Bay
Kawau Bay
Kawau Island
Motuora Island
Mahurangi Harbour
Waiwera
Whangaparaoa Peninsula

Jellicoe Channel
Craddock Channel

Hauturu / Little Barrier Island

Port Fitzroy
Kaikoura I (Selwyn I)
Broken Is (Pig Is)
Okiwi
Claris
Tryphena

Rakitu Island (Arid Island)
Great Barrier Island (Aotea Island)

HAURAKI GULF

Colville Channel
Cape Colville

Cuvier Island (Repanga Island)

Tiritiri Matangi Island
Whangaparaoa Bay
Rangitoto Island
The Noises
Rakino I
Motutapu I
Waiheke Island

Moehau 892

Little Bay
Colville
Amodeo Bay
Papaaroha
Whangapoua
Matarangi
West
Kennedy Bay
Kuaotunu
Opito

Mercury Islands (Iles D'Haussez)
Great Mercury Island (Ahuahu)
Red Mercury Island (Whakau)
Ohinau Island

AUCKLAND
Piha
Karekare
Little Huia
Whatipu
Wattle Bay
Matakawau
Pollok
Glenbrook Beach
Waipipi
Patumahoe
Waiuku

Oneroa
Onetangi
Cowes
Rotoroa I
Orapiu
Kawakawa Bay
Clevedon
Manurewa
Papakura
Drury
Grahams Beach
Karaka
Kingseat
Ramarama
Bombay
Pukekohe
Pokeno
Tuakau
Te Kohanga
Meremere
Mercer
Maramarua
Otaua
Onewhero
Pukekawa

Tamaki Strait
Pakihi Island
Ponui Island (Chamberlins Island)
Coromandel
Te Kouma
Manaia
Te Mata
Tapu
Te Puru

Whitianga
Cooks Beach
Hahei
Hot Water Beach
Coroglen
Tairua

COROMANDEL PENINSULA
Shoe Island
The Alderman Islands
Mercury Bay

Kohukohunu 688
FIRTH OF THAMES
Kaiaua
Miranda
Kopu
Matatoki
Puriri

Ruamahunga
Waiomu
COROMANDEL
FOREST
Pauanui
Slipper Island (Whakahau)
Opoutere

Waikato River
Port Waikato
Glen Murray
Rangiriri
Naike
Te Kauwhata
Taniwha
Lake Waikare
Ngaruawahia
Huntly
Taupiri
Horotiu
Hamilton
Whatawhata
Raglan

Thames
Turua
Ngatea
Kerepehi
Mangatarata
Patetonga
Mackaytown
Tirohia
Paeroa
Waikino
Karangahake
PARK
Whangamata
Whiritoa

Waihi
Waihi Beach
Mayor Island (Tuhua)

BAY OF PLENTY
Karewa Island

Morrinsville
Springdale
Te Hoe
Orini
Whitikahu
Tauhei
Gordonton
Horsham Downs
Eureka
Tauwhare
Te Miro
Matamata
Whitehall
Hinuera

Te Aroha
Waihou
Te Aroha West
Waitoa
Manawaru
Waharoa
Turangaomoana
Okauia
McLaren Falls
Oropi

KAIMAI
Omokoroa Beach
Opureora
Mount Maunganui
TAURANGA
Te Puke
Maketu
Motiti Island

Cambridge
Karapiro
Ohaupo
Rotoorangi
Te Awamutu
Kihikihi
Tokanui
Pukeatua
Arapuni
Puketurua
Putaruru
Lichfield
Tirau
Te Poi
MAMAKU
FOREST PARK

PIRONGIA FOREST PARK
Pirongia 959
Pirongia
Ohaupo
Horahora
Lake Karapiro

Raglan Harbour (Whaingaroa)
Mt Karioi 756
Te Uku
Te Mata
Ngahinapouri
Te Pahu
Te Papatapu

Karewa/ Gannet Island
Aotea Harbour
Kawhia
Kawhia Harbour
Albatross Point
Taharoa
Oparau
Aotea
Te Kawa
Tihiroa
Waikeria
Otorohanga
Waitomo Caves

Horahora
Putaruru
Mamaku
Ngongotaha
Mourea
Haparu
Lake Rotoma
Lake Rotoiti
Lake Rotoehu
L Rototii
L Rotoma

ROTORUA
Whakarewarewa
Tokoroa
Lichfield
Te Ngae
Lake Okareka
Mt Tarawera 1111+
Te Wairoa
Lake Tarawera
Kawerau
Putauaki 821
Lake Rotoma

Otaramarae
Okere Falls
Pongakawa Valley
Paengaroa

© TERRALINK INTERNATIONAL LIMITED 2006

Joins map 59

WAIKATO

Jet boating on the Waikato River

The lush green farming region of the Waikato is the epitome of pastoral New Zealand, with its sheep, cattle and deer farms and horse breeding industry. The majestic **Waikato River**, New Zealand's longest, winds its way through the Waikato and through the main city of **Hamilton**, a centre for students which offers cafés, cinemas, theatres and lovely themed riverside gardens.

Appealing small towns dot the Waikato countryside, and for nature lovers the region has bush-clad mountains, beautiful waterfalls and hot thermal pools, with surf beaches on the west coast. The **Waitomo Caves**, part of a subterranean network of caves over hundreds of kilometres, are the biggest natural attraction, and visitors can explore the underground river, starry glow-worm caves and limestone formations by boat and foot.

Long occupied by Maori descended from the ancestral Tainui canoe, the Waikato was the scene of fierce battles between Maori and European settlers in the mid 19th century. Defensive earthworks from the 1863–64 fighting can be seen at **Rangiriri**. **Turangawaewae Marae** in the small town of **Ngaruawahia** is the official residence of the Maori Queen.

Pureora Forest Park

Saved from logging in the 1970s by tree-dwelling protesters, this magnificent forest area has giant totara trees and a 12m observation tower which gets visitors up among the treetops. The park's spectacular bird life includes the endangered kokako, kaka (native parrot) and parakeets.

main attractions

◈ **Kaimai-Mamaku Forest Park**

This 45 000ha park offers visitors luxuriant forests, plunging waterfalls, old gold-mining trails and many walking tracks.

◈ **Kawhia**

Kawhia, a fishing port on a pretty harbour, is sacred to Waikato Maori as the final landing place of their ancestral Tainui canoe.

◈ **Mangapohue Natural Bridge**

This stalactite-studded 17m limestone arch is a relic from an ancient underground river system. 30-million-year-old oyster fossils can be seen nearby.

◈ **Otorohanga Kiwi House**

Kiwi are bred in captivity at the Kiwi House, where a nocturnal viewing house allows visitors to watch active kiwi digging for food.

◈ **Raglan**

Internationally known for its left-hand surf break, this appealing character town on a peaceful harbour is also home to many artists.

◈ **Te Aroha**

A spa town in Victorian days, Te Aroha has hot springs, the 3.5m soda water Mokena Geyser, and elegant buildings.

◈ **Tirau**

An array of creative corrugated iron buildings and sculptures, along with arts and crafts outlets, make Tirau worth a visit.

◈ **Waikato River**

New Zealand's longest river, of great importance to Waikato Maori, offers many chances for recreation as it flows from Lake Taupo to the Tasman Sea.

◈ **Waitomo Caves**

These 30-million-year-old caves have beautiful limestone formations and glow-worms. Boat trips take visitors through the 18m Cathedral cavern.

 Visitor information

Hamilton i-SITE Visitor Centre
Cnr Bryce and Anglesea Sts, Hamilton
Ph: (07) 839 3580
www.waikatonz.co.nz

Balloon Festival over the city of Hamilton

North Island

TASMAN SEA

BAY OF PLENTY

© TERRALINK INTERNATIONAL LIMITED 2006

Joins maps 59 & 61

BAY OF PLENTY

The Bay of Plenty was named by English navigator Captain James Cook, who sailed into the bay in 1769 aboard his ship the *Endeavour*. The area has long been home to Maori; the landing places of ancestral canoes which brought migrants across the Pacific can be seen at **Maketu**, **Mauao** and **Whakatane**, and the region is dotted with the sites of historic pa (fortified villages).

One of New Zealand's sunniest regions, the Bay of Plenty is a thriving horticultural area with a particular focus on kiwifruit. Gorgeous white-sand beaches, fringed by red-flowering pohutukawa trees, stretch along the coastline. Water activities on offer include surfing, swimming, boating and deep sea fishing. Visitors can swim with dolphins; dive or snorkel in the fascinating undersea environment of **Mayor Island (Tuhua) Marine Reserve**; or visit the unique volcanic landscape of **Whakaari/White Island**. Walking trails lead through areas of beautiful forest, and adventure activities include white water rafting, jet boating and skydiving.

Fast-growing **Tauranga**, the region's main city, has excellent shopping and restaurants, and the associated town of **Mount Maunganui** is a relaxed beach resort.

main attractions

◈ **Kaimai-Mamaku Forest Park**

Many walking tracks lead through this 45 000ha park, which has luxuriant forests, plunging waterfalls and old gold-mining trails.

◈ **Katikati**

Murals of pioneer life and a walkway featuring haiku carved into river stones make Katikati worth a visit.

◈ **Mount Maunganui**

'The Mount' is a thriving beach resort with a beautiful white-sand beach, rocky islands, hot saltwater springs and the historic mountain of Mauao.

◈ **Nga Tapuwae o Toi Walkway**

This beautiful 16km walkway, close to Whakatane, passes sea cliffs, historic sites of Maori settlement, bird colonies, forest and secluded bays.

◈ **Paengaroa**

Paengaroa and adjacent area 'The Junction' offer adventure tourism, fishing, wildlife parks, a theme park, craft and honey shops.

◈ **Papamoa Beach**

This lovely white-sand beach is great for swimming and surfing.

◈ **Tauranga**

The energetic city of Tauranga has restaurants, shopping, cultural activities and an attractive waterfront.

◈ **Mayor Island (Tuhua)**

This beautiful island, a dormant volcano, has interesting geological forms of lava and black obsidian, and rich marine life in a marine reserve.

Crater Lake, Whakaari/White Island

Whakaari/White Island

This 324ha island, 50km off shore, is New Zealand's most active volcano, and its extraordinary landscape bubbles, steams and rumbles with thermal activity. Attempts to mine the island's sulphur have all been abandoned due to eruptions and mud flows. 'Whakaari is privately owned, but guided tours visit the island by boat or helicopter.

 Visitor information

Tauranga i-SITE Visitor Centre
95 Willow St, Tauranga
Ph: (07) 578 8103
www.bayofplentynz.com

View of beach and historic mountain of Mauao, Mount Maunganui

North Island

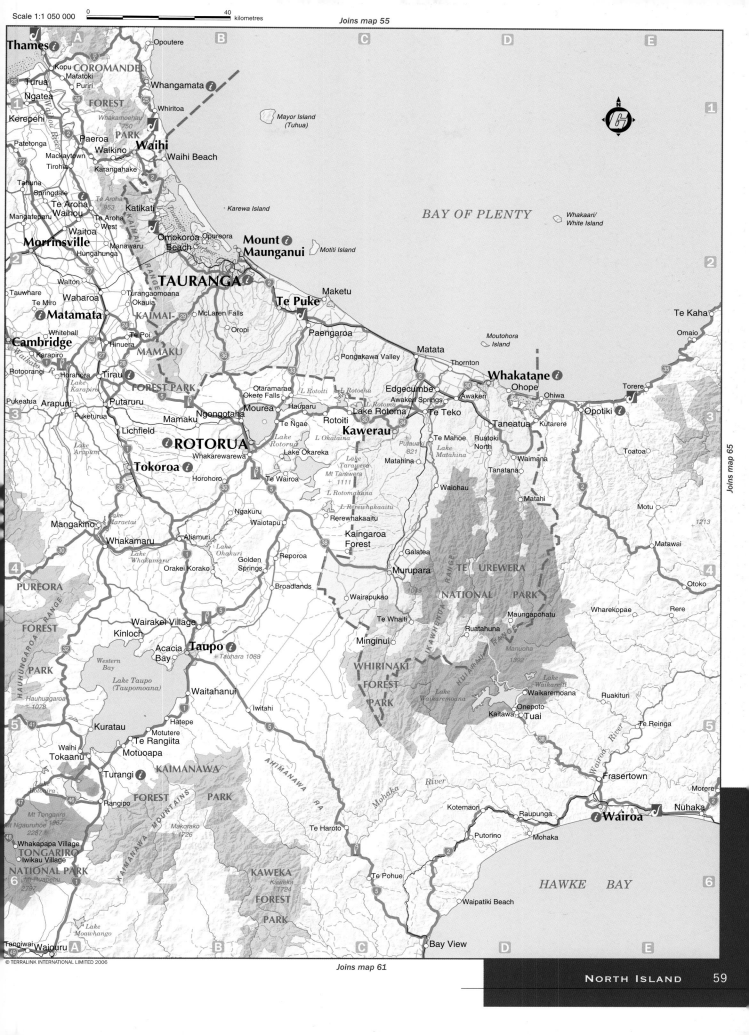

Scale 1:1 050 000

0   40
kilometres

BAY OF PLENTY

Whakaari/
White Island

Thames

Kopu COROMANDEL
Matatoki
Turua   Puriri
Ngatea   FOREST
Kerepehi

Opoutere

Whangamata

Whiritoa
Patetonga
Mackaytown   Waikino   Waihi
Tirohia   Karangahake   Waihi Beach
Tahuna
Springdale
Te Aroha   Katikati
Mangateparu   Waihou
Waitoa   Te Aroha
West
Morrinsville
Hungahunga   Omokoroa
Manawaru   Beach   Opureora

Karewa Island

Mayor Island
(Tuhua)

Mount
Maunganui

Motiti Island

Moutohora
Island

Te Kaha
Omaio

Tauwhare   Waharoa   Turangaomoana
Te Miro   Okauia
Matamata   McLaren Falls
Whitehall   Te Poi   Oropi
Cambridge   Hinuera
Karapiro   KAIMAI-
Rotoorangi   MAMAKU
Horahora   Tirau
Arapuni   Putaruru   FOREST PARK
Pukeatua   Puketurua
Lichfield   Mamaku   Ngongotaha
Whakarewarewa
ROTORUA

TAURANGA

Te Puke   Maketu

Paengaroa
Pongakawa Valley
Matata
Thornton
Edgecumbe
Awakeri Springs   Whakatane
Otaramarae   Lake Rotoma   Awakeri   Ohope
Okere Falls   Rotoiti   Te Teko   Ohiwa
Hauparu   Taneatua
Te Ngae   Kawerau   Kutarere
Mourea   Te Mahoe   Opotiki
Lake   Ruatoki
Okataina   North
Waimana

Torere

Toatoa

Tokoroa
Horohoro
Te Wairoa
Whakamaru   Atiamuri
Mangakino   Ngakuru   Waiotapu
Waioeka   Reporoa
Orakei Korako   Golden
Springs   Rerewhakaaitu
Broadlands   Kaingaroa
Forest
Galatea
Murupara
Wairapukao
Te Whaiti
Minginui
Ruatahuna

Matahina
Waiohau
Tanatana
Matahi

Motu
Matawai

Otoko

Wharekopae   Rere

Maungapohatu

TE UREWERA
NATIONAL PARK

PUREORA
FOREST
PARK
Wairakei Village   WHIRINAKI
Kinloch   FOREST
Acacia   PARK
Bay   Taupo
Waitahanui
Kuratau   Hatepe   Iwitahi
Motutere
Waihi   Te Rangiita
Tokaanu   Motuoapa   KAIMANAWA
Turangi   FOREST   PARK
Rangipo
KAIMANAWA
MOUNTAINS

Western
Bay

Lake Taupo
(Taupomoana)

Te Haroto

Waikaremoana
Onepoto
Kaitawa   Tuai

Te Reinga

Frasertown
Morere
Wairoa
Nuhaka

TONGARIRO
NATIONAL PARK
Whakapapa Village
Iwikau Village

KAWEKA
FOREST
PARK

AHIMANAWA RA

Mohaka River

Kotemaori
Raupunga
Putorino   Mohaka

Te Pohue
Waipatiki Beach

HAWKE
BAY

Bay View

Waiouru

© TERRALINK INTERNATIONAL LIMITED 2006

ROTORUA

Main street, Rotorua

Set 297m above sea level on the North Island's central volcanic plateau, the Rotorua region has long been the scene of volcanic activity. This geothermal activity manifests itself in hot pools, volcanically-formed lakes, and uniquely beautiful thermal landscapes with geysers, coloured mineral terraces, boiling mud and steaming vents.

Home to Maori since the 14th century, the Rotorua area became a major tourist destination in the 19th century. Visitors from around the world were drawn there by the **Pink and White Terraces**, two beautiful silica terraces of multi-levelled pools. The terraces were destroyed in 1886 when **Mount Tarawera** erupted, devastating the surrounding area and killing more than 150 people. Despite the destruction, visitors have continued to flock to the area's thermal attractions, beautiful lakes and adventure activities.

Rotorua is also a major centre for Maori culture, and the local Te Arawa tribe has been involved with tourism for more than a century. Maori concerts, performances, food and arts and crafts are all on offer; expert carvers and weavers demonstrate their craft at **Te Puia**.

 Visitor information

Rotorua i-SITE Visitor Centre
1167 Fenton St, Rotorua
Ph: (07) 348 5179
Freephone: 0800 768 678
www.rotoruanz.com

Rotorua lakes

The region's 16 beautiful lakes were formed and shaped by volcanic activity. Most offer swimming, boating, kayaking and fishing; scenic walks lead around **Lake Okataina** and **Lake Tikitapu (Blue Lake)**. Informative cruises take passengers out on **Lake Tarawera**, including to thermal **Hot Water Beach**.

main attractions

◈ **Adventure activities**

White water rafting and sledging are popular on nearby rivers, and there are luge rides and adventure activities at Mount Ngongotaha and the Agrodome.

◈ **Maori cultural attractions**

Rotorua offers Maori cultural performances and concerts, as well as exhibitions and demonstrations of traditional arts and crafts.

◈ **Mt Tarawera & the Buried Village**

Displays at the Buried Village focus on the devastating 1886 eruption of Mt Tarawera. Excavated buildings can also be seen.

◈ **Polynesian Spa**

Spa treatments, massage and hot thermal pools on Lake Rotorua's shores are all on offer at this award-winning spa complex.

◈ **Rotorua Museum of Art and History**

This excellent museum, in a historic spa building, features beautiful Maori artworks and displays about Mount Tarawera's eruption.

◈ **Tamaki Maori Village**

Visitors can take in a concert and hangi (traditionally cooked meal) at this replica pre-European village.

◈ **Wai-O-Tapu Thermal Wonderland**

Craters, blowholes, mineral terraces and the Lady Knox Geyser can all be seen at Wai-O-Tapu.

◈ **Waimangu Volcanic Valley**

There are lovely walks in this thermally active valley, created by the eruption of Mount Tarawera.

◈ **Whakarewarewa**

Rotorua city's largest thermal reserve features geysers, including world-famous Pohutu, and is also home to Maori cultural activities.

Whakarewarewa, Rotorua

North Island

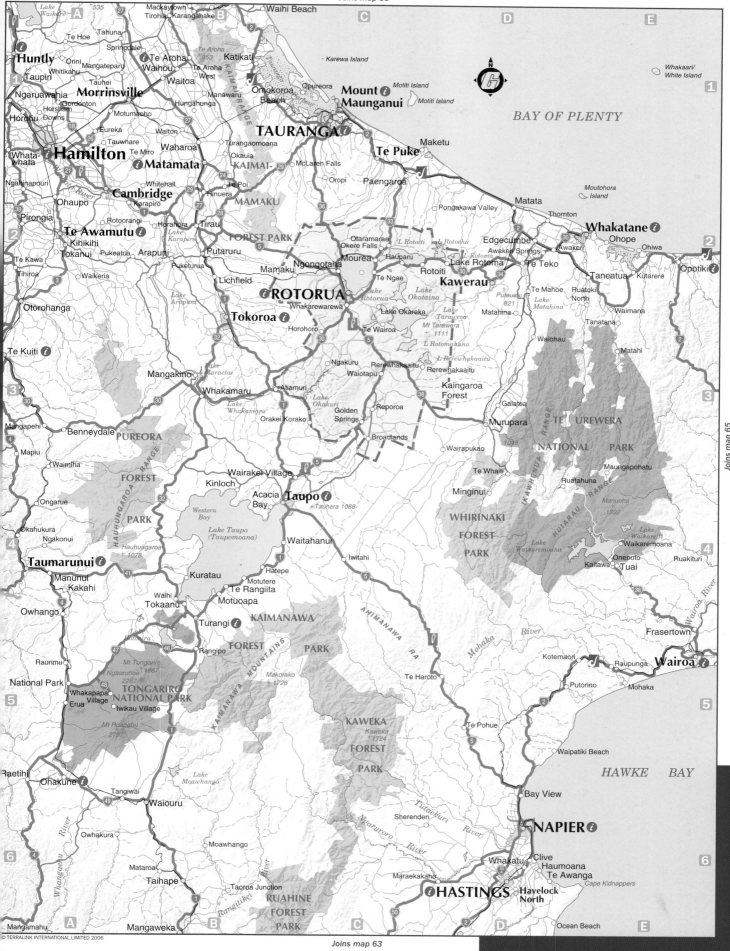

Scale 1:1 050 000

0   40
kilometres

BAY OF PLENTY

Whakaari/
White Island

Huntly
Lake Waikare
Te Hoe
Tahuna
Mackaytown
Tirohia
Karangahake
Waihi Beach
Springdale
Orini
Mangateparu
Whitikahu
Te Aroha
Katikati
Taupiri
Waihou
Te Aroha West
Morrinsville
Waitoa
Omokoroa Beach
Opureora
Motiti Island
Ngaruawahia
Gordonton
Motumaoho
Manawaru
Mount
Motiti Island
Horsham Downs
Hungahunga
Maunganui
Horotiu
Eureka
Walton
TAURANGA
Whata-whata
Tauwhare
Te Miro
Waharoa
Hamilton
Te Mapara
Te Puke
Maketu
Ngahinapouri
Te Poi
Matamata
Turangaomoana
Okauia
McLaren Falls
Oropi
Paengaroa
Matata
Whitehall
Hinuera
Moutohora
Cambridge
KAIMAI-
Pongakawa Valley
Island
Ohaupo
Rotoorangi
Horahora
Tirau
Thornton
Pirongia
Lake Karapiro
MAMAKU
Whakatane
Te Awamutu
Arapuni
Putaruru
FOREST PARK
Otaramarae
Edgecumbe
Ohope
Kihikihi
Pukeatua
Okere Falls
Awakeri Springs
Ohiwa
Tokanui
Puketurua
Mamaku
Ngongotaha
Mourea
Hauparu
Awakeri
Te Kawa
Lichfield
L Rotoiti
L Rotoehu
Kawerau
Te Teko
Opotiki
Tihiroa
ROTORUA
Te Ngae
Lake Rotoma
Waikeria
Whakarewarewa
Te Mahoe
Ruatoki North
Waimana
Otorohanga
Tokoroa
Lake Okareka
Pukaki
Taneatua
Kutarere
Horohoro
Lake Okataina
Matahina
Mt Tarawera
L Matahina
Tanatana
Te Kuiti
Mangakino
Ngakuru
Rerewhakaaitu
Matahi
Reporoa
L Rotomahana
Waiotapu
Rerewhakaaitu
Waiohau
Mangapehi
Whakamaru
Atiamuri
Golden Springs
Kaingaroa Forest
Galatea
Benneydale
PUREORA
Lake Whakamaru
Orakei Korako
Murupara
TE UREWERA
Mapiu
Lake Ohakuri
Broadlands
Maungapohatu
Waimiha
FOREST
Wairapukao
Te Whaiti
NATIONAL PARK
Ruatahuna
Ongarue
PARK
Wairakei Village
Te Whaiti
Manuoha
Okahukura
Kinloch
Minginui
Ngakonui
Acacia Bay
Taupo
WHIRINAKI
Lake Waikareiti
Taumarunui
Western Bay
Tauhara 1068
FOREST
Waikaremoana
Manunui
Waitahanui
PARK
Onepoto
Kakahi
Lake Taupo (Taupomoana)
Iwitahi
Kaitawa
Tuai
Ruakituri
Kuratau
Hatepe
Owhango
Waihi
Motutere
Te Rangiita
AHIMANAWA RA
Frasertown
Tokaanu
Motuoapa
Raurimu
Turangi
KAIMANAWA
Mohaka River
Wairoa
National Park
FOREST
Rangipo
Mt Tongariro 1967
PARK
Makorako 1726
Kotemaori
Raupunga
Mt Ngauruhoe 2287
KAIMANAWA MOUNTAINS
Te Haroto
Putorino
Mohaka
TONGARIRO NATIONAL PARK
Whakapapa Village
Erua
Iwikau Village
Mt Ruapehu 2797
KAWEKA
Kaweka 1724
Te Pohue
FOREST
Waipatiki Beach
Raetihi
PARK
HAWKE BAY
Ohakune
Tangiwai
Lake Moawhango
Bay View
Waiouru
Owhakura
Sherenden
NAPIER
Moawhango
Ngaruroro River
Whakatu
Clive
Mataroa
Haumoana
Taihape
Te Awanga
Cape Kidnappers
Taoroa Junction
Maraekakaho
HASTINGS
Havelock North
RUAHINE
Mangamahu
FOREST
Ocean Beach
Mangaweka
PARK

© TERRALINK INTERNATIONAL LIMITED 2006

LAKE TAUPO

Lake Taupo and its surrounding landscape, in the central North Island, were created by awesome volcanic forces. The lake itself is the caldera of a huge volcano which erupted with incredible force around 181AD; the resulting pillar of ash was more than 50km high, and the eruption's effects were noted as far away as Italy and China. Volcanic activity continues in the area today, with thermal areas and hot springs dotting the region, and electricity produced by geothermal steam at **Wairakei**.

World famous for its trout fishing, the resort town of **Taupo** is busy in summer, and activities on offer for the adventurous include skydiving, jet boating, abseiling, and bungy jumping from a platform high above the **Waikato River**. Water sports on the lake include swimming, waterskiing, kayaking and sailing.

Turangi, at Lake Taupo's southern end, is a centre for adventure activities and trout fishing, with fishing particularly good on the **Tongariro River**; there are also many beautiful walks. Turangi is a base for trips into **Tongariro National Park**, an important and spectacular World Heritage Area.

 Visitor information

Taupo i-SITE Visitor Centre
Tongariro St, Taupo
Ph: (07) 376 0027
www.laketauponz.com

Lake Taupo

New Zealand's largest lake at 616km², Lake Taupo was created by a huge, week-long volcanic eruption around 181AD. The lake offers excellent trout fishing, and is a popular spot for many water sports; there are Maori rock carvings at **Mine Bay**.

main attractions

◈ **Adventure activities**

Thrill seekers can enjoy bungy jumping, skydiving, abseiling, jet boating, kayaking and white water rafting.

◈ **Aratiatia Rapids**

Water rushes through these rapids at 90 000 litres per second when the control gates are opened on the hydro-electric Aratiatia Dam.

◈ **Craters of the Moon**

Mud pools, bubbling craters and steam make this thermal area worth visiting.

◈ **Huka Falls**

A huge volume of water hurtles through a narrow channel at these impressive falls on the Waikato River.

◈ **Kaimanawa Forest Park**

Walks lead through beautiful beech forest and tussock grassland in this forest park.

◈ **Orakei Korako**

This lovely thermal area, with its coloured silica terraces and beautiful pools, is reached by boat across a lake.

◈ **Thermal hot springs**

Thermal mineral springs in Taupo and Tokaanu provide relaxing hot bathing; at Tokaanu, a walk leads among bubbling mud and hot pools.

◈ **Tongariro National Trout Centre**

This trout hatchery features interpretive displays and an underwater trout viewing chamber.

◈ **Trout fishing**

The Taupo region is known internationally for its excellent trout fishing. Visitors can fish independently, with a guide, or from a boat on the lake.

◈ **Volcanic Activity Centre**

At this interactive educational centre, visitors can learn about the region's geothermal features. The centre has seismographs, an earthquake simulator, a shop and more.

◈ **Wairakei Geothermal Power Project**

5% of NZ's electricity is produced here geothermally, from what was originally one of the world's most thermally active areas.

Maori cliff carvings, Mine Bay, Lake Taupo

North Island

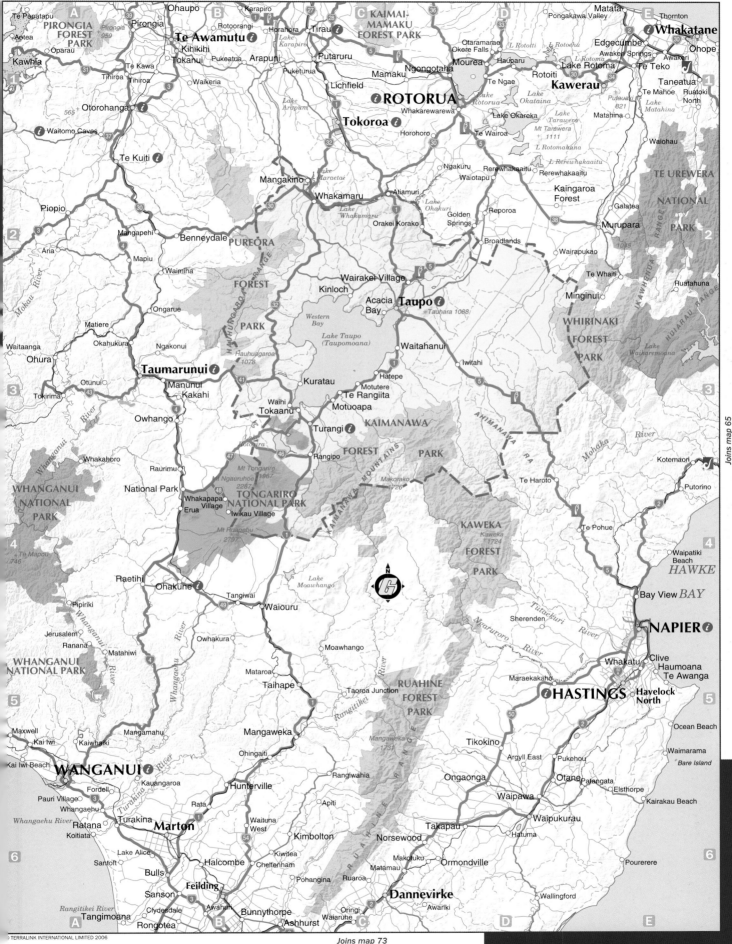

EASTLAND

Sunny, friendly and extremely laid back, the unspoilt region of Eastland has stunning beaches and forests, and is the first part of New Zealand to see the sun each day. Known locally as the East Coast, the region was the first landing place in New Zealand for early Maori migrants from the Pacific, and the first point seen by British explorer Captain James Cook. It remains strongly Maori and rural in character.

Eastland's biggest city, **Gisborne**, is home to the outstanding **Tairawhiti Museum**, and the first landing spots of both Maori arrivals and Captain Cook are nearby. Some of New Zealand's best chardonnay-producing wineries are in the countryside surrounding Gisborne. Inland is remote **Te Urewera National Park**, which has beautiful native forests and stunning **Lake Waikaremoana**.

The coast north of Gisborne is dotted with small villages; this is an area rich in history and natural beauty. There are unspoilt beaches and good fishing along most of the coast, an ornate Maori church at **Tikitiki**, the lighthouse at **East Cape**, and a fabulous drive between the cape and **Opotiki**.

East Cape Lighthouse

Visitor information

Gisborne i-SITE Visitor Centre
209 Grey St, Gisborne
Ph: (06) 868 6139
www.gisbornenz.com

Te Urewera National Park

One of the most stunning parts of New Zealand, lush native forests and beautiful lakes give this 212 672ha park a haunting, ethereal feel. Home to the Tuhoe iwi (Maori tribe), the park is rich in wildlife and history. **Lake Waikaremoana** is especially popular for fishing and hiking.

main attractions

◈ **Cook Landing Site National Historic Reserve**

This important historic reserve was the landing place of British explorer Captain James Cook in 1769, and of two ancestral Maori canoes, centuries earlier.

◈ **East Cape Lighthouse**

There are stunning sea views from this 154m lighthouse at the country's most easterly point.

◈ **Gisborne wineries**

Grapes have been grown in the area since the 1850s, and chardonnay is a specialty today.

◈ **Lake Waikaremoana**

The 46km walk around this beautiful lake in Te Urewera National Park is considered one of New Zealand's 'Great Walks'.

◈ **Mahia Peninsula**

There are forest walks, rock pools and beaches at this windswept, atmospheric coastal peninsula.

◈ **Pacific Highway**

The route around the coast from Opotiki to Gisborne offers spectacular views.

◈ **St Mary's Church**

Tikitiki's Anglican church is one of New Zealand's most ornate Maori churches.

◈ **Tairawhiti Museum**

This Gisborne museum houses an extensive collection reflecting the area's Maori and European heritage.

◈ **Tolaga Bay Wharf**

Built in 1936, Tolaga Bay's 660m wharf is one of the longest in the world.

◈ **Wainui Beach**

This outstanding beach near Gisborne offers some of the country's best surfing.

◈ **Waioeka Scenic Reserve**

New Zealand's largest scenic reserve is great for trout fishing, swimming and hiking.

Captain Cook statue, Gisborne

North Island

0   40
kilometres

BAY OF PLENTY

Whakaari/
White Island

Cape Runaway

Matakaoa Point

Hicks Bay
Hicks Bay

Waihau Bay

Te Araroa

Whanarua Bay

Awatere

East Cape

East Island

Matata
Thornton
Te Kaha
Edgecumbe
Whakatane
Ohope
Awakeri Springs
Ohiwa
Awakeri
Opotiki
Lake Rotoma
Te Teko
Taneatua
Kutarere
Kawerau
Te Mahoe
Ruatoki North
Waimana
Matahina
Tanatana
Waiohau
Matahi

Moutohora
Island

Omaio

Torere

Tikitiki

RAUKUMARA
FOREST PARK

Hikurangi
1752

Ruatoria

Hiruharama

Ihungia

Te Puia Springs

Waipiro Bay
Waipiro Bay

Tokomaru Bay
Tokomaru Bay

Toatoa

Motu

Motuoroi Island

1213

Kaingaroa Forest
Galatea
Murupara
Wairapukao
Te Whaiti
Minginui

TE UREWERA
NATIONAL PARK

Maungapohatu

Ruatahuna

Manoha
1392

Matawai

Whatatutu

Tolaga Bay
Tolaga Bay

Pourewa Island

WHIRINAKI
FOREST PARK

Wharekopae
Rere
Otoko
Te Karaka

Waipaoa

Waihau Bay

Lake Waikareiti

Waikaremoana
Ruakituri
Ngatapa
Waituhi
Ormond
Waiherere
496
Whangara

Lake Waikaremoana
Onepoto
Kaitawa
Tuai
Te Reinga

Patutahi

GISBORNE

Makorori

Manutuke

Poverty Bay
Tuaheni Point

Muriwai
Waingake

Young Nicks Head (Te Kuri)

Bartletts

Te Haroto

Frasertown

Morere

Mahanga Beach

Nuhaka
Oputama
Mahia

Kotemaori
Raupunga
Wairoa
Mahia Beach
Whangawehi

Putorino
Mohaka
Table Cape (Kahutara Point)

Te Pohue

MAHIA PENINSULA

Waipatiki Beach

HAWKE BAY

Portland Island

Bay View

N
G

NAPIER

Whakatu
Clive
Haumoana
Te Awanga
HASTINGS
Maraekakaho
Havelock North

Cape Kidnappers

Ocean Beach

RUAPEHU

Whakapapa Ski area

The Ruapehu region, on the North Island's Central Plateau, is a stunningly beautiful place with lush forests, snow-topped volcanic mountains and rushing rivers laden with trout. The area is dominated by the dramatic landscape of **Tongariro National Park**, New Zealand's first national park and a World Heritage Area, given to the nation by the area's Maori people.

The park's three active volcanoes, **Mount Ruapehu**, **Mount Ngauruhoe** and **Mount Tongariro**, offer first-rate scenery, snow sports, hiking and trout fishing. Mount Ruapehu is home to New Zealand's two biggest ski areas, and extraordinary walking routes lead through the park's unique volcanic landscapes. Scenes for *The Lord of the Rings* were filmed on the barren slopes of Ruapehu, acting as the forbidding realm of Mordor.

Winding through the wild lowland forests of the diverse **Whanganui National Park**, the historic **Whanganui River**, at 290km, is New Zealand's longest navigable river. River trips, fishing, bushwalking and visiting historic sites are popular activities here.

The small friendly settlements of **Ohakune**, **Waiouru**, **Raetihi** and **Taumarunui** are good places from which to explore the region's many treasures.

 Visitor information

Taumarunui i-SITE Visitor Centre
Hakiaha St, Taumarunui
Ph: (07) 895 7494

Ruapehu Information Centre
Clyde St, Ohakune
Ph: (06) 385 8427
www.visitruapehu.com

Tongariro National Park

This 79 598ha National Park and World Heritage Area was gifted to the country in 1887 by the Ngati Tuwharetoa tribe. The slopes of its three volcanic peaks — **Mounts Ruapehu**, **Tongariro** and **Ngauruhoe** — and the surrounding forests and rivers offer year-round adventure. Snow sports, cycling, hiking, climbing and fishing are popular, depending on the season.

main attractions

◈ **Army Museum Waiouru**
This fascinating Waiouru landmark explores New Zealand's military history.

◈ **Bayview Chateau Tongariro**
Built in the 1920s, this recently refurbished Georgian-style hotel offers stylish dining and accommodation facilities.

◈ **Pureora Forest Park**
There are long and short walks through this magnificent podocarp forest, saved from logging in the 1970s by tree-dwelling protesters.

◈ **Raurimu Spiral**
Regular scheduled services and vintage steam train rides are available on this engineering masterpiece, a stretch of railway line climbing 215m in just 11km.

◈ *The Lord of the Rings* **locations**
Mount Ngauruhoe stood in for menacing Mount Doom, and Pinnacle Ridge is where the Orcs attacked Elrond and his army.

◈ **Tongariro Crossing**
This strenuous 17km hike passes through a moon-like landscape, featuring the spectacular Red Crater and the gorgeous Blue and Emerald Lakes.

◈ **Turoa Ski Area**
This steep and exciting field has good chairlifts, a safe learner's area and panoramic views of forests and mountains.

◈ **Whakapapa Ski Area**
New Zealand's biggest and busiest ski field has 550ha of ski area and 400ha more terrain accessible by lift.

◈ **Whanganui National Park**
A trip down the mighty, historic Whanganui River is a good way to explore the park's unspoilt lowland forest.

Mount Ruapehu with reflection of Mount Ngauruhoe in mirror from the Desert Road

North Island

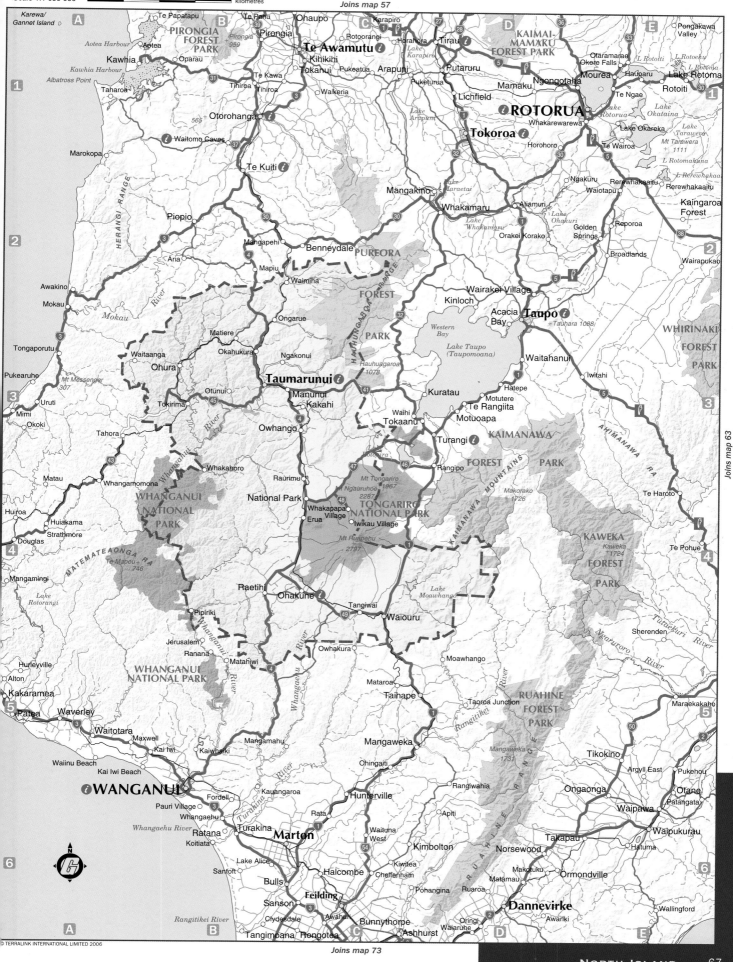

Scale 1:1 050 000

0   40
          kilometres

© TERRALINK INTERNATIONAL LIMITED 2006

HAWKE'S BAY

On the east coast of the North Island, Hawke's Bay is a thriving agricultural area, with a varied landscape of lovely rivers, fertile plains and dramatic coastal scenery.

Blessed with a hot, sunny climate, Hawke's Bay is a leading wine producer, and home to many gourmet food producers; weekends see farmers' markets selling fresh produce in some towns. Arts, crafts and culture are another focus, and the region offers a variety of arts festivals and the chance to visit artists at work.

The lively main cities of **Napier** and **Hastings** feature art deco architecture, and also offer excellent restaurants, shopping and cultural attractions.

Plenty of outdoor activities are available, with lovely beaches for swimming and surfing; there are walking tracks through scenic forest areas and along the coast. Visitors with more of an adrenalin bent may want to try jet boating, paragliding, caving or hot air ballooning.

The traditional Maori New Year festival of **Matariki** is celebrated with particular enthusiasm in Hastings, and on the **Clive River**, visitors can paddle an 18m carved waka (Maori canoe). Maori cultural tours are also available.

Art deco architecture

Napier and **Hastings** were rebuilt in the 1930s after a devastating earthquake and fires. As a result the two cities have a unique assemblage of art deco buildings; some feature Maori motifs. Visitors can explore on guided or self-guided tours, and Napier's annual **Art Deco Weekend**, in February, celebrates the decorative style.

ⓘ Visitor information

Hastings i-SITE Visitor Centre
Russell St, Hastings
Ph: (06) 873 5526
www.hastings.co.nz

Napier i-SITE Visitor Centre
100 Marine Pde, Napier
Ph: (06) 834 1911
www.hawkesbaynz.com

Marine Parade, Napier

main attractions

◈ **Arts & crafts**

Many of Hawke's Bay's artists and craftspeople welcome visits to their studios and galleries.

◈ **Boundary Stream Mainland Island**

This scenic reserve has threatened native plants and birds, and Hawke's Bay's highest waterfall.

◈ **Cape Kidnappers gannet colony**

The world's largest mainland gannet colony has around 20 000 birds and sweeping sea views.

◈ **Hawke's Bay food producers**

A Food Trail guides visitors around the many artisan food producers, and farmers' markets sell fresh produce.

◈ **Kaweka Forest Park**

This remote, scenic wilderness area offers great walking, picnicking, fishing and hunting.

◈ **Te Mata Peak**

There are panoramic views from this mountain, one of the first places in the world to see the sun each day.

◈ **Waimarama and Ocean Beach**

These two golden-sand beaches are popular for surfing and picnicking.

◈ **Wineries**

Hawke's Bay's many wineries welcome visitors and offer tastings.

◈ **World's longest place name**

Taumatawhakatangihangakoauauotamate-aturipukakapikimaungahoronukupokai-whenuakitanatahu, the world's longest place name, can be seen on an AA sign.

Te Mata Peak, Havelock North

North Island

0   40 kilometres

A   B   C   D   E

Te Whaiti
Maungapohatu
Wharekopae
Rere
Waipaoa
Ormond
Minginui
Ruatahuna
Ngatapa
Waituhi
Waiherere
Wairakei Village
Kinloch
WHIRINAKI
Manuoha 1392
Patutahi
GISBORNE
Acacia Bay
Taupo
Tauhara 1088
FOREST
Lake Waikaremoana
Waikaremoana
Ruakituri
Manutuke
Muriwai
Waitahanui
PARK
Kaitawa
Onepoto
Tuai
Waingake
Poverty Bay
Kuratau
Iwitahi
HUIARAU RANGE
Te Reinga
Bartletts
Motutere
Hatepe
Te Rangiita
Motuoapa
KAIMANAWA
AHIMANAWA RA
Mohaka River
Kotemaori
Raupunga
Frasertown
Nuhaka
Morere
Mahanga Beach
Tokaanu
Turangi
Te Haroto
River
WAIROA
Wairoa
Mahia Beach
Mahia
Rangipo
FOREST
PARK
Putorino
Mohaka
Opoutama
Whangawehi
KAWEKA
Kaweka 1724
Te Pohue
MAHIA PENINSULA
Makorako 1726
FOREST
PARK
Waipatiki Beach
HAWKE BAY
Portland Island
Lake Moawhango
Tutaekuri River
Bay View
Moawhango
Sherenden
NAPIER
Taoroa Junction
Ngaruroro River
Whakatu
Clive
Haumoana
Te Awanga
RUAHINE
FOREST
Maraekakaho
HASTINGS
Havelock North
Cape Kidnappers
Mangaweka
Mangaweka 1731
PARK
Tikokino
Ocean Beach
Rangiwahia
Argyll East
Pukehou
Waimarama
Bare Island
Apiti
Ongaonga
Otane
Patangata
Elsthorpe
Kairakau Beach
Waipawa
Takapau
Waipukurau
Hatuma
Pourerere
Norsewood
Makotuku
Matamau
Ormondville
Ruaroa
Wallingford
Dannevirke
Awarki
Oringi
Woodville
Waiaruhe
Kumeroa
Waitahora
Porangahau
Mangatainoka
Pahiatua
Weber
PUKETOI RANGE 803
Makuri
Pongaroa
Cape Turnagain
N

Tinui
Castlepoint

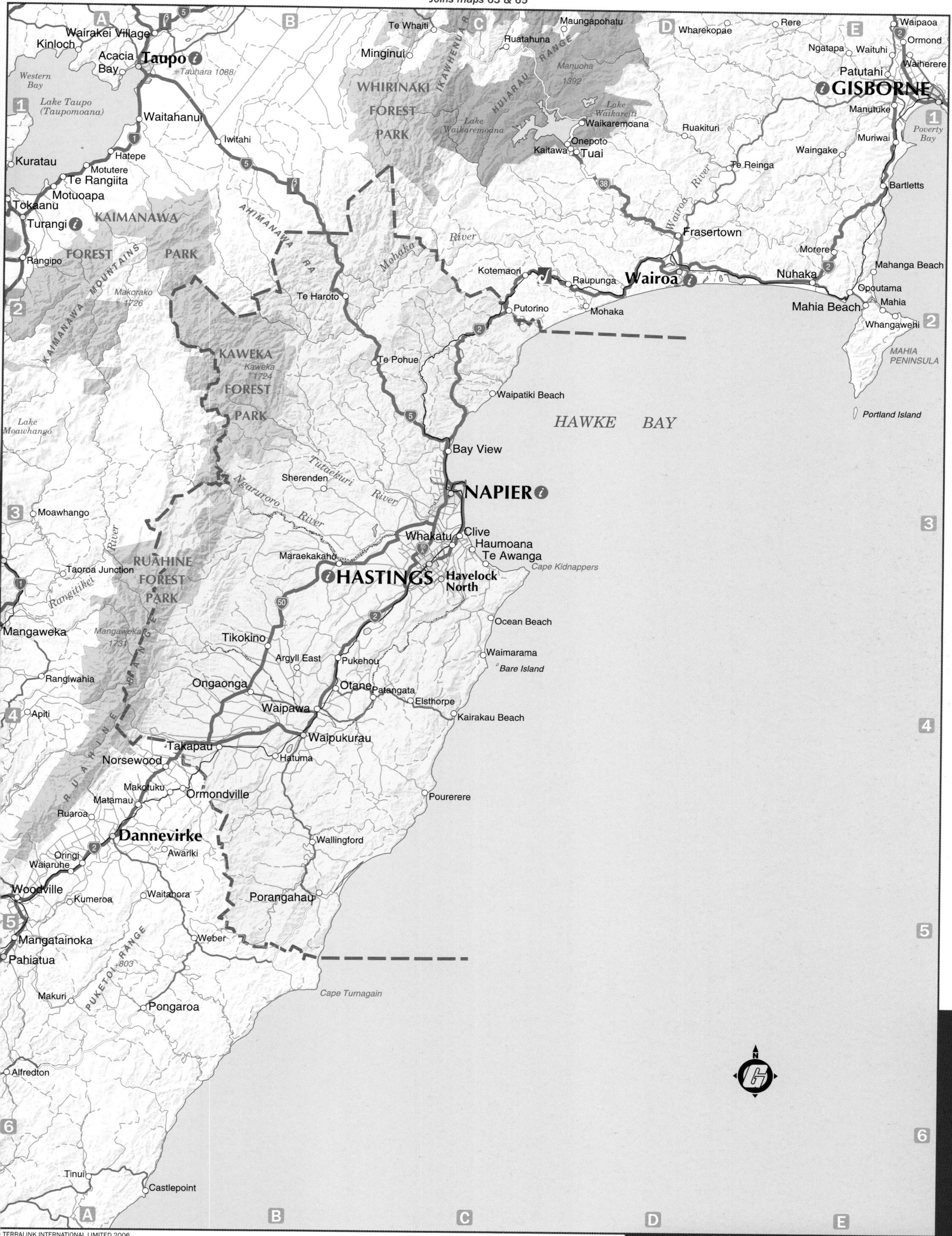

TERRALINK INTERNATIONAL LIMITED 2006

TARANAKI

Puke Ariki, New Plymouth

Dominated by the volcanic cone of beautiful **Mount Taranaki**, the pastoral region of Taranaki is a centre for sheep and dairy farming, and energy production. Because of inter-tribal warfare, there were few Maori in Taranaki when Europeans first moved into the region; after tribes who had fled the area returned, conflict over land ownership and sovereignty led to war from 1860 to 1870.

For visitors today, Taranaki offers wonderful coastal, mountain and rural scenery, historic sites, excellent hiking and long stretches of surf beach. **Egmont National Park**, created in 1900, surrounds Mount Taranaki. There are more than 300km of tracks in the park, which offers excellent hiking, climbing and skiing. The mountain is only a 30-minute drive from the coast, so it's possible to surf and ski on the same day.

Overlooked by the mountain, Taranaki's main centre of **New Plymouth** is a relaxed coastal city with quality galleries, museums, restaurants, parks and walks. As a result of the region's mild climate and volcanic soils, there are many beautiful gardens; rural Taranaki has many peaceful small towns.

Mount Taranaki

This stunning 2518m dormant volcano has long been sacred to Maori, and in legend was once part of the cluster of volcanoes at **Tongariro**, but was cast out for falling in love with Tongariro's lover. Also known as **Mount Egmont**, the mountain is the centre of Egmont National Park, and offers great walking, climbing and skiing.

 Visitor information

New Plymouth i-SITE Visitor Centre
1 Ariki St, New Plymouth
Ph: (06) 759 6060
www.taranaki.info

main attractions

◈ **Dairyland**
Dairyland has interactive displays about the dairy industry, and a simulated milk tanker ride.

◈ **Egmont National Park**
New Zealand's second oldest national park has a network of excellent walking tracks.

◈ **Forgotten World Highway**
This historic, remote route between Stratford and Taumarunui is rich in Maori and European heritage sites.

◈ **Govett-Brewster Art Gallery**
This excellent contemporary gallery has a collection of works by modernist artist Len Lye.

◈ **New Plymouth Coastal Walkway**
A 7km walkway from Lake Rotomanu to Port Taranaki passes sculptures, beaches and rivers.

◈ **Oakura Beach**
Peaceful Oakura is great for swimming, surfing and windsurfing.

◈ **Parihaka**
This Maori village, once a centre of peaceful resistance to confiscation of Maori land, is open to the public on the 18th and 19th of each month.

◈ **Parks and gardens**
Taranaki's beautiful gardens feature rhododendrons, azaleas, roses, fuchsias and native plants.

◈ **Puke Ariki**
An interactive library, museum and visitor centre, Puke Ariki has a wonderful collection of Maori taonga (treasures).

◈ **Surf Highway 45**
The coastal route west of Mount Taranaki leads past scenic, world-class surf beaches.

Mount Taranaki from Lake Mangamahoe

North Island

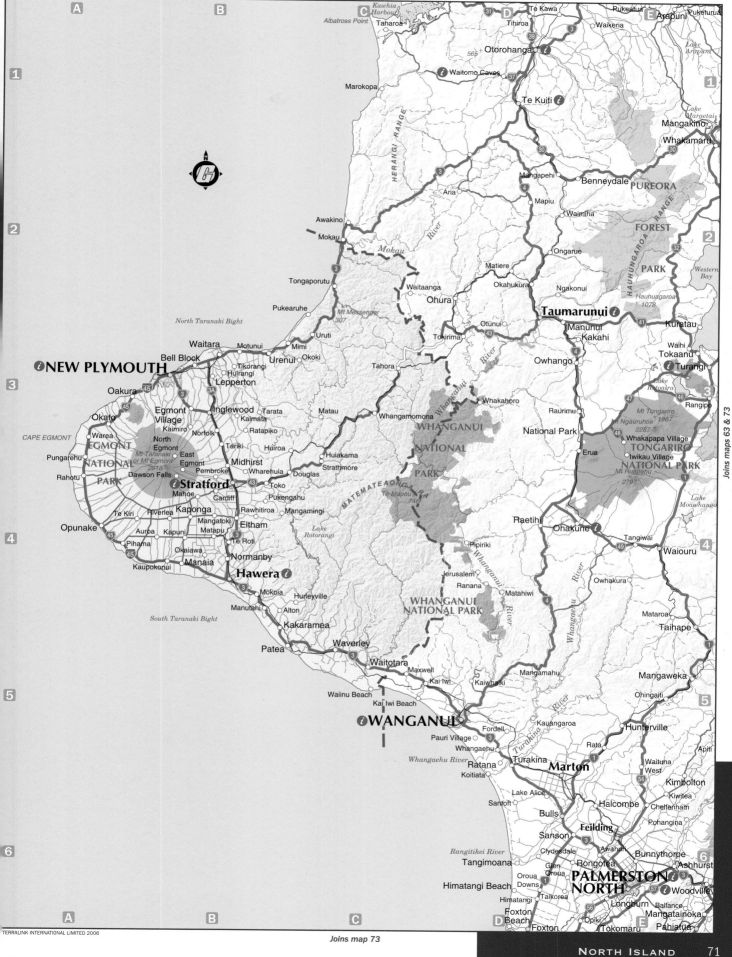

Scale 1:1 050 000
0   40   kilometres

A   B   C   D   E

Albatross Point
Kawhia Harbour
Taharoa
Te Kawa
Rukeatua
Puketurua
Arapuni
Arapuni

Tihiroa
Pukeatua
Waikeria
Lake
Arapuni

Otorohanga
565

Mangakino
Whakamaru

Marokopa
Waitomo Caves
Waikeria

Te Kuiti
Mangapehi
Benneydale   PUREORA

Aria
Mapiu   FOREST

North Taranaki Bight
Awakino
Mokau
Waimiha   PARK

Mokau River
Matiere
Ongarue   HAUHUNGAROA RANGE   Western
Bay

Tongaporutu
Waitaanga
Okahukura   Ngakonui   Hauhuagaroa
1078

Pukearuhe
Ohura   Otunui   Taumarunui

Mt Messenger
307
Tokirima   Manunui
Kakahi   Kuratau

Uruti
Mimi   Tahora   Owhango   Waihi
Tokaanu

Waitara   Motunui   Okoki   Whangaihu River   Turangi

NEW PLYMOUTH
Bell Block   Tikorangi   Hurangi   Whakahoro   National Park   Lake
Rotoaira   Rangipo

Oakura   Lepperton   Matau   Raurimu   Mt Tongariro
1967

Egmont   Inglewood   Tarata   Whangamomona   WHANGANUI   Mt Ngauruhoe
2287
Village   Kaimata   Erua   Whakapapa Village   TONGARIRO

Okato   Kaimiro   Ratapiko   NATIONAL   Iwikau Village   NATIONAL

CAPE EGMONT   Warea   Norfolk   Huiroa   Huiakama   Mt Ruapehu
2797   PARK

Okato   North   Tariki   Wharehuia   Strathmore   Lake
Moauhango

EGMONT   Egmont
or Mt Egmont   Midhirst   Douglas   Te Mapou
746   Raetihi
Pungarehu   2518   East   Ohakune

NATIONAL   Egmont   Toko   Tangiwai

Rahotu   Dawson Falls   Pembroke   MATEMATEAONGA   Waiouru
PARK   Stratford   Pukengahu

Mahoe   Cardiff   Rawhitiroa   Mangamingi   Pipiriki

Te Kiri   Riverlea   Kaponga   Lake   Owhakura

Opunake   Aupara   Kapuni   Rotorangi   Jerusalem   Mataroa

Pihama   Matapu   Eltham   Ranana   Taihape

Kaupokonui   Okaiawa   Te Roti   WHANGANUI   Matahiwi

Manaia   Normanby   NATIONAL PARK   Mangaweka

Hawera   Whangaehu River

South Taranaki Bight   Mokoia   Hurleyville   Mangamahu   Ohingaiti

Manutahi   Alton   Waitotara   Maxwell   Huntervile

Kakaramea   Kai Iwi   Kaiwhaiki   Rata   Apiti

Patea   Waverley   WANGANUI   Fordell   Kauangaroa   Waituna
West

Waiinu Beach   Kai Iwi Beach   Pauri Village   Turakina River   Kimbolton

Whangaehu   Rata   Kiwitea
Ratana   Turakina   Marton   Cheltenham

Koitiata   Lake Alice   Pohangina

Santoft   Halcombe   Feilding
Bulls   Sanson   Awahuri   Bunnythorpe   Ashhurst

Rangitikei River   Clydesdale   Rongotea   PALMERSTON
Tangimoana   Glen   Oroua   NORTH   Woodville

Himatangi Beach   Oroua Downs   Longburn   Mangatainoka
Himatangi   Taikorea   Foxton   Opiki   Pahiatua
Foxton
Beach   Tokomaru

TERRALINK INTERNATIONAL LIMITED 2006

NORTH ISLAND   71

MANAWATU

Agriculture is a major focus in this large North Island region, which encompasses the **Wanganui**, **Rangitikei**, **Horowhenua**, **Tararua** and **Manawatu** districts. The area's main industries include beef, sheep and deer farming; farmstays and visits allow visitors to experience New Zealand rural life, and there are many historic houses and beautiful gardens.

The fascinating **Whanganui River**, rich in Maori and European history, is at the centre of **Whanganui National Park**, and can be explored by boat, road or walking. Historic **Wanganui**, built on the river, is a thriving centre for the arts; the region's major city, **Palmerston North**, is a busy university town with good restaurants, cafés, galleries, museums and theatre.

Wild rivers, bush-clad mountain ranges, deep gorges and dramatic surf beaches offer many outdoor activities across the region. White water rafting, kayaking and jet boating are popular on the **Rangitikei River**.

Peaceful small towns are dotted around the area; visitors can find intriguing history in the Whanganui River's villages, brewery tours at **Mangatainoka**, rhododendron gardens at **Kimbolton**, a gumboot festival at **Taihape**, wind farms near **Woodville** and Scandinavian heritage in **Norsewood**.

Visitor information

i-SITE Palmerston North Visitor Centre
The Square, Palmerston North
Ph: (06) 350 1922
www.manawatunz.co.nz

Wanganui i-SITE Visitor Centre
101 Guyton St, Wanganui
Ph: (06) 349 0508
www.wanganuinz.com

Whanganui River

New Zealand's longest navigable river, the Whanganui River flows 290km from **Mount Tongariro** to the Tasman Sea, and was once an important travel and trade route for both Maori and European settlers. Today it offers visitors a wonderful mix of scenic beauty, history and outdoor adventure, including a multi-day canoe trip.

main attractions

◈ **Manawatu Gorge**
Spectacular Manawatu Gorge offers hiking, kayaking and jet boating.

◈ **New Zealand Rugby Museum**
A must for rugby fans, this Palmerston North museum has exhibits about the national obsession, from the first New Zealand game in 1870 to today.

◈ **Outdoor activities**
Hiking, kayaking, jet boating, trout fishing and even bungy jumping are all possible in the region, with its many beautiful rivers, gorges and forests.

◈ **Pukaha Mount Bruce National Wildlife Centre**
This native wildlife sanctuary has many endangered birds, including kiwi in a nocturnal house.

◈ **Ruahine Forest Park**
Hiking and hunting are good in this 94 000ha forest park, where tracks lead through unspoilt forest and spectacular alpine areas.

◈ *The Lord of the Rings* **locations**
The Rangitikei and Moawhanga Rivers were both used for filming scenes in Peter Jackson's film trilogy, as was Waitarere Forest.

◈ **Wanganui**
This historic city on the Whanganui River is a centre of excellence for the arts, and has many lovely buildings.

◈ **Whanganui National Park**
Rugged valleys, beautiful forests, fascinating history and the important Whanganui River make this national park a must-see.

◈ **Whanganui River Road**
This back road along the Whanganui River allows visitors to experience rich history, tiny villages, historic Maori buildings and beautiful scenery.

Whanganui River, Wanganui

North Island

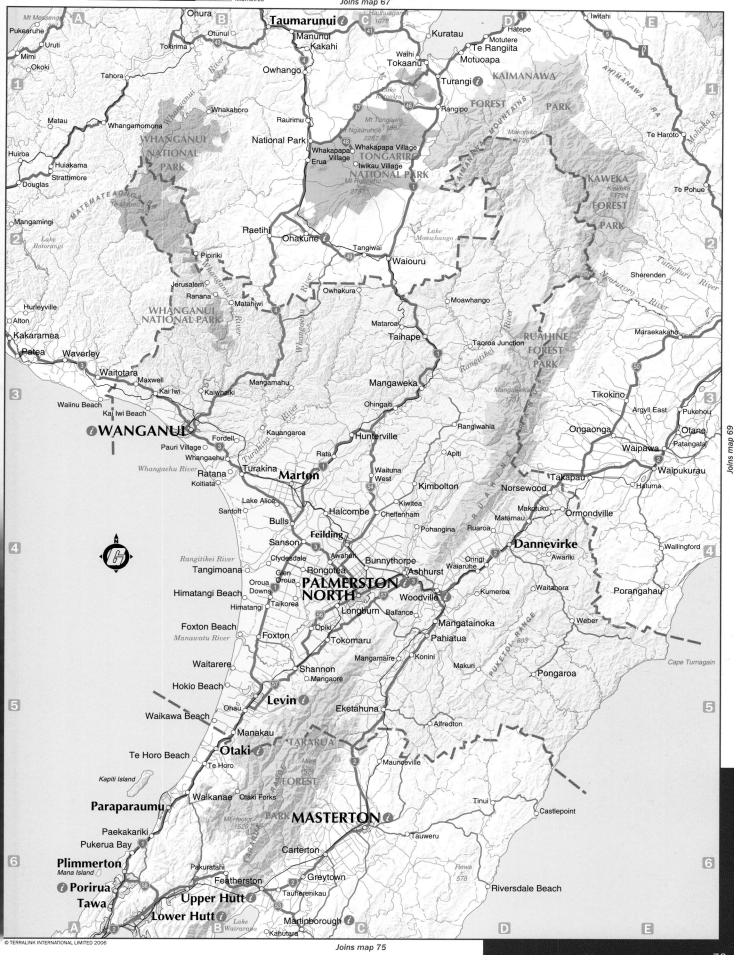

Scale 1:1 050 000

0   40 kilometres

Joins map 69

WAIRARAPA

In the south-east corner of the North Island, the Wairarapa region is a popular weekend getaway for visitors from Wellington, just over an hour's drive away. Bordered to the west by the dramatic **Tararua Range**, and by rugged coastline to the east, parts of the Wairarapa have been home to Maori for centuries; Europeans first settled there in the mid-19th century.

Today, the Wairarapa is a relaxed pastoral area, its countryside dotted with appealing small towns, sheep farms and orchards, as well as an increasing number of vineyards and olive groves. The burgeoning wine area around **Martinborough** is known for its award-winning pinot noir, and there are also wineries to the north, including around **Gladstone** and the main town of **Masterton**. Martinborough is a popular spot for visitors; it offers cafés, restaurants and boutique accommodation, as does the pretty village of **Greytown**.

Sandy beaches on the east coast offer surfing and swimming; the rugged southern coastline is home to wildlife and to sites of early Maori occupation. To the west, there are beautiful walks through unspoilt forest in **Tararua Forest Park**.

Visitor information

Wairarapa i-SITE Visitor Centre
316 Queen St, Masterton
Ph: (06) 370 0900

Martinborough i-SITE Visitor Centre
18 Kitchener St, Martinborough
Ph: (06) 306 9043
www.wairarapanz.com

Palliser Bay

This dramatic, rugged bay was occupied early by Maori, and there are many archaeological sites. Young seals can be seen frolicking at the North Island's largest fur seal breeding colony; **Cape Palliser**'s red-and-white striped lighthouse is a steep walk up 250 steps.

main attractions

◈ **Aratoi Wairarapa Museum of Art & History**

This excellent museum explores the Wairarapa's cultural, natural and artistic heritage.

◈ **Castlepoint**

Great swimming, surfing and fishing, rare plants, a spectacular limestone reef and historic lighthouse make Castlepoint a delight to visit.

◈ **Greytown**

Greytown has NZ's most complete main street of Victorian architecture, interesting shops, good food, gardens and boutique accommodation.

◈ **Holdsworth**

Short and long walks lead into rich native forest at the eastern gateway to Tararua Forest Park.

◈ **Lake Ferry**

This popular fishing spot offers great views over Lake Onoke and the wild waters of Palliser Bay.

◈ **Martinborough**

Once a sleepy farming settlement, Martinborough is now a boutique wine village and popular weekend getaway for Wellingtonians.

◈ **Putangirua Pinnacles**

These spectacular rain-eroded landforms, formed over 120 000 years, were used for filming *The Lord of the Rings*.

◈ **Tararua Forest Park**

This 120 000ha park offers great hiking and hunting in the Tararua Range's lush forest and alpine areas.

◈ **Wineries**

A versatile and expanding wine region, the Wairarapa is known particularly for its pinot noir.

Southern Wairarapa coast

North Island

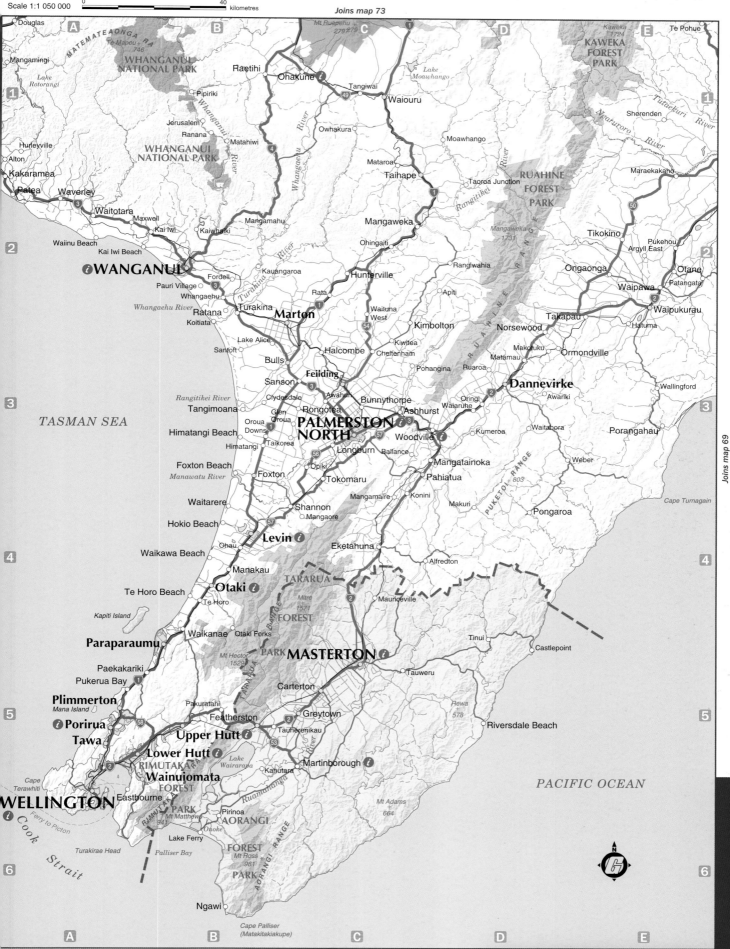

Scale 1:1 050 000

0   40

kilometres

Joins map 69

WELLINGTON

attractions

main attractions

◈ **Cultural attractions**

The Wellington region offers excellent live theatre, dozens of galleries and an almost constant series of arts festivals and events.

◈ **Days Bay**

This pretty seaside suburb on the east side of Wellington Harbour can be reached by ferry from central Wellington.

◈ **Kaitoke Regional Park**

Camping, swimming and picnicking are all popular in this lovely area of riverside native forest.

◈ **Kapiti Coast**

This stretch of coast has appealing small towns and great beaches.

◈ **Matiu/Somes Island**

This island wildlife sanctuary in Wellington Harbour can be visited by ferry.

◈ **Paekakariki**

A peaceful seaside village, Paekakariki is a lovely place to relax.

◈ **Parliament Buildings**

The seat of government in Wellington has iconic buildings in 1960s, 1920s and 1890s styles.

◈ **Red Rocks**

Wellington's rugged southern coast is home to a colony of fur seals near a red-hued rocky outcrop.

◈ **Tararua Forest Park**

The magnificent Tararua Range has great hiking and hunting opportunities.

◈ **Te Papa**

New Zealand's national museum offers interactive exhibits about the country's culture and heritage.

◈ *The Lord of the Rings* locations

Kaitoke Regional Park became 'Rivendell', and the Hutt River did duty as the 'River Anduin'.

◈ **Wellington waterfront**

Historic port buildings line the city's beautiful waterfront, a popular spot for walking and jogging.

Vibrant urban life, cultural sophistication, heritage attractions and natural beauty all come together in the Wellington region, at the south-west of the North Island.

Wellington, New Zealand's lively capital city, is the main centre of the region, and is rich in both natural and cultural attractions. Beautifully located on green hills around a dramatic harbour, Wellington is also a major travel crossroads between the North and South Islands. Maori call the area around Wellington city **Te Upoko o Te Ika**, 'the Head of the Fish', a reference to the myth in which legendary trickster Maui fished up the North Island.

The **Kapiti Coast**, to the city's north, is home to a number of picturesque seaside towns which look out onto **Kapiti Island**, an important offshore wildlife sanctuary which can be visited by boat. The coast has long stretches of sandy beach, and, to the east, there are beautiful walks in the **Tararua Forest Park**.

The studios of film maker Peter Jackson, director of *The Lord of the Rings*, are in Wellington, and the city was a base for making the movie trilogy.

Kapiti Island

One of New Zealand's most important conservation sites, 10km-long Kapiti Island is a protected sanctuary where wildlife flourishes and visitor numbers are limited. The island is rich in history, having been occupied by various Maori tribes, warrior chief Te Rauparaha and a European whaling station. The surrounding marine reserve offers dramatic underwater scenery.

 Visitor information

Wellington i-SITE Visitor Centre
Cnr Wakefield and Victoria Sts, Wellington
Ph: (04) 802 4860
www.WellingtonNZ.com

Wellington Harbour and city

North Island

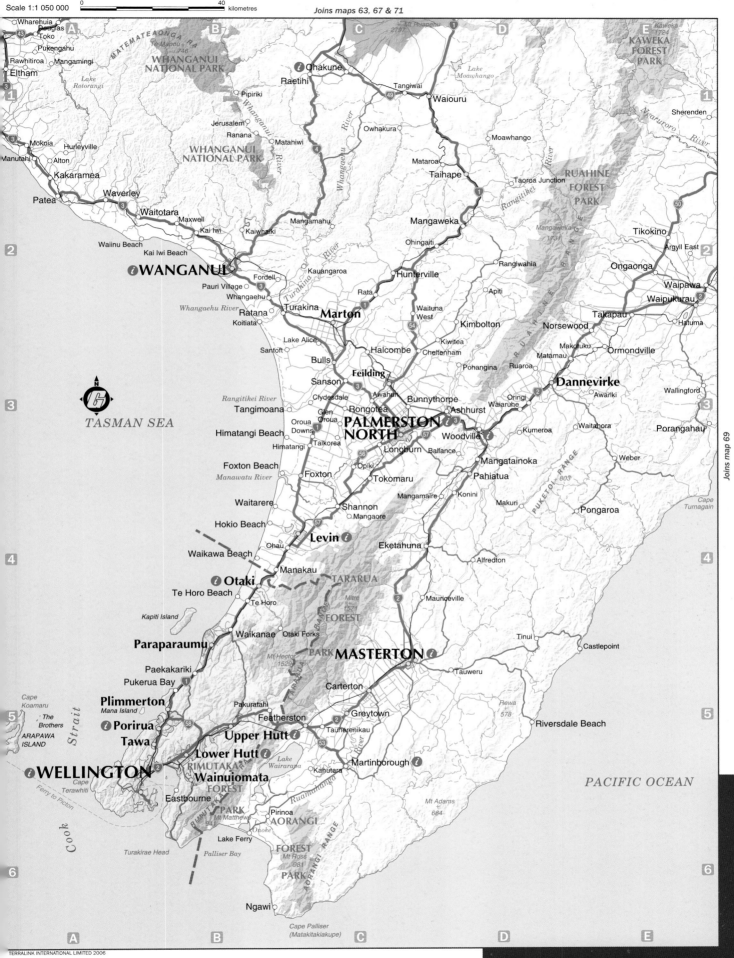

0   40 kilometres

Wharehuia
Douglas
Toko
Pukengahu
Rawhitiroa
Mangamingi
Eltham
Mokoia
Hurleyville
Manutahi
Alton
Kakaramea
Waverley
Patea
Waitotara
Maxwell
Kai Iwi
Kaiwhaiki
Waiinu Beach
Kai Iwi Beach
Kai Iwi

MATEMATEAONGA
Te Mapou 746
WHANGANUI
NATIONAL PARK
Lake Rotorangi
WHANGANUI
NATIONAL PARK
Pipiriki
Jerusalem
Ranana
Matahiwi

Ohakune
Raetihi
Mt Ruapehu 2787
Tangiwai
Waiouru
Owhakura
Moawhango
Mataroa
Taihape
Taoroa Junction

Lake Moawhango

KAWEKA FOREST PARK
Kaweka 724
Sherenden
Ngaruroro River

RUAHINE FOREST PARK
Mangaweka 1731
Tikokino
Argyll East
Ongaonga
Waipawa
Waipukurau
Hatuma
Takapau
Norsewood
Makotuku
Ormondville
Matamau
Wallingford

WANGANUI
Pauri Village
Fordell
Whangaehu
Whangaehu River
Ratana
Koitiata
Turakina
Marton
Rata
Hunterville
Rangiwahia
Apiti

Lake Alice
Santoft
Bulls
Sanson
Clydesdale
Tangimoana
Oroua Downs
Himatangi Beach
Himatangi
Foxton Beach
Manawatu River
Waitarere
Hokio Beach
Waikawa Beach

Rangitikei River
Halcombe
Feilding
Awahuri
Rongotea
Glen Oroua
Talkorea
Opiki
Foxton
Shannon
Mangaore
Ohau
Levin
Manakau

Kimbolton
Cheltenham
Kiwitea
Waituna West
Pohangina
Ruaroa
Bunnythorpe
Ashhurst
PALMERSTON NORTH
Woodville
Longburn
Ballance
Tokomaru
Mangamaire
Konini
Makuri

Dannevirke
Oringi
Waiaruhe
Kumeroa
Waitahora
Weber
Porangahau
Mangatainoka
Pahiatua
Pongaroa
Cape Turnagain

PUKETOI RANGE 803

RUAHINE RANGE

TASMAN SEA

Foxton
Eketahuna
Alfredton

TARARUA
Waikanae
Otaki Forks
Te Horo
Kapiti Island
Paraparaumu
Paekakariki
Pukerua Bay
Plimmerton
Mana Island
Porirua
Tawa

FOREST
Mt Hector 1529
PARK
Mt Holdsworth
Mitre 1571

Masterton
Mauriceville
Tauweru
Tinui
Castlepoint

Carterton
Greytown
Featherston
Pakuratahi
Tauherenikau
Upper Hutt
Lower Hutt
WELLINGTON
Wainuiomata
Eastbourne
RIMUTAKA FOREST PARK
Mt Matthews 941

RIMUTAKA
Lake Wairarapa
Martinborough
Kahutara
Pirinoa
AORANGI
Onoke
Lake Ferry
FOREST
Mt Ross 981
PARK
Ngawi

Rewa 578
Riversdale Beach

Ruamahanga River
AORANGI RANGE
Mt Adams 664

PACIFIC OCEAN

Cape Koamaru
The Brothers
ARAPAWA ISLAND
Cook Strait
Cape Terawhiti
Turakirae Head
Palliser Bay
Cape Palliser
(Matakitakiakupe)

WELLINGTON CITY

New Zealand's capital city, and the world's southernmost capital, Wellington is beautifully situated between green hills and a magnificent harbour at the south-west tip of the North Island, with residential areas spreading north to **Porirua** and the **Hutt Valley**. The early Polynesian explorer Kupe is credited with discovering Wellington's harbour centuries ago, and European settlers first arrived in 1840.

Wellington today is a lively and sophisticated city which brings together an eclectic mix of cultural and natural attractions. Wellington offers visitors great shopping, an array of theatres and galleries, the national museum **Te Papa**, the excellent biennial **International Festival of the Arts**, and a thriving arts and film-making scene.

Many of New Zealand's most important heritage attractions can be found in Wellington; the city is also home to more cafés, bars and restaurants per head than New York, yet its urban appeal is balanced by great natural beauty. The harbour is surrounded by tree-clad hills dotted with historic wooden houses, and Wellington's rugged southern coast, home to seals, seabirds, surfers and marine life, is just a short drive from the city centre.

main attractions

⬥ **Botanic Gardens**

These lovely 25ha gardens feature native forest, rose gardens, plant collections and sculptures.

⬥ **Cable Car**

Wellington's iconic cable car runs from downtown Lambton Quay to hilly Kelburn, offering great views.

⬥ **Cuba Street**

This lively street is home to funky cafés, galleries, bars and shops.

⬥ **Karori Wildlife Sanctuary**

Native plants and rare wildlife are regenerating in this unique sanctuary area, only 2km from the city's centre.

⬥ **Lambton Quay**

Wellington's main shopping street, historic Lambton Quay was originally on the waterfront before land reclamation.

⬥ **Mount Victoria**

This lookout offers panoramic 360-degree views over Wellington.

⬥ **Oriental Bay**

Waterfront strolls are popular along this elegant bay with its golden-sand beach.

⬥ **Parliament Buildings**

The centre of government, these buildings include the modernist Beehive, 1922 Parliament House and 1899 Parliamentary Library.

⬥ **Te Papa**

The national museum is a rich repository of New Zealand culture and heritage.

⬥ **Thorndon**

New Zealand's oldest suburb is home to historic buildings and lovely gardens.

facts

⬥ Population: 420 000
⬥ Date founded: 1840
⬥ Tallest building: Majestic Centre (116m)
⬥ Oldest building in central city: Colonial Cottage Museum (1858)
⬥ Average temperature: 20.3°C (January), 11.3°C (July)

ℹ️ Visitor information

Wellington i-SITE Visitor Centre
Cnr Wakefield and Victoria Sts, Wellington
Ph: (04) 802 4860
www.WellingtonNZ.com

Places of Interest

Archives New Zealand **A** C2
Beehive **B** C2
Botanic Gardens **C** B3
Cable Car **D** C3
Capital E **E** D4
Carter Observatory & Planetarium **F** C3
Circa Theatre **G** D4
City Gallery Wellington **H** D3
Civic Square **I** D4
Colonial Cottage Museum **J** C5
Downstage Theatre **K** D4
Embassy Theatre **L** D4
Frank Kitts Park **M** D3
Government Buildings **N** D2
Katherine Mansfield Birthplace **O** D1
Mount Victoria Lookout **P** E5
Museum of Wellington City and Sea **Q** D3
National Library of New Zealand **R** D2
Old St Paul's **S** D2
Oriental Bay **T** E4
Otari–Wilton's Bush **U** A1
Parliament Buildings **V** D2
Te Papa **W** D4
The Film Archive **X** D4
Tomb of the Unknown Warrior **Y** D5
Westpac Stadium **Z** E2

Bucket Fountain, Cuba Street, Wellington

Scale 1:20 000

0 750 metres

Continued on map 82

WILTON BUSH

OTARI-WILTON'S BUSH
Otari School

WILTON PARK

WILTON

KARORI CEMETERY

IAN GALLOWAY PARK

Cardinal McKeefry School

WESTERN SLOPES RESERVE

STELLIN MEMORIAL PARK

Crematorium

NORTHLAND

Northland Park

Northland School

BOTANIC GARDENS

Carter Observatory & Planetarium

Cable Car Museum

KELBURN PARK

KELBURN

Kelburn School

Northland Tunnel

Kelburn Viaduct

Karori Tunnel

Karori Wildlife Sanctuary

TAITVILLE

Victoria University

HIGHBURY

Airport Seatoun

Te Aro School

Athena Montessori College

MITCHELLTOWN

Polehill Reserve

Colonial Cottage Museum

MT COOK

TANERA PARK

CENTRAL PARK

NAIRN ST PARK

BROOKLYN

Brooklyn School

Fire stn

Library

St Bernards School

PRINCE OF WALES PARK

GEORGE DENTON PARK

THORNDON

PIPITEA

Katherine Mansfield Birthplace

Queen Margaret College

Westpac Stadium

Thorndon School

Wellington Girls College

St Mary's College

Sacred Heart Sch

Nat Library of NZ

Parliament Bldgs

Beehive

Old Government Bldgs

Wellington Railway Stn

Whitireia Community Polytech

LAMBTON

Bluebridge Ferry Terminal

Lynx Ferry Terminal

Inter-Island Wharf

Waterloo Wharf

Old St Paul's Archives

Interislander Ferry Terminal

Thorndon Container Wharf

Queens Wharf

East by West Ferry Terminal

Museum of Wgtn City & Sea

Events Centre

Lambton Harbour

Frank Kitts Park

City Gallery Wgtn

Capital E

Michael Fowler Centre

Civic Square

Circa Theatre

Chaffers Marina

Te Papa

Oriental Bay

Freyberg Pool

ORIENTAL BAY

The Film Archive

Downstage

Embassy

MT VICTORIA

Mount Victoria Lookout

Te Aro School

TE ARO

Mt Cook School

Wellington High School & Comm Ed Centre

Tomb of the Unknown Warrior

BASIN RESERVE

St Marks School

Massey University Wellington Campus

Wellington College

Wellington East Girls College

NEWTOWN

Wellington Hospital

EWART HOSPITAL

Alexandra Park

HATAITAI PARK

Kilbirnie School

SOUTHERN CROSS HOSPITAL

Mt Victoria Tunnel

Continued on map 82

© TERRALINK INTERNATIONAL LIMITED 2006

Only 2km wide, nestled between the harbour and hills, central Wellington is easily explored by foot, or on the yellow City Circular buses. Wellington's suburbs can be reached by bus. Public transport links central Wellington to the outlying **Hutt Valley** and **Porirua**, but a car is probably best for reaching more isolated spots.

Walking tour of central Wellington

Wellington Railway Station, built in the 1930s, is a good starting point for exploring the city. Heading north on Mulgrave Street, **Thistle Inn** is one of New Zealand's oldest pubs; before land reclamation, it was only a few metres from the water, and drinkers often arrived by boat. **Archives New Zealand** displays the original Treaty of Waitangi, the 1840 agreement between Maori and the British which is seen as the country's founding document. **Old St Paul's** is a beautiful Gothic-style church built from native timber.

To the west in Molesworth St, the **National Library** is home to a rich collection of historical material. Across the road is the three-building complex of **Parliament**: the modernist **Beehive**, Victorian Gothic **Parliamentary Library** and Edwardian neo-classical **Parliament House**. Tours are available. On the corner of **Lambton Quay**, the small park of **Wai-titi Landing** was once a beach and a landing place for Maori canoes; to the right, the **Cenotaph** is a memorial to New Zealand's war dead. Beautiful **Government Buildings**, opposite, is the world's second largest wooden building. Completed in 1876, it anticipated current laws by 130-odd years by banning smoking inside when it was opened!

Lambton Quay, once the shoreline, is Wellington's bustling main shopping street. The city's red **cable car** has taken commuters up and down to **Kelburn** since 1902, and the ride offers wonderful views. Further south, **Civic Square** is a large public space featuring a number of sculptures. It's bordered by the **City Library**, the excellent **City Gallery Wellington**, the 1904 **Town Hall** and the children's entertainment centre **Capital E**. The bridge across to the waterfront and **Frank Kitts Park** is a work of art in itself.

The area around **Cuba Street**, leading south from Civic Square, is home to a host of bohemian cafés, bars, shops and galleries, and is great for a wander and a coffee. To the east, **Te Aro Park** was once the site of Te Aro Pa, a Maori village; the **Opera House** is an ornate Edwardian theatre, as is the **St James Theatre**, further east on **Courtenay Place**. This broad street and its surrounding area make up Wellington's main entertainment district; there are dozens of bars and restaurants, as well as theatres and cinemas. The restored 1924 **Embassy Theatre**, on Kent Terrace, was the venue for 2003's world premiere of *The Return of the King*.

On the harbour front, the imposing building of **Te Papa**, New Zealand's national museum, is bursting with lively interactive displays, and has a wonderful collection of Maori taonga (treasures). The waterfront is popular for walking and jogging, and has gorgeous sea views; heading north, the **Wellington Writers' Walk** is a series of sculptures celebrating New Zealand writers. The **Museum of Wellington City and Sea** showcases the city's maritime heritage; a number of historic port buildings are now home to restaurants.

Suburban attractions

Historic **Thorndon**, New Zealand's oldest suburb, has many lovely old wooden houses. The **Katherine Mansfield Birthplace** is a restored historic house where New Zealand's most famous writer spent her early years. The 25ha **Botanic**

Te Papa, Wellington

Wellington

FESTIVALS AND EVENTS

Wellington's calendar bursts with festivals and events throughout the year. The month-long **International Festival of the Arts**, held biennially, offers a dazzling array of theatre, music, dance and writers; **Summer City** has cultural events throughout summer. The delightful **Cuba Street Carnival**, in February, features a night parade, music and stalls in the city's hippest street; each July, Wellingtonians brave the winter cold for the **International Film Festival**. September's **World of WearableArt Awards Show** showcases fabulously creative costumes. Wellington also hosts the yearly **International Jazz Festival** and **Comedy Festival**, and events reflecting the city's ethnic diversity are popular, including celebrations for **Waitangi Day**, **Diwali** and **Chinese New Year**.

One of the displays from the International Festival of the Arts, Wellington

Gardens, established in 1868, have native forest, rose gardens, a duck pond and some beautiful walks; the **Carter Observatory** offers planetarium shows. **Bolton Street Memorial Park** is a fascinating historic cemetery.

The unique **Karori Wildlife Sanctuary** is a protected 252ha area of regenerating native forest, only 2km from the central city. A specially designed fence keeps out predators, and some rare species are breeding in the sanctuary, including kiwi, and the delightful native parrot kaka. **Otari–Wilton's Bush** is New Zealand's only native botanic garden.

The elegant suburb of **Oriental Bay** is popular for walking and rollerblading along the harbour front; above it, the **Mount Victoria Lookout** offers wonderful views in

all directions. Scenes for *The Lord of the Rings* were filmed in the town belt here.

Further south, in **Newtown**, **Wellington Zoo** is New Zealand's oldest zoo. To the east, the **Miramar Peninsula** is home to film maker Peter Jackson's studios. There's good swimming for those who can brave cold water at picturesque **Scorching Bay**; the bay's café was popular with cast and crew of *The Lord of the Rings*. Some scenes for the film trilogy were shot at **Seatoun**'s old army base; filming locations can also be found at **Upper Hutt**'s **Harcourt Park** (the 'Gardens of Isengard') and the nearby **Hutt River** ('River Anduin'). Continuing along Wellington's wild southern coast, home to sea birds and penguins, **Lyall Bay** is a surfing beach; at

Island Bay, the **Marine Education Centre** has fascinating displays about local marine life. From quaint **Owhiro Bay**, a track for walkers or 4WD leads to the fur seal colony at **Red Rocks**.

Leaving from the central city, harbour ferries stop at the wildlife sanctuary of **Matiu/Somes Island**, formerly a quarantine station. The ferries continue to lovely **Days Bay**, a pretty spot for swimming, fishing and picnicking; **Eastbourne** is a seaside suburb with a village feel.

Further north in **Lower Hutt**, **The Dowse** is a wonderful contemporary gallery specialising in applied arts; art aficionados will also want to visit **PATAKA** in **Porirua**, an excellent gallery and museum with a strong community basis and a focus on Maori and Pacific cultures.

TASMAN SEA

Cook Strait

MANA ISLAND
Shingle Point
South Point
Rocky Bay
The Bridge
Mt Cooper (Whitireia)
Goat Point
Onehunga Bay
Deepwater Point
WHITIREIA PARK RESERVE
CAMBORNE
MANA
GOLDEN GATE
Te Paokapo
Titahi Bay
Round Point
Te Korohiwa Rocks
Green Point
Pararauma
Rukutane
STUART PARK
TITAHI BAY
Paremata
PAREMATA
PAPAKOWHAI
ASCOT PARK
WAITANG
ASCOT

Angapaua
Wairere
Te Anapaura
Rock Point
TAKAPUWAHIA
ELSDON
PORIRUA SCENIC RESERVE
PROSSER
PATAKA
PORIRUA
PORIRUA HOSPITAL
CHAMPION
PORIRUA EAST
CANNONS CREEK
WARSPITE

Kiakia
Pipinui Point
Boom Rock

COLONIAL KNOB RESERVE
KENEPURU HOSPITAL
KENEPURU DR
RANUI HEIGHTS
CARDIFF PARK
TRUST PORIRUA PARK

Mill Creek
LINDEN
LINDENVALE
WESTHAVEN
GREENACRES
TAKAPU VALLEY
BELMONT REGIONAL PARK

TAWA
Redwood North
REDWOOD
SUNDALE
GRENADA NORTH
GRENADA NORTH PARK
Redwood South
SOUTHGATE
Takapu Road

OHARIU VALLEY
GLENSIDE
CHURTON PARK
GRENADA VILLAGE
SETON NOSSITER PARK
WOODRIDGE
HOROKIWI
HARBO NORMAN
MAUNGARA
Western Hut
PERCY KOROKORO RECREA RESERVE
KOROKORO
Korokoro Stream

Oharui Bay
OHARIU VALLEY ROAD
PAPARANGI
JOHNSONVILLE
JOHNSONVILLE EAST
GILBERD BUSH RESERVE
NEWLANDS PARK
PETONE
Petone
MAKARA BEACH
JOHNSONVILLE PARK
Kaukau
NEWLANDS
Petone Wharf
JACKSON
THE ESPLANADE

Opau Bay
Te Ikaamaru Bay
Ohau Bay
OPAU ROAD
MAKARA RD
Makara Stream
TAKARAU
GORGE
ROAD
KHANDALLAH PARK
BURMA RD
RAROA
Raroa
NGAURANGA
HUTT 2
WARARAPA LINE

BROADMEADOWS
KHANDALLAH RESERVE
Awarua St
Simla Cres
Khandallah
RANGOON HEIGHTS
Ngauranga

South Point
HUNTLEIGH PARK
Ngaio
KHANDALLAH
Fox Hill
CASHMERE
WELLINGTON URBAN MOTORWAY

NGAIO
TE KAINGA
NGAIO GORGE RD
HUTT RD

Matiu / Somes Island
Mokopuna Island

CROFTON DOWNS
Crofton Downs
HIGHLAND PARK
KAIWHARAWHARA
Kaiwharawhara

Wellington Harbour
(Port Nicholson)

CHARTWELL
Wilton Bush
WADESTOWN
WADESTOWN
WILTON
TOWN BELT
THORNDON
Wellington - Picton ferry (Interislander)

KARORI WEST
JOHNSON HILL RESERVE
KARORI CEMETERY
NORTH LAND
BOTANIC GARDENS
Wellington
LAMBTON
City - Matiu / Somes Island - Days Bay ferry
City - Picton ferries (Bluebridge & Lynx)
Point Jerningham
Point Halswell
Kau Bay
RONA
Point Well

KARORI RD
KARORI
KELBURN
THE TERRACE
Point Jerningham
Balaena Bay
Mahanga Bay
Makaro/Ward Island
EASTBOURN

WRIGHTS HILL RESERVE
TAITVILLE
HIGHBURY
TE ARO
GHUZNEE
VIVIAN ST
ORIENTAL BAY
MT VICTORIA
ROSENEATH
Shelly Bay
SCORCHING BAY DOMAIN
Point Gordon
Scorching Bay
Robinson Bay
Point Arthur

KARORI WILDLIFE SANCTUARY
MITCHELLTOWN
ARO ST
MT COOK
HATAITAI
MAUPUIA PARK
MAUPUIA
Greta Point
Point Arthur

BROOKLYN
NEWTOWN
WGTN HOSP
Evans Bay
MIRAMAR
Worser Bay
Camp Bay

KOWHAI PARK
VOGELTOWN
CONSTABLE
KILBIRNIE
EVANS BAY PDE
COBHAM DR
SEATOUN HEIGHTS
BROADWAY
SEATOUN
"Bree" Fort Dorset

MORNINGTON
BERHAMPORE
MELROSE
RONGOTAI
CALABAR
STRATHMORE PARK
Point Dorset

KINGSTON
Wellington Zoo
TOWN BELT
LYALL BAY
RONGOTAI
WELLINGTON INTERNATIONAL AIRPORT
BREAKER BAY
Breaker Bay
Hinds Point

HAPPY VALLEY
SOUTHGATE
ISLAND BAY
HOUGHTON BAY
Lyall Bay
MOA POINT
ATATURK PARK
Ranger Point
Palmer Head

OWHIRO BAY
THE PARADE
Marine Education Centre
Island Bay
Arthurs Nose
Te Raekaihau
Moa Point
Chaffers Passage
Inconstant Point

Owhiro Bay

82

Wellington

le 1: 120 000

0   5 kilometres

F **G** **H** **J** **K**

PAEKAKARIKI HILL RD
ROAD
PAUATAHANUI
58
ROAD
PAREMATA
FLIGHTYS ROAD
MURPHYS ROAD
MULHERN ROAD
HAYWARDS
BELMONT ROAD
JUDGEFORD
58
ROAD

MOONSHINE
MOONSHINE
MOONSHINE
ROAD
ROAD

Whakatikei River

ROAD

TE MARUA
KAITOKE REGIONAL PARK
2
AKATARAWA CEMETERY
Speedway Te Marua
GEMSTONE DRIVE RESERVE
RATA PARK
BIRCHVILLE
EMERALD HILL RESERVE
THE PLATEAU
MANGAROA HILL SCENIC RESERVE
"Isengard Gardens"
HARCOURT
BROWN OWL
MAIN
ROAD
MOUNT MARUA
TUNNEL GULLY RECREATION AREA
1
RIVERSTONE TERRACES
TOTARA PARK
GIBBONS ST
Hutt River
AWA KAIRANGI PARK
TOTARA PARK DR.
TIMBERLEA
MAORIBANK
MAYMORN
PAKURATAHI FOREST

TRENTHAM SCENIC RESERVE
TRENTHAM MEMORIAL PARK
2
HAYWARDS
SILVERSTREAM SCENIC RESERVE
WHAKATIKI ST
MOONSHINE RD
TRENTHAM LINE
Upper Hutt
FERGUSSON
WAIRARAPA
KINGSLEY HEIGHTS
WALLACEVILLE
MAIDSTONE PARK
MANGAROA
Training Stables
PARKS LINE RD
FLUX RD
MANGAROA VALLEY ROAD
Cooleys Stream
Caldera Stream

KEITH GEORGE MEMORIAL PARK
SILVERSTREAM
HERETAUNGA
Heretaunga
Trentham
Racecourse
WALLACEVILLE RD
WALLACEVILLE CEMETERY
KATHERINE MANSFIELD DR
WHITEMANS VALLEY
PAKURATAHI FOREST
2

MANOR PARK
Manor Park
PINEHAVEN
WHITEMANS RD
PINEHAVEN RD
WITAKO SCENIC RESERVE
DAVIS FIELD
Black Stream
Mangaroa
Huia Stream
3

HOLBORN
HAYWARDS HILL ROAD
STOKES VALLEY RD
Pomares
AVRO RD
BLUE MOUNTAINS
VALLEY ROAD
Narrow Neck Stream
Pakuratahi River

KELSON
KELSON SPORTS GROUND
TAITA DRIVE
2
EASTERN
TAITA
Taita
STOKES VALLEY
FRASER PARK
JOHNSONS RD
RUSSELLS RD
WHITEMANS ROAD

BELMONT
SPEEDYS RESERVE
BELMONT DOMAIN
FAIRWAY DRIVE
MAJOR DRIVE
WESTERN
HUTT
AVALON
Naenae
TAITA TERRACE
TAITA CEMETERY
RECREATION RESERVE
3

ANGA
BOULCOTT HIGH
HARCOURT
DAYS
NAENAE
CAMBRIDGE
NAENAE
NAENAE PARK
KINGS CREEK
HUTT HOSPITAL
EPUNI
FAIRFIELD
WATERLOO
Epuni
Hutt Central (Waterloo)
KNIGHTS RD

RIK WAIWHETU
Woburn
TE WHITI PARK
HAYWARD EASTERN HILLS SCENIC RESERVE
UTT ARK
RACEFIELD
WAINUIOMATA
WELLINGTON ROAD
ARAKURA
WISE STREET
RECREATION RESERVE

FRANCIS BELL RESERVE
POINT HOWARD
PARKWAY
GLENDALE
WAINUIOMATA
WAINUIOMATA SCENIC RESERVE
MOORES VALLEY RD
Wainuiomata River
4

LOWRY BAY
YORK BAY
MAHINA BAY
AYS BAY
PLANTATION RESERVE

HOMEDALE
HARRY TODD RECREATION RESERVE
Big Huia Creek
Orongorongo River
Orore Stream
RIMUTAKA FOREST PARK
Waiorongomai River
Lake Wairarapa
5

Sewage treatment plant
COAST ROAD
COAST ROAD
EAST HARBOUR REGIONAL PARK
Gollans Stream
Wainuiomata River

RIMUTAKA FOREST PARK
Orongorongo River
Whangaroa River
Mangaua Stream
EAST WEST ACCESS ROAD
WESTERN LAKE ROAD

Lake Pounui
River
6

Croziers Creek
Skull Gully Stream
Wet Branch
East Branch

Continued on map 178

NK INTERNATIONAL LIMITED 2006

■ Awhitu   POP 420

Map 158, B5

Positioned at the southern head of **Manukau Harbour** south-west of Auckland, the **Awhitu Peninsula** was an important strategic point for early Maori settlers. Today Awhitu is a small community closely connected to **Awhitu Regional Park**, while close by are galleries, beaches, historic Maori and European sites, and scenic walks.

Cow beside welcome sign, Bulls

MAIN ATTRACTIONS: Awhitu Regional Park includes historic **Brook Homestead**, dating back to the 1870s. The park also features two fine sandy beaches and a regenerating wetlands area. Also nearby is **Earthtalk**, a progressive organic farm that caters for visitors. **NEARBY ATTRACTIONS:** About 8km north-west is the strategic **Manukau Heads Signal Station**, where the HMS *Orpheus* ran aground in 1863. It offers terrific views. On the north of the peninsula is **Orua Bay Bird Park**, where a wide variety of exotic birds can be seen in park surroundings. **Matakawau**, south-west of Awhitu, hosts the **Awhitu Country Market**; **Matakawau Scenic Reserve** offers relaxing walks in regenerated bush. To the west is **Waimatuku Walks**, where visitors can walk through an award-winning bush property with historic sites and panoramic views. **VISITOR INFORMATION:** 2 Queen St, Waiuku, Ph: (09) 235 8924, www.aucklandnz.com

■ Bulls   POP 1755

Map 176, C3

The small town of Bulls, 150km north of Wellington, is the southern gateway to the peaceful, rural **Rangitikei** district, and was named after founder James Bull. **MAIN ATTRACTIONS:** Bulls has many antique and curio shops, and is known for its punning signs, illustrated with a cartoon bull, which describe the town as 'Unforget-a-Bull'. The **Rangitikei River** is popular for trout fishing. **NEARBY ATTRACTIONS:** At **Ohakea**, 3km south-west, the **Ohakea Air Force Museum** has hands-on interactive displays about New Zealand's servicemen and women and the planes they flew in the RNZAF. The **Amazing Maze 'n Maize**, 8km north, is a maze cut into a field of corn, and is open seasonally. The small coastal village of **Tangimoana**, 23km south-west at the Rangitikei River estuary, is set in sand dunes, and the beach offers fishing and swimming. Tangimoana was the site of early Maori settlements, and, after Europeans arrived, the site of a ferry which took passengers across the river to **Scott's Ferry**. The ferry has been restored and is on display. **Himatangi Beach**, to the south, is the site of New Zealand's largest sand dune field; the dunes grew so large in the 1990s that they began to encroach on neighbouring houses.

Visitor Information: 113 Bridge St, Ph: (06) 322 0055, www.rangitikei.com

■ Cambridge   POP 13 890
Map 160, E4

This charming rural **Waikato** town, 22km south-east of Hamilton, is considered to be New Zealand at its most English, and has elegant buildings, tree-lined streets and a tranquil village green. The **Waikato River** meanders through the town, which services a lush farming district and is the heart of New Zealand's equestrian and thoroughbred industry.

Main Attractions: Cambridge is centred around attractive **Victoria Square**, a park modelled on an English village green and lined with oak and elm trees. Visitors can learn more about the area's horse breeding industry at the **New Zealand Horse Magic Show**, or by touring a stud farm. Art and craft and antique shops, including the **Cambridge Country Store** in a converted 1898 Gothic-style church, provide enjoyable shopping. A heritage trail leads visitors around the town's historic buildings; **St Andrew's Anglican Church** is worth a visit for its stained glass windows and beautiful wooden interior. **Cambridge Museum** features displays of pioneer life. **Lake Te Koutu** is surrounded by a domain and bird sanctuary.

Nearby Attractions: Scenic jet boat rides are available along the Waikato River to **Lake Karapiro**,

Maori spirits departure point, Cape Reinga

8km east of Cambridge, which offers waterskiing and yachting, and is a world-class rowing venue. The hands-on **Karapiro Hydro Museum** explores how the river's power is harnessed to produce electricity.

Visitor Information: Cnr Victoria & Queen Sts, Ph: (07) 823 3456, www.cambridge.net.nz

■ Cape Reinga   POP 165
Map 152, A1

Cape Reinga, at the North Island's northern tip, overlooks the waters where the **Tasman Sea** meets the **Pacific Ocean**. A place of great spiritual significance to Maori, it is seen as the departure point for the spirits of the dead.

Main Attractions: Dramatic sea views, with waves sometimes as high as 10m, can be seen from Cape Reinga's windswept lighthouse. The pohutukawa tree on the very tip of the cape is sacred to Maori as the place where spirits depart the earth for their return to the legendary homeland of Hawaiki.

Nearby Attractions: The trip to Cape Reinga along **Ninety Mile**

Beach is spectacular. The giant sand dunes at **Te Paki**, 16km south-east, are popular for surfing and tobogganing, and there are wild horses in the **Aupouri Forest**. The walk from Cape Reinga to **Cape Maria van Diemen** takes about five hours return; to the east, lovely **Tapotupotu Bay** is a two-hour walk, and **Kapowairua** is a further eight hours. **Parengarenga Harbour** is a huge, shallow harbour; **Henderson Bay** and **Rarawa Beach** are beautiful white-sand beaches.

Visitor Information: South Rd, Kaitaia, Ph: (09) 408 0879, www.northlandnz.com

■ Carterton   POP 4100
Map 179, F3

Carterton, 85km north-east of Wellington in the **Wairarapa**, is in a farming area with a beautiful unspoilt landscape and burgeoning wine industry. The town has interesting antique and craft shops, and there are lovely walks in **Tararua Forest Park**, to the west.

Main Attractions: Carterton is known as New Zealand's **Daffodil Capital**, and hosts a popular daffodil festival every spring. A donation to charity allows visitors to pick daffodils at a farm east of the town; this has been a regular event since the 1920s. The **Paua Shell Factory** makes jewellery and souvenirs from iridescent blue-green paua shell; guided tours are available. From **Clareville**, just north of the town, the triangle formed by Chester Rd, Norfolk Rd and State Highway Two is home to antique shops, gardens, an animal park and a potter.

NEARBY ATTRACTIONS: East of Carterton, there are wineries around the pretty farming settlement of **Gladstone**; **Gladstone Vineyard** has an excellent café. There are pleasant walks in **Carter Scenic Reserve**, 12km south-east by the **Ruamahanga River**. Spectacular **Waiohine Gorge**, 15km west, is popular for camping, swimming

Lighthouse, Castlepoint

and recreation; it's also a gateway to hikes in the Tararua Forest Park, accessed via a dramatic swingbridge. Spectacular views over the area can be seen from the summit of **Mount Dick**.

VISITOR INFORMATION: 316 Queen St, Masterton, Ph: (06) 370 0900, www.wairarapanz.com

Castlepoint   POP 95
Map 179, J2

Located on the **Wairarapa**'s east coast, 68km from Masterton, this lovely coastal settlement is a base for fishing and popular with holiday makers. Castlepoint was visited by New Zealand's two most illustrious early explorers; reputedly first discovered by the Maori explorer Kupe, it was given its English name in 1770 by the British navigator Captain James Cook, who thought the majestic 162m rock formation resembled a castle. One of New Zealand's earliest sheep stations was established at Castlepoint in 1848.

MAIN ATTRACTIONS: Sport fishing charters, surfing and swimming are popular, and the sheltered lagoon offers safe swimming. Castlepoint's iconic lighthouse first began operation in 1913, and is now fully automated. The spectacular limestone reef is dotted with fossils, and offers good fishing and wonderful views. Walkers should take care on the lower reef. There is an easy half-hour return walk to the lighthouse, and a one-hour walk to a limestone cave; the climb to the top of **Castle Rock** offers great views. **Castlepoint Reserve** is home to the rare Castlepoint daisy, *Brachyglottis compactus*. There are many seals and sea birds in the area, and small whales have been seen on occasion. Regular horse races have been run on the beach since the 19th century, and are still held today.

NEARBY ATTRACTIONS: The remote coastal area of **Mataikona**,

20km north, has sandy and rocky beaches. There is a golf course at **Whakataki**.

VISITOR INFORMATION: 316 Queen St, Masterton, Ph: (06) 370 0900, www.wairarapanz.com

Clevedon   POP 455
Map 158, D4

Located on the plains south-east of Auckland city, Clevedon has a surprisingly rustic feel for a place so close to Auckland, and offers a leisurely rural lifestyle.

MAIN ATTRACTIONS: **Clevedon Animal Farm** showcases the district's rural way of life, with pony rides, farm walks and animal performances. **McNichol Homestead and Museum** has artefacts and displays which highlight early settler and farm life in the region. **Clevedon Scenic Reserve** is a 100ha reserve of native bush around the **Wairoa River** and includes numerous walking tracks. The district's craftspeople show off their wares each Sunday in the **Clevedon Market**, while for horse enthusiasts there is the **New Zealand Polo Open**, which draws good crowds every February.

NEARBY ATTRACTIONS: The Clevedon area is becoming a popular area for wineries. Tours are available; Clevedon also hosts the annual **Clevedon Wine and Food Festival**. Another spot that should appeal to food lovers is **Clevedon Coast Oysters**, about 10km north-east of the town, where visitors can watch export-quality oysters being processed. North of the town is **Duder Regional Park**, notable for its seabird colonies, coastal walks and scenic **Hauraki Gulf** views. To the south-east, about 25km along the **Pacific Coast Highway**, is the **Miranda Shorebird Centre**, one of New Zealand's best spots for bird watching.

VISITOR INFORMATION: 9 North Rd, Ph: (09) 292 8660, www.clevedon.co.nz

North Island

Sailor's Grave, Coromandel Peninsula

◼ Coromandel POP 1435
Map 159, G3

Coromandel township, 50km north of Thames on the west coast of the **Coromandel Peninsula**, was established in 1862 during the area's gold mining and timber milling boom. Today it is a popular holiday destination, and the central port for the region's green-lipped mussel aquaculture industry.

MAIN ATTRACTIONS: **Coromandel School of Mines and Historical Museum** features displays of gold mining and logging artefacts, geological specimens and photographs. The old Coromandel jailhouse at the rear of the museum is popular with visitors. New Zealand's only narrow gauge railway leads through regenerating forest at **Driving Creek Railway and Potteries**, 3km north; there's also a craft shop. Visitors can watch as real gold is processed at the **Coromandel Goldfields and Stamper Battery**, 2km north of the town.

NEARBY ATTRACTIONS: The winding, unsealed 26km **309 Road** between Coromandel and **Whitianga** features many sites of interest, including a walk up the eroded volcano of **Castle Rock**, the whimsical playground of **Waiau Waterworks**, swimming holes at **Waiau Falls** and a grove of giant kauri trees. Around **Kuaotunu**, 29km east of Coromandel, are remote and lovely beaches, including **Otama Beach** and **Opito Bay**. **Colville** is a small settlement 25km north with a charming general store. At the Coromandel Peninsula's northern tip, remote **Fletcher Bay** has secluded beaches, beautiful forests and great sea views. The **Coromandel Coastal Walkway** between Fletcher Bay and **Stony Bay** is an easy grade 7km hike through stunning coastal scenery.
VISITOR INFORMATION: 355 Kapanga Rd, Ph: (07) 866 8598, www.thecoromandel.com

◼ Dannevirke POP 5350
Map 177, G3

A service centre for the farming industry, Dannevirke is located in the **Tararua** district, 207km north-east of Wellington. The town was first settled by a handful of Danish and Norwegian families in the 1870s; the settlers' cemetery includes the graves of these pioneers, and many street names reflect Dannevirke's Scandinavian heritage. The 20ha **Domain** has a Viking ship children's playground.
MAIN ATTRACTIONS: Local **Makirikiri Marae** (Maori community meeting-place) has a meeting-house with beautiful carvings; the **Gallery of History** has displays of historical material. **Fantasy Cave** features storybook and nursery rhyme characters, and at Christmas, Santa Claus is in residence.
NEARBY ATTRACTIONS: The character village of **Norsewood**, 21km north-east, has a heritage trail and pioneer museum exploring its Scandinavian history. Norsewood also has a small award-winning cheese factory, a glass bevellers and the clothing label **Norsewear**. To the west, the steep ranges of the 94 000ha **Ruahine Forest Park** offer walking, hunting and camping in podocarp forests, tussock grasslands and alpine meadows. The forest is rich in wildlife, including some rare species. **Ngapaeruru Scenic Reserve**, 15km east, has a giant totara tree. Spectacular **Waihi Falls**, 45km east, are well worth a visit; **Akitio** and **Herbertville** are long stretches of surf beach, offering good fishing.
VISITOR INFORMATION: 156 High St, Ph: (06) 374 4167, www.tararua.com

◼ Dargaville POP 4530
Map 154, E6

Dargaville, 55km south-west of Whangarei in the **Northland** region, was founded in 1872 on the **Wairoa River**, and was once an important port exporting timber and kauri gum as the surrounding kauri forests were milled. Now known as the **Kumara Capital**, Dargaville today is a service centre for the nearby agricultural district, which produces two-thirds of New Zealand's kumara (sweet potato).
MAIN ATTRACTIONS: **Dargaville Museum** displays relics from the days of kauri milling and gum-digging, and from some of the many ships wrecked on the nearby coast. Products made from timber and kauri gum are on sale in local craft stores, and a paper mill produces paper using rice grass from the river.
NEARBY ATTRACTIONS: **Ripiro Beach**, 100km long, is the longest driveable beach in New Zealand, and extends from **Maunganui Bluff** in the north to **Pouto Point** in the south. Beach tours are available to Pouto Point, the entrance to the **Kaipara Harbour**, where visitors can see the

(CONTINUED P.89)

The Coromandel Peninsula lies on the eastern shore of the **Hauraki Gulf**, an hour and a half's drive (115km) from Auckland, or two hours (55km) by ferry across the Gulf. The peninsula is dominated by the rugged **Coromandel Range**, which forms the greater part of the **Coromandel Forest Park**, running north for 85km and rising to almost 900m at its highest point, **Mt Moehau**.

Famous for its unspoilt beaches and coastal scenery, the peninsula is also known for the sense of escape and relaxation offered by its 'alternative lifestyle' communities.

Thames is the largest town, with smaller but important settlements at **Coromandel** town, **Whitianga** and **Tairua**.

Fishing, diving and hiking opportunities abound for adventurous visitors; the peninsula's gold mining and kauri logging past features in a number of good museums. Most towns offer art and craft galleries and good dining and accommodation.

main attractions

◈ 309 Road
◈ Coromandel Coastal Walkway
◈ Coromandel Forest Park
◈ Coromandel town
◈ Goldmine Experience
◈ Hahei
◈ Hot Water Beach
◈ Opoutere Beach
◈ Te Whanganui-A-Hei Marine Reserve

Visitor information

Coromandel Information Centre
355 Kapanga Rd, Coromandel
Ph: (07) 866 8598

Thames i-SITE Visitor Centre
206 Pollen St, Thames
Ph: (07) 868 7284
www.coromandelnz.com

Hot Water Beach, Coromandel Peninsula

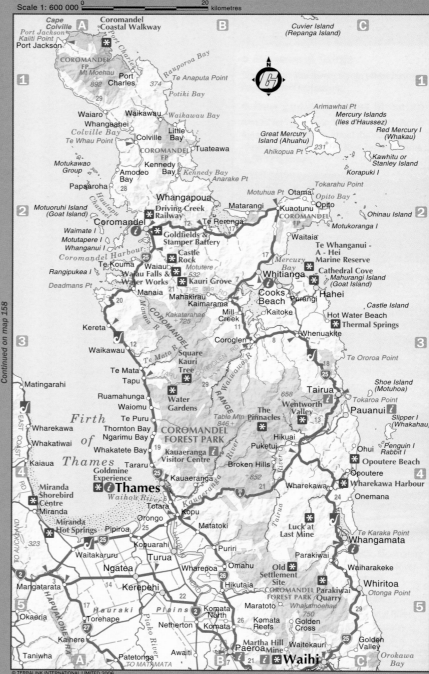

Continued on map 158

Continued on maps 160 & 161

© TERRALINK INTERNATIONAL LIMITED 2006

North Island

remote 1884 **Kaipara Lighthouse**, spectacular sand dunes and old shipwrecks. **Baylys Beach**, 12km west of Dargaville, offers cafés, sand dunes and surf; a 20-minute climb leads up **Tokatoka Peak**, the core of an old volcano. The three **Kai Iwi Lakes**, 34km north, are fresh water sand dune lakes offering fishing, swimming, sailing, wind surfing and kayaking. A half-hour walk leads from the lakes to the coast. The **Trounson Kauri Park**, 40km from Dargaville, has walks through beautiful forest, including some impressive stands of kauri trees. Guided night-time walks are an opportunity for visitors to see and hear kiwi. **Waipoua Kauri Forest** has superb, ancient kauri, including the 51m tree **Tane Mahuta**. The **Kauri Museum** at Matakohe, 44km south-east, has fascinating displays on kauri in all its facets.

VISITOR INFORMATION: Cnr Normanby & Poto Sts, Ph: (09) 439 8360, www.kauricoast.co.nz

Kai Iwi Lakes, north of Dargaville

Eketahuna   POP 580
Map 176, E6

This peaceful rural town, 142km north-east of Wellington at the south of the **Tararua** farming district, was settled by pioneers from Sweden, Germany and Norway.

MAIN ATTRACTIONS: Located close to the beautiful **Tararua Range**, Eketahuna is a good base for hiking, hunting or fishing. The town is known for its locally made, high quality woodcraft products; there are also interesting historic buildings and a pioneer cemetery.

NEARBY ATTRACTIONS: The **Pukaha Mount Bruce National Wildlife Centre**, 9km south, is an important native wildlife sanctuary, with breeding programmes for endangered native species. There are walks through the remnants of a beautiful ancient forest; among the plentiful wildlife are kiwi and the prehistoric native

reptile tuatara. The centre has daily feeding sessions for eels and for kaka, and guided tours are available. West of Eketahuna at the end of the **Mangatainoka River**, tracks lead into the **Tararua Forest Park**. Further south, the pretty **Kiriwhakapapa Valley** has walks along an old timber logging tramline; the area is home to many birds. There's an easy loop track, and a longer three-hour walk over a saddle into the neighbouring **Mikimiki Valley**; mountain biking is also possible.

VISITOR INFORMATION: 42 Vogel St, Woodville, Ph: (06) 376 1023, www.tararua.com

Eltham   POP 2100
Map 172, D4

Situated inland in central **Taranaki**, 50km south of New Plymouth, Eltham has a long history of dairy farming. New Zealand's first dairy factory was built there in 1887 by enterprising Chinese businessman Chew Chong, who had exported the country's first butter to England three years earlier. Eltham's other 'firsts' include New Zealand's first tar-sealed street and first concrete-floored milking shed.

MAIN ATTRACTIONS: Settled by Europeans in the 1870s, Eltham has many appealing heritage buildings, and historic walks lead around these. The 1911 **Municipal Buildings** contain a collection of early photos of the town; the **Town Hall** and 1904 **Post Office** are also impressive. Dairying is still a focus in Eltham, and the town's cheese factory specialises in gourmet cheeses, which can be sampled and bought at the **Cheese Bar**. The **Eltham Bird Centre** offers walks through native bush, with many birds. A quirky attraction is the **Eltham Toy Wall**, a wall with thousands of toys cemented to it.

NEARBY ATTRACTIONS: **Rotokare Scenic Reserve**, to the east, has a 4.2km walk through the forest around **Lake Rotokare**. Bird life is plentiful at the spring-fed lake, and kiwi can sometimes be heard at night. **Lake Rotorangi** is New Zealand's longest man-made lake; 46km long, it's popular for boating and fishing. From **Stratford**, 11km north, the remote **Forgotten World Highway** leads past fascinating historic sites.

VISITOR INFORMATION: 55 High St, Hawera, Ph: (06) 278 8599, www.taranaki.info

Racing at Manfeild Park, Feilding

■ **Featherston**   POP 2325

Map 178, D3

The small town of Featherston, at the base of the **Rimutaka Range** 63km north-east of Wellington, is the southern gateway to the **Wairarapa**.

MAIN ATTRACTIONS: The **Featherston Heritage Museum** commemorates the World War I military camp which was used as a prisoner of war camp in World War II; the **Fell Locomotive Museum** displays the world's only fell locomotive. This was used on the **Rimutaka Incline**, a steep section of railway which formed part of the original line into the area until the Rimutaka Tunnel was completed in 1955. Featherston has some good antique shops and historic buildings.

NEARBY ATTRACTIONS: **Lake Wairarapa**, south of the town, has attractive picnic spots and many birds. At the far end of the Western Lake Road, 39km south, is the intriguing small settlement of **Ocean Beach**, with its ramshackle array of baches (small holiday homes) across from an untamed beach, good for fishing and surfing. On the cliffs above, the luxury resort of **Wharekauhau** is quite a contrast. A two- to three-hour walk along the **Lake Onoke** spit leads to the lake outlet, opposite the settlement of **Lake Ferry**. The spit is a great spot for bird watching. Walkers and mountain bikers can follow the 18km route of the old Rimutaka railway to **Kaitoke**, north of **Upper Hutt**; the walk is signposted from **Cross Creek**, 10km south of Featherston.

VISITOR INFORMATION: The Old Courthouse, SH2, Ph: (06) 308 8051, www.wairarapanz.com

■ **Feilding**   POP 13 640

Map 176, D3

The attractive rural town of Feilding is located 20km north of Palmerston North on the **Oroua River**. Feilding is the **Manawatu**'s second largest centre, and is known for its renovated Edwardian architecture and lovely gardens; the town has been 12 times winner of 'New Zealand's Most Beautiful Town'. Feilding is also home to the southern hemisphere's largest stock sale yards.

MAIN ATTRACTIONS: The **Clock Tower** in central **Manchester Square** features the town's original, restored 1902 clock. A **Heritage Walk** takes visitors around the town's interesting buildings. The **Horse-Drawn Era Museum** has coaches, wagons and gigs, and visitors can ride in some of the vehicles; the **Steam Rail Museum** has a restored historic engine. **Manfeild Park** is home to one of New Zealand's largest motorsport venues. The **Fragrant Garden** is a nursery specialising in herbs and lavender, with attractive gardens.

NEARBY ATTRACTIONS: The pretty town of **Kimbolton**, 27km north-east, has spectacular views as far south as **Kapiti Island**. Kimbolton is home to the 7.2ha **Cross Hills Gardens**, where more than 2000 varieties of rhododendrons and azaleas put on an impressive display in spring; in the **Heritage Park** there are still more rhododendrons. The 30km-long **Pohangina Anticline**, beside the **Ruahine Range**, is a new mountain range rising at least a millimetre a year — very fast in geological terms. **Ohakea Air Force Museum**, 19km west at **Ohakea**, explores the history of the RNZAF through interactive displays, simulators and heritage aircraft. **Himatangi Beach** is part of the largest sand dune field in New Zealand, and was once an important place for Maori gathering seafood and shellfish; in the 1990s, the dunes grew so large they threatened nearby houses. **Tangimoana** is another sandy beach, popular for swimming and fishing.

VISITOR INFORMATION: 10 Manchester Square, Ph: (06) 323 3318, www.manawatunz.co.nz

■ **Foxton**   POP 4615

Map 176, B5

Located 112km north-east of Wellington in the **Horowhenua** district, Foxton was once a centre for milling native flax, with 50 mills operating within

North Island

16km at one point. Today carpet is the town's main industry.

MAIN ATTRACTIONS: Foxton's museums and galleries include the **Foxton Flax Stripping Museum**, the **Doll Gallery** and the **Trolley Bus Museum**. **Foxton Beach**, 5km to the west at the mouth of the **Manawatu River**, is a popular spot for fishing and water sports; the river estuary is home to many waterbirds, including migratory species from Siberia and Alaska.

NEARBY ATTRACTIONS: **Waitarere Forest**, to the south near **Waitarere**, was the setting for scenes in 'Osgiliath Wood' and 'Trollshaw Forest' in *The Lord of the Rings* films; the forest is also used for mountain biking and orienteering. At **Shannon**, 17km south-east, **Owlcatraz** is a native wildlife park with a focus on owls, including a large collection of owl ornaments. **Tokomaru**, north-east of Shannon, has a **Steam Museum** with heritage engines and its own railway station. **Himatangi Beach**, north of Foxton, is the site of New Zealand's largest sand dune field.

VISITOR INFORMATION: Main St, Ph: (06) 363 8940, www.foxton.org.nz

■ Gisborne   POP 32 700
Map 180, C4

The largest city in the **Eastland** region, Gisborne holds a highly significant place in New Zealand history for both Maori and Pakeha. British explorer Captain James Cook landed there in 1769 in his ship the *Endeavour*, the first time a European had set foot in New Zealand. The ancestral Maori canoes Horouta and Te Ikaroa-a-Rauru had landed at the same site, centuries earlier. Gisborne today is known for its great surf beaches; it's also the first city in the world to see the rising sun each day.

MAIN ATTRACTIONS: **Tairawhiti Museum** is one of the best regional museums in New Zealand; it has excellent displays of Maori, colonial and natural history. **Te Moana Maritime Museum** has displays on Maori canoes, Cook's journeys and early whaling, as well as a collection of early surfboards. **Cook Landing Site National Historic Reserve** commemorates the place by the mouth of the **Turanganui River** where both Captain Cook and the early Maori canoes landed. At the foot of **Titirangi (Kaiti Hill)**, the impressively carved **Te Poho-o-Rawiri meeting house** can be viewed with permission; behind the marae is a small Maori church. Titirangi also offers great views over the area. North of the river mouth are statues of Cook and *Endeavour* crew member Young Nick. **Waikanae Beach** is a popular swimming beach.

NEARBY ATTRACTIONS: Gisborne is an important area for wineries; the region is particularly known for its chardonnay. Historic **Manutuke**, 13.5km west, has some beautifully decorated Maori buildings, including **Toko Toru Tapu Maori Church**. **Eastwoodhill Arboretum**, 35km west, contains a fine collection of northern hemisphere trees and shrubs. **Rere Falls**, 15km further west, is a pretty waterfall and swimming hole, with a natural rock slide. There are excellent beaches around Gisborne; perhaps the most popular is **Wainui Beach**, 8km south-east. **Whangara**, 29km north, was the setting for the popular 2002 film *Whale Rider*; tours related to the film are available.

VISITOR INFORMATION: 209 Grey St, Ph: (06) 868 6139, www.eastlandnz.com

■ Greytown   POP 2000
Map 178, E3

Located in the **Wairarapa**, 76km north-east of Wellington, Greytown was New Zealand's first planned inland town, and was established in 1854. Fruit-growing is a focus in the surrounding countryside. Greytown has recently become a popular getaway spot for Wellingtonians, and has an increasing range of boutique accommodation.

MAIN ATTRACTIONS: Greytown's delightful main street is lined with stately trees and wooden Victorian buildings, including rose-covered cottages. The town has excellent cafés, restaurants, gift and antique shops and gourmet food outlets; nearby orchards sell fruit and

Victorian buildings in main street, Greytown

GISBORNE WINERIES

Grapes were first planted around Gisborne in the 1850s, and the region's first wines were made some 70 years later by German winemaker Friedrich Wohnsiedler. **Montana** went on to plant chardonnay around Gisborne in the 1970s.

Today the area is a major wine producer, and is known as New Zealand's chardonnay capital. Gisborne's hot sunny climate and clay loam soils are key factors in the success of the wines. These are known for their great drinkability at an early age, due to the hot weather which ripens grapes to a high sugar level.

Chardonnay accounts for just over half of the plantings, but excellent gewürztraminer, semillon, merlot and chenin blanc are also being produced, and pinot gris and viognier have a promising future in the area.

Events for wine lovers include **Taste Gisborne** in January and the **Wine and Food Festival** in October. The annual **International Chardonnay Challenge** draws hundreds of competitors from Australia, New Zealand and beyond.

Sunset over vineyards, Gisborne

 Visitor information

Gisborne i-SITE Visitor Centre
209 Grey St, Gisborne
Ph: (06) 868 6139
www.gisbornenz.com

---

vegetables at roadside stalls. **Cobblestones Museum** displays Victorian memorabilia in an early settlers' cottage; there are beautiful totara trees and a children's playground in **Soldiers' Memorial Park**. **Papawai Marae**, just east of the town, was once the centre of the Maori Parliament or Kotahitanga movement, which worked for Maori self-determination in the late 19th and early 20th century. The marae (community meeting-ground) features statues carved in the early 1900s to represent ancestors, and an 1888 meeting-house; it's possible to arrange a visit.
NEARBY ATTRACTIONS: There's good camping, swimming and recreation in the **Waiohine Gorge**, 15km north-west; the gorge is also a gateway to hikes in the **Tararua** Forest Park. **Mount Dick** offers spectacular views. **Lake Wairarapa**, to the south-east, is the lower North Island's largest wetland area, and is home to many birds. Jet boat rides and kayaking are available on the **Ruamahanga River**.
VISITOR INFORMATION: 316 Queen St, Masterton, Ph: (06) 370 0900, www.greytown.co.nz

■ **Hamilton** POP 138 800
Map 181, C3
New Zealand's fourth largest city, 129km south of Auckland, Hamilton is the main centre of the **Waikato** region. The city is one of New Zealand's major centres of learning, and has a considerable student population. The **Waikato River** flows through Hamilton, which offers a youthful, contemporary lifestyle, with cafés, bars, cinemas and theatres.
MAIN ATTRACTIONS: Stretching along the banks of the Waikato River, Hamilton has numerous riverside walks and parks, and a three-hour cruise on the historic paddleboat **MV Waipa Delta** is a fun way of exploring the river. The 58ha riverside **Hamilton Gardens** offer a series of themed gardens, including a garden of contemplation, a Chinese scholar's garden and a Victorian flower garden. The **Waikato Museum of Art and History** has an exceptional collection of Maori treasures, with a permanent display about local tribe Tainui. Nearby **Exscite** features a changing programme of science and technology exhibits, and the contemporary **ArtsPost**

North Island

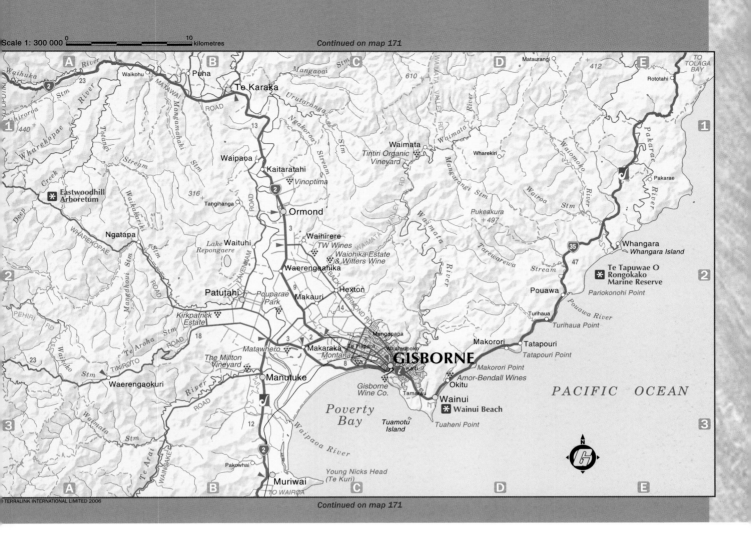

Continued on map 171

Scale 1: 300 000

Continued on map 171

gallery focuses mainly on local artists. **SKYCITY Hamilton** is the city's casino, based in the riverside entertainment centre. On Victoria Street, a statue of *Rocky Horror Picture Show* character 'Riff Raff' pays tribute to the movie's creator, ex-Hamiltonian Richard O'Brien. Award-winning **Hamilton Zoo**, 8km from the city, has dozens of native birds in Australasia's largest free flight aviary. South-west of the city, the 57ha **Lake Rotoroa** offers yachting, boating and swimming. NEARBY ATTRACTIONS: **Woodlands** is a historic estate with an 1872 homestead and lovely gardens, to the north-east at **Gordonton**. **Ngaruawahia**, 19km north of Hamilton, is a centre of great importance to Waikato Maori, and the Maori Queen's official home

is at the town's **Turangawaewae Marae**. **Waingaro Hot Springs**, 42km north-east, is a complex of pools and water attractions based around a natural thermal spring. VISITOR INFORMATION: Cnr Bryce and Anglesea Sts, Ph: (07) 839 3580, www.waikatonz.com

■ Hastings   POP 59 140
Map 182, C3
Located in the fertile agricultural area of **Hawke's Bay**, 293km north-east of Wellington, Hastings is surrounded by orchards and vineyards. The city is busy in apple harvest season as a base for fruit pickers. MAIN ATTRACTIONS: Like nearby **Napier**, Hastings was rebuilt after the devastating earthquake in 1931, and as a result is a showcase of Spanish Mission and art deco

architecture. The **Westerman's Building** and **Hawke's Bay Opera House** are highlights. Hastings is a good starting point for wine and food trails and tours, or for visiting artists and craftspeople, particularly around the coastal settlements of **Haumoana** and **Te Awanga**, to the east. A Sunday morning farmers' market brings fresh local produce and organic foods to town, and **Pernel Fruitworld**, in the area's orchard district, has more than 12 000 fruit trees. Each June, the city hosts New Zealand's most extensive celebrations for **Matariki**, the Maori New Year. The week-long festival includes performance, art, special events and fireworks. September brings the **Blossom Festival**, a spring celebration with parades, crafts and visiting artists.

The **Hawke's Bay Exhibition Centre** has contemporary and historical art exhibitions; **Splash Planet** is a water park with water slides, hot pools and a miniature castle. **Frimley Park** has an impressive rose garden.

NEARBY ATTRACTIONS: **Cape Kidnappers**, at the southern tip of Hawke's Bay, is home to the world's largest mainland gannet breeding colony, and an excellent golf course. **Waimarama** and **Ocean Beach** are sandy beaches popular for surfing; at Waimarama, cultural Maori tours are available, based around a local marae (Maori community meeting-place). At **Clive**, 10km north-east, visitors can go paddling on the **Clive River** in an 18m traditionally carved Maori canoe. West of Hastings in the **Mangatahi** wine growing area, a lavender farm offers tours.

VISITOR INFORMATION: Russell St, Ph: (06) 873 5526, www.hastings.co.nz

■ **Havelock North**   POP 9660
Map 175, J3
The **Hawke's Bay** town of Havelock North, surrounded by wineries, has a peaceful village atmosphere, and is home to three elite boarding schools.
MAIN ATTRACTIONS: Many top wineries are close to Havelock North, and offer tastings and sometimes fine dining. The **Village Growers Market** is held on Saturday mornings at **Black Barn Vineyard** through spring and summer, showcasing fresh Hawke's Bay produce. Havelock North is also known for its cafés and art galleries. Stately homesteads include **Duart House** and **Chesterton** homestead. Free tours take visitors through **Arataki Honey**, one of the southern hemisphere's biggest beekeeping enterprises with over 21 000 hives.
NEARBY ATTRACTIONS: **Te Mata Peak**, 16km south, is one of the first places in the world to see the light

each day, and has wonderful views over Hawke's Bay and the North Island. The coastal villages of **Te Awanga** and **Haumoana** are home to wineries, artists and craftspeople; there are golden sand beaches south-east at **Waimarama** and **Ocean Beach**, and Maori cultural tours are available at Waimarama. The world's largest mainland gannet breeding colony is at **Cape Kidnappers**, at the southern tip of Hawke's Bay.
VISITOR INFORMATION: The Roundabout, Ph: (06) 877 9600, www.hawkesbaynz.com

■ **Hawera**   POP 10 945
Map 172, D5
Located 70km south of New Plymouth, Hawera is the largest town in southern **Taranaki**. The service centre for a farming area blessed with rich volcanic soils, Hawera is 2km north of the southern hemisphere's largest single-site dairy factory.
MAIN ATTRACTIONS: **Hawera Water Tower** was built in 1914 to store water for fire fighters after a devastating 1912 fire, but shortly after its completion was hit by an earthquake which tipped it

sideways. Climbing the tower affords great views over the area. Elvis lives on in Hawera at the **Elvis Presley Memorial Record Room**, a huge collection of Elvis memorabilia and records. **Tawhiti Museum** is a private museum with extraordinary displays and dioramas, including life-size figures made on the premises using casts from real people. In **King Edward Park**, the **Wendy statue** is an antipodean counterpart to the Peter Pan statue in Kensington Gardens; the biennial **Wendy Festival** is a celebration for Wendies from around the world! **Dairyland**, 2km south of the town, has themed exhibits about dairy farming; visitors can ride on a simulated milk tanker. A reserve featuring the remains of the early **Turuturumokai Pa** (Maori fortified village) is 2km north.
NEARBY ATTRACTIONS: The coastline north-west of Hawera is known for its excellent surfing. Adventure activities on the **Waingongoro River**, to the west, include dam dropping and white water sledging; trips on the river pass **Okahutiti Pa**, where Maori prophet Tohu Kakahi was born. **Parihaka Pa**, about 65km

Hang gliding off Te Mata Peak, near Havelock North

North Island

Tawhiti Museum, Hawera

north-west of Hawera, is a site of great historical importance, and was a base for Maori who practised passive resistance against Taranaki land confiscations in the 1870s. Parihaka was razed by government troops in 1881, and protest leaders Te Whiti and Tohu were imprisoned without trial. Parihaka is open to visitors on the 18th and 19th of each month.

VISITOR INFORMATION: 55 High St, Ph: (06) 278 8599, www.taranaki.info

■ Helensville   POP 2215
Map 158, A2

Helensville, 47km north-west of Auckland, is at the southern tip of **Kaipara Harbour**, the largest enclosed harbour in the southern hemisphere. Helensville is an ideal base to explore the nearby waterways and surrounding rural area.

MAIN ATTRACTIONS: The region's early colonial past is showcased at the **Helensville Pioneer Museum**. A colonial kitchen, parlour and bedroom are among the leading displays. Close to the museum is the original **Helensville Courthouse**, preserved in its original 1870s style. The annual **Helensville A&P Show**, held in February, has a variety of displays showcasing the region's rural industry.

NEARBY ATTRACTIONS: **Parakai Springs Aquatic Park**, 2km north-west, has thermal pools and private spas. From **Parakai**, **Kaipara Cruises** take tourists out on Kaipara Harbour. Some cruises also depart from **Shelly Beach**. **MacNut Farms**, 11km north of Parakai, is a working macadamia nut farm which welcomes visitors. Further north is **South Head**, which can be explored by car and on horse treks. South of Helensville is **Woodhill Forest**, a good spot for picnics, mountain biking and walking; quad biking is also popular in the forest. Many of the Auckland region's leading wineries can be found in the **Kumeu–Huapai** area, about 30km south of Helensville around State Highway 16, while to the south-west is **Muriwai Regional Park**, famous for its gannet colony.

VISITOR INFORMATION: 40 Commercial Rd, Ph: (09) 420 7468, www.helensville.co.nz

■ Hunterville   POP 505
Map 176, D1

Hunterville, founded in 1884 as a timber and railway town, is located in the **Rangitikei** district, and is on both State Highway One and the main trunk railway line from Auckland to Wellington.

MAIN ATTRACTIONS: Hunterville is in sheep farming country, and the town features an impressive sculpture of a sheep-herding huntaway dog, in tribute to all the hard-working dogs of Hunterville and New Zealand. The **Hunterville Huntaway Festival** each November features a barking competition for dogs, and a dog-and-owner race which culminates in the spectacle of owners pushing their dogs in wheelbarrows. Horse treks allow visitors to explore the spectacular hill country on horseback, and the beautiful **Rangitikei River** offers trout fishing, rafting and jet boating. The **Hunterville Districts Settlers Museum and Art Gallery** has displays of pioneer equipment.

NEARBY ATTRACTIONS: The pretty, historic town of **Mangaweka** is 21km north-east of Hunterville, scenically positioned high above the Rangitikei River. Mangaweka is a centre for outdoor activities, including rafting and kayaking on the river. Rafting possibilities include trips to the ancient **Ohingaiti Boulders**, or night-time trips amidst glow-worms. **Vinegar Hill**, 40km north on the Rangitikei River, is a popular spot for picnicking, swimming and camping.

VISITOR INFORMATION: 113 Bridge St, Bulls, Ph: (06) 322 0055, www.rangitikei.com

■ Huntly   POP 6820
Map 160, D2

Located 93km south of Auckland, Huntly is surrounded by rich **Waikato** farmland and beautiful lakes. The town is known for its long history of coal mining, and for the production of bricks, which have been made there since 1884 and feature prominently in Huntly buildings. The coal- and gas-fired **Huntly Power Station** is New Zealand's largest thermal power station. The **Waikato River**

Stonyridge Vineyard, Waiheke Island

In the 1960s, Auckland became one of the first regions in New Zealand to seriously take up wine making, and it remains a quality wine-producing area. Names like **Villa Maria**, **Kumeu River**, **Babich**, **Matua Valley**, **Goldwater** and **Stonyridge** all hail from the Auckland region.

North-west Auckland produced New Zealand's first high-quality sauvignon blancs, but today this region, which includes **Henderson** and **Kumeu–Huapai**, is also a producer of quality chardonnay and reds. The **Matakana Coast** to the north-east is a new wine-producing area noted for its Bordeaux-style wines, chardonnay and pinot gris. The prolific **Waiheke Island** vineyards are known for their high-quality red wines, and the **South Auckland** area centred on **Clevedon** is developing its own reputation for reds. Most vineyards are open to the public at some time during the year, and wine tours are available.

> ### ⓘ Visitor information
> **New Zealand i-SITE Visitor Centre**
> 137 Quay St, Princes Wharf, Auckland
> Ph: 0800 AUCKLAND
> www.aucklandnz.com

Oak wine barrels at Matua Valley

New Zealand's largest thermal power station, Huntly Power Station

flows through the town, bordered by wetlands.

MAIN ATTRACTIONS: The **Waikato Coalfields Museum**, in a historic 1890 homestead within a scenic reserve, explores Huntly's mining and cultural history and includes a reconstructed mine tunnel. A walkway leads around **Lake Hakanoa**, a popular spot for boating and fishing. The **Hakarimata Walkway**, 2km south of Huntly on the west bank of the Waikato River, leads through a native bush reserve, including a grove of giant kauri trees.

NEARBY ATTRACTIONS: Vintage steam trains run on the former **Rotowaro** to **Glen Afton** railway, 12km west of Huntly; the line was established for transporting coal. A 14km walking trail along the west side of the Waikato River leads from Huntly north to **Rangiriri**, the site of a decisive 1863 battle between Maori warriors and British troops. The **Rangiriri Battle Site Heritage Centre** has displays about the battle, and the defensive earthworks are still visible. **Waingaro Hot Springs**, 25km south-east, has thermally heated pools and water attractions; guided tours are available through **Nikau Cave**, a limestone glow-worm cave on a private farm to the west.

VISITOR INFORMATION: 160 Great South Rd, Ph: (07) 828 6406, www.waikatonz.com

◼ Inglewood   POP 2930
Map 172, D2

Located 13km south-east of New Plymouth in the **Taranaki** region, Inglewood is picturesquely sited in rich dairying pasture, with majestic **Mount Taranaki** as a backdrop.

MAIN ATTRACTIONS: The **Fun Ho! National Toy Museum** has more than 3000 toys from the iconic New Zealand toy company, which was based in Inglewood for

(CONTINUED P.98)

North Island

Scale 1 : 300 000

0   10   kilometres

Tarahiki I (Shag I)

Thumb Point (Te Patu Point)
Horohoru Rock
Hooks Bay
Pakatoa Island
Rotoroa Island

Ponui Island (Chamberlins Island)

Pakihi Island (Sandspit Island)
Karamuramu Island

Waiheke Island
Ouhiti Bay
Cowes
Passage Rock
Orapiu
Waiheke

Onetangi
Thompsons Pt
Peninsula Estate
Nani I
Palm Beach
Obsidian
Onetangi Estate
Saratoga Estate
Stonyridge
Te Motu
Ridgeview Estate
Te Whau
Omiha

Oneroa
Cable Bay
Mudbrick
Goldwater
Kennedy Point

Tamaki Strait

Raukura Point

Orere Point
Orere

Kawakawa Bay

HUNUA RANGES

Hunua Ranges Regional Park
Upper Mangatawhiri Reservoir
Moumoukai

Kohukohunui

Koheruahi Point
Whakakaiwhara Pt

Waikopua Bay
Clevedon

Omana Beach
Puhinui Stm
Inverness
Ness Valley
Arahura

Hunua
Hunua Falls

Happy Valley
Paparimu

Mangatangi
Mangatawhiri

Waitoa River

Whitford
Brookby
Ardmore
Alfriston

Ponga

Bombay

Motukaraka Island

Rakino Island
Motutapu Island Recreation Res
Home Bay
Emu Point

Browns Island (Motukorea)
Musick Point

Buckland's Beach
Howick
Howick Historical Village
Pakuranga
East Tamaki
Otara

Rainbow's End Adventure Park

Papakura
Drury
Opaheke
Runciman

Ramarama

Paparata

Billy Goat Point

Rangitoto Island Scenic Reserve
Rangitoto

Rangitoto Channel

North Head

Kelly-Tarlton's Underwater World

AUCKLAND

One Tree Hill
Stardome Observatory

Manukau City Centre

Manurewa

Paerata
Helvetia
Pukekohe East

Pukekohe

North Shore
Ihesay Bay
Castor Bay
Marangi Bay
Milford
Devonport

Waitemata Harbour

Auckland

Manukau's Pollen Island

Villa Maria
Ihumatao

Ellets Beach
Kataka
Te Hihi
Kingseat

Glenbrook
Mauku
Sedgebrook
Glenbrook Vintage Railway

Albany Heights
Albany Village
Coatesville
Patenemoremo

Riverhead
Huapai
Kumeu
Taupaki
Swanson
Henderson
Babich
Pleasant Valley

West Harbour
Massey
Te Atatu

New Lynn

Mangere Bridge
Cape Horn
Pukekohe
Island

Manukau Harbour

Grahams Beach
Awhitu

Clarks Beach
Waiau Pa
Waiau Beach

Te Toro
Waipipi

Kohekohe
Lake Pokorua

Waikato River

Wharepapa
Woodhill
Rewiti
Waimauku
Wainui

Waitakere

WAITAKERE RANGES

Waitakere Ranges Regional Park

Bethells Resvr
Lower Nihotupu Resvr
Upper Nihotupu Resvr
Huia Resvr
Lower Huia Resvr

Parau
Cornwallis
Laingholm
Little Huia
Huia

Big Bay
Orua Bay
Mako Pt

Awhitu Central
Matakawau
Pollok

Waiuku River

Waikato River

Waiuku

Te Henga (Bethells Beach)
Piha
Tautomo I
Karekare
Anawhata
Panatahi Island

Whatipu

South Head
Whiatu Stm

Manukau Entrance

TASMAN SEA

NORTH ISLAND   97

Matakana Wineries

Omaha Flats
The Antipodean
Takatu

Matakana
Matakana Estate
Ascension
Heron's
Hyperion
Eldon

Warkworth
Sandspit
Snells Beach
Algies Bay

Mahurangi

Ransom

TO WELLSFORD

TO HAMILTON

TERRALINK INTERNATIONAL LIMITED 2006

almost 50 years. A magnificent rhododendron in the middle of town is reputed to be one of New Zealand's largest; Inglewood also has New Zealand's oldest standing original railway station.

NEARBY ATTRACTIONS: Inglewood is a base for trips to **Egmont National Park**, which has over 300km of walking trails on and around beautiful Mount Taranaki, through sub-alpine forest and to waterfalls and lookouts. **Pukeiti Rhododendron Trust**, west of Inglewood, is internationally renowned for its impressive collection of rhododendrons. **Everett Park Scenic Reserve**, 9km north-east, has swimming holes, native bush and glow-worms. **Lake Mangamahoe**, 10km north-west, has tracks for walking and mountain biking; beautiful reflections of Mount Taranaki can often be seen in the lake.

VISITOR INFORMATION: 1 Ariki St, New Plymouth, Ph: (06) 759 6060, www.taranaki.info

■ Kaikohe   POP 4025

Map 154, D2

Located in the centre of **Northland**, Kaikohe provides shopping and service facilities for the surrounding farming, horticultural and forestry district. Kaikohe is a centre for the northern Maori tribe of Ngapuhi, and the chief Hone Heke, known for his challenges to British sovereignty in the 1840s, spent his last years in the town.

MAIN ATTRACTIONS: **Monument Hill** has a memorial to another Hone Heke, one of New Zealand's earliest Maori MPs, who was named after his warrior great-uncle. The **Kaikohe Pioneer Village** is a re-created 19th century village. **Rawiri Taiwhanga Park** commemorates New Zealand's first Maori commercial farmer, who ran a dairy farm on the outskirts of town in the 1840s.

NEARBY ATTRACTIONS: The Kaikohe

Ahipara rock pools, Ninety Mile Beach

district was the scene of fighting between Maori and British troops during the Northland wars of the 1840s. **St Michael's Church**, 7km north-east, marks the site of the 1845 **Ohaeawai** battle in which the British were defeated by warrior chief Hone Heke. The Maori fighters repelled the British from a pa (fortified village) with highly innovative fortifications and entrenchment. The **Mission House** at **Waimate North**, built in 1832, features period furnishings. **Ngawha**, 6km east of Kaikohe, has hot springs. To the north, **Puketi and Omahuta Forests** are home to majestic kauri trees and native wildlife.

VISITOR INFORMATION: State Highway 12, Omapere, Ph: (09) 405 8869, www.northlandnz.com

■ Kaitaia   POP 5150

Map 152, E5

The main town in the **Far North**, Kaitaia services an area of farming, fruit and avocado growing. The town was once a centre for **Northland**'s kauri gum industry, which exported gum to make varnish, linoleum and other products. Many Dalmatians came to the area as gum diggers, and Kaitaia still has a strong Dalmatian

community, as well as many Maori.

MAIN ATTRACTIONS: The **Far North Regional Museum** has displays on kiwi, moa and gum digging. Maori cultural attractions include arts and crafts demonstrations, and traditional herbal medicines. **Okahu Estate Winery**, 3km south-west, is an award-winning winery; the **Kaitaia Walkway**, 3km south-east, leads to a kauri grove and lookout.

NEARBY ATTRACTIONS: The beautiful beach at **Ahipara**, 14km south-west, offers fishing, surfing and horse riding, and has massive sand dunes. Ahipara was once the site of a kauri gum field worked by 2000 diggers. The **Te Houtaewa Challenge** is a marathon held each March on **Ninety Mile Beach**, and celebrates the legendary Maori runner Te Houtaewa, who was sent out by his mother to get kumara (sweet potato) from nearby gardens, but instead ran the length of the beach to steal it from another village. The **Herekino Forest Track**, which starts 16km from Kaitaia, is a 15km walk through forest, including groves of large kauri. At the **Ancient Kauri Kingdom** at **Awanui**, 7km north, furniture made from 50 000-year-old swamp kauri stumps is on display. **Lake Ngatu** is a freshwater dune lake and popular

North Island

picnic spot. **Gumdiggers Park**, 35km north of Kaitaia, is the site of a historic gum field, with relics including an original gum digger's hut, holes and shafts.

VISITOR INFORMATION: Jaycee Park, South Rd, Ph: (09) 408 0879, www.northlandnz.com

■ **Katikati** POP 2915
Map 161, H2
Katikati is located on the **Uretara River**, in the western **Bay of Plenty** 34km north-west of Tauranga. The town is in a horticultural area producing avocados, lavender, kiwifruit, citrus and flowers, and is known for its many murals.

MAIN ATTRACTIONS: The information centre has a map of the murals, and tours are also available. The **Haiku Pathway** is a walk leading to a peaceful riverside park, past a series of river boulders with haiku carved into them. The **Katikati Heritage Museum** explains local history, starting with the arrival of Maori, then telling the stories of the town's 19th century Ulster pioneers.

NEARBY ATTRACTIONS: **Morton Estate**, 8km south, is one of New Zealand's larger wineries, and offers tastings and door sales. **Sapphire Springs** is a complex of hot thermal pools; there are also hot springs at **Athenree**, 12km north. **Katikati Bird Gardens** have lovely gardens populated by peacocks and other birds. **Omokoroa Beach**, on a promontory in **Tauranga Harbour**, is a popular spot in summer; it has lovely harbour views and hot springs. A ferry from Omokoroa crosses the harbour to peaceful **Matakana Island**, where there are white-sand surf beaches. **Kauri Point Historic Reserve**, 5km north of Katikati, has historic Maori fortifications and beautiful pohutukawa trees on the shoreline, and its jetty is popular for fishing. From **Te Kura a Maia (Bowentown Heads)**, a former pa site, there are spectacular views of Matakana Island and the harbour. There are also many lovely walks in the nearby **Kaimai-Mamaku Forest Park**.

VISITOR INFORMATION: 36 Main Rd, Ph: (07) 549 1658, www.katikati.org.nz

■ **Kawakawa** POP 1400
Map 155, F2
Once a coal mining town, the small town of Kawakawa is the southern gateway to the **Bay of Islands**. The internationally known Austrian architect and artist Friedensreich Hundertwasser made his home near the town from the mid-1970s till his death in 2000.

MAIN ATTRACTIONS: Kawakawa is known for its public toilets designed by Hundertwasser in inimitable 'organic' style, featuring curves and spirals, colourful mosaics, a roof planted in grass, and embedded recycled bottles which serve as windows.

NEARBY ATTRACTIONS: The **Kawiti Caves** at **Waiomio**, 4km south, feature white limestone formations and glow-worms, and the Maori meeting-house and marae there are a memorial to Kawiti, an important figure in the 1840s Northland wars between Maori and Europeans. Earthworks from Kawiti's **Ruapekapeka Pa** (fortified village) can still be seen, 18km south of Kawakawa. This impressively fortified pa was occupied by the British in 1846. The small town of **Moerewa**, 6km west, has a collective of Maori-owned businesses, including a café and gallery.

VISITOR INFORMATION: The Wharf, Marsden Rd, Paihia, Ph: (09) 402 7345, www.northlandnz.com

■ **Kawerau** POP 6975
Map 163, J4
The forestry town of Kawerau, surrounded by pine plantations, is located on the inland plains of the eastern **Bay of Plenty**. Kawerau was founded in 1954 to accommodate workers at the huge, then-newly-established pulp and paper mill, which processes wood from vast **Kaingaroa Forest**.

MAIN ATTRACTIONS: Kawerau has a free thermally heated swimming pool. Visitors can book for a two-hour tour of the **Norske Skog Tasman/ Carter Holt Harvey Tasman Mills**. The dormant volcano of **Putauaki (Mount Edgecumbe)** contrasts strikingly with the plains

Hundertwasser-designed public toilets, Kawakawa

which surround it, and there are panoramic views from the summit; visitors need an access permit. A beautiful walk leads from the town along the **Tarawera River** to the **Tarawera Forest**.

NEARBY ATTRACTIONS: From a road in the forest, a 15-minute walk through native bush leads to the magnificent **Tarawera Falls**. The falls emerge from a lava cave in the canyon wall; a further walk continues to the top of the falls, and onward to **Lake Tarawera**, with beautiful views of the lake and **Mount Tarawera** en route. A permit is needed to access the walk. To the west, **Lake Rotoma** and **Lake Rotoehu** offer trout fishing, swimming and boating.

VISITOR INFORMATION: Plunkett St, Ph: (07) 323 7550, www.kaweraudc.govt.nz

■ Kawhia   POP 505

Map 160, B5

The quiet town of Kawhia is a fishing port on a pretty harbour on the western **Waikato** coast. Kawhia is hugely important to the Waikato's Maori people as the final landing spot and resting place of the Tainui canoe, in which their ancestors migrated to New Zealand during the 14th century.

MAIN ATTRACTIONS: Two large upright stones in the grounds of Kawhia's **Maketu Marae** (Maori meeting-ground) mark the stern and prow of the canoe, buried there by the canoe's leaders after their epic journey across the Pacific. The pohutukawa tree to which they tied the canoe still grows on the beachfront. The marae also features an impressive carved meeting-house, though permission is needed to visit. **Ocean Beach**, a windswept spot 6km west, is home to the thermally heated **Te Puia Springs**, which well up through the sand. **Kawhia Museum** displays historic photos, Maori carvings and Jurassic fossils. Kawhia hosts an annual festival of traditional Maori food in February. The town also offers kayaking, swimming, walking and horse trekking; heritage cruises on the harbour visit Maori and European historic sites.

NEARBY ATTRACTIONS: The back roads to **Raglan**, 55km north, are mostly unsealed, but scenic. West of Kawhia, there are walking trails in the 13 000ha **Pirongia Forest Park**, and panoramic views from the top of **Mount Pirongia**.

VISITOR INFORMATION: 4 Wallis St, Raglan, Ph: (07) 825 0556, www.waikatonz.com

■ Kerikeri   POP 4855

Map 153, H6

The relaxed town of Kerikeri, at the northern end of the **Bay of Islands**, offers orchards, arts and crafts, a café culture and historic attractions. Kerikeri was once a base for the Maori chief Hongi Hika, who fought many other tribes in the early 19th century, but encouraged European settlement and trading. As a result, a missionary station — New Zealand's second — was established at Kerikeri in 1819.

MAIN ATTRACTIONS: The 1832 **Stone Store** is New Zealand's oldest stone building, and the 1821 **Mission House** is the country's oldest house. Both are open to visitors, and the Stone Store displays the types of goods that were once bartered there. A ten-minute historical walk leads to the terraces of **Kororipo Pa**, once the fortress of Hongi Hika. Across the river, a 4km track through the scenic reserve leads to the 27m **Rainbow Falls**, passing some lovely spots for swimming and picnicking. An **Arts and Crafts Trail** guides visitors around the studios and galleries of the area's many artisans. **Rewa's Village** is a re-creation of a pre-European Maori village. Steamboat cruises are available on the **Kerikeri River**. A 20km walking track links Kerikeri to the historically important town of **Waitangi**, partly following old Maori trails. The track is one section of the partly developed **Te Araroa trail**, which when complete will be a walking trail the length of New Zealand.

NEARBY ATTRACTIONS: The area around Kerikeri has wineries and gourmet food producers, and roadside stalls offer fresh produce from the area's

Locals outside the Kawhia Rowing Regatta Club, Kawhia

North Island

orchards. **Aroha Island**, 12km north-east, is a 5ha island with many native birds, including kiwi. Beautiful **Matauri Bay** is home to the 17 **Cavalli Islands**, which offer secluded beaches for swimming, snorkelling and fishing. Diving is excellent around the submerged wreck of the *Rainbow Warrior*; **Motukawanui Island** has many pre-European archaeological sites.
VISITOR INFORMATION: Cobham Rd, Ph: (09) 407 9297, www.northlandnz.com

■ Lake Ferry   POP 130
Map 178, C5

The small coastal settlement of Lake Ferry, situated at the outlet of **Lake Onoke** in the southern **Wairarapa**, offers beautiful views over **Palliser Bay**, and to the South Island on a clear day. New Zealand's first sheep station was established 28km north of Lake Ferry in 1844. At that time, sheep were herded around the coast from Wellington; the publican at Lake Ferry had the men and animals ferried across the lake mouth, hence the name Lake Ferry.
MAIN ATTRACTIONS: Lake Ferry is a popular spot for surf casting, and there is good fishing in Lake Onoke. The historic **Lake Ferry Hotel** has wonderful views over the lake and sea, and is a great spot for a seafood meal.
NEARBY ATTRACTIONS: Lake Ferry is a base for visiting **Cape Palliser**, the North Island's southernmost area. Early archaeological sites are common in the area, which was home to Maori over a number of centuries; legend has it that the early navigator Kupe lived here, and the massive rock slabs **Nga-Ra-a-Kupe** (Kupe's sails) are named for him. Cape Palliser also has an 1897 lighthouse, nattily painted with red stripes, and a fur seal breeding colony where seal pups can often be seen frolicking in a pool. The **Putangirua Pinnacles**, dramatic landforms eroded by rain, are a

Fishing from jetty, Point Wells, south of Leigh

three-hour return walk in **Aorangi Forest Park**. The spit across Lake Onoke's mouth was accessible from Lake Ferry by ferry in days gone by; today it can only reached by a 40km drive around the lake, but offers an interesting walk with many sea birds. The tiny settlement of **Ocean Beach** has many rustic baches (small holiday homes).
VISITOR INFORMATION: 18 Kitchener St, Martinborough, Ph: (06) 306 9043, www.wairarapanz.com

■ Leigh   POP 425
Map 157, F3

A tiny community on the east coast, 86km north of downtown Auckland, Leigh is the gateway to a series of natural attractions.
MAIN ATTRACTIONS: Offshore **Goat Island**, the first marine reserve in New Zealand, is abundant with marine life, including snapper, crayfish, sponges, and sometimes dolphins and orca; the water is usually beautifully clear. Those who don't want to get wet can get great views from glass-bottomed tour boats. Close by is **Seafriends**, an educational field centre with an

aquarium, library and restaurant.
NEARBY ATTRACTIONS: **Pakiri**, 9km north-west, is a relaxing white sand beach with good surf and horse trekking. **Ti Point Reptile Park**, about 5km south, is New Zealand's only reptile zoo and features the tuatara, an ancient relative of lizards which has survived for 200 million years. Another 10km south in **Point Wells** is the **Longreach Estate Ostrich Farm**, featuring hatchery tours, ostrich walks and ostrich products. Further south is the **Matakana Coast** winery district. East of this area is **Sandspit**, where ferries leave for historic **Kawau Island**, featuring **Mansion House**, Governor George Grey's former stately house that is now a museum.
VISITOR INFORMATION: 3 Takatu Rd, Matakana, Ph: (09) 422 7433, www.warkworth-information.co.nz

■ Levin   POP 19 045
Map 176, C6

A thriving provincial town servicing a horticultural area with many orchards and berryfruit growers, Levin is the largest town in the

Horowhenua district. It is located 94km north-east of Wellington at the base of the magnificent **Tararua Range**.

Main Attractions: Around Levin, roadside stalls offer fresh produce from the market gardens and orchards. Levin is also home to a garment manufacturing industry, and factory shops have clothing bargains on sale. **Lake Horowhenua**, to the west, offers yachting and rowing. **Waitarere** and **Hokio Beach** are pleasant sandy beaches with good swimming and fishing. Scenes for *The Lord of the Rings* films were shot in **Waitarere Forest**; the forest's pine plantation did duty as 'Osgiliath Wood' and 'Trollshaw Forest'.

Nearby Attractions: Tiny **Manakau**, 12km south, was once a busy sawmilling and flax milling town, and has a number of historic buildings. **Waikawa Beach**, 5km west of Manakau, was the site of the first pa (Maori fortified village) established in the area by Te Rauparaha, an expansionist Maori warrior chief who controlled a considerable portion of New Zealand in the early 19th century. Further south, **Otaki Forks** is the main western entrance to the

beautiful **Tararua Forest Park**; there are a number of short walks, and also a four-day walk leading across the ranges to **Kaitoke**. At **Shannon**, 18km north-east, **Owlcatraz** is a nature park featuring native owls.

Visitor Information: 93 Oxford St, Ph: (06) 367 8440, www.naturecoast.co.nz

■ **Mahia Beach**   POP 400
Map 171, G5

A coastal settlement 85km south of Gisborne, at the northern end of **Hawke's Bay**, Mahia Beach is a holiday town and the gateway to **Mahia Peninsula**.

Main Attractions: Windswept, beautiful 374ha Mahia Peninsula was originally an island, but has been joined to the mainland by sand accumulation. **Mahia Peninsula Scenic Reserve** is one of the east coast's last remaining large tracts of lowland coastal forest. It can be walked in about two hours on a 3.5km loop track that goes through a variety of native vegetation. Swimming, fishing, surfing and diving are also popular.

Nearby Attractions: **Clonkeen Caves**, north of **Nuhaka**, are 6.3km-long caves which feature stalactites, stalagmites, glow-worms and

limestone formations. **Morere**, 26km north-west of Mahia Beach, is a sedate town; it is most popular for **Morere Hot Springs**, thermal pools in a scenic reserve. About 100km north-west is **Lake Waikaremoana** at the southern tip of **Te Urewera National Park**, an area of spectacular scenery and lush native forests. The 46km track around Lake Waikaremoana is classed as one of New Zealand's 'Great Walks'.

Visitor Information: Cnr SH2 and Queen St, Wairoa, Ph: (06) 838 7440, www.wairoanz.com

■ **Manaia**   POP 950
Map 172, C4

The peaceful small town of Manaia is located near the southern coast of **Taranaki** at the foot of beautiful **Mount Taranaki**. Manaia is a service centre for the local farming area, and is also home to New Zealand's largest privately owned bakery.

Main Attractions: A walkway through the **Manaia Domain** leads past historic sites from the 19th century Taranaki wars, including a historic redoubt, and 1880 blockhouses built by the armed constabulary. New Zealand country singers are the focus of displays at the **Taranaki Country Music Hall of Fame**.

Nearby Attractions: **Kaupokonui Beach**, 7km west, is a good swimming beach; swimming and surfing are also popular at **Ohawe Beach**, 8km east. The **Ohawe Military Cemetery** has the graves of British soldiers who died in the 1866 Battle of Otapawa. Near **Okaiwa**, **Te Ngutu o Te Manu** is a scenic reserve which was once the site of historical battles between Maori and Europeans; today it's a picnic spot with bush walks. There is good trout fishing on the **Waingongoro River**. At **Kapuni**, 7km north of Manaia, the flares from the **Natural Gas Corporation Kapuni Treatment**

"Bread Capital" sign, Manaia

North Island

Station are an impressive sight from the road; the station is not open to the public. At **Kaponga**, 15km north, the **Hazelwood Horse Ornament Collection** is a house filled with horse paraphernalia. The 10ha **Hollard Gardens**, 4km north of Kaponga, feature a significant collection of native and exotic plants. Further north is the southern entrance to **Egmont National Park**, and the visitor centre at **Dawson Falls**.

VISITOR INFORMATION: 55 High St, Hawera, Ph: (06) 278 8599, www.taranaki.info

■ Mangawhai　POP 655
Map 156, E2

The small twin villages of Mangawhai Heads and Mangawhai Point, 121km north of Auckland, are popular with visitors for their beaches, bush walks, beautiful views and cafés.

MAIN ATTRACTIONS: Mangawhai is nestled around a harbour bordered by huge sand dunes on one side, and mangroves and pohutukawa trees on the other. Several threatened bird species nest in the estuary's bird sanctuary. **Mangawhai Heads Beach** offers excellent surfing, and fishing from its rocky headlands. The **Mangawhai Cliffs Walkway** has spectacular views inland and over the **Hauraki Gulf** and **Hen and Chicken Islands**. There are five white-sand beaches within 15 minutes' drive. Mangawhai also features galleries, cafés and a historic hotel.

NEARBY ATTRACTIONS: The road to **Langs Beach** and **Waipu Cove** has beautiful views, particularly in summer when the pohutukawas are in full crimson flower. **Waipu**, 20km north-west, was settled from the 1850s by a religious community of Scottish Highlanders, who were previously based in Nova Scotia but driven further afield by hardship and difficult

Heritage buildings at Mangonui

weather. **Highland Games** are held in the town every New Year's Day, and **Waipu Heritage Centre** has displays on the settlers' lives. There are glow-worms and limestone formations in the **Waipu Caves**, and a walkway offers views over **Bream Bay**. The **Brynderwyn Walkway** is a demanding hike offering spectacular views.

VISITOR INFORMATION: Moir St, Ph: (09) 431 5090, www.mangawhai.co.nz

■ Mangonui　POP 1585
Map 153, F5

The fishing port of Mangonui is the main town in the **Far North**'s **Doubtless Bay**, an area of lovely beaches and rocky coves. The bay was named in 1769 by Captain Cook, who noted in his logbook that it was 'doubtless a bay'. Doubtless Bay was a centre for whaling from the late 18th century, and Mangonui — the name means 'Great Shark' in Maori — was once a thriving port used by whalers and traders.

MAIN ATTRACTIONS: Mangonui's waterfront is lined with historic buildings from its days exporting flax, kauri wood and gum, and many of the buildings are now home to cafés, galleries and art shops. A **Heritage Trail** leads visitors around the town's historic sites. There are walks to **Mill Bay** and **Rangikapiti Pa Historic Reserve**, which has early Maori terracing and spectacular views over Doubtless Bay. Mangonui's award-winning fish and chip shop is reputed to be one of New Zealand's best.

NEARBY ATTRACTIONS: West of the town, 2.5km-long **Coopers Beach** is a safe swimming beach edged with pohutukawa trees. **Cable Bay** offers good surfing; **Taipa**, where the early Maori explorer Kupe reputedly landed, has open ocean and a sheltered estuary. The **Karikari Peninsula** has ocean beaches on its east side and quiet inlets on the west, with a golf resort and winery on the road to **Maitai Bay**. **Tokerau Beach** offers excellent surfcasting; **Whatuwhiwhi** features a swimming beach, and **Rangiputa** is a pretty village. **Butler Point**, east of Mangonui (15km by car or 150m by boat), has a whaling museum, restored early homestead, gardens and Maori pa site. **Whangaroa Harbour**, to the east, is a base for game fishing and trips to the **Cavalli Islands**.

VISITOR INFORMATION: Waterfront Rd, Ph: (09) 406 2046, www.doubtlessbay.com

■ Martinborough   POP 1355
Map 178, E4

Founded in 1881 near New Zealand's first sheep station in the southern **Wairarapa**, the small town of Martinborough is the centre of a winery area, internationally known for its pinot noir. The first vines were planted here in the late 1970s; since then, Martinborough has been transformed from a sleepy farming town to a self-styled wine village which attracts many visitors. Olive groves are also being planted around the town, and produce some excellent olive oils.

MAIN ATTRACTIONS: Martinborough's streets radiate out from its historic central **Square** in a Union Jack pattern. There are around 30 wineries surrounding the Square, most of which welcome visitors and offer tastings. The

Wairarapa Growers Market, every Sunday, sells produce, crafts and food. **Toast Martinborough**, held each November, is a highly popular festival showcasing wine, food and music.

NEARBY ATTRACTIONS: The back roads via the **Ponatahi Valley** north-east to **Gladstone** — another wine growing area — are a scenic drive through pretty countryside dotted with early buildings. **Tora Hau Nui Wind Farm**, 21km south-east, was New Zealand's first commercial wind farm. The wild coastal areas of **Tora** and **White Rock**, to the south-east, offer good surfing and fishing; the **Tora Coastal Walk** is a three-day guided hike which takes in farmland, native bush and dramatic coastal scenery. **Lake Ferry**, 36km south-west at the mouth of **Lake Onoke**, has a historic hotel with expansive sea and lake views, and is popular for surfcasting. **Palliser Bay**, further south, has Maori archaeological sites, rugged coastline, a seal colony and the dramatic **Putangirua Pinnacles**.

VISITOR INFORMATION: 18 Kitchener St, Ph: (06) 306 9043, www.wairarapanz.com

■ Marton   POP 4750
Map 176, C2

Marton, 170km north of Wellington in the southern **Rangitikei** basin, is an educational centre and a service town for the local farming district.

MAIN ATTRACTIONS: Marton has many lovely heritage homes and gardens; restored buildings at **Marton Historical Village** include a pioneer cottage, a police cell block and a barn. There is good trout fishing in the **Rangitikei River**. To the east on State Highway One, the **Amazing Maze 'n Maize** is a maze cut into a field of corn, and is open seasonally.

NEARBY ATTRACTIONS: The **Ohakea Air Force Museum**, 16km south, is an interactive museum with a focus on the planes and people of the RNZAF. The small Maori town of **Ratana**, 20km west, is the home of the Ratana faith, a prophetic Maori Christian movement founded in the 1920s. Thousands of people descend on the tiny township every year in a pilgrimage of Ratana followers.

VISITOR INFORMATION: 113 Bridge St, Bulls, Ph: (06) 322 0055, www.rangitikei.com

■ Masterton   POP 19 500
Map 179, F2

The main town of the **Wairarapa** region, Masterton is 100km north-east of Wellington and is the service centre for the surrounding farming area.

MAIN ATTRACTIONS: **Aratoi Wairarapa Museum of Art & History** is a stylish gallery and museum with art and historical exhibitions. **Queen Elizabeth Park** has beautiful gardens, a lake, a children's playground, a skate park and miniature train. The recreation centre has one of New Zealand's longest hydroslides. The **Wairarapa International Balloon Fiesta**, held annually in March, is a five-day showcase of hot air ballooning, including a magical evening event featuring tethered, lighted balloons

Main street, Martinborough

North Island

and fireworks. New Zealand's national shearing contest, the **Golden Shears**, is also held in March. Man-made **Henley Lake** is popular for walking and picnicking.
NEARBY ATTRACTIONS: There are a growing number of wineries in the countryside around Masterton, to the north at **Opaki** and south around **Gladstone**. **Holdsworth**, 17km west, is the main eastern gateway to the **Tararua Forest Park**; there are short and long walks through beautiful native forest. The **Pukaha Mount Bruce National Wildlife Centre**, 30km north, is a wildlife sanctuary where rare native species are bred. Visitors can walk among the remnants of a beautiful ancient forest, see kiwi and the prehistoric native reptile tuatara, or watch feeding sessions (held separately) for eels and kaka. **Castlepoint** and **Riversdale**, both east of Masterton on the Pacific coast, are popular swimming and surfing beaches.
VISITOR INFORMATION: 316 Queen St, Ph: (06) 370 0900, www.wairarapanz.com

■ Matakana   POP 265
Map 157, F4

The small town of Matakana, 73km north of Auckland, hosted an exotic plant nursery for Governor George Grey in the 1860s. Today it's the hub of a notable wine, craft and tourism area.
MAIN ATTRACTIONS: Matakana and the immediate surrounding area is best known today for its wineries, which have an increasing reputation, particularly for chardonnay, pinot gris and Bordeaux-style blends. Wine tours are available. Saturday morning's **Matakana Village Farmers Market** is a good place to sample the region's culinary products. Close to the village is **Matakana Country Park**, a relaxing slice of farm life.
NEARBY ATTRACTIONS: Tile company **Morris & James** offers daily tours

'Hobbiton', film set for *The Lord of the Rings*, near Matamata

of their pottery, several kilometres east. Farmland, forest, walkways and pristine harbour views can be seen at **Tawharanui Regional Park**, about 10km east. Native plants have flourished thanks to a regeneration project, and the area is now predator-free. At **Goat Island Marine Reserve** a huge variety of marine life can be seen from boats or while snorkelling. The unique lizard-like tuatara is an attraction at **Ti Point Reptile Park**, about 5km south of Goat Island. **Kawau Island**, featuring the historic **Mansion House** built for Governor Grey in the 1860s and some quality walks, is accessible by ferry from **Sandspit**, 10km south-east. Just west is **Warkworth**, home of rural attractions such as **SheepWorld** and Honey Centre, while 5km north of Matakana is **Longreach Estate Ostrich Farm** at **Point Wells**. The area can be viewed by helicopter via **Skywork Helicopters**, based about 5km east of Matakana.
VISITOR INFORMATION: 3 Takatu Rd, Ph: (09) 422 7433, www.matakanacoast.com

■ Matamata   POP 6080
Map 161, G4

Known for its gracious Edwardian buildings, Matamata is set in the lush farmland of the eastern **Waikato**, at the base of the scenic **Kaimai Range**. The town is one of the world's top centres for horse breeding, and has produced many champion thoroughbreds.
MAIN ATTRACTIONS: The '**Hobbiton**' set for *The Lord of the Rings* film trilogy was built on a local 10ha sheep farm, and fans can visit on a guided tour to see where filming took place. **Firth Tower**, built in 1882 by businessman Josiah Firth, is now a museum with Maori and European historical relics, surrounded by pioneer buildings. Matamata offers adventure activities, including kayaking and jet-boating on the **Waihou River**, and skydiving and gliding at **Waharoa Airfield**.
NEARBY ATTRACTIONS: **Opal Hot Springs** and an 18-hole golf course are 6.5km east of Matamata. The **Kaimai-Mamaku Forest Park** has many walking tracks, including the

(CONTINUED P.107)

WAIRARAPA WINERIES

The **Wairarapa** region, just over an hour's drive from Wellington, is a relative newcomer to New Zealand's wine production scene. In the late 1970s, scientists searched for a new area with wine making potential, and discovered the farming area around **Martinborough**.

Many vineyards now surround Martinborough's village square; it's possible to walk around the wineries, and the town has become a popular spot for visitors. More recently, the wine-growing region has expanded north to **Gladstone** and **Masterton**.

Some of New Zealand's most prestigious and impressive pinot noirs are made around Martinborough. This versatile region also produces good merlot, chardonnay, gewürztraminer, sauvignon blanc, riesling and pinot gris. **Ata Rangi** is known particularly for its pinot noir; **Palliser Estate** has produced a series of award-winning sauvignon blancs.

Each November, Martinborough hosts the annual **Toast Martinborough**, a festival of wine, food and music.

Visitor information

Martinborough i-SITE Visitor Centre
18 Kitchener St, Martinborough
Ph: (06) 306 9043

Wairarapa i-SITE Visitor Centre
316 Queen St, Masterton
Ph: (06) 370 0900
www.wairarapanz.com

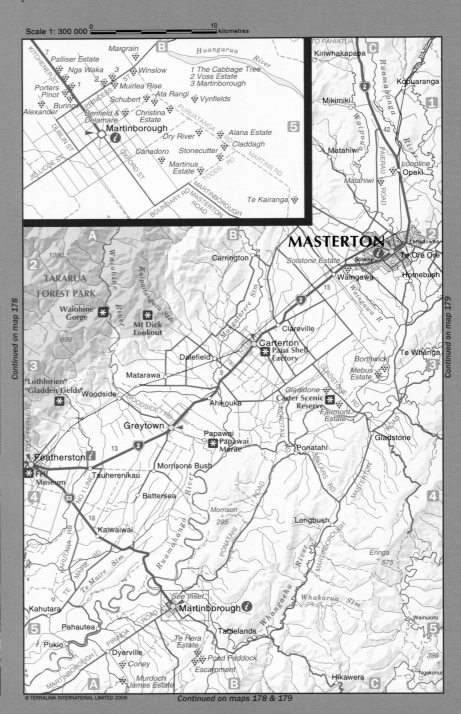

Palliser Estate Vineyard, Martinborough

Continued on map 178
Continued on map 179
Continued on maps 178 & 179

North Island

Wairere Track, an old Maori trading trail which leads to the beautiful 153m **Wairere Falls**. Fishing is good in the area, with plenty of rainbow trout in the lower Waihou River.

VISITOR INFORMATION: 45 Broadway, Ph: (07) 888 7260, www.waikatonz.com

■ Miranda   POP 160

Map 159, F6

Located about 90 minutes' drive south-east of Auckland, Miranda is one of the highlights of the scenic **Pacific Coast Highway** drive along the **Shorebird Coast**.

MAIN ATTRACTIONS: Miranda is home to one of New Zealand's most notable shorebird migrating grounds, with birds from the Arctic as well as New Zealand birds. The **Miranda Shorebird Centre** offers good viewing spots and information. **Miranda Hot Springs**, about 5km south of the shorebird centre, has a huge hot spring swimming pool, saunas and spas.

NEARBY ATTRACTIONS: Just west of Miranda is the **Hunua Ranges Regional Park**, a popular area for walking, mountain biking, horse riding, fishing, the **Hunua Falls**

and further bird watching. It is the only northern mainland habitat of the endangered kokako. The scenic **Pacific Coast Highway** has numerous bird-watching spots. **Kaiaua**, a beach settlement 9km north of Miranda, is a popular weekend relaxation spot. **Thames**, 34km east, is a former gold mining town with museums and displays showcasing its history.

VISITOR INFORMATION: SH1, Mill Rd, Bombay, Ph: (09) 236 0670, www.franklindistrict.co.nz/tourism

■ Muriwai Beach   POP 2040

Map 158, A3

A small settlement on the west coast, 41km west of Auckland, Muriwai Beach is known for its surf lifestyle and natural attractions.

MAIN ATTRACTIONS: **Muriwai Regional Park** is home to one of New Zealand's two onshore gannet colonies. About 1200 pairs of adult gannets nest here each summer; the colony is within walking distance of the park entrance. Fur seals feed and rest at **Oaia Island**, 1.6km off the coast. The black sand beach and offshore islands are also

home to white-fronted terns and blue penguins. Several picturesque walks are available in the park; the outstanding beach is also a popular spot for surfing, swimming and fishing.

NEARBY ATTRACTIONS: **Woodhill Forest**, to the north, is a good spot for picnics, mountain biking and walking. Many of the Auckland region's leading wineries can be found in the **Kumeu–Huapai** area east of Muriwai Beach; some of New Zealand's first commercial wineries were established there. About 30km north is the southern edge of the **Kaipara Harbour**, the largest enclosed harbour in the southern hemisphere; boat tours are available. To the south is **Waitakere Ranges Regional Park** and some top quality beaches, including **Te Henga (Bethells Beach)**, **Piha** and **Karekare**.

VISITOR INFORMATION: Main Rd, Kumeu, Ph: (09) 412 9886, www.muriwai.com

■ Murupara   POP 1960

Map 163, J6

The timber town of Murupara, 61km south-east of Rotorua, is a service centre for the forestry workers of the **Kaingaroa Forest**. Pine trees were first planted in the area in the early 20th century, and there are now 140 000 hectares of plantations. Murupara is also the western gateway to **Te Urewera National Park**.

MAIN ATTRACTIONS: **Covell Estate Wines**, 12km north at Galatea, is one of New Zealand's most unusually sited wineries, growing grapes organically on 5ha of volcanic soils, and is open for tastings and visits. Early Maori cave drawings can be seen in a rock shelter 8km west of Murupara.

NEARBY ATTRACTIONS: **Te Urewera National Park**, to the south-east, is home to the Tuhoe tribe, and is replete with unspoilt forests,

Gannet flying over colony, Muriwai Beach

HAWKE'S BAY WINERIES

Long hot summers and cool winters have helped make **Hawke's Bay** one of New Zealand's premier wine regions, producing particularly good chardonnay, merlot, cabernet sauvignon and syrah.

Some of New Zealand's earliest wines were made in Hawke's Bay by wealthy farmers in the 1890s, and the country's oldest surviving wine producer, **Mission Vineyards**, has operated there for over 150 years.

A number of wineries are clustered around **Havelock North**, with others west and north of **Napier**. Many wineries have restaurants, and **Church Road Winery** has an excellent wine museum. Visitors can do guided or self-drive tours of the vineyards, and cycling is an enjoyable way to explore the flat terrain.

Hawke's Bay is host to many wine festivals and vineyard events throughout the year, including **Hawke's Bay Harvest**, and an international concert at **Mission Estate**, both in February.

Ripening grapes, Hawke's Bay vineyard

Hawke's Bay vineyard

 Visitor information

Hastings i-SITE Visitor Centre
Russell St, Hastings
Ph: (06) 873 5526
www.hastings.co.nz

Napier i-SITE Visitor Centre
100 Marine Pde, Napier
Ph: (06) 834 1911
www.hawkesbaynz.com

---

lakes, rivers and plentiful bird life. The township of **Aniwaniwa**, 76km from Murupara, has a visitor centre, a museum and a motor camp. The 46km walk around **Lake Waikaremoana** offers impressive lake views, and the short walk from Aniwaniwa to **Lake Waikareiti** is also very beautiful. South of Murupara, the 55 000ha **Whirinaki Forest Park** was a conservation battleground in the 1970s as protesters fought to prevent logging of the native forest. The park is the site of massive, awe-inspiring trees, and there are many walking trails, including to a lagoon with many frogs, and to **Whirinaki Waterfall**.
VISITOR INFORMATION: Quay St, Whakatane, Ph: (07) 308 6058

■ **Napier**   POP 54 540
Map 183, D4
The coastal city of Napier, 313km north-east of Wellington in **Hawke's Bay**, is one of the world's best examples of an art deco city. Napier was essentially rebuilt in the 1930s, after a huge earthquake in 1931 devastated the city and killed 258 people there and in nearby **Hastings**.
MAIN ATTRACTIONS: Napier's city centre and the suburb of **Marewa** have many fine examples of art deco architecture. The seafront **Marine Parade**, lined with Norfolk Island pines and character wooden buildings, features parks, sunken gardens, the art deco **Soundshell**, and a statue of Maori folklore figure **Pania of the Reef**. The **National Aquarium of New Zealand** has sharks, piranha, saltwater crocodiles, kiwis, the native prehistoric reptile tuatara, and other animals; it's possible to dive in the main tank. Nearby **Marineland** has performing dolphins and seals, and a penguin recovery programme. **Hawke's Bay Museum**

(CONTINUED P.110)

Cape Kidnappers, Napier

North Island

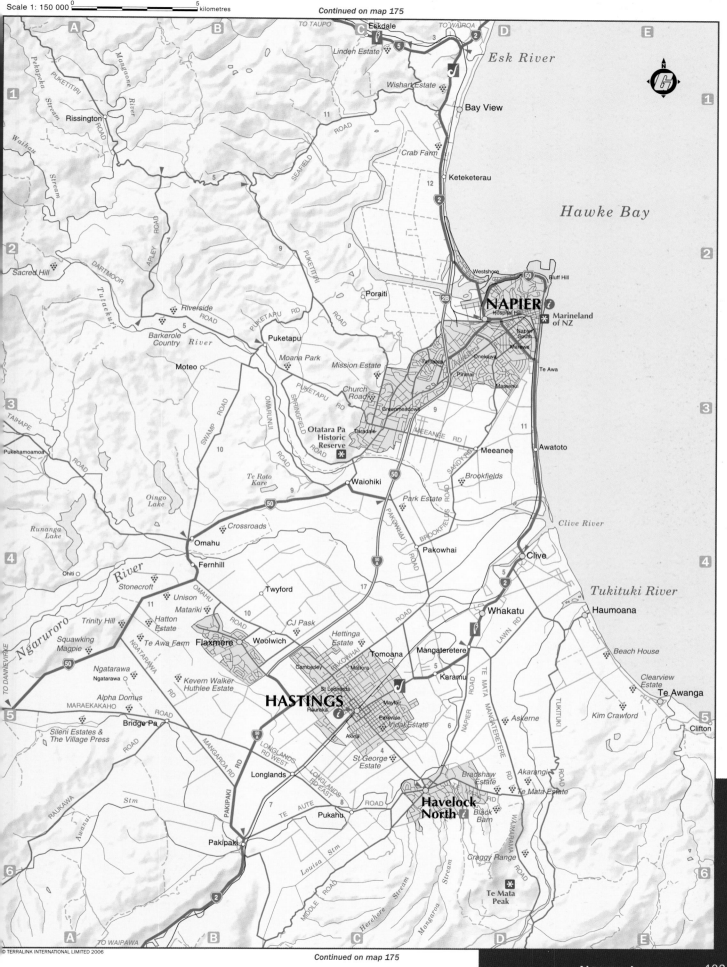

Scale 1: 150 000

Continued on map 175

A   B   C   D   E

TO TAUPO

TO WAIROA

Eskdale

Linden Estate

Esk River

Wishart Estate

Bay View

Hawke Bay

Crab Farm

Rissington

Keteketerau

Sacred Hill

DARTMOOR

Poraiti

Westshore

Bluff Hill

NAPIER

Hospital Hill

Marineland of NZ

Riverside

Napier South

Marewa

Te Awa

Barkerole Country

Puketapu

Moana Park

Mission Estate

Tamatea

Onekawa

Pirimai

Maraenui

Moteo

Church Road

Greenmeadows

MEEANEE RD

Otatara Pa Historic Reserve

Taradale

Waiohiki

Meeanee

Awatoto

Te Roto Kare

Brookfields

Oingo Lake

Clive River

Runanga Lake

Crossroads

Park Estate

Pakowhai

Clive

Tukituki River

Ohiti

Omahu

Fernhill

Twyford

Whakatu

Haumoana

Stonecroft

Unison

Matariki

CJ Pask

Hettinga Estate

Tomoana

Mangateretere

Beach House

Trinity Hill

Hatton Estate

Te Awa Farm

Woolwich

Flaxmere

Mashora

Karamu

Clearview Estate

Squawking Magpie

Ngatarawa

Kevern Walker Huthlee Estate

Cambedey

St Leonards

Te Awanga

Alpha Domus

MARAEKAKAHO

HASTINGS

Mayfair

Kim Crawford

Clifton

Sileni Estates & The Village Press

Bridge Pa

Akina

Parkvale

Vidal Estate

Askerne

TO DANNEVIRKE

Longlands

St George Estate

Bradshaw Estate

Te Mata Estate

Akarangi

Pukahu

Havelock North

Black Barn

Pakipaki

Louisa Stm

Craggy Range

Te Mata Peak

TO WAIPAWA

TO WAIPAWA

© TERRALINK INTERNATIONAL LIMITED 2006

Coastal walkway with Wind Wand sculpture, New Plymouth

has exhibitions on Maori art and culture, including local tribe Ngati Kahungunu. Other displays feature art deco and earthquakes. Good swimming and surfing can be found at the beach past the port. **Bluff Hill Lookout** offers great views over the area. Napier makes a good base for visiting the area's many vineyards, food producers and artists; a farmers' market is held on Saturday mornings.

NEARBY ATTRACTIONS: The **Esk Valley**, around 12km north, is home to wineries and a lavender farm. **Tangoio Falls Scenic Reserve** has a pretty walk through native bush to a waterfall. **Lake Tutira**, 40km north, has a bird sanctuary, a walkway and the remains of early Maori settlements; the 16km **Hawke's Bay Coastal Walkway** passes below cliffs and over beaches, and seals can sometimes be seen. **Boundary Stream Mainland Island**, 60km north-west, is a wildlife sanctuary with rare birds and plants. At **Clive**, 11km south of Napier, visitors can paddle a traditionally carved 18m waka (Maori canoe). **Cape Kidnappers**, at the southern tip of Hawke's Bay, is home to the world's largest mainland gannet breeding colony, and to an excellent golf course. The **Kaweka Forest Park**, 50km west, is a wilderness area with thermal areas, unspoilt rivers, trout fishing and bird life. The **Ruahine Forest Park**, also 50km west of Napier, has good hunting, fishing and scenic walks.

VISITOR INFORMATION: 100 Marine Pde, Ph: (06) 834 1911, www.hawkesbaynz.com

■ **New Plymouth**　POP 47 765

Map 184, B2

The main city of the **Taranaki** region, New Plymouth is located on the North Island's west coast, overlooked by majestic **Mount Taranaki**. New Plymouth is a relaxed, interesting city in an area known for farming and energy production.

MAIN ATTRACTIONS: The **Govett-Brewster Art Gallery** is an excellent contemporary gallery; it's home to the Len Lye collection, works by the ground-breaking modernist artist. The **Puke Ariki** complex aims to tell Taranaki's stories through an information centre, library and impressive museum. The **Richmond Cottage**, next door, is an 1853 stone cottage with a heritage garden. Maori arts and crafts are displayed at the **Rangimarie Maori Arts and Crafts Centre**. On the waterfront, the **Wind Wand** is a 45m-high Len Lye-designed kinetic sculpture, and is the centrepiece of the **New Plymouth Coastal Walkway**, a 7km coastal route which passes sculptures, beaches and rivers. Beautiful 49ha **Pukekura Park** has gardens, native bush, streams and waterfalls, and in summer hosts the **Festival of Lights**; it adjoins **Brooklands Park**, home to a small but excellent zoo. **St Mary's Church** is New Zealand's oldest stone church; the **New Plymouth Observatory** has a planetarium programme. Carved **Fitzroy Pole** marks what was once the boundary of European land after a decision in 1844. The **Sugar Loaf Islands Marine Protected Area** includes a number of eroded volcanic islands, and is home to sea birds, fur seals and rich marine life.

NEARBY ATTRACTIONS: South of New Plymouth, **Egmont National Park** surrounds the spectacular dormant volcano of Mount Taranaki, and offers some excellent walks. The historic homestead **Tupare**, 7km south, has beautiful 3.6ha gardens. The **Taranaki Aviation, Transport and Technology Museum** is 9.5km south of New Plymouth, opposite pretty **Lake Mangamahoe**. **Pukeiti Rhododendron Trust**, 20km south, is internationally known for its rhododendrons. **Surf Highway 45**, the coastal route south from New Plymouth, has surf beaches and beautiful scenery; **Oakura** is an interesting small town with resident artists and a great beach. Further south, **Parihaka Pa** was the site of a massive Maori campaign of passive resistance to land confiscations, and can be visited on the 18th and 19th of each month.

VISITOR INFORMATION: 1 Ariki St, Ph: (06) 759 6060, www.taranaki.info

North Island

Ngaruawahia   POP 385

Map 160, D3

The **Waikato**'s oldest settlement, this small town 18km north of Hamilton is the meeting place of two major rivers, the **Waikato** and **Waipa**. These were once canoe routes of great importance to Maori, and were used later for transport by European settlers. Ngaruawahia is still a place of central importance to Waikato Maori, and beautiful **Turangawaewae Marae** is the official residence of the Maori Queen, Dame Te Arikinui Te Atairangikaahu.

MAIN ATTRACTIONS: The annual **Ngaruawahia Regatta**, held in March, features waka (Maori canoe) races, wood chopping, hurdle races and water skiing. Major celebrations are held each May for **Coronation**, the anniversary of the Queen's coronation day. **Taupiri Mountain**, 8km north-east, was once a pa (fortified village) and is a sacred burial ground for Waikato Maori. Kings Potatau, Tawhiao and Te Rata, and Princess Te Puea, are all buried on the mountain.

NEARBY ATTRACTIONS: Walking tracks in the **Hakarimata Scenic Reserve** lead through native forest, including rimu and kauri trees, and offer views over the **Waikato River**. **Waingaro Hot Springs**, 23km west, have three thermal mineral pools and New Zealand's longest open hot water hydroslide in a park-like setting. **Nikau Cave**, a limestone glow-worm cave on a private farm to the west, offers guided tours.

VISITOR INFORMATION: Cnr Bryce and Anglesea Sts, Hamilton, Ph: (07) 839 3580, www.waikatonz.com

Ngawi   POP 55

Map 178, D6

The quiet village of Ngawi, on the coast of rugged **Palliser Bay** in the southern **Wairarapa**, is a base for commercial fishing operators.

MAIN ATTRACTIONS: Fishing charter trips are available from Ngawi; a three-day fishing contest is held each February.

NEARBY ATTRACTIONS: **Cape Palliser**, 10km south-east, is the southernmost point of the North Island. It boasts a breeding colony of fur seals, where pups can often be seen playing in a pool; a steep climb up 250 steps leads to the red and white lighthouse, erected in 1897. **Nga-Ra-a-Kupe** (Kupe's sails), named after the early Polynesian explorer, are massive slabs of rock which resemble sails slanting into the wind. The **Putangirua Pinnacles**, in **Aorangi Forest Park** 20km north, are dramatic landforms created by rain washing away silt and sand. A two- to three-hour walk leads to the Pinnacles, where filming took place for scenes at **'Dimholt Road'** in *The Lord of the Rings*. There are many other tracks leading further into the park. Some of New Zealand's earliest Maori occupation sites can be found at Palliser Bay; the remains of terracing and food storage pits are visible.

VISITOR INFORMATION: 18 Kitchener St, Martinborough, Ph: (06) 306 9043, www.wairarapanz.com

Ohakune   POP 1295

Map 173, K4

This pretty town at the south-western corner of **Tongariro National Park**, on the North Island's central plateau, is a base for snow sports at the nearby **Turoa Ski Area** on **Mount Ruapehu**. Ohakune is also famous for its locally grown vegetables, particularly carrots. Quiet in summer, it becomes a bustling ski resort over winter.

MAIN ATTRACTIONS: The **Ohakune Mountain Mardi Gras**, held annually in August, is a huge street party with fireworks, bands and street performers.

NEARBY ATTRACTIONS: Snow sport enthusiasts flock to Ohakune in winter to take advantage of New Zealand's two biggest ski areas, the Turoa and **Whakapapa** ski fields on Mount Ruapehu. Spectacular Tongariro National Park offers wonderful scenery, walks and snow sports on and around the three active volcanoes of Ruapehu, **Ngauruhoe** and **Tongariro**. The 17km **Ohakune Mountain Road** is a beautiful drive through native forest to Turoa Ski Area, and is also great for mountain biking. From the road, some lovely walks lead into the park, including the **Rimu Track**, the **Mangawhero Forest Walk**, and a 1½-hour walk to 39m **Waitonga Falls**, the park's highest waterfall. Scenes for *The Lord of the Rings* were filmed near **Mangawhero Falls**; the rocky stream bed was used to portray **'Ithilien'**. Scenic flights and tours from Ohakune allow tourists to visit some of the sites used as **'Mordor'** in the films. Other activities around Ohakune include horse trekking, golf, fishing, kayaking, jet boating and canoeing. The **Karioi Lakes**, 12km south-east, are two lakes in mountain beech forest, with plentiful bird life. The adjacent area is a 'Mainland Island' which aims to restore the native forest habitat; there is a pest eradication programme, and kiwi have been

Giant carrot welcome sign, Ohakune

A national park since 1900, Egmont National Park protects the beautiful dormant volcano of **Mount Taranaki**, sacred to local Maori, and the two older volcanoes of **Kaitake** and **Pouakai**. The 33 534ha park has more than 300km of walking tracks through rich forest, to waterfalls, wetlands and lookouts; more adventurous walkers may want to head for the mountain's summit, independently or with a guide, or do the 55km **Around Mountain Circuit**. Walkers should remember to respect the highly changeable weather.

From **Dawson Falls** there are many lovely walks, including to **Wilkies Pools**, a series of eroded rock pools, through the sub-alpine forest often called 'goblin forest' because of its gnarled trees and trailing moss. The **Pouakai Circuit** is a two-day walk through beautiful areas and historic sites; visitors can stay the night in a restored historic camphouse, originally military barracks in the 1860s land wars.

Dawson Falls, Egmont National Park, Taranaki

 Visitor information

DOC North Egmont Visitor Centre
Egmont Rd, Egmont Village
Ph: (06) 756 0990
www.doc.govt.nz

main attractions

- Ahukawakawa Swamp
- Dawson Falls
- Historic Camphouse
- Manganui Ski Field
- Mount Taranaki
- Pouakai Circuit
- Wilkies Pools

---

reintroduced. The disused logging trails in **Rangataua Conservation Area** are great for mountain biking through scenic forests.
VISITOR INFORMATION: Clyde St, Ph: (06) 385 8427, www.ohakune.info

■ Omapere & Opononi   POP 595
Map 154, B3
These two peaceful towns sit on the southern side of the **Hokianga Harbour**, on the west coast of **Northland**. The ancestral Polynesian navigator Kupe is believed to have first made landfall in the Hokianga, and later to have made his home there. Many northern Maori trace their ancestry to the harbour's discovery and settlement. Opononi became famous in 1955–56 for the presence of Opo, a wild dolphin which

befriended local humans.
MAIN ATTRACTIONS: The white sand beaches of Omapere and Opononi offer safe swimming. A statue in Opononi commemorates Opo the dolphin, who is buried beside it, and the **Hokianga Heritage Centre** has displays about the area's history. The harbour's **North Head** has vast 300m-high golden sand dunes. **Arai-Te-Uru Recreation Reserve**, on the harbour's **South Head**, has excellent views of the sand dunes, and a swimming beach. From the reserve, the **Hokianga–Waipoua Coastal Track** leads south along the coast.
NEARBY ATTRACTIONS: **Waipoua Kauri Forest**, 26km south, is a superb and important forest area with many impressive kauri, including the 51m tree **Tane Mahuta**, and the massive

Te Matua Ngahere, which has a trunk diameter of more than 5m and is estimated to be 2000 years old. **Waiotemarama** has a craft store and a maze through maize plants.
VISITOR INFORMATION: SH12, Omapere, Ph: (09) 405 8869, www.northlandnz.com

■ Opotiki   POP 7070
Map 164, C4
This peaceful coastal town in the eastern **Bay of Plenty**, 151km east of Tauranga, is the gateway to the **East Cape**. Opotiki features a main street lined with the works of master Maori carvers.
MAIN ATTRACTIONS: The **Hukutaia Domain** has a fine collection of native plants, many of them rare or endangered; it

North Island

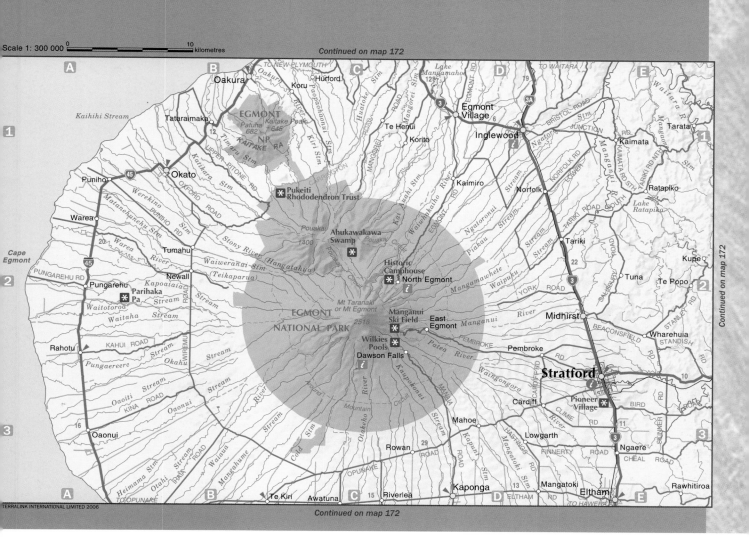

Continued on map 172

Scale 1: 300 000

Continued on map 172

TERRALINK INTERNATIONAL LIMITED 2006

also has a massive hollow puriri tree estimated to be over 2000 years old. Historic **Hiona St Stephens Church** is where the missionary Carl Volkner, believed by local Maori to be a government spy, was murdered in 1865. There is good swimming, fishing, surfing and boating at **Ohiwa** and **Waiotahi** beaches.

NEARBY ATTRACTIONS: The **Waioeka Gorge Scenic Reserve**, south of Opotiki, and **Raukumara Forest Park** to the east are wilderness areas offering beautiful walks through native bush, along with trout fishing, swimming and hunting. Bird life is plentiful, including some rare species. Opotiki is also a base for jet boating and rafting trips on the **Motu River**. About 60km by road

to the west is **Whakatane**, the main town in the eastern Bay of Plenty, and beautiful **Ohope Beach**. About 50km south-west of Opotiki is **Te Urewera National Park**, one of the North Island's most spectacular areas of native forest and wildlife; there are some beautiful walks, and **Lake Waikaremoana** at the south of the park is a particular highlight.

VISITOR INFORMATION: Cnr St John St and Elliott St, Ph: (07) 315 8484, www.opotikinz.com

■ **Opunake**   POP 1500

Map 172, B4

Opunake, on the western coast of **Taranaki** 64km from New Plymouth, is set on a beautiful surf beach, and is popular with summertime holidaymakers.

MAIN ATTRACTIONS: Opunake's

(CONTINUED P.116)

Totem poles, Opotiki

TONGARIRO NATIONAL PARK

Located on the North Island's central plateau, the 79 598ha Tongariro National Park was New Zealand's first, established in 1887. The park preserves three active volcanic peaks — **Mount Tongariro**, **Ngauruhoe** and **Ruapehu** — which were gifted to the people of New Zealand by Ngati Tuwharetoa, the local Maori tribe. The park is a dual World Heritage Area, in recognition of its outstanding geological features and its spiritual significance to Maori. Ngauruhoe and Ruapehu erupt frequently; the dramatic 1995 eruption of Ruapehu covered the surrounding countryside in a thick layer of ash.

Ruapehu boasts two commercial ski fields, **Whakapapa** and **Turoa,** which usually operate from June until September. Tongariro features the **Tongariro Crossing,** an immensely popular one-day walk. The **Northern Circuit Great Walk** on Tongariro (three to four days) and the **Round the Mountain** track on Ruapehu (four to six days) are longer, more challenging hikes. A reasonable level of fitness is required for the walks, and sun block, water, food, sturdy footwear and warm and waterproof clothing are essential on all mountain excursions.

Red Crater and Mount Ngauruhoe, Tongariro Crossing

Tongariro Crossing

This strenuous 17km hike between the **Mangatepopo** and **Ketetahi** huts takes walkers through a barren landscape featuring the steaming **Red Crater** and the astounding **Blue** and **Emerald Lakes**. The walk takes an average of six to seven hours. Drop-off and pick-up bus services operate to and from all parts of the district.

main attractions

❖ Mt Ngauruhoe

Conical and steep-sided, the 2287m Ngauruhoe can be scaled, but only by experienced climbers.

❖ Mount Ruapehu

The highest and most active of the park's three volcanoes, 2797m Ruapehu features excellent ski fields and hiking tracks.

❖ Mount Tongariro

Active but quieter than its neighbours, 1967m Tongariro features coloured lakes, hot springs and the Tongariro Crossing.

❖ Round the Mountain track

A map is required for this four- to six-day tramp on a poled track around Ruapehu, which takes in beech forests and scree slopes.

❖ Turoa Ski Area

This exciting field featuring steep advanced runs and good back country conditions is most easily accessible from Ohakune.

❖ Whakapapa Ski Area

New Zealand's biggest ski field, with a large beginner's area and good intermediate and advanced runs, is accessible from Whakapapa Village.

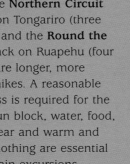

ℹ Visitor information

Ruapehu Information Centre
Clyde St, Ohakune
Ph: (06) 385 8427

DOC Whakapapa Visitor Centre
Whakapapa Village, Mount Ruapehu
Ph: (07) 892 3729
www.visitruapehu.com
www.doc.govt.nz

Tongariro National Park

North Island

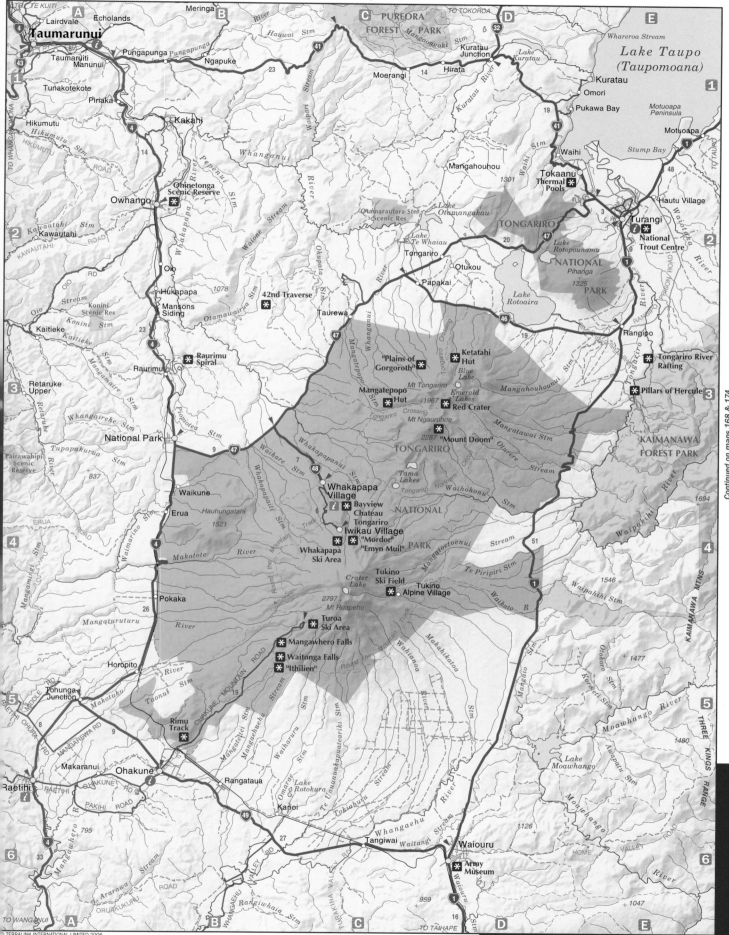

Te Kuiti

A Lairdvale
Echolands
Meringa

Taumarunui
Taumaruiti
Manunui
Pungapunga
Ngapuke

Tunakotekote

Piriaka

Hikumutu

Kakahi

Kawautahi

Owhango

Ohinetonga
Scenic Reserve

Oio

Hukapapa

Mansons
Siding

42nd Traverse

Raurimu
Spiral

Taurewa

Kaitieke

Raurimu

Retaruke
Upper

"Plains of
Gorgoroth"

Ketatahi
Hut

Blue
Lake

National Park

Mangatepopo
Hut

Emerald
Lakes
Red Crater

Waikune

Whakapapa
Village

Erua

Bayview
Chateau
Tongariro

Iwikau Village
"Mordor"
"Emyn Muil"

Whakapapa
Ski Area

Tukino
Ski Field

Tukino
Alpine Village

Pokaka

Crater
Lake

Mt Ruapehu

Turoa
Ski Area

Mangawhero Falls

Horopito

Waitonga Falls
"Ithilien"

Tohunga
Junction

Rimu
Track

Makaranui

Ohakune

Raetihi

Rangataua

Karioi

Tangiwai

Waiouru

Army
Museum

PUREORA
FOREST PARK

Moerangi

Hirata

Kuratau
Junction

Kuratau

Omori

Pukawa Bay

Mangahouhou

Tokaanu
Thermal
Pools

Waihi

Lake Taupo
(Taupomoana)

Whareroa Stream

Motuoapa
Peninsula

Motuoapa

Stump Bay

Hautu Village

TONGARIRO

Turangi
National
Trout Centre

Tongariro

Otukou

Papakai

NATIONAL

PARK

Pihanga

Lake
Rotoaira

Rangipo

Tongariro River
Rafting

Pillars of Hercule

KAIMANAWA
FOREST PARK

TONGARIRO

Mt Tongariro

"Mount Doom"

Mt Ngauruhoe

Tama
Lakes

NATIONAL

PARK

THREE KINGS RANGE

Lake
Moawhango

Lake
Rotokura

To Wanganui

To Taihape

Marina Villas, Gulf Harbour

beach is great for swimming and surfing, and hosts a **Beach Carnival** each January. The 7km **Opunake Walkway** leads around the **Opunake Lake** and to historic **Te Namu Pa**; it offers beautiful scenery, **Mount Taranaki** views and historic sites.

NEARBY ATTRACTIONS: Unspoilt surf beaches stretch along the coastline around Opunake. The **Maui Production Station Display Centre**, 8km north at **Oaonui**, is the visitor centre at New Zealand's largest gas processing plant; it has displays and models of the station and offshore installations. **Parihaka Pa**, about 20km north, is a site of major cultural and historical importance. In the 1870s it was a large and successful Maori village, and the base for a peaceful protest movement against confiscation of Maori land. In 1881 Parihaka's leaders were arrested and the town was razed by government troops. Today Parihaka is open to the public on the 18th and 19th of each month. **Cape Egmont Lighthouse**,

at Taranaki's most western point, is a great subject for photographs, with Mount Taranaki as a backdrop. At **Pihama**, 10km south, the **Lizzie Bell Memorial Cemetery** has the graves of 12 men who died in a 1901 shipwreck.

VISITOR INFORMATION: 55 High St, Hawera, Ph: (06) 278 8599, www.taranaki.info

■ Orewa   POP 5610
Map 158, B2

A relaxed outer suburban area 38km north of downtown Auckland, Orewa is the main town of the **Hibiscus Coast** and is a popular relaxation and holiday spot.

MAIN ATTRACTIONS: Orewa is the gateway to the **Whangaparaoa Peninsula**, a popular playground for Aucklanders. On the tip of the peninsula is fine walking around **Shakespear Regional Park**. Nearby is **Gulf Harbour**, which has a high-quality golf course and boat marinas. Just south of Orewa is **Silverdale**, which has factory bargain stores and the artificial

ski field **Snowplanet**. **Alice Eaves Scenic Reserve** has walks through native bush just north of the town, and the nearby **Waiwera Infinity Thermal Spa** features pools, slides and spa treatment facilities.

NEARBY ATTRACTIONS: **Tiritiri Matangi Island** is a wildlife sanctuary just east of the Whangaparaoa Peninsula. Many of New Zealand's rare native birds can be found here; the island can be accessed from Gulf Harbour and Auckland city. The historic town of **Puhoi**, 12km north, has buildings going back to the 1880s, when it was settled by Bohemian peasants. Highlights include the **Bohemian Museum**, the **Catholic Church**, and the **Art of Cheese**, a cheese factory and café. Nearby on the coast, **Wenderholm Regional Park** is popular for walkers and features the period museum **Couldrey House**. **Warkworth**, 27km north, is home to rural attractions such as **SheepWorld**, and is the gateway to the **Matakana Wine Country**.

VISITOR INFORMATION: 214A Hibiscus Coast Hwy, Ph: (09) 426 0076, www.orewa-beach.co.nz

■ Otaki   POP 5645
Map 178, D1

Located in the **Kapiti** region, 74km north of Wellington, Otaki is flanked by hills to the east and the Tasman Sea to the west. Maori culture is strong in the town, which is home to **Te Wananga-o-Raukawa**, a Maori centre of higher learning. The famed Ngati Toa warrior chief Te Rauparaha was originally buried here; his body was later taken to **Kapiti Island**. Market gardening is a focus around the town.

MAIN ATTRACTIONS: **St Mary's Pukekaraka Church**, built in 1851, is New Zealand's oldest Catholic church still in use; **Rangiatea** is the oldest surviving Anglican Maori church, and has recently been rebuilt after its tragic destruction

North Island

by fire in 1995. **Otaki Beach**, 3km west, is a long stretch of surf beach edged with sand dunes.

NEARBY ATTRACTIONS: **Otaki Forks**, 19km south-east, is the main western entrance to the beautiful **Tararua Forest Park**, and a popular spot for picnicking, swimming, walking and camping. Otaki Forks is also the entrance point for a major four-day walk across the ranges to **Kaitoke**. Scenes for *The Lord of the Rings* were filmed in the **Otaki Gorge**, although the actual locations aren't accessible to the public. Kayaking, rafting and adventure activities are popular in the gorge. Offshore Kapiti Island is a protected wildlife sanctuary, and can be visited by boat from **Paraparaumu Beach**. **Lake Papaitonga**, north of Otaki, is a tranquil dune lake and home to many waterbirds.

VISITOR INFORMATION: Centennial Park, SH1, Ph: (06) 364 7620, www.WellingtonNZ.com

Otorohanga   POP 2630
Map 160, D6

A service town for the local farming community, Otorohanga is 58km south of Hamilton in the **King Country**. Otorohanga was the site of major Maori settlement in the mid-19th century, with 3000–4000 people living on the site of the present town and in terraced pa on the hills around the river. European access to the King Country was prohibited by the Maori King Tawhiao until 1884, but from 1887 timber millers began to settle around Otorohanga.

MAIN ATTRACTIONS: New Zealand's national symbol, the kiwi, is bred in captivity at the **Kiwi House and Bird Sanctuary**. A nocturnal viewing house allows visitors to watch active kiwi digging for food; the sanctuary is home to other native birds and the native reptile tuatara. Otorohanga's main street is decorated with 'Kiwiana' murals and displays, featuring iconic New Zealand institutions such as the All Blacks, pavlovas, gumboots and sheep. **Otorohanga Museum** covers local history.

NEARBY ATTRACTIONS: **Waitomo Caves**, 16km south-west, are a collection of vast limestone caves with beautiful stalactites and stalagmites, and thousands of glow-worms. The caves are accessible by boat or by walking, and adventure activities include abseiling and black-water rafting. **Mangapohue Natural Bridge**, 26km west of Waitomo, is a 17m limestone arch in a scenic reserve; **Piripiri Caves Scenic Reserve** features a large cave with ancient fossils of giant oysters. The beautiful three-tier **Marokopa Falls**, 5km further west, plunge 36m from a limestone precipice.

VISITOR INFORMATION: 57 Maniapoto St, Ph: (07) 873 8951, www.otorohanga.co.nz

Paekakariki   POP 1730
Map 178, C2

This appealing small town on the **Kapiti Coast**, 40km north of Wellington, has a long stretch of sandy beach, and a peaceful village atmosphere.

MAIN ATTRACTIONS: **Queen Elizabeth Park** features sand dunes, remnant forest, early Maori pa sites and regenerating wetlands; it was also the site of a World War II US Marine camp. The park offers good swimming, fishing, walking, horse riding and picnicking.

NEARBY ATTRACTIONS: There are walking tracks through **Battle Hill Farm Forest Park**, the site of a several-day siege between Maori and European forces in 1846. The **Wellington Tramway Museum**, 5km north, showcases the historic wooden trams which carried Wellington commuters around the city until 1964; visitors can ride on a restored tram. The drive over the **Paekakariki Hill Road** offers panoramic views over the coast.

VISITOR INFORMATION: Cnr Wakefield and Victoria Sts, Wellington, Ph: (04) 802 4860, www.WellingtonNZ.com

Paeroa   POP 3880
Map 161, G1

Located 130km south-east of Auckland, south of the **Coromandel** region, Paeroa was established in 1870 and was once the major port on the **Ohinemuri River**. Today it is most famous as the birthplace of

(CONTINUED P.118)

Queen Elizabeth Park, Paekakariki

the soft drink Lemon and Paeroa, usually known as 'L&P'.

MAIN ATTRACTIONS: In the 19th century, Paeroa's therapeutic local spring water began to be bottled, with the addition of lemon, and sold. The drink is no longer manufactured in Paeroa, but a **7m replica Lemon and Paeroa bottle** stands as a tribute near the town centre. Paeroa has many antique stores; **Paeroa & District Historical Society Museum** explores the district's early history. The **Paeroa Historical Maritime Park**, 2km north, displays restored vessels, including the double paddle steamer *Kopu*.

NEARBY ATTRACTIONS: Between Paeroa and **Waihi**, State Highway Two traverses the dramatic **Karangahake Gorge**. The **Karangahake Gorge Historic Walkway**, following part of an old railway line, has good swimming and picnic spots; walkers can see beautiful **Owharoa Falls** and **Waikino Station**, from which a vintage train runs to Waihi. Five minutes' walk from Waikino Station, the remains of the **Victoria Crown Battery** are on display among other gold mining relics. The **Captain Cook Memorial** at **Netherton** marks the landing place of the great British explorer and his crew in 1769.

VISITOR INFORMATION: Belmont Road, Ph: (07) 862 8636, www.thecoromandel.com

■ **Pahiatua**   POP 2610

Map 177, F5

Located in the **Tararua** district, 168km north-east of Wellington, Pahiatua is a service centre for the local farming area, and offers good fishing, hunting and hiking in the surrounding countryside.

MAIN ATTRACTIONS: At Pahiatua's north end, a World War II Harvard plane has been converted into a children's slide. The **Polish Memorial**, 2km south, commemorates the refugee camp which was home to 700-odd Polish refugee children from 1944

to 1952. Pahiatua hosts a week-long trout fishing carnival every October.

NEARBY ATTRACTIONS: **Mangatainoka**, 6km north-east, is home to the **Tui Brewery**, established in 1889 to supply 'export quality brews to beer drinkers around the colony', and still pumping out the brown liquid today. The brewery's striking seven-storey art deco tower is an impressive sight in the rural countryside; visitors can book for a guided tour. West of **Woodville**, 16km north, a four-hour walkway leads through the dramatic **Manawatu Gorge**; jet boating and kayaking are also possible in the gorge. On the south-east edge of the gorge is the **Tararua Wind Farm**, the southern hemisphere's largest wind farm. Rare native species are bred in captivity at the **Pukaha Mount Bruce National Wildlife Centre**, 35km south of Pahiatua, and there are walks through an area of ancient forest. East at the small settlement of **Horoeka** are the picturesque **Waihi Falls**; there is good swimming and surfing at the beaches of **Akitio** and **Herbertville**.

VISITOR INFORMATION: 121 Main St, Ph: (06) 376 6619, www.tararua.com

■ **Paihia**   POP 1835

Map 155, F1

The seaside town of Paihia is a base for exploring the **Bay of Islands**. First settled by Europeans as a mission station in 1823, the town's population increases dramatically over summer.

MAIN ATTRACTIONS: Water-based activities are a focus in the Bay of Islands, including sailing, jet boating, marlin fishing, swimming with dolphins and sea kayaking. Cruises take visitors out and about in the bay, including to the **Hole in the Rock** at **Cape Brett** and to archaeologically significant **Urupukapuka Island**, where visitors can walk around many sites of pa (Maori fortified villages), storage

pits, drains and terraces. There are also walking tracks on **Moturua** and **Motuarohia Islands**. Passenger ferries leave Paihia's wharf for the historic town of **Russell**, across the harbour. Native forest is regenerating in nearby **Opua Forest**, which has some large kauri trees, walking tracks and lookouts.

NEARBY ATTRACTIONS: Just north of Paihia, **Waitangi** is a place of great historic significance to New Zealanders, as the 1840 Treaty between European and Maori leaders was signed here. **Opua**, 5km south, is an attractive port town with a marina and charter yachts. The ferry from Opua takes cars across the bay to the road to Russell.

VISITOR INFORMATION: The Wharf, Marsden Rd, Ph: (09) 402 7345, www.northlandnz.com

■ **Palmerston North**   POP 72 680

Map 185, C4

The main city of the **Manawatu** region, 145km north of Wellington, Palmerston North is a centre for education and research; it also has excellent shopping, restaurants and cultural attractions.

Lemon & Paeroa monument, Paeroa

North Island

MAIN ATTRACTIONS: **Te Manawa** is a museum, art gallery and science centre featuring contemporary art, interactive science exhibits and Maori taonga (treasures). At the **New Zealand Rugby Museum**, visitors can explore the history of this popular sport. On the banks of the **Manawatu River** is **Victoria Esplanade**, a lovely park with a playground and miniature railway; its **Duguld McKenzie rose breeding and trialling centre** was voted one of the world's top five rose gardens in 2003. The early homestead of **Wharerata** is a well-used cafe and function centre. **The Square**, surveyed in 1866 as a focal point for the new town, is a meeting and events venue.

NEARBY ATTRACTIONS: The dramatic **Manawatu Gorge**, to the east, is one of just a few places in the world where a river runs east to west through a main divide. The large red rock in the gorge's centre was considered to be a guardian spirit by the local Maori tribe, Rangitane. The **Manawatu Gorge Walk** is a four-hour walk through the gorge, offering spectacular views; jet boating and kayaking are also possible. At the **Ashhurst Domain**, an observation platform offers great views of the **Tararua Wind Farm**, the largest in the southern hemisphere. The 30km **Pohangina Anticline**, running along the base of the **Ruahine Range**, is a mountain range growing by at least a millimetre a year. At **Himatangi Beach**, 29km west, is New Zealand's biggest sand dune field.

VISITOR INFORMATION: The Square, Ph: (06) 350 1922, www.manawatunz.co.nz

■ **Paraparaumu**   POP 21 375
Map 178, C2

The main town on the **Kapiti Coast**, fast-growing Paraparaumu is 51km north of Wellington. It has a lovely beach, and is the base for boat trips to **Kapiti Island**.

MAIN ATTRACTIONS: **Paraparaumu Beach**, 4km west of the town centre, offers good swimming and fishing. The **Lindale Centre**, just north, is a complex of shops and attractions, including an award-winning cheesemaker, craft shops, a honey shop and an olive shop; there are also farm shows. **Southward Vintage Car Museum**, 3km north, has a huge collection of vintage and unusual cars. Scenic flights are available from Paraparaumu's airfield.

NEARBY ATTRACTIONS: Offshore Kapiti Island, a wildlife reserve since 1897, is one of New Zealand's most important sites for bird recovery, and offers some beautiful walks and wonderful bird life. Boat trips leave daily from Paraparaumu; visitor numbers are limited, and permits must be booked from the Department of Conservation. Kapiti Island is rich in Maori and European history; the surrounding **Kapiti Island Marine Reserve** has wonderful underwater scenery.

VISITOR INFORMATION: Coastlands Pde, SH1, Ph: (04) 298 8195, www.WellingtonNZ.com

■ **Patea**   POP 1300
Map 172, E6

The small coastal town of Patea, in southern **Taranaki**, is 61km north-west of Wanganui. The area was first settled by Maori in the 14th century; it was a military settlement during the 19th century Taranaki wars.

MAIN ATTRACTIONS: Patea is known for the Patea Maori Club, which had a massive hit in 1984 with the song 'Poi E', and gave new life to the town after the closure of the local freezing works. The impressive roadside **Aotea Memorial Waka**, a town landmark, is a replica waka (Maori canoe). Built in 1933, it commemorates the journey across the Pacific of the early Polynesian navigator Turi. **South Taranaki District Museum** explores the

Sculpture outside Te Manawa, Palmerston North

area's culture and heritage; Patea also has some beautiful heritage buildings. The **Patea River Walkway** leads along the riverside past several historic sites. Nearby beaches offer good swimming, surfing and fishing, and there are lookouts with spectacular views over the Taranaki coastline.

NEARBY ATTRACTIONS: The **Rotorangi Hydro Walk**, 10km north, is a lakeside walkway through native bush at **Lake Rotorangi**.

VISITOR INFORMATION: 55 High St, Hawera, Ph: (06) 278 8599, www.taranaki.info

■ **Piha**   POP 730
Map 158, A4

Piha is just 40km west of Auckland, but this small beach town surrounded by wild natural beauty feels as if it's in another country.

MAIN ATTRACTIONS: **Piha Beach** is the most popular beach near Auckland for surfers. Numerous surf contests are held out here, as unfortunately are surf rescues: the beach can be dangerous, and swimmers should stay between the flags. Walks include the **Tasman Lookout Track** at the south of the beach, **Lion Rock** to the north and the **Laird Thompson Track** to neighbouring **White's Beach** further north.

NEARBY ATTRACTIONS: Beautiful **Karekare Beach**, just south of

(CONTINUED P.122)

HAURAKI GULF

Minutes away from the bustle of downtown Auckland, the **Hauraki Gulf** islands seem a world away. Easily accessible, the islands are one of the most popular spots in the Auckland region for a day trip.

The islands offer a wide range of attractions for visitors. **Rangitoto** was the last volcano to erupt in the region and has a fantastic pohutukawa forest, and adjoining **Motutapu** has signs of early Maori settlement. **Waiheke** is a playground in itself with numerous wineries, cafés, galleries and beaches. Further afield, the more remote **Great Barrier Island** is a great spot for outdoor recreation such as diving, horse trekking and hiking, while **Little Barrier Island** and **Tiritiri Matangi Island** are pristine wildlife sanctuaries. Off the North Shore coast, **Goat Island** is a marine reserve with spectacular snorkelling and **Kawau Island** has historic places to go with its great scenery.

Many of the islands are within an hour of Auckland by ferry, while flights are available to Great Barrier and Waiheke Island.

Summer dining, Mudbrick Vineyard Restaurant, Waiheke Island

ℹ️ Visitor information

New Zealand i-SITE Visitor Centre
137 Quay St, Princes Wharf, Auckland
Ph: 0800 AUCKLAND
www.aucklandnz.com

Waiheke Island Wine Festival

Most of Waiheke Island's 20-plus wineries are open to the public, but this two-day festival weekend in late January or early February provides a great opportunity to sample the best of them, along with great food. Festival tickets include buses that allow visitors to sample the offerings of the wineries and restaurants at their leisure.

main attractions

◈ **Dolphin & Whale Safari**

These cruises take visitors to view the dolphins and whales of the Hauraki Gulf in their natural habitat.

◈ **Goat Island**

Located just off the North Shore coast, about an hour from Auckland, Goat Island was New Zealand's first marine reserve and offers fantastic snorkelling.

◈ **Great Barrier Island**

A perfect spot to relax, Great Barrier Island is renowned for its forests, wildlife, hiking, diving and beaches.

◈ **Kawau Island**

In addition to its wildlife, this island has former Governor George Grey's 1860s stately mansion, Maori pa sites and old copper mines.

◈ **Little Barrier Island**

One of New Zealand's most valuable nature sanctuaries, this island features rare birds, reptiles and plants. Department of Conservation permits are required to land.

◈ **Rangitoto Island**

This volcano erupted 600 years ago and numerous relics from the eruption are still evident.

◈ **Tiritiri Matangi Island**

Many of New Zealand's rare native birds, including the takahe, kokako, stitchbird and little spotted kiwi, can be found at this wildlife sanctuary.

◈ **Waiheke Island**

The most popular island in the Gulf includes wineries, fine restaurants and art galleries in addition to fabulous walks and beaches.

Mansion House, Kawau Island

North Island

Scale 1 : 600 000

0   20   kilometres

© TERRALINK INTERNATIONAL LIMITED 2006

Continued on map 159

Continued on maps 160 & 161

TO WHANGAREI
Waipu
Braigh
Waipu River
Waipu Cove
Taranga I
Bream Bay
Bream Tail
Sail Rock
Fanal Island
(Motukino)

Langs Beach
Bryderwyn
Tara
Molesworth
Mangawhai
Heads
Mangawhai Point
Pukekaroro
Hakaru
Te Arai
Point
Kaiwaka
Te Arai
Topuni
Te Hana
Port Albert
Waiteitei
Wellsford
Hoteo
North
Wayby Valley
Wayby
Whangaripo
Pakiri
Goat Island
Cape Rodney
Leigh
Ti Point
Point Wells
Omaha
Takatu
Tawharanui
Takatu Point

Needles Point
Aiguilles Island
Rangiwhakaea Bay
Miners Head
Ahuriri Point
Maunganui Point
(Separation Point)
Katherine Bay
Motairehe
Kawa
Great Barrier Island
(Aotea Island)
Waikaro Point
Whangapoua
Beach
Rakitu Island
(Arid Island)
Port
Abercrombie
Kaikoura Island
(Selwyn Island)
Port
Fitzroy
Glenfern Sanctuary
Okiwi
Windy
Canyon
Kauri Dams
Whakatautuna Point
Mt Hobson
627
Tramline Track
Broken Islands
(Pig Islands)
Kaitoke Hot Springs
Whangaparapara
Claris
Whangaparapara Har
Blind Bay
Okupu
Medlands Beach
Shag Point
Tryphena
Tryphena
Harbour
Cape Barrier

Little Barrier Island
(Hauturu Island)
Hauturu
722
Jellicoe Channel
Craddock Channel

Tauhoa
Hoteo
Streamlands
Matakana
Dome
Valley
Waiwhiu
Warkworth
Big Omaha
Omaha
Flats
Mangakura
Woodcocks
Kaipara
Flats
Kourawhero
Hepburn
Creek
Algies Bay
Snells
Beach
Sandspit
North Channel
Mansion
House
Kawau Island
Channel
Glorit
Ahuroa
Komokoriki
Pohuehue
Pukapuka
Mahurangi
Motuketekete Island
Channel Island
Colville Channel

Araparera
Kakanui
Makarau
Puhoi
Mahurangi
West
Motuora Island
Cape
Jackson
Port
Jackson
Kaiiti Point
Port Jackson
COROMANDEL
FP
Mt Moehau
892
Port
Charles

Kanohi
Waiwera
Hot Springs
Whangaparaoa
Bay
Hauraki Gulf
Port Charles
374
Te Anaputa Point
Potiki Bay

Kaukapakapa
Waitoki
Orewa
Silverdale
Waiau
Bay
Whangaparaoa
Passage
Tiritiri Matangi Island
Waiaro
Whangaahei
Waikawau
Waikawau Bay

Parakai
Helensville
Te Pua
Loch Norrie
Dairy Flat
Stillwater
Okura
Whangaparaoa
Peninsula
Piripiri Pt
Long Bay
Toroa Point
(Gull Point)
Whangaparaoa
The Noises
Rakino Channel
Rakino Island
Colville Bay
Te Whau Point
Colville
Little
Bay
COROMANDEL
FP

Wharepapa
Woodhill
Rewiti
Riverhead
Redvale
Glenvar
Coatesville
Albany
Heights
Paremoremo
Albany
Village
Cuthill
North
Harbour
North Shore
Rangitoto
Island
Motutapu
Island
Thumb Point
(Te Patu Point)
Owhiti
Bay
Waiheke
Island
Motukawao
Group
Kennedy
Bay
Amodeo
Bay
Papaaroha
Anarake Pt

Waimauku
Huapai
Kumeu
Taupaki
West Harbour
Te Atatu
Peninsula
Birkenhead
Takapuna
Rangitoto
260
Oneroa
Onetangi
Bay
Onetangi
Motuoruhi Island
(Goat Island)
Whangapoua
Driving Creek
Railway
Te Rerenga

Muriwai
Beach
Waitakere
Swanson
Henderson
Valley
Henderson
New Lynn
Devonport
St Heliers
Howick
Motuihe I
Browns Bay
(Motukorea)
Musick Point
Omiha
Cowes
Pakatoa
Island
Rotoroa Island
Waimate I
Motutapere I
Whanganui I
Coromandel
Coromandel Harbour
Te Kouma
Waiau
Motutere
532
Te Henga
(Bethells Beach)
Anawhata
Piha
Karekare
Huia
Parau
Laingholm
Ihumatao
Mt Wellington
Otahuhu
Orapiu
Rangipukea I
Deadmans Pt
Ponui Island
(Chamberlins Island)
Rangipuketai I
Manaia
Mahakirau
Kaimarama
Mill
Creek

WAITAKERE
RANGES
474
Whatipu
Little
Huia
Big Bay
Cornwallis
Grahams
Beach
Puponga Pt
Manukau
Harbour
Waiatarua
Titirangi
Mangere
AUCKLAND
Whitford
Brookby
Kawakawa
Bay
195
Orere
Point
Pakihi Island
(Sandspit Island)
Raukura Point
Orere
Kereta
Waikawau
Square
Kauri
Tree
Te Mata
Tapu
Coroglen
Te Mata River
Kakatarahae
725
COROMANDEL
RANGE

South
Head
Wattle Bay
Orua
Bay
Awhitu
Central
Matakawau
Pollok
Seagrove
Ellett's
Beach
Clarks
Beach
Karaka
Runciman
Manurewa
Papakura
Alfriston
Ardmore
Clevedon
Ness
Valley
Cosseys
Reservoir
Kohukohunui
688
Hunua
Falls
Wairoa
Resr
Upper
Mangatawhiri
Reservoir
Matingarahi
Ruamahunga
Waiomu
Thornton Bay
Te Puru
Water
Gardens
Table Mtn
846
COROMANDEL
FOREST PARK

Waiau
Beach
Glenbrook
Beach
Waipipi
Kohekohe
Te Toro
Patumahoe
Raerata
Helvetia
Pukekohe
East
Opaheke
Drury
Hunua
Ponga
Paparata
Papakura
Mangatangi
Reservoir
Wharekawa
Whakatiwai
Kaiaua
Miranda
Shorebird
Centre
Miranda
Firth
of
Thames

TASMAN
SEA
Mauku
Sedgebrook
Glenbrook
Vintage
Railway
Mission
Bush
Pukekohe
Puni
Buckland
Happy
Valley
Papakura
Ararimu
Paparimu
Moumoukai
Mangatawhiri
Maramarua
Mangatangi
Miranda
Hot Springs
Pipiroa
Thames
Waihou River
Piako
Totara
Kadaeranga
Orongo
Matatoki

Waiuku
Kariotahi
Whiriwhiri
Aka Aka
Tuakau
Harrisville
Kingseat
Pokeno
Kellyville
Pokeno
Bombay
Whangarata
Mercer
Kopuku
Island Block
Mangatarata
Kerepehi
Pipiroa
Waitakaruru
Turua
Ngatea
323
Kopuarahi
Wharepoa
Puriri
Omahu
Hikutaia

Taurangaruru
Maioro
Otaua
Te Kohanga
HAMILTON
TO HAMILTON
TO MATAMATA
TO TAIRUA
TO PAEROA

GREAT BARRIER ISLAND (AOTEA ISLAND)

Rugged, beautiful Great Barrier Island lies about 100km north-east of Auckland in the **Hauraki Gulf**, and can be accessed by air or ferry. A peaceful, sparsely populated place, the island is known for its lovely white-sand beaches and lush native forests. Much of Great Barrier is wilderness; over 60% of the island is administered by the Department of Conservation.

Great Barrier's east coast has beautiful white-sand beaches pounded by surf; on the west, richly forested hills meet the coast. The possum-free island is a haven for rare wildlife species. Historic sites include Maori pa and settlement sites, as well as relics from its days as a European whaling, mining and logging centre.

Popular activities include walking, camping, kayaking, swimming, surfing, horse trekking, exploring historic spots, and soaking in thermal hot springs — or just enjoying the laid-back atmosphere.

Camping on Great Barrier Island

i **Visitor information**

Great Barrier Island Visitor Information Centre
Hector Sanderson Rd, Claris
Ph: (09) 429 0033
www.greatbarrier.co.nz

main attractions

- Glenfern Sanctuary
- Great Barrier Forest
- Hirakimata (Mt Hobson)
- Kaitoke Hot Springs
- Kauri dams
- Medlands Beach
- Tramline Track
- Tryphena
- Whangapoua Beach
- Windy Canyon

Piha, became iconic after it was used for the beach scenes of Jane Campion's 1992 movie *The Piano*. Other notable beaches are **Te Henga (Bethells Beach)** and **Anawhata Beach** to the north and **Whatipu Beach** to the south. Just east of Piha is **Waitakere Ranges Regional Park**, a picturesque park full of native trees and numerous walking tracks. The **Arataki Visitors Centre**, about 15km east, has some fine views and walks.
VISITOR INFORMATION: Scenic Drive, Titirangi, Ph: (09) 817 0077, www.piha.co.nz

■ Port Waikato   POP 465
Map 160, A1
Located 89km south-west of Auckland on the west coast, Port Waikato was once a bustling and important port for early settlers, especially during the New Zealand Wars of the 1860s. Today it is more noted as a place to relax.
MAIN ATTRACTIONS: Port Waikato is on the southern side of the mouth of the **Waikato River**, New Zealand's longest river. The area can be viewed by walking along spectacular sand dunes to the beach, or on an off-road tour along the beach and the nearby hills. **Sunset Beach** is popular with surfers, and features a seal colony.
NEARBY ATTRACTIONS: The farmland setting used for the '**Weathertop Hollow**' scenes in *The Lord Of The Rings* films, about 10km south, can be viewed on a guided tour. **Nikau Cave**, about 25km south, is a fine cave complex with glow-worms, stalactites and stalagmites, and without the crowds. Another 15km further south is **Waingaro Hot Springs**, a popular spot with hot mineral pools, hot water slides and boats. About 25km east near **Tuakau** is **Mark Vette's Rescue Zoo**, a haven for at-risk exotic animals.
VISITOR INFORMATION: 4C Roulston St, Pukekohe, Ph: (09) 238 4081, www.franklindistrict.co.nz/tourism

Lion Rock, Piha Beach

North Island

Entrance sign to Raetihi

Pukekohe   POP 18 825
Map 158, D6

A thriving town 52km south of Auckland, Pukekohe was originally a rural service centre, and provides a quieter lifestyle for Auckland commuters.

MAIN ATTRACTIONS: The most-visited place by far is **Pukekohe Raceway**, the home of car racing in New Zealand. A round of the Australian **V8 Supercar** series is held annually; the raceway also hosts several other notable motorsport events. **Pukekohe training track** for thoroughbred racehorses is set to become the main training track for the Auckland region. The **Pioneer Memorial Cottage**, built in 1859, is redone in 1860s period style, when it was garrisoned by British troops during the land wars. It's open Saturdays.

NEARBY ATTRACTIONS: About 8km west is **Wrights Watergardens**, a 3ha garden complex featuring numerous waterlilies and lotus ponds. The café on the premises overlooks the **Mauku Waterfall**. A little further west is the **Glenbrook Vintage Railway**, a popular 6km steam carriage railway. **Glenbrook Farm Park**'s residents include Arabian horses, cattle, goats, sheep, alpaca and talking cockatoos. Tours are possible at the **Glenbrook Steel Mill**. The historic town of **Waiuku**, 19km west, is home to 19th century hotels and boats, and is the gateway to the **Awhitu Peninsula**. To the east is **Bombay**; the **Simunovich Olive Estate** is New Zealand's largest olive farm. South near **Tuakau**, **Mark Vette's Rescue Zoo** is a haven for exotic animals.

VISITOR INFORMATION: 4C Roulston St, Ph: (09) 238 4081, www.franklindistrict.co.nz/tourism

Putaruru   POP 3785
Map 161, G5

A service centre for the surrounding forestry and dairy farming region, Putaruru is 65km south-east of Hamilton.

MAIN ATTRACTIONS: The **Putaruru Timber Museum**, on the site of an early pine tree nursery, has displays on the North Island's timber and logging industries. Putaruru is a venue for national woodturning exhibitions. The **Te Waihou Walkway**, 5km north-east off State Highway 28, is a lovely walk along the **Waihou River** to the **Blue Spring**, a source of crystal clear water which is bottled and sold commercially. The river was once a travelling route for the second Maori King. **Putaruru Waterpark** has an interactive water sculpture in the colour of the Te Waihou spring. Fishing is also a focus in the area, with plentiful trout in the many nearby rivers.

NEARBY ATTRACTIONS: **Lake Arapuni**, 16km west, is a man-made lake popular for swimming, boating, water-skiing and fishing. Completed in 1929, **Arapuni** is the oldest government-built hydro-electric power station on the Waikato River. A historic swingbridge, suspended 54m above the power station, crosses the bush-lined gorge below. Not for those with a fear of heights, it offers wonderful views of the gorge. **Lichfield**, 8km south of Putaruru, has a historic stone store and 1886 brick water tower, and the southern hemisphere's largest cheese factory.

VISITOR INFORMATION: 75 Tirau St, Ph: (07) 883 7284, www.swktodc.govt.nz

Raetihi   POP 1070
Map 173, K4

The farming and forestry town of Raetihi, in the western central North Island's **Ruapehu** district, is located between **Tongariro National Park** and **Whanganui National Park**. The first Europeans settled at Raetihi in 1893, but development was hampered by the difficulty of access to the area — for many years by steamer up the **Whanganui River** and then by dray road.

MAIN ATTRACTIONS: Raetihi's **Theatre Royal** is reputedly the oldest purpose-built theatre in the southern hemisphere.

NEARBY ATTRACTIONS: West of Raetihi, the **Whanganui River Road** is a fascinating riverside route through picturesque historic villages and lush forests; there are many beautiful marae (Maori community meeting-places), which may be visited with permission. Quiet **Pipiriki**, 26km west, was a busy port during the Whanganui River's days as a major North Island travel route. North of Pipiriki, Whanganui National Park can be explored by boat or walking. East of Raetihi is the World Heritage Area of **Tongariro National Park**, where the three active volcanoes of **Mount Ruapehu**, **Tongariro** and **Ngauruhoe** offer stunning scenery, snow sports, hiking and trout fishing. From the ski town of **Ohakune**, the **Ohakune Mountain Road** leads up through lush forests to the **Turoa Ski Area** on Ruapehu. **Whakapapa Ski Area**, further north, is New Zealand's largest ski field.

VISITOR INFORMATION: Clyde St, Ohakune, Ph: (06) 385 8427, www.visitruapehu.com

Raglan POP 2665
Map 160, B4

The character harbour town of Raglan, 45km west of Hamilton, attracts surfers from around the world to **Manu Bay**'s famous left-hand break and the international surfing competitions held over summer. Raglan also has a reputation for its artisans.

MAIN ATTRACTIONS: The **Arts and Crafts Trail** allows visitors to buy crafts and watch artists at work. Raglan's sheltered harbour offers fishing, swimming, windsurfing and boating; harbour cruises are available. There is safe swimming at **Te Kopua Recreational Reserve**, **Cox Bay** and **Puriri Park**.

NEARBY ATTRACTIONS: **Ngarunui Beach**, 7km west, is a surf beach with impressive cliffs, and **Manu Bay**, 8km west, reputedly has the world's longest left-hand break. **Whale Bay**, further west, is another famous surf beach. **Bridal Veil Falls** is a spectacular 55m waterfall in a native bush reserve; two trails lead to the summit of **Mount Karioi**, which offers a panoramic outlook. The unsealed back road between Raglan and the harbour town of **Kawhia**, 45km south, is a scenic route with coastal and bush views. Densely forested **Pirongia Forest Park**, home to two extinct volcanoes, offers a wide range of walks, including the easy three-hour **Nikau Walk**, and a track to **Kaniwhaniwha Caves**. There are beautiful views from the summit of **Mount Pirongia**.

VISITOR INFORMATION: 4 Wallis St, Ph: (07) 825 0556, www.raglan.org.nz

Rawene POP 460
Map 154, C2

The lovely small town of Rawene, on the southern shore of **Northland**'s **Hokianga Harbour**, is the departure point for a car ferry across the harbour. Rawene was New Zealand's third European settlement, and the area had thriving ship-building and timber milling industries in the 19th century. Rawene was the site of the 1898 Dog Tax Rebellion, when Maori marched on the town in protest at a tax on dogs, and government troops were sent in response.

MAIN ATTRACTIONS: A **Heritage Trail** leads visitors around Rawene's many historic buildings, including the 1860s kauri homestead **Clendon House** and six churches. The **Mangrove Walkway**, built on the former site of a century-old timber mill, explores the unique mangrove habitat.

NEARBY ATTRACTIONS: **Horeke**, 40km north-east, was once home to a busy ship-building industry. The nearby **Mangungu Mission House** was established in 1838–9, and was the scene of the largest gathering to discuss and sign the 1840 Treaty of Waitangi. **Wairere Boulders Park** has unusual boulder formations and kauri trees. **Kohukohu**, 4km from the ferry, was once the largest town in the north, and a **Heritage Trail** leads around its historic buildings. The village of **Motuti** has a strong focus on Maori arts and crafts, and the marae (meeting-ground) features impressive carvings. **Warawara Forest**, 25km west of Kohukohu, is a large area of kauri forest. **Mitimiti**, west of the forest, is an isolated coastal Maori settlement where visitors can take a Maori culture or beach tour.

VISITOR INFORMATION: SH12, Omapere, Ph: (09) 405 8869, www.hokianga.co.nz

Rotorua POP 52 610
Map 186, C2

Rotorua, 234km south-east of Auckland on the shores of **Lake Rotorua**, has been a tourist destination since the 19th century, drawing visitors with its many geothermal attractions and therapeutic hot pools.

MAIN ATTRACTIONS: **Rotorua Museum of Art and History**, in the former Bath House building, has displays on the **Mount Tarawera** eruption, the bath house's history and local Maori tribe Te Arawa; the nearby **Blue Baths** are a restored 1930s swimming pool complex. The lake-edge **Polynesian Spa** has outdoor hot mineral pools, and health and

Raglan surf

North Island

Champagne Pool, Wai-O-Tapu Thermal Wonderland, south of Rotorua

beauty treatments; the thermal village area of **Whakarewarewa** features expert Maori carvers and weavers at **Te Puia**. **St Faith's Anglican Church**, at the historic lakeside thermal village of **Ohinemutu**, features Maori carvings and panels. **Mokoia Island**, in the lake's centre, is the setting of the well-known Maori love story of Hinemoa and Tutanekai. Maori performances, concerts and hangi (food cooked in an underground oven) are on offer around Rotorua. Fishing, jet boating, swimming, kayaking and scenic cruises are all popular activities. A gondola ride to the summit of **Mount Ngongotaha** offers extensive views, and adventure activities are available there and at the nearby **Agrodome**, which also has shows and displays about sheep and farming. **Rainbow Springs** and **Paradise Valley Springs** have fresh water springs full of trout.

Nearby Attractions: The region's 16 lakes offer fishing, boating and swimming; there are walkways around **Lake Okataina** and **Lake Tikitapu (Blue Lake)**. The **Buried Village**, 15km south-east, has displays about Mount Tarawera's 1886 eruption, and excavated buildings which were buried by debris. Mount Tarawera, now under the guardianship of the Ngati Rangitihi tribe, can be visited on a guided 4WD tour. Thermal areas include **Hell's Gate and Wai Ora Spa**, 16km north-east, which has a hot waterfall, and **Waimangu Volcanic Valley**, 24km south, created during the Tarawera eruption. The thermal attractions at **Wai-O-Tapu Thermal Wonderland**, 29km south, include coloured mineral terraces and the Lady Knox Geyser; beautiful **Orakei Korako**, further south, is a thermal valley accessed by boat. **Tamaki Maori Village**, 15km south of Rotorua, is a replica pre-European village.

Visitor Information: 1167 Fenton St, Ph: (07) 348 5179, 0800 768 678, www.rotoruanz.com

■ Ruatoria   POP 840
Map 165, J3

The main town in the northern part of **Eastland**, 123km north of Gisborne, Ruatoria is a stronghold of Maori culture in the region.

Main Attractions: Ruatoria is home to the Ngati Porou iwi (tribe), who welcome visitors wanting to learn more about Maori culture. Ruatoria is also the base of the Ngati Porou East Coast rugby team; the townspeople are among New Zealand's most passionate supporters of the national sport, and watching a game with them is an experience not to be missed. Nearby are several high quality beaches, and fishing is also popular.

Nearby Attractions: **Mount Hikurangi**, about 25km west of Ruatoria at the east of the **Raukumara Forest Park**, is the highest peak in Eastland at 1752m, and an important landmark for the Ngati Porou people. It's also the first mainland place in the world to see the sun. Permission is needed from the tribe to visit the mountain. **Te Puia Springs**, 29km south, is a pleasant town with relaxing hot springs. **Tikitiki**, 22km north-east, is a small town steeped in Maori tradition; it's home to **St Mary's Anglican Church**, one of the country's most ornate Maori churches.

Visitor Information: 209 Grey St, Gisborne, Ph: (06) 868 6139, www.eastlandnz.com

■ Russell   POP 805
Map 155, F1

Russell, in the **Bay of Islands**, started life as a fortified Maori settlement called **Kororareka**. Before 1840 it was New Zealand's largest town, and first permanent European settlement. Known as 'the hell hole of the Pacific' due to the rough behaviour of whalers, traders and sailors on shore leave, it was also the site of Maori rebellion against encroaching European settlement. The flagpole displaying the Union Jack was chopped down four times by the chief Hone Heke, and the town was sacked and burnt in 1845. Russell today is a peaceful town with lovely colonial buildings and pohutukawa trees lining its waterfront.

(CONTINUED P.128)

VOLCANIC PLATEAU THERMAL ATTRACTIONS

Geothermally active for millennia, the North Island's volcanic plateau is dotted with volcanoes, hot springs, beautiful thermal landscapes, and lakes formed by collapsed volcanic caldera.

Thermal activity around **Rotorua** was the drawcard for its original Maori settlers, and has attracted tourists since the 19th century. Spa resorts have also been popular since the early days, and visitors can bathe in thermally-heated mineral pools throughout the region, with massage and pampering treatments available at a number of spa complexes.

Rotorua is permeated by the smell of sulphur; within the city limits, the thermal areas of **Kuirau Park**, **Sulphur Point** and the historic Maori village **Ohinemutu** can all be visited for free. **Rotorua Museum of Art and History**, in the city's old Bath House building, has displays of the early 20th century's sometimes eccentric spa therapies.

Geothermal **Rainbow Mountain** has unique plants adapted to volcanic conditions, and walks to see crater lakes, steaming cliffs and the mountain's summit. Further south, near **Taupo**, the **Wairakei Geothermal Power Project** produces electricity from thermal steam, and visitors can learn about geothermal activity at the **Volcanic Activity Centre**.

Mt Tarawera & the Buried Village

The Pink and White Terraces, once known as the eighth wonder of the world, were destroyed in 1886 when Mt Tarawera erupted, killing more than 150 people and permanently changing the landscape. Buildings excavated after the eruption can be seen at the Buried Village, and visitors can explore the mountain on guided 4WD trips.

main attractions

◈ **Orakei Korako**

A boat trip across a lake takes visitors to this thermal valley with its mud pools, geysers, beautiful coloured terraces and pools.

◈ **Polynesian Spa**

Hot pools offer bathing in a lovely outdoor setting on the shores of Lake Rotorua. Spa treatments and massage are also available.

◈ **Hell's Gate and Wai Ora Spa**

A spa complex offers traditional Maori massage and mud treatments at Hell's Gate, also known for the southern hemisphere's largest hot waterfall.

◈ **Wai-O-Tapu Thermal Wonderland**

Brilliantly coloured pools and mineral terraces, and the Lady Knox Geyser, are features of this thermal area.

◈ **Waimangu Volcanic Valley**

Formed during Mt Tarawera's 1886 eruption, this thermal area has the largest hot spring in the world.

◈ **Wairakei Geothermal Power Project**

This power station produces 5% of NZ's electricity from what was originally one of the world's most thermally active areas.

◈ **Whakarewarewa Thermal Reserve**

Also a major Maori cultural area, this well-known thermal area is home to the 20m Pohutu Geyser.

ⓘ **Visitor information**

Rotorua i-SITE Visitor Centre
1167 Fenton St, Rotorua
Ph: (07) 348 5179
Freephone: 0800 768 678
www.rotoruanz.com

Taupo i-SITE Visitor Centre
Tongariro St, Taupo
Ph: (07) 376 0027
www.laketauponz.com

Wai-O-Tapu Thermal Wonderland, south of Rotorua

North Island

Scale 1: 300 000

0   10
kilometres

KAIMAI-MAMAKU FP

TO TAURANGA

TO TE PUKE

Mamaku

OTUROA

Te Pu
Kaharoa
Rotongata
Hamurana
Awahou
Okere Falls
Tokerau
Okere Falls
Whangamarino
Otaramarae
Pikiao Marae

Mourea

Lake Rotoiti
Hinehopu
Rotoehu
Lake Rotoehu
Haparu
Gisborne Point
Rotoiti
Lake Rotoma

Agrodome Adventure Park
Waiteti
Ngongotaha
Hell's Gate (Tikitere) & Wai Ora Spa
Tikitere
Ruato
Te Ngae
Lake Rotokawau
Lake Rotoiti
L Rotoma Scenic Res

Arahiwi Scenic Reserve
Arahiwi
Mamaku

Dansey's Rd Scenic Res
Tarukenga
Ngongotaha Valley
Paradise Valley Springs

Gondola & Luge
Rainbow Springs
Ohinemutu
Lake Rotorua
Mokoia Island
Rotokawa
Lake Okataina
Lake Okataina Walkway
Lake Okataina Scenic Reserve

ROTORUA
Western Heights
Mt Ngongotaha 757 Scenic Res
Mangakakahi
Whakarewarewa Thermal Reserve
Owhata
Lynmore
Makatiti Dome Scenic Reserve
Tarawera Falls

Springfield
Glenholme
Tihiotonga
Lake Okareka
Lake Okareka
Lake Tarawera

Utuhina Stm
Whakarewarewa Forest Park
Lake Rotokakahi (Green Lake)
Lake Tikitapu (Blue Lake)
Te Wairoa
Buried Village
Wairere Falls
Punaromia
Lake Tarawera Scenic Res

Horohoro
Haparangi 688
Kapenga
Mt Tarawera 1111

Waireka
Rotohouhou Stm
Tamaki Maori Village
Tumunui
Earthquake Flat
Hot Water Beach
Lake Rotomahana

Guthrie
Karapiti Stm
761
Waimangu
Waimangu Volcanic Valley
Waimangu Scenic Res
Lake Rerewhakaaitu

Ngakuru
Rotomahana
Rerewhakaaitu

Waikite Valley
Rainbow Mountain Scenic Reserve
Waikite
Rainbow Mountain
Waiotapu Village

Upper Atiamuri
Lake Atiamuri
Te Kopia Scenic Reserve
Paeroa 979
Waiotapu
Wai-O-Tapu Thermal Wonderland

Atiamuri
Ohakuri
Wharepaina
Kaingaroa Forest

Lake Ohakuri
Parekarangi
Reporoa
Maori Cave Art

Orakei Korako Hidden Valley
Golden Springs
Mihi

Maroanui 897
Ohaaki
Broadlands
Wairapukao

Te Pouwhakatutu
Oruanui
Tahorakuri

Wairakei Thermal Valley
Wairakei Village
Aratiatia
Aratiatia Rapids
Lake Rotokawa

Wairakei
Geothermal Power Project
Wairakei Terraces
Craters of the Moon
Volcanic Activity Centre
Huka Falls
Rotokawa

TO TAUPO

TERRALINK INTERNATIONAL LIMITED 2006

Continued on maps 163 & 169

BAY OF ISLANDS

The beautiful Bay of Islands has 144 islands, gorgeous coastal scenery and many secluded beaches. Sea kayaking, sailing, cruising, diving, marlin fishing and swimming with dolphins are all popular activities.

The area is also of major historical significance, and has been described as the birthplace of the nation. It was the site of New Zealand's first permanent European settlement, and the Treaty of Waitangi was signed at **Waitangi** between Maori chiefs and European leaders in 1840. Many historic sites can be seen, including the **Treaty House** at Waitangi, and the Catholic mission of **Pompallier** in **Russell**. This elegant, historic township was once known as 'hell hole of the Pacific', due to sailors, whalers and traders using it for shore leave. The relaxed town of **Kerikeri** has citrus orchards, cafés and historic attractions.

main attractions

❖ 'Hole in the Rock', Cape Brett
❖ Mission House and Stone Store, Kerikeri
❖ Paihia
❖ Russell
❖ Waitangi National Reserve

ⓘ Visitor information

Bay of Islands i-SITE Visitor Centre
The Wharf, Marsden Rd, Paihia
Ph: (09) 402 7345
www.northlandnz.com

Mission House and Stone Store, Kerikeri

MAIN ATTRACTIONS: **Christ Church**, New Zealand's oldest church, is scarred with musket ball holes from the 1845 fighting. The Catholic mission building of **Pompallier**, built from rammed earth, was home to a print shop which printed 40 000 books in Maori. **Russell Museum** has interesting displays about the area's history. There are excellent views over the town from **Maiki (Flagstaff Hill)**, the site of Hone Heke's assaults on the flagpole.

NEARBY ATTRACTIONS: The **Cape Brett Tramping Track**, north-east of Russell, is an eight-hour walk offering spectacular views over the Bay of Islands. From the **Rawhiti–Ngaiotonga** road, 28km east, a one-hour walk leads to the **Whangamumu Harbour** site of New Zealand's last shore-based whaling station. The boiler and vats that once held whale oil can still be seen. **Urupukapuka Island** has an archaeological trail leading around a series of Maori sites.

VISITOR INFORMATION: The Wharf, Marsden Rd, Paihia, Ph: (09) 402 7345, www.northlandnz.com

Christ Church, New Zealand's oldest church, Russell

North Island

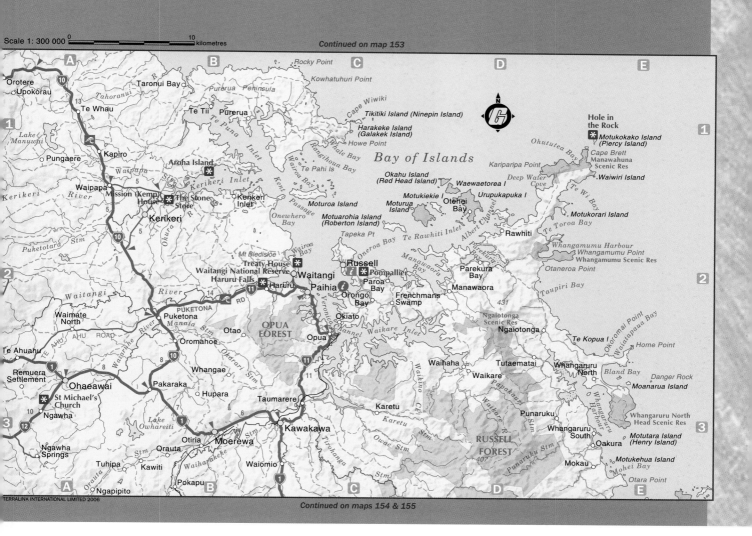

Continued on map 153

Scale 1 : 300 000

Continued on maps 154 & 155

TERRALINK INTERNATIONAL LIMITED 2006

Stratford POP 5230

Map 172, D3

Stratford is a rural service centre in inland **Taranaki**, nestled below beautiful **Mount Taranaki** 39km south of New Plymouth. Named after Shakespeare's birthplace, Stratford was originally called Stratford-on-Patea, and 67 of its streets are named for Shakespearean characters.

MAIN ATTRACTIONS: The **Taranaki Pioneer Village**, 1km south of the town centre, is an outdoor museum with 50 heritage buildings. Peaceful **Carrington Walkway** leads through bush along the banks of the **Patea River**; 8ha **King Edward Park** has a pretty rhododendron dell. Stratford's central clock tower has New Zealand's first glockenspiel; like much in the town, it takes

its theme from Shakespeare, and features performances by models of characters from *Romeo and Juliet*. The **Percy Thomson Gallery** has touring and local art exhibitions.

NEARBY ATTRACTIONS: State Highway 43 from Stratford to **Taumarunui** is known as the **Forgotten World Highway**. This remote and fascinating 155km route passes many historic places, including old coal mines, waterfalls, Maori pa sites and **Whangamomona** village. **Cardiff Centennial Walkway**, 6km west, is a 3km riverside walkway along the **Waingongoro River**. The **Manganui Skifield**, 20km west on the slopes of **Mount Taranaki**, is open from June to August and has steep terrain for advanced skiers. Stratford is also a base for visits to **Egmont**

National Park, where there are many walks through lovely forest.

VISITOR INFORMATION: 1 Ariki St, New Plymouth, Ph: (06) 759 6060, www.taranaki.info

Taihape POP 1805

Map 174, C3

At the northern border of the **Rangitikei** district, the appealing small town of Taihape is a popular stop for travellers on State Highway One, and has some good cafés. Taihape is famously known as the Gumboot Capital of the world, and celebrates the black rubber farmers' boots with a yearly festival.

MAIN ATTRACTIONS: The annual **Taihape Gumboot Throwing Festival** includes gumboot-throwing competitions and gumboot art. Abseiling, tramping and horse

Corrugated iron gumboot sculpture, Taihape

trekking are all popular activities around Taihape, and visitors can go jet boating, kayaking and white water rafting on the **Rangitikei River**, with its dramatic cliffs and gorges.
NEARBY ATTRACTIONS: For lovers of adrenalin, there are extreme adventure activities in the spectacular **Mokai Canyon**, including the North Island's highest bungy jump (80m) and a flying fox that hurtles above the river at speeds of more than 160km/h. Scenes for the **'River Anduin'** in *The Lord of the Rings* movies were filmed here and at the river's junction with the **Moawhango River**. At **Pukeokahu**, to the east, there is white water rafting over boulders in a spectacular canyon; the rapids further south are good for rafting and kayaking. Quieter types might prefer to check out the four beautiful gardens within half an hour's drive of Taihape; **Titoki Point**, **Rongoiti**, **Waitoka** and **Kiri Kiri** gardens all welcome visitors. The pretty settlement of **Mangaweka**, 21km south, is home to a café in a converted old DC3 plane, and is also a centre for adventure tourism based around

the Rangitikei River. In the army town of **Waiouru**, 31km north, the **Army Museum Waiouru** tells the story of the New Zealand Army in peacetime and wartime.
VISITOR INFORMATION: 90 Hautapu St, Ph: (06) 327 5143, www.rangitikei.com

■ Tairua   POP 1460
Map 159, J4
Tairua is a popular seaside holiday resort, two hours' drive from Auckland on the east coast of the **Coromandel Peninsula**. Tairua's twin town of **Pauanui** is accessible by ferry across **Tairua Harbour**.
MAIN ATTRACTIONS: Boat charters offer fishing, diving, sightseeing and expeditions to offshore islands, including privately-owned **Slipper Island**. There are spectacular views from the summit of **Paku** volcano, which is a 30-minute walk and the site of a historic pa (Maori fortified village).
NEARBY ATTRACTIONS: Pauanui, south across the harbour, has white sand beaches with good swimming, surfing and fishing. The steep 387m **Pauanui Summit Track** offers panoramic views along the coast. Some 8km north of Tairua, an excellent half-day hike leads from **Te Karo Bay** to the historic **Sailor's Grave** coastal area. Visitors can dig their own open-air seaside spa at fabulous **Hot Water Beach**, which has thermally-heated mineral springs that bubble through the sand at the low tide mark, but is unsafe for swimming. **Hahei**, 20km north, has a lovely white-sand beach; the famous **Cathedral Cove** is a beautiful beach with a huge limestone arch, accessible only by walking or boat. **Te Whanganui-A-Hei Marine Reserve** is a marine reserve area along this dramatic limestone coast, scattered with islands and offering wonderful snorkelling and diving. South of Tairua, the **Broken Hills Recreation Area** has

plentiful native bird life and walks through a historic gold mining area. Beautiful **Opoutere Beach**, 3.5km from the turnoff south of **Hikuai**, is a secluded, unspoilt surf beach. The **Wharekawa Harbour** features a stunning natural sandspit and many birds.
VISITOR INFORMATION: Main Rd, Ph: (07) 864 7575, www.tairua.info

■ Taumarunui   POP 5135
Map 167, G5
Situated on the North Island's central plateau, Taumarunui is a service centre for the farming and forestry industries of the **Ruapehu** district, and is the northern gateway to the **Whanganui River**.
MAIN ATTRACTIONS: Activities for visitors include hiking, hunting, fishing, swimming and scenic flights. A scenic one-hour walk leads along the bank of the Whanganui River.
NEARBY ATTRACTIONS: Taumarunui is the starting point for the five-day, 145km canoe trip down the Whanganui River, New Zealand's longest navigable waterway. Surrounded by lush forests, the river is rich in Maori and European history; **Whanganui National Park** has walking tracks, and the intriguing **Bridge to Nowhere**. A two-hour climb up 771m **Mount Hikurangi**, north-east of Taumarunui, offers panoramic views over the mountains of **Tongariro National Park**. This famous national park, 30 minutes' drive away, is a World Heritage Area offering magnificent forest, volcanic scenery, unforgettable walks and snow sports. The **Raurimu Spiral**, 21km south, is a unique feat of railway engineering through dense native forest, completed in 1908; it can be viewed from the lookout at **Raurimu**. East of Raurimu in the **Tongariro Forest**, the **42nd Traverse** is a mountain biking trail which descends 570m on old bush tracks. A beautiful

North Island

walk through **Ohinetonga Scenic Reserve** passes through forest, and there is a lagoon with waterlilies. Further east, **Pureora Forest Park** is a magnificent area of podocarp forest, with rich bird life. There are long and short walks, and a 12m observation tower. The **Forgotten World Highway** is a fascinating 155km trip down remote State Highway 43 to **Stratford**. The route passes many historic sites, including old coal mines, waterfalls, Maori pa sites and **Whangamomona** village.
VISITOR INFORMATION: Hakiaha St, Ph: (07) 895 7494, www.visitruapehu.com

■ **Taupo**   POP 20 310
Map 187, B3
Located on the north-eastern shores of **Lake Taupo** in the central North Island, the resort town of Taupo looks out across the lake to the mountains of **Tongariro National Park**.
MAIN ATTRACTIONS: Volcanically-formed Lake Taupo is known for its trout fishing, and is also popular for sailing, kayaking, waterskiing and swimming. Lake cruises are available; some visit the modern Maori rock carvings at **Mine Bay**, accessible only by boat. Taupo is a centre for adventure activities, including bungy jumping over the **Waikato River**, skydiving, jet boating and white water rafting on local rivers. Lake Taupo is the venue for some of New Zealand's biggest cycling events. The area's many walks include a track along the **Waikato River** to **Aratiatia**, which crosses a hot thermal stream and passes the impressive, thunderous **Huka Falls**. Water rushes through the **Aratiatia Rapids** at a rate of 90 000 litres per second when the **Aratiatia Dam**'s spillway is opened (three to four times daily). **Taupo Hot Springs Spa** has hot mineral pools for bathing, and **Lake Taupo Museum and Art Gallery** features an impressive Maori meeting-house.

Taupo also has good shopping and restaurants.
NEARBY ATTRACTIONS: There are spectacular views from the summit of **Mount Tauhara**, a two-hour walk off State Highway 5. At thermally-active **Wairakei**, 10km north, the **Wairakei Geothermal Power Project** generates about 5% of New Zealand's electricity from geothermal steam; nearby is a thermally heated prawn farm, and shops featuring honey and fruit wines. The **Craters of the Moon** is a thermal area with mud pools, bubbling craters and steam; at the **Volcanic Activity Centre**, visitors can learn about New Zealand's geothermal activity. **Wairakei Terraces** offers a Maori cultural experience, and the man-made silica terraces reproduce the original ones at Wairakei. Jet boat rides are available on the Waikato River to the Huka Falls. Further north, thermal **Orakei Korako**'s lovely silica terraces, mud pools and geysers can be reached by a boat ride across a lake.
VISITOR INFORMATION: Tongariro St, Ph: (07) 376 0027, www.laketauponz.com

■ **Tauranga & Mt Maunganui**
POP 95 700
Map 161, J3
Tauranga, 201km south-east of Auckland, is the main city of the **Bay of Plenty**. Beachside Mount Maunganui is just five minutes away, and together the two offer a great combination of urban lifestyle and beach relaxation. One of New Zealand's largest export ports, Tauranga is among the country's fastest growing cities. Mount Maunganui, across the harbour, offers lovely beaches.
MAIN ATTRACTIONS: There are thermal mineral pools at Tauranga's **Fernland Spa**. **Gate Pa** marks the site where Maori defeated the British in a fierce 1864 battle. In Mount Maunganui, the 360m volcanic mountain of **Mauao** was the landing place of the ancestral Maori Takitimu canoe, and has been important to Maori for centuries. Walkways lead around the mountain's base and to its summit, where historic fortifications can be seen. Nearby are hot salt water pools. **Moturiki Island**, connected to the main beach,

Downtown Tauranga

Beautiful Lake Taupo, New Zealand's largest lake at 616km², is the result of a massive volcanic eruption around 181AD. The eruption produced a 50km-high column of ash; reports from Rome and China mentioned its effects on the skies. In Maori legend, the lake was created by Ngatoirangi, a tohunga (priest), who threw a totara tree into a barren basin to seed a new forest. The tree's branches pierced the ground, and water gushed up to fill the basin.

Lake Taupo is fed by 47 rivers and streams, and the massive **Waikato River** is its only outlet. Hot springs still exist around the lake edge, and the trout fishing is world famous. The lake is also a popular spot for water sports, including waterskiing, swimming, kayaking, sailing and parasailing. Modern Maori rock carvings at **Mine Bay** can only be reached by boat.

Trout fishing, Lake Taupo

main attractions

❖ Mine Bay rock carvings
❖ Taupo
❖ Thermal attractions
❖ Trout fishing
❖ Water sports

Lake Taupo

i Visitor information

Taupo i-SITE Visitor Centre
Tongariro St, Taupo
Ph: (07) 376 0027
www.laketauponz.com

has a blowhole which produces geyser-like displays; further east, **Papamoa Beach** is another fine white-sand beach. Water-based activities include diving, snorkelling, deep-water fishing, scenic cruises and swimming with dolphins. The airport offers scenic flights, including over the active volcano of **Whakaari/White Island**. Tauranga plays host to a number of festivals, including a jazz festival in March and an arts festival in October.

NEARBY ATTRACTIONS: **Mayor Island (Tuhua)**, 40km north of Tauranga, is a dormant volcano, with fascinating geology which includes lava flows and black obsidian. Diving and snorkelling are excellent around the island, as a marine reserve protects the abundant sea life. The **Wairoa River** is a popular spot for white water rafting, and has some of New Zealand's best falls. **McLaren Falls**, a 170ha lakeland park 15km south-west of Tauranga, has walking tracks, bird life, hostels and camp sites. Peaceful **Matakana Island**, in **Tauranga Harbour**, has white-sand surf beaches and offers good windsurfing, kayaking and fishing. **Omokoroa**, 22km west of Tauranga, is a popular holiday spot, and has hot thermal pools.

VISITOR INFORMATION: 95 Willow St, Tauranga, Ph: (07) 578 8103, www.bayofplentynz.com

■ Te Araroa   POP 175
Map 165, J2

A beautifully situated small town near **East Cape** on the scenic **Pacific Coast Highway**, 162km north of Gisborne, Te Araroa is an important place for the Ngati Porou iwi (tribe). The legendary ancestor Paikea, who reputedly came to New Zealand on the back of a whale, and inspired the book and 2002 film *Whale Rider*, landed nearby. Te Araroa was also the birthplace of Sir Apirana Ngata, an important Maori leader and MP of the early 20th century.

MAIN ATTRACTIONS: In Te Araroa's school grounds, **Te Waha-o-Rerekohu** is one of the largest pohutukawa trees in New Zealand, and is reputed to be 600 years old. Overlooking the town is the historic **Whetumatarau pa site**, which offers superb views. Maori heritage tours can be organised locally. Close by is outstanding **Punaruku Beach**; fishing is good here, and on **Haupara Point**, which can be accessed via a bush walk.

(CONTINUED P.134)

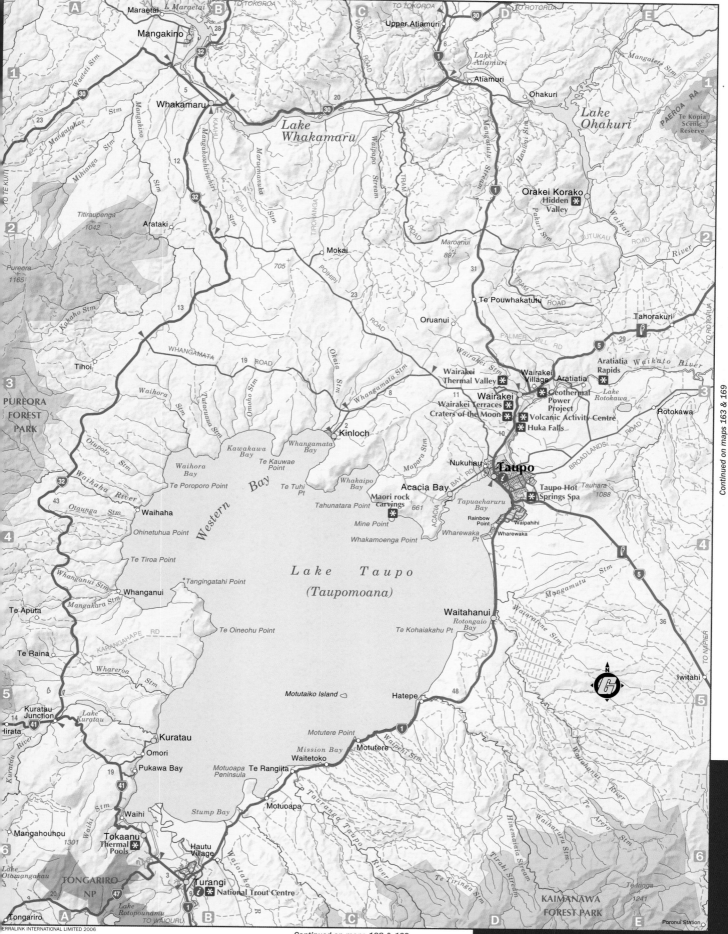

0
10
kilometres

1

Maraetai

L. Maraetai

TO TOKOROA

Upper Atiamuri

TO ROTORUA

Mangakino

28

Lake
Atiamuri

Ohakuri

Lake
Ohakuri

Paeroa Ra.

Te Kopia
Scenic
Reserve

30

Atiamuri

Whakamaru

5

30

Lake
Whakamaru

Orakei Korako
Hidden Valley

2

Titiraupenga
1042

Arataki

Mokai

Maroanui
897

31

Te Pouwhakatutu

Tahorakuri

29

Pureora
1165

705

Oruanui

3

PUREORA
FOREST
PARK

Tihoi

Waihora

Kinloch

Wairakei
Thermal Valley

Wairakei
Village

Aratiatia

Aratiatia
Rapids

Rotokawa

2

Wairakei

Wairakei Terraces
Craters of the Moon

Geothermal
Power
Project

Volcanic Activity Centre

Huka Falls

Lake
Rotokawa

Rotokawa

32

43

Waihaha

Te Kauwae
Point

Whakaipo
Bay

Nukuhau

Taupo

Acacia Bay

Taupo Hot
Springs Spa

Tauhara
1088

4

Ohinetuhua Point

Mine Point

Whakamoenga Point

Rainbow
Point

Waipahihi

Wharewaka

Wharewaka
Pt

5

Whanganui

Te Aputa

Te Raina

Lake   Taupo
(Taupomoana)

Waitahanui

Rotongaio
Bay

Te Kohaiakahu Pt

Iwitahi

36

Motutaiko Island

Hatepe

48

TO NAPIER

Kuratau
Junction

14

41

Hirata

Kuratau

Omori

Pukawa Bay

Motutere Point

Mission Bay

Waitetoko

Motutere

Te Rangiita

Motuoapa
Peninsula

6

Mangahouhou

Waihi

Tokaanu
Thermal
Pools

Hautu
Village

Motuoapa

Stump Bay

TONGARIRO
NP

47

Turangi

National Trout Centre

KAIMANAWA
FOREST
PARK

Te Iringa
1241

Tongariro

Lake
Rotopounamu

TO WAIOURU

Poronui Station

TERRALINK INTERNATIONAL LIMITED 2006

NEARBY ATTRACTIONS: The inland **Karakatuwhero Valley** is a good place for picnicking and river swims. **East Cape Lighthouse**, 21km east, marks the most easterly tip of New Zealand; the lighthouse is up 500-odd steps. **Hicks Bay**, 12km north-west, was named by Captain Cook in 1769, after a crew member on the *Endeavour*; it has beautiful beaches and early pa sites. **Tikitiki**, 23km south, is a small town where Maori culture is strong; it's home to the ornately decorated **St Mary's Anglican Church**. Further south-west is **Raukumara Forest Park** and **Mount Hikurangi**, the first mainland place in the world to see the sun.

VISITOR INFORMATION: 209 Grey St, Gisborne, Ph: (06) 868 6139, www.eastlandnz.com

■ Te Aroha   POP 3685
Map 161, G2

In the eastern **Waikato**, 55km north-east of Hamilton, Te Aroha is nestled at the base of bush-clad **Mount Te Aroha**. It was a flourishing spa town in the 1890s, with visitors attracted by the therapeutic hot springs.

MAIN ATTRACTIONS: **Te Aroha Domain** has gracious Edwardian buildings, and the town's museum is in the historic bathhouse building. Soda and mineral pools are available for a relaxing warm soak, and behind the pools is the **Mokena Geyser**, which spouts soda water to a height of 3.5m every 40 minutes. A three-hour walk up Mount Te Aroha gives walkers magnificent views of the **Bay of Plenty** and Waikato, and, on a clear day, as far as **Mount Ruapehu** and **Mount Taranaki**. Tracks in the foothills are popular with mountainbikers. The **Howarth Wetlands Reserve** offers an easier one-hour walk and plenty of birds.

NEARBY ATTRACTIONS: The 45 000ha **Kaimai-Mamaku Forest Park** was once home to Maori, for whom it was a resource for hunting, food and medicine. The forests with their mighty kauri trees were later milled by the European settlers, who also mined for gold in the area. There are many short walks, including into the **Waiorongomai Valley**. The valley has many relics of the gold mining days, among them mines and shafts, water races, stamping batteries and tramway tracks. An old Maori trail, 26km south, leads to the beautiful 153m-high **Wairere Falls**.

VISITOR INFORMATION: 102 Whitaker St, Ph: (07) 884 8052, www.tearoha-info.co.nz

■ Te Awamutu   POP 13 450
Map 160, D5

Te Awamutu, 29km south-west of Hamilton in the southern **Waikato**, is a service town for a dairy farming region. The town is New Zealand's self-proclaimed **Rose Capital**.

MAIN ATTRACTIONS: Over 2000 rose bushes provide a spectacular display in the town's **Rose Gardens** and **Memorial Park Gardens**, and an annual rose show is held in November, when the blooms are at their best. The town is in an area of historical interest, with old churches, pa sites, redoubt sites and battlegrounds nearby. The **Te Awamutu Heritage Trail** leads visitors around some important sites, including the 1854 **St John's Anglican Church**, which has one of New Zealand's oldest stained-glass windows. Te Awamutu is famous as the birthplace of musician brothers Tim and Neil Finn of Split Enz and Crowded House fame, and their exploits are featured in an exhibition at **Te Awamutu Museum**. The museum also displays Maori and local European history, including the ancient Maori artefact of Uenuku.

NEARBY ATTRACTIONS: **Pirongia Forest Park**, to the west, has walking trails, and there are impressive views from the top of **Mount Pirongia**. **Lake Ngaroto** offers yachting and windsurfing, and has a floating boardwalk skirting the reserve of restored native bush. **Vilagrad Wines**, at **Ohaupo**, 11km north, is Waikato's oldest vineyard. The rock-climbing centre of **Wharepapa South**, 23km to the south-east, has some world-class climbs. The small rural community of **Kihikihi**, 4km south, can be explored on its 17-stop heritage trail.

VISITOR INFORMATION: 1 Gorst Ave, Ph: (07) 871 3259, www.teawamutu.co.nz

■ Te Kaha   POP 375
Map 164, E2

Located 68km north-east of Opotiki, Te Kaha is the main town on the picturesque **Pacific Coast Highway** on the way to **East Cape**. Te Kaha is on a stretch of coast where many of the ancestral Maori waka (canoes) landed with the first Maori settlers, probably around 1200AD.

MAIN ATTRACTIONS: At **Te Kaha marae** is **Tukaki meeting-house**, an ornately carved building; permission is needed to view it. **Te Kaha Beach** is rocky but provides spectacular views. The town's pub is a local icon, and was also the setting for the 2004 Oscar-nominated short film *Two Cars, One Night*. Sailing and fishing are popular.

NEARBY ATTRACTIONS: The **Haparapara**

Rose gardens, Te Awamutu

North Island

River at **Omaio Bay**, 13km south-west, is believed to be the only river in New Zealand without introduced fish. Historic **Raukokore Anglican Church**, on the seafront about 30km north-east, is a major landmark. Several scenic bays can be seen from the highway to the north-east, including **Whanarua Bay**, **Whangaparaoa Bay** and **Cape Runaway**. East Cape, 111km east, is the easternmost mainland spot in New Zealand; the lighthouse can be accessed by foot. Inland is **Raukumara Forest Park**, which has beautiful native forest and wildlife.
VISITOR INFORMATION: Cnr St John St and Elliott St, Opotiki, Ph: (07) 315 8484, www.eastlandnz.com

■ Te Kauwhata POP 1095
Map 160, D1
Located 80km south of Auckland in the northern **Waikato**'s rolling countryside, Te Kauwhata is a service town for a farming, fruit growing and winemaking area. Grape-growing in the area started early, with the 1901 appointment of an Italian viticulturist to a government farming research facility, and vineyards are now well established.
MAIN ATTRACTIONS: **Rongopai Wines**, based in the picturesque research station developed by Italian viticulturist Romeo Bragato in 1902, is known for botrytised dessert wines. **Cook's Landing Winery** has wine tasting, a café with a sunny deck and lovely views over the countryside. The **Rangiriri Battle Site Heritage Centre**, 3km south-east of Te Kauwhata on State Highway One, has displays about the important 1863 battle between Maori and British troops. The defensive earthworks from the battle site can be seen across the road. **Rangiriri** also has a historic hotel.
NEARBY ATTRACTIONS: An 18km walking trail between Rangiriri and **Meremere** skirts the edge of the Waikato River. The track is one section of the partly developed **Te Araroa trail**, which when complete will be a walking trail the length of New Zealand.
VISITOR INFORMATION: 5A Main Rd, Ph: (07) 826 4303, www.waikatonz.com

■ Te Kuiti POP 4375
Map 167, G1
The small town of Te Kuiti, 78km south of Hamilton in the **King Country**, is known as New Zealand's shearing capital, and is home to many champion sheep shearers. Te Kuiti is also of historic importance, as the Maori King Tawhiao and his people took refuge in the area after defeat by the British in the 1863–64 land war. Rebel leader Te Kooti also sought refuge in the town from 1872 and accepted the Maori King's pacifist philosophy.
MAIN ATTRACTIONS: Te Kuiti has a **'Big Shearer' statue** in prominent position. The first weekend of April sees celebrations at the **Te Kuiti Muster**, a lively array of events including shearing championships, sheep races and Maori cultural performances. The magnificently carved Maori meeting-house **Te Tokanganui-a-Noho**, at the southern entrance to the town, was built by Maori leader Te Kooti as a gift to the local Ngati Maniapoto people. The pavilion **Te Kuititanga o Nga Whakaaro** illustrates the town's history, and **Brook Park** has a café and a hillside walk to the site of a historic pa (Maori fortified village). Pleasant walks skirt the edge of the **Mangaokewa Stream** and lead to a scenic reserve.
NEARBY ATTRACTIONS: The 30-million-year-old **Waitomo Caves**, 19km north-west, feature limestone formations, glow-worms and an underground river. Adventure activities include abseiling and

Sheep shearer statue, Te Kuiti

black-water rafting. West of Waitomo, attractions include the limestone arch of **Mangapohue Natural Bridge**, **Piripiri Caves Scenic Reserve** and beautiful three-tier **Marokopa Falls**. The coastal fishing village of **Mokau**, 79km south-west, has good surfing and fishing, and interesting displays at the **Tainui Museum**. River cruises in a historic boat explore the **Mokau River**. Several kilometres north, the **Maniora Marae** contains the anchor stone of the ancestral Tainui canoe.
VISITOR INFORMATION: Queen St, Ph: (07) 878 8801, www.waitomo.govt.nz

■ Te Puke POP 6770
Map 163, G2
Located in rich horticultural country in the **Bay of Plenty**, 23km south-east of Tauranga, Te Puke was the starting place for New Zealand's booming kiwifruit industry. The town is known as the world's kiwifruit capital, and there are hundreds of growers locally.
MAIN ATTRACTIONS: Each year the

WAITOMO CAVES

Entrance to Waitomo Caves

The Waitomo Caves are part of a subterranean cave network formed more than 30 million years ago. The caves are popular for their beautiful limestone formations and glow-worms, and activities for the adventurous include black-water rafting, abseiling, waterfall climbs and rock climbing.

An underground river runs through the **Waitomo Glow-worm Cave**, and boat trips take visitors through the 18m high **Cathedral** cavern — where opera diva Kiri Te Kanawa has sung — and the **Glow-worm Grotto**.

Aranui Cave is a dry cave known for its unusual formations; **Ruakuri Cave** has an ancient Maori burial ground at its entrance and giant oyster fossils.

Adventure trips in the **Lost World Cave** and **Haggas Honking Holes** take visitors abseiling and rock climbing. The **Museum of Caves** offers information on the region's geology; the **Waitomo Walkway** is a three-hour walk to a scenic reserve.

main attractions

❖ Aranui Cave
❖ Cathedral cavern
❖ Glow-worm Cave
❖ Lost World Cave
❖ Museum of Caves
❖ Ruakuri Cave
❖ Waitomo Walkway

 Visitor information

Waitomo i-SITE Visitor Centre
21 Waitomo Caves Rd, Waitomo Caves
Ph: (07) 878 7640
www.waitomo.govt.nz

Aranui Cave stalactites

---

town hosts a week-long **Kiwifruit Festival**, with a ball, the crowning of a Kiwifruit Queen, and showcasing of kiwifruit products.

NEARBY ATTRACTIONS: **Papamoa, Pukehina** and **Maketu** are all surf beaches within 10 minutes' drive of Te Puke. The small beach settlement of **Maketu**, 15km north-east, was the landing place of the ancestral Maori Arawa canoe more than 600 years ago, and a foreshore monument commemorates this. Maketu is also famous for its locally produced pies. 'The Junction', 6km east near **Paengaroa**, is an area rich in attractions, including **Kiwi 360**, a kiwifruit orchard and theme park, and vintage car displays at the **Te Puke Auto Barn**. Honey and related health products are another local industry, and the **Comvita Visitor Centre** has tours, a gallery and a shop. **Longridge Park**'s adventure activities include jetboating and 4WD trips; there is also a petting farm. The **Papamoa Hills Cultural Heritage Regional Park**, off State Highway Two 5km north of Te Puke, has walkways through native bush and farmland. The park offers panoramic views over the coastline, and includes some significant sites of early Maori settlement.

VISITOR INFORMATION: 130 Jellicoe St, Ph: (07) 573 9172, www.tepuke.co.nz

■ **Thames**   POP 6705

Map 159, G5

The historic town of Thames, once a busy gold mining and kauri logging centre, is located 115km south-east of Auckland at the foot of the majestic **Coromandel Range**.

MAIN ATTRACTIONS: The **Thames School of Mines Museum** was set up to instruct gold miners in the 1880s, and is now a mineralogical museum. **Thames Historical Museum** features period rooms, shops and other exhibits. **The Butterfly and Orchid Garden** displays exotic orchids and living butterflies. Visitors to the **Goldmine Experience** can tour an operating gold mine and watch gold being produced by the **Stamper Battery**. Stout-hearted visitors may enjoy the colony of cave weta (giant native insects) nearby.

NEARBY ATTRACTIONS: The **Kauaeranga Valley** in the **Coromandel Forest Park** offers walking tracks, huts and camping grounds, and is accessible from the **Kauaeranga Visitor Centre**, 15km south-east of

North Island

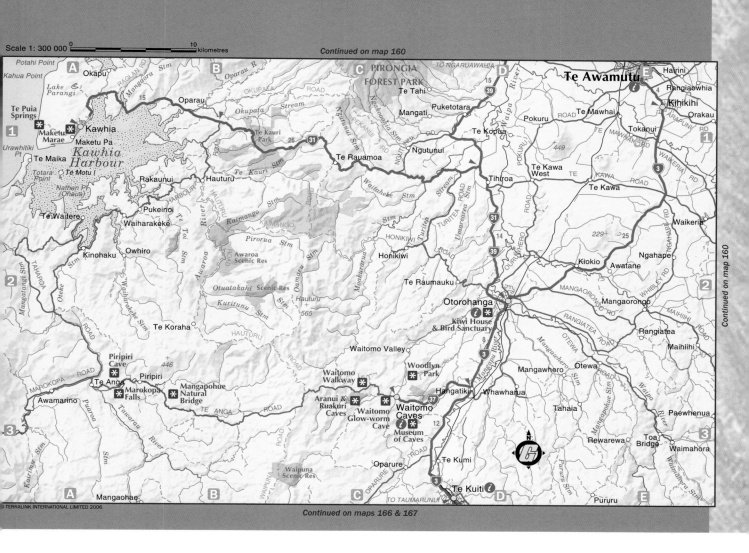

Continued on map 160

Scale 1: 300 000

Continued on map 160

Continued on maps 166 & 167

© TERRALINK INTERNATIONAL LIMITED 2006

Thames. A 3½-hour walk leads up the dramatic 759m **Pinnacles**, and there are many old kauri dams in the valley. The **Karaka Bird Hide**, accessible from a board walk, is a great place to watch shore birds in the mangrove swamps. State Highway 25 north of Thames takes travellers along the scenic **Pohutukawa Coast**, named for the beautiful trees lining the roadside, which are covered in brilliant scarlet blossoms throughout the summer. On the unsealed road from **Tapu** to **Coroglen**, a short walk leads to a unusual square-shaped kauri tree, estimated to be 1200 years old; **Rapaura Water Gardens** have native bush walks, waterlilies and a three-level waterfall. **Miranda**, a 30-minute drive west of Thames, is a bird-watcher's paradise. The

huge mudflats attract thousands of shorebirds each winter, and there are hides for bird viewing. Visitors can swim in natural hot mineral water at **Miranda Hot Springs**.
VISITOR INFORMATION: 206 Pollen St, Ph: (07) 868 7284, www.thecoromandel.com

■ **Tirau**   POP 725

Map 161, G5
The small town of Tirau, 54km south-east of Hamilton, has revitalised itself as a tourist attraction with its array of creative corrugated iron buildings and sculptures. Tirau means 'many cabbage trees', and the native cabbage tree is a symbol of the town.
MAIN ATTRACTIONS: Tirau's unique **Big Dog Information Centre** is housed in a building shaped like a huge

dog. The **Big Sheep Wool Gallery**, in a sheep-shaped building, sells a range of wool products; other quirky sculptures include a large cheese, pukeko birds and a cow pushing a shopping trolley. The town also has many craft shops, antique outlets and cafés; the

Firth of Thames coastline

Tolaga Bay Wharf, one of the world's longest

Museum of Early New Zealand has pioneer relics and a honey shop.
NEARBY ATTRACTIONS: The **Okoroire Hot Springs Hotel**, 6km north-east, is an 1889 hotel close to thermal pools. The pools are picturesquely situated among ferns and glow-worms on the banks of the **Waihou River**. The **Three Kauri Tree Walk** leads to massive kauri trees. The **Oraka Deer Park**, 5km north, is a working deer farm which welcomes visitors. **Lake Karapiro**, to the west, is a man-made lake popular for waterskiing, yachting and rowing.
VISITOR INFORMATION: 63 Main Rd, Ph: (07) 883 1202, www.tirauinfo.co.nz

■ **Tokomaru Bay**   POP 460
Map 165, H5
Situated on the coast of **Eastland**, 83km north of Gisborne, Tokomaru Bay is home to many craftspeople and fishermen.
MAIN ATTRACTIONS: Tokomaru Bay sits along a golden beach, between rocky headlands, and is great for swimming, surfing and fishing. Many of the local craftspeople are happy to open their doors to the public. The town was once much

larger and had a sizeable freezing works; the old site can be visited today. Also worth a look is the old wharf at the northern end of the bay, at **Waima**.
NEARBY ATTRACTIONS: **Te Puia Springs**, 11km north, has natural hot springs for bathing. **Anaura Bay Walking Track**, about 10km south, is a 3.5km walking track through coastal forest, grassed hillside and production pine forest. **Mount Hikurangi**, about 40km north-west, on the east side of **Raukumara Forest Park**, is Eastland's highest mountain, and of great importance to the local Ngati Porou tribe. It's also the first mainland place in the world to see the sun each day. Visitors need permission from Ngati Porou to access the mountain.
VISITOR INFORMATION: 209 Grey St, Gisborne, Ph: (06) 868 6139, www.eastlandnz.com

■ **Tokoroa**   POP 14 425
Map 162, D5
Located between the dairy farming area of the **Waikato** and the forests of the central North Island, Tokoroa is 10km north of the massive **Kinleith Pulp and Paper Mill**,

which processes timber from the region's 140 000ha forests. The town is named for the Maori chief Tokoroa, who was killed leading his people against the British.
MAIN ATTRACTIONS: Tokoroa is home to the **Talking Poles** project, a trail of pole sculptures celebrating the various cultures of its residents. The project is ongoing, and there are plans to eventually have 50 poles. There are native bush reserves within the commercial forest areas; visitors need a permit to enter. **Colson's Hill Lookout** offers great views of the area — as far as **Mount Ruapehu** on a clear day. Man-made **Lake Moananui** is a popular walking and picnicking spot. The yearly **Golden Axe and Logger Sports Carnival** allows local axemen and woodsmen to compete with one another and demonstrate their skills with an axe.
NEARBY ATTRACTIONS: **Whakamaru**, **Maraetai** and **Ohakuri** hydro lakes and dams are popular places for swimming, boating and fishing, and there is plentiful trout in the area's rivers.
VISITOR INFORMATION: SH1, Ph: (07) 886 8872, www.swktodc.govt.nz

■ **Tolaga Bay**   POP 870
Map 165, H6
This small town on **Eastland**'s coast, 47km north of Gisborne, was once an important port; today it's a popular beach resort.
MAIN ATTRACTIONS: Completed in 1929, the 660m **Tolaga Bay Wharf** is one of the longest in the world, and was constructed so boats could be loaded at all tides. Nearby is the entrance to **Cook's Cove Walking Track**, which takes walkers to a cove where British explorer Captain James Cook landed in 1769. The local beaches offer good swimming and fishing.
NEARBY ATTRACTIONS: About 20km south, the small settlement of **Whangara** was the setting for the

North Island

much-loved 2002 film *Whale Rider*. Tours related to the film and Witi Ihimaera's original novel can be arranged locally. Between Whangara and nearby **Pouawa** to the south is **Te Tapuwae O Rongokako Marine Reserve**, a popular spot for diving; dolphins, seals and whales are frequent visitors.

Gisborne, 47km south, is Eastland's largest city. It has many historic attractions highlighting the area's Maori heritage and Captain Cook's early ventures to New Zealand; they include **Tairawhiti Museum**, **Te Moana Maritime Museum** and **Cook National Historic Reserve**.

Near Gisborne are popular **Wainui Beach** and chardonnay-producing wineries. North of Tolaga Bay, the **Anaura Bay Walking Track** is a scenic walk.

VISITOR INFORMATION: 209 Grey St, Gisborne, Ph: (06) 868 6139, www.eastlandnz.com

■ Turangi POP 3440
Map 168, C4

Located at the southern end of **Lake Taupo**, Turangi is a centre for world-class trout fishing on the **Tongariro River**, and is also a base for trips into the beautiful World Heritage Area of **Tongariro National Park**. The river offers excellent rafting, and there are many interesting walks in the vicinity.

MAIN ATTRACTIONS: Leading south from Turangi, the **Tongariro River Walkway** is a popular three-hour return walk which follows the river. **Tongariro National Trout Centre**, 5km south, has an interpretive centre, a scenic walk and an underwater viewing chamber offering excellent views of rainbow trout in their natural habitat. The 20-minute **Tokaanu Thermal Walk**, 6km north-west of Turangi, leads through a natural thermal area with hot mineral pools and bubbling mud; the **Tokaanu Thermal Pools** are hot pools for bathing. Tokaanu also has a historic wharf, popular

for picnicking.

NEARBY ATTRACTIONS: **Tongariro National Park** was gifted to the nation in 1887 by Te Heuheu Tukino IV, paramount chief of the Ngati Tuwharetoa tribe, and is known for its cultural importance to Maori and extraordinary volcanic landscape. Walking, climbing and skiing are all possible, and the 17km **Tongariro Crossing** passes through stunning, unique volcanic and glacial landforms. Beautiful **Lake Rotopounamu** (which translates as 'Greenstone Lake'), 11km west of Turangi, is a great spot for walkers, swimmers, bird watchers and picnickers. There are some interesting walks in the **Kaimanawa Forest Park**, including to the **Pillars of Hercules**, a spectacular gorge, and to a lookout with views of the Tongariro River and mountains. From **Pukawa**, a 15-minute drive west, there are walks through bush and along the lakefront.

VISITOR INFORMATION: Ngawaka Pl, Ph: (07) 386 8999, www.laketauponz.com

■ Tutukaka POP 545
Map 155, J4

Tutukaka, 27km north-east of Whangarei on the **Tutukaka Coast**, is a base for dive trips to the **Poor Knights Islands**. The area is also famous for its deep-sea game fishing, with marlin, tuna and kingfish in the waters. Beautiful white-sand beaches offer swimming, snorkelling and surfing.

MAIN ATTRACTIONS: The sunken wrecks of the frigates *Tui* and *Waikato* are interesting sites for divers. The **Tutukaka Head Walkway**, accessible only at low tide, is a one-hour walk to a lighthouse. **Tutukaka Wild**, 3km north of Tutukaka's marina, has adventure activities and a zoo. **Ngunguru**, 2km south, is a holiday resort with a good surf break and an estuary. **Scow Landing** is a picnic spot in native bush on the

Ngunguru River, where sailing ships once tied up to trade.

NEARBY ATTRACTIONS: The **Poor Knights Islands** marine reserve, 24km off the coast, offers wonderful diving. Very clear water, warm subtropical currents, plentiful marine life and underwater caves and tunnels make the waters around the islands a spectacular dive location. Visitors are not permitted to land on the islands, which have been tapu (forbidden) since a massacre of the Maori inhabitants in the early 1800s, and are now a wildlife sanctuary. **Matapouri Bay**, 8km north, is a beautiful bay with classic Kiwi baches (beach huts), and a walking track leads to **Whale Bay**, an idyllic beach lined with trees. **Sandy Bay** is a renowned surfing spot.

VISITOR INFORMATION: Tarewa Park, 92 Otaika Rd, Whangarei, Ph: (09) 438 1079, www.whangareinz.org.nz

Red moki with yellow and red sponges, Poor Knights Island

Waiheke Island   POP 7140

Map 158, E3

This attractive island, about 35 minutes by ferry east of Auckland city, has lovely beaches, vineyards and olive groves. Home to many artists, it's increasingly a base for commuters from Auckland.

MAIN ATTRACTIONS: Waiheke's main town of **Oneroa** is an appealing village full of artistic vitality. **Whittaker's Musical Experience** is a museum featuring antique instruments; these are demonstrated and discussed every day. Whittaker's is part of the **Artworks** complex, which includes galleries, theatres and a cinema. **Waiheke Sculpture Studio & Gallery** is one of many fine art galleries in and around Oneroa; its artists focus on stonework, especially with cream-white limestone. Oneroa also hosts the **Waiheke Island Wine Festival** in February and the **Waiheke Jazz Festival**, usually held over Easter. Waiheke is known for its wineries;

their red wines are highly regarded. The island also has numerous art galleries, with an art trail linking them. On the road east to **Onetangi** is **Waiheke Island Historic Village and Museum**, which includes a woolshed museum and a restored 1930s island cottage. **Stony Batter Historic Reserve**, about 15km east of Oneroa in the island's north-east, has extensive tunnels and gun emplacements dating back to 1941. **Onetangi Reserve**, just east of Onetangi, is a peaceful spot of native forest. Waiheke also has numerous beaches to relax on. **Connells Bay Sculpture Park**, on the island's east coast, has sculptures by New Zealand artists in a park setting, and is open by appointment.

VISITOR INFORMATION: 2 Korora Rd, Oneroa, Ph: (09) 372 1234, www.waiheke.co.nz

Waihi   POP 4525

Map 161, G1

Less than two hours' drive south-east of Auckland, the township of Waihi lies at the southern end of the **Coromandel Peninsula**. Waihi has been a mining town since 1878, and still boasts a fully operational gold and silver mine.

MAIN ATTRACTIONS: Guided tours of the **Martha Mine** are available, and a viewing platform overlooks the mine. The **Goldfields Railway** in Wrigley Street offers rides on a vintage train between Waihi and **Waikino**. **Waihi Gold Mining Museum & Arts Centre** in Kenny Street has displays of the town's gold mining history.

NEARBY ATTRACTIONS: **Waihi Beach**, 5km south-east, has a 9km white sand surf beach, leading to an inlet into **Tauranga Harbour**; boating and game fishing are popular. A 45-minute walk leads through bush to peaceful **Orokawa Bay**, which has no road access, passing mine tunnels and historic Maori sites.

A further walk leads to the 30m **William Wright Falls**. Boats can be chartered to visit **Mayor Island (Tuhua)**, a dormant volcanic island offering walks through the crater valley and around the island. A half hour's drive leads through the spectacular **Karangahake Gorge**, once the site of gold mining and kauri logging; the **Karangahake Gorge Historic Walkway** follows the route of the old railway, and passes gold mining relics and beautiful **Owharoa Falls**. There are hot springs at **Athenree**, and **Bowentown Domain** is a 128ha reserve on the rocky headland at Tauranga Harbour's northern entrance. Walks in the reserve lead to several historic sites of Maori pa (fortified villages) with superb views.

VISITOR INFORMATION: Seddon St, Ph: (07) 863 6715, www.thecoromandel.com

Waikanae   POP 9370

Map 178, C2

The peaceful town of Waikanae is located on the **Kapiti Coast** 58km north of Wellington. Waikanae is on the **Waikanae River**, and has a pretty beach and impressive estuary.

MAIN ATTRACTIONS: **Nga Manu Nature Reserve** is a 15ha reserve featuring native wildlife and pretty bush walks. Visitors can watch eels being fed, and there are many native birds, including kiwi in a nocturnal house. Peaceful **Waikanae Beach** is a beautiful stretch of sand, and offers good swimming, fishing and relaxing. **Waikanae Estuary** is a nationally significant estuary, providing a habitat for many waterbirds. The estuary area is part of the **Kapiti Island Marine Reserve**; in earlier days, the river mouth was home to a large Maori settlement. **Mahara Gallery** showcases local artists.

NEARBY ATTRACTIONS: **Mangaone Walking Track** is a three-hour walk along a former bush tramway in

Old pump house, Martha mine, Waihi

North Island

Sunset over Waikanae River

low hill country east of the town, passing through farmland and regenerating forest. The 330ha native forest to the east of Waikanae is the **Hemi Matenga Memorial Park Scenic Reserve**, protecting one of the largest remaining stands of kohekohe forest and offering beautiful walks and wonderful views over the coast and **Reikorangi Valley**. **Reikorangi Potteries Park & Café** has pottery for sale in a pretty bush setting. There is a great collection of vintage cars at **Southward Car Museum**, 4km south. The **Lindale Centre**, 5km south, features farm shows and an animal petting area, along with an award-winning cheesemaker, craft shops and a honey shop. **Staglands**, 20km south on the Akatarawa Rd, is a 10ha wildlife reserve with native and exotic birds and animals, including some rare species. North of Waikanae, **Otaki Forks** is the eastern gateway to walks in the **Tararua Forest Park**, including a four-day crossing of the range.
VISITOR INFORMATION: Mahara Pl, Ph: (04) 904 5768, www.WellingtonNZ.com

◼ Waiouru POP 1645
Map 174, B1
Located in the central North Island's **Ruapehu** district, 814m above sea level in the **Rangipo Desert**, Waiouru is home to New Zealand's largest army base.
MAIN ATTRACTIONS: The **Army Museum**

Waiouru chronicles New Zealand's military history and heritage in times of peace and war. West of Waiouru, **Tangiwai** has a memorial to the 151 train passengers killed in 1953's Christmas Eve rail disaster, when the railway bridge was swept away by a lahar from **Mount Ruapehu**.
NEARBY ATTRACTIONS: To the north, the **Desert Road** section of State Highway One is a windswept area with tussock vegetation and an awe-inspiring outlook onto the active volcanic peaks of Mount Ruapehu, **Mount Tongariro** and **Mount Ngauruhoe**. These three are the jewels of **Tongariro National Park**, a World Heritage Area which offers extraordinary scenery, skiing, snowboarding and hiking. The **Tongariro Crossing**, known as New Zealand's best one-day walk, leads through a surreal, seemingly lunar landscape; **Whakapapa** and **Turoa Ski Areas** have the largest skiable terrain in New Zealand.
VISITOR INFORMATION: Clyde St, Ohakune, Ph: (06) 385 8427, www.visitruapehu.com

◼ Waipukurau POP 3910
Map 175, G5
Waipukurau, inland in southern **Hawke's Bay**, 53km south-west of Hastings, is a service centre for the surrounding farming district.
MAIN ATTRACTIONS: The **Electra Gallery** features work from local artists. Gliding and hot air ballooning are available from the **Waipukurau airfield**, and many of the area's gardens are open for visiting.
NEARBY ATTRACTIONS: The coastal settlement of **Porangahau**, 40km south-east, is known for seafood meals at its historic hotel, as well as secluded beaches offering fishing charters, surfcasting, walks and 4WD safaris. The area also boasts the world's longest place name, **Taumatawhakatangihangakoauauotamateaturipukakapikimaungahoronukupokaiwhenua-**

kitanatahu, which is a shortened form (!) of 'The hilltop where Tamatea, the man with big knees, conqueror of mountains, eater of land, traveller over land and sea, played his flute to his loved one'. **Te Angiangi Marine Reserve** offers interesting viewing of the reserve's protected marine life. The area around **Takapau**, 22km west, is an emerging wine region, proving suitable for cool-climate varieties such as pinot noir and sauvignon blanc because of the land's elevation and distance from the sea. The character village of **Norsewood**, 34km west, was originally settled by Scandinavians, and has a heritage trail, a pioneer museum and an award-winning cheese factory. Further west, the **Ruahine Forest Park** offers good walking, hunting and fishing.
VISITOR INFORMATION: Railway Esplanade, Ph: (06) 858 6488, www.hawkesbaynz.com

◼ Wairoa POP 5230
Map 170, D5
Wairoa is located in northern **Hawke's Bay** on the banks of the **Wairoa River**, 100km south-west of Gisborne. The town was once a river port exporting wool, flax, fibre, meat and dairy products; today it's noteworthy for its natural attractions and Maori character.
MAIN ATTRACTIONS: The relocated riverside **Portland Lighthouse**, built of solid kauri, was used on **Portland Island** at the tip of the **Mahia Peninsula** from 1878 to the mid-1950s. Maori have lived in the Wairoa area for hundreds of years, and to the west, in the alluvial **Wairoa Valley**, there are many historic Maori sites. **Whakamahi Lagoon**, about 10km east of Wairoa at the river's mouth, is an important wetland with plentiful bird life. The **Waiatai Scenic Reserve**, 4km east, is home to an impressive giant puka tree. In June 2005 Wairoa

This remote and beautiful 212 672ha National Park is home to the Tuhoe, or 'Children of the Mist', a Maori tribe with deep cultural connections to the area. The park contains lush, unspoilt forests, lakes and rivers, and there is plentiful bird life, including kiwi and kaka. There are many tracks and huts for walkers; the township of **Aniwaniwa** has a visitor centre, a motor camp and a museum.

The 46km walk around **Lake Waikaremoana** is considered one of New Zealand's 'Great Walks'; it leads through fern groves, beech and podocarp forest, and offers impressive lake views, particularly from the **Panekiri Bluff**. The short walk from Aniwaniwa to **Lake Waikareiti** is very beautiful, and rowboats at the track's end allow visitors to explore the lake, including **Rahui Island**, which has its own small lake. Another interesting walk leads to the **Onepoto Caves**.

Lake Waikaremoana

main attractions

- Aniwaniwa Museum
- Boating & fishing
- Lake Waikareiti
- Lake Waikaremoana
- Onepoto Caves
- Panekiri Bluff
- Rahui Island

 Visitor information

DOC Aniwaniwa Visitor Centre
State Highway 38, Aniwaniwa
Ph: (06) 837 3803
www.doc.govt.nz

---

hosted the first **Wairoa Maori Film Festival**; organisers are hoping to make it an annual event. There is water-skiing, jet boating and rowing on the sheltered river.
NEARBY ATTRACTIONS: About 50km north-west of Wairoa is **Lake Waikaremoana** at the southern tip of **Te Urewera National Park**. This area of spectacular scenery and rich native forests can be explored by the 46km track around the lake, and there are many other excellent walks; the **Aniwaniwa Museum** has interesting displays.
Te Reinga Falls Scenic Reserve, 35km north-east of Wairoa, has a spectacular 35m waterfall. Just north-east of Te Reinga is **Hackfalls Arboretum** in **Tiniroto**, which has a large collection of imported trees and shrubs in a lake setting. The **Clonkeen Caves**, near **Nuhaka**, are 6.3km-long limestone and glow-worm caves.
VISITOR INFORMATION: Cnr SH2 and Queen St, Ph: (06) 838 7440, www.wairoanz.com

■ **Waitangi**   POP 130
Map 155, F1
The small town of Waitangi, in the **Bay of Islands**, is of huge historic importance to New Zealanders. The Treaty of Waitangi — known as the country's founding document — was signed there in 1840 between Maori chiefs and representatives of Queen Victoria's government, making New Zealand formally a British colony.
MAIN ATTRACTIONS: **Waitangi National Reserve** is rich in cultural icons. The Treaty of Waitangi was signed in the colonial-style **Treaty House**, and across the lawn, the beautifully carved whare runanga (Maori meeting-house) was completed in 1940, the centenary of the Treaty. Built for the same occasion from two massive kauri logs, the 35m waka taua (war canoe) is New Zealand's largest. The reserve has a visitors' centre and gallery, and regular Maori cultural performances. A walking track leads past mangroves to **Haruru Falls**, where the water falls in an unusual horseshoe shape. In Maori legend, the lagoon below is home to a taniwha (water monster). The **Haruru River** had more than 100 Maori villages along its banks in the 19th century. **Mount Bledisloe** offers impressive views over the area.
NEARBY ATTRACTIONS: Nearby **Paihia** is a base for visitors to

North Island

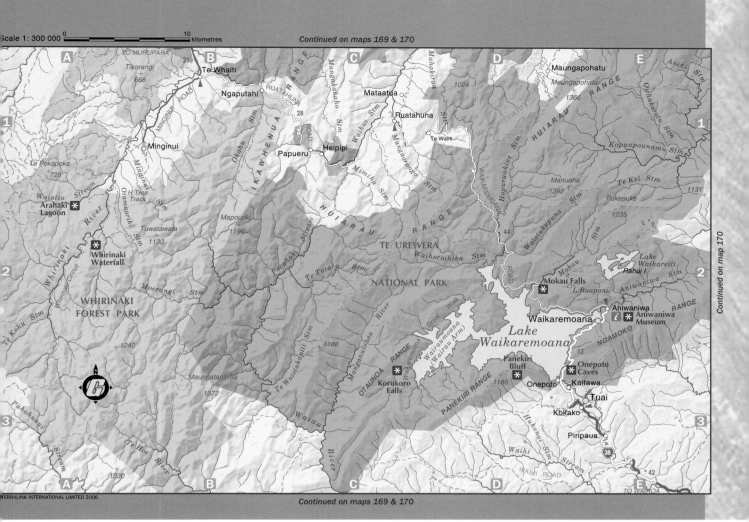

Continued on maps 169 & 170

Continued on maps 169 & 170

Treaty House, Waitangi

the Bay of Islands, and offers cruises, dolphin swimming, kayaking and visits to islands.

VISITOR INFORMATION: The Wharf, Marsden Rd, Paihia, Ph: (09) 402 7345, www.northlandnz.com

■ Waitara   POP 6245

Map 166, B6

The largest town in north **Taranaki**, 16km north-east of New Plymouth, Waitara was settled early by Maori. The first of the Taranaki wars broke out in 1860 over the disputed ownership of a block of land at Waitara. Today, dairy farming and energy production are the main industries in the area.

MAIN ATTRACTIONS: At **Manukorihi Pa**, the impressive meeting-house **Te Ikaroa-a-Maui** is a memorial to Sir Maui Pomare, a Maori leader of the

Virginia Lake Scenic Reserve, Wanganui

early 20th century who worked to improve the lot of the tribes whose land had been confiscated. The **Waitara River** is popular for boating and fishing. Train trips are available on a restored 7km branch railway line from Waitara to **Lepperton**.

NEARBY ATTRACTIONS: **Urenui**, 16km north, has a great surf beach. Further north, starting from **Pukearuhe**, the five-hour **Whitecliffs Walkway** leads through open farmland and coastal forest, and offers great views of the coastline and **White Cliffs (Paraninihi)**. The **Three Sisters** are towering 25m rock formations at **Tongaporutu**, about 55km north; **Elephant Rock** resembles an elephant, and there are rock drawings in a nearby cave. A few minutes' drive further north are the remains of **Te Kawau pa** (Maori fortified village), on an islet only accessible at low tide. The site is now a burial ground and is not open to visitors. The mouth of the **Mohakatino River** was the landing spot of one of the ancestral Maori

canoes which migrated across the Pacific. The quiet fishing village of **Mokau**, 69km north of Waitara at the mouth of the **Mokau River**, was once a busy port shipping coal and timber; the town's **Tainui Museum** has interesting historical material, and the black sand beach offers good surfing and fishing. Cruises are available on the river, which was once an important route for early Maori, and later provided access to inland coal mines, sawmills and farms. **Maniora Marae**, several kilometres north, is home to the anchor stone of the ancestral Tainui canoe, and offers cultural experiences for visitors.

VISITOR INFORMATION: 1 Ariki St, New Plymouth, Ph: (06) 759 6060, www.taranaki.info

■ Waiuku   POP 6670
Map 158, B6

Established in 1851 at the southern tip of the **Manukau Harbour**, 63km south-west of Auckland, Waiuku is a thriving modern town which retains some of its

19th century atmosphere.

MAIN ATTRACTIONS: The **Kentish Hotel** is one of the oldest pub houses in New Zealand, dating back to 1854, and still operates as a bar today. Across the road is a reminder of Waiuku's early maritime history, the *Jane Gifford*, which in its glory days took people and produce across the harbour to southern Auckland. Nearby on the **Tamakae Reserve** is **Waiuku Museum**, which honours the town's early history.

NEARBY ATTRACTIONS: **Glenbrook Vintage Railway**, about 5km north-east, is a popular 6km steam carriage railway, while those looking for a farming experience can visit adjoining **Glenbrook Farm Park**. A further 10km east is **Pukekohe**, home of the **V8 Supercars** racing. South of Waiuku is **Waiuku Forest**, which offers drives and walks through the southern part of the forest. About 5km north is **Waipipi Bird Park**, home to 50 aviaries featuring hand-reared parakeets, lorikeets, parrots, cockatoos and conures. Further north is the pleasant **Awhitu Peninsula** and the southern entrance to Manukau Harbour.

VISITOR INFORMATION: 4C Roulston St, Pukekohe, Ph: (09) 238 4081, www.franklindistrict.co.nz/tourism

■ Wanganui   POP 39 425
Map 189, D3

Located on the North Island's west coast, Wanganui is 190km from Wellington at the mouth of the **Whanganui River**. As New Zealand's longest navigable waterway, the river was an important route for both Maori and Europeans. Maori settlements were well established along the river from the 14th century; Europeans developed a town at Wanganui from 1840, leading to several years of strife with the Maori inhabitants. Today Wanganui services the surrounding agricultural region; it is

North Island

also known for its historic buildings and artists, and is a base for trips up the river.

MAIN ATTRACTIONS: The **Whanganui Riverboat Centre** has displays about the riverboat era, and offers river cruises on the restored paddle steamer PS *Waimarie*. **Whanganui Regional Museum** has colonial and Maori exhibits, including a 22m waka taua (war canoe); the **Sarjeant Gallery**, in an elegant stone building, has historical and contemporary art. Wanganui's many artists open their studios to visitors in the yearly **Open Studios Weekend**. **Durie Hill Elevator**, built in 1919, takes visitors up 65m **Durie Hill**. There are walks at pretty **Virginia Lake Scenic Reserve**, and at **Queens Park**. **Kowhai Park** has a quirky children's playground; **Moutoa Gardens** was once the site of the Maori fishing village **Pakaitore**. **Putiki Church**, plain outside, has a richly decorated interior of Maori carvings and panelling. At the river mouth, **Castlecliff Beach** is popular for swimming, surfing and fishing.

NEARBY ATTRACTIONS: The fascinating Whanganui River can be explored by paddle steamer, jet boat or canoe. The **Whanganui River Road** follows the lower reaches of the river for 79km, passing through the grandly-named small Maori settlements of **Koriniti** (Corinth), **Hiruharama** (Jerusalem) and

SheepWorld cafe, Warkworth

Ranana (London). There are some beautiful historic marae (Maori community meeting-places); these may be visited with permission from the owners. Early Catholic mission buildings remain at Hiruharama and Ranana. **Pipiriki**, a once busy river port 78km from Wanganui, has the **Colonial House** museum. Pipiriki is also a popular exit point for canoeists travelling the river. Further north in **Whanganui National Park**, the remote 42km **Matemateaonga Track** passes through rich forests; the intriguing **Bridge to Nowhere** was built in the 1930s to access farms which never eventuated.

VISITOR INFORMATION: 101 Guyton St, Ph: (06) 349 0508, www.wanganuinz.com

■ **Warkworth**   POP 2825
Map 156, E4
One of the main towns on the **Kowhai Coast**, Warkworth, 64km north of Auckland, is a historic town with a variety of country lifestyle attractions.

MAIN ATTRACTIONS: Warkworth is at the heart of the Kowhai Coast, named for the yellow-flowering native tree, and its biggest yearly event is the **Kowhai Festival**, held in October. Just north of the town is **SheepWorld**, a theme park focusing on New Zealand's most iconic imported animal. Visitors can see shearing and sheepdogs in action, and get a chance to feed the lambs. Just south of the town is the **Honey Centre**, with New Zealand's largest display of live honey-making bees, and plenty of honey available to taste. Nearby is the **Satellite Station**, from where New Zealand gets its overseas television feeds.

Warkworth & District Museum provides an insight into the district's pioneering families; several rooms are recreated in a 1920s style, and there are artefacts from the 1890s to the 1950s. Connected to

the museum is **Parry Kauri Park**, which features two huge kauri trees believed to be 1000 years old.

NEARBY ATTRACTIONS: Just to the east of Warkworth is **Snells Beach**, and two beautiful parks, **Scandrett** and **Mahurangi**. Immediately to the north-east is the **Matakana Wine Country**, with several wineries noted for their red wines and pinot gris. **Kawau Island**, accessible by ferry from **Sandspit**, is home to **Mansion House**, built by former Governor George Grey in the 1860s and now a museum. **Goat Island Marine Reserve**, 20km north, is renowned for its marine life and snorkelling.

VISITOR INFORMATION: 1 Baxter St, Warkworth, Ph: (09) 425 9081,
www.warkworth-information.co.nz

■ **Waverley**   POP 905
Map 173, F6
The southernmost town in **Taranaki**, Waverley is a peaceful small town in a dairy farming area, 44km north-east of Wanganui.

MAIN ATTRACTIONS: A heritage walk leads around Waverley's historic buildings, including the majestic 1908 **Town Hall**, the striking **Post Office Building**, and the lovely 1881 railway station. The **Waverley Railway Museum** features railway memorabilia; there are pioneer items on display at the **Woolshed Museum**, open by appointment.

NEARBY ATTRACTIONS: **Waverley Beach** is popular for camping and picnicking. At **Waitotara**, 10km south-east, visitors can get up close and personal with farm animals at **Ashley Park**. In the remote **Waitotara Valley**, to the north-east, jet boating and bush walks are available. The **Kohi Rock Carvings** are rare rock carvings, on private land outside Waverley; a wooden replica can be seen in the **South Taranaki Museum** at **Patea**.

VISITOR INFORMATION: 55 High St, Hawera, Ph: (06) 278 8599, www.taranaki.info

WHANGANUI RIVER

New Zealand's longest navigable waterway, the Whanganui River flows 290km from its source on **Mount Tongariro**, through the city of **Wanganui** to the **Tasman Sea**. The river's sheltered valleys were settled early by Maori, whom it provided with an important travel and trade route; from the late 19th century it did the same for Europeans.

Wonderful for canoeing, the river has 239 listed rapids, yet is suitable for beginners. The 145km trip from **Taumarunui** to **Pipiriki** takes five days; shorter journeys are also possible. The river runs through the heart of **Whanganui National Park**, which has unspoilt forests, rich wildlife and lovely walks.

Picturesque villages along the river include **Hiruharama (Jerusalem)**, once home to the poet James K Baxter, and Pipiriki. The **Bridge to Nowhere** was built in the 1930s for farming developments which were later abandoned. A number of beautifully preserved marae (Maori community meeting-places) may be visited with permission.

Whanganui River

main attractions

- ❖ Bridge to Nowhere
- ❖ Canoeing & kayaking
- ❖ Jet boating
- ❖ Matemateaonga Track
- ❖ Pipiriki
- ❖ St Joseph's Church, Jerusalem
- ❖ Tieke Kainga
- ❖ Wanganui
- ❖ Whanganui River Road
- ❖ Whanganui Journey

 Visitor information

Wanganui i-SITE Visitor Centre
101 Guyton St, Wanganui
Ph: (06) 349 0508
www.wanganuinz.com

Aerial view of Wellsford

■ Wellsford   POP 1740

Map 156, E3

The quiet historic town of Wellsford, 83km north of Auckland, is a gateway to the **Kaipara Harbour** and a favourite stop for travellers heading towards the sunny **Northland** region.

MAIN ATTRACTIONS: The **Albertland & Districts Museum** pays homage to a group of settlers who arrived from Britain in the 1860s, aiming to create a classless, nonconformist society in New Zealand. This became the last organised colonisation of New Zealand, and this well-run museum tells their story. **EnviroNZ Sculptures** makes bronze representations of indigenous fauna and flora.

NEARBY ATTRACTIONS: West of Wellsford, **Minniesdale Chapel** is a place of worship built by the Albertlanders in the 1860s. Close by is **Kaipara Harbour**, the largest enclosed harbour in the southern hemisphere. The harbour is a good spot for fishing and swimming.

Lovely **Pakiri Beach**, 26km east of Wellsford, offers swimming and horse trekking; further south-east is **Goat Island Marine Reserve**, a great place for looking at local marine life, either from a boat or by snorkelling. **Warkworth**, 19km south-east, is the focal point of the **Kowhai Coast** and home to the leading rural attraction **SheepWorld**.
VISITOR INFORMATION: 1 Baxter St, Warkworth, Ph: (09) 425 9081,
www.warkworth-information.co.nz

■ Whakatane   POP 17 780

Map 190, E2

Sunny Whakatane, 94km east of Tauranga, is a service centre for the eastern **Bay of Plenty**. Whakatane, on a natural harbour, was the 13th century landing place of the Mataatua Maori

(CONTINUED P.148)

North Island

Scale 1 : 600 000
0   20
kilometres

Continued on maps 168 & 174

WANGANUI

Taumarunui

Marton

TASMAN SEA

Whanganui R

Whanganui River

Whangaehu River

Lake Taupo

TONGARIRO NATIONAL PARK

WHANGANUI NATIONAL PARK

MATEMATEAONGA RANGE

UREORA FOREST PARK

Tongaporutu, Ahititi, Okau, Kotare, Waitaanga, Ohura, Mangaparo, Tatu, Aukopae, Te Whakarae, Otunui, Tokirima, Heao, Opatu, Koiro, Kirikau, Tahora, Moki Tunnel, Fangarakau, Tawhata, Whakahoro, Maungaroa, Retaruke, Kohuratahi, Marco, Whangamomona, Pohokura, Makahu, Aotuhia, Puniwhakau, Tangahoe, Parinui, Ramanui, Tieke Kainga, Whakatina, Takou, Moeroa, Taumatatahi, Ngamatapouri, Makakaho, Taunoko, Pipiriki, Waipuna, Tanupara, Moeawatea, Tawhiwhi, Makakaho Junction, Orangimea, Mangawhio, Puao, Paparangi, Te Tuhi Junction, Jerusalem, St Joseph's Church, Ranana, Matahiwi, Operiki Pa, Koriniti Pa, Kakatahi, Kohi, Waverley, Ngutuwera, Rangitatau, Waitotara, Nukumaru, Maxwell, Kai-Iwi, Brunswick, Rapanui, Westmere, Okoia, Marybank, Fordell, Waiinu Beach, Kai-Iwi Beach, Upokongaro, Kauangaroa, Whangaehu, Ratana, Turakina, Bonny Glen, Fern Flat, Koitiata, Makirikiri South, Crofton, Tutaenui, Porewa, Tokorangi, Dunolly, Beaconsfield, Komako, Kimbolton, Apiti, Mangarimu, Peep-o-Day, Pakihikura, Rangiwahia, Marton Block, Hinau, Pemberton, Livingstone, Walpuru, Orangipongo, Mangaonoho, Otamakapua, Ruahine, Pouwhakaura, Ohingaiti, Poukiore, Kaikarangi, Rataiti, Mangaweka, Lower Kawhatu, Manui, Omatane, Utiku, Ohotu, Taihape, Winiata, Mataroa, Rongoiti Junction, Koeke Junction, Papanui Junction, Ruanui, Te Horoa, Colliers Junction, Owhakura, Rangiwaea Junction, Irirangi, Bells Junction, Hihitahi, Raketapauma Pa, Hihitahi, Moawhango, Turangarere, Te Moehau, Whitikaupeka Pa, Ngawaka, Opaea, Kaiewe Junction, Pungataua, Wainui Junction, Waiouru, Army Museum, Tangiwai, Karioi, Rangataua, Ohakune, Makaranui, Raetihi, Mangaeturoa, Horopito, Tohunga Junction, Orautoha, Pokaka, Erua, Pokaka, Iwikau Village, "Mordor", "Emyn Muil", Whakapapa Skifield, Whakapapa Village, "Ithilien", "Plains of Gorgoroth", "Mount Doom", Mt Ngauruhoe 2287, Mt Tongariro 1967, Tukino Skifield, Tukino Alpine Village, Turoa Skifield, Mt Ruapehu 2797, Haukungatahi 1521, National Park, Waikune, Raurimu, Raurimu Spiral, Retaruke Upper, Riamaki (Upper Ruatiti), Ruatiti, Waikune, Kaitieke, Mansons Siding, Hukapapa, Oio, Kawautahi, Owhango, Hikumutu, Kakahi, Te Maire, Piriaka, Tunakotekote, Taumaruiti, Manunui, Ngapuke, Pungapunga, Moerangi, Hirata, Mangahouhou, Taurewa, Otukou, Papakai, Tongariro, 42nd Traverse, Tokaanu, Thermal Pools, Hautu Village, Turangi, National Trout Centre, Rangipo, Waihi, Kuratau, Omori, Pukawa Bay, Motuoapa, Kuratau Junction, Te Apuata, Te Raina, Whanganui, Te Oineohu Point, Tangingatahi Pt, Kurutau, Oruaiwi, Meringa, Echolands, Taringamotu, Taringamotu Valley, Mangakahu Valley, Te Koura, Tuhua, Matiere, Okahukura, Ngakonui, Lairdvale, Nihoniho, Waitaanga

TE KUITI, TO TE KUITI, TO TOKOROA, TO WAITARA, TO STRATFORD, TO HAWERA, TO BULLS, TO FEILDING

Whakatane river mouth

canoe, which brought settlers across the Pacific; there was already a Maori settlement on the site when they landed.

MAIN ATTRACTIONS: Nearby beaches offer surfing and swimming, and Whakatane is a base for dive tours, swimming with dolphins, windsurfing and fishing. The riverside **Mataatua Reserve** includes the original landing place of the Mataatua canoe. A bronze statue at **Whakatane Heads** commemorates Wairaka, a young woman who paddled the drifting Mataatua canoe to safety in defiance of tradition, and gave the town its name by saying she would act 'whakatane', like a man. The **Red Barn**, 7km from Whakatane, sells a wide range of work from local artists. The 16km **Nga Tapuwae o Toi Walkway** starts and finishes in Whakatane, and takes in sea cliffs, historic Maori pa sites, bird colonies, pohutukawa forest and secluded bays. **Whakatane Museum** has exhibits

about Maori and European history.

NEARBY ATTRACTIONS: Boat trips take visitors to the active marine volcano of **Whakaari/White Island**, 50km offshore, with its continual steaming, bubbling and rumbling geothermal activity. The volcanic island of **Moutohora (Whale Island)** is a wildlife refuge with hot springs and historic sites, but public access is highly restricted. **Ohope**, 7km east, has a beautiful 11km beach; **Ohiwa Harbour** attracts many migratory wading birds. **Awakeri Hot Springs**, 16km south-west of Whakatane, has thermally heated pools. Near **Edgecumbe**, 19km west, the **Amazing Maze 'n Maize** is a 6ha maze cut into a paddock of corn plants, and is open seasonally. To the south, walking tracks lead through spectacular forest in the **Waimana/Tauranga River Valley**, in the northern part of **Te Urewera National Park**.

VISITOR INFORMATION: Quay St, Ph: (07) 308 6058, www.whakatane.com

■ **Whangamata**　POP 3860
Map 159, J6
Whangamata, 165km from Auckland on the **Coromandel Peninsula**'s south-eastern coast, has long been home to Maori. European miners and squatters settled in the area from the mid-19th century. The hills around Whangamata were logged for kauri trees in the 1880s, and gold mining developed in the surrounding valleys. Today it is known for its beautiful surf beaches.

MAIN ATTRACTIONS: Whangamata offers the appealing combination of beaches and rainforest. Its 4km white sand beach, with excellent surf breaks, fishing, snorkelling and swimming, attracts crowds in summer. The **Whangamata Craft Trail** leads visitors around the studios of local artists.

NEARBY ATTRACTIONS: There are many walking tracks in the nearby **Coromandel Forest Park** and **Tairua Forest**, past old gold mining sites. Walks in the **Wentworth Valley**, off State Highway 25, 3km south of town, lead to historic mines (30 minutes) and spectacular **Wentworth Falls** (two hours); there is also a five-hour traverse of the **Coromandel Range**. An easy walk leads through riverside bush into the **Parakiwai Valley**, originally a horse tramway to a gold mine, and passes gold mining relics. Historic Maori pa sites can be seen around the **Otahu Estuary**. **Whiritoa**, 15km south, is a pretty beach with surfing, fishing and safe swimming in a tidal lagoon.

VISITOR INFORMATION: 616 Port Rd, Ph: (07) 865 8340, www.whangamatainfo.co.nz

■ **Whangamomona**　POP 24
Map 173, G2
The tiny, remote village of Whangamomona, in north-east **Taranaki** on State Highway 43, was first settled in 1895, and has a Historic Places Trust precinct

North Island

rating. Once a flourishing town, Whangamomona's decline began after massive floods in 1924.

MAIN ATTRACTIONS: Whangamomona is best known for its biennial **Republic Day**, which draws thousands of visitors to celebrate the town's 1989 protest against local government boundary changes; the community declared itself a republic as a result. The town is rich in historic buildings; a heritage trail leads walkers around 17 of these, including the impressive hotel.

NEARBY ATTRACTIONS: The **Forgotten World Highway** is a fascinating, remote 155km drive leading from **Stratford** to **Taumarunui** and featuring many historic and scenic sites, including the **Moki Tunnel**, bush walks, waterfalls, old coal mines, and historic Maori war and peace poles at **Maraekowhai Reserve**. There are panoramic views from the **Tahora Saddle** and **Whangamomona Saddle**; spectacular **Mount Damper Falls** is the North Island's highest waterfall. The **Matemateaonga Track**, a 42km walk through beautiful **Whanganui National Park** to the historic **Whanganui River**, can be accessed by turning off SH43 at **Strathmore**.

VISITOR INFORMATION: 1 Ariki St, New Plymouth, Ph: (06) 759 6060, www.taranaki.info

■ **Whangarei**   POP 46045
Map 191, D4
Northland's main city, and New Zealand's warmest, Whangarei is located at the head of **Whangarei Harbour**. Home to cafés, galleries and museums, it is also a base for visiting the **Tutukaka Coast**.

MAIN ATTRACTIONS: Whangarei's **Town Basin**, a harbour area with yachts and fishing boats, has stylish restaurants and galleries, including **Clapham's Clocks**, which has a huge collection of clocks and watches. The **Fernery and Conservatory** offers excellent displays of native ferns; **Whangarei Art Museum** showcases local arts and crafts. **Northland Craft Trust** is an artists' co-operative set in gardens. **Whangarei Museum**, 5km west of the town, has a kiwi house, an 1885 homestead and some beautiful Maori cloaks; beside the museum is a centre which cares for sick and injured native birds. **Whangarei Falls**, 5km north, are a spectacular 26m waterfall; north-east of the city at the **AH Reed Kauri Park**, visitors can view 500-year-old kauri trees from a treetop boardwalk, and visit a waterfall. **Mount Parihaka**, once the site of New Zealand's largest pa (Maori fortified village), offers walks through native bush and views over the city. The **Waimahanga Walkway** passes through estuarine mangrove swamps.

NEARBY ATTRACTIONS: The 35km drive to **Whangarei Heads** passes peaceful harbour bays; a one-hour walk up **Mount Manaia** leads through native bush to impressive views. **Bream Head Scenic Reserve**, culturally significant to Maori, has some of the North Island's best coastal forest. The reserve features an impressive array of wildlife, World War II gun emplacements and early Maori sites. **Bream Bay**, south of Whangarei Harbour, has lovely beaches, including the surf beaches of **Ruakaka** and **Uretiti**. New Zealand's only oil refinery at **Marsden Point**, 35km south-west, has a visitors' centre. To the north-east, the **Tutukaka Coast** has beautiful beaches and spectacular diving around the **Poor Knights Islands**. Walks through rugged **Tangihua Forest**, to the south-east, pass groves of mature kauri and an old timber dam.

VISITOR INFORMATION: Tarewa Park, 92 Otaika Rd, Ph: (09) 438 1079, www.whangareinz.org.nz

■ **Whitianga**   POP 3080
Map 159, H3
Whitianga is located on the east coast of the **Coromandel Peninsula**, on the shore of **Mercury Bay**. This attractive deep water

Orca whales breaching off the Whangarei coast

harbour was named by the British explorer Captain James Cook, who anchored there to observe the transit of Mercury in 1769. The bay is believed to have been occupied since its early discovery by the Maori explorer Kupe. Europeans settled there in the 19th century, and the industries of kauri and flax milling, gold mining, gum digging and boat building flourished until the resources on which they depended were exhausted. Whitianga today is a farming, fishing and tourism centre.

MAIN ATTRACTIONS: Numerous companies offer fishing charters for snapper, groper, broadbill swordfish and all species of marlin. There are also opportunities for diving, scenic cruises, kayak trips, windsurfing and sailing. The **Mercury Bay Historical Museum** has early artefacts on display.

NEARBY ATTRACTIONS: A ferry trip from the Whitianga wharf takes visitors across the harbour to the **Stone Steps Wharf**, built in 1837 and the oldest stone wharf in Australasia. Several lovely beaches are accessible from this point, including **Front Beach**, **Flaxmill Bay** and **Cooks Beach**. Further south-east, the small town of **Hahei** has a lovely white-sand beach facing onto a bay dotted with islands, and offers great snorkelling and diving in **Te Whanganui-A-Hei Marine Reserve**. Beautiful **Cathedral Cove**, accessible only by foot or boat, is famous for its huge, spectacular limestone arch. The **309 Road** is a scenic drive to **Coromandel** town, passing a kauri grove and **Waiau Falls**.

VISITOR INFORMATION: Albert St, Ph: (07) 866 5555, www.whitianga.co.nz

View through rock arch at Cathedral Cove

■ **Woodville**   POP 1480
Map 177, F4
Located at the junction of State Highways Two and Three, 28km east of Palmerston North in the Tararua district, the town of Woodville is home to a growing number of antique shops.

MAIN ATTRACTIONS: The renowned Bohemian-born artist Gottfried Lindauer, who painted many portraits of Maori in the 19th and early 20th centuries, settled in Woodville from 1890, and is buried in the **Old Gorge Cemetery**. The unique **Gottfried Lindauer Replica Studio** has prints of Lindauer's work and historical memorabilia.

NEARBY ATTRACTIONS: Woodville is the eastern gateway to the spectacular **Manawatu Gorge**, just west of the town. A four-hour walk leads through the gorge, and takes hikers through forests with plentiful bird life and spectacular views. Jet boating, kayaking and rides on a steam train are also possible; on the north side of the gorge is the **Te Apiti Wind Farm**. Tracks lead into the **Ruahine Forest Park** from the end of Coppermine Road, 15km from Woodville; walkers can see old copper mining shafts, native orchids, cave wetas and a waterfall. A winding unsealed road leads up **Wharite Peak**, 12km to the west. This is the gateway to many walks in the forest park, and there are great views. **Mangatainoka**, 10km south, is home to the **Tui Brewery**, established there in 1889. The brewery's seven-storey art deco tower is a striking sight, and guided tours are available. **Akitio** and **Herbertville**, on the Pacific coast to the east, are sandy beaches with safe swimming and good surfing.

VISITOR INFORMATION: 42 Vogel St, Ph: (06) 376 1023, www.tararua.com

North Island

NORTH ISLAND KEY MAP

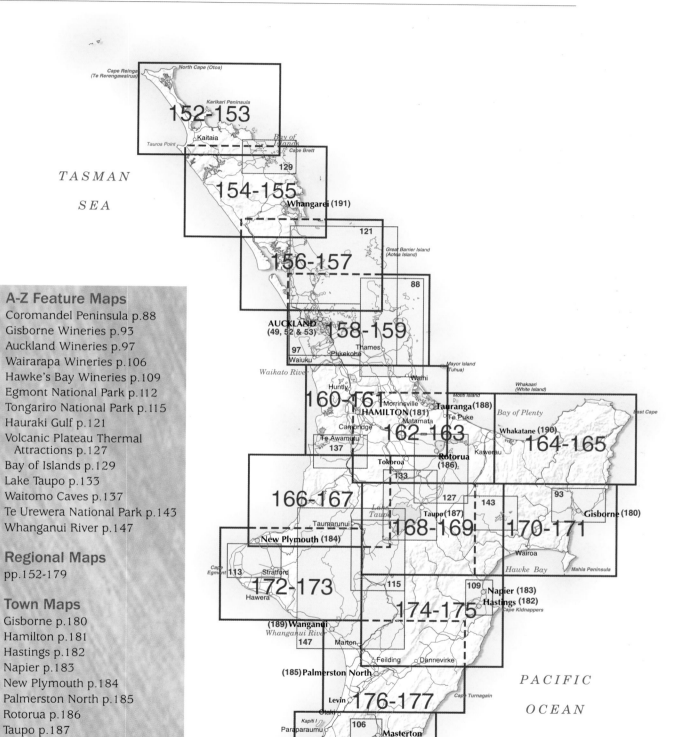

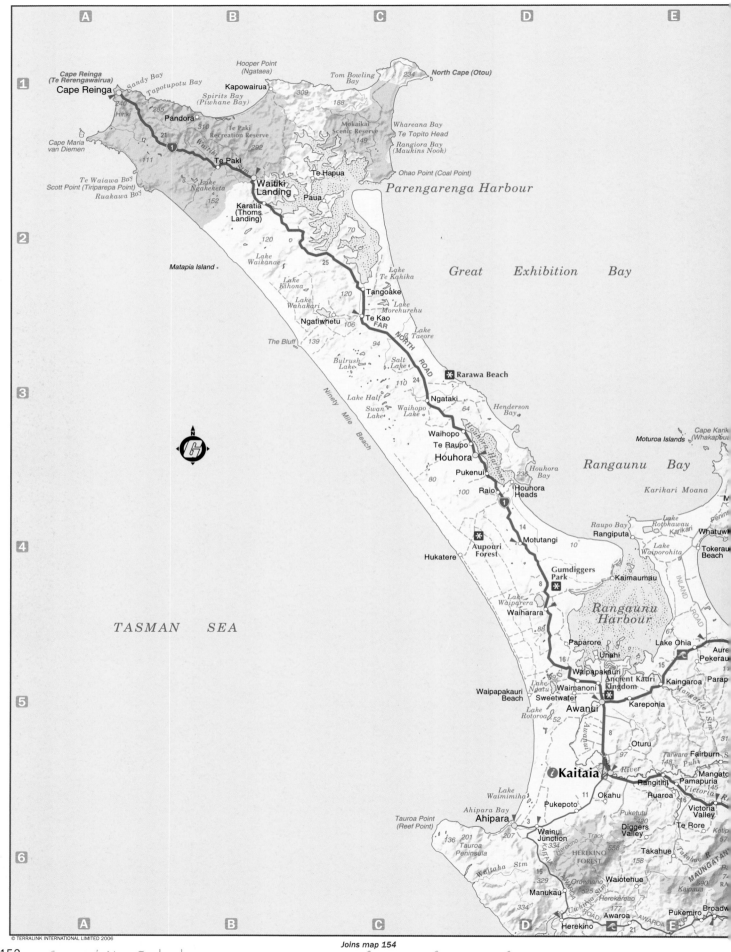

Cape Reinga
(Te Rerengawairua)
Cape Reinga
Sandy Bay
Tapotupotu Bay

Hooper Point
(Ngataea)
Kapowairua

Tom Bowling
Bay
North Cape (Otou)
234

Spirits Bay
(Piwhane Bay)

Hiriki

Pandora

309

188

Cape Maria
van Diemen

285

Te Paki
Recreation Reserve

21

Mokaikai
Scenic Reserve
149

Whareana Bay
Te Topito Head

292

Te Paki

111

Waitiki

Te Hapua

Rangiora Bay
(Maukins Nook)

Te Waiawa Bay
Scott Point (Tiriparepa Point)
Ruakawa Bay

152

Lake
Ngakeketa

**Waitiki
Landing**

Paua

Ohao Point (Coal Point)

Parengarenga Harbour

Karatia
(Thoms
Landing)

120

Matapia Island

Lake
Waikanae

70

25

Great   Exhibition   Bay

Lake
Kihona

Lake
Te Kahika

Lake
Wahakari

120

Tangoake

Lake
Morehurehu

Ngatiwhetu

106

Te Kao
FAR

Lake
Taeore

The Bluff

139

94

NORTH
ROAD

Bulrush
Lake

Salt
Lake

Lake Half

110

24

✳ **Rarawa Beach**

Swan
Lake

Waihopo
Lake

Ngataki

Henderson
Bay

Ninety   Mile   Beach

64

Moturoa Islands

Cape Karik
(Whakapua)

Waihopo
Te Raupo

Houhora

Houhora Harbour

Rangaunu   Bay

Houhora
Bay

Pukenui

236

Karikari   Moana

Raio

Houhora
Heads

80

100

Raupo Bay

Lake
Rotokawau
Karikari

Rangiputa

Whatuw

1

14

Motutangi

10

Lake
Waiporohita

Tokerau
Beach

Hukatere

✳
Aupouri
Forest

TASMAN   SEA

8

✳
Gumdiggers
Park

Kaimaumau

**Rangaunu
Harbour**

67

INLAND   ROAD

Lake
Waiparera

Waiharara

88

Lake Ohia

Aure
Pekerau

Paparore

16

Unahi

15

Kaingaroa

Parap

Waipakauri

59

Ancient Kauri
Kingdom
✳

Waipakauri
Beach

Lake
Ngatu

Waimanoni

Kareponia

Sweetwater

8

Lake
Rotoroa

Awanui

Oturu

97

Talware Fairburn

148
Te Puh

31

Mangato

ℹ **Kaitaia**

River

Rangitihi

Victoria

Pamapuria

145

Lake
Waimimiha

11

Okahu

Ruaroa

16

Ahipara Bay

Pukepoto

Puketutu

Victoria
Valley

Tauroa Point
(Reef Point)

Ahipara

3

Diggers
Valley

Te Rore

Ketip
57

136

201
Tauroa
Peninsula

207

Wainui
Junction

Track

HEREKINO
FOREST

558

Takahue

158

MAUNGATAN

590

RA

Waitaha Stm

15
329

Orowhaio
525 stm

Waiotehue

Kaipaua

Manukau

334

Herekareao

177

74
Be

Uwhitua Road

AWAROA

Pukemiro

Broadw

Herekino

Awaroa

21

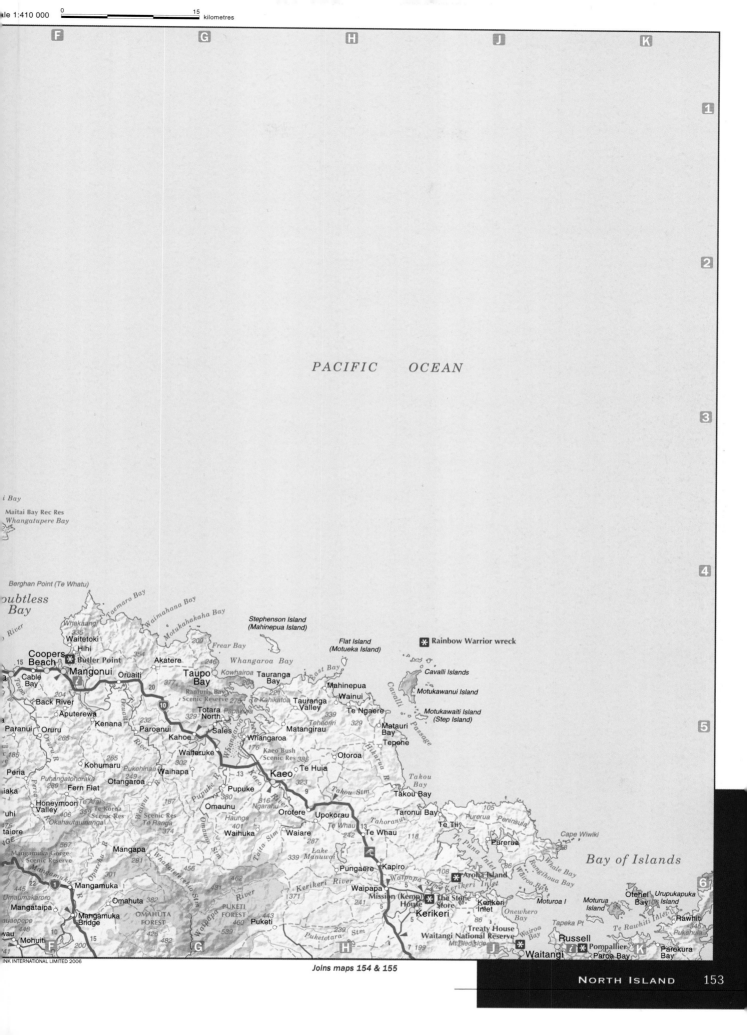

F   G   H   J   K

1

2

3

PACIFIC OCEAN

4

i Bay

Maitai Bay Rec Res
Whangatupere Bay

Berghan Point (Te Whatu)

Taemaro Bay

*Doubtless
Bay*

Waimahana Bay

Whakaangi 335

Motukahakaha Bay

*Stephenson Island
(Mahinepua Island)*

*Flat Island
(Motueka Island)*

✳ Rainbow Warrior wreck

Waitetoki
Hihi

Coopers
Beach

✳ Butler Point

354   Akatere

246 *Frear Bay*

Whangaroa Bay

Cavalli Islands

Mangonui

Cable
Bay

Oruaiti

Taupo
Bay

Kowhairoa

Tauranga
Bay

East Bay

Mahinepua

Cavalli Passage

Motukawanui Island

204   *River*

20   377

Ranfurly Bay
Scenic Reserve 275

221

204

Wainui

Motukawaiti Island
(Step Island)

Back River

Totara
North 329

Kahikatoa

Tauranga
Valley

Te Ngaere

Aputerewa

232

Kahoe

Sales

Papatara

339

Teheoriri

329

Matauri
Bay

Paranui

Oruru

265

Kenana

Paroanui

176

Whangaroa

Matangirau

Tepene

Waitaruke

302

385

Otoroa

Peria

Kohumaru

Pukehinau 249

Waihapa

Kaeo Bush
Scenic Res

Te Huia

*Takou
Bay*

185

Otangaroa

Pupuke

380

Kaeo

323

Takou Stm

Takou Bay

Honeymoon
Valley 359

Te Arai

187

Omaunu

816

9

Fern Flat

Te Korna
Scenic Res
Te Ranga

Orotere

Ngarahu

Taronui Bay

105

Mangamuka Gorge
Scenic Reserve

Mangapa

Hauaga
401

Waiare

Upokorau

242

Te Tii

Purerua

Te Whau

Tahoranui

118

Purerua

Purerua Peninsula

Cape Wiwiki

Whale Bay

Bay of Islands

Mangamuka

Omahuta

Waihuka

287

*Lake
Manuwai*
339

Te Whau

13

Te Puna Inlet

86

*Rangihoua
Bay*

Mangataipa

Mangamuka
Bridge

OMAHUTA
FOREST

462

Pungaere

Kapiro

108

✳ Aroha Island

Waipapa Stm

86

Moturua I

Otehel
Bay

*Urupukapuka
Island*

Mohuiti

200

PUKETI
FOREST

460

Puketi

Kerikeri River

Waipapa

241

Puketotara Stm

Mission (Kemp)
House

239

Kerikeri

239

✳ the Stone
store

86

Kerikeri
Inlet

*Onewhero
Bay*

Tapeka Pt

Moturua
Island

Te Rawhiti Inlet

345

Rawhiti

Pukehua

Treaty House

*Wairoa
Bay*

7 199

Waitangi National Reserve
Mt Bledisloe

Russell

Parekura
Bay

Waitangi

Pompallier

Paroa Bay

A | B | C | D | E

Ahipara Bay
Ahipara
Pukepoto
Puketutu
Mangataiore
Waihuka
Waiare
Te Whau
118

Wainui Junction
Diggers Valley
Te Rore Kotipu
Mangamuka Gorge Scenic Reserve
Mangapa
Mangamuka
Omahuta
Whakatetereha Stm
Pungaere
Lake Manuwai
Kapiro

1
Waiha Stm
Manukau
HEREKINO FOREST
Takahue
MAUNGATANIWHA RANGE
Raetea RAETEA FOREST
Umaumakaroro
Mangamuka Bridge
Mangamuka
Omahuta
OMAHUTA FOREST
PUKETI FOREST
Puketi
Waipapa
Mission
Keri

Waiotehue
Mangataipa
Mohuiti
Tutekehua
Umawera
Rahiri
Waihou Valley
Waimate North
Puketon
Keri

Herekino
Awaroa
Pukemiro
Broadwood
Orawau
Kahikatoa
Rawhia
Rangiahua
Okaihau
Lake Omapere
Te Ahuahu
Remuera Settlement
Ohaeawai

Puhata
Pareokawa
Paponga
Te Karae
Urungaio
Orira
Okaka
Utakura
Maraeroa
St Michael's Church
Ngawha
Pakaraa

Kohe
Runaruna
Mata
Te Huahua
Motukaraka Scenic Res
Mangungu
Mission House
Horeke
Ivydale
Wairere Boulders Park
Mangataraire
Kaikohe
Ngawha Springs
Tuhipa

2
Whangape Harbour
WARAWARA FOREST
Panguru
Tapuwae
Motuti
Motukaraka
Rangiora
Matawhera
Rawene
Papua
Motukiore
Kaikohe
Rakautao
Ngapipito

Mitimiti
Waireia
Lower Waihou
Onoke
Opata
Ohuri
Moehau
Te Iringa
Ngapuhi
Punakitere Valley
Tautoro

Matihetihe
Reena
Te Karaka
Punehu
Karuhiruhi
Omanaia
Waima Valley
Taheke
Punakitere
Kirioke
Tautoro

Rangi Point
Waitapu
Koutu
Whirinaki
Oue
Waima
Otaua
Mataraua
Matawaia

3
Hokianga Harbour
Motutoa
Pakanae
Ononi
Opononi
WAIMA FOREST Te Raupua
Wahaotetupua Scenic Res
Three Bridges
Hikurangi Scenic Res

North Head
South Head
Omapere
Oraora
Waimamaku
Wekaweka
MATARAUA FOREST
Orowhana
Awarua
Pukemiro
Kaiko

Waiotemarama
PARATAIKO RANGE
Kohekohe
WAIPOUA KAURI FOREST
Waimatenui
Nukutawhiti
Twin Bridges

Tane Mahuta (Giant Kauri)
Waipoua Forest Sanctuary
Toetoehatiko
Pakotai

4
Kawerua
Waipoua Settlement
Waipoua Forest
Tutamoe
MARLBOROUGH FOREST
TUTAMOE RANGE
Opouteke

Waipoua River
Kaitui Katui Scenic Res
Oranoa
Donnellys Crossing
Mangatu
Opouteke

Maunganui Bluff Scenic Res
Trounson Kauri Park
Four Sisters (Giant Kauris)
KAIHU FOREST
Pekape

Maunganui Bluff
Aranga
Whatoro
Awakino

Aranga Beach
Shag Lake
Kaihu
Ahikiwi
Maropiu
Kairara
Avoca
Waihue

5
TASMAN SEA
Lake Waikere
Lake Taharoa
Kai Iwi Lakes
Lake Kaiiwi
Mamaranui
Maitahi
Pukewharariki
Tangowahine
Hoanga
Te Wharau
Awakino Point

Omamari
Tangowahine
Parore
Dargaville
Turiwiri

Mangatara
Baylys Beach
BAYLYS COAST RD
Mt Wesley
Sunny Nook
Arapohue

6
Rehutai
Mahuta
Aratapu
Mititai

Te Kopuru
Redhill
Tatarariki
Tokatoka

A | B | C | D | E

Gregory's New Zealand

North Island

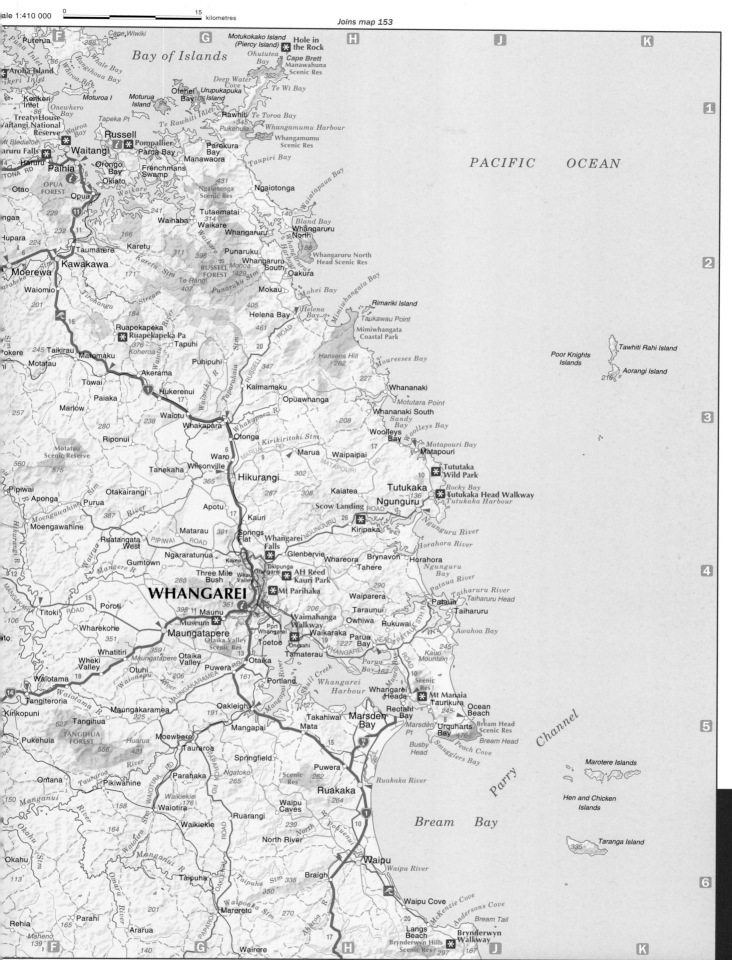

F G H J K

Cape Wiwiki
Puterua
Cape Wiwiki
Whale Bay
Motukokako Island
(Piercy Island)
Hole in
the Rock
258
Aroha Island
Rangihoua Bay
Ohutuea
Bay
Cape Brett
Manawahuna
Scenic Res
Bay of Islands
Moturoa I
Otehei
Bay
Urupukapuka
Island
86
Waikuri
Deep Water
Cove
362
Te Wi Bay
Kerikeri
Inlet
Onewhero
Bay
Moturua
Island
Tapeka Pt
Te Rawhiti Inlet
Rawhiti
345
1
Waitangi National
Reserve
Treaty House
86
Russell
Pompallier
Parekura
Bay
Pukehuia
52
Whangamumu Harbour
Whangamumu
Scenic Res
Waitangi
Paroa Bay
Manawaora
Taupiri Bay
Paihia
Frenchmans
Swamp
431
Ngaiotonga
Haruru Falls
Orongo
Bay
Okiato
Ngaiotonga
Scenic Res
PACIFIC OCEAN
Otao
Opua
OPUA
FOREST
Opua
241
Tutaematai
314
140
Bland Bay
Whangaruru
North
11
Waihaba
Waikare
Whangaruru
186
Whangaruru North
Head Scenic Res
229
Taumarere
232
11
Karetu
166
398
Punaruku
Whangaruru
South
Moerewa
Kawakawa
224
6
171
RUSSELL
FOREST
425
Oakura
Waiomio
201
Tirohanga
Te Rangi
407
Monoa
Stm
Mokau
Mohei Bay
Rimariki Island
184
405
Helena Bay
Helena
Bay
Taukawau Point
16
Ruapekapeka
461
Mimiwhangata
Coastal Park
Mimiwhangata Bay
245 Taikirau
Ruapekapeka Pa
376
Tapuhi
347
Hansens Hill
262
Moureeses Bay
Poor Knights
Islands
Tawhiti Rahi Island
Motatau
Maromaku
Koheroa
20
227
Aorangi Island
216
Towai
Akerama
Puhipuhi
Whananaki
257
Paiaka
Hukerenui
17
Kaimamaku
208
Motutara Point
Whananaki South
Sandy
Bay
Marlow
Waiotu
238
Opuawhanga
Woolleys
Bay
Woolleys Bay
280
Whakapara
Matapouri Bay
Matapouri
Riponui
Otonga
Kirikiritoki Stm
Marua
Waipaipai
17
Tututaka
Wild Park
Motatau
Scenic Reserve
560
575
Waro
9
302
10
Rocky Bay
Tutukaka Head Walkway
Tanekaha
Wilsonville
365
Hikurangi
287
308
Kaiatea
136
Tutukaka Harbour
Pipiwai
Aponga
Otakairangi
Purua
387
Apotu
17
Kauri
Scow Landing
Tutukaka
Ngunguru
26
Kiripaka
Moengawahine
Ruatangata
West
391
Springs
Flat
Ngunguru River
Moengawahine
Gumtown
Matarau
Horahora River
Ngararatunua
288
Whangarei
Falls
Glenbervie
Whareora
Brynavon
Horahora
Three Mile
Bush
Kamo
Tikipunga
AH Reed
Kauri Park
Tahere
Ngunguru
Bay
15
Poroti
Otangarei
Pataua River
Titoki
395
11
Maunu
361
Mt Parihaka
290
Waiparera
Taraunui
Taiharuru River
Pataua
Taiharuru Head
Museum
Waimahanga
Walkway
206
Owhiwa
Rukuwai
Taiharuru
WHANGAREI
Maungatapere
351
Port
Whangarei
Waikaraka
19
Parua
Bay
227
Awahoa Bay
Whatitiri
Maungatapere
359
Otaika Valley
Scenic Res
Toetoe
Onerahi
Parua
Bay
162
245
Otuhi
Otaika
Valley
13
Tamaterau
10
Kauri
Mountain
Wheki
Valley
Otaika
Waiotama
18
Puwera
161
Skull Creek
Whangarei
Harbour
Scenic
Res
Ocean
Beach
Tangiteroria
206
Portland
Whangarei
Heads
Mt Manaia
Taurikura
245
Kirikopuni
Waiotama R
Maungakaramea
225
Oakleigh
191
127
Reotahi
Bay
Marsden
Pt
Bream Head
Scenic Res
Bream Head
Tanihua
Takahiwai
Mata
Marsden
Bay
Urquharts
Bay
476
Peach Cove
Pukehuia
TANGIHUA
FOREST
627
Mangapai
15
Busby
Head
Smugglers Bay
Parry Channel
556
421
Marotere Islands
Omana
Tauraroa
Moewhare
Springfield
Puwera
262
Ruakaka River
Hen and Chicken
Islands
Parahaka
Ngatoko
265
Scenic
Res
264
Ruakaka
Pikiwahine
Ruakaka
Bream Bay
Taranga Island
335
150
Waikiekie
176
Waiotira
Waipu
Caves
239
Manganui
158
Ruarangi
Okahu
164
Waikiekie
North River
1
10
Okahu
Okahu
Stm
113
Taipuha
338
Braigh
Waipu
Waipu River
Rehia
Parahi
201
Marereku
350
270
Waipu Cove
McKenzie Cove
Andersons Cove
Maheno
139
Ararua
Taipuha Stm
20
Langs
Beach
Bream Tail
Waipooka Stm
Wairere
Brynderwyn
Walkway
Brynderwyn Hills
Scenic Res
297
167

A · B · C · D · E

Tangowahine
Hoanga
Parore
Te Wharau
Mangatara
Awakino
Point
Dargaville
Turiwiri
Mt Wesley
Rehutai
Sunny
Nook
Arapohue
Mahuta
Aratapu
Mititai
Te Kopuru
Redhill
Tatarariki
Glinks Gully
Repia
Koremoa
Tikinui
Taingaehe
Ruawai
Mapau
Te Kowhai

Pukehuia
Omana
Pikiwahine
Windy Hill
Okahu
Rehia
Parahi
Arapohue
Tokatoka
Peak
Tokatoka
Naumai
Whenuanui
Raupo

Moewhare
Tauraroa
Springfield
Parahaka
Waiotira
Waikiekie
Ruarangi
Ruarangi
North River
Taipuha
Maraetai
Ararua
Paparoa
Wairere
Huarau
Maungaturoto
Pahi
Whakapirau
Marohemo
Tanoa
Batley
Oruawharo
Oneriri
Port Albert
Tapora
Wharehine
Minniesdale
Chapel

Puwera
Ruakaka
Waipu
Caves
Waipu
Braigh
Waipu Cove
Langs
Beach
Brynderwyn Hills
Brynderwyn
Bryderwyn
Molesworth
Tara
Pukekaroro
Kaiwaka
Te Arai
Point
Hakaru
Te Arai
Topuni
Te Hana
Wellsford
Albertland
Museum
Hoteo
North
Wayby
Valley
Wayby
Tauhoa
Hoteo
Streamlands
Kaipara
Flats
Kourawhero
Woodcocks

Bream Bay
Mangawhai
Heads
Mangawhai F
Spectacle
Lake
Tomara
Lake
Tom
Whangaripo
Waiteitei
Whangar
Waiwhiu
SheepWorld
Waiwhiu
Do
Val
Warkwo
Hon
Cent
Pohuehu
Puh

Kauri
Museum
Matakohe

TASMAN SEA

Kaipara

Harbour

Lake
Rototuna
Rototuna
Kellys Bay
Lake
Wairere
Lake
Karaka
Lake
Mokeno
Lake
Humuhumu
Lake
Rotokawau
Lake
Karoro/
Mathews
Lake
Kanono
Pouto Point
Kaipara
Lighthouse
North Head
Kaipara
Head

Okaro Ck

Otamatea Channel

Tinopai
Coates
Bay

Kaipara
Entrance
South Head

Tauhoa Channel

South Head
Lake
Otatoa
Lake
Kuwakatai
Waioneke
Shelly
Beach
Lake
Kereta

Mangakura
Glorit
Ahuroa
Komokoriki
Araparera
Kakanui
Makarau
Kanohi
Wainui
Waitoki

Kaukapakapa

Mt Harriet
Atuanui
Scenic Res
Woodcocks

Parakai Aquatic Park,
Kaipara Cruises
Parakai
Parkhurst
Te Pua
Helensville
Wharepapa
Woodhill
Woodhill
Forest
Rewiti
Waimauku
Loch
Norrie
Waikoukou
Valley
Riverhead
Huapai
Kumeu
Coatesville
Dairy Flat

North Island

© TERRALINK INTERNATIONAL LIMITED 2006

0 15
kilometres

F G H J K

Marotere Islands

Hen and Chicken
Islands

Taranga Island
335

PACIFIC OCEAN

N

Burgess Island (Pokohinu)

Mokohinau Islands

Fanal Island (Motukino)

1

Aiguilles Island

Miners Head
526
450

Rangiwhakaea Bay

2

340 Rakitu Island
(Arid Island)

Motairehe

Maunganui Point
(Separation Point)
Mohunga
Kawa 335 Whangapoua Creek

Whangapoua
Beach
222

Katherine Bay

Port Abercrombie 185
Kaikoura Island
(Selwyn Island)

Glenfern Sanctuary

Port
Fitzroy

Okiwi

Windy Canyon

365 Whakatautuna
Point

Kauri Dams
Mt Hobson
627

Great Barrier
Forest 205
Great Barrier Island
(Aotea Island) 398

Tramline Track

Awana Bay

Broken Islands
(Pig Islands)

310

Kaitoke Hot Springs
398 Kaitoke Ch

Craddock Channel

Jellicoe Channel

Hauturu /
Little Barrier Island

Ngamanauraru Bay

Te Ananuiarau Bay

Waimaomao Bay

Mt Hauturu
722

Whangaparapara

Whangaparapara Har

Claris

Okupu

Blind Bay

406

Medlands Beach

3

Pakiri River

Pakiri Beach

Pakiri

Goat I Goat Island
Marine Reserve

Seafriends

335 Cape Rodney

Leigh

11

Whangateau

437

l Peak

g Omaha

11

Point
Wells

Omaha

Omaha Flats

Takatu

Skywork
Helicopters

Buckleton
Beach

Snells
Beach

Algies Bay

Mahurangi

Ti Point

Omaha Bay

Whangateau Harbour

Tawharanui
Regional Park

117

Takatu Point

Tawharanui

North Channel

Mt Taylor
164

Kawau
Bay

Mansion
House

182

Scandrett
Regional Park

100

Martins
Bay

Rosbaquet Bay

Kawau
Island

Big Bay

Motuketekete Island

Motuora Island

Tryphena

Shag Point

Windy Hill
361

Tryphena
Harbour 402

Cape
Barrier

Colville Channel

Channel Island

Cape Colville
Port
Jackson

Kaiiti Point

Port Jackson

Fantail Bay
Rec Res

Fletcher
Bay

Pahi Stm

Coromandel
Coastal Walkway

353

Stony Bay

Port Charles

COROMANDEL
FP
856

Port Charles

892

Rauporoa
Bay

4

5

urangi
est

Mahurangi
Regional Park

Puhoi River
Wenderholm
Regional Park

Waiwera

Waiwera
Hot Springs

Hatfields Beach

Orewa

Whangaparaoa
Bay

Red Beach

Stanmore
Bay

dale

Okura
Redvale

Glenvar

Torbay

Browns Bay
Rothesay Bay

Mairangi Bay

Castor Bay

Milford

North
Shore

Glenfield

Haven

14

Long Bay

Army Bay

107

Shakespear
Regional Park

Okoromai Bay

80

Whangaparaoa
Peninsula

Whangaparaoa Passage

eiti River

27

Okura River

Rakino Channel

The Noises

Tiritiri Matangi Island

Hauraki Gulf

Rakino Island

Thumb Point
(Te Patu Point)

Motutapu
Island

Rangitoto
Island

Motutapu Island
Recreation Res

Rangitoto Island
Scenic Reserve
121
260

Historic Village,
Onetangi Reserve

Oneroa

Onetangi

Waiheke
Island

Home Bay

Owhiti
Bay

Hooks Bay

Stony Batter
Reserve

617

29

323

Waiaro

Whangaahei

238

Waikawau

Waikawau
Bay

Little
Bay

Colville Bay

Colville

Waikawau Bay
Farm Park

COROMANDEL
FP

6

Motukawao Group

Waitete Bay

Papaaroha

Amodeo
Bay

524

Kennedy Bay

28 514

501

Motuoruhi Island
(Goat Island)

Waimate Island

Coromandel

Goldfields &
Stamper Battery

Driving Creek
Railway
586

573

12

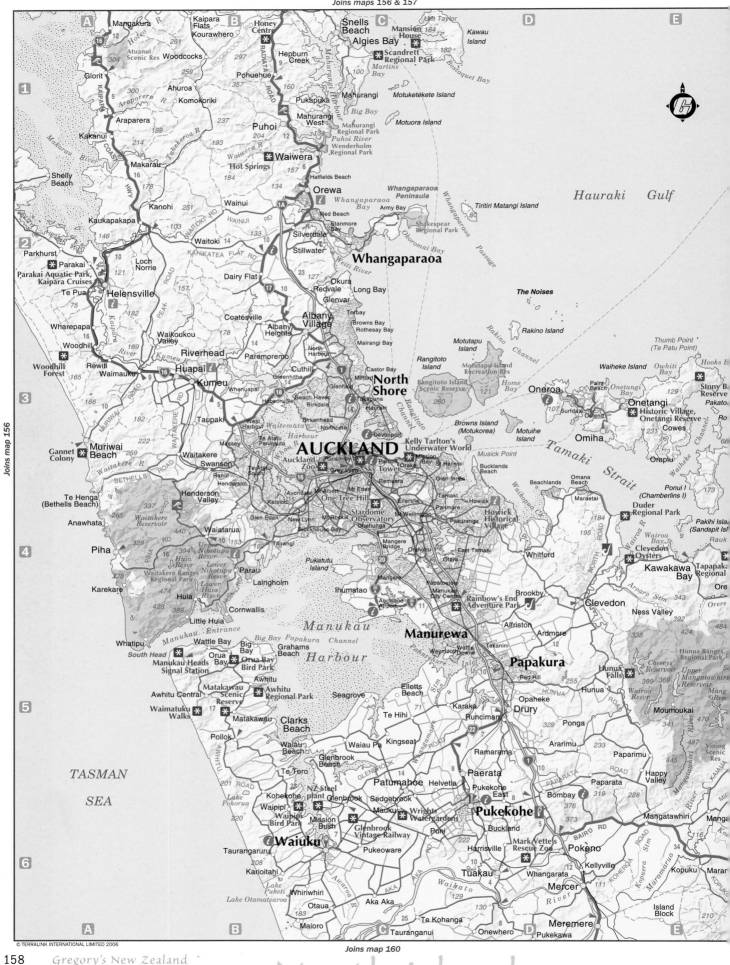

158 Gregory's New Zealand

North Island

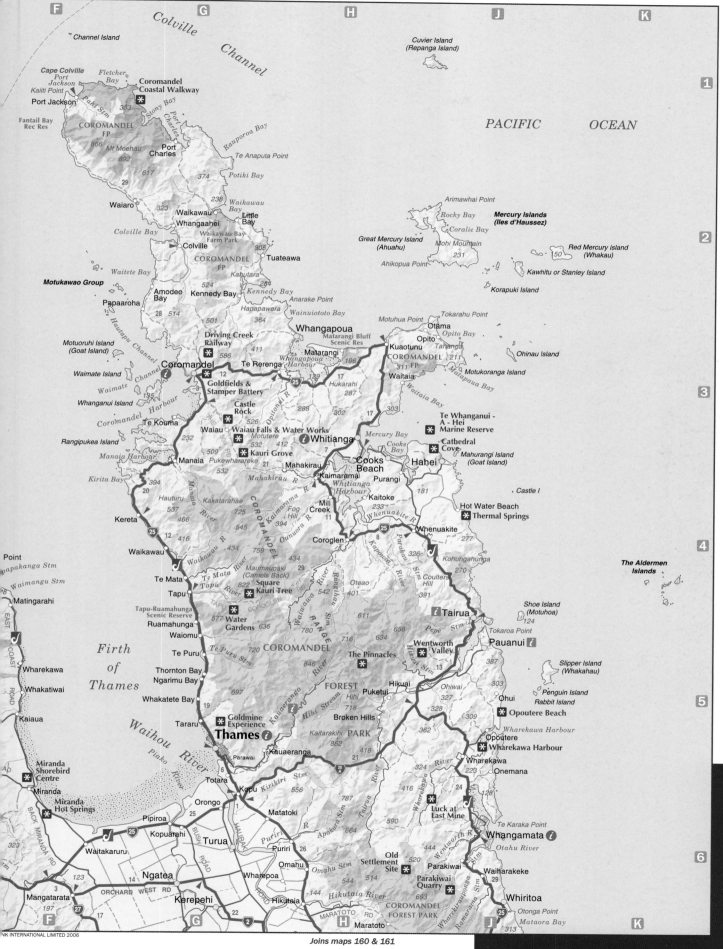

Colville *Channel*

PACIFIC OCEAN

Cuvier Island
(Repanga Island)

Channel Island

F   **G**   **H**   **J**   **K**

Cape Colville
Fletcher
Bay
Port Jackson
Kaiiti Point
Port Jackson

COROMANDEL FP
866 Mt Moehau 892
617
29
323
Waiaro
Waikawau
Whangaahei
Colville Bay
Colville
238 Waikawau Bay
Little Bay
Waikawau Bay Farm Park
305
Tuateawa
COROMANDEL FP
524
Kahutara
284
Motukawao Group
Amodeo Bay Kennedy Bay Kennedy Bay
Papaaroha
28 514
501
Hapapawera Anarake Point
364 Wainuiototo Bay

Arimawhai Point
Rocky Bay Mercury Islands (Iles d'Haussez)
Great Mercury Island (Ahuahu) Mohi Mountain Coralie Bay 231
Ahikopua Point Red Mercury Island (Whakau) 150
Kawhitu or Stanley Island
Korapuki Island Ohinau Island

Motuoruhi Island (Goat Island)
Driving Creek Railway
Whangapoua
Matarangi Bluff Scenic Res
Matarangi
Coromandel
411 586
Te Rerenga Whangapoua Harbour 196
Goldfields & Stamper Battery
12 25 129 Hukarahi 17 287
Waimate Island
Waimate Channel 195
Whanganui Island Castle Rock 526
Te Kouma 288 302 17
Waiau Waiau Falls & Water Works 532 412
Whitianga
Rangipukea Island 232 Motutere 7
Manaia Harbour Kauri Grove 509
Manaia Pukewhararareke Mahakirau 21
532
Kirita Bay 394 Kakatarahae Mahakirau R Kaimarama
20 537 725
Hauturu 466 545 Fog Hill 394 Mill Creek
Kereta COROMANDEL 759 11
12 416 434
Waikawau Waikawau River Maumaupaki (Camels Back) 434
Te Mata Te Mata River 822 Square Kauri Tree 29 542 401
Tapu Tapu River Water Gardens 636 780
Tapu-Ruamahunga Scenic Reserve 577
Ruamahunga COROMANDEL RANGE 716 634
Waiomu
Te Puru Te Puru Stm 720 COROMANDEL 846
Thornton Bay The Pinnacles
Ngarimu Bay 697 FOREST
Whakatete Bay 19 Hihi 718
Tararu Goldmine Experience
Thames Kaitarakihi 852 PARK
Kauaeranga 418
Parawai 21
6 Totara
Kopu Kirikiri Stm 556
Orongo 1
Pipiroa Matatoki 787
Kopuarahi 25
Waitakaruru Turua Puriri 26
123 Puriri 664
Ngatea 14 Omahu 590
Kerepehi Wharepoa 544 514
ORCHARD WEST RD Hikutaia 144 Hikutaia River 693
Mangatarata 197 27 17 2 MARATOTO RD Maratoto

Otama Opito Bay
Opito Tahanga
Kuaotunu COROMANDEL 211
Waitaia 311 FP Motukoranga Island
Waitaia Bay Matapaua Bay
303 Te Whanganui - A - Hei Marine Reserve
Mercury Bay Cathedral Cove
Cooks Bay Mahurangi Island (Goat Island)
Cooks Beach Hahei
Whitianga Harbour Purangi 181 Castle I
Kaitoke 233 Hot Water Beach
Coroglen Whenuakite R Thermal Springs
8 25 Whenuakite 277
Kappuni R 326 Kohungahunga 270
Coulters Hill 391
Oteao The Aldermen Islands
611 Shoe Island (Motuhoa) 124
Tairua
Pepe Stm Tokaroa Point
Wentworth Valley 658 Pauanui
13 387 Slipper Island (Whakahau)
Ohiwai 303 Penguin Island
Hikuai 327 Ohui Rabbit Island
Puketui 328 Opoutere Beach
362 309
Old Settlement Site Opoutere
520 Wharekawa Harbour
Parakiwai 324 Wharekawa
418 416 Onemana
324 24 128
Luck at Last Mine Te Karaka Point
590 Whangamata Otahu River
Parakiwai Quarry 444 29 Waiharakeke
520 Whangamata Whiritoa
COROMANDEL Otonga Point
FOREST PARK 313 Mataora Bay

Firth of Thames

Point
Waimangu Stm
Matingarahi
EAST COAST ROAD
Wharekawa
Whakatiwai
Kaiaua
Waihou River
Miranda Shorebird Centre
Miranda
Miranda Hot Springs
Piako River
BACK MIRANDA RD
323

1 **2** **3** **4** **5** **6**

TASMAN SEA

Port Waikato

Meremere

Rangiriri

Ohinewai

Te Kauwhata

Huntly

Taupiri

Ngaruawahia

HAMILTON

Raglan

Temple View

Cambridge

Pirongia

Te Awamutu

Kihikihi

Ohaupo

Kawhia

Kawhia Harbour

Otorohanga

PIRONGIA
FOREST PARK

Kiwi House
& Bird Sanctuary

Gregory's New Zealand

North Island

Huntly A B C D **Katikati** E

Netherby
Taupiri
Mountain
Taupiri

Mangateparu
Waiorongomai
Waiorongomai
Heritage
Museum
Wairakau
Katikati
Heritage
Museum
Katikati
Bird
Gardens

Hopuhopu
Komakorau
Whitikahu
Tauhei
Te Aroha
West
Shaftesbury
Sapphire
Hot Springs
Aongatete

Kainui
Woodlands
Historic
Homestead
Gordonton
Waitoa
Tatuanui
Manawaru
Whakamarama
Pahoia
Apata

Horotiu
Horsham
Downs
Kuranui
Morrinsville
Ngarua
Hungahunga
Gordon
Mauriroho
Scenic Res

Rototuna
Puketaha
Motumaoho
Kereone
Wardville
Wairere
Falls
Whakamarama

Te Rapa
Eureka
Tahuroa
Kiwitahi
Walton
Turangaomoana
Gordon Park
Scenic Reserve

St Andrews
Zoo
Forest
Lake
Tauwhare
Pa
Tauwhare
Tamihana
Waharoa
Okauia
Opal Hot
Springs
KAIMAI -
MAMAKU

HAMILTON
Newstead
Matangi
Pukemoremore
Te Miro
Scenic Res
Richmond
Downs
Peria
Firth Tower
Historic
Museum
Te Ohaki Pa
Okauia Pa
FOREST

Temple
View
Fitzroy
Glenview
Tamahere
Te Miro
Sanatorium
Hill
Whitehall
Te Tapui
Scenic Reserve
Matai "Hobbiton"
Matamata
PARK

Koromatia
Bruntwood
Fencourt
Hautapu
French
Pass
Buckland
Hinuera
Te Poi

Tuhikaramea
Vilagrad
Wines
Kaipaki
Pukeroro
Taotaoroa
Selwyn

Ngahinapouri
Cambridge
Pukerimu
Karapiro
Piarere
Oraka
Deer Park
Waiomou
Okoroire

Ohaupo
Monavale
Pukekura
Lake
Karapiro
Maungatautari
Karapiro
Hydro
Museum
Hot
Springs

Te Rore
Paterangi
Rotoorangi
Horahora
Tirau
Tapapa

Pirongia
Mangapiko
Ngaroto
Te Rahu
Kairangi
Whanake
Te Akatarere
Te Waihou
Walkway

Te Awamutu
Hairini
Rangiaowhia
Puahue
Pukeatua
Arapuni
Puketurua
Putaruru
Pinedale

Puketotara
Pokuru
Kihikihi
Orakau
Tokanui
Parawera
Puniu
Owairaka
Valley
Pukewhakaahu
Panitutu
Hodderville
Lichfield
Ngatira
Arahiwi
Scenic Reserve

Te Kopua
Te Kawa
West
Te Kawa
Waikeria
Rotongata
Waotu
Wiltsdown

Tihiroa
Ngahape
Korakonui
Panetapu
Wharepapa
South
Lake
Arapuni
Arohena
Tokoroa
Colson's Hill
Lookout

Otorohanga
Kiwi House
& Bird Sanctuary
Awatane
Mangaorongo
Rangiatea
Maihiihi
Wharepuhunga
Waipapa
Big Rock
Mountain Bike Park
Lake
Moananui
Kinleith

Mangawhero
Whawharua
Otewa
Mangatutu
Waipapa
Lake
Waipapa

Hangatiki
Tahaia
Toa
Bridge
Paewhenua
Tauraroa
Rewarewa
Waimahora
Ngaroma
Waipapa
Maraetai

Pururu
Rangitoto
PUREORA
FOREST
PARK
Mangakino
Wawa
Upper Atiamuri

Puketutu
Mangaokewa
Waipa Valley
Horokino
Whakamaru
Lake
Whakamaru

Kopaki
Arataro
Barryville
Lake
Atiamuri

A B C D E

North Island

0 15 kilometres

F G H J K

Bay of Plenty

Matakana Island

Opureora

Tauranga Entrance

231

Mount Maunganui

Omanu
Omanu Arataki
Omanu Beach

Matua
Otumoetai
Te Maunga

TAURANGA

Wairoa Pa

Fernland Spa
Tauranga South
Gate Pa
Greerton
Welcome Bay

Matapihi
Maungatapu

Kairua
Waitao

Papamoa Beach

Barkes Corner
Reef

Ngapeke

16

Waimapu
Kaitemako

Papamoa
Papamoa Hills
Cultural Heritage
Regional Park

Maketu

Te Ranga
Ohauiti

Kaiate Falls
Kaiate Falls

Te Puke

Rangiuru
Te Tumu

Little Waihi

Pyes Pa

Mt Misery
476

Manoeka

Otawa Scenic Res

Rangiuru
Te Matai

Vintage Auto Barn
Kiwi 360

Motiti Island
57

Tumu Bay

Motuhaku Island

Okurei Point

Hidden Gorge Scenic Res

Oropi

Waiari

The Junction

Comvita Visitors Centre

Paengaroa

Pongakawa

Pukehina

Ohinepanea

Otamarakau

Hauone
Pikowai

35

Motunau Island

Omanawa Falls

Douglas Corner
248

Rangiuru
946

Pongakawa Valley

91

Tokata I.
Rurima I
Moutoki I

36
372

Mangatoi

Te Ranga

33

209

Pongakawa

220

264

147

Matata
Matata Scenic Res
370

Moutohora Island
(Whale Island)

Puwhenua
622

Torehapa
Stream

466

Ngawaro

Mangorewa River

Kaituna River

Pokopoko Stm

Oeutheithea Stm

226

305

456

366

Awakaponga

9

THORNTON ROAD

Thornton

Red Barn

Paroa

Whakatane

Te Pu
Kaharoa

Rotongata

Okere Falls
Tokerau

384

Pikiao Marae

345

Lake Rotoehu
229

510

Manawahe

Otakiri

Edgecumbe
6

Poroporo
Pahou

Awaheu Stm

Oturoa

Hamurana

Okere Falls
Whangamarino

Otaramarae

412

Lake Rotoma

Lake Rotoiti

Rotoehu

Lake Rotoma
Scenic Res

Mangaone Mangaone
Scenic Res

Amazing Maze 'n' Maize

10

Awakeri

White Pine Bush

Agrodome Adventure Park

Mourea
Tikitere 'Hell's Gate'

Haparu

Gisborne Point

Hinehopu

Rotoiti

Mangaone

Awakeri Springs

13

Tarukenga

Awahou
Waiteti

Lake Rotorua

Tikitere
Te Ngae

Ruato

36

Lake Rotokawau

Rotomahana

Hinehopu Track
4817

Rotoehu

817

L Rotoma
Scenic Res

Onepu

Te Teko

293

Ngongotaha

Rainbow Springs

Mokoia Island

Rotokawa

534

Lake Rotoatua

Lake Okataina Walkway

7

34

Puteuaki
(Mt Edgecumbe)
821

Te Mahoe

262

Gondola & Luge

Western Heights

Ohinemutu

728

Kawerau

Lake Otumahi

363

Paradise Valley Springs

Mt Ngongotaha Scenic Res
757

Mangakakahi

ROTORUA

Owhata
Lynmore

Lake Okareka

Lake Okataina Scenic Res

934
Makatiti Dome
Scenic Reserve

Tarawera

Lake Matahina

351

Glenholme
Springfield

Whakarewarewa

WHAKAREWAREWA FOREST PARK

Tihiotonga

L Tikitapu
(Blue Lake)
699

Lake Tarawera

Matahina

478

Horohoro

Kapenga

Buried Village

Te Wairoa
Wairere Falls

626

Tarawera Falls

Mt Tarawera
1111
1024

358

Waiohau

Tamaki Maori Village

Tumunui

Earthquake Flat
597

Hot Water Beach

380

431

Guthrie

Tumunui Hill
761

Waimangu

448

Waiohau

Ngakuru

Rainbow Mountain
Scenic Reserve

Waimangu
Volcanic Valley

Waimangu Scenic Res

L Okaro

Lake Rotomahana

506

Pokairoa

457

Waikite Valley

Rainbow Mountain

Waikite
826

Waiotapu Village

Rerewhakaaitu

472

Kopuriki

Waiotapu

Wai-o-tapu Thermal Wonderland

541

453

Horomanga

205

Te Kopia Scenic Reserve

Wharepaina

17

Ngatamawahine Stream

930

TE UREWERA
NATIONAL PARK

Parekarangi

Reporoa

470

425

Galatea
Covell Estate Wines

945

825

Golden Springs

Tokiaminga Stm

Wharekaunga Stm

546

546

Kaingaroa Forest

20

Maori Cave Art

Murupara

Joins map 164

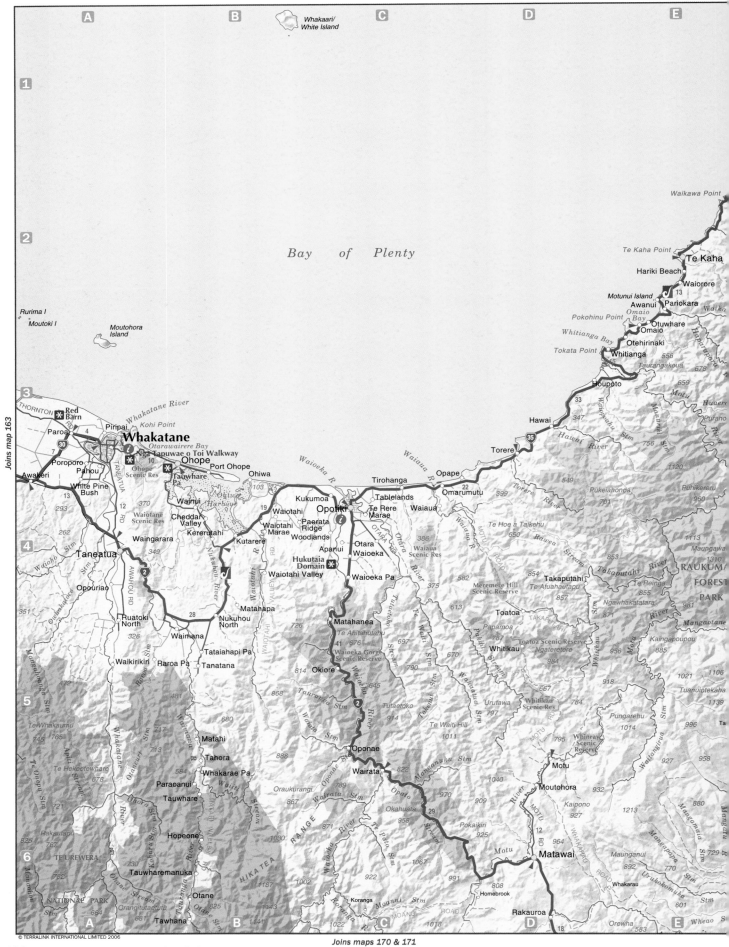

Bay of Plenty

Whakaari/White Island

Waikawa Point

Te Kaha Point

Te Kaha
Hariki Beach
Waiorore
Motunui Island
Awanui   Pariokara
Pokohinu Point   Omaio   Otuwhare
Omaio Bay   Omaio
Whitianga Bay   Otehirinaki
Tokata Point   Whitianga   556
Tautangakoua   678
Houpoto   859
33   Huarei
Hawai   347   Purahou
35   Hawai River   756   Puhikereru
Torere   549   960
Torere   Pukelahonda
Opape   701   1120
Omarumutu   399   707
22
Tirohanga   Te Hoe a Taikehu   1113
Tablelands   650   853   Maungawa   1310
Opotiki   Waiaua   854   Te Afuahaulapu   857   RAUKUMA
Te Rere   386   Meremere Hill   857   FOREST
Marae   Scenic Reserve   Te Reinga   855   PARK
Waioeka   582   Toatoa   871   Mangaotane
375   613   Papamoa   Ngawhakatatara   981
Waioeka Pa   Whitikau   787   Toatoa Scenic Reserve   956   Kaingapoupou
676   Ngateretere   984   885
697   670   918   Tuanuiotekaha   1106
Matahanea   790   667   Whitikau   1021   1139
41   Waioeka Gorge   Urutawa   Scenic Res   784   Ta
Scenic Reserve   Scenic Res   797   Pungarehu
814   Okiore   645   Whinray   1014   996
868   914   Te Waiti Hill   795   Scenic Reserve   927   958
680   1011   1040   Motu   1213   880
Oponae   822   Moutohora   932   Mangapapa   770
Wairata   970   Kaipono   Maunganui   729
867   789   Opato   909   927   892   601
1090   Wairata   958   29   Matawai   Whakarau
Okahuata   Pokaikiri   12   964   Maunganui
871   922   925   RD   Manaanui Stm   Uruokomuha   Stm
1002   991   Motu   808   Matawai   Orewha
1443   1018   Homebrook   18   583
Koranga   Rakauroa

THORNTON
Red Barn
Paroa   Piripai   Whakatane River
4   Kohi Point
Whakatane   Otarawairere Bay
30   10   Ohope   Nga Tapuwae o Toi Walkway
7   Poroporo   Pahou   Ohope   Port Ohope
Awakeri   White Pine   Scenic Res   Ohiwa
Bush   Tauwhare   Pa   Ohiwa Harbour
13   12   Wainui   103   Waioeka R.
293   370   Cheddar   19   Kukumoa
262   Waiotane   Valley   Waiotahi   Opotiki
Scenic Res   Kererutahi   Waiotahi   Paerata
Waingarara   Kutarere   Marae   Ridge
349   Woodlands   Otara
Taneatua   Aparui   Waioeka
2   Hukutaia
Opouriao   Domain   Waiotahi Valley
351   Ruatoki   Matahapa   726
North   Nukuhou
28   North   Matahanea
326   Waimana
472   Waikirikiri   Raroa Pa   Tanatana
Matahi   Tataiahapi Pa   814
481   Tahora
Te Whakaumu   Whakarae Pa   888
745   765   584
Paraoanui   Tauwhare
721   Te Hekeotewhare
678   Hopeone   RANGE
Te Onepu Stm   730   1090
825   767   Tauwharemanuka   HIKATEA
Hakautapu   782   1187
TE UREWERA
NATIONAL PARK   Otane   1002
664   Orangitutaetutu   825   922
681   Tawhana   1441
1443

Joins map 163

© TERRALINK INTERNATIONAL LIMITED 2006

0   15 kilometres

F   G   H   J   K

1

Cape Runaway
Lottin Pt
(Wakatiri)
Midway Pt
378
474
510
460
Matakaoa Pt
Whangaparaoa
Bay
Potaka
Wharekahika River
Whangaparaoa
210
240
Mohai Stream
Oueha Stm
Hicks Bay
Haupara Pt
Otamaroa
27
Hicks Bay
Orete Point
Waihau Bay
Waihau
Bay
Oruati Beach
12
istoric Anglican Church
Raukokore
402
396
338
744
867
Pukeamaru
Scenic Reserve
673
Te Araroa
TE ARAROA
Horoera
Horoera Point
Papatea
Bay
Papatea
289
17
480
Waikura
492
990
Karakatuwhero
Te Waha-o-Rerekohu
(Largest Pohutukawa Tree)
384
21
EAST CAPE RD
Whanarua Bay
488
Mangairoa
495
762
Kokomuka
553
Tapatu
254
Awatere
Awatere River
East Cape
eheretaunga
686
785
Pohueroro Stm
Te Kumi
580
Kopuapounamu
666
23
393
368
313
East Cape Lighthouse
Kaikoura
684
810
Taumaoteawhengaroa
1166
781
255
Te Hue
305
Maraehara
329
East Island
(Whangakeno Island)
565
ahore
836
er
River
766
1258
1413
1185
539
Maraehara
382
942
944
Ahiapurua
1173
Komapara
1005
467
476
Poroporo River
312
Rangitukia
1036
Potts Peak
1405
1618
Pungarehunui
1013
Ohinepoutea
Pakihiroa
TAPUAEROA
539
VALLEY
Whakawhitira
19
Kakariki
Wairoa
339
Waiapu River
Tikitiki
St Mary's Church
Waiomatatini
Port Awanui
Whakariki Point
1109
1320
1475
1106
678
387
Takamore
RD
320
Reporua
1156
Puketauhinu
Hikurangi
1752
1272
Rotokautuku
Papawera
3
Ruatoria
Mahora
Kaimoho Point
RAUKUMARA
1387
Aorangi
Whakapourangi
Pohatukura
Tuparoa
FOREST
1426
Aorangiwai
Scenic Reserve
1089
Hiruharama
484
Otuauri
507
PARK
1173
RANGE
Aorangi
Waikohu Stm
928
1467
1186
26
Tutuwhinau
506
Whareponga
1253
1294
910
35
Kopuaroa
1342
Mata River
710
Thungia
420
Takapau
Ohineakai
4
997
Ihungia
Whakoau
537
Waipiro Bay
Waipiro Bay
1325
910
523
Koutunui Head
1439
MATA
Te Puia
Springs
Waimahuru Bay
Scenic Reserve
927
728
473
11
520
Moutahiauru I
Huiarua
Mangatarata
563
Maungaroa
539
Hautanoa
Waima
Te Ariuru
Koutunui Point
ARNDALE
RD
964
Wairangi
Tauwhareparae
689
ROAD
Tuatini
Te Puka
5
Arowhana
Ongaruru
Tokomaru Bay
976
Tokomaru Bay
671
1078
615
470
Hikuwai
Mawhai Point
1073
1010
597
36
Nuhiti Q
Scenic Res
533
Waipare
Scenic Res
Motuhina I
829
998
637
489
Arero
Anaura Bay
Scenic Res
Anaura Bay
531
Puakato
675
443
Motuoroi I
Anaura Bay
Walking Track
683
The Three Bridges
282
Tauwhareparae
Mangatokerau R
555
Mangatokerau
473
Huanui
Parariki Stm
601
Te Kaho
Mangatuna
Kaiaua
Marau Pt
Pareheka
Scenic Res
479
Whakakiauanga
Kaiaua Bay
428
Waipage
Hokoroa
Wharekaka
6
The Five
Bridges
Karaka Bay
Whatatutu
439
Takapau
Uawa River
Tolaga Bay
Tolaga Bay
Tolaga Bay Wharf
Kanakanaia
472
Manga
430
Paremata
Hauiti
Pourewa I
Cook's Cove
Walking Track
Mangaheia

F   G   H   J   K

PACIFIC
OCEAN

INK INTERNATIONAL LIMITED 2006

Joins map 171

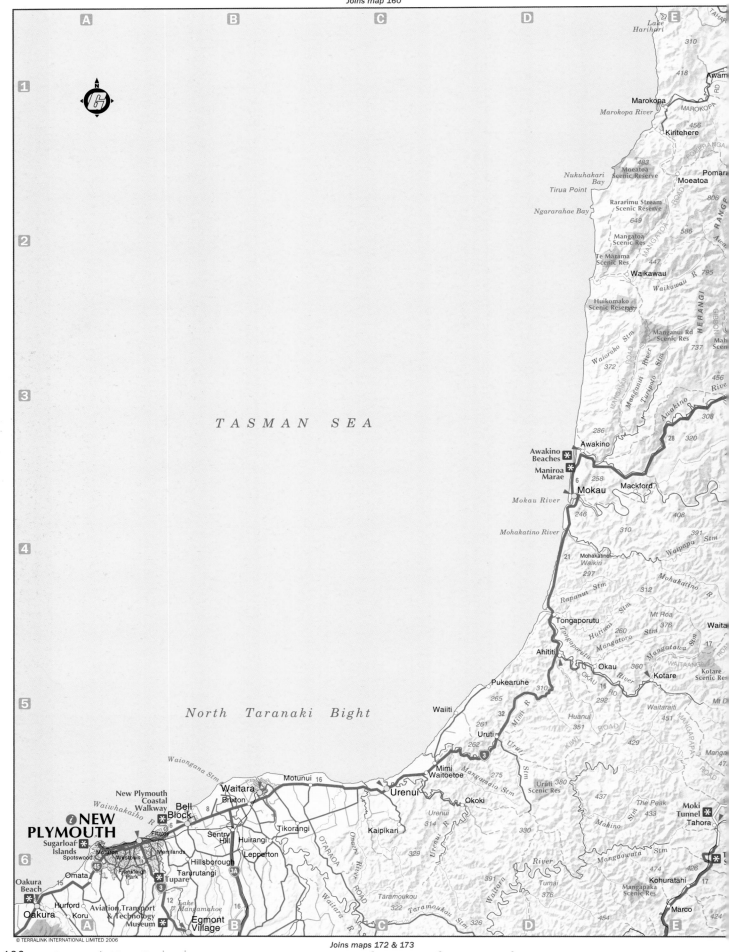

TASMAN SEA

North Taranaki Bight

Marokopa
Marokopa River
MAROKOPA
310
418
Awam
456
Kiritehere

Nukuhakari Bay
Moeatoa
Scenic Reserve
483
649
Pomara
Moeatoa
806
Tirua Point
Rararimu Stream
Scenic Reserve
Ngararahae Bay
Mangatoa
Scenic Res
586

Te Marama
Scenic Res
447
Waikawau
795

Huikomako
Scenic Reserve
Waiorako Stm
Manganui Rd
Scenic Res
737
Mah
Scen

372
Turipaho Stm
456
Rive

286
308
Awakino
28
320
Awakino
Beaches
258
Maniroa
Marae
6
Mokau
Mackford
Mokau River
246

Mohakatino River
310
408

21
Mohakatino
Waikiri
297
312
Mohakatino R.
Wapapa Stm
391 Stm

Rapanui Stm
260
376
Mt Roa
Hutiwai Stm
Tongaporutu
Tongaporutu R.
Mangatoro
Waita
Ahititi
Okau
360
Okau River
Kotare
292
Kotare
Scenic Res
Pukearuhe
310
16
Waiiti
265
Mimi R.
Huanui
351
Waitaraiti
451
Mt D
Uruti
32
261
Uruti Stm
429
Manga
262
3
Mimi
Waitoetoe
275
Uruti 380
Scenic Res
The Peak
433
Moki
Tunnel
Motunui 16
Urenui
Mangapapa Road
437
Tahora
Waitara
New Plymouth
Coastal
Walkway
Brixton
Okoki
Urenui R.
314
330
Bell
Block
8
Tikorangi
Kaipikari
Makino Stm
NEW
PLYMOUTH
Waiwhakaiho R.
Sentry
Hill
Huirangi
6
Fitzroy
Merrilands
Lepperton
Otaraoa Road
329
391
River
Mangaowata Stm
474
Kohuratahi
426
Sugarloaf
Islands
Spotswood
45
Westown
Frankleigh
Park
Tupare
9A
Tarurutangi
Hillsborough
Onaero River Road
Waitara R.
Taramoukou R.
322
Taramoukou Stm
326
Mangapaka
Scenic Res
454
424
Oakura
Beach
15
Omata
3
12 *Lake Mangamahoe*
16
Marco
Oakura
Hurford
Koru
Aviation, Transport
& Technology
Museum
Egmont
Village

North Island

© TERRALINK INTERNATIONAL LIMITED 2006

Scale 1:410 000

0   15 kilometres

F   Te Koraha

Piripiri
Cave
e Anga   Piripiri   446
Mangapohue
Natural   559   299
Marokopa   Bridge   Waitomo Valley   Woodlyn
Falls   Waitomo   Park
River   Walkway   37   Woodlyn
ANGA   Aranui &   Park
Tawarau   Ruakuri Caves   7   Hangatiki
River   Glow Worm Cave   198   Te Kumi
Cathedral Cavern   12
Waipuna   Lost World Cave   i   Museum
Scenic Res   Oparure   of Caves

Kikooterangi   476   Te Kuiti   i
aohae   401   Mangatea
Ngapaenga   398
434   391
Waitanguru   Mairoa   274   11
Tanehopuwai   Waiteti   346
410   331   364   23
Mangaotaki   404   Eight Mile   Puketutu
Mangaotaki R   361   Junction   407
383   3   11   356   402
Te Mapara   378   Kopaki
Piopio   8
255   Aratoro   411   RD
Paemako   356   Mangapehi   11
294   290   12   Mangapehi
Aria   MOKAUITI   RD   Benneydale
234   448   4   Porootarao   571
324   430   611
Puketehi   642
Scenic Res   564   Mapiu   Waimiha
465   608   Tangitu
Waitaka   719   Waihuka
Scenic Reserve   Scenic Res
498   17
Mangatupoto   408
Otangiwai   Ongarue   544
Matiere   12   Te Koura   569
Nihoniho   Tuhua   Okahukura   771   26

Ohura   494   564
Te Araohakere   551   Mahoe
565   323   460   563
556   Mangaparo   418   Taumarunui
Waiaraia   500   i   Taumaruiti
Scenic Res   Otunui   Manunui
Tatu   Aukopae   13   Tunakotekote
Tokirima   27   Piriaka
Heao   Te Whakarae   464
Koiro   Hikumutu   Kakahi
Opatu   Te Maire   Tutumai   14
Kirikau   632   462
439   Kawautahi   Owhango
Tawhata   Te Ruahine   Porere
518   Scenic Reserve   575
393   Pukerata   585   Ojo
585   529   Konini   Hukapapa
Whakahoro   Scenic Res   Mansons
Maungaroa   Retaruke   Kaitieke   Siding 42nd Traverse
Raurimu
Raurimu
Spiral

A   B   C   D   E

1
Mangapehi   540   486   Horokino   + 586   393   12   692   730   652   Lake Ohaki
Benneydale   22   560   Barryville   470   Titiraupenga   Mangakino   512   777   808   571
Porootarao   582   Tiroa   Pureora   1042   Arataki   500   Mokai   897   618   680   706   Orakei Korako   Hidden Valley
611   571   Piropiro   Maraeroa   705   543   565   634   746   Te Pouwhakatutu   31   Wairakei Thermal Valley   657   455
544   408   Waimiha   Okauaka Stm   598   Pureora 1165   13   705   524   23   Oruanui   Ngangiho   575   472   Aratiat
2   PUREORA   Ketemaringi   953   892   730   595   Whangamata   19   ROAD   733   Nukuhau   591 16   635   Taupo   Aratiatia   Lake Rotokawe
FOREST PARK   939   1088   839   Tihoi   579   WHANGAMATA   647   POIHIPI   794   638   Wairakei Terraces   10   Craters of the Moon   Roto
528   517   905   885   Waihora   585   592   707   Acacia Bay   Wairakei Village   Volcanic Activity Centre
666   750   662   895   Whanganui   477   Maori rock carvings   661   Huka Falls   Huka Falls
Mangakahu Valley   991   675   695   564   Waihaha   472   Mine Pt   Tuhingamata   16   Wharewaka   631
1042   Te Hiapo   950   Ruahine   801   Lake Taupo   Whakamoenga Point   Rainbow Point   Waipahihi

Lake Taupo
(Taupomoana)

National Park   Tongariro National Park

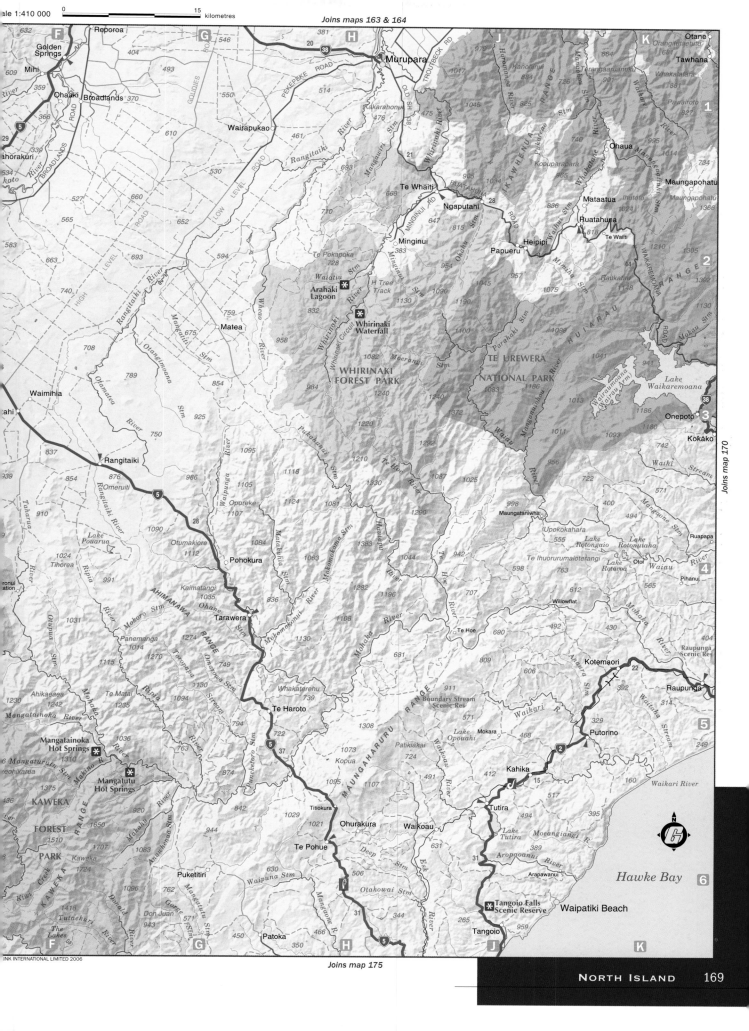

Joins map 170

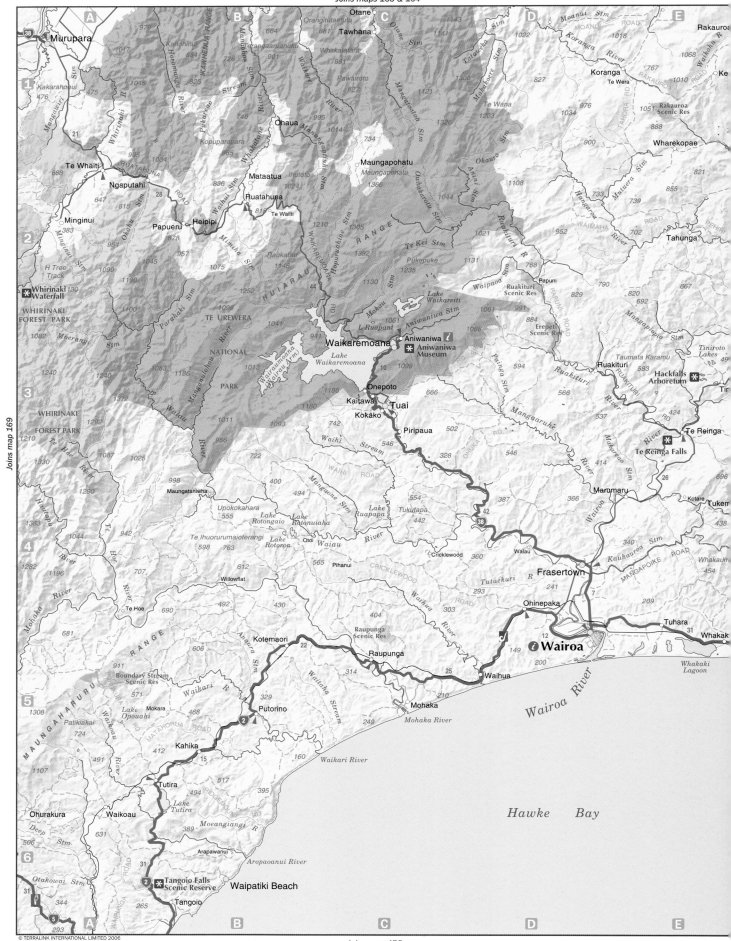

Gregory's New Zealand

North Island

© TERRALINK INTERNATIONAL LIMITED 2006

ale 1:410 000

0   15

kilometres

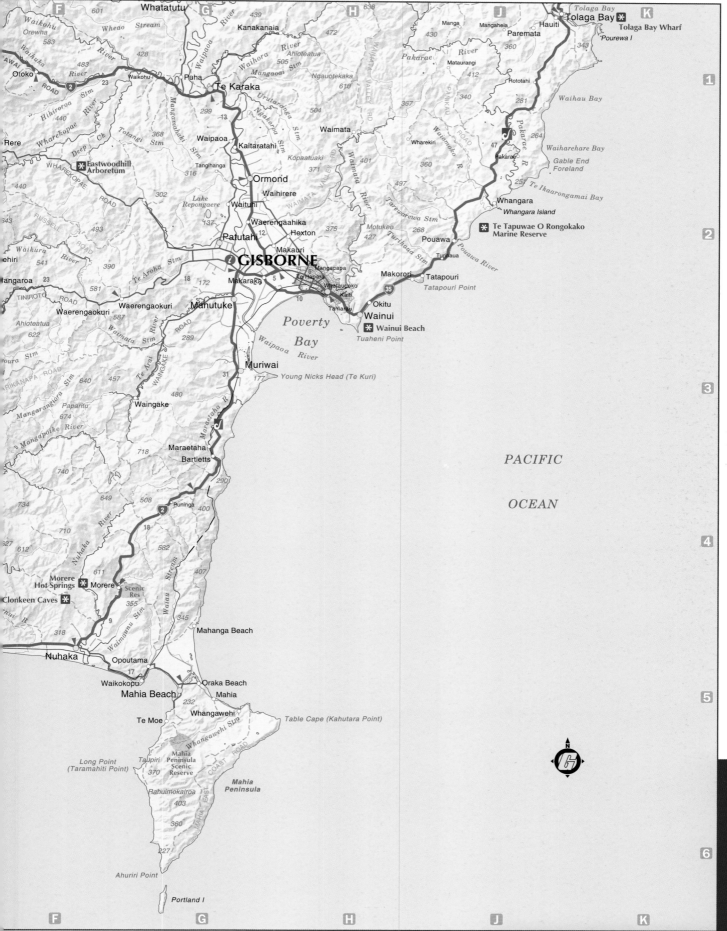

Whatatutu

Orewha

Otoko

Rere

Eastwoodhill
Arboretum

Patutahi

Waerengaokuri

Manutuke

GISBORNE

Makaraka

Poverty
Bay

Muriwai

Young Nicks Head (Te Kuri)

Maraetaha
Bartletts

Puninga

Morere
Hot Springs   Morere

Clonkeen Caves

Nuhaka

Opoutama

Waikokopu

Mahia Beach   Mahia

Oraka Beach

Whangawehi

Te Moe

*Long Point
(Taramahiti Point)*

Mahia
Peninsula
Scenic
Reserve

*Mahia
Peninsula*

Ahuriri Point

Portland I

Te Karaka

Puha

Kanakanaia

Waipaoa

Kaitaratahi

Tanghanga

Ormond

Waihirere

Waituhi

Waerengaahika
Hexton

Makauri

Waimata

Te Hapara

Mahanga Beach

Whangara
Whangara Island

Te Tapuwae O Rongokako
Marine Reserve

Pouawa

Tupuraua

Makorori   Tatapouri
Tatapouri Point

Okitu

Wainui

Wainui Beach

Tuaheni Point

Tolaga Bay
Hauiti
Paremata
Tolaga Bay Wharf
Pourewa I

Manga
Mangaheia

Matyaurangi

Rototahi

Waihau Bay

Waiharehare Bay

*Gable End
Foreland*

Te Ikaarongamai Bay

Pakarae

PACIFIC

OCEAN

Table Cape (Kahutara Point)

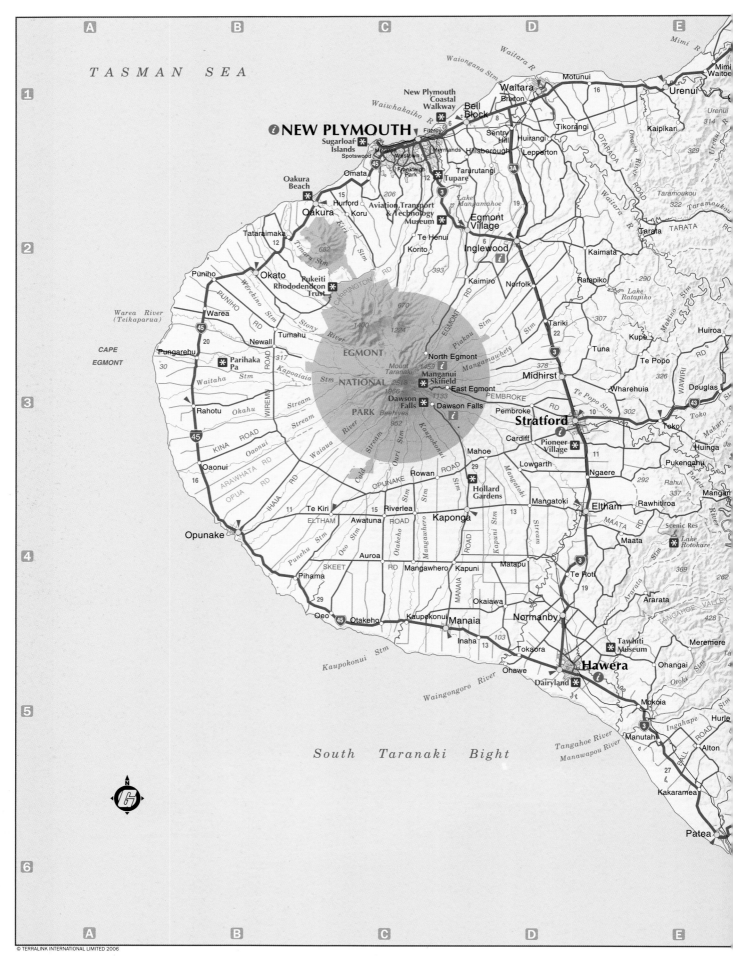

North Island

Scale 1:410 000

0   15 kilometres

Huanui 351

Tatu

Aukopae

Te Whakarae

Hikumutu
Te Maire

Piriaka

Kakahi

Forgotten
World
Highway

Mangapapa 473

Tokirima

Koiro

Puheki 434

Opatu

Kirikau

Kawautahi

Porere 575

Owhango

Ōio

The Peak 433

Moki
Tunnel ✳
Tahora

Tangarakau
Scenic Reserve

Heao

Ohura

Tawhata

Te Ruahine
Scenic Reserve
Pukerata

Taungawha

Konini
Scenic Res

Kaitieke

Hukapapa

Mansons
Siding

Tahora
Saddle ✳
Kohuratahi

Tangarakau

Whakahoro

Maungaroa

Retaruke

Rotokahu
Scenic Res

Retaruke
Scenic Res

Retaruke
Upper

Raurimu
Spiral ✳

Marco

Whangamomona

Te Mata

WHANGANUI

Riamaki
(Upper Ruatiti)

Pairawahipi
Scenic Reserve

National Park

Pohokura

Waiamaru

Riarlaki

Ruatiti

Waikune

Te Wera

Pohokura Knob

Bridge to
Nowhere ✳

Manearoa

Pehu

Erua

Huiakama
Strathmore
Makahu

NATIONAL

Paritea

Tangahoe

Murumuru

Orautoha

Pokaka

Horopito

Tututawa

Puniwhakau

PARK

Parinui

Ramanui

Piraruhe

Tohunga
Junction

MATEMATEAONGA

Taurakawa

RANGE

Puteore

Whakatina

Manganui o te Ao

Ngatauhao Ameku

Pipipi

Makaranui

Raetihi

Ohakune

Omoana

Takou

Moeroa

Karikarirua

Mangaone Stm

Maungarau

Poutahi

Kiekie

Mangaeturoa

Otiranui

Moeawatea

Rotokohu
Scenic Res

Puraroto

Tuanuiotakou

Whaharangi

Taunoko

Pipiriki

Kaukore Stm

Waipuna

Tanupara

Papahaua

Taumatatahi

Makakaho

Rakaumahi

Jerusalem

Ngarakauwhakarara

Ngamatapouri

Makakaho
Junction

Ranana

Patukino
Scenic Res

Tawhiwhi

Te Tuhi
Junction

Powaiaunga
Scenic Reserve

Matahiwi

Te Konia

Maukuku

Lake
Mangawhio

Orangimea

Kakatahi

Pukekiwi

Kohi

Mangawhio

Puao

Paparangi

WHANGANUI
NATIONAL
PARK

Koriniti Pa

Operiki Pa

Pitangi
Scenic Res

Tauakira

Maewa

Pukewharariki

Waverley
Ngutuwera

Rangitatau

Okiwa

Otawaki
Scenic Res

Whakaihuwhaka

Wharemata

Waitotara

Nukumaru

Maxwell

Kai-Iwi

Pungarehu

Parikino

Mangamahu

Kaiwhaiki

Brunswick

LINK INTERNATIONAL LIMITED 2006

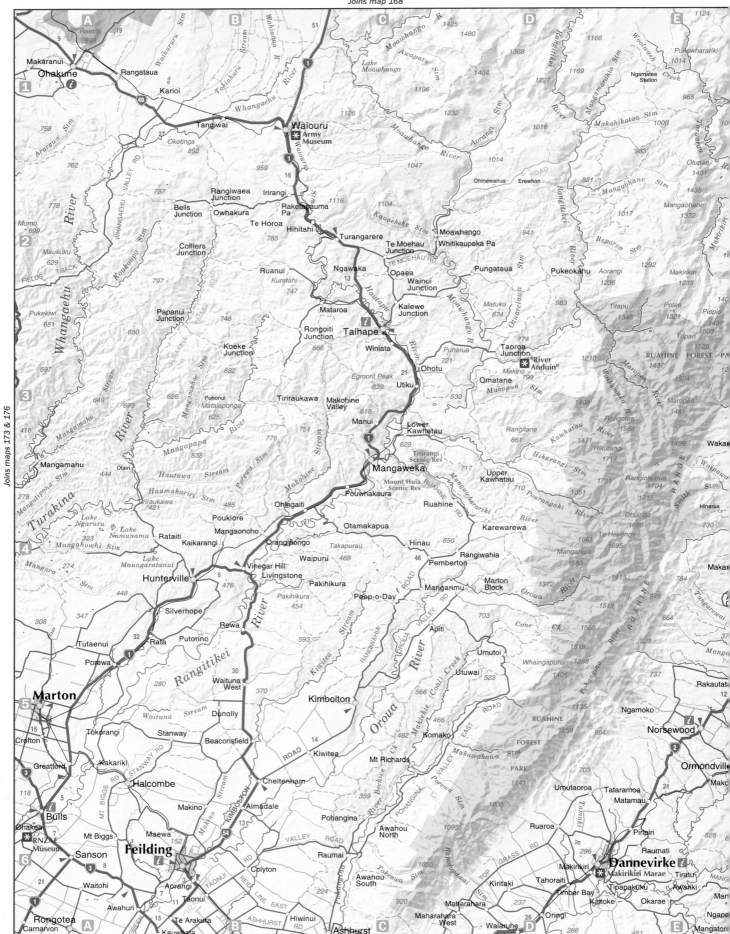

Gregory's New Zealand

North Island

Joins maps 173 & 176

© TERRALINK INTERNATIONAL LIMITED 2006

ale 1:410 000

0   15
kilometres

F   **G**   **H**   **J**   **K**

Tangoio
Whirinaki
Eskdale
Bay View
Keteketerau
Westshore
Bluff Hill
NAPIER
Marineland
Poraiti
Puketapu
Moteo
Otatara Pa Historic Reserve
Omahu
Twyford
Pernel Fruitworld
Clive
Haumoana
Fernhill
Woolwich
Whakatu
Te Awanga
Insalata Verde
Flaxmere
Tomoana
Mangateretere
Clifton
Ngatarawa
HASTINGS
Maraekakaho
Bridge Pa
Arataki Honey
Gannet Colony
Longlands
Havelock North
Pukahu
Growers Market
Pakipaki
Kereru
Te Mata Peak
Cape Kidnappers
Te Hauke
Poukawa
Ocean Beach
Te Aute
Lake Poukawa
Tikokino
Pukehou
Waimarama
Argyll East
Bare I (Motukura)
Ongaonga
Otane
Ruataniwha
Patangata
Elsthorpe
Waipawa
Kairakau Beach
Maharakeke
Hatuma
Mangakuri Beach
Waipukurau
Omakere
Wanstead
Queroa
Pourerere
Flemington
Paoanui Point
Aramoana
Wallingford
Blackhead
Te Uri
Blackhead Point

Hawke Bay

KAWEKA FOREST PARK

PACIFIC OCEAN

Tukituki River

LINK INTERNATIONAL LIMITED 2006

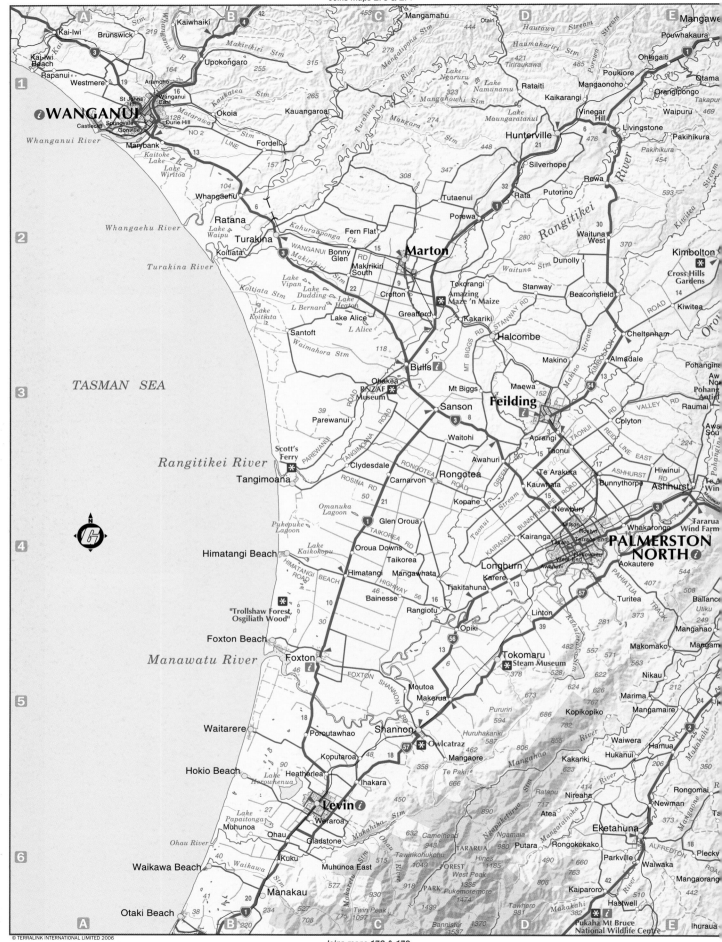

TASMAN SEA

WANGANUI

Rangitikei River

Manawatu River

Ohau River

PALMERSTON NORTH

Feilding

Marton

Hunterville

Levin

Foxton

Shannon

North Island

ale 1:410 000

0   15   kilometres

Titirangi Scenic Res
F   G   H   J   K

Upper Kawhatau
Ruahine
Hinau   650
Pemberton   46   Rangiwahia
Mangarimu   Marton Block
eep-o-Day   703   Apiti
Umutoi
Utuwai   523
Komako   466
chards
Maharahara West
Woodville
Hopelands
hata   Ngawapurua
Mangatainoka
Tui Brewery
hiatua
Ngaturi
Kaitawa
Mangaone
Pori
Mt Marchant   578
Haunui
redton
Castlehill

Karewarewa
Ruahine
FOREST PARK
Umutaoroa   Tataramoa
Matamau
Ruaroa   Piripiri
Makirikiri   Raumati
Dannevirke
Makirikiri Marae   Tiratu
Tahoraiti   Tipapakuku
Timber Bay   Kaitoke   Okarae
Oringi   Awariki
Waiaruhe
Papatawa
Kumeroa   Waitahora
Kohinui
Coonoor
Horoeka   Waimiro
Korora
Makuri   Puketoi
Mangatiti
Kohiku
Rakaunui
Tiraumea   Waihoki Valley
Mara
Owahanga

Tikokino
Blackburn   Springhill
Ongaonga   Argyll East
Ashcott   Ruataniwha
Takapau   Waipawa
Rakautatahi   Maharakeke   Hatuma   Waipukurau
Ngamoko   Whenuahau   Hatuma Lake
Norsewood   Kopua
Makotuku   Ormondville
Whetukura   Flemington   Wanstead
Mangahei
Mangatoro   Te Uri   Wallingford
Ngapaeruru   Mangatuna
Ngapaeruru Scenic Reserve   Mangaorapa   Porangahau
Motea   Toi Flat   Homebush
Waipatiki   Weber   Ti Tree Point
Waihi Falls   Wimbledon
Waione   Herbertville   Cape Turnagain
Kaituna
Pongaroa   Akaroa   Akitio

PACIFIC OCEAN

NK INTERNATIONAL LIMITED 2006

NORTH ISLAND   177

Joins map 175

TASMAN

SEA

Cook Strait

Wellington - Picton Ferry

Kapiti Island

Mana Island

Otaki Beach
Otaki
Manakau
Te Horo Beach
Te Horo
Peka Peka
Nga Manu Nature Reserve
Waikanae Beach
Waikanae
Otaihanga
Paraparaumu Beach
Car Museum
Lindale Centre
Paraparaumu
Raumati Beach
Raumati South
Queen Elizabeth Park
"Pelennor Fields"
Paekakariki
McKays Crossing
Pukerua Bay
Te Rewarewa Point
Plimmerton
Titahi Bay
Karehana Bay
Pauatahanui
Judgeford "River Anduin"
Battle Hill
Porirua
PATAKA
Colonial Knob
Pipinui Point
Tawa
Redwood
Ohariu Valley
Oharu Bay
Makara Beach
Ohau Point
Makara
Cape Terawhiti
Oteranga Bay
Outlook Hill
Mt Misery
Quartz Hill
WELLINGTON
Eastbourne
"Outer Shire"
Wellington Zoo
"Dunharrow"
Red Rocks Seal Colony
Sinclair Head
Pencarrow Head
Fitzroy Bay
Baring Head
Seal Colony
Turakirae Head

"Isengard Gardens" "Orc Tree"
"Rohan River"
Birchville
Totara Park
Brown Owl
Te Marua
Maymorn
Upper Hutt
Mangaroa
Silver Stream Railway Museum
Trentham
Silverstream
Pinehaven
Whitemans Valley
Stokes Valley
"Helm's Deep"
"Minas Tirith"
Belmont Regional Park
Haywards
Avalon
Naenae
Waterloo
Lower Hutt
Petone Settlers Museum
Gracefield
Wainuiomata
East Harbour Regional Park
Days Bay

Reikorangi
Maungakotukutuku Scenic Reserve
Cloustonville
Staglands Wildlife Reserve
"Rivendell" "Fords of Isen"
Kaitoke
Kaitoke Regional Park
"Lothlorien" "Gladden Fields"
Woodside
Mt Dick Lookout
Waiohine Gorge
Matarawa
Greytown
Morrisons Bush
Featherston
Fell Museum
Tauherenikau
Battersea
Kaiwaiwai
Rimutaka Incline Walk
Cross Creek
Pigeon Bush
Lake Wairarapa
Martinborough
Dyerville
Kahutara
Pahautea Pukio
Kohunui Maori Settlement
Tuhitarata
Ruakokoputuna
Pirinoa
Whangaimoana
Ocean Beach
Lake Ferry
Lake Onoke
Palliser Bay
"Dimholt Road"
Putangirua Pinnacles
Whatarangi
Ngawi
White Rock
White Rock Station
Te Kaukau (Mungaroa)
Cape Palliser (Matakitakiakupe)
Nga-Ra-a-Kupe, Seal Colony, Lighthouse

TARARUA
FOREST PARK
Holdsworth
Mt Holdsworth
RIMUTAKA RANGE
FOREST PARK
AORANGI RANGE
FOREST PARK

North Island

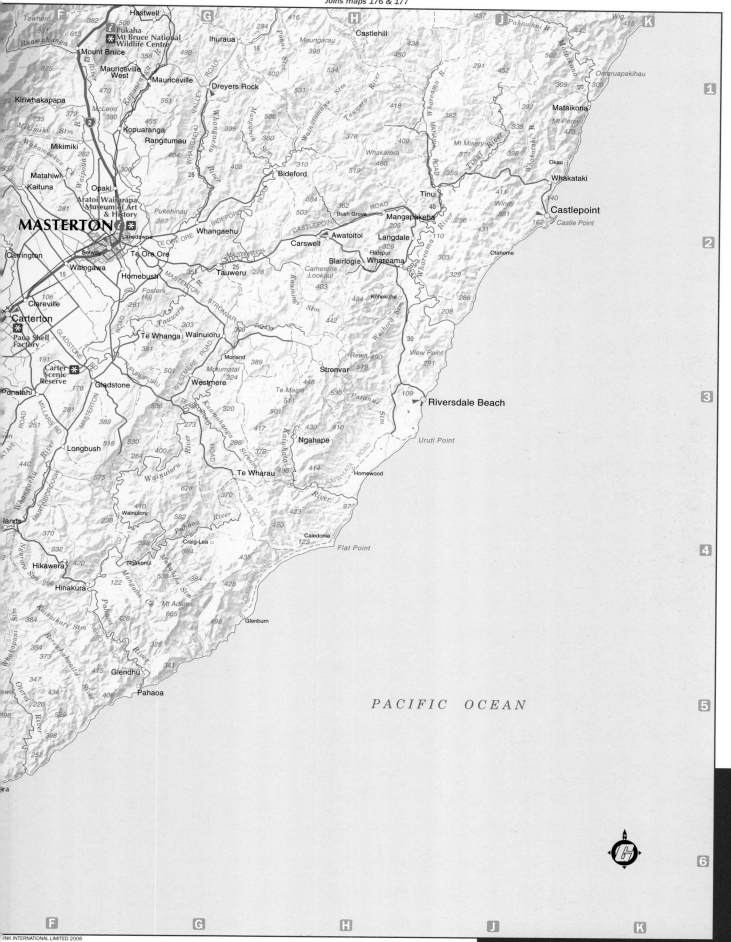

Scale 1:410 000

0   15 kilometres

PACIFIC OCEAN

INK INTERNATIONAL LIMITED 2006

Scale 1:20 000

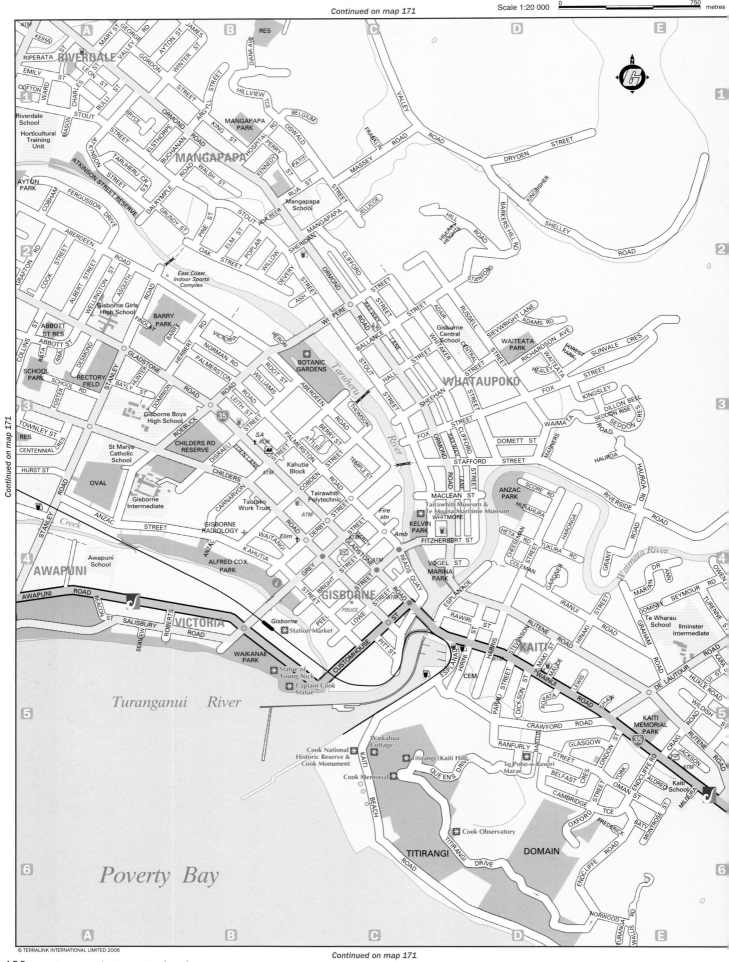

Gisborne

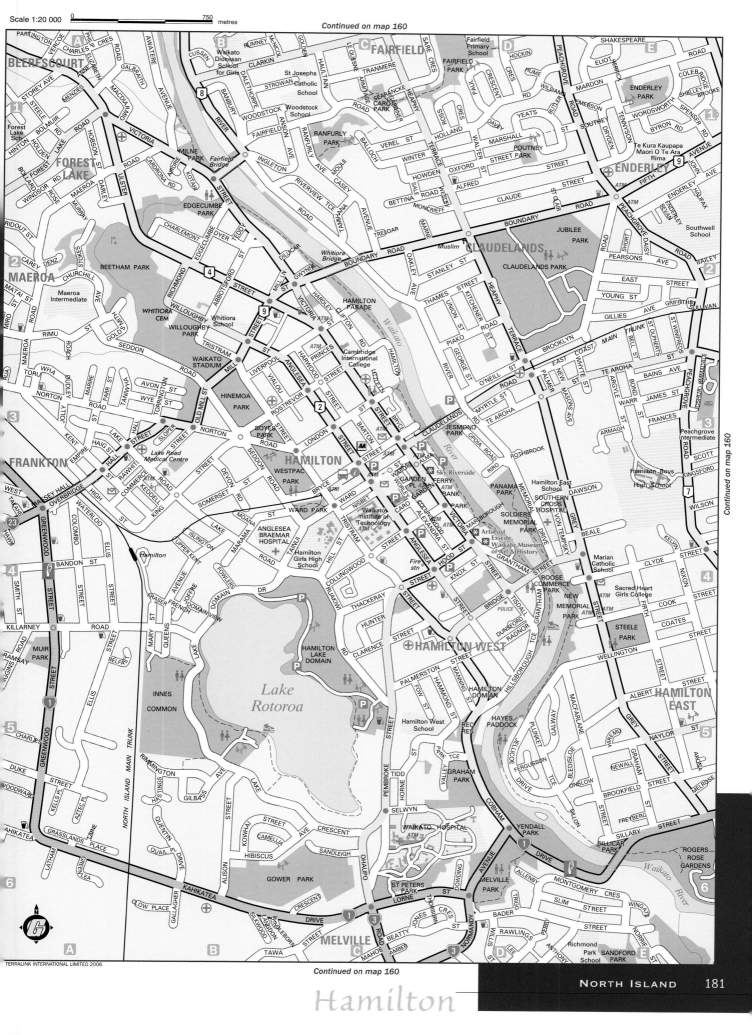

Scale 1:20 000

750 metres

BEERESCOURT

FOREST LAKE

MAEROA

FRANKTON

FAIRFIELD

ENDERLEY

CLAUDELANDS

HAMILTON

HAMILTON WEST

HAMILTON EAST

Lake Rotoroa

MELVILLE

TERRALINK INTERNATIONAL LIMITED 2006

Hamilton

Scale 1:20 000

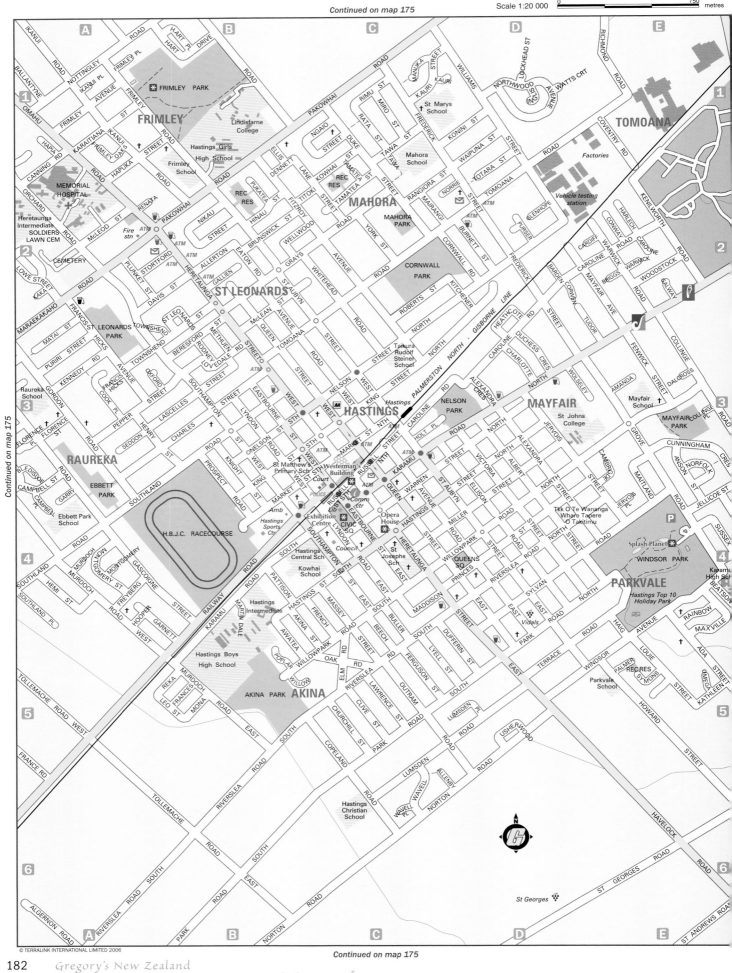

Hastings

Scale 1:20 000

0   750   metres

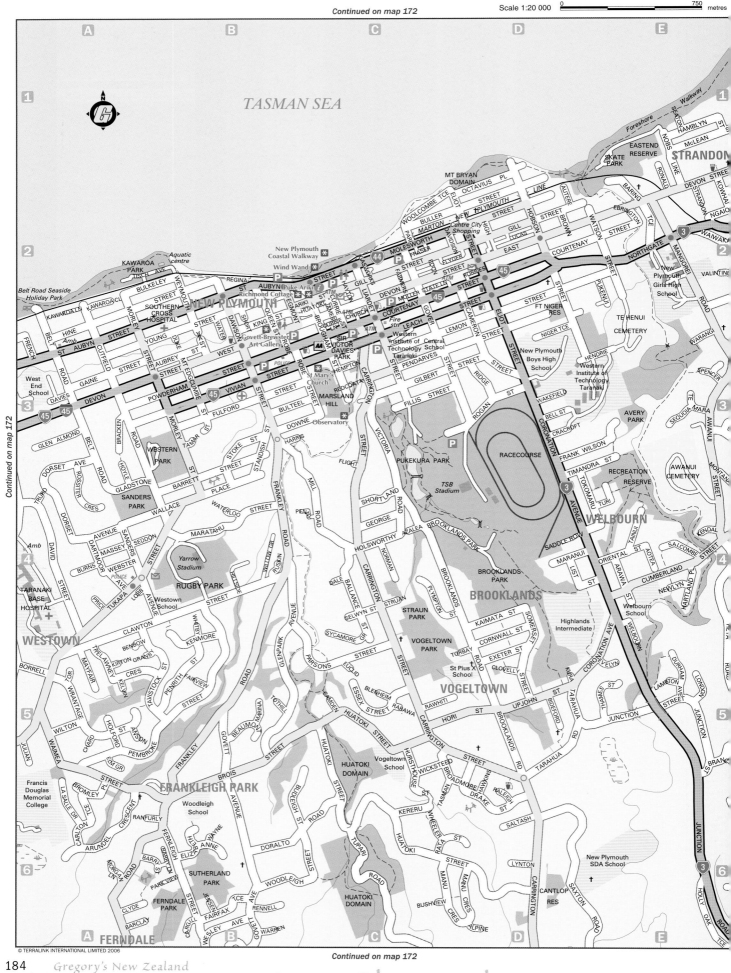

TASMAN SEA

New Plymouth

© TERRALINK INTERNATIONAL LIMITED 2006

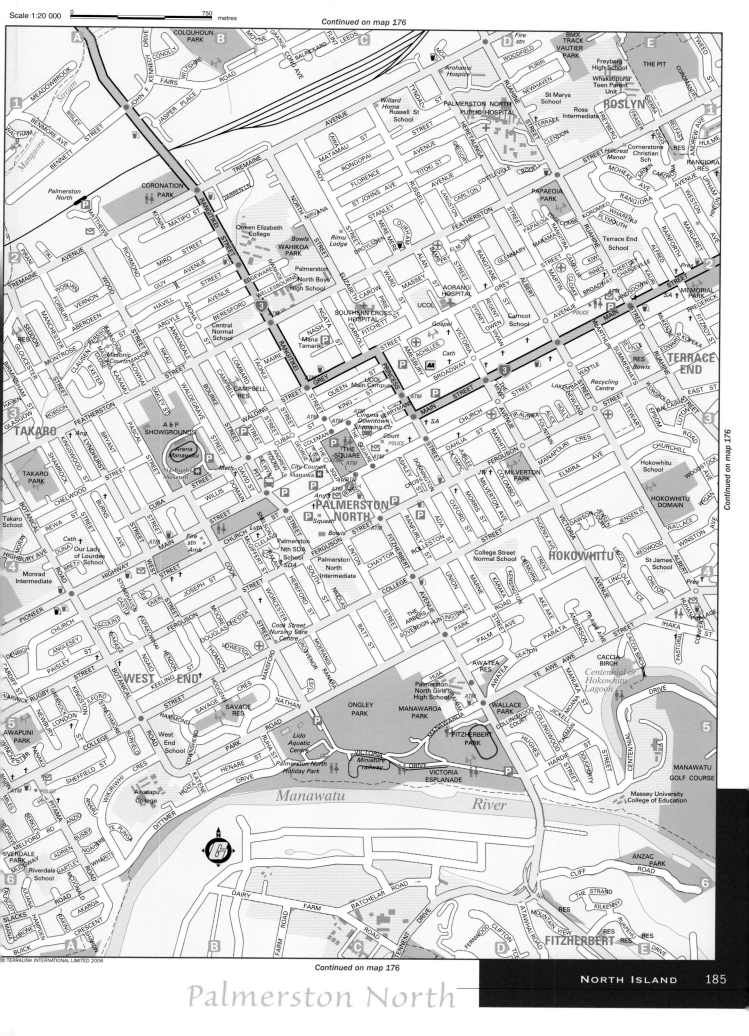

Palmerston North

© TERRALINK INTERNATIONAL LIMITED 2006

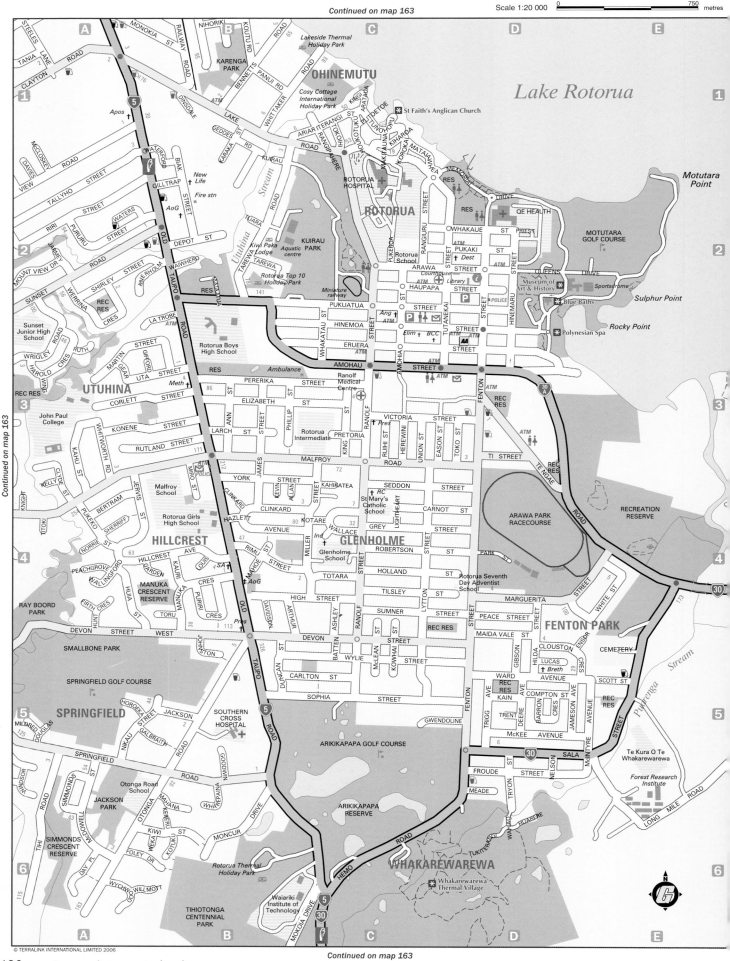

Scale 1:20 000

0   750   metres

Lake Rotorua

Motutara Point

A   **B**   **C**   **D**   **E**

1

MONOKIA ST

NIHORIKI

KOUTU RD

RAILWAY ROAD

KARENGA PARK

BENNETTS ST

PANUI ST

WHITTAKER

Lakeside Thermal Holiday Park

OHINEMUTU

Cosy Cottage International Holiday Park

St Faith's Anglican Church

Apos

WATERFORD

GILLTRAP

BIAK STREET

GEDDES

KARAKA RD

KUIRAU

LAKE

ROAD

ARIARI ITERANGI

RANGIPI AHERE

TOKOHU

KOTUKU

TUNOHO

MAKITAUNAOPU

KIHAROA

KOROKA

MATAWHAEA

2

New Life

Fire stn

AoG

WATERS STREET

DEPOT ST

WAIWHERO

MATAKTUA

TAREWA

TAREWA

Kiwi Paka Lodge

Aquatic centre

KUIRAU PARK

Rotorua Top 10 Holiday Park

Miniature railway

ROTORUA HOSPITAL

WHAKAUE

PUKEROA

Rotorua School

PUKAKI

Dest

ARAWA STREET

HAUPAPA

MEMORIAL DRIVE

RES

RES

QE HEALTH

PRIEST ST

MOTUTARA GOLF COURSE

QUEENS DRIVE

Museum of Art & History

Sportsdrome

Sulphur Point

Rocky Point

Blue Baths

Polynesian Spa

3

Continued on map 163

RES

Ambulance

PERERIKA ST

ELIZABETH ST

PHILLIP ST

LARCH ST

ANN ST

UTUHINA

Meth

CORLETT STREET

KONENE

RUTLAND STREET

John Paul College

Rotorua Boys High School

Ranolf Medical Centre

PUKUATUA

WHAKATAU ST

HINEMOA

ERUERA

AMOHAU STREET

VICTORIA STREET

RUIHI ST

HEREWINI ST

UNION ST

EASON ST

TOKO ST

Pretoria

KING

MALFROY ROAD

FENTON STREET

TE NGAE ROAD

RES

4

Malfroy School

Rotorua Girls High School

HILLCREST

YORK ST

JAMES ST

KEVIN ST

ALLAN ST

CLINKARD

CLINKARD

AVENUE

RIMU STREET

MAHOE

HAZLETT

MIRO ST

KAHIKATEA

SEDDON STREET

St Mary's Catholic School

WALLACE

GREY ST

Glenholme School

ROBERTSON

HOLLAND

TOTARA

TILSLEY

GLENHOLME

LIGHTHEART

CARNOT ST

LYTTON ST

PARK ST

ARAWA PARK RACECOURSE

RECREATION RESERVE

MARGUERITA

WHITE ST

FENTON PARK

CEMETERY

5

PEACHGROVE AVE

WALLINGFORD

HILLCREST AVE

GARDEN

KAURI

PURIRI CRES

TORU

MANUKA CRESCENT RESERVE

RAY BOARD PARK

DEVON STREET WEST

SMALLBONE PARK

SPRINGFIELD GOLF COURSE

SPRINGFIELD

HOROHIA

JACKSON

SOUTHERN CROSS HOSPITAL

AoG

TAUPO ROAD

DUNCAN ST

DAVIDSON ST

ARTHUR ST

HIGH STREET

CARLTON ST

SOPHIA STREET

DEVON

BATTEN ST

ASHLEY ST

RANOLF STREET

WYLIE

McLEAN ST

KOWHAI ST

SUMNER

REC RES

Rotorua Seventh Day Adventist School

MAIDA VALE

CLOUSTON

HILDA ST

LUCAS ST

Breth

WARD AVE

GIBSON ST

COMPTON ST

BARRON CRES

JAMESON AVENUE

PEACE STREET

KAIN ST

TRENT DR

DEERE AVE

SCOTT ST

REC RES

EXSIOR CRES

6

MILDRED ST

DOUGLAS

WINDSOR ROAD

SIMMONDS ST

NIKAU ST

GALBRAITH ST

GOODWIN

SPRINGFIELD ROAD

OTONGA ROAD

Otonga Road School

Jackson Park

MAHANA

KERENU

KIWI ST

WEKA ST

FOLEY DR

WYCHW

WILLMOTT

SIMMONDS CRESCENT RESERVE

Rotorua Thermal Holiday Park

TIHIOTONGA CENTENNIAL PARK

Waiariki Institute of Technology

MONCUR

MOKOIA DRIVE

HEMO ROAD

ARIKIKAPAPA GOLF COURSE

ARIKIKAPAPA RESERVE

GWENDOLINE

FENTON ST

NELSON ST

SALA STREET

McKEE AVENUE

FROUDE ST

TRYON ST

MEADE

WANAKA

HUARERE

TUKITERANGI

WHAKAREWAREWA

Whakarewarewa Thermal Village

Te Kura O Te Whakarewarewa

Forest Research Institute

LONG MILE ROAD

Rotorua

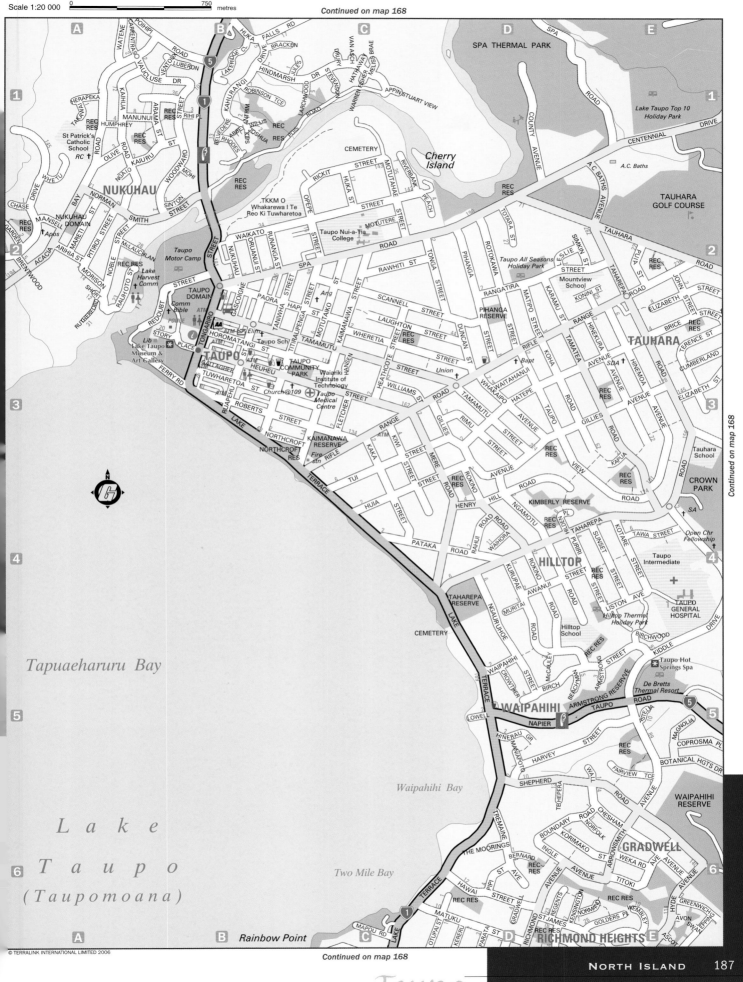

Taupo

Scale 1:20 000

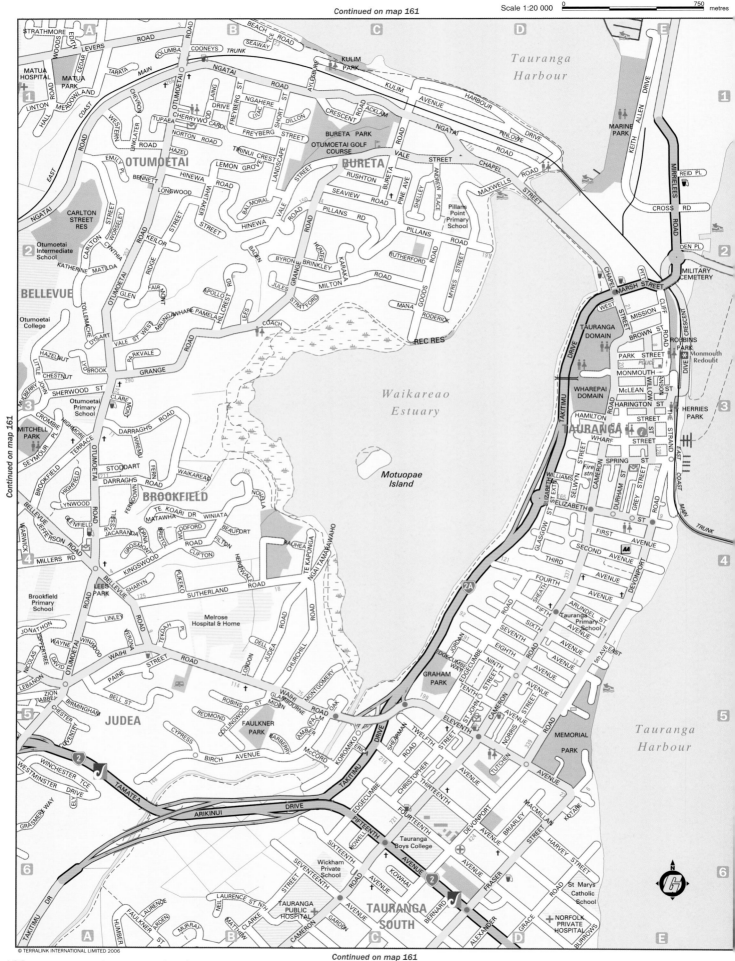

Continued on map 161

© TERRALINK INTERNATIONAL LIMITED 2006

Tauranga

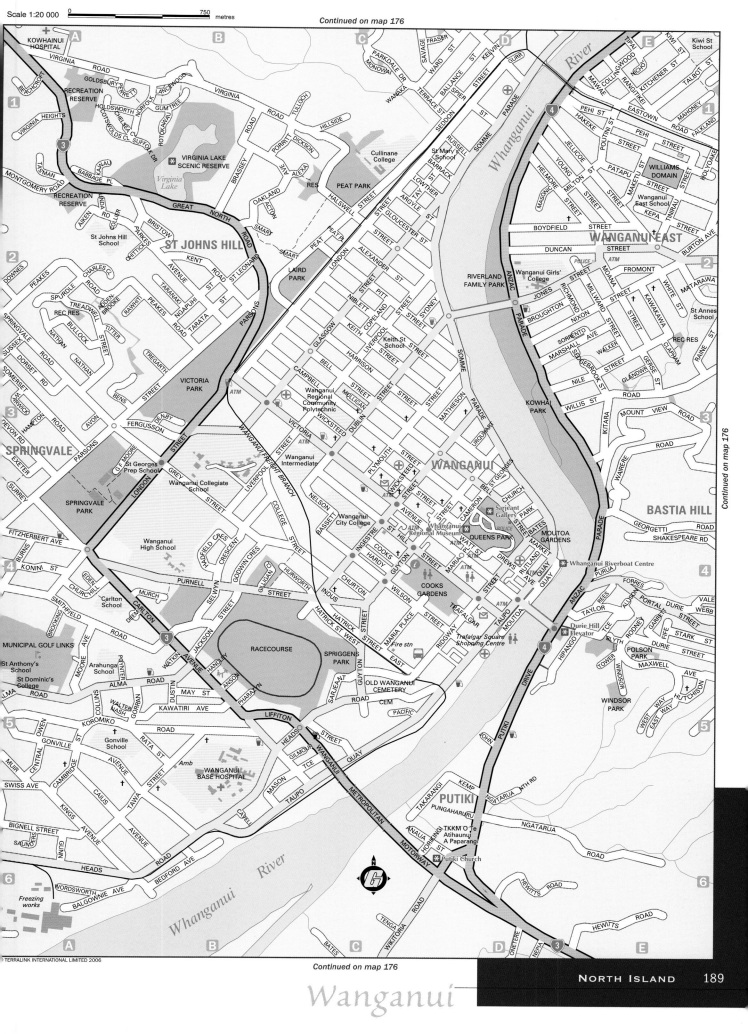

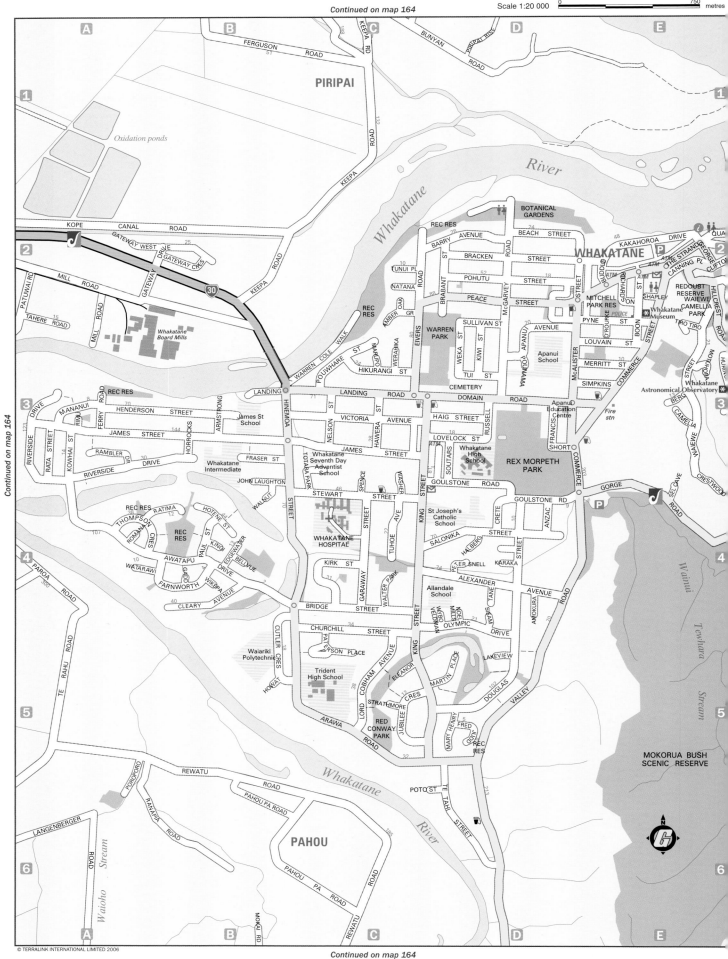

Scale 1:20 000

0 750 metres

PIRIPAI

Oxidation ponds

Whakatane

Continued on map 164

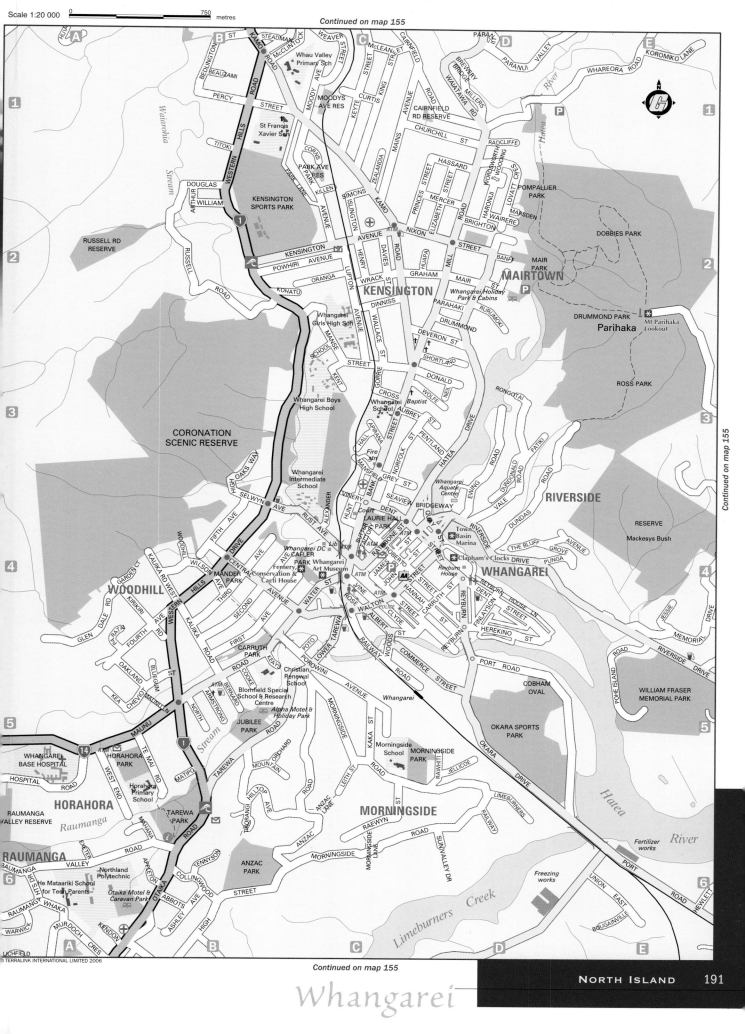

Scale 1:20 000

0   750   metres

A   B   C   D   E

1

2

3

4

5

6

Whau Valley Primary Sch

St Francis Xavier Sch

KENSINGTON SPORTS PARK

RUSSELL RD RESERVE

Watarohia Stream

PARK AVE RES

KENSINGTON

Whangarei Girls High Sch

CORONATION SCENIC RESERVE

Whangarei Boys High School

Whangarei Intermediate School

WOODHILL

Whangarei DC
CAFLER PARK
Conservation & Cacti House

Whangarei Art Museum

CARRUTH PARK

Christian Renewal School

Blomfield Special School & Research Centre

Alpha Motel & Holiday Park

JUBILEE PARK

HORAHORA

WHANGAREI BASE HOSPITAL

Horahora Park

Horahora Primary School

TAREWA PARK

RAUMANGA VALLEY RESERVE

Raumanga

RAUMANGA

He Mataariki School for Teen Parents

Northland Polytechnic

Otaika Motel & Caravan Park

ANZAC PARK

MORNINGSIDE

Morningside School

MORNINGSIDE PARK

OKARA SPORTS PARK

COBHAM OVAL

WILLIAM FRASER MEMORIAL PARK

WHANGAREI

Town Basin Marina

Clapham's Clocks

Reyburn House

Whangarei Aquatic Centre

RIVERSIDE

RESERVE
Mackesys Bush

MAIRTOWN

MAIR PARK

DOBBIES PARK

DRUMMOND PARK

Parihaka

Mt Parihaka Lookout

ROSS PARK

Whangarei Holiday Park & Cabins

Pohe Island

Hatea River

Limeburners Creek

Fertilizer works

Freezing works

© TERRALINK INTERNATIONAL LIMITED 2006

SOUTH ISLAN

Bigger than the North Island, yet home to only about a quarter of New Zealand's population, the South Island has a slower pace of life, and many remote and beautiful areas. For visitors seeking unspoilt wilderness, awe-inspiring scenery and a chance to get away from it all, the South Island is a truly magnificent destination. Its contrasting landscapes include towering snowy mountains, dramatic glaciers, deep fiords, lush forests, dramatic limestone formations, glacier-carved lakes, wild coastline and beautiful beaches.

Some of the world's best walking tracks can be found in the 10 national parks, four of which make up the important Te Wahipounamu South-west New Zealand World Heritage Area. Many areas are home to extraordinary native wildlife, including whales, Hector's dolphins, penguins, seals, kiwi, the rare kakapo, kotuku (white herons) and many more species.

Christchurch, known as New Zealand's most English city, is centred around Cathedral Square and the pretty Avon River, and has excellent galleries and theatres;

Dunedin, further south, is more Scottish in nature, and is home to easily accessible wildlife around the Otago Peninsula.

The wine regions of Marlborough, Nelson, Canterbury and Central Otago welcome visitors to their

South Island:

Population: 970 000

Total area: 150 437km^2

% of New Zealand: 55.6

Highest mountain: Aoraki/Mount Cook, 3754m

Maori name: Te Waka a Maui (Maui's canoe); Te Wahipounamu (The Place of Greenstone)

Castle Hill, Arthur's Pass

scenically-located wineries. There are also many historic sites and buildings, including evocative relics from the 19th century gold rush around Otago and the West Coast.

The South Island is a place of climatic extremes, with much of the Southern Alps in permanent snow and ice. Rainfall is generally high to the west of the Alps, and low to the east; Nelson and Marlborough have long sunshine hours.

Car travel is easy, although some remote roads are winding and narrow, and in sparsely populated areas there can be a long drive between service centres. Buses cover most of the South Island, and the larger cities have airports, but independent transport is the best way to access more isolated areas.

ⓘ Visitor information

Christchurch i-SITE Visitor Centre
Old Chief Post Office, Cathedral Sq West, Christchurch
Ph: (03) 379 9629

Dunedin i-SITE Visitor Centre
48 The Octagon, Dunedin
Ph: (03) 474 3300

www.newzealand.com
www.i-site.org

Main ATTRACTIONS

◈ **Abel Tasman National Park**
Golden beaches, turquoise waters, forests and wildlife make this park wonderful for walking or kayaking.

◈ **Aoraki/Mount Cook**
New Zealand's highest peak, mighty Aoraki/Mount Cook is seen as a sacred mountain and ancestor by the South Island's Ngai Tahu tribe.

◈ **Catlins**
This gorgeous, remote area has forests, waterfalls, historic sites, beaches, rugged coastline and great wildlife viewing.

◈ **Central Otago**
'Central' is home to dramatic landscapes, historic villages, gold mining relics and stylish wineries producing award-winning pinot noir.

◈ **Fiordland**
This important, remote wilderness area has snowy peaks, untouched forests, lakes and glacier-carved fiords, including famous Milford Sound.

◈ **Fox and Franz Josef Glaciers**
These two massive glaciers reach from the Southern Alps into bush-clad valleys just 250m above sea level.

◈ **Kaikoura**
Whale watch tours, plentiful wildlife and a wonderful setting between mountains and sea make this small town popular with visitors.

◈ **Marlborough Sounds**
Forest-clad hills rise straight out of the sea in this beautiful area of flooded river valleys.

◈ **Mount Aspiring National Park**
Some of New Zealand's best walking tracks lead through this spectacular park of towering mountains, unspoilt forests and river valleys.

◈ **Queenstown**
Adventure tourism, skiing, wineries, mountain scenery and a beautiful lakeside location make Queenstown an important visitor destination.

◈ **Stewart Island**
New Zealand's third largest island is mostly occupied by the remote wilderness of Rakiura National Park, which offers great walking and much bird life.

SOUTH ISLAND

Often jokingly called 'the mainland' by its residents today, the South Island was given two different names by Maori. One name is **Te Waka a Maui**, 'the Canoe of Maui', based on the legend in which the mischievous demi-god Maui hauled up the massive fish of the **North Island**; **Stewart Island**, also called Rakiura, was the canoe's anchor. Maori also know the South Island as **Te Wahipounamu**, the 'Place of Greenstone', as the island's **West Coast** provided its early inhabitants with a rich source of prized greenstone.

From pre-European times Maori traversed the South Island in search of greenstone, which they prized greatly for its beauty and usefulness. The first European arrival was Dutch navigator Abel Tasman in 1642; next was the British explorer Captain James Cook, who anchored at **Ship Cove** in 1770, then sailed through **Cook Strait** and down the South Island's east coast.

European sealers and whalers arrived from the late 18th century, with considerable interaction between sealers and Maori residents around **Foveaux Strait**. By 1850, British settlements had been founded in **Nelson**, **Otago**

West Coast sunset

and **Canterbury**, but the South Island's hilly interior remained largely uncharted by Europeans until the discovery of gold in the 1860s. The ensuing gold rush drew thousands of settlers, Chinese as well as British; **Dunedin** became the country's largest and most prosperous city.

Today, the South Island is home to only a quarter of New Zealand's population, and more than half of those are in Canterbury. Just 10% of Maori today live south of Cook

Strait. Most are from the Ngai Tahu iwi (tribe); Ngai Tahu's tribal area covers most of the South Island, and is the largest of any tribes.

Almost two-thirds of the South Island is mountainous. The massive **Southern Alps** stretch most of the island's length, rising to more than 3000m and including New Zealand's highest peak, 3754m **Aoraki/Mount Cook**. West of the mountains, where rainfall is high, are lush rainforests; to the drier east is Otago and **Southland**'s rolling farmland, and the huge, flat **Canterbury Plains**. The southern lakes, and the fiords which cut into the island's south-western corner, were formed by glaciers gouging the land.

Wool and gold first made the South Island prosperous, and the trade in shipping frozen meat to Britain developed from the 1880s. Today sheep and dairy farming, wine production, hydro-electric power production, fishing and tourism are all important industries.

Poolburn, Central Otago

South Island

TOURISM REGION HIGHLIGHTS

The South Island is famous for its extraordinary wilderness areas, including the high peaks of the Southern Alps, 10 of New Zealand's 14 national parks, spectacular glaciers, beautiful lakes and amazing native wildlife. It's also home to award-winning wineries in spectacular settings, interesting cities and a rich array of historic and cultural attractions.

A Canterbury (pp.206–213)

Akaroa; Aoraki/Mount Cook; Aoraki/Mount Cook National Park; Avon River; Arthur's Pass National Park; Banks Peninsula; Cathedral Square; Christchurch Botanic Gardens; Hanmer Springs Thermal Reserve; International Antarctic Centre; Kaikoura; Lake Pukaki; Lake Tekapo; Mt Hutt Skifield; *TranzAlpine* train journey; Waipara Valley wineries

B Central Otago (pp.218-219)

Bannockburn; Bendigo; Central Otago wineries; Clyde; Danseys Pass; Kawarau Gorge; Lake Dunstan; Maniototo; Naseby; Nevis Valley; Ophir; Otago Central Rail Trail; Poolburn Reservoir; Ranfurly; Ripponvale; St Bathans

C Dunedin (pp.220-227)

Cadbury World; Golden Point Historic Reserve; Larnach Castle; Matanaka Farm Buildings; Moeraki Boulders/Kaihinaki; Oamaru; Otago Museum; Otago Peninsula; Penguin Place; Royal Albatross Centre; Taieri Gorge Railway

D Fiordland (pp.228–229)

Doubtful Sound; Fiordland National Park; Hollyford Track; Homer Tunnel; Kepler Track; Lake Manapouri; Milford Deep underwater observatory; Milford Road; Milford Sound; Milford Track; Piopiotahi Marine Reserve; Te Ana-au Glow-worm Caves

E Lake Wanaka (pp.214–215)

Cardrona; Lake Hawea; Lake Wanaka; Makarora; Mount Aspiring National Park; Mount Aspiring/Tititea; Rippon Vineyard; Rob Roy Track; Treble Cone Skifield; Warbirds Museum

F Marlborough (pp.202–203)

Havelock; Long Island–Kokomohua Marine Reserve; Marlborough Sounds; Marlborough wineries; Molesworth Station; Motuara Island; Nydia Track; Queen Charlotte Drive; Queen Charlotte Track; Rangitoto ke te tonga (D'Urville Island); Te Aumiti (French Pass)

G Nelson (pp.200–201)

Abel Tasman National Park; Abel Tasman Coastal Track; Farewell Spit; Golden Bay; Kahurangi National Park; Kaiteriteri; Mapua; Nelson Lakes National Park; Nelson wineries; Pupu Springs; Totaranui; World of WearableArt & Collectable Cars Museum

H Queenstown (pp.216–217)

Arrowtown; Chinese miners' settlement; Coronet Peak Skifield; Dart River; Gibbston Valley; Glenorchy; Kingston Flyer; Lake Hayes; Lake Wakatipu; Macetown; Queenstown; Routeburn Track; Skippers Canyon; *TSS Earnslaw*

I Southland (pp.230–231)

Catlins; Codfish Island; Eastern Southland Gallery; Gabriel's Gully; Lake Waihola/Sinclair Wetlands; Lawrence Chinese Camp; Nugget Point; Rakiura National Park; Rakiura Track; Riverton/Aparima; Stewart Island; The Paua Shell House; Tuatapere Hump Ridge Track; Ulva Island Open Sanctuary

J West Coast (pp.204–205)

Cape Foulwind; Fox Glacier; Franz Josef Glacier; Heaphy Track; Jackson Bay; Kahurangi National Park; Kotuku Sanctuary; Lake Matheson; Maruia Springs; Okarito Lagoon; Oparara Arches; Paparoa National Park; Punakaiki Pancake Rocks and Blowholes; Shantytown; Wangapeka Track; Westland/Tai Poutini National Park

Looking towards Queenstown from Crown Range, Central Otago

PARKS & RESERVES

The South Island is home to 10 of New Zealand's 14 national parks. These encompass some extraordinary and highly significant landscapes, including the towering peaks of the **Southern Alps**, glacier-carved fiords, lush rainforests, dramatic limestone formations, vast glaciers, alpine meadows, caves, wild coastline, remote beaches and beautiful lakes. These wilderness areas are also home to much wildlife, including some rare and endangered species.

Together, **Aoraki/Mount Cook**, **Westland/Tai Poutini**, **Fiordland** and **Mount Aspiring National Parks** make up 2.6 million hectare Te Wahipounamu South-west New Zealand World Heritage Area, which covers 10% of New Zealand's land area.

A Abel Tasman National Park

(Map 281, F3)

New Zealand's smallest national park at 22 530ha, idyllic Abel Tasman National Park has golden-sand beaches, turquoise sea, granite cliffs, lush forest and plenty of wildlife. Located about 65km north-west of Nelson, it's home to one of the country's 'Great Walks', the 51km **Abel Tasman Coastal Track**, which leads through native bush overlooking beautiful beaches. Sea kayaking is popular, and many visitors explore by a mix of walking, kayaking and boat transport.

B Aoraki/Mount Cook National Park

(Map 294, C3)

This 70 696ha alpine park in the central South Island has New Zealand's highest mountains and largest glaciers. There are 19 peaks over 3000 metres, including New

Aoraki/Mount Cook National Park

Zealand's highest mountain, 3754m **Aoraki/Mount Cook**, sacred to the Ngai Tahu tribe. Skiing is possible on the 28km **Tasman Glacier**, NZ's largest. Aoraki/Mount Cook National Park is a mecca for experienced climbers from around the world; it also offers accessible day walks among beautiful alpine flora.

C Arthur's Pass National Park

(Map 289, H4)

This 114 500ha park is located in the Southern Alps on a historic road between **Canterbury** and the **West Coast**, and was the South Island's first national park. Arthur's Pass National Park has braided rivers, steep gorges, native bush and mountains; it's also home to the inquisitive kea, the great spotted kiwi and many other birds. The park's tracks offer long and short hikes, and its mountains have drawn climbers since the 19th century.

D Fiordland National Park

(Map 304, E4)

The remote wilderness area of 1.2 million ha Fiordland National Park, in the south-western corner of the South Island, is an extraordinarily beautiful landscape of snow-capped mountains, deep lakes, virgin forests and tussock grasslands. Its fourteen glacier-carved fiords are edged by sheer cliffs with cascading waterfalls, and the park is home to plants and wildlife from the ancient Gondwana super-continent. The 500km network of walking trails includes three of New Zealand's 'Great Walks', the **Milford**, **Kepler** and **Routeburn Tracks**.

E Kahurangi National Park

(Map 280, C4)

Ecologically significant 452 002ha Kahurangi National Park, in the north-western South Island, has rugged mountains, glacial valleys, remote rivers, unspoilt forest, cave systems and pristine coastline. The

South Island

park's rich flora and fauna includes a huge range of species; the **Oparara Basin** features dramatic limestone formations. There are more than 570km of walking tracks, including the 82km **Heaphy Track**, a 'Great Walk'.

F Mount Aspiring National Park

(Map 299, G3)

New Zealand's third largest national park at 355 543ha, Mount Aspiring National Park stretches from **Fiordland**'s rainforests across alpine areas and river valleys to the Southern Alps. Its beautiful valleys have attracted tourists since the 19th century; the park offers wonderful walking and mountaineering, including on 3033m **Mount Aspiring/Tititea**, and the 'Great Walk' of the **Routeburn Track**. Jet boating is possible on the remote rivers.

G Nelson Lakes National Park

(Map 285, H4)

About 100km south of Nelson, 102 000ha Nelson Lakes National Park has beech forest, mountains, alpine meadows, rich bird life and beautiful lakes. There are lovely walks around glacially-formed **Lake Rotoiti** and **Lake Rotoroa**; the lakes are also popular for boating and fishing. The park's many tracks include a three-day walk to alpine **Lake Angelus**, and in spring, the alpine areas are bright with flowers.

H Paparoa National Park

(Map 284, B5)

On the northern West Coast, about 35km north of Greymouth, 30 000ha Paparoa National Park has rich forests, limestone cliffs, caves and a spectacular coastline. The area is most famous for **Punakaiki**'s limestone **Pancake Rocks and Blowholes**; the blowholes spout sea water dramatically when sea and weather conditions are right. Walking, canoeing and caving are popular.

I Rakiura National Park

(Map 315, H4)

New Zealand's newest national park, 157 000ha **Rakiura National Park** covers about 85% of **Stewart Island**. Its many walking tracks lead through unspoilt native forest

with much bird life, including some rare species. The 29km **Rakiura Track**, one of New Zealand's 'Great Walks', passes through coastal areas and over a forested ridge; **Ulva Island Open Sanctuary** is a pest-free 250ha island with a huge bird population.

J Westland/Tai Poutini National Park

(Map 293, J3)

This 127 541 ha park on the southern West Coast stretches from the high Southern Alps to wild coastal beaches. The park is home to spectacular **Fox** and **Franz Josef Glaciers**, which descend into rainforested valleys only 250m above sea level; near the coast are lakes, wetlands and wide river mouths with many water birds. Walking, mountaineering, ski touring and scenic flights over the glaciers are all popular.

National Park Information

Christchurch Conservation Information Centre
133 Victoria St, Christchurch
Ph: (03) 371 3706
www.doc.govt.nz

Mount Aspiring National Park

WINERIES

The South Island is home to the world's southernmost wineries. It also has New Zealand's largest wine region — **Marlborough** — and the country's fastest growing region, **Central Otago**.

It was Marlborough which put New Zealand on the international wine map in the 1980s with its intensely-flavoured sauvignon blanc, and the region still has a huge profile internationally. Over 45% of New Zealand's vineyards are in Marlborough, and more than 50% of the country's wine exports are Marlborough-grown sauvignon blanc.

Winemaking in the South Island has a history almost as long as the country's European occupation, with German winemakers in **Nelson** in the 1840s, French pioneers planting vineyards on **Banks Peninsula** around the same time, and wines made in Central Otago during the 19th century gold rush.

Today the South Island's main wine regions — Nelson, Marlborough, **Waipara**, **Canterbury** and Central Otago — are home to many wineries, often in highly scenic locations. A large number of wineries welcome visitors and offer tastings, and many have restaurants. Informative wine tours are available in most of the wine regions, and wine festivals are popular.

A Canterbury
(p.276)

The first vines in the Canterbury region were planted on Banks Peninsula by French settlers in the 1840s. The region's current wine industry got started in the 1970s, after a Lincoln University research project which trialled vineyards and winemaking in the sheep farming country of the **Canterbury Plains**. Today there are a number of wineries on the plains, and east of Christchurch on Banks Peninsula. Most of the plantings are chardonnay and pinot noir; riesling and sauvignon blanc are also grown. The area has long dry summers, plentiful sunshine and cool conditions, with the plains sheltered from rain by the **Southern Alps**. **French Farm Vineyards** on Banks Peninsula has great views over beautiful **Akaroa Harbour**; **Kaituna Valley**'s wines have won many awards. Christchurch hosts the annual **Canterbury Wine and Food Festival** each February.

B Central Otago
(pp.268-269)

The world's most southerly wine production area is also New Zealand's fastest growing wine region. Many of the vineyards are in spectacular locations, with beautiful mountain and lake scenery as a backdrop. The region's wineries fall into four main areas: **Gibbston Valley**, east of **Queenstown**; **Lake Wanaka**; the **Cromwell Basin**, around **Cromwell** and the old gold mining areas of **Bannockburn** and **Bendigo**; and around **Alexandra**. The area, with its cold winters and hot summers, is particularly well suited to pinot noir; the emphasis on a single variety is unique in New Zealand, and the region's pinot noirs have met with international acclaim. Good pinot gris is also produced. **Felton Road**, at Bannockburn, has an international reputation for its pinot noir and riesling; **Rippon Vineyard** overlooks a gorgeous vista of Lake Wanaka. **Gibbston Valley Wines**, New Zealand's most visited winery, has a tunnel into the hillside for storing wine, and also produces cheeses. January sees Queenstown play host to the two-day **Central Otago Pinot Noir Celebration**, and February's **Central Otago Wine and Food Festival**, held in the **Queenstown Botanical Gardens**, brings together food, wine, jazz and entertainment.

Gibbston Valley wine cave, Central Otago

South Island

C Marlborough

(pp.260-261)

The region around **Blenheim** brought New Zealand wine to the international stage in the early 1980s with its now iconic sauvignon blanc; today, Marlborough is the country's largest wine production area, producing more than half of all NZ wine in some years. The region's hot sunny days and chilly nights have proved perfect for sauvignon blanc; the stony soils of the former riverbeds provide extra warmth and help the grapes ripen. There's an increasing emphasis on pinot noir, and Marlborough also produces excellent chardonnay, riesling, gewürztraminer and sparkling wines. The one-time farming area of the **Wairau Valley**, west of Blenheim, is home to many wineries with a beautiful mountain backdrop. The flat terrain lends itself to exploring by bicycle. The **Awatere Valley** — drier and warmer than Blenheim — is also a burgeoning wine area. **Cloudy Bay Vineyards** was one of the first Marlborough wineries to impress the world with its sauvignon blanc; **Montana Brancott Winery**, New Zealand's largest wine producer, has a visitor centre and offers tours. **Herzog Winery** has an impressive restaurant with a tremendous wine list; **Tohu Wines** is the country's first winery with Maori ownership and branding. The popular **Wine Marlborough Festival** draws thousands of visitors to this picturesque area each February.

D Nelson

(p.260)

The Nelson region's first winemaking experiment was by German arrivals in the mid-19th century; the current wineries got started in the 1970s. Vineyards are dotted on the **Waimea Plains** and **Upper Moutere**, taking advantage

of the long sunshine hours and the western hills which shelter the area from rain. The Waimea Plains are blessed with plentiful sun, crisp cool winters and alluvial soils; the Upper Moutere has hot days, cool nights and clay gravel soils. There are also plantings in **Golden Bay**. Aromatic whites are a focus here; Nelson's vineyards are set among hop farms, apple orchards and olive groves, and produce pinot noir, chardonnay, sauvignon blanc, pinot gris and riesling.

E Waipara (p.276)

The first significant plantings in the **Waipara Valley**, about 60km north of Christchurch, were made in the early 1980s. Originally a dairy and cattle farming area, today it's a fast growing wine region, producing premium quality wines. Plantings are dominated by sauvignon blanc, pinot noir, riesling and chardonnay. Sheltered by the **Teviotdale Hills** to the east, the region has less frost and rain than the Canterbury Plains, and the vines do well in its silty alluvial soils and silty loams. Fragrant riesling, good pinot noir and chardonnay are all made in Waipara. The annual **Waipara Wine and Food Celebration** is held each March.

Crowds enjoying the Wine Marlborough Festival

NELSON

Boasting both cultural and natural attractions, the Nelson region has a sunny climate, great beaches and three national parks. It's also home to a vibrant mix of artists, craftspeople, wineries and orchards.

Occupied by Maori for centuries, Nelson was visited early by European explorers. The Dutch seafarer Abel Tasman — the first European to visit New Zealand — anchored his ship in **Golden Bay** in 1642; **Tasman Bay** and **Abel Tasman National Park** are both named after him. The next European arrival was British explorer Captain James Cook, who sailed across the mouth of Tasman and Golden Bays 128 years later.

Nelson city is a lively centre with plenty of galleries, cafés, wineries and breweries. To the west, Golden Bay is a beautiful and relaxed coastal area known for its alternative lifestylers and artists.

The three national parks all have their own distinct character. Abel Tasman National Park is a coastal playground with golden beaches, popular for walking and kayaking; **Nelson Lakes National Park**, to the south, has pristine glacial lakes and beech forests; and **Kahurangi National Park**, stretching south to Westland, has unspoilt forests and deep cave systems.

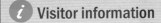

Golden sand beach at Abel Tasman National Park

Nelson Lakes National Park

Pristine Nelson Lakes National Park has beech forest, craggy mountains, clear streams and beautiful lakes, including glacier-formed **Lake Rotoiti** and **Lake Rotoroa**. The park's alpine areas are thick with flowers in spring, and the forests are full of birds. Picturesque **St Arnaud**, on Lake Rotoiti's shore, is the gateway to the park.

ℹ Visitor information

Nelson i-SITE Visitor Centre
77 Trafalgar St, Nelson
Ph: (03) 548 2304
www.nelsonnz.com

main attractions

◈ **Abel Tasman National Park**

Sea kayaking and walking are popular in this beautiful coastal park, which has golden beaches, turquoise sea, forests and wildlife.

◈ **Arts & crafts**

Home to many artists and craftspeople, the Nelson region has excellent galleries and markets.

◈ **Farewell Spit**

This 26km sandspit is an internationally significant wetland and bird sanctuary, and has a historic lighthouse.

◈ **Golden Bay**

Golden sand beaches, rocky headlands and arty small towns are a feature of this relaxed coastal area.

◈ **Kahurangi National Park**

NZ's second largest national park has rugged mountains, limestone caves, unspoilt coastline, native forests and rich bird life.

◈ **Kaiteriteri**

A pretty golden beach and clear waters make Kaiteriteri a popular resort spot.

◈ **Mapua**

This seaside township has galleries, cafés and an aquarium in its old port buildings.

◈ **Nelson wineries**

Wineries are dotted around the Upper Moutere, Waimea Plains and Golden Bay.

◈ **Pupu Springs**

New Zealand's largest fresh water spring has incredibly clear water and an underwater observation window.

◈ **World of WearableArt & Collectable Cars Museum**

Extraordinary, creative and often humorous wearable artworks are showcased in this fascinating museum.

Lake Rotoiti, Nelson Lakes National Park

South Island

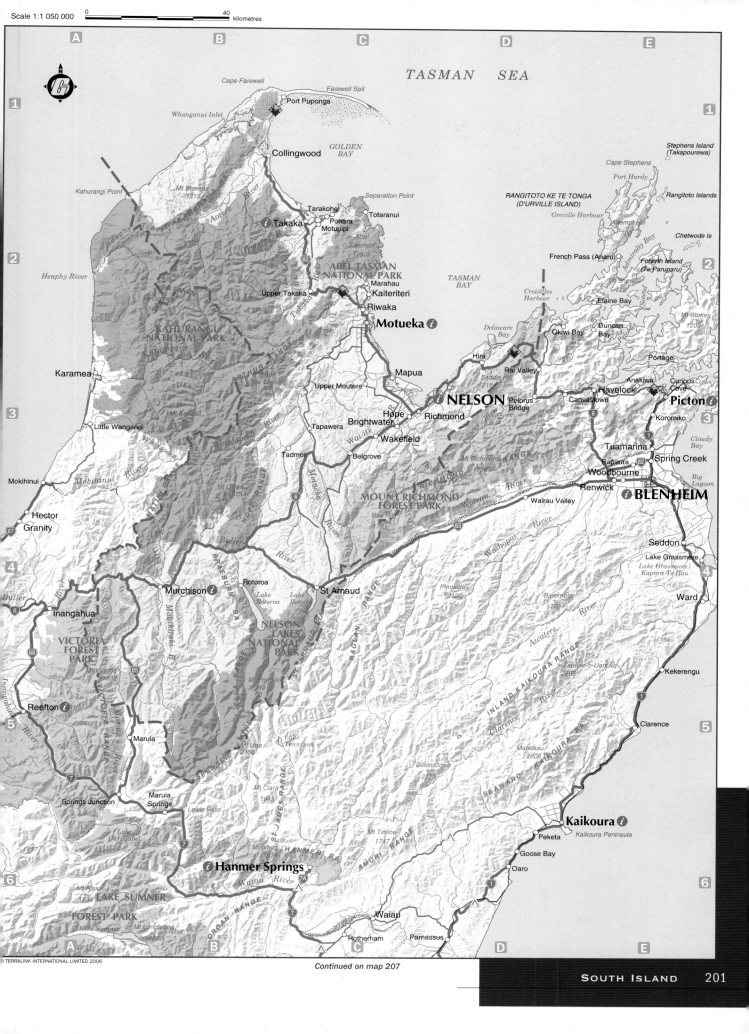

TASMAN SEA

Cape Farewell
Farewell Spit
Whanganui Inlet
Port Puponga

GOLDEN
BAY
Collingwood

Kahurangi Point

Mt Stevens
1213
Tarakohe
Takaka
Pohara
Motupipi
Totaranui

Separation Point

Heaphy River

Upper Takaka

ABEL TASMAN
NATIONAL PARK
Marahau
Kaiteriteri
Riwaka

Stephens Island
(Takapourewa)

Cape Stephens
Port Hardy

RANGITOTO KE TE TONGA
(D'URVILLE ISLAND)

Greville Harbour

Rangitoto Islands

Attempt Hill
725

Chetwode Is

Forsyth Island
(Te Paruparu)

French Pass (Anaru)

Admiralty Bay

Mt Stevens

TASMAN
BAY

Motueka

KAHURANGI
NATIONAL PARK

Mt Domett
1675

Mt Kendall

Karamea

Little Wanganui

Mt Arthur
1795

Mapua

Upper Moutere

Hira

Croisilles
Harbour

Delaware
Bay

Elaine Bay

Okiwi Bay

Duncan
Bay

Mt Stokes
1203

Rai Valley

Saddle Hill
215

NELSON

Pelorus
Bridge

Canvastown

Havelock

Portage

Anakiwa

Curious
Cove

Picton

Koromiko

Cloudy
Bay

Tuamarina

Spring Creek

Rapaura

Woodbourne
Renwick

BLENHEIM

Seddon

Lake Grassmere
Kapara Te Hau

Ward

Kekerengu

Clarence

Kaikoura

Peketa
Goose Bay
Oaro

Hector
Granity

Mokihinui

Inangahua

VICTORIA
FOREST PARK

Reefton

Maruia

Springs Junction

Maruia
Springs

Lewis Pass

Hanmer Springs

Waiau River

Waiau

Rotherham
Parnassus

Richmond
Hope
Brightwater
Wakefield
Belgrove

Tapawera

Tadmor

Murchison

Rotoroa

Lake
Rotoroa

Lake
Rotoiti

St Arnaud

NELSON
LAKES
NATIONAL
PARK

MOUNT RICHMOND
FOREST PARK

Wairau Valley

Pinnacle
2190

Barometer
1780

Tapuae-o-Uenuku
2885

INLAND KAIKOURA RANGE

Dillon Cone
2170

Manakau
2608

SEAWARD KAIKOURA RA

Kaikoura Peninsula

Mt Una
2300

Lake
Tennyson

Mt Clara
1945

Mt Franklin
2240

Mt Owen
1875

Mt Tinline
1747

LAKE SUMNER
FOREST PARK

Mt Ajax
1834

Lake Sumner

MARLBOROUGH

Sunny Marlborough, at the north-east of the South Island, is home to the lovely maritime playground of the **Marlborough Sounds**. Reputedly discovered by the famed Polynesian navigator Kupe, the Sounds were also visited by early European explorers. Dutch seafarer Abel Tasman sailed past **Rangitoto ke te tonga (D'Urville Island)** in 1642, and British explorer Captain James Cook arrived in the area in 1770, landing at **Ship Cove** and then on Rangitoto ke te tonga.

Today, fishing, swimming, walking, diving, sea kayaking and wildlife viewing are all popular activities in the area. The town of **Picton**, at the head of **Queen Charlotte Sound**, was originally a Maori settlement. Today it's a thoroughfare for travellers to and from the North Island, and a base for exploring the Sounds.

Wine is also a major focus in Marlborough, with the country's largest wine-producing area in the pretty countryside around **Blenheim**. The area's wineries are internationally famous for their sauvignon blanc, but also produce chardonnay, pinot noir, riesling and sparkling wines. Wineries can be explored on guided tours, or independently by cycling, walking or car.

main attractions

◈ **Havelock**

This historic small town, the gateway to Pelorus and Kenepuru Sounds, is known for its greenshell mussels.

◈ **Long Island–Kokomohua Marine Reserve**

Diving is excellent in the clear waters of this protected marine area.

◈ **Marlborough wineries**

New Zealand's biggest wine-producing area is feted for its sauvignon blanc, which put New Zealand on the world wine map in the 1980s.

◈ **Molesworth Station**

Open only in summer, this high country cattle station has dramatic landscapes and fascinating history.

◈ **Motuara Island**

Captain James Cook proclaimed British sovereignty over the South Island on Motuara Island, now a bird sanctuary.

◈ **Nydia Track**

This remote eight- to nine-hour track leads through regenerating bush, and offers excellent views over the Sounds.

◈ **Queen Charlotte Drive**

This beautiful scenic route leads from Picton to Havelock, and has wonderful views.

◈ **Queen Charlotte Track**

A popular three- to four-day walk leads through lush coastal forest, farmland and historic coves.

◈ **Rangitoto ke te tonga (D'Urville Island)**

Many birds, dolphins and seals can be seen at this secluded island; it also has waterfalls and glow-worm grottoes.

◈ **Te Aumiti (French Pass)**

Rich in wildlife, this remote, turbulent stretch of water was once home to the famous dolphin Pelorus Jack.

Queen Charlotte Sound, Marlborough

Marlborough Sounds

This beautiful area of drowned river valleys — **Queen Charlotte**, **Pelorus** and **Kenepuru Sounds** — features bush-clad hills rising from the water's edge, and beautiful bays and coves. Wildlife includes dolphins, seals and penguins; there are also many historic sites. **Picton** and **Havelock** are good bases for exploring the Sounds.

 Visitor information

Blenheim i-SITE Visitor Centre
Railway Station, Sinclair St, SH1, Blenheim
Ph: (03) 577 8080

Picton i-SITE Visitor Centre
The Foreshore, Picton
Ph: (03) 520 3113

www.destinationmarlborough.com

Shifting stock, Molesworth Station, Marlborough

South Island

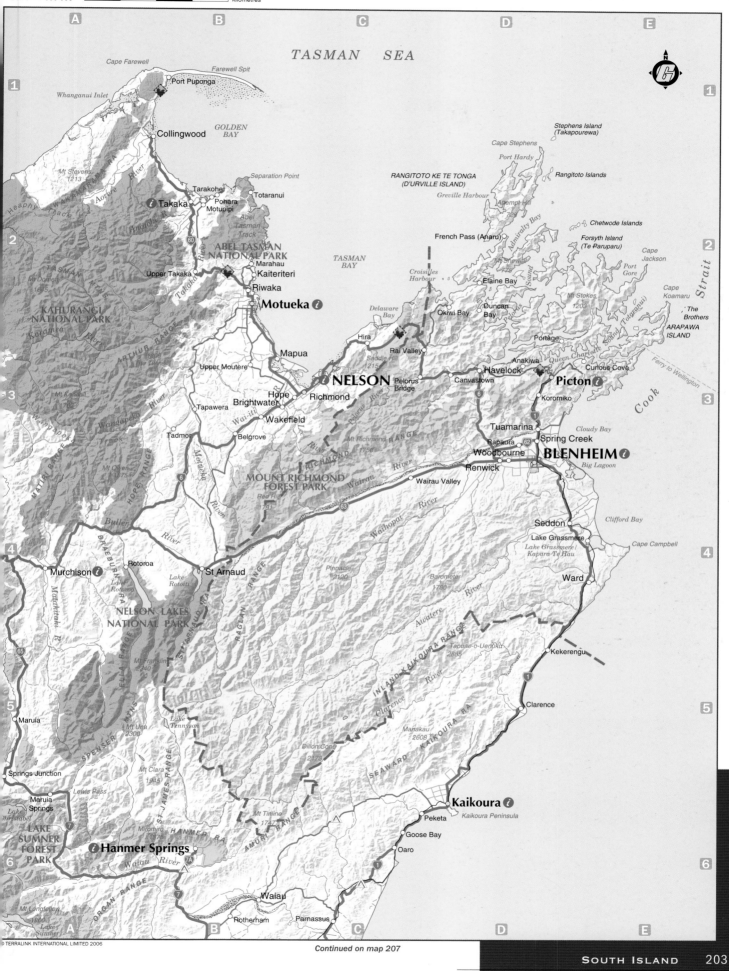

0   40
kilometres

TASMAN SEA

Cape Farewell
Whanganui Inlet
Port Puponga
Farewell Spit

Collingwood

GOLDEN BAY

Mt Stevens
1213

Tarakohe
Separation Point
Totaranui

Takaka
Pohara
Motupipi

Upper Takaka

ABEL TASMAN
NATIONAL PARK

Marahau
Kaiteriteri
Riwaka

Motueka

RANGITOTO KE TE TONGA
(D'URVILLE ISLAND)

Stephens Island
(Takapourewa)

Cape Stephens

Port Hardy

Greville Harbour

Attempt Hill

Rangitoto Islands

Chetwode Islands

KAHURANGI
NATIONAL PARK

Mt Domett
1615

Heaphy Track

Aorere River

TASMAN BAY

French Pass (Anaru)

Croisilles Harbour

Delaware Bay

Hira

Rai Valley

Saddle Hill
1215

Okiwi Bay

Duncan Bay

Elaine Bay

Admiralty Bay

Forsyth Island
(Te Paruparu)

Cape Jackson

Port Gore

Mt Stokes
1203

Cape Koamaru

ARAPAWA ISLAND

The Brothers

Cook Strait

Mapua

Upper Moutere

Hope
Brightwater

Richmond

Wakefield

Tapawera

Belgrove

Tadmor

NELSON

Pelorus Bridge

Portage

Canvastown

Havelock

Anakiwa

Picton

Curious Cove

Ferry to Wellington

Koromiko

Tuamarina

Spring Creek

Cloudy Bay

MOUNT RICHMOND
FOREST PARK

Red Hill
731

Mt Richmond
1750

Wairau River

Waihopai River

Wairau Valley

Rapaura
Woodbourne

Renwick

BLENHEIM

Big Lagoon

Seddon

Lake Grassmere /
Kapara Te Hau

Clifford Bay

Cape Campbell

Murchison

Rotoroa

St Arnaud

Lake Rotoroa

Lake Rotoiti

Pinnacle
2120

Barometer
1780

Awatere River

Ward

NELSON LAKES
NATIONAL PARK

Mt Franklin
2340

Mt Una
2300

Lake Tennyson

Tapuae-o-Uenuku
2885

Clarence River

Kekerengu

Maruia

Mt Oliver
1675

Mt Clara
1945

Dillon Cone
2175

Manakau
2608

Clarence

Springs Junction

Lewis Pass

Miromiro

Mt Tinline
1747

SEAWARD KAIKOURA RA

Kaikoura

Peketa

Kaikoura Peninsula

Maruia Springs

LAKE SUMNER
FOREST PARK

Hanmer Springs

Waiau River

Goose Bay

Oaro

Mt Longfellow

Waiau

Rotherham

Parnassus

© TERRALINK INTERNATIONAL LIMITED 2006

WEST COAST

The wild and beautiful West Coast of the South Island is home to only 31 000 people. This long, narrow region, bordered to the west by the **Tasman Sea** and to the east by the **Southern Alps**, has a rich landscape of unspoilt rivers, rainforests, beaches and glaciers, and provides access to five of New Zealand's 14 national parks.

From early times, the West Coast was a source of pounamu (jade) for Maori, who travelled long distances for the precious stone and traded it with tribes around the country. European settlement of the area began after a gold find in 1864; within two years, there were 30 000 people on the coast. Coal mining and timber milling were also important industries, and coal mining continues today.

The West Coast's gold rush has left it with many heritage buildings, historic relics, and tiny settlements that are little more than ghost towns. But it's the coast's natural beauty that draws visitors: huge and beautiful glaciers only 250m above sea level, wild beaches, rainforests, dramatic limestone formations, and fascinating wildlife, including rare giant land snails, seals, and kotuku (white herons).

Fox Glacier

main attractions

◈ **Cape Foulwind**

Cape Foulwind has a fur seal breeding colony and a coastal walkway.

◈ **Heaphy Track**

This 82km 'Great Walk' leads through beautiful Kahurangi National Park, from the West Coast to Golden Bay.

◈ **Kahurangi National Park**

This 452 002ha park is ecologically significant for its many plant and bird species; it also has a karst landscape and beautiful forests.

◈ **Kotuku Sanctuary**

New Zealand's only breeding colony of the beautiful kotuku (white heron) can be visited near Whataroa.

◈ **Lake Matheson**

On clear days, Aoraki/Mount Cook can be seen dramatically reflected in this pretty lake.

◈ **Okarito Lagoon**

New Zealand's largest unmodified wetland is home to more than 70 species of birds, and offers wonderful kayaking.

◈ **Oparara Arches**

The largest of these dramatic limestone arch formations is 200m long and 49m wide.

◈ **Punakaiki Pancake Rocks**

These layered rocks have a pancake-like appearance, and spout water from blowholes when sea conditions are right.

◈ **Shantytown**

Visitors can ride on a historic train and pan for gold at this re-created pioneer town.

◈ **Westland/Tai Poutini National Park**

This important 127 541ha park has dramatic mountains, forests, lakes, glaciers and remote beaches.

Glaciers

Fox Glacier and **Franz Josef Glacier** reach down from the high Southern Alps into rainforest valleys only 250m above sea level; nowhere else in the world's temperate zones do glaciers advance so close to the sea. Guided glacier walks and climbs, heli-hikes and scenic flights let visitors get great views of these huge tongues of ice.

Visitor information

Westland i-SITE Visitor Centre
7 Tancred St, Hokitika
Ph: (03) 755 6166

Westport i-SITE Visitor Centre
1 Brougham St, Westport
Ph: (03) 789 6658

www.west-coast.co.nz

Pancake Rocks, Punakaiki

South Island

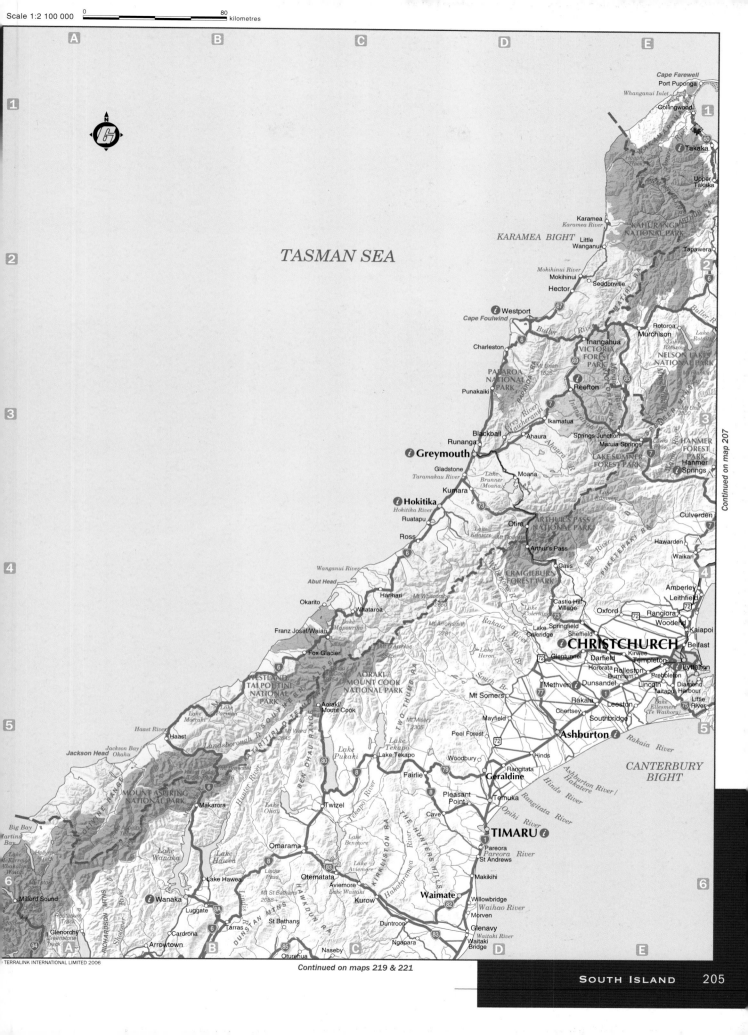

CANTERBURY

Canterbury sweeps from its east coast shoreline lapped by the **Pacific Ocean** across the fertile **Canterbury Plains** to the peaks of the **Southern Alps**. It incorporates some of New Zealand's favourite adventure playgrounds, including **Aoraki/Mount Cook National Park** and **Arthur's Pass National Park**, and combines nine spectacular districts, from **Kaikoura** in the north to **Waimate** at its southern end, with the volcanic grandeur of **Banks Peninsula** to the east.

South Canterbury has an impressive collection of Maori rock art, particularly in the **Opihi** and **Pareora** river areas. The smooth walls of limestone outcrops in South Canterbury provided an ideal canvas for early Maori. Many of the rock drawings have survived the elements and can be clearly seen.

More than half of the South Island's population live in Canterbury, many of them in **Christchurch**, the most English of New Zealand's cities. Between 1858 and 1870, Canterbury attracted almost a fifth of all New Zealand's immigrants. The influence of these largely English settlers is evident today in the architecture and immaculate parks of the South Island's biggest city.

Visitor information

Christchurch i-SITE Visitor Centre
Old Chief Post Office, Cathedral Sq West, Christchurch
Ph: (03) 379 9629
www.christchurchnz.net

TranzAlpine train trip

One of the world's great train journeys, the renowned *TranzAlpine* leaves Christchurch on the east coast, crosses the Canterbury Plains, winds its way over massive viaducts and through the stunning **Waimakariri Gorge**, and crosses the Southern Alps before descending through beech rainforests to arrive in the **West Coast** town of **Greymouth** some 4½ hours later.

main attractions

◈ **Akaroa**

This pretty town flanking beautiful Akaroa Harbour has French origins, evident in its street names, architecture and cuisine.

◈ **Aoraki/Mount Cook National Park**

This inspiring glacial park has the greatest concentration of mountains in the country, including New Zealand's highest peak, Aoraki/Mount Cook.

◈ **Arthur's Pass National Park**

Wide, meandering rivers, steep gorges, native forest and the mountains of the Southern Alps offer visitors boundless outdoor experiences.

◈ **Banks Peninsula**

Birds and marine life are plentiful around this scenic volcanically-formed peninsula.

◈ **Christchurch Botanic Gardens**

Spanning the Avon River, the Botanic Gardens boast a fine collection of exotic and indigenous plants.

◈ **Hanmer Springs Thermal Pools & Spa**

The South Island's main thermal resort has natural hot pools known to Maori as Waitapu (sacred waters).

◈ **Kaikoura whale watching**

Whale watch tours by air or boat allow visitors to see sperm whales, dolphins, seals and orcas.

◈ **Lake Tekapo**

This vividly turquoise-coloured lake is perfectly framed by the majestic Southern Alps.

◈ **Mt Hutt Ski Area**

A fabulous location in the Southern Alps overlooking the Canterbury Plains, Mt Hutt claims the longest ski season in Australasia.

◈ **Waipara Valley wineries**

Pinot noir, riesling, chardonnay and sauvignon blanc dominate plantings in Canterbury's premier wine growing region.

Aoraki/Mount Cook - New Zealand's highest peak

South Island

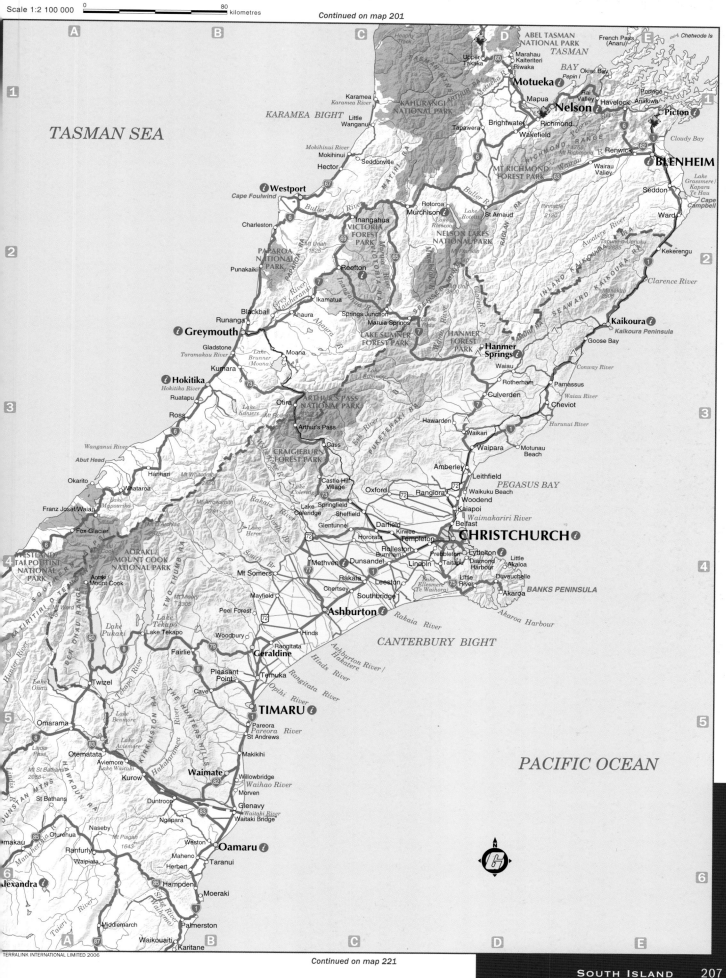

Scale 1:2 100 000

0   80
kilometres

TASMAN SEA

KARAMEA BIGHT

ABEL TASMAN
NATIONAL PARK

TASMAN
BAY

Heaphy
Track

Upper
Takaka

Marahau
Kaiteriteri
Riwaka

French Pass
(Anaru)

Chetwode Is

Motueka *i*

Okiwi Bay

Pepin I

Mapua

Rai
Valley

Havelock

Portage
Anakiwa

Nelson

Picton *i*

Karamea

Karamea River

Little
Wanganui

KAHURANGI
NATIONAL PARK

Brightwater

Richmond

Wakefield

Renwick

Tapawera

Cloudy Bay

Mokihinui River

Mokihinui

Seddonville

Hector

MT RICHMOND
FOREST PARK

Wairau Valley

BLENHEIM

Lake
Grassmere /
Kapara
Te Hau

Seddon

Cape
Campbell

Ward

Rotoroa

Murchison *i*

Lake
Rotoroa

St Arnaud

NELSON LAKES
NATIONAL PARK

Kekerengu

Westport *i*

Cape Foulwind

Charleston

Inangahua

VICTORIA
FOREST
PARK

Mt Uriah
1525

Punakaiki

PAPAROA
NATIONAL
PARK

Reefton *i*

Clarence River

Ikamatua

Springs Junction

Maruia Springs

Lewis
Pass

Mt Una
2300

HANMER
FOREST
PARK

Kaikoura *i*

Kaikoura Peninsula

Blackball

Ahaura

Goose Bay

Runanga

LAKE SUMNER
FOREST PARK

Greymouth *i*

Gladstone

Taramakau River

Lake
Brunner
(Moana)

Moana

Hanmer
Springs

Waiau

Conway River

Kumara

Lake
Sumner

Rotherham

Parnassus

Hokitika *i*

Culverden

Cheviot

Hokitika River

Otira

Ruatapu

ARTHUR'S PASS
NATIONAL PARK

Lake
Kaniere

Hawarden

Waiau River

Hurunui River

Ross

Arthur's Pass

Cass

Waikari

Waipara

Motunau
Beach

Wanganui River

CRAIGIEBURN
FOREST PARK

Amberley

PEGASUS BAY

Abut Head

Mt Whitcombe
2650

Castle Hill
Village

Leithfield

Harihari

Lake
Coleridge

Oxford

Rangiora

Waikuku Beach

Whataroa

Mt Arrowsmith
2781

Lake
Heron

Springfield

Sheffield

Woodend

Kaiapoi

Franz Josef/Waiau

Lake
Mapourika

Glentunnel

Darfield

Waimakariri River

Belfast

Fox Glacier

Lake
Coleridge

Hororata

Kirwee

Templeton

CHRISTCHURCH *i*

Rolleston

Lyttelton

WESTLAND
TAI POUTINI
NATIONAL
PARK

AORAKI
MOUNT COOK
NATIONAL PARK

Mt Cook
3754

Methven

Dunsandel

Lincoln

Taitapu

Little
Akaloa

Diamond
Harbour

Duvauchelle

Aoraki
Mount Cook

Mt Somers

Rakaia

Leeston

Little
River

Akaroa

BANKS PENINSULA

Mt Misery
3305

Mayfield

Chertsey

Lake
Ellesmere
Te Waihora

Southbridge

Peel Forest

Ashburton *i*

Rakaia River

Akaroa Harbour

Lake
Tekapo

Lake Tekapo

Woodbury

Hinds

CANTERBURY BIGHT

Twizel

Fairlie

Rangitata

Geraldine

Temuka

Ashburton River /
Hakatere

Lake
Ohau

Pleasant
Point

Cave

Opihi
River

Hinds
River

Rangitata
River

Omarama

Lake
Benmore

TIMARU *i*

PACIFIC OCEAN

Pareora

Pareora River

St Andrews

Otematata

Aviemore

Kurow

Lake Aviemore

Makikihi

Duntroon

Waimate

Willowbridge

Waihao River

Morven

St Bathans

Mt St Bathans
2088

Lake Waitaki

Ngapara

Glenavy

Weston

Waitaki River

Waitaki Bridge

Oturehua

Naseby

Mt Pisgah
1643

Maheno

Oamaru *i*

Ranfurly

Taranui

Waipiata

Herbert

Alexandra *i*

Hampden

Moeraki

Middlemarch

Palmerston

Waikouaiti

Karitane

TERRALINK INTERNATIONAL LIMITED 2006

CHRISTCHURCH CITY

Named after the cathedral college of Christ Church at Oxford University, Christchurch is New Zealand's most English city. It reflects its English origins with wooded parks, punts gliding down the **Avon River**, neo-Gothic architecture and wooden villas. However, the South Island's largest city (New Zealand's oldest) is set in the middle of premier New Zealand landscape, between the volcanic grandeur of **Banks Peninsula** to the east, and the vast, fertile **Canterbury Plains** to the west. The city has a vibrant culture with its art galleries, arts festivals, shops, restaurants and cafés.

Christchurch has had a significant role in the history of Antarctic exploration. Both Robert Falcon Scott and Ernest Shackleton used the port of **Lyttelton** as the final departure point for expeditions, and there is a statue of Scott in the central city.

Christchurch city is pleasant to explore; its flat terrain lends itself to biking, or visitors can sightsee from the comfort of a historic tram. A good starting point for tourists is the city's **Cathedral Square**, home to Neil Dawson's **Chalice** sculpture and the impressive Gothic **Christchurch Cathedral**.

main attractions

◈ **Arts Centre**

Visitors can enjoy theatre, arts and crafts outlets and fine dining at this dynamic centre for the arts.

◈ **Avon River**

Christchurch's iconic river winds through the city and extensive Botanic Gardens, and is popular for punting.

◈ **Botanic Gardens**

These 30 riverside hectares in the city centre have a huge range of plants and a magnificent rose garden, and are surrounded by 161ha Hagley Park.

◈ **Canterbury Museum**

Built in 1877, this museum is renowned for its collection of Maori artefacts and the Hall of Antarctica.

◈ **Cathedral Square**

This gathering place for locals and tourists has the 18m high metal Chalice sculpture and soaring, Gothic Christchurch Cathedral.

◈ **Christchurch Casino**

The casino has popular table games and the Grand Café.

◈ **Christchurch Pier**

One of the city's main coastal landmarks, this pier stretches more than 300m into the water.

◈ **Christchurch Tramway**

These historic trams follow an inner city loop that takes in local features and shopping areas.

◈ **International Antarctic Centre**

This interesting centre recreates Antarctica's atmosphere, including icy weather in the 'Antarctic Storm' chamber and rides in the all terrain 'Hägglund' vehicle.

◈ **The Gondola**

Take the Gondola to the summit of the Port Hills for panoramic views from the city to the Southern Alps.

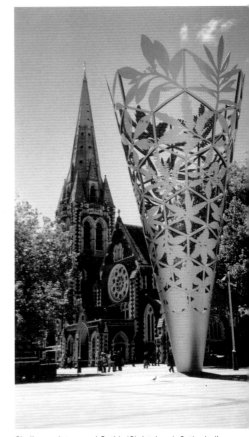

Chalice sculpture and Gothic 'Christchurch Cathedral'

Places of Interest

Antigua Boatsheds **A** C4
Arts Centre **B** C3
Canterbury Brewery **C** C4
Cathedral of the Blessed Sacrament **D** E4
Cathedral Square **E** D3
Centennial Leisure Centre **F** D3
Centre of Contemporary Art **G** C3
Christchurch Cathedral **H** D3
Christchurch Art Gallery **I** C3
Christ's College **J** B3
City Winery **K** C4
Fudge Cottage **L** C3
Jade Stadium **M** E5
Mona Vale **N** A2
New Regent Street **O** D3
Our City O-Tautahi **P** C3
Oxford Terrace **Q** C3
Science Alive! **R** D5
Southern Encounter Aquarium & Kiwi House **S** C3

ℹ️ Visitor information

Christchurch i-SITE Visitor Centre
Old Chief Post Office, Cathedral Sq West, Christchurch
Ph: (03) 379 9629
www.christchurchnz.net

facts

◈ Population: 334 000
◈ Date founded: 1856
◈ Tallest building: Price Waterhouse (76.3m)
◈ Oldest building: Deans Cottage (1843)
◈ Average temperature: 22°C (Jan), 11°C (July)

Christchurch

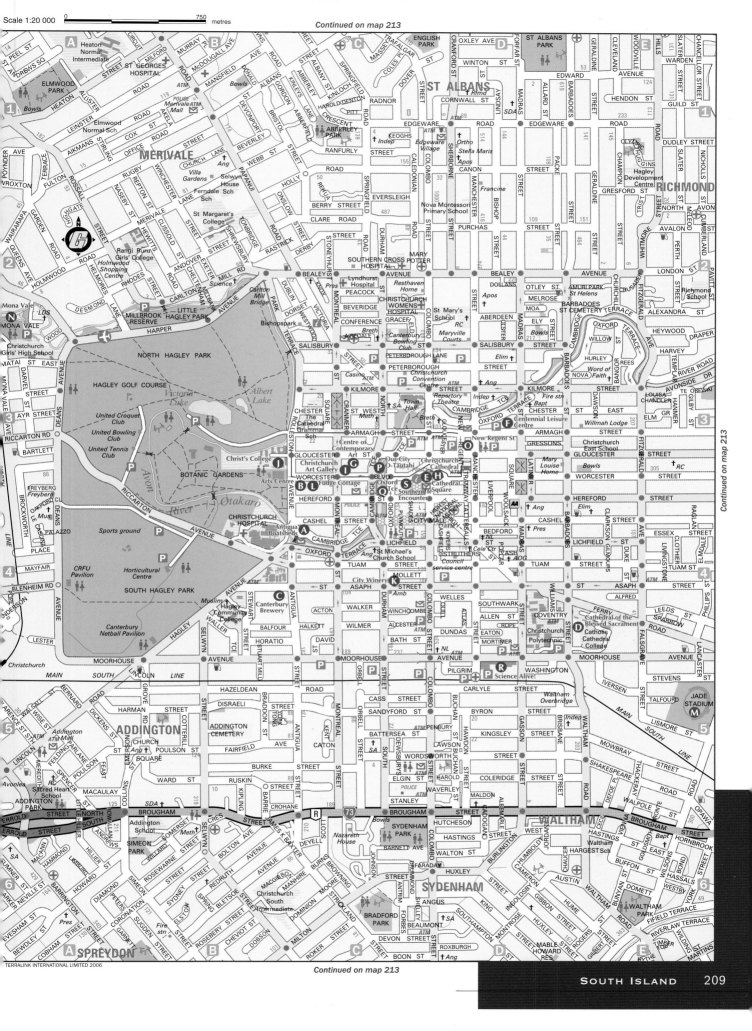

Scale 1:20 000

0   750 metres

TERRALINK INTERNATIONAL LIMITED 2006

CBD & SUBURBS

Christchurch is a pleasant, compact city, easy to explore on foot although its flat terrain inspires some tourists to hire a bike and see the city that way. Another option is to take one of **Christchurch Tramway**'s beautifully restored trams, which do an inner city loop that takes in the local features and shopping areas. Public transport links the city to outlying suburbs, or take a car and create your own itinerary.

Walking tour of central Christchurch

A popular starting point for tourists is the city's **Cathedral Square** in the centre of town. **Christchurch Cathedral**, consecrated in 1881, dominates the square with its Gothic grandeur yet sits well with the modern 18m high **Chalice**, a Neil Dawson metal sculpture, marking the centre of the square. Also at hand is the **Southern Encounter Aquarium & Kiwi House** with a variety of marine life, a touch tank for the kids and a kiwi enclosure.

From Cathedral Square, head north up Colombo Street; turn right onto Gloucester Street, then left up New Regent Street and along the restored tracks of the Tramway, enjoying the pastel painted Spanish mission-style architecture. Turn left

down Armagh Street until you reach **Victoria Square**, a beautiful park with a bridge over the **Avon River** leading to the fragrant **Floral Clock**. Turn left down Durham Street North and left again onto **Oxford Terrace**, a lively centre for nightlife with its restaurants and bars.

Backtracking from Oxford Terrace to Worcester Street, go west to Montreal Street, which will take you to the eye-catching **Christchurch Art Gallery** with its lively programme of local, national and international exhibitions. From Worcester Boulevard, head west to the city's famous **Arts Centre** housed in Gothic Revival buildings that were the original Canterbury College (now **Canterbury University**). The Arts Centre has six galleries, 40 specialty shops and, each weekend, a **Weekend Market** with more than 80 colourful stalls. It also boasts the **Court Theatre**, New Zealand's longest running professional theatre company, and various other performance venues. Nobel Prize winner Lord Ernest Rutherford was a student at Canterbury College, and the Arts Centre's **Rutherford's Den** offers an innovative multimedia glimpse into his life.

From the Arts Centre, turn left down Rolleston Avenue to reach the historic **Antigua Boatsheds**. From there you can rent canoes, rowboats and paddle boats or sit back and relax on a punt and enjoy the serene Avon River. A walk back to the corner of Rolleston Avenue and Worcester Boulevard leads to the **Canterbury Museum** with its stunning **Maori Gallery** and **Antarctic Hall**. No visit to Christchurch is complete without a walk around the famous

Punting on the Avon River, Christchurch

Botanic Gardens, which boast the finest single collection of exotic and indigenous plants in New Zealand. There is also an excellent children's playground and swimming pool. To quench a thirst after a long walk around Christchurch, head south to St Asaph Street where you can enjoy a lively **Canterbury Brewery Heritage Tour** and sample the beers brewed on site.

Suburban attractions

A short drive from the central city, in **Fendalton**, is picturesque **Mona Vale**, an Elizabethan-style homestead on 5.5ha of landscaped gardens, ponds and fountains. **Science Alive!**, housed in the city's old railway station in Moorhouse Avenue, is full of constantly changing interactive exhibits for adults and children with a scientific bent.

Further west from the city centre, **Riccarton House and Bush** has impressive historic buildings (including the oldest on the Canterbury Plains) and 12ha of parkland and native forest. The **Air Force Museum** at **Wigram** has nearly 30 classic aircraft and extensive information about New Zealand's military aviation history. **Orana Wildlife Park** in **McLeans Island** is New Zealand's

Restored tram, Christchurch

Christchurch

FESTIVALS AND EVENTS

Stretching from New Year's Eve to March, **SummerTimes** is a festival of free outdoor entertainment. Each January the **World Buskers Festival** creates a carnival atmosphere around Cathedral Square and the Arts Centre; February's **Flowers & Romance Festival** is set amidst Christchurch's gardens.

The biennial mid-winter **Christchurch Arts Festival** is the South Island's largest arts event and a leading showcase of New Zealand arts and culture, featuring theatre, dance, music, opera, literary and visual arts.

The South Island's foremost gardening show, **Gardenz**, takes place in Hagley Park each Labour Weekend; November's **New Zealand Cup and Show Week** includes fashion shows.

Fireworks display at New Brighton Pier, New Zealand Cup and Show Week, Christchurch

New Brighton Pier, Christchurch

largest open range wildlife and conservation centre.

Reputed to be the world's best Antarctic attraction, the **International Antarctic Centre** is just a few minutes from Christchurch Airport. See the kiwi in its natural environment at the **Willowbank Wildlife Reserve**, and get up close to alpacas, wallabies and deer. Maori cultural performances are also held here.

Heading east from the city centre is **Nga Hau E Wha**, the country's largest marae (Maori tribal meeting-place). This is a multi-cultural facility where visitors can see carvings, weavings and paintings; there's also a nightly concert with the option of a mouth-watering hangi (traditional Maori feast). The **Queen Elizabeth II Park** in **Burwood** is a huge sports complex with indoor pools, waterslides, a gym and squash courts.

For a panoramic view of Christchurch, take the 15-minute drive from the city centre to Bridle Path Road and let the **Gondola** transport you to the summit of the **Port Hills** for breathtaking views of Christchurch, **Lyttelton Harbour** and the **Southern Alps**.

Christchurch's favourite beach is **Sumner**, just south-east of the city. Here you can enjoy a swim, a stroll along its promenade, a coffee at a beachside café and the quirky architecture of the area. Closer to the city are **New Brighton** and **South Brighton** beaches. The **New Brighton Pier** at New Brighton is one of the city's main coastal landmarks and stretches for more than 300m into the water; it's a great place to take photos or settle in with a fishing line. After all that relaxation, get the adrenalin racing with a jet boat ride down the lower **Waimakariri River**.

The perfect way to finish a day exploring Christchurch is to drive over the Port Hills to Christchurch's port, beautiful Lyttelton Harbour. Get a photo at sunset — it will be worth framing.

MANDEVILLE NORTH

SWANNANOA

TRAM

ROAD

TWO CHAIN ROAD

SOUTH

EYRE

ROAD

EYRETON

Kaiapoi

EYREWELL FOREST

Eyre River Diversion

Waimakariri

Continued on map 297

TEMPLERS ISLAND

Lake Tani

Willi Wild Rese

McLEANS ISLAND

McLEANS ISLAND

ROAD

Orana Park

Orana Wildlife Park

JOHNS

SAWYERS ARMS

GARDINERS RD

CASEB

Stu Rd

HAREWOOD

NORT

HAREWOOD

ROAD

ROAD

BISHOPDALE

Bishopdale Shopping Centre

CHRISTCHURCH INTERNATIONAL AIRPORT

Antarctic Centre

BURNSIDE

GRAHAMS ROAD

WAIRAKEI

Wairak Shoppi

BRYND

OLD

WEST

MEMORIAL

Warr Shopping Centre

HALKETT

WEST COAST

ROAD

RUSSLEY

AVONHEAD CEMETERY

Avonhead Shopping Centre

AVENUE

WAIMAIRI

PEER

FENDALTON

HALKETT

ROAD

YALDHURST CEMETERY

ROAD

YALDHURST

HYDE PARK

AVONHEAD

Waimairi Shopping Centre

ILAM

FENDALTON MALL

FENDAL

Fendalton Mall

CHATTERTONS

MINERS ROAD

BUCHANANS

YALDHURST ROAD

RUSSLEY

MASHAM

Riccar House and Mu

UPPER RICCARTON

Bush Inn Shopping Centre

Wes Rice

WEST MELTON

WEST

MASHAM

BROOMFIELD

RICCARTON RACECOURSE

RICCARTO

73

DAWSONS

HASKETTS ROAD

KIRK

RICCARTON RACECOURSE

SOCKBURN

BLENHEIM

COAST

ROAD

HEI HEI

WATERLOO

CARMEN

MIDDLETON

ADD STH

ROAD

RUAPUNA PARK

ISLINGTON

LINE

Hornby Mall

MAIN

SOUTH

Wild West Mini Golf

THEFFERS

CHCH

75

WEST MELTON

SANDY KNOLLS

ROAD

TEMPLETON

HORNBY

WIGRAM AERODROME

Air Force Museum

CANTERBURY AGRICULTURAL PARK

WIGRAM

MAIN

SOUTH

HALSWELL

HORNBY INDUSTRIAL

AWATEA RD

HILLMORTON

WEST MELTON

MIDLAND

MADDISONS

WEEDONS

SOUTH

ROAD

HAMPTONS

SHANDS

SPRINGS

JUNCTION

WIGRAM

DUNBARS RD

WESTLAKE

75

HALSWELL

HENDERSONS RD

SPARKS

LINE

CEM

ROAD

PREBBLETON

CEM

Halswell Shopping Centre

CEM

HALSWELL

HOSKYNS RD

MAIN

Rolleston

BIRCHS

ROAD

HALSWELL QUARRY RESERVE

LINE

Shopping Centre

ROLLESTON

SPRINGSTON

ROBINSONS

ROAD

ROAD

HALSWELL ROAD

OLD TAI TAPU ROAD

LINE

SOUTH

MAIN

WATERHOLES

BROADFIELD

SHANDS

ROAD

ROAD

TAI TAPU ROAD

MAIN

ROLLESTON

ROAD

SHANDS

LADBROOKS

ESMERE

75

CEMETERY

Christchurch

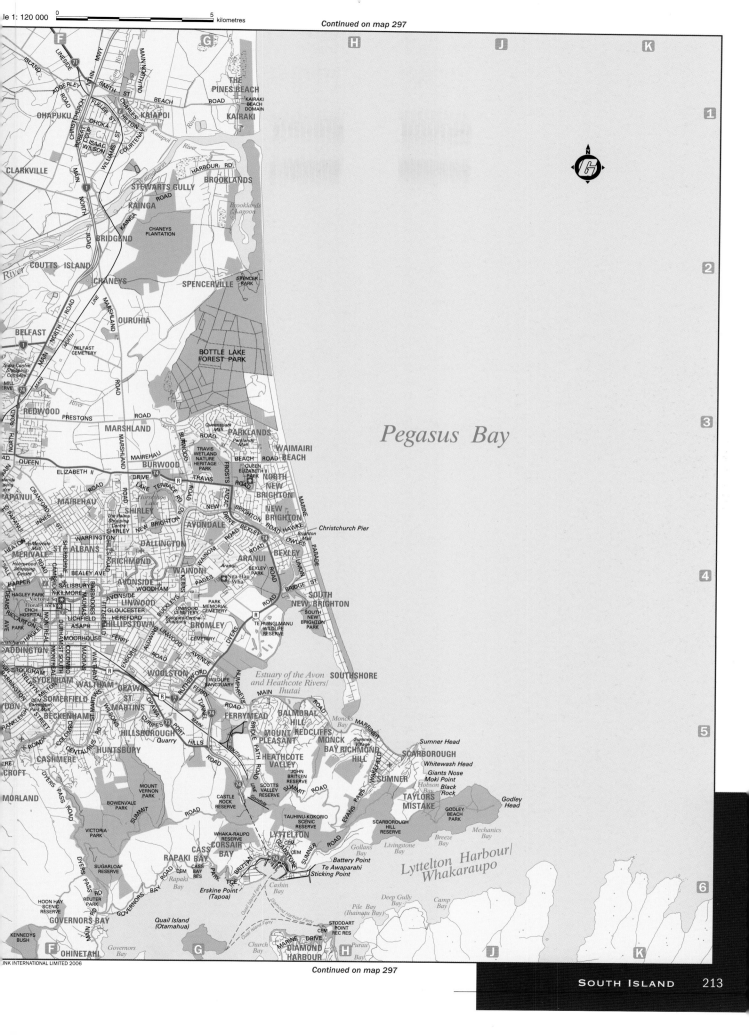

0   5
kilometres

Pegasus Bay

F **G** **H** **J** **K**

N
G

1

2

3

4

5

6

CLARKVILLE

OHAPUKU
KAIAPOI
KAIRAKI
THE PINES BEACH

BROOKLANDS
STEWARTS GULLY
KAINGA
BRIDGEND
CHANEYS PLANTATION
Brooklands Lagoon

COUTTS ISLAND
CHANEYS
SPENCERVILLE
SPENCER PARK
BELFAST
BELFAST CEMETERY
OURUHIA

BOTTLE LAKE
FOREST PARK

REDWOOD
PRESTONS
MARSHLAND
PARKLANDS
Queenspark Mall
Parklands Mall
WAIMAIRI BEACH

BURWOOD
TRAVIS WETLAND NATURE HERITAGE PARK
Queen Elizabeth II Park
NORTH NEW BRIGHTON

APANUI
MAIREHAU
SHIRLEY
TRAVIS
NEW BRIGHTON
Brighton Mall

MERIVALE
ST ALBANS
DALLINGTON
RICHMOND
AVONDALE
BEXLEY
Christchurch Pier
HAWKE

WAINONI
ARANUI
BEXLEY PARK
Nga Hau E Wha

AVONSIDE
WOODHAM
LINWOOD
PHILLIPSTOWN
LINWOOD CEMETERY
PARK MEMORIAL CEMETERY
SOUTH NEW BRIGHTON
SOUTH NEW BRIGHTON PARK

BROMLEY
Te Huingi Manu Wildlife Reserve

ADDINGTON
SYDENHAM
WALTHAM
WOOLSTON
SOUTHSHORE
Estuary of the Avon and Heathcote Rivers / Ihutai

SOMERFIELD
MARTINS
HILLSBOROUGH
FERRYMEAD
BALMORAL HILL
MOUNT PLEASANT
Moncks Bay

BECKENHAM
HUNTSBURY
Quarry
REDCLIFFS
MONCK BAY
RICHMOND HILL
Sumner Village
Sumner Head
SCARBOROUGH

CASHMERE
MOUNT VERNON PARK
HEATHCOTE VALLEY
JOHN BRITTEN RESERVE
Whitewash Head
Giants Nose
Moki Point
Black Rock
SUMNER

MORLAND
BOWENVALE PARK
CASTLE ROCK RESERVE
SCOTTS VALLEY RESERVE
TAYLORS MISTAKE
GODLEY BEACH PARK
Godley Head
Mechanics Bay

CROFT
VICTORIA PARK
SUMMIT
TAUHINU-KOKORIO SCENIC RESERVE
SCARBOROUGH HILL RESERVE
Breeze Bay

SUGARLOAF RESERVE
WHAKA-RAUPO RESERVE
LYTTELTON
Gollans Bay
Livingstone Bay

HOON HAY SCENIC RESERVE
GOVERNORS BAY
RAPAKI BAY
CORSAIR BAY
CASS BAY
Battery Point
Te Awaparahi
Sticking Point
Lyttelton Harbour / Whakaraupo

KENNEDYS BUSH
Erskine Point (Tapoa)
Cashin Bay
Pile Bay (Ihainapu Bay)
Deep Gully Bay
Camp Bay

OHINETAHI
Governors Bay
Quail Island (Otamahua)
Church Bay
DIAMOND HARBOUR
Purau Bay
STODDART POINT REC RES

LAKE WANAKA

This beautiful region of spectacular mountain scenery, glacier-formed lakes and unspoilt forests has attracted tourists since the 19th century, with paddle steamer cruises available to the head of **Lake Wanaka** from 1881.

The area's two signature lakes, Lake Wanaka and **Lake Hawea**, were gouged out of solid rock by glaciers. Both dramatically blue, they are fed by melt water from snow fields and glaciers. The two lakes are surrounded by mountains, and deciduous trees at the water's edge are showy in autumn. The area draws visitors in all seasons, with great skiing at **Treble Cone**

and **Cardrona** in the winter, and jet boating, rafting, fishing, hiking and adventure activities year round.

The relaxed town of **Wanaka**, on the southern shore of Lake Wanaka, has a strong arts community and offers good accommodation, shopping, restaurants and winery visits. It's also a base for trips to **Mount Aspiring National Park**; the park's pinnacle, pyramid-shaped 3033m **Mount Aspiring/Tititea**, can be seen from **Glendhu Bay**, ten minutes' drive from Wanaka. The

road south over the **Crown Range** to **Arrowtown** offers wonderful views, and historic sites in the **Cardrona Valley**.

 Visitor information

Lake Wanaka i-SITE Visitor Centre
100 Ardmore St, Wanaka
Ph: (03) 443 1233
www.lakewanaka.co.nz

Lake Wanaka

Glacially formed Lake Wanaka, New Zealand's fourth largest lake, is more than 300m deep; in Maori mythology, the chief Te Rakaihautu dug the lake with his digging stick. The mighty **Clutha River**, NZ's largest river by volume, has its origins at the south end of the lake.

main attractions

◆ **Adventure activities**

Jet boating, rafting, canyoning, river sledging, rock climbing and abseiling are all on offer around Wanaka.

◆ **Cardrona**

This historic area has old gold mining sites, Cardrona Skifield and the 1863 Cardrona Hotel; there are dramatic views from the Crown Range Road.

◆ **Lake Hawea**

A narrow isthmus separates this lovely glacial lake from Lake Wanaka.

◆ **Makarora**

Tiny Makarora is a base for trips into the national park, and for the Siberia Experience, an adventure experience involving jet boating, hiking and a plane flight.

◆ **Mount Aspiring National Park**

This World Heritage Area offers long and short walks, and lovely mountain scenery.

◆ **Rippon Vineyard**

Rippon Vineyard, on the shores of Lake Wanaka, is one of New Zealand's most beautifully sited wineries.

◆ **Rob Roy Track**

This easy 1.5-hour walk in Mount Aspiring National Park offers alpine scenery and views of the Rob Roy Glacier.

◆ **Treble Cone Skifield**

The largest ski field in the South Island, Treble Cone has some of New Zealand's longest groomed runs.

◆ **Warbirds Museum**

Wanaka's Warbirds Museum has WWII fighter planes, flight simulators and displays.

◆ **Warbirds Over Wanaka**

Visitors throng to Wanaka for this biennial air show at Easter, featuring historic aircraft.

Dusk at Lake Wanaka

South Island

Scale 1:1 050 000

0   40   kilometres

Continued on map 205

A B C D E

1

Bruce Bay

WESTLAND
TAI POUTINI
NATIONAL PARK

Aoraki/
Mt Cook

Aoraki/
Mount Cook

Lake
Paringa

Mt Ward
2645

Dun Fiunary
2500

Open Bay
Islands

Haast

Haast River

Mt Macfarlane
2057

SOLUTION RA

BANNOCK BRAE RA

STRACHAN RA

NEUMANN RANGE

BEN OHAU RANGE

Lake
Pukaki

Mt Sefton
3151

KA TIRITIRI O TE MOANA

2

Hannahs Clearing

Jackson Head

Jackson Bay

Jackson Bay /
Okahu

Neils Beach

Haast Pass
Haipai

Mt Brewster
2516

Mt Huxley
2505

SOUTHERN ALPS

YOUNG RANGE

BARRIER RA

Lake
Ohau

Lake Ohau
Alpine Village

Twizel

MOUNT ASPIRING

Mt Alba
2360

Mt Fowler
2606

Makarora

Mt Melina
1925

Lake
Hawea

Omarama

Lake
Benmore

NATIONAL PARK

OLIVINE RANGE

ASPIRING RANGE

AWARUA RANGE

Awarua Point

Big Bay

Martins Bay

Mt Aspiring /
Tititea
3038

Mt Alta
2339

Lake
Wanaka

Lake
Wanaka

Lindis Pass

Otematata

ST BATHANS RA

HAWKDUN RANGE

Lake
McKerrow
Whakatipu
Waitai

Mt Tutoko
2723

Lake Alabaster
Wawahi Waka

Mt Earnslaw
Pikirakatahi
2820

HARRIS MOUNTAINS

HUMBOLDT MOUNTAINS

ROUTEBURN TRACK

Lake Hawea

Albert Town

Wanaka

Luggate

Lindis Peak
1226

Mt St Bathans
2088

Mt Ida
1690

3

Milford Sound

Mila Peak
1683

EARL MTS

DARRAN MTS

North River

LIVINGSTONE MTNS

AILSA MTNS

RICHARDSON MTNS

GREENSTONE TRACK

Greenstone River

Shotover River

Glenorchy

Mt Cardrona
1954

Cardrona

Mt Pisa
1963

PISA RANGE

Tarras

Cloudy Peak
1526

St Bathans

DUNSTAN MOUNTAINS

Becks

Oturehua

Naseby

4

Arrowtown

Coronet Peak
1651

Arthurs Point

Queenstown

Kawarau River

Double Cone
2319

Bannockburn

Cromwell

Omakau

Ophir

Manuherikia River

Wedderburn

Ranfurly

Waipiata

ROUGH RIDGE

5

THOMSON MOUNTAINS

EYRE MOUNTAINS

Lake
Wakatipu

North
Mavora
Lake

Ben Nevis
2234

Nevis River

Clyde

Alexandra

Lake
Dunstan

Lake
Roxburgh

Pinelheugh
1124

TAIERI RIVER

Summit Rock
1452

Orangapai

Patearoa

Middlemarch

Lake
Te Anau

Snowdon Peak
1573

Jane Peak
2022

Kingston

GARVIE MOUNTAINS

HECTOR MTNS

Rocky Mount
1885

Lake Roxburgh

Roxburgh

Teviot

UMBRELLA MTNS

Whitecoomb
1455

6

Te Anau

TAKITIMU MTNS

Spence Peak
1634

Oreti River

Aparima R.

Mossburn

Mid Dome
1478

Garston

Athol

Lumsden

Mataura R.

Balfour

Waikaia

Waikaia River

Heriot

Ettrick

Millers Flat

Lammermoor
1160

LAMMERMOOR

Lake
Mahinerangi

Lawrence

Waipori
Falls

A B C D E

Joins map 221

QUEENSTOWN

With magnificent mountain scenery, beautiful lakes, wineries in spectacular settings, intriguing gold mining history and the bustling town of **Queenstown**, the Queenstown region is deservedly hugely popular with visitors. Beautiful year-round, in winter it's a major centre for skiing and snow sports.

In an extraordinarily scenic setting on the shores of **Lake Wakatipu**, surrounded by the dramatic **Eyre Mountains** and **Remarkables**, Queenstown is a busy resort town with dozens of bars, restaurants and visitor activities on offer. It's known as 'Adventure Capital of the World', and adrenalin aficionados can get their fix from bungy jumping, white water sledging, jet boating, canyon swinging, skydiving and more.

Those of a more peaceful bent can explore historic gold mining sites around **Arrowtown**, visit gloriously sited wineries in the **Gibbston Valley**, walk among unspoilt forests and glacial lakes in the World Heritage Area of **Mount Aspiring National Park**, or relax at peaceful **Glenorchy**, near Lake Wakatipu's northern tip. Glenorchy is the gateway to the national park and to some of New Zealand's best walks, including the famous **Routeburn Track**.

 Visitor information

Queenstown i-SITE Visitor Centre
Clocktower Bldg, Queenstown
Ph: (03) 442 4100,
Freephone: 0800 668 888
www.queenstown-vacation.com

main attractions

◈ **Adventure activities**
A huge array of activities are on offer, many of them in beautiful, dramatic settings.

◈ **Coronet Peak Skifield**
The region's oldest ski field offers great skiing and snowboarding.

◈ **Gibbston Valley**
This gorgeous valley is home to picturesque wineries in dramatic settings, including New Zealand's most visited winery.

◈ **Glenorchy**
The lakeside village of Glenorchy is a base for trips into Mount Aspiring National Park.

◈ **Lake Wakatipu**
This zigzag-shaped lake was formed by glaciers, and is bordered on all sides by mountains.

◈ **Queenstown**
Lively Queenstown is one of New Zealand's most important holiday destinations.

◈ **Routeburn Track**
This 32km 'Great Walk' features waterfalls, lakes, beech forest and gorgeous mountain scenery.

◈ **Skippers Canyon**
This spectacular canyon, once a centre for gold mining, offers adventure activities.

◈ *The Lord of the Rings* **filming locations**
Settings from all around the Queenstown region were used in the film trilogy.

◈ *TSS Earnslaw*
Cruises on Lake Wakatipu and to Walter Peak High Country Farm are available on this historic coal-fired steamer.

Arrowtown
Established after a gold find on the **Arrow River** in 1862, Arrowtown today has beautiful old wooden buildings, historic sites and a restored Chinese miners' settlement. The town is beautiful in autumn, when the deciduous trees on its streets and nearby hills turn gold and red.

Shotover River, Queenstown

South Island

Scale 1:1 050 000

0 _____ 40 kilometres

Continued on map 205

A　　　　B　　　　C　　Jackson Head　Jackson Bay /　Hannahs Clearing　D　　　　E

TASMAN SEA

Jackson Bay　Okahu

Neils Beach

1

Awarua Point

MOUNT ASPIRING

Mt Brewster
2515

Mt Huxley
2505

Big Bay

Mt Alba
2360

NATIONAL PARK

Makarora

Lake Ohau
Alpine Village

Martins Bay

Mt Pollux
2536

2

Lake
McKerrow /
Whakatipu
Waitai

Lake Alabaster
Waiwhakiki Waka

Mt Aspiring /
Tititea
3033

Lake
Wanaka

Mt Melina
1925

Milford Sound /
Piopiotahi

Mt Tutako
2723

Mt Earnslaw /
Pikirakatahi
2830

Mt Alta
2339

Lake
Hawea

Lake Hawea

Lindis Pass

Mitre Peak
1683

Lake
Wanaka

Albert Town

Mt St
Bathans
2088

Poison Bay

Wanaka

Lindis Peak
1226

Sutherland Sound

Luggate

Tarras

Cloudy Peak
1526

St Bathans

Bligh Sound

Milford Sound

Glenorchy

Mt Cardrona
1964

Mt Pisa
1963

3

FIORDLAND

Mt Irene
1859

Arthurs Point

Cardrona

Lake
Dunstan

Becks

NATIONAL PARK

Coronet Peak
1651

Arrowtown

Cromwell

Omakau

Mt Balloon
1992

Queenstown

Kawarau River

Double Cone
2319

Cromwell

Ophir

Clyde

Lake
Wakatipu

Bannockburn

Alexandra

4

Showdon Peak
1573

Ben Nevis
2234

Lake
Roxburgh

North
Mavora
Lake

Kingston

Rocky Mount
1885

Jane Peak
2022

Lake
Te Anau

Lake Roxburgh

Roxburgh

Pinelheugh
1124

Te Anau

Garston

Teviot

5

Athol

Millers Flat

Monowai

Mid Dome
1478

Whitecomb
1455

Ettrick

1159

Lake
Manapouri

Mossburn

Heriot

Lawrence

Lake
Monowai

Lumsden

Waikaia

Waitahuna

Ohai

Balfour

Waikaka

Tapanui

Tuapeka Mouth

Clifden

Nightcaps

Wairio

Dipton

Riversdale

Mandeville

Pukerau

Clydevale

Pukemaori

Papatotara

Tuatapere

Otautau

Drummond

Winton

Gore

Waipahi

Clinton

Waiwera
South

Balclutha

6

Fairfax

Mataura

Wyndham

Mokoreta
713

Orepuki

Thornbury

Edendale

A　　　　B　　　　C　　　　D　　　　E

© TERRALINK INTERNATIONAL LIMITED 2006

Continued on map 231

SOUTH ISLAND 217

Joins map 219

CENTRAL OTAGO

Beautiful Central Otago is a golden heartland of dramatic landscapes and climatic extremes. This was gold mining country in the late 19th century, and many of the region's towns owe their existence to the gold boom. The first finds were in 1861, and within a few months thousands of people were at work on the diggings. There are many historic gold mining sites to be seen, and miners' trails wander through the hills.

Central Otago today is a peaceful place of evocative old stone and mud-brick buildings, historic towns, gold mining relics, dramatic rock formations, lush fruit orchards and beautifully-sited vineyards; the region is particularly lovely in autumn, when golden-leaved trees and tussock contrast with the intense blues and turquoises of the rivers and lakes.

'Central' has long been home to many orchards, which grow cherries, apricots, apples, nectarines, plums and pears. Today, wine is a burgeoning industry; hot summers and cold winters make the region particularly suited to pinot noir, and vineyards stretch across former farmland around **Cromwell**, **Bannockburn** and **Alexandra**.

 Visitor information

Alexandra i-SITE Visitor Centre
Centennial Ave, Alexandra
Ph: (03) 448 9515

Cromwell and Districts i-SITE Visitor Centre
47 The Mall, Cromwell
Ph: (03) 445 0212
www.centralotagonz.com

Otago Central Rail Trail

This unique 150km trail for walkers, cyclists and horse riders was once the Central Otago rail branch line, which closed in 1990. The re-surfaced trail allows users to explore the area's remote scenery and history in a peaceful setting without cars; it crosses historic bridges and viaducts and goes through tunnels.

main attractions

◈ **Bannockburn**
Dramatically-sited vineyards and old gold mining areas dot the beautiful Bannockburn countryside.

◈ **Bendigo**
At these abandoned gold towns, visitors can see ruined cottages, mine shafts and tailings.

◈ **Central Otago wineries**
Pinot noir is the main focus in this thriving cool-climate wine region.

◈ **Clyde**
This historic small town is dotted with beautiful old stone buildings from the gold rush days.

◈ **Kawarau Gorge**
There are dramatic rapids and a gold mining centre in this spectacular gorge.

◈ **Lake Dunstan**
Peaceful Lake Dunstan, created when the Cromwell Gorge was flooded, offers water sports and eco-tourism.

◈ **Maniototo**
The vast, spacious plain of the Maniototo, known as 'Big Sky Country', offers outdoor activities and gold mining relics.

◈ **Ophir**
Once a bustling gold-rush centre, this quiet village has lovely historic stone buildings.

◈ **Ranfurly**
Blessed with many art deco buildings, Ranfurly has reinvented itself as a rural art deco capital.

◈ **St Bathans**
Tiny St Bathans, once home to 2000 people, has a historic hotel and lovely old mud-brick buildings.

Blue Lake, Saint Bathans

South Island

Scale 1:1 050 000

0 40 kilometres

Continued on map 205

Jackson Head
Jackson Bay Okahu
Jackson Bay
A **B** **C** **D** Lake Tekapo **E** Kimbell

Neils Beach

Burkes Pass
Fairlie

MOUNT ASPIRING
Mt Brewster 2515
Mt Huxley 2505

Tengawai

NATIONAL PARK
Mt Alba 2360
YOUNG RANGE

Mt Pollux 2536

HUXLEY RANGE
BARRIER RA
Lake Pukaki

Lake Ohau

Albury

1 Makarora **1**

BEN OHAU R

Twizel

Mt Aspiring/Tititea 3033

Lake Ohau Alpine Village

GRAMPIAN MTNS

Mt Melina 1925

HAAST RANGE

THE HUNTERS HILLS

Hakataramea River

DALGETY RA

Lake Wanaka

2 Omarama **2**

Mt Ramslaw/Pikirakatahi 2830

Lake Hawea

ST BATHANS RA

Lindis Pass

Lake Benmore

Mt Sutton 1916

KIRKLISTON RANGE

Otematata

Aviemore
L Aviemore

Lake Waitaki

Lake Hawea

Mt St Bathans 2088

HAWKDUN RANGE

Albert Town

Lindis Peak 1226

L Waitaki

Wanaka

Luggate

Kurow

Waitaki River

Glenorchy

Mt Cardrona 1936
Mt Pisa 1963

Tarras

St Bathans

Kohurau 2015

Duntroon

Cardrona

Cloudy Peak 1526

Mt Ida 1690

Ngapara

3 Arrowtown Becks Oturehua Kyeburn Diggings **3**

Arthurs Point

Coronet Peak 1651

PISA RANGE

Lake Dunstan

DUNSTAN MOUNTAINS

Naseby

Maheno

Queenstown

Kawarau River

Cromwell

Omakau

Wedderburn

Mt Pisgah 1643

Reidston

Double Cone 2319

Bannockburn

Ophir

Ranfurly

Herbert

Lake Wakatipu

Ben Nevis 2234

Clyde

Manuherikia River

Waipiata

Hampden

Jane Peak 2022

Alexandra

Orangapai

Hyde

Moeraki

4 Kingston Patearoa Dunback **4**

Rocky Mount 1885

Lake Roxburgh

Summit Rock 1450

Macraes Flat

HECTOR MTNS

Nevis River

Middlemarch

Palmerston

Garston

Pinelheugh 1124

ROUGH RIDGE

Taieri River

Waikouaiti

Athol

Lake Roxburgh

ROCK AND PILLAR RA

Karitane

Mid Dome 1478

Whitecoomb 1455

Roxburgh

Teviot

Taieri River

Hummock 736

Seacliff

GARVIE MOUNTAINS

UMBRELLA MTNS

Ettrick

Millers Flat

Otago Harbour

5 Waikaia 1159 Outram Port Chalmers **5**

Lumsden

Mosgiel

Cape Saunders

EYRE MOUNTAINS

Heriot

Lake Mahinerangi

Allanton

Balfour

Tapanui 1019

Lawrence

Waipori Falls

DUNEDIN

Dipton

Riversdale

Waikaka

Tapanui

Berwick

Brighton

HOKONUI HILLS

Mandeville

Pomahaka River

Tuapeka Mouth

Waitahuna

Lake Waihola

Waihola

Mataura River

Clutha River

Taieri Mouth

6 Gore Pukerau Waipahi Clydevale Milton **6**

Winton

Waiwera South

Balclutha

PACIFIC OCEAN

Edendale

Mataura

Clinton

Kaitangata

Wyndham

Mokoreta 715

Mata Au

Wallacetow

A **B** **C** **D** **E**

Molyneux Bay
Kaka Point

Joins map 221

SOUTH ISLAND 219

© TERRALINK INTERNATIONAL LIMITED 2006

DUNEDIN

Fascinating history, plentiful wildlife, great natural beauty and the interesting city of **Dunedin** draw visitors to this region in the south-east South Island. The Dunedin region is bounded to the east by the Pacific coast, and inland by mountain ranges, the **Waitaki River** and a string of man-made lakes for hydro-electric power production.

Moeraki

The small coastal settlement of Moeraki is known for the fascinating **Moeraki Boulders/ Kaihinaki**, spherical 65-million-year-old boulders up to four metres in circumference, which lie scattered along the beach. A walk through native bush leads to a viewing platform overlooking the boulders, or visitors can walk among them on the beach.

Maori settled the coastal area around Dunedin four centuries ago, and European settlement began in the 1830s. Dunedin city, driven by the 1860s gold mining boom, was New Zealand's main commercial and industrial centre in the late 19th century; as a result, it has a rich legacy of Edwardian and Victorian buildings.

The port town of **Oamaru**, to the north, also became prosperous due to the 19th century trade in shipping frozen meat to Britain; its harbour area was developed with grand buildings built from the local cream-coloured limestone. These elegant, imposing buildings still stand today, many of them now home to cafés, shops and galleries.

For those with an interest in wildlife, the region's beautiful coastline is well populated with seals, penguins, sea lions and birds, including some rare species.

i Visitor information

Dunedin i-SITE Visitor Centre
48 The Octagon, Dunedin
Ph: (03) 474 3300
www.dunedinnz.com

main attractions

◈ Dunedin
The 'Edinburgh of the south' has vibrant culture, elegant historic buildings, natural beauty and a lively student scene.

◈ Gabriel's Gully
Gabriel's Gully was the site of a massive gold rush in 1861; visitors can still pan for gold today.

◈ Golden Point Historic Reserve
Historic gold mining relics and a working battery can be seen at this site of an 1889 gold mine.

◈ Lake Waihola/Sinclair Wetlands
Lake Waihola is popular for boating, fishing and swimming; the nearby Sinclair Wetlands have rich bird and fish life.

◈ Matanaka Farm Buildings
New Zealand's oldest surviving farm buildings date from the 1840s.

◈ Oamaru
Beautiful heritage buildings, penguin colonies and an interesting arts scene make Oamaru worth a visit.

◈ Otago Peninsula
Close to Dunedin, scenic Otago Peninsula is home to a rich array of wildlife.

◈ Royal Albatross Centre
The majestic royal albatross can be viewed at the world's only mainland breeding colony.

◈ Taieri Gorge Railway
This trip on a historic section of railway line leads through the rugged, spectacular Taieri Gorge.

◈ Wildlife
Seals, blue penguins, yellow-eyed penguins, sea lions and albatrosses can all be seen around the region.

Moeraki Boulders/Kaihinaki, Moeraki

South Island

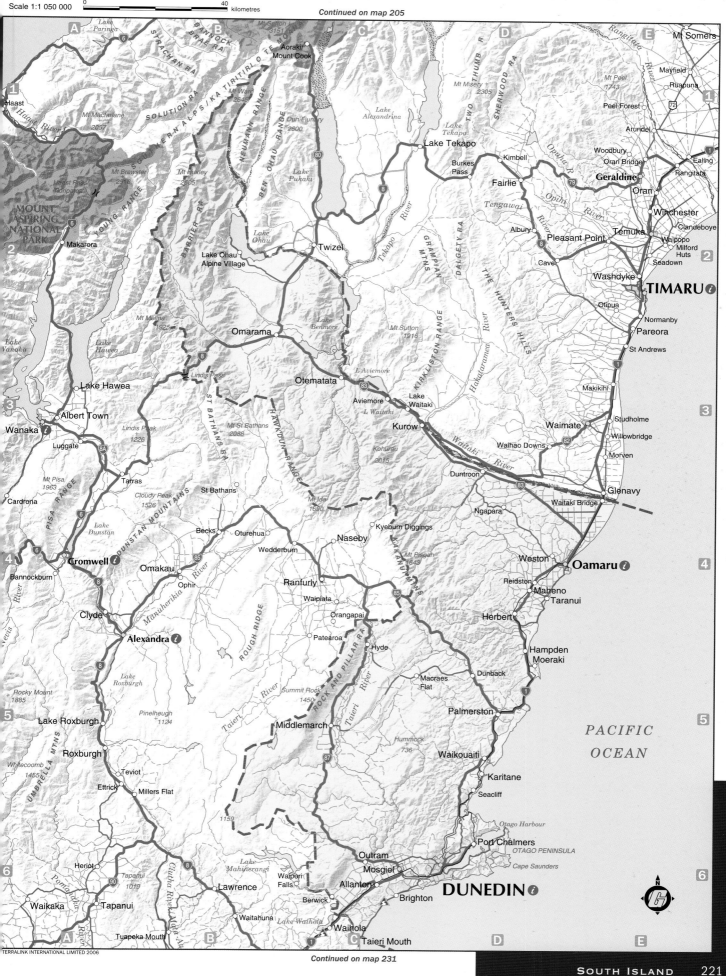

0   40 kilometres

Continued on map 205

A   B   C   D   E

Lake Paringa
Mt Sefton
3151
Aoraki/
Mount Cook
Mt Somers
Mayfield
Ruapuna
1
Haast
Mt Macfarlane
2057
Mt Ward
2645
Lake
Alexandrina
Mt Misery
2305
Mt Peel
1743
Peel Forest
Arundel
Dun Fiunary
2500
Lake
Tekapo
Woodbury
Orari Bridge
Ealing
2
Mount
Aspiring
National
Park
Mt Brewster
2516
Mt Huxley
2505
Lake Tekapo
Burkes
Pass
Kimbell
Geraldine
Orari
Rangitata
Makarora
Lake
Ohau
Fairlie
Winchester
Temuka
Clandeboye
Waipopo
Milford
Huts
Seadown
Lake Ohau
Alpine Village
Twizel
Albury
Pleasant Point
Cave
Washdyke
TIMARU
3
Lake
Hawea
Omarama
Lake
Benmore
Mt Sutton
1916
Otipua
Normanby
Pareora
St Andrews
Makikihi
Lake Hawea
Albert Town
Lindis Pass
Otematata
L Aviemore
Aviemore
L Waitaki
Lake
Waitaki
Waimate
Studholme
Willowbridge
Wanaka
Mt St Bathans
2088
Kurow
Kohurau
2015
Duntroon
Walhao Downs
Morven
Glenavy
Waitaki Bridge
4
Luggate
Lindis Peak
1226
St Bathans
Mt Ida
1690
Becks
Oturehua
Kyeburn Diggings
Naseby
Ngapara
Mt Pisgah
1643
Weston
Oamaru
Reidston
Maheno
Taranui
Cromwell
Omakau
Ophir
Wedderburn
Ranfurly
Waipiata
Herbert
Cardrona
Mt Pisa
1963
Tarras
Cloudy Peak
1526
Clyde
Orangapai
Patearoa
Hyde
Hampden
Moeraki
Dunback
Alexandra
Bannockburn
Lake
Roxburgh
Summit Rock
1450
Macraes
Flat
5
Rocky Mount
1885
Pinelheugh
1124
Middlemarch
Hummock
736
Waikouaiti
PACIFIC
OCEAN
Lake Roxburgh
Karitane
Roxburgh
Teviot
Seacliff
Ettrick
Millers Flat
Whitecoomb
1455
1159
Port Chalmers
OTAGO PENINSULA
6
Heriot
Tapanui
1019
Lawrence
Lake
Mahinerangi
Waipori
Falls
Outram
Mosgiel
Allanton
Brighton
Otago Harbour
Cape Saunders
DUNEDIN
Waikaka
Tapanui
Waitahuna
Berwick
Waihola
Tuapeka Mouth
Lake Waihola
Waihola
Taieri Mouth

A   B   C   D   E

Continued on map 231

DUNEDIN CITY

main attractions

◈ **Baldwin Street**

Featured in the *Guinness Book of Records* as the world's steepest street, Baldwin Street has a gradient of 1 in 1.266.

◈ **Cadbury World**

Chocolate aficionados will relish the Cadbury World tour and chocolate shop.

◈ **Dunedin Public Art Gallery**

This excellent gallery features New Zealand art and changing exhibitions.

◈ **Dunedin Railway Station**

The ornate Flemish Renaissance-styled railway station is one example of Dunedin's rich historic architecture.

◈ **Larnach Castle**

New Zealand's only castle is an ornately decorated building on Otago Peninsula, and has great harbour views.

◈ **Mount Cargill**

There are impressive views over Dunedin from the summit of Mount Cargill.

◈ **Otago Museum**

This excellent museum has Maori, historical and nature exhibits.

◈ **Royal Albatross Centre**

At the world's only mainland breeding colony for the royal albatross, visitors can see and learn about these majestic birds.

◈ **St Kilda**

St Kilda is a popular beach for swimming and surfing.

◈ **Tunnel Beach**

An interesting walk leads to Tunnel Beach, which has a hand-hewn stone tunnel, rock arches and caves.

facts

◈ Population: 120 000
◈ Date founded: 1848
◈ Oldest building: Ferntree House, 1849
◈ Average temperature: 19°C (January), 9°C (July)

Education, arts and culture, historic architecture and wildlife are all a focus in the interesting city of Dunedin. The city is sited on dramatic hills at the south-west end of a long natural harbour, in an area first settled by Maori more than four centuries ago. Whalers, gold miners and other immigrants — many of them from Scotland and China — followed in the 19th century. Scottish settlers gave Dunedin much of its character, and its name, which is Gaelic for Edinburgh.

With the advent of the 1860s **Otago** gold rush, Dunedin became New Zealand's most populous and prosperous city. Today it's comparatively quiet, but remains one of the southern hemisphere's best preserved Edwardian and Victorian cities. The **University of Otago**, New Zealand's first university, was founded there in 1869, and students ('scarfies', in local parlance) still make up a strong part of the city's culture.

Peaceful **Otago Peninsula**, only 20 minutes' drive away on the south-east side of **Otago Harbour**, is home to an impressive array of wildlife, including albatrosses, fur seals, sea lions, blue penguins and rare yellow-eyed penguins.

Places of Interest

Cadbury World **Ⓐ** C3
Dunedin Botanic Gardens **Ⓑ** D1
Dunedin Casino **Ⓒ** B4
Dunedin Public Art Gallery **Ⓓ** B4
Dunedin Public Libraries **Ⓔ** B3
Dunedin Railway Station **Ⓕ** C4
First Church of Otago **Ⓖ** B4
Fortune Theatre **Ⓗ** B4
Hocken Collections **Ⓘ** D3
Knox Church **Ⓙ** C3
Moana Pool **Ⓚ** B3
New Zealand Sports Hall of Fame **Ⓛ** C4
Olveston **Ⓜ** B3
Otago Museum **Ⓝ** C2
Otago Settlers Museum **Ⓞ** C4
Speight's Brewery **Ⓟ** B4
St Joseph's Cathedral **Ⓠ** B4
St Paul's Cathedral **Ⓡ** B4
The Octagon **Ⓢ** B4
University of Otago **Ⓣ** C3

---

i **Visitor information**

Dunedin i-SITE Visitor Centre
48 The Octagon, Dunedin
Ph: (03) 474 3300
www.dunedinnz.com

University of Otago, Dunedin

Dunedin

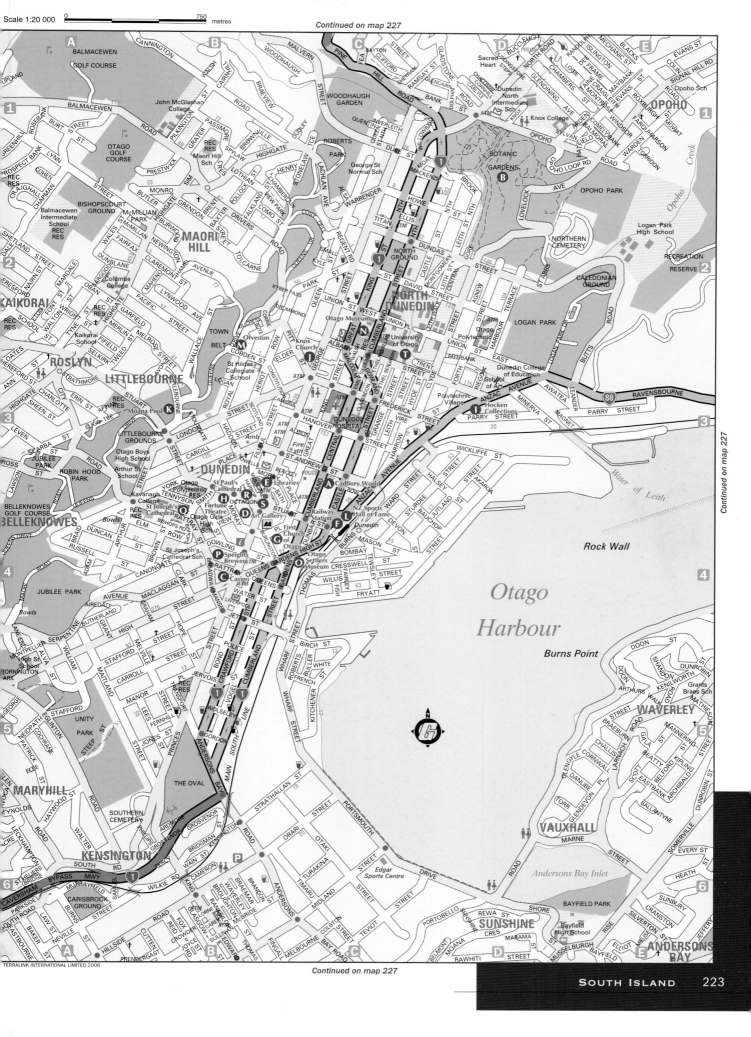

CBD & SUBURBS

Dunedin Railway Station

Many of Dunedin's central attractions are close together and can be easily explored by walking; the Dunedin City Explorer is a bus service which loops around the main attractions. Dunedin is a hilly city, but distances are not great, and the central city is flat and relatively compact. Buses serve the outlying suburbs; for visits to **Otago Peninsula**, a car is recommended.

Walking tour of central Dunedin

Dunedin Railway Station is a good starting point for a walking tour; opened in 1906, it's an imposing building with glorious Flemish Renaissance-styled architecture. Trips leave the station daily on the **Taieri Gorge Railway**, a journey on a historic railway line which passes over high viaducts and through hand-carved rock tunnels, and heads through the spectacular **Taieri Gorge**. Also at the railway station, the **New Zealand Sports Hall of Fame** explores New Zealand's greatest sporting achievements.

West of here on Cumberland Street, chocolate factory tours are on offer at **Cadbury World**; the factory has operated since the 1930s. Head south to Queens Gardens and the **Otago Settlers Museum** to find out about the Maori, Scots, Chinese and others who have made Otago their home. Wildlife cruises around **Otago Peninsula** leave from the wharf to the east. To the west on Moray Place, the 1873-built Gothic **First Church of Otago** has beautiful stained glass and a tapestry of the region's early settlement. Further west, on Rattray Street, the famous southern **Speight's Brewery** offers guided tours and beer tasting; **St Joseph's Cathedral** is an ornate Catholic cathedral. There's more impressive early architecture at **Otago Boys' High School** on Arthur Street, and around the corner in Stuart Street are Edwardian terrace houses.

Head back down Stuart Street to the city's central hub, the **Octagon**, which features a statue of the 18th century Scottish poet Robbie Burns. **Dunedin Public Art Gallery** has excellent fine arts exhibitions; **St Paul's Cathedral** is an imposing church built in Oamaru stone. There are interesting shops, galleries and cafés on and around the Octagon.

A walk north up Great King Street leads to the excellent displays at **Otago Museum**, which include the **Southern Land, Southern People Gallery**. **Discovery World**, part of the museum, is an interactive science centre. To the east is the **University of Otago**, founded in 1869, and the centre of Dunedin's lively student culture; its Gothic-style clocktower was built in 1878. East of the university on Anzac Avenue are the wonderful **Hocken Collections**, a historical research library and treasure trove of manuscripts, paintings, drawings, photographs and more. Further north-east are the 28ha **Dunedin Botanic Gardens**, where the 4ha **Rhododendron Dell** puts on a bright display in spring, and there's a bird-filled aviary.

South-west on Royal Terrace, the historic Jacobean-style mansion **Olveston** was built in 1904–06, and contains artefacts from around the world; today, it's open to the public, and lets visitors see how a prosperous Dunedin family would have lived in the early years of the 20th century.

Suburban attractions

A 2km drive north of the central city is the world's steepest street, **Baldwin Street**, which has a gradient of 1 in 1.266, and is the venue for events including the 'Gutbuster' race and a Jaffa-rolling race. To the north, the **Signal Hill Lookout** has wonderful views over the city, **Otago Harbour** and **Otago**

Dunedin

FESTIVALS AND EVENTS

Dunedin's calendar is busy with festivals and events; the year kicks off with the week-long **Dunedin Summer Festival** and the student festivities of **Orientation Week**. Dunedin Railway Station's extravagant architecture is the backdrop (and its 110m platform is the catwalk) for the **Vodafone id Dunedin Fashion Show**, held each March to showcase Dunedin's fashion designers. May sees New Zealand's largest book sale at the **Regent Theatre 24 Hour Book Sale**, a full 24 hours of books and entertainment; July's **Cadbury Chocolate Carnival** includes a Jaffa race down the world's steepest street. The biennial **Otago Festival of the Arts** brings a rich array of cultural events to the city every second October.

Jaffa race, Cadbury Chocolate Carnival, Dunedin

Peninsula. Further north-east, historic **Port Chalmers** is home to many artists; the peaceful settlement of **Careys Bay** has a historic 1874 hotel.

South of the central city, picturesque **St Kilda** and **St Clair** beaches are popular for swimming and surfing, if somewhat chilly; there's a heated salt water pool at St Clair. **Tunnel Beach**, just south of St Clair on the coastal road to **Brighton**, has rock arches, caves, a hand-carved tunnel and a 45-minute walkway.

From here head east onto beautiful Otago Peninsula, a haven of wildlife, scenery and history. There are 12ha of beautiful gardens at **Glenfalloch Woodland Garden** on Portobello Road, the peninsula's 'low road'. The seaside village of **Portobello** has craft studios, and

the **New Zealand Marine Studies Centre**, run by the university, displays local marine life. **Fletcher House** is a 1909 villa furnished in period style.

At the far end of the peninsula is dramatically-sited **Taiaroa Head**; the **Royal Albatross Centre** has interpretive displays and a viewing area where these huge, majestic birds can be seen at the world's only mainland breeding colony. Taiaroa Head is also home to military installations, including the **Armstrong Disappearing Gun**. On Harington Point Road, **Penguin Place** is a conservation project with the aim of saving the world's rarest penguin, the yellow-eyed penguin; visitors can view a colony of these beautiful, shy birds, and learn about the attempt to protect them. To the south of the peninsula, there

are some lovely walks around the **Chasm** and **Sandfly Bay**, also a penguin nesting spot. Fur seals, blue penguins and sea lions can also be seen around the beaches.

The drive along **Highcliff Road** (Otago Peninsula's 'high road') offers dramatic views over the Pacific Ocean and Otago Harbour. On Camp Road, built between 1871 and 1887 by the MP and Minister William Larnach, ornate **Larnach Castle** is New Zealand's only castle.

Larnach Castle, Otago Peninsula

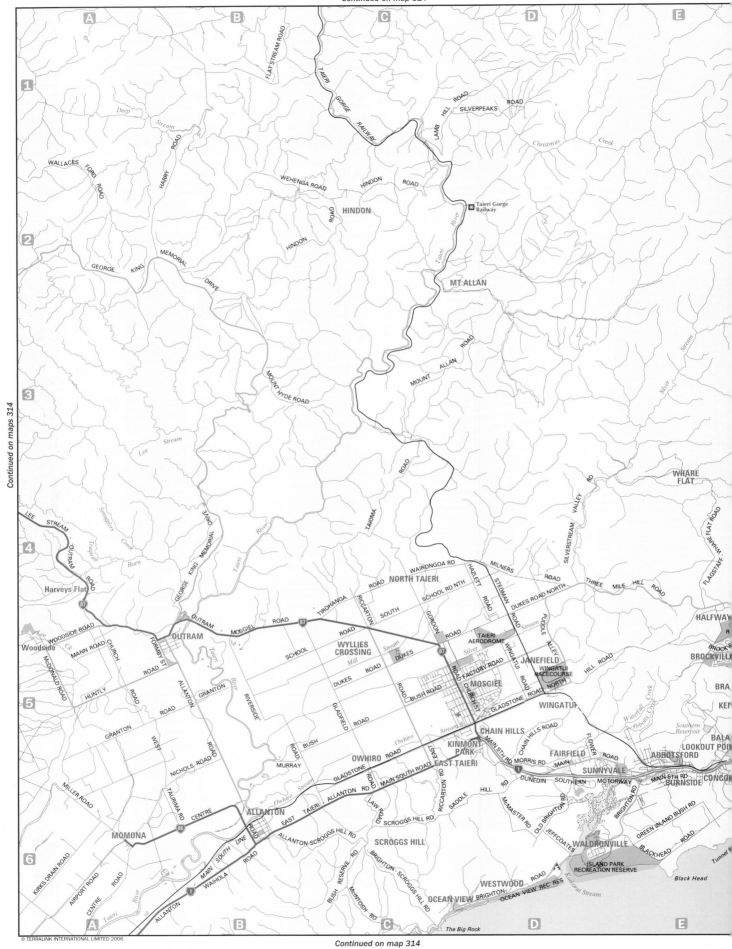

Gregory's New Zealand

Dunedin

© TERRALINK INTERNATIONAL LIMITED 2006

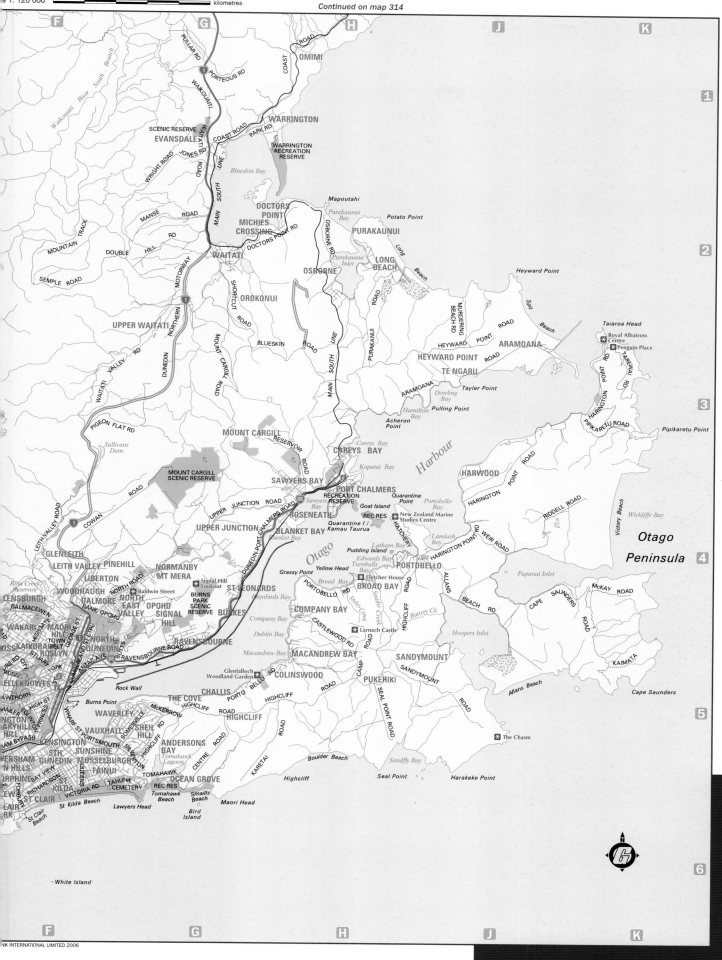

F   G   H   J   K

1

2

3

4

5

6

OMIMI

WARRINGTON

SCENIC RESERVE
EVANSDALE

WARRINGTON
RECREATION
RESERVE

Blueskin Bay

DOCTORS
POINT
MICHIES
CROSSING

Mapoutahi

*Purakaunui
Bay*   Potato Point

PURAKAUNUI

WAITATI

OSBORNE

*Purakaunui
Inlet*

LONG
BEACH

Beach

UPPER WAITATI

OROKONUI

BLUESKIN

Heyward Point

MURDERING
BEACH RD

Spit

Beach

Taiaroa Head

Royal Albatross
Centre
Penguin Place

HEYWARD   POINT

ARAMOANA

HEYWARD POINT

TE NGARU

PIGEON FLAT RD

*Sullivans
Dam*

MOUNT CARGILL

RESERVOIR

ARAMOANA

*Dowling
Bay*   Tayler Point

Pulling Point

*Hamilton
Bay*

Acheron
Point

HARINGTON POINT RD
TAREWAI RD

PIPIKARETU ROAD

Pipikaretu Point

MOUNT CARGILL
SCENIC RESERVE

Careys Bay

CAREYS   BAY

Harbour

HARWOOD

SAWYERS BAY

PORT CHALMERS

RECREATION
RESERVE

Koputai Bay

HARINGTON

RIDDELL ROAD

Victory Beach

Wickliffe Bay

COWAN

UPPER   JUNCTION

ROSENEATH

*Sawyers
Bay*

Quarantine
Point

*Portobello
Bay*

HARINGTON POINT

WEIR ROAD

*Otago
Peninsula*

UPPER JUNCTION

Quarantine I I
Kamau Taurua

Goat Island

REC RES

New Zealand Marine
Studies Centre

*Lamlash
Bay*

BLANKET BAY

Blanket Bay

Otago

HATCHERY

*Latham
Bay*

LEITH VALLEY ROAD

GLENLEITH

LEITH VALLEY   PINEHILL

NORTH ROAD

NORMANBY
MT MERA

Signal Hill
Lookout

BURNS
PARK
SCENIC
RESERVE

Pudding Island

Edwards Bay
Turnbulls
Bay

PORTOBELLO

McKAY   ROAD

KAIMATA

LIBERTON

*Ross Creek
Reservoir*

Baldwin Street

ST LEONARDS

Grassy Point   Yellow Head

Broad Bay

Papanui Inlet

WOODHAUGH

DALMORE

NORTH
EAST
VALLEY

OPOHO

SIGNAL
HILL

BUTKES

Graynbirds Bay

PORTOBELLO RD

BROAD BAY

BEACH   RD

CAPE   SAUNDERS

LENSBURGH

BALMACEWEN

BANK OPOHO

Company Bay

COMPANY BAY

Snley Creek

Battery Ck

HIGHCLIFF

Hoopers Inlet

ROAD

WAKARI MAORI
HILL

TOWN BELT

Dublin Bay

CASTLEWOOD RD

Larnach Castle

CAPE SAUNDERS

OSS KAIKORAI

ROSLYN

NORTH
DUNEDIN

RAVENSBOURNE

Macandrew Bay

MACANDREW BAY

CAMP

SANDYMOUNT

Allans Beach

Cape Saunders

ELLEKNOWES

RAVENSBOURNE
ROAD

Glenfalloch
Woodland Garden

COLINSWOOD

SANDYMOUNT

PUKEHIKI

HAWTHORN

THE COVE

CHALLIS

PORTO BELLO

HIGHCLIFF

SEAL POINT ROAD

The Chasm

WAVERLEY

Rock Wall

Burns Point

McKERROW

HIGHCLIFF
ROAD

HIGHCLIFF

KARETAI

Boulder Beach

Sandfly Bay

VAUXHALL

SHEIL
HILL

ANDERSONS
BAY

CENTRE

ROAD

Highcliff

Seal Point

Harakeke Point

KENSINGTON
STH

SUNSHINE

MUSSELBURGH

TAINUI

*Tomahawk
Lagoon*

OCEAN GROVE

EVERSHAM
N HILLS

DUNEDIN

ST
KILDA

TAHUNA
CEMETERY

Tomahawk
Beach

RPHINE

ST CLAIR

St Kilda Beach

Lawyers Head

*Smaills
Beach*

Maori Head

St Clair
Beach

Bird
Island

~White Island

N
G

FIORDLAND

One of New Zealand's most spectacular — and most visited — areas, this south-western corner of the South Island is a place of tremendous natural beauty, with vast areas of wilderness in the World Heritage Area of **Fiordland National Park**. The unspoilt mountains, rivers, lakes and forests are home to a rich array of wildlife, including some rare native fauna — and a great many sandflies!

Fiordland takes its name from the deep, glacier-carved fiords which cut into the richly forested landscape. Most famous among these is **Milford Sound**, which draws thousands of visitors each year to explore its beauty by cruising, kayaking, diving or walking; the **Milford Track** has been described as the world's best walk. Milford Sound and **Doubtful Sound** have wonderful underwater life; seals, dolphins and penguins also make their home here.

Human settlement in the area has always been limited by the steep terrain, isolation and wet climate, although early Maori hunted birds, fish and greenstone, and European sealers and whalers based themselves in the fiords. Today, Fiordland is still a remote area with only one town of any real size, lakefront **Te Anau**.

main attractions

◈ **Doubtful Sound**

Fiordland's deepest fiord has cascading waterfalls, towering mountains, seals, dolphins and penguins.

◈ **Fiordland National Park**

This wilderness area has snow-capped mountains, unspoilt beech forest, peaceful lakes and 14 glacier-carved fiords.

◈ **Hollyford Track**

This 56km track offers dramatic views of mountains, lakes and the Hollyford River, and windswept St Martins Bay.

◈ **Kepler Track**

The 60km Kepler Track traverses lake edges, beech forest, alpine mountain tops and a glacial valley.

◈ **Lake Manapouri**

Beautiful Lake Manapouri is dotted with forest-clad islands.

◈ **Milford Road**

This stunning alpine road through the World Heritage Area to Milford Sound passes the Mirror Lakes and waterfalls and goes through the 1.2km Homer Tunnel.

◈ **Milford Track**

This famous 54km track is renowned for its glacial valleys, rainforest, mountain views, alpine flowers and waterfalls.

◈ **Te Ana-au Glow-worm Caves**

These huge limestone caverns, only accessible by boat, have underground waterfalls, whirlpools and a glow-worm grotto.

◈ **Te Anau**

Beautifully located on Lake Te Anau's shores, Te Anau is known for its good restaurants.

Waterfall, Milford Sound

Milford Sound

This beautiful fiord is surrounded by steep cliffs and mountains, with many waterfalls tumbling into the sea. Diving is wonderful, due to the unusual phenomenon of 'deep water emergence' which allows deep-water marine species to thrive close to the surface; the **Milford Deep Underwater Observatory** allows non-diving visitors to get a look at the undersea life.

 Visitor information

Fiordland i-SITE Visitor Centre
Lakefront Drive, Te Anau
Ph: (03) 249 8900
www.fiordlandnz.com

Lake Te Anau, Fiordland National Park

South Island

Continued on maps 205 & 231

0   40 kilometres

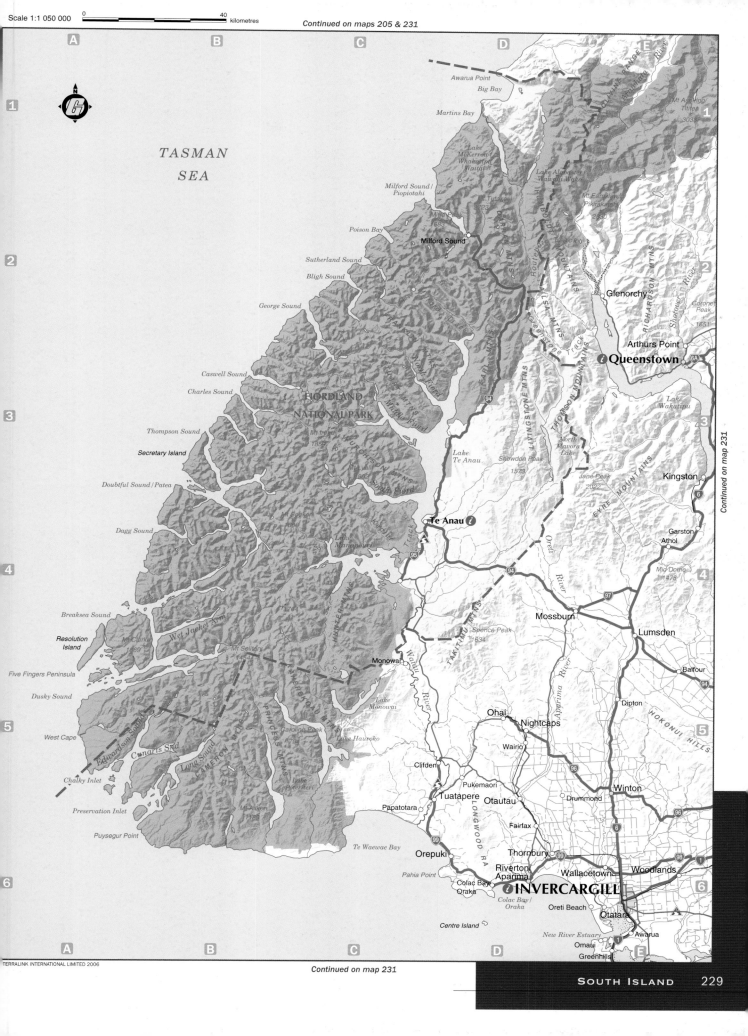

A   B   C   D   E

1

Awarua Point

Big Bay

TASMAN
SEA

Martins Bay

Mt Aspiring
Tititea
3038

Lake
McKerrow /
Whakatipu
Waitai

Milford Sound /
Piopiotahi

Lake Alabaster /
Wawahi Waka

2

Poison Bay

Mitre Peak
1683

Milford Sound

Mt Earnslaw
Pikirakatahi
2830

Sutherland Sound

Glenorchy

Bligh Sound

Coronet
Peak
1651

George Sound

Arthurs Point

ⓘ **Queenstown** GA

3

Caswell Sound

FIORDLAND
NATIONAL PARK

Lake
Te Anau

North
Mavora
Lake

Lake
Wakatipu

Kingston

Charles Sound

Thompson Sound

Mt Tutoko
1853

Snowdon Peak
1573

Secretary Island

Jane Peak
2022

Doubtful Sound / Patea

4

Dagg Sound

Lake
Manapouri

ⓘ **Te Anau**

Garston
Athol

Mid Dome
1478

94

Oreti

95

Breaksea Sound

Mt Clerke
1669

River

Mossburn

Lumsden

Resolution
Island

Mt Solitary

Monowai

94

97

Spence Peak
1634

Balfour

94

Five Fingers Peninsula

Lake
Monowai

Dipton

Dusky Sound

5

Lake Hauroko

Ohai

Nightcaps

HOKONUI
HILLS

West Cape

Caroline Peak

Wairio

Edwardson Sound

Cunaris Snd

Long Sound

Lake
Poteriteri

Clifden

96

Chalky Inlet

Mt Allen
1165

Pukemaori

Winton

Tuatapere

Otautau

Drummond

Preservation Inlet

Papatotara

Fairfax

96

Puysegur Point

Te Waewae Bay

Orepuki

Thornbury

99

Wallacetown

Woodlands

98

1

6

Pahia Point

Riverton
Aparima

ⓘ **INVERCARGILL**

Colac Bay
Oraka

Oreti Beach

Otatara

E

Colac Bay /
Oraka

Omaui

Centre Island

New River Estuary

Awarua

1

Greenhills

A   B   C   D   E

Continued on map 231

SOUTHLAND

Lush and green, New Zealand's most southern region is a peaceful place of surf-pounded beaches, rolling plains, wide rivers and unspoilt forests. For visitors it offers beautiful scenery, great hiking, trout fishing and a huge array of native wildlife. Dotted with friendly small towns, Southland has the longest daylight hours in New Zealand.

Southland's main city of **Invercargill** has appealing parks and gardens, historic buildings and a growing student population; **Bluff** is famous for its oysters, and is the jumping-off point for ferry trips to **Stewart Island**.

The **Catlins** region, in the south-east, is a fascinating area where early Maori artefacts have been found, and which was later occupied by European sealers, whalers and timber millers. Today it's a mix of historic sites, native bush, waterfalls and unspoilt beaches, with an amazing range of marine and bird life to be seen.

In Maori lore, remote Stewart Island is the anchor of the canoe which belonged to the legendary demi-god Maui. The island is home to **Rakiura National Park**, New Zealand's southernmost — and newest — national park, another great area for viewing wildlife.

Visitor information

Invercargill i-SITE Visitor Centre
108 Gala St, Invercargill
Ph: (03) 214 6243

DOC Stewart Island Visitor Information Centre
Main Rd, Halfmoon Bay
Ph: (03) 219 0009
www.visit.southlandnz.com

Rakiura National Park

New Zealand's newest national park, on **Stewart Island**, is a peaceful place of virgin native forests and much wildlife. Rare bird species include the kakapo, Cook's petrel and the South Island saddleback; Stewart Island kiwi can be seen in the park, and there are long and short walks.

main attractions

◈ **Catlins**
This remote, beautiful area has rich wildlife, forests, waterfalls, isolated beaches and historic sites.

◈ **Eastern Southland Gallery**
This stylish gallery in Gore's old library building displays a terrific collection of New Zealand art and African artefacts.

◈ **Nugget Point**
This promontory with its 1869 lighthouse is a great place to see a vast array of wildlife, including seals, gannets, shags, penguins and the rare Hector's dolphin.

◈ **Riverton/Aparima**
A picturesque beach town, Riverton/ Aparima has an arty, relaxed ambience and beachfront cafés.

◈ **Southland Museum and Art Gallery Niho o te Taniwha**
Housed in a pyramid, this museum features art and historical exhibitions, and a collection of live tuatara.

◈ **Stewart Island**
The country's third largest island offers remote beauty, natural attractions and great hiking.

◈ **The Paua Shell House**
The walls and garden of this Bluff house have been gloriously, lovingly decorated with hundreds of iridescent blue-green paua shells.

◈ **Tuatapere Hump Ridge Track**
A spectacular walk leads from the sea to the mountains, through forest and over historic viaducts.

◈ **Ulva Island Open Sanctuary**
This pest-free 250ha island has walking tracks, golden beaches and fantastic bird life, including some rare species.

Nugget Point, Catlins

South Island

Scale 1:1 680 000
0   80 kilometres

TASMAN SEA

Continued on maps 205, 207 & 221

Open Bay Islands
Jackson Head
Jackson Bay / Okahu
Jackson Bay
Neils Beach
Haast
Hannahs Clearing
Haast Pass / Tioripatea
Brewster
Mt Huxley 2505
Mt Ward 2645
Lake Pukaki
Aoraki / Mount Cook
MT COOK NATIONAL PARK
HALL RANGE
Lake Tekapo

MOUNT ASPIRING NATIONAL PARK
Mt Aspiring / Tititea 3033
Mt Pollux 2536
Makarora
Mt Maclarlane 2057
Mt Huxley
SOLUTION RA
STRACHAN RA
ANNOCK BRAE RA
YOUNG RA
BARRIER RA
HUXLEY RA
BEN OHAU RA
NAUMANN RA
Duc Fluney 2500

Awarua Point
Big Bay
Martins Bay
Lake McKerrow / Whakatipu Waitai

Milford Sound / Piopiotahi
Milford Sound
Poison Bay
Sutherland Sound
Bligh Sound
George Sound
Caswell Sound
Charles Sound
Thompson Sound
Secretary Island
Doubtful Sound / Patea
Dagg Sound
Breaksea Sound
Resolution Island

FIORDLAND NATIONAL PARK

Mt Tutoko
Lake Ada
Lake Alabaster / Wawahi Waka
EARL MTNS
DARRAN MTNS
HARRIS MTNS
RICHARDSON MTNS
LIVINGSTONE MTNS
THOMSON MTNS
EYRE MOUNTAINS
GARVIE MTNS
HECTOR MTNS
Mt Alta 2339
Lake Wanaka
Lake Hawea
Mt Melina 1925

Wanaka
Albert Town
Luggate
Lake Hawea
Lindis Peak 1226
Tarras
Cloudy Peak 1526
Lindis Pass
St Bathans 2088
Mt St Bathans
HAWKDUN RA
ST BATHANS RA
DUNSTAN MTNS
Mt Ida
Kohurau 2015

Lake Ohau
Lake Ohau Alpine Village
Omarama
Lake Benmore
Mt Sutton 1916
Otematata
Aviemore
Lake Waitaki
Lake Aviemore
Twizel

Glenorchy
Arrowtown
Arthurs Point
Queenstown
Cardrona
Mt Cardrona 1936
Mt Pisa 1963
Coronet Peak
Kawarau
Double Cone 2319
Ben Nevis 2234
Lake Wakatipu
Cromwell
Omakau
Opir
Becks
Oturehua
Wedderburn
Kyeburn Diggings
Naseby
Mt Pisgah 1643
Clyde
Alexandra
Ranfurly
Waipiata
Orangapai
Pataroa
Hyde
Patearoa
Naseby
ROUGH RIDGE
RAGGEDY RANGE
MANUHERIKIA R
Middlemarch
Hummock 736
Summit Rock 1450
Taieri R

Snowdon Peak
North Mavora Lake
Jane Peak 2022
Lake Te Anau 1573
Kingston
Athol
Garston
Rocky Mount 1885
Lake Roxburgh
Whitecomb 1455
Roxburgh
Teviot
Ettrick
Millers Flat
UMBRELLA MTNS
Pinelheugh 1124
Lake Roxburgh
1159

Te Anau
Manapouri
Mossburn
Lumsden
Waikaia
Heriot
Tapanui
Lawrence
Outram
Waipori Falls
Allanton
Berwick
Brighton

Mid Dome 1476
Spence Peak 1634
Dipton
Balfour
Riversdale
Mandeville
Waikaka
Waitahuna
Tuapeka Mouth
Lake Waihola
Waihola
Taieri Mouth

Monowai
Lake Monowai
Lake Hauroko
Ohai
Nightcaps
Wairio
Clifden
Winton
Drummond
Pukerau
Waipahi
Clydevale
Milton
Lake Waihola
Lake Mahinerangi

Gore
Mataura
Clinton
Balclutha
Kaitangata

Tuatapere
Otautau
Papatotara
Fairfax
Thornbury
Wallacetown
Edendale
Wyndham
Waiwera South
Kaka Point

Orepuki
Colac Bay / Oraka
Riverton Aparima
INVERCARGILL
Woodlands
Glenham
Mt Pye 720
Owaka
Nugget Point
CATLINS FOREST PARK
Tahakopa
Papatowai
Molyneux Bay

Pahia Point
Te Waewae Bay
Colac Bay / Oraka
Centre Island
New River Estuary
Oreti Beach
Otatara
Awarua
Omaui
Greenhills
Mataura Island
Gorge Road
Waimahaka
Tokanui
Fortrose
Waikawa

Bluff
Bluff Harbour
Toetoes Bay
Foveaux Strait

Solander Island (Hautere)
Bishop and Clerks Islands
Rugged Islands
Codfish Island (Whenuahou)
RAKIURA NATIONAL PARK
Mt Anglem / Hananui 980
Ruapuke Island
Breaksea Islands
Hazelburgh Group
Titi / Muttonbird Islands

Mason Bay
Halfmoon Bay (Oban)
Ernest Islands
Chew Tobacco Bay
STEWART ISLAND / RAKIURA
Mt Allen 750
Port Adventure
Breaksea Islands
Titi / Muttonbird Islands

Titi / Muttonbird Islands
Taukihepa / Big South Cape Island
Port Pegasus / Pikihatiti
Broad Bay

© TERRALINK INTERNATIONAL LIMITED 2006

■ Akaroa   POP 580

Map 297, J5

The harbourside town of Akaroa is **Canterbury**'s oldest European settlement. Located on **Banks Peninsula**, an 82km drive south-east of Christchurch, Akaroa was settled by the French as well as British; this dual heritage is still evident today in its architecture and French street names.

MAIN ATTRACTIONS: Akaroa is home to plentiful bird and marine life, including blue penguins and the Hector's dolphin. Cruises are offered for viewing the beautiful volcanic harbour and its wildlife. Possibly the best example of how early French colonialists lived is in the immaculately preserved **Langlois Eteveneaux House**, thought to have been prefabricated in France and built in Akaroa in the 1840s. The **Akaroa Museum** explores comprehensive local history. **The Custom House** at **Daly's Wharf** is a remnant from Akaroa's days as a Port of Entry; there are also relics from the days when Akaroa was a whaling depot.

NEARBY ATTRACTIONS: There are many walks around the area, including the popular **Banks Peninsula Track**, which is on private land. There's a beautiful stony beach at **Birdlings Flat**, to the south-west; gourmet cheeses are on offer at the **Barrys Bay Cheese Factory**. To the north-west, **Lyttelton Harbour** with its three islands, **Quail**, **Ripapa** and **King Billy**, is well worth a visit.

VISITOR INFORMATION: 80 Rue Lavaud, Ph: (03) 304 8600, www.akaroa.com

■ Alexandra   POP 4410

Map 307, H3

Summers are hot and rainfall low in prosperous Alexandra, a service centre for the local farming district in inland **Central Otago**, located at the juncture of the **Manuherikia** and **Clutha Rivers**.

MAIN ATTRACTIONS: Alexandra is surrounded by orchards, and fresh fruit is for sale from roadside stalls. Recently the area has benefited from a wine-making boom, with pinot noir a specialty. Most wineries offer tastings. The **Alexandra Historical Museum** has historical photos and artefacts from gold mining days. Two impressive stone piers are all that remain of the original **Alexandra Bridge** across the Clutha River; **Shaky Bridge** is a historic suspension bridge now only

Akaroa Harbour and town

used by pedestrians. A one-hour walk leads to the 11m-diameter hillside **Alexandra Clock**.

NEARBY ATTRACTIONS: Mountain biking and walking are popular in the surrounding hills, with many old gold trails weaving through the **Old Man, Dunstan, Raggedy** and **Knobby Ranges**. The rugged **Dunstan Trail** is popular with mountainbikers, as is the **Otago Central Rail Trail**, a 150km trail for walkers, cyclists and horse riders on the old railway route from **Clyde** to **Middlemarch**. **Earnscleugh Flat Tailings**, 4km west, protects an impressive area of dredge tailings. The **Lake Roxburgh Walkway**, which starts from the pioneer cemetery on **Graveyard Gully Road**, leads through an old gold mining area, and has Otago's best-preserved examples of Chinese miners' rock shelters. In winter, the frozen **Manorburn Dam**, about 6km south-east, is popular for skating and curling on the natural ice.

VISITOR INFORMATION: Centennial Ave, Ph: (03) 448 9515, www.centralotagonz.com

■ **Aoraki/Mount Cook Village**

POP 235

Map 294, B4

Aoraki/Mount Cook Village is located at the southern end of **Aoraki/Mount Cook National Park**. This tiny village provides accommodation, information and sustenance to thousands of visitors who flock there to experience the alpine wilderness.

MAIN ATTRACTIONS: Aoraki/Mount Cook National Park officially came into existence in 1953. This exceptional piece of New Zealand is part of Te Wahipounamu South-west New Zealand World Heritage Area. There are many beautiful short walks around the village, and hikers may get to see the goat-like thar, the delicate chamois and the shy red deer. The **Hermitage Hotel** is famous for its barstool views of

Aoraki/Mount Cook Village

Aoraki/Mount Cook, New Zealand's highest peak at 3754m.

NEARBY ATTRACTIONS: **Twizel**, 63km south, is home to the only breeding ground for the world's rarest wading bird, the New Zealand native kaki/black stilt. During winter, **Ohau Snow Fields**, between Twizel and **Omarama**, are very popular. Excellent terrain and snow conditions have made this high country alpine ski area a growing attraction.

VISITOR INFORMATION: Bowen Drive, Ph: (03) 435 1186, www.doc.govt.nz

■ **Arrowtown**   POP 1690

Map 306, E1

This pretty historic town 20km north-east of Queenstown was established after an 1862 gold find on the **Arrow River**. A rough and unruly mining settlement in its early days, Arrowtown now offers stylish shopping and restaurants in its historic wooden buildings.

MAIN ATTRACTIONS: The humble settlement of the Chinese gold miners — who were subject to much prejudice at the time — can be seen on the banks of the Arrow River; some of the tiny huts have been

restored, and there are excellent interpretive panels. The **Lakes District Museum** explores the town's gold mining and early Maori history; the self-drive **Wakatipu Arts Trail** leads visitors around local artists and craftspeople. The many deciduous trees in the town and on the surrounding hills put on a colourful display in autumn. Scenes for *The Lord of the Rings* film trilogy were filmed in Arrowtown; **'Ford of Bruinen'** scenes were shot only minutes from the town centre on the Arrow River, and the **'Gladden Fields'** location is a short walk from **Wilcox Green**.

NEARBY ATTRACTIONS: **Macetown**, 14km north, is a ghost town from the gold rush days, and can be reached by 4WD via the original miners' wagon track. There are spectacular views and historic sites on the **Crown Range Road** north-east to **Wanaka** through the **Cardrona Valley**. Pretty **Lake Hayes**, several kilometres south of Arrowtown, is popular for kayaking, fishing and walking; in autumn the trees which line its shores turn golden. The historic 1880 suspension bridge across the spectacular **Kawarau Gorge** is the

BANKS PENINSULA

Scenic Banks Peninsula, south-east of Christchurch, was formed by huge volcanic eruptions. Nestled in the centre of an ancient volcano is the historic town of **Akaroa**. Originally a French settlement,

Akaroa (Maori for 'long harbour') has the feel of a French provincial village and is a haven for artists and craftspeople. The volcanic crater provides a rich environment for birds and marine life, including the world's smallest dolphin, the Hector's dolphin.

Banks Peninsula has a fascinating Maori and European history. The Ngai Tahu Maori tribe occupied the peninsula long before James Cook sighted it in 1770; **Lyttelton**'s scenic harbour, Banks Peninsula's northern major sea inlet, was the port of entry for English settlers coming to Canterbury in the 1850s.

A journey down the spine of the peninsula allows panoramic views of the hills and inlets of an area rich in beauty, history, artistry and adventure.

Diver and Hector's dolphin, near Akaroa

main attractions

- ◈ Akaroa
- ◈ Akaroa Museum
- ◈ Barry's Bay Cheese Factory
- ◈ Birdlings Flat
- ◈ French Farm Winery
- ◈ Harbour cruises
- ◈ Hector's dolphins
- ◈ Lyttelton Timeball Station
- ◈ Pohatu Marine Reserve
- ◈ Quail Island

ⓘ Visitor information

Lyttelton i-SITE Visitor Centre
20 Oxford St, Lyttelton
Ph: (03) 328 9093

Akaroa Information Centre
80 Rue Lavaud, Akaroa
Ph: (03) 304 8600
www.akaroa.com

---

site of a bungy jump. To the east en route to **Cromwell**, the **Gibbston Valley** has many wineries in a dramatic setting.
VISITOR INFORMATION: 49 Buckingham St, Ph: (03) 442 1824, www.arrowtown.com

◼ Arthur's Pass   POP 85
Map 289, H5

The tiny settlement of Arthur's Pass is the highest-altitude town in New Zealand. Situated 4km from the pass the town is named for, it is set in the icy heart of the **Southern Alps** on the road connection between **Canterbury** and the **West Coast**. This route was originally used by Maori heading for the West Coast in search of greenstone; the pass was first discovered by Europeans in 1864, who in the wake of the

West Coast gold rush were keen to find a crossing from Canterbury.
MAIN ATTRACTIONS: Beautiful **Arthur's Pass National Park** was the South Island's first national park. The 114 500ha park has wide, meandering braided rivers, steep gorges, native forest and the mountains of the Southern Alps, offering visitors boundless outdoor experiences. The park is also famously home to the mischievous kea (an inquisitive native alpine parrot), and there are great spotted kiwi and many more birds. **DOC Arthur's Pass Visitors Centre** has information on all park walks, including route guides for longer hikes. The centre shows a short video on the history of Arthur's Pass.
NEARBY ATTRACTIONS: Day walks are

possible to the beautiful **Otira Valley**, **Temple Basin**, **Mt Bealey** and **Avalanche Peak**. Longer hikes include the two-day **Goat Pass Track**, the difficult **Harman Pass** and **Harper Pass Track**; these tracks pass through wonderful alpine areas, but are only for the experienced. An easier way to enjoy

Lake Hayes, south of Arrowtown

South Island

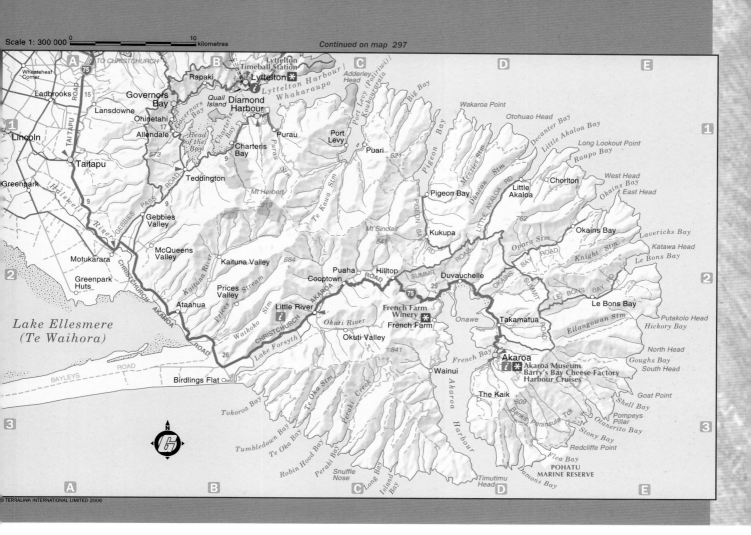

the grandeur of the Southern Alps is on the world-famous *TranzAlpine* train journey from Christchurch to Greymouth, a spectacular trip which passes through Arthur's Pass.

Visitor Information: SH73, Ph: (03) 318 9211, www.doc.govt.nz

■ Ashburton   POP 15 770
Map 316, C4

Ashburton is located 84km south-west of Christchurch on the **Canterbury Plains**, and has stunning views of the **Southern Alps**. The town is the gateway to outdoor attractions, including the **Rakaia Gorge** and South Island ski areas.

Main Attractions: The **Ashburton Art Gallery** features local and national artists and touring exhibitions, and presents performing arts events. The **Ashford Craft Village** is the home of the famous **Ashford Spinning Wheels and Weaving Looms**. The town has many heritage attractions, including the **Ashburton Vintage Car Museum**, the **Plains Railway and Historical Village** and **Lyn Historical Woodworking Trust**. The **Ashburton Aviation Museum** has a huge collection of heritage planes and displays from its years as an air force training base during World War II.

Nearby Attractions: **Lake Hood**, five minutes from town, is a good spot for recreational activities. Ashburton is situated about halfway between the **Rakaia** and **Rangitata Rivers**, famous for their salmon fishing. The Rangitata River also has world class white water rafting, and the

Castle Hill, Arthur's Pass

upper river valley has spectacular alpine and high country scenery. It also boasts the filming location for Peter Jackson's *The Lord of the Rings* fortress city, '**Edoras**'. **Mt Somers**, 40km west, has a 17km sub-alpine

AORAKI/MT COOK NATIONAL PARK

Aoraki/Mount Cook National Park has the greatest concentration of mountains in the country. There are 19 peaks over 3000 metres, including the highest, 3754m **Aoraki/Mount Cook**, which is sacred to the Ngai Tahu tribe, and attracts climbers from around the world.

A national park since 1953, and part of Te Wahipounamu South-west New Zealand World Heritage Area, the area is surrounded by the **Southern Alps**, **Two Thumb**, **Liebig** and **Ben Ohau** ranges. Over a third of the area is in permanent snow and glacial ice, including the country's largest glacier, the 29km **Tasman Glacier**.

Aoraki/Mount Cook

Accessible walks such as the **Kea Point Track** and the **Hooker Valley Track** offer breathtaking proximity to glacial lakes, the grandeur of mountains and the delicate beauty of the Mount Cook buttercup. Guided heli-ski trips can be taken down the Tasman Glacier, and scenic flights offer a bird's-eye view.

Sightseeing plane on the Tasman Glacier

main attractions

- ◈ Aoraki/Mount Cook
- ◈ Heli-skiing
- ◈ Hooker Valley Track
- ◈ Kea Point Track
- ◈ Mountaineering
- ◈ Scenic flights
- ◈ Tasman Glacier
- ◈ The Hermitage

ⓘ Visitor information

DOC Aoraki/Mount Cook Visitor Centre
Bowen Drive, Aoraki/Mount Cook Village
Ph: (03) 435 1186
www.doc.govt.nz

---

walkway, and near **Methven**, 34km north of Ashburton, there's excellent skiing at **Mt Hutt**.
VISITOR INFORMATION: East St, Ph: (03) 308 1050, www.ashburtontourism.co.nz

■ Balclutha   POP 4110
Map 313, H3
Balclutha, on the mighty **Clutha River** 81km south-west of Dunedin, is south **Otago**'s largest town, and a gateway to the beautiful **Catlins** area. The Clutha, known as **Mata-Au** to Maori, is New Zealand's biggest river by volume, and has been a major source of gold and of hydro-electric power. Scottish settlers named it Clutha, the Gaelic word for Clyde.
MAIN ATTRACTIONS: An impressive arched concrete bridge, built in 1935, crosses the river. Just south of Balclutha, the island of **Inchclutha** divides the river in two. The river is a site for trout and salmon fishing, and guided fishing trips are available. Riverside **Naish Park** is a good place for a picnic; the **Blair Athol Walkway** leads along the river. The **Awakiki Walkway** leads through podocarp forest, including some 300-year-old totara trees.
NEARBY ATTRACTIONS: On the road to **Milton**, 24km north-east, is the 1860s **Old Sod Cottage**; Milton has historic buildings including the old flour mill and the textile mill. There are glow-worms in the old **Manuka Gorge** railway tunnel, and fishing is excellent at **Toko Mouth**. **Lake Waihola**, 41km north-east of Balclutha, is a tidal fresh water lake, and the **Sinclair Wetlands** are a privately managed wetland conservation area with many waterbirds, walking tracks and a visitor centre. Nearby **Taieri Mouth** is a picturesque fishing village with a safe swimming beach; **Taieri Island/Moturata** is a nature reserve. The scenic **Taieri Mouth Road** north crosses the historic 1891 **Taieri Ferry Bridge** and follows the water's edge back to **Dunedin**.
VISITOR INFORMATION: 4 Clyde St, Ph: (03) 418 0388, www.cluthadistrict.co.nz

■ Blenheim   POP 26 550
Map 317, D3
Sunny Blenheim is the main town in the **Marlborough** region, 28km south of Picton, and is a base for exploring New Zealand's largest wine production area.
MAIN ATTRACTIONS: There are more

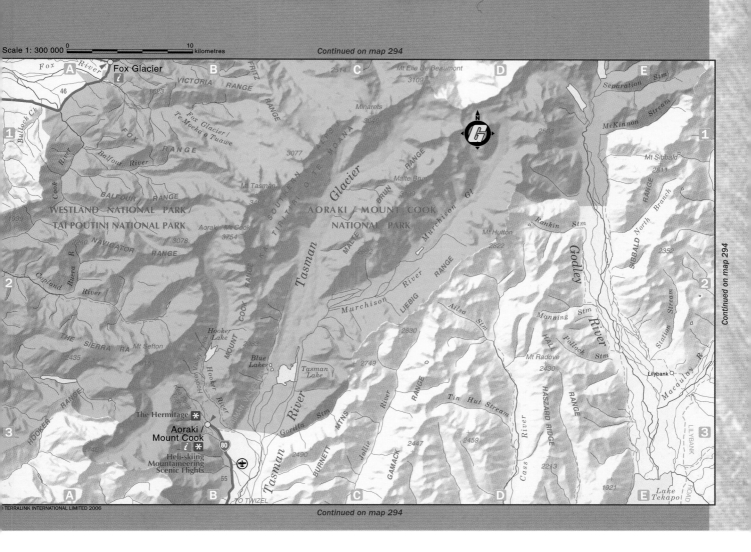

Continued on map 294

Scale 1: 300 000

Continued on map 294

than 70 wineries in the pretty countryside around Blenheim and the satellite town of **Renwick**, 8km west. **Montana Brancott Winery** is New Zealand's largest winery, and hosts the **Wine Marlborough Festival**, a popular yearly wine festival. Blenheim has a farmers' market on Sunday mornings in summer. The **Millennium Public**

Southern Blenheim countryside

Art Gallery is a contemporary gallery with changing exhibitions. **Brayshaw Museum Park** has a reconstructed colonial village; **Pollard Park** and **Seymour Square** are pretty gardens. The **Wither Hills Farm Park** has walkways and mountainbike trails through rolling hills.

NEARBY ATTRACTIONS: Cherries, olives and lavender are all grown in the surrounding countryside. To the west, the braided **Wairau River** provides excellent fishing; further west, there are hiking trails in beautiful **Mount Richmond Forest Park** and **Nelson Lakes National Park**. The cemetery at **Tuamarina**, 9km north, has a memorial to the settlers killed in the Wairau Massacre, a disastrous encounter between Maori and Europeans

in 1843. The rural township of **Seddon**, 25km south-east, has craftspeople, gardens and colonial homesteads; west of Seddon, the **Awatere Valley** has a developing wine and olive industry. **Tapuae-o-Uenuku**, important to Maori of the area, was the first mountain ever climbed by Everest conqueror Sir Edmund Hillary. High country **Molesworth Station**, 130km south-west of Blenheim, is New Zealand's largest farm; visits are possible in summer. From State Highway One south of Seddon, the settling ponds of the **Lake Grassmere Saltworks** can be seen. Nearby **Marfells Beach** has wonderful views.

VISITOR INFORMATION: Railway Station, Sinclair St, SH1, Ph: (03) 577 8080, www.destinationmarlborough.com

Bluff POP 1935
Map 312, A6

The port town of Bluff, 31km south of Invercargill on **Southland**'s south coast, is the gateway to **Stewart Island**. Historically Bluff was a centre for whaling and sealing; industries today include fishing, fish processing and the aluminium smelter at **Tiwai Point**.

MAIN ATTRACTIONS: The unique **Paua Shell House** was a labour of love for its late residents, Fred and Myrtle Flutey, who decked the place out with hundreds of iridescent blue-green paua shells. Bluff is famous for its iconic Bluff oysters; the **Bluff Oyster and Southland Seafood Festival** celebrates the succulent shellfish each April. **Bluff Maritime Museum** has displays about shipwrecks, whaling and oysters. **Stirling Point**, 1.5km south, is the southernmost termination point for State Highway One, which runs (as per the popular saying) from **Cape Reinga** to Bluff; the route's finish point is marked by a signpost with distances to the South Pole and other places. Walks from here include the two-hour coastal **Foveaux Walk** and the 30-minute **Glory Track**. From the summit of 265m **Bluff Hill**, there are expansive views; the hill is supposedly the burial site of two important chiefs from the Kati Mamoe tribe.

NEARBY ATTRACTIONS: The **Greenpoint Walkway**, 5km north, offers great views of the sea and of wrecked ships which litter the shore. The wetlands at **Awarua Bay**, 29km north-east on the east side of **Bluff Harbour**, are an important breeding ground for migratory wading birds. Tours are available of the **Tiwai Point Aluminium Smelter**.

VISITOR INFORMATION: 108 Gala St, Invercargill, Ph: (03) 214 6243, www.bluff.co.nz

Clyde POP 825
Map 307, G2

This appealing small town in **Central Otago** on the banks of the mighty **Clutha River** was once the centre of the Dunstan gold fields, until a bridge was built across the Clutha at **Alexandra**, which took over Clyde's administrative functions. Clyde sits below the mammoth **Clyde Dam**, New Zealand's third largest capacity hydro power station.

MAIN ATTRACTIONS: Clyde's streets are lined with historic stone buildings, and a number of museums explore the town's past, including the **Clyde Station Museum**, which displays heritage engines, and the **Briar Herb Factory Museum Complex**. Thyme grows wild on the nearby hills, and the herb factory was operational in the 1930s. The unique **Otago Central Rail Trail** for walkers, cyclists and horse riders was once the Central Otago rail branch line, which closed permanently in 1990; the re-surfaced 150km trail from Clyde to **Middlemarch** allows users to explore the area's remote scenery and history in a peaceful setting inaccessible to cars.

NEARBY ATTRACTIONS: The controversial Clyde Dam development flooded the **Cromwell Gorge** river valley in the early 1990s, creating **Lake Dunstan**, north of Clyde, which is used for water sports and has plentiful bird and fish life, including rainbow and brown trout. There are wineries to explore around Clyde, and around Alexandra, 11km south.

VISITOR INFORMATION: Centennial Ave, Alexandra, Ph: (03) 448 9515, www.centralotagonz.com

Collingwood POP 185
Map 280, D2

This small coastal town in **Golden Bay**, 26km north-west of Takaka, is built on the site of an old Maori pa (fortified village); the area was the scene of New Zealand's first gold rush in 1857. Collingwood is the gateway to **Kahurangi National Park**, and a base for walkers setting out on the famous **Heaphy Track**.

MAIN ATTRACTIONS: **Collingwood Museum** has pioneer relics on display; the **Rosy Glow Chocolate House** sells hand-made chocolates.

NEARBY ATTRACTIONS: Ecologically important 452 002ha Kahurangi National Park can be explored on the Heaphy Track, one of New Zealand's 'Great Walks'. The park entrance in the **Aorere Valley**, 34km south, is a starting point for the 82km track, which finishes north of **Karamea** on the West Coast. Shorter walks in the park include the **Aorere Goldfields Walk**, which leads past historic relics of New Zealand's first major goldfield, and the two- to three-hour **Kaituna Track**. 4WD tours are available to 26km **Farewell Spit**, an internationally significant wetland and bird sanctuary with huge sand dunes. **Wharariki Beach**, 29km north, is a remote and lovely West Coast beach with sand dunes, rock formations and a seal colony. Horse treks are on offer, and kayaking is possible in the **Whanganui Inlet**. There are interesting rock formations at **Rockville**, 8km south; **Te Anaroa Caves** are extensive limestone caves with stalactites and stalagmites.

VISITOR INFORMATION: Willow St, Takaka, Ph: (03) 525 9136, www.nelsonnz.com/golden

The Paua Shell House, Bluff

South Island

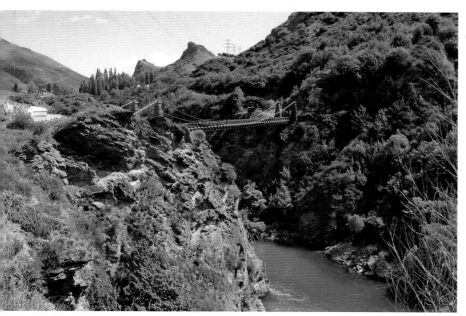
The historic Kawarau Gorge bridge, near Cromwell, Otago

■ Cromwell   POP 2665
Map 307, G1
This busy **Central Otago** town on the shores of **Lake Dunstan** is the service centre in a fruit growing area, and is New Zealand's furthest inland town. Cromwell was originally known as 'The Junction' due to its position at the confluence of the **Kawarau** and **Clutha Rivers**. Part of the town was flooded by the **Clyde Dam** project in the 1990s.
MAIN ATTRACTIONS: A number of Cromwell's old stone buildings have been moved and restored to form a historic precinct, **Old Cromwell Town**. **Jackson's Lookout** overlooks the site of the original bridge into the main street, now under 11m of water. **Lake Dunstan** is rich in bird and fish life; fishing, kayaking, waterskiing and jet boating are all possible on the lake, and eco-tours are available.
NEARBY ATTRACTIONS: The abandoned **Bendigo** gold towns, 20km north-east, are a fascinating array of ruined stone cottages, mine shafts and tailings. Around **Bannockburn**, 8km south, is a burgeoning wine area with wineries open to visitors. There are also some interesting

walks through old mining areas, past the remnants of water races, dams, tunnels and buildings; the landscape was dramatically sculpted by the miners sluicing for gold. The old gold fields of the remote **Nevis Valley**, about 80km south-west, are perhaps New Zealand's best representation of a working gold field, and are a great place for picnicking, mountain biking, fishing and exploring. The orchards at **Ripponvale**, 5km west, are especially pretty in autumn. Visitors can pan for gold at the **Goldfields Mining Centre**. Further west, rugged **Kawarau Gorge** has dramatic rapids, and near the **Roaring Meg** power station, the river pushes through a 1.2m gap.
VISITOR INFORMATION: 47 The Mall, Ph: (03) 445 0212, www.cromwell.org.nz

■ Fox Glacier   POP 260
Map 293, J3
Fox Glacier village, inland from the southern **West Coast** 164km south-west of Hokitika, is a base for visits to nearby **Fox Glacier** in **Westland/Tai Poutini National Park**.
MAIN ATTRACTIONS: Fox Glacier, named

in 1872 after a visit by Prime Minister William Fox, is about 6km east of the township, and can be accessed by walking or heli-hikes. Walks around the glacier include the moraine walk, the **Minnehaha Walk** and the **River Walk**. The 1½-hour **Chalet Lookout Track** takes walkers to a lookout with views over the terminal face. The short **Glow Worm Forest Walk** leads to a glow-worm grotto.
NEARBY ATTRACTIONS: Beautiful **Lake Matheson**, about 9km west, offers stunning reflections of **Mount Tasman** and **Aoraki/Mount Cook**; an hour-long walk leads around the lake. **Gillespies Beach**, 15km west, is a remote black-sand beach with magnificent forest, a seal colony, and impressive views of the mountains. The drive south is very scenic; the **Copland Valley**, about 26km south-west in the national park, is an entrance point to an impressive three-day walk. A six-hour walk in the valley leads to thermal springs at **Copland Flat**. **Lake Paringa**, about 60km south-west, is surrounded by rainforest, and popular for boating, fishing and walking.
VISITOR INFORMATION: SH6, Ph: (03) 751 0807, www.west-coast.co.nz

■ Franz Josef/Waiau   POP 320
Map 293, J2
This small inland township on the southern **West Coast**, 136km south-west of Hokitika, provides accommodation and facilities for visitors to **Franz Josef Glacier**.
MAIN ATTRACTIONS: Franz Josef Glacier, 5km south, is one of two glaciers which reach down from the **Southern Alps** into the West Coast rainforests; in Maori legend it's the frozen tears of a young woman whose lover died climbing the nearby mountains. Good views of the glacier can be had from **Sentinel Rock** (a 10-minute walk) or the 40-minute **Ka Roimata o**

GOLDEN BAY

This beautiful, relaxed area features golden-sand beaches, rocky headlands and arty small towns; it was named not for its golden beaches, but for the 1857 gold find near **Collingwood**. The road to Golden Bay leads over **Takaka Hill**, known as the marble mountain, which offers magnificent views over **Tasman** and **Golden Bays**, and an intriguing landscape of karst formations.

Many artists and craftspeople are based in Golden Bay, and the relaxed town of **Takaka** has galleries and cafés. Collingwood is a base for trips to **Kahurangi National Park**.

Popular beaches include **Pohara Beach**, **Tata**, **Wharariki Beach** and **Wainui Inlet**; **Ligar Bay** has a memorial to Dutch explorer Abel Tasman. The 26km beach of **Farewell Spit** is an internationally important wetland and bird sanctuary. **Pupu Springs**, sacred to Maori, are New Zealand's largest fresh water spring, and have incredibly clear water.

 Visitor information

Golden Bay i-SITE Visitor Centre
Willow St, Takaka
Ph: (03) 525 9136
www.nelsonnz.com/golden

main attractions

- ◈ Bencarri Farm
- ◈ Farewell Spit
- ◈ Kahurangi National Park
- ◈ Ligar Bay
- ◈ Pohara Beach
- ◈ Pupu Springs
- ◈ Rawhiti Cave
- ◈ Takaka
- ◈ Wharariki Beach

Pupu Springs, Golden Bay

Hine Hukatere Walk. Longer walks include the one-hour **Douglas Walk**, and a five-hour walk to **Roberts Point** which gets walkers quite close to the terminal face.

NEARBY ATTRACTIONS: The small town of **Whataroa**, 32km north-east, is a base for trips to the kotuku (white heron) breeding colony. About 150 of these beautiful birds nest each summer at New Zealand's only known breeding ground. Boat tours and walks through rainforest are also available in the **Waitangi Roto Nature Reserve**; beautiful **Okarito Lagoon**, to the west, has many waterbirds, and is wonderful for kayaking.

VISITOR INFORMATION: Main Rd SH6, Ph: (03) 752 0796, www.west-coast.co.nz

■ **French Pass (Anaru)**   POP 40
Map 282,E2
The small fishing and farming village of French Pass (Anaru) is located in the western part of the **Marlborough Sounds**, 56km north of **Rai Valley**, and is the gateway to remote **Rangitoto ke te tonga (D'Urville Island)**.

MAIN ATTRACTIONS: French Pass (Anaru) is a base for wildlife watching; this beautiful, isolated area is home to king shags, terns, gannets, penguins, seals and dolphins. Walking, fishing, diving, sea kayaking and swimming with dolphins and seals are all popular. There are walks to a sandy beach, and to the lookout over **Te Aumiti (French Pass)** passage, a turbulent, dangerous stretch of water with many whirlpools and eddies, long feared by mariners. In the late 19th century it was famous for the presence of Pelorus Jack, a white dolphin who regularly met and accompanied passing vessels. In Maori oral tradition, the passage is the resting place of Te Kawau-a-Toru, the early explorer Kupe's pet shag, which

(CONTINUED P.244)

Franz Josef Glacier reflected in Peters Pool

South Island

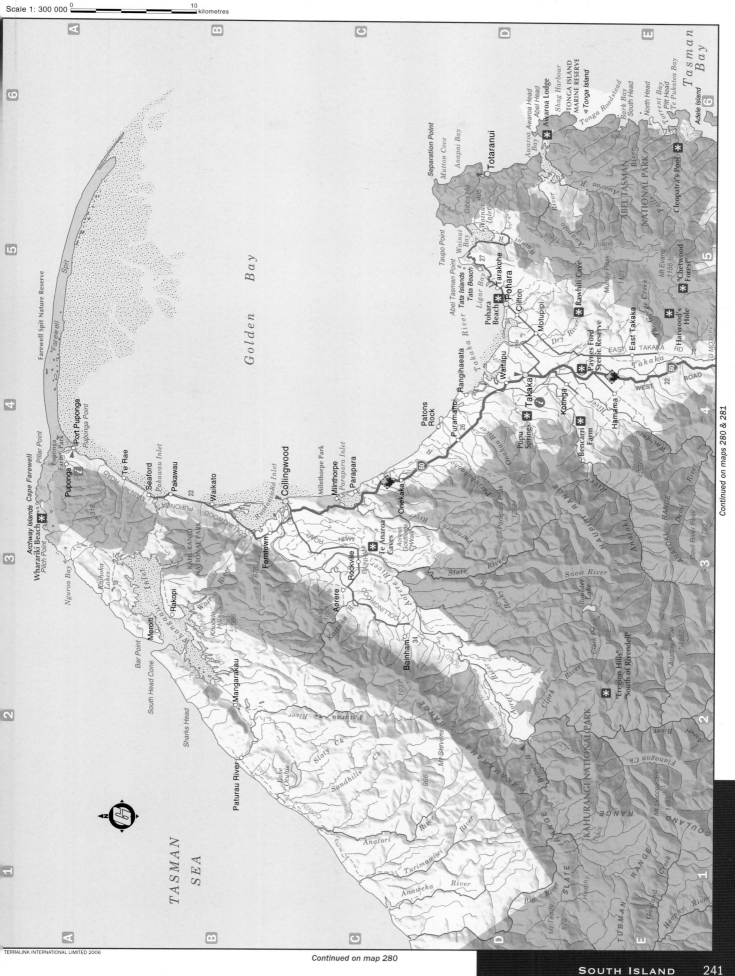

Scale 1: 300 000

0   10
kilometres

TERRALINK INTERNATIONAL LIMITED 2006

Continued on map 280

Continued on maps 280 & 281

Tasman Bay

ABEL TASMAN NATIONAL PARK

Golden   Bay

Separation Point

Totaranui

Awaroa Lodge

TONGA ISLAND MARINE RESERVE
◄Tonga Island

Anaroa Awaroa Head
Abel Head
Shag Harbour
Tonga Roadstead

Tonga Island

North Head
Bark Bay
South Head

Torrent Bay
Pit Head
Te Pukatea Bay

Adele Island

Cleopatra's Pool

Mt Evans 1156 m

Anapai Bay
Mutton Cove
Gibbs Hill

Wainui 405

Taupo Point
Wainui Inlet
Wainui Bay

Abel Tasman Point
Ligar Bay 27
Tata Islands
Tata Beach

Pohara Beach
Pohara
Clifton
Motupipi

Rawhiti Cave

"Chetwood Forest"

Murray Peak 1101

Mt Evans

Dry River

Harwood's Hole

Takaka River

Rangihaeata
Paramaroa
Wattapu

East TAKAKA
East Takaka

Takaka   Takaka   ROAD

Patons Rock

Pupu Springs

Payne's Ford Scenic Reserve

Kotinga
Hamama

WEST   60   22
WEST   ROAD

Bencarri Farm

Anatoki River

TO MOTUEKA

Wangapeka River

ARTHUR RANGE

Parapara Peak 1264

Parapara Inlet
Parapara

Milnthorpe Park
Milnthorpe

Collingwood

Ruataniwha Inlet

Waikato

Pakawau
Pakawau Inlet

Seatord

Te Rae

PUPONGA   22

MAIN   ROAD

COLLINGWOOD

Puponga
Port Puponga
Puponga Point
Puponga Farm Park

Pillar Point

Cape Farewell
Archway Islands
Wharariki Beach
Pilch Point

Farewell   Spit

Farewell Spit Nature Reserve

Golden   Bay

Ngaroa Bay
Kahoka Lakes

KAHURANGI NATIONAL PARK

Rakopi

Meroiti

Mangarakau

Paturau River

Bar Point
South Head Cone

Sharks Head

TASMAN   SEA

Te Anaroa Caves

Aorere Goldfields Walk

Ferntown

Rockville

Aorere

Bainham   34

Aorere River

COLLINGWOOD   ROAD

Kaituna Track

Kaihoka Hills 585

Knuckle Hills 506

Whanganui Inlet

Wangapeka   River
Kaituna   River

GOULAND RANGE

SLATE RANGE

ANATOKI RANGE

HAUPIRI RANGE

WAKAMARAMA RANGE

TUBMAN RANGE

"Fregion Hills"
"South of Rivendell"

Snow River
Slate River
Boulder Lake
Clark River
Brown R
Devil River
Devil River Peak 1780

Slaty Ck
Sandhills
Mt Stevens 966
Lake Otuhie

Paturau River
Anatori River
Turimawiwi River
Anaweka River
Big River
Healthy River
Gouland Creek
Heaphy River

Mt Teddy 870
Mt Likocogs head
Clark Peak 1622
Agate Peak 1562

Aorere Peak 1495

Flanagan Ck
Brown R
Aorere River

WEST   HAAST   ROAD

SOUTH ISLAND

GLACIER COUNTRY

This area of spectacular natural beauty on the southern **West Coast** is a place of huge contrasts. Its towering snowy peaks, dramatic glaciers, lush rainforests, wild beaches and wildlife-rich wetlands draw many visitors, for whom the area offers wonderful sightseeing, walking, hiking, climbing, kayaking and wildlife viewing.

Westland/Tai Poutini National Park, part of Te Wahipounamu South-west New Zealand World Heritage Area, shares a boundary with **Aoraki/Mount Cook National Park** to the east, but the high rainfall west of the **Southern Alps** means the two parks look dramatically different. The permanent snow fields of the Southern Alps feed dozens of glaciers; among them are **Fox** and **Franz Josef Glaciers**. These two huge cascades of ice are the most accessible glaciers found anywhere in the world's temperate zones, descending into rainforested valleys only 250m above sea level.

Close to the coast are pretty lakes, wetlands and wide river mouths, populated by many water birds; this is a breeding area for the crested grebe, and for the beautiful kotuku, or white heron, a bird of great symbolic importance to Maori.

 Visitor information

Franz Josef DOC Visitor Centre
Main Rd, SH6, Franz Josef/Waiau
Ph: (03) 752 0796
www.doc.govt.nz
www.glaciercountry.co.nz

Franz Josef Glacier

main attractions

❖ **Copland Flats thermal springs**

A seven-hour walk up the Copland Valley leads to lovely natural thermal springs.

❖ **Copland Track**

This difficult three-day walk into Aoraki/ Mount Cook National Park is spectacular, but only for experienced hikers.

❖ **Fox Glacier**

Glacier walks, heli-hikes and scenic flights let visitors get close to this spectacular glacier.

❖ **Franz Josef Glacier**

Beautiful Franz Josef Glacier can be accessed by helicopter, or by guided and independent walks.

❖ **Kotuku Sanctuary**

Guided tours take visitors to New Zealand's only breeding colony of the kotuku (white heron).

❖ **Lake Matheson**

Dramatic reflections of Mount Tasman and Aoraki/Mount Cook can be seen in this pretty lake.

❖ **Okarito**

There are many lovely walks around this peaceful coastal village.

❖ **Okarito Lagoon**

Kayaking is popular on this lagoon, New Zealand's largest unmodified tidal inlet and an important feeding area for many birds.

Westland/Tai Poutini National Park

Reaching from the towering **Southern Alps** to the **West Coast**'s wild beaches, this 127 541 ha national park offers short walks around the glaciers and lakes; longer back country walks require good fitness levels. The park's peaks are a mecca for experienced climbers.

Southern Alps, Westland/Tai Poutini National Park

South Island

TASMAN SEA

Kotuku Sanctuary *

Saltwater Lagoon Scenic Reserve

Saltwater Lagoon

Abut Head

Whataroa

Waitangitaona River

207

Waitahi Bluff
L Windemere
Waitangi Roto Nature Reserve

Waitangitaona River

Okarito Lagoon

Otatoki Ck

Ohutua Ck

Rotokino

347

Okarito

Kohuamarua Bluff

Three Mile Lagoon

Oroho Creek

Okarito

Lake Wahapo

The Forks

FORKS OKARITO ROAD

Blanchards Bluff

Cockabulla Creek

32

Zalas Ck

Okarito River

Whataroa

6   31

Rohuta Scenic Res

Five Mile Lagoon

Company Creek

Alpine Lake Ata Puai

Waiho River

462

Lake Mapourika

MacDonalds Creek

Waitangitaona R

Gaunt Creek

Gunn Peak

1753

Omoeroa Bluff

Waiho Flat

Lake Pratt

Potters Creek

Damfey Ck

PRICE RD

Tatare

Stony Ck

Omoeroa River

Docherty Creek

169

Franz Josef / Waiau
i *

2188

Gillespies Point / Kohaihai

Galway Point

Waikukupa River

Hauroa Creek

Lake Gibbs

Lake Mueller

L Wombat

Glow Worm Grotto

Tatare Stm

BURSTER RANGE

2559

Gillespies Beach

Otorokua Point

Waikowhai Bluff

Whelan Creek

Waitapi Ck

Waihapi Creek

Lake Lyttle

Lake Gault

462

6

"Lighting of the Beacons" *

Fritz Josef Glacier / Ka Roimata o Hine Hukatere

BAIRD RANGE

Callery River

MAXIMILLIAN RANGE

Cook Bluff

Ohinetamatea River (Saltwater Ck)

Cook River

Waikowhai Stm

GILLESPIES BEACH

Lake Matheson

23

1742

FRITZ RANGE

2514

Mt Elie De Beaumont 3109

Fox Glacier *i*

Fox River

VICTORIA RANGE

Fox Glacier / Te Moeka o Tuawe

Minarets

Karangarua

Nicholson Ck

46

Cook River

FOX RANGE

3077

Malte Brun

BRUN RANGE

Havelock Creek

Balfour River

Mt Tasman

Tasman Glacier

Murchison Gl

Karangarua

1939

BALFOUR RANGE

Aoraki/Mt Cook 3754

AORAKI / MOUNT COOK

Murchison River

LIEBIG RANGE

Rough Creek

6

COPLAND RANGE

WESTLAND NATIONAL PARK / TAI POUTINI NATIONAL PARK

5078

NATIONAL PARK

Hermann Ck

Architect Creek

Copland River

NAVIGATOR RANGE

MOUNT COOK RANGE

Tasman Lake

2830

Ailsa Stm

Thermal Springs *

Regina Creek

THE SIERRA RA

Mt Sefton

Blue Lakes

2749

Makawhio River

Lake Rototekoiti

Jumbo Ck

Douglas River

435

Hooker River

Tasman Lake

Jollie River

1977

Karangarua River

HOOKER RANGE

Gorilla Stm

GAMACK RANGE

2080

BARE ROCKY RANGE

2746

The Hermitage *

Aoraki / Mount Cook *i*

TO TWIZEL

BANNOCK BRAE RANGE

Jacobs River

2459

Continued on maps 288 & 294
Continued on maps 293 & 294

MOUNT ASPIRING NATIONAL PARK

New Zealand's third largest national park, part of Te Wahipounamu South-west New Zealand World Heritage Area, stretches from **Fiordland**'s rainforests across alpine meadows and braided river valleys to the **Southern Alps**. Tourism began early there, with guided walks into the **Routeburn Valley** available by the 1880s.

Mount Aspiring/Tititea, the region's highest point at 3033m, is a mecca for climbers and photographers. The **Routeburn Track**, one of New Zealand's 'Great Walks', crosses into **Fiordland National Park**; the **Greenstone/Caples** circuit is another beautiful walk.

The **Matukituki Valley** has some excellent short walks, and the massive **Rob Roy Glacier** can be seen after an easy 2½ hour walk to the **Rob Roy Valley**. The 1.8km walk to **Lake Sylvan** is also very pretty. There are many huts offering accommodation for walkers, and jet boating is spectacular on the remote **Dart**, **Wilkin** and **Makarora Rivers**.

main attractions

- ❖ Dart River
- ❖ Greenstone & Caples Tracks
- ❖ Lake Sylvan
- ❖ Matukituki Valley
- ❖ Mount Aspiring/Tititea
- ❖ Rees–Dart Track
- ❖ Rob Roy Glacier
- ❖ Routeburn Track
- ❖ Wilkin Valley

ⓘ Visitor information

DOC Glenorchy Visitor Centre
Cnr Mull and Oban Sts, Glenorchy
Ph: (03) 442 9937
www.doc.govt.nz

Mount Aspiring National Park

---

broke a wing in the treacherous waters and was drowned.
NEARBY ATTRACTIONS: Secluded, peaceful Rangitoto ke te tonga (D'Urville Island) is home to many birds, including the rare king shag; dolphins and seals swim in the surrounding waters. The island has some lovely walks to waterfalls and glow-worm grottoes, and nature tours are available to off-shore islands. Rangitoto ke te tonga is also rich in history; Dutch seafarer Abel Tasman sailed past in 1642, and Captain Cook landed in 1770. The 56km drive from Rai Valley to French Pass, while partially unsealed, is extremely scenic, leading through forest and farmland and offering wonderful sea views.
VISITOR INFORMATION: The Foreshore, Picton, Ph: (03) 520 3113, www.frenchpass.com

■ **Geraldine** POP 2205
Map 303, H1
Geraldine is a pretty, rural **Canterbury** town with a friendly village atmosphere. Located 136km south of **Christchurch**, it's on the main highway to top tourist areas **Aoraki/Mount Cook** and **Queenstown**.
MAIN ATTRACTIONS: Five minutes' walk from the main street is **Talbot Forest**, a rare remnant of lowland podocarp native forest, which offers great views over the plains and mountains. The town's long established parks have exotic trees which give a brilliant display in autumn. Many artists and craftspeople sell their work locally, including at the **Bélanger-Taylor Glass Studio**; there's also a cheesemaker and chocolatier, and **Barker's Shop** in the **Berry Barn Complex** has fruit products. Geraldine's **Vintage Car & Machinery Museum** has over 30 vintage and veteran cars, and 100 tractors from 1912. There's also a rare 1929 Spartan Biplane on display.
NEARBY ATTRACTIONS: **Peel Forest**, 19km north, is an important indigenous podocarp forest.

Village of Glenorchy

South Island

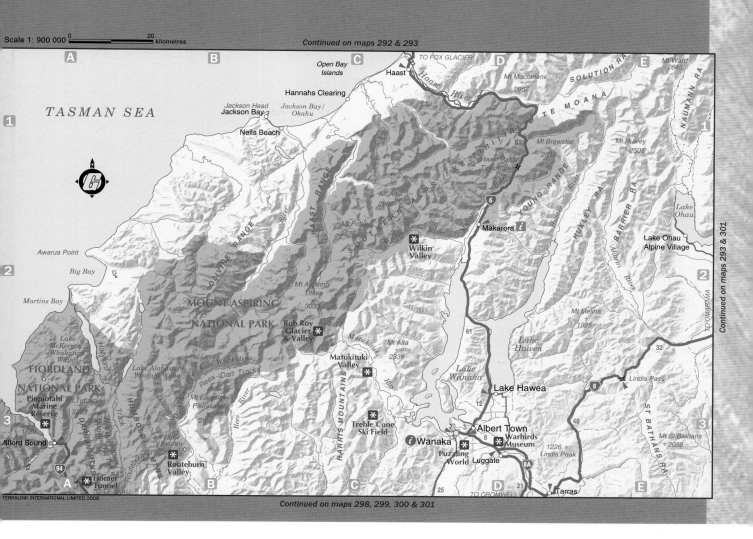

Continued on maps 292 & 293

Scale 1: 900 000

TO FOX GLACIER

TASMAN SEA

Open Bay Islands

Hannahs Clearing

Jackson Head
Jackson Bay

Jackson Bay/ Okahu

Neils Beach

Haast

Awarua Point

Big Bay

Martins Bay

Lake McKerrow Whakatipu Waitai

FIORDLAND

NATIONAL PARK

Piopiotahi Marine Reserve

Milford Sound

Homer Tunnel

Lake Alabaster Wawahi Waka

MOUNT ASPIRING

NATIONAL PARK

Mt Aspiring Tititea 3033

Rob Roy Glacier & Valley

Mt Earnslaw Pikirakatahi 2830

Rees - Dart Track

Matukituki Valley

Mt Alta 2339

Treble Cone Ski Field

Routeburn Valley

Lake Sylvan

Wanaka

Puzzling World

Luggate

Albert Town

Warbirds Museum

Lake Wanaka

Lake Hawea

Lake Hawea

Makarora

Mt Brewster 2516

Mt Huxley 2505

Lake Ohau

Lake Ohau Alpine Village

Mt Melina 1925

Lindis Pass

Lindis Peak 1226

Mt St Bathans 2088

ST BATHANS RA

Tarras

TO CROMWELL

Continued on maps 298, 299, 300 & 301

Continued on maps 293 & 301

TERRALINK INTERNATIONAL LIMITED 2006

The nearby **Rangitata River** has world class white water rafting and salmon fishing opportunities, with spectacular alpine and high country scenery in the upper river valley. *The Lord of the Rings* director Peter Jackson chose **Mt Potts Station** in the Rangitata River valley as the filming location for 'Edoras'.

VISITOR INFORMATION: Cnr Talbot and Cox Sts, Ph: (03) 693 1006, www.southisland.org.nz

■ Glenorchy   POP 225

Map 299, G6

This village at the northern tip of **Lake Wakatipu**, 45km north-west of **Queenstown**, is surrounded by mountains, glacier-fed rivers and beech forest. Glenorchy has been a tourist destination since the 1890s; it's a gateway to the nearby

World Heritage Area and to many important hiking tracks, but is an appealing stop in its own right due to its lovely setting.

MAIN ATTRACTIONS: Walking, scenic flights, fishing and horse trekking are all possible, and jet boats head up the wild **Dart River** and deep into **Mount Aspiring National Park**. The road between Queenstown and Glenorchy is very beautiful, with spectacular views of Lake Wakatipu and glacial rock formations, including sheer mountain sides and hanging valleys.

NEARBY ATTRACTIONS: The valleys north of Glenorchy are worth exploring; 15km from Glenorchy is the wonderfully-named small settlement of **Paradise**, where part of *The Lord of the Rings* was shot, including scenes in '**Lothlorien**',

'**Isengard**' and '**Amon Hen**'. Peaceful **Kinloch**, 26km by car or a few minutes by boat across the lake, is a lovely spot for lakeside relaxing. The popular 32km **Routeburn Track**, one of New Zealand's 'Great Walks', can be walked independently or with a guide. The **Greenstone** and **Caples Tracks** can be linked with the Routeburn; there's also a 1.8km walk to pretty **Lake Sylvan**.

VISITOR INFORMATION: Cnr Mull and Oban Sts, Ph: (03) 442 9937, www.glenorchy.com

■ Gore   POP 9930

Map 312, D2

Gore, located 68km north-east of Invercargill on the **Mataura River**, is a service town for the local farming district. The town — **Southland**'s second largest — is famous for

country music and trout fishing.
MAIN ATTRACTIONS: The wonderful
Eastern Southland Gallery, in
Gore's old library building, has
exhibitions of significant New
Zealand art, including works by
Ralph Hotere and Rita Angus; it
also has a substantial collection
of African artefacts. The **Hokonui
Moonshine Museum** explores the
historic illicit whisky industry which
produced the infamous Hokonui
Moonshine, brewed during 51 years
of prohibition from 1902. **Gore
Historical Museum** has displays
about Maori history, trout fishing,
and pioneers; **Hokonui Pioneer
Park** has heritage buildings and
vintage farming paraphernalia. The
Mataura River has the highest trout
catch rates of any New Zealand
river, and guides for fishing trips are
available. The annual **New Zealand
Gold Guitar Awards** are a 10-day
festival of country music.
NEARBY ATTRACTIONS: Tracks lead
through native forest and up to
lookouts at **Croydon Bush Scenic
Reserve**, 10km north-west; in
summer, flowering rata put on
a wonderful scarlet display.
Croydon Aircraft Company, 15km
north-west, has restored vintage

Haast River

aeroplanes; rides are available in a
Tiger Moth. An aviation museum is
being developed at the site.
VISITOR INFORMATION: Norfolk St,
Ph: (03) 203 9288, www.gorenz.com

■ Greymouth   POP 9530
Map 318, C3
Located at the mouth of the **Grey
River**, Greymouth is the largest
town on the **West Coast**, and
is a base for outdoor activities.
Originally the site of a Maori pa
(fortified village), it has a long
history as a gold mining centre.
MAIN ATTRACTIONS: Tours are on offer at
Monteith's Brewing Company, well
known in New Zealand for its array
of boutique beers. Greymouth's
galleries and studios produce arts
and crafts, including from local
greenstone. **History House Museum**
explores the town's gold mining and
pioneer past; the **Quay Walk** leads
along the river front. Mountain
biking, rafting, canoeing, caving,
climbing and walking are all popular
in surrounding wilderness areas.
NEARBY ATTRACTIONS: Greymouth
is the start or end point for the
TranzAlpine train journey, a
spectacular 4½ hour trip between
the South Island's west and east
coast which passes through
a staggering array of scenery,
including the **Southern Alps** and
Waimakariri Valley, and ends up in
Christchurch. The **Brunner Mine
Industrial Site**, 11km north-east,
has coal mining relics and a historic
suspension bridge; the mine was
the scene of an infamous accident
in which 65 people died. The
historic mining town of **Blackball**,
28km north-east, is known for its
locally produced salami, and for
its heritage hotel, now known as
Formerly the Blackball Hilton after
a challenge by the hotel chain. The
18km **Croesus Track**, 1km from
Blackball, crosses the **Paparoa
Range**. **Shantytown**, 11km south
of Greymouth, is a replica 1890s

town with more than 30 buildings;
visitors can pan for gold, or ride on
an 1877 locomotive. At **Kumara**,
about 25km south-east on SH73,
the foundations of colourful
1893–1906 premier 'King Dick'
Seddon's house can be seen. There
are surf beaches at **Cobden Beach**
and **Rapahoe**. **Lake Brunner
(Moana)**, 29km south-east, is a
pretty lake offering great trout
fishing and beautiful forest walks.
VISITOR INFORMATION: Cnr Herbert and
Mackay Sts, Ph: (03) 768 5101,
www.west-coast.co.nz

■ Haast   POP 155
Map 292, D6
The small settlement of Haast
is in the southern **West Coast**
area near the mouth of the **Haast
River**, 117km south-west of **Fox
Glacier**. The area is rich in natural
attractions, with huge stands of
rainforest, major wetlands, sand
dune forests, wild beaches and
plentiful wildlife.
NEARBY ATTRACTIONS: Haast is near the
northern boundary of the World
Heritage Area of **Mount Aspiring
National Park**. Opened in 1965,
the road south to **Wanaka** (145km
away) follows the route of an old
Maori greenstone trail through
the national park; a number of
walks lead from the road to scenic
waterfalls, including **Roaring Billy**,
the **Fantail Falls** and **Thunder Falls**.
The **Haast Pass**, 63km south-east,
is a beautiful alpine pass reaching
a height of 563m at its summit.
The road south-west from Haast to
Jackson Bay is a starting point for
many wilderness walks, including
the **Hapuka Estuary Walk**; jet
boating trips are available on the
Waiatoto River. Jackson Bay, 51km
south-west, attracted European
settlers in the 1870s, but their plans
to establish farms came to nought.
Now a remote fishing village,
Jackson Bay has wonderful views of
the **Southern Alps**, and colonies of

South Island

Thermal pools, Hanmer Springs

Fiordland crested penguins; there are some interesting coastal walks. The unsealed road up the **Jackson River** offers wonderful views of the **Cascade River Valley**. Peaceful **Lake Moeraki**, 30km north of Haast, has good trout fishing; at nearby **Monro Beach**, a 40-minute walk through bush, there's a penguin colony.

VISITOR INFORMATION: Cnr SH6 and Jackson Bay Rd, Ph: (03) 750 0809, www.west-coast.co.nz

■ Halfmoon Bay (Oban)   POP 350
Map 315, J3

This small township is the only real settlement on **Stewart Island**, where the main industries are fishing, marine farming, conservation and tourism. The island has archaeological evidence of Maori habitation from around the 13th century; the British explorer Captain James Cook sighted it in 1770, mistakenly mapping it as a peninsula. European settlement began in the early 19th century, and intermarriage with local Maori women was common. In the 1920s, Norwegians settled on the island as part of a whaling enterprise.

MAIN ATTRACTIONS: Volunteer-run

Rakiura Museum explores Stewart Island's history, both Maori and European; **Oban Presbyterian Church** was built in 1904.

NEARBY ATTRACTIONS: **Rakiura National Park** was declared a national park in 2002, and has 245km of walking tracks, including the 'Great Walk' of **Rakiura Track**. The rich coastal wildlife includes sooty shearwaters (muttonbird/titi), mollymawks and penguins. Forest birds include tui, kaka, bellbirds and Stewart Island kiwi; these, unlike other kiwi species, are active during the day.

VISITOR INFORMATION: Main Rd, Ph: (03) 219 0009, www.stewartisland.co.nz

■ Hanmer Springs   POP 665
Map 290, E2

Hanmer Springs, the South Island's premier thermal resort, is situated 130km north of Christchurch, 10km off SH7. On the **Alpine Pacific Triangle Touring Route**, Hanmer is a favourite weekend destination for Christchurch residents with its hot pools, forest walks and skiing.

MAIN ATTRACTIONS: At **Hanmer Springs Thermal Pools & Spa**, the therapeutic thermal waters known to Maori as 'Waitapu' (sacred waters) have been working their magic on visitors for many years; the reserve has a range of public and private pools, and spa facilities. A great winter experience is to lounge in a hot pool while snow falls around you. For a change of pace there are more adrenaline pumping activities such as jet boating, rafting, and bungy jumping at **Thrillseekers Canyon**; visitors can also explore the area by horse or mountain bike, or cruise above it all in a helicopter. There are some pretty walks in nearby forest, including the **Woodland Walk** and **Conical Hill Lookout**.

NEARBY ATTRACTIONS: **Hanmer Springs Ski Area** is 17km north of town. **Molesworth Station**, 8km north of Hanmer Springs, is New Zealand's

biggest farm at 180 500ha; it also boasts the country's largest cattle herd. Independent visits can be made to the stunning farm between December and February, and 4WD tours are available. **Acheron Accommodation House**, 22km from Hanmer, is a historic cob building constructed in 1863 to provide accommodation to travellers. **Mount Lyford Ski Field** is 60km east of Hanmer. Like Hanmer Springs Ski Area, this popular and picturesque ski field is less expensive than the larger resorts. The **Lewis Pass Highway** leads to spectacular 907m-high **Lewis Pass**, 62km north-west of Hanmer at the northern end of the **Southern Alps**. This beautiful area has snow-topped mountains, alpine areas, lakes and rivers; there are some lovely walks, including the **St James Walkway**, and tracks in **Lake Sumner Forest Park**, to the south. **Maruia Springs**, west of Lewis Pass, has thermal springs and a Japanese-styled bath house.

VISITOR INFORMATION: 42 Amuri Ave West, Ph: (03) 315 7128, www.hurunui.com

■ Havelock   POP 475
Map 282, D5

This historic small town in the **Marlborough Sounds** is located at the westernmost tip of scenic **Queen Charlotte Drive**, 35km west of Picton. The gateway to **Pelorus** and **Kenepuru Sounds**, Havelock was once a busy gold-mining town, and a centre for milling and exporting timber.

MAIN ATTRACTIONS: Havelock is famous for its greenshell mussels, and visitors can try these in a restaurant or take a cruise to a nearby mussel farm. The town's colonial-era buildings are home to galleries, cafés and restaurants; from the harbour, boat cruises allow visitors to explore the beautiful waters of the Marlborough Sounds. Diving, boating, swimming, kayaking and

(CONTINUED P.250)

STEWART ISLAND

The smallest of New Zealand's three main islands, separated from the South Island by **Foveaux Strait**, Stewart Island is known in Maori as **Rakiura**, usually translated as Glowing Skies. In Maori legend, the South Island was the canoe of mythical trickster Maui, and Stewart Island was the anchor.

A 20-minute flight from **Invercargill**, or an hour's ferry trip from **Bluff**, Stewart Island draws many nature-loving visitors to experience its rich forests, wetlands, beaches and plentiful wildlife. The island is about 75km long and 45km wide, but has only about 400 residents, most of them in the main town of **Halfmoon Bay (Oban)**. There are around 245km of walking tracks; Stewart Island is also a great place for kayaking, diving, snorkelling, boating and relaxing.

Rakiura National Park is New Zealand's newest national park, and offers excellent walking through unspoilt native bush. The forest is rich in birds, including good numbers of Stewart Island kiwi and some other rare species. **Codfish Island** is a significant bird sanctuary and a focus for recovery efforts for the endangered kakapo, but is not open to visitors.

main attractions

◈ Fuchsia Walk
This easy walk leads through native fuchsia forest which attracts many birds.

◈ Moturau Moana
A 30-minute walk leads to a pretty native garden on a historic site, with views over Halfmoon Bay.

◈ Observation Rock
A popular spot for watching the sun set over Paterson Inlet, this lookout spot is a 15-minute walk from the visitors centre.

◈ Paterson Inlet
Paterson Inlet's 100km² of sheltered water has 20 islands and is great for kayaking.

◈ Rakiura Museum
This museum explores Stewart Island's past, including muttonbirding, whaling, mining, fishing and Maori history.

◈ Rakiura National Park
This 157 000ha national park, the country's newest, covers about 85% of Stewart Island and offers great walking.

◈ Rakiura Track
One of New Zealand's 'Great Walks', this easy 29km track passes through coastal areas, climbs a 300m-high forested ridge, and includes historic sites.

◈ Southern Circuit
A multi-day 56km wilderness track, the Southern Circuit is a challenging walk for experienced hikers.

◈ Ulva Island/Te Wharawhara Marine Reserve
This 1075ha marine sanctuary has rich marine life, including a huge variety of seaweed species.

Ulva Island Open Sanctuary

This pest-free 250ha island, a bird sanctuary since 1922, has a huge abundance of bird life in its beautiful forests. Rare species which breed here include the Stewart Island robin, the saddleback, the yellowhead and the rifleman; there are also walking tracks, picnic spots and golden beaches.

 Visitor information

DOC Stewart Island Visitor Information Centre
Main Rd, Halfmoon Bay (Oban)
Ph: (03) 219 0009
www.stewartisland.co.nz

Halfmoon Bay, Stewart Island

South Island

0 10 kilometres

A B C D E

1

Foveaux
Strait

Bishop and Clerks
Islands

Cave Point
Black Rock Point
White Rock Point
Lucky Point
Saddle Point

Rugged
Islands

Mt Anglem /
Hananui
980

Christmas
Village Bay

Ferry to Picton

North Island

The Knobbies
North West
Bay
North Red Head
Roger Head
Sealers
Bay

Little Mt Anglem
738

Garden Point

Womens
Island

2

Codfish Island
(Whenuahou)
250

Waituna
Bay

Murray R

Gull Rock Point

Edwards I
(Motunui)

Big Bight

Freshwater

610

Port William /
Potirepo

Jacky Lee Island
(Pukeokaoka)

Titi / Muttonbird
Islands

Richards Point

L Sheila

THOMSON RIDGE
549

Bobs Point

Herekopare I
(Te Marama)

Shark Island

Rocky Mount

Mamaku Pt

Bunker
Islets

Mason Head

399

Scott Burn

River

Horseshoe Bay
Horseshoe Point

Bench
Island

STEWART ISLAND /
RAKIURA

Tolson R

Moturau Moana
Halfmoon Bay
(Oban)
Observation Rock
Fuchsia Walk
Rakiura Museum

Halfmoon Bay
Ackers Point

Duck Ck

Southern

Mt Rakeahua
681

North Arm

Dynamite Pt

Prices Pt

Native
Island

Bullers Point
(Anglem)

Carter

3

Mason
Bay

South West Arm

Paterson Inlet /
Whaka a Te Wera

Ulva I

Ulva Island
Open Sanctuary

Passage

Ernest
Islands

Abrahams
Bay

ULVA ISLAND /
TE WHARAWHARA
MARINE RESERVE

Cow Island

Southern

River

Bald Hill
514

Steep Head

Rakeahua

Bravo I

RAKIURA

Big Glory
Bay

Lauras Leg

Chew Tobacco
Point

446

Crail

NATIONAL PARK

Gorge Creek

Heron River

Chew Tobacco
Bay

Table Hill
716

East Cape /
Koromere

4

Doughboy Bay

Adventure Hill
265

Pikaroro Pt
Pikaroro Bay

Deceit Peaks

Doughboy
Creek

Blakies Ck

Pegasus Nature Reserve

Laird River / Tutaekawetoweto

Port Adventure
Scenic Reserve

Sinbads
Mistake

Weka I

South Red
Head Point

563

Mt Allen
750

Newton Ck

Toitoi River

Stirling
Head

Tia I
(Entrance)

TIN RANGE

Koneka River

Pegasus Ck

Tikotatahi
Bay

Shelter Pt

Kundy I

Seal Creek

372

Breaksea Is
Titi /
Muttonbird Is

Betsy I
Boat Group

John Point

Big I
Rat I

503

Robertson R

Kuri
Point

Big Kuri Bay

Owen
Head

Horomamae /
Owen Island

Chimneys I

Basin Ck

5

The Sisters
Easy
Harbour

North Arm

185

Seal Point

Tutaepawhati Bay

Goose I

407
Gog

Pearl I

The
Brothers

Cook Arm

Anchorage I

Smooth Point

PACIFIC

Noble
Island

Port Pegasus / Pikihatiti

Smiths
Lookout
474

South
Arm

140

Ernest Island

OCEAN

493

Broad Bay

6

Broad Head

Wilsons Point

Kaninihi Point

N
G

Murphy
Island

South Cape / Whiore

A B C D E

wildlife viewing are all popular.
NEARBY ATTRACTIONS: The **Nydia Track** is a remote eight- to nine-hour track through regenerating forest, offering excellent views over the Sounds, and passing **Nydia Bay**, once the site of a Maori pa (fortified village). Havelock is a base for trips to remote **French Pass (Anaru)**, which has abundant bird and marine life, and a turbulent tidal passage; visitors can reach it by boat or via a scenic 56km drive from **Rai Valley**. Wildlife on peaceful **Rangitoto ke te tonga (D'Urville Island)** includes gannets, penguins, the rare king shag, dolphins and seals, and there are walks to waterfalls and glow-worm grottoes. Historic **Canvastown**, 10km west of Havelock, started life as a tent city during 1864's Wakamarina gold rush. **Pelorus Bridge** scenic reserve, 27km west, has impressive native forest with towering trees.
VISITOR INFORMATION: The Foreshore, Picton, Ph: (03) 520 3113, www.destinationmarlborough.com

■ **Hokitika**   POP 3480
Map 288, D3
On the **West Coast**, 43km south-west of Greymouth, Hokitika's first European building was erected from calico and saplings in 1864. The next year, a gold rush began, and by 1866 Hokitika was a bustling town with at least 6000 residents; that year, almost half of all immigrants to New Zealand arrived through its port! Today it's New Zealand's main centre for working greenstone (jade), and is home to many artists.
MAIN ATTRACTIONS: Outdoor activities are popular, including rafting, kayaking and river cruises. Every March, the **Hokitika Wildfoods Festival** draws crowds from around New Zealand who come to sample bush foods, both sublime and bizarre. The town has many arts and crafts outlets, with greenstone a

particular focus. Fish and freshwater eels are on display at **Westland's WaterWorld**; the **National Kiwi Centre** has a nocturnal house with kiwi. **West Coast Historical Museum** features the town's gold mining history, and a self-guided walk leads around the town's historic sites. There's a glow-worm dell near the northern outskirts.
NEARBY ATTRACTIONS: Scenic **Lake Kaniere**, about 20km east, is skirted by a 13km walkway; there are shorter walks to **Dorothy Falls** and **Canoe Cove**. The walkway at **Lake Mahinapua**, 10km south-west, leads through a scenic reserve to sand dunes. Both lakes offer water sports and fishing. **Ross**, 27km south-west, is a historic gold mining town; gold is still mined there today. Walkways lead past the old gold fields, and it's possible to pan for gold. The giant matai tree near pretty **Lake Ianthe**, 22km further south, is reputedly over 1000 years old.
VISITOR INFORMATION: 7 Tancred St, Ph: (03) 755 6166, www.west-coast.co.nz

■ **Invercargill**   POP 46 300
Map 319, B3
Southland's largest town, and New Zealand's southernmost city, Invercargill is 215km south-west of Dunedin; it was an early centre for meat and wool exports, which made it prosperous. The city is home to a thriving student population.
MAIN ATTRACTIONS: Invercargill is centred around 80ha **Queens Park**, which has duck ponds, rose gardens, an aviary and a golf course. The **Southland Museum and Art Gallery Niho o te Taniwha**, in a pyramid building at the entrance to Queens Park, features Southland's natural and human history, including Maori artefacts and the Subantarctic Islands. The museum also has New Zealand's largest collection of live tuatara (prehistoric native reptiles), including the centenarian tuatara Henry. The

Hokitika Beach

42.5m-high red-brick **Water Tower**, completed in 1889, offers great views over the city to those who climb its 112 steep steps. **Anderson Park Art Gallery** displays New Zealand art in a 1925 Georgian-style house surrounded by 24ha of lovely gardens. Invercargill also has some beautiful historic buildings.
NEARBY ATTRACTIONS: **Sandy Point Domain**, 7km west, has totara forest, sand dunes and lookouts with views over the **New River Estuary**, where there are many wading birds; a good spot for walking and mountain biking, this area was inhabited by early Maori. **Oreti Beach**, 10km west, is popular for water sports. The wetlands at **Waituna Lagoon**, 20km south-east, are an important breeding ground for migratory wading birds. **Waipapa Point**, 63km south-east of Invercargill, was the site of an 1881 shipwreck

South Island

which killed 130; as a result, a lighthouse was built in 1884.

VISITOR INFORMATION: 108 Gala St, Ph: (03) 214 6243, www.visitinvercargillnz.com

■ Kaikoura   POP 2110

Map 320, C3

Located 183km north of **Christchurch**, Kaikoura sits at the edge of the **Pacific Ocean** and is the most northern of the three main destination points in the **Alpine Pacific Triangle Touring Route**.

MAIN ATTRACTIONS: Kaikoura was once a major whaling area, but is now famous for whale watching; dolphin and seal swimming are also popular. While it draws thousands of tourists every year, in many ways Kaikoura is still a gritty little fishing town, and that's very much part of its charm. There's a fur seal colony with two adjacent walkways, one along the coast and one on the clifftops. Guided tours let visitors see albatross and other seabirds. Kaikoura has excellent diving, snorkelling and surfing conditions, with a vibrant underwater world well worth exploring. Kaikoura means 'eat crayfish', and the delicious crustacean is on offer at many of the town's restaurants and takeaway bars. **Kaikoura Museum** explores the area's Maori and whaling history. Maori cultural tours are available from the local sub-tribe Kati Kuri; their base, **Takahanga**

Kaikoura coastline

Marae, has contemporary artworks, but can only be visited when invited and formally welcomed. **Fyffe House** is the only surviving colonial whalers' cottage; the **Kaikoura Wine Company** has an impressive cellar and delicious vineyard platters. The **Kaikoura Art Trail** is a journey through the inspiration and creativity of local artists. There are limestone formations in **Maori Leap Cave**, 3km south.

NEARBY ATTRACTIONS: **Mount Lyford Skifield**, one hour's drive west, is a popular skiing area; there are daily shuttle buses to the mountain. The route north from Kaikoura to **Blenheim** is a beautiful coastal drive with wonderful views over the wild sea.

VISITOR INFORMATION: West End, Ph: (03) 319 5641, www.kaikoura.co.nz

■ Kaiteriteri   POP 365

Map 281, F4

The small town of Kaiteriteri, on the west side of **Tasman Bay** 60km from Nelson, is a popular resort spot and a base for visits to **Abel Tasman National Park**.

MAIN ATTRACTIONS: Kaiteriteri's gorgeous golden sand beach offers safe swimming; **Kaka Pah Point** has lovely walks to secluded coves. **Withell's Walk** leads through native bush to some spectacular views over the bay. Launch and kayak tours head from Kaiteriteri into the national park, and tours led by Maori guides give visitors the chance to paddle a traditionally carved waka (canoe) and learn about Maori culture.

NEARBY ATTRACTIONS: Abel Tasman National Park is New Zealand's smallest national park, and has golden beaches, turquoise water, interesting rocky outcrops, plentiful wildlife and native bush. The tiny township of **Marahau**, 5km north of Kaiteriteri, is the gateway to the beautiful **Abel Tasman Coastal Track**, one of New Zealand's 'Great

Walks'; Marahau is the main base for booking kayaks, water taxis and guided tours.

VISITOR INFORMATION: Wallace St, Motueka, Ph: (03) 528 6543, www.abeltasmangreenrush.co.nz

■ Karamea   POP 440

Map 280, A5

Karamea is located on a remote part of the **West Coast** 100km north of Westport. Set between forested hills and rugged coastline, Karamea is a base for trips into **Kahurangi National Park**, and is the southern exit or entrance point for the **Heaphy Track**.

MAIN ATTRACTIONS: **Karamea Centennial Museum** has displays about the town's history. Nearby estuaries are rich in bird life, and the long sandy beaches are great for surfcasting (but unsafe for swimming). The **Karamea River** offers good swimming, fishing and kayaking.

NEARBY ATTRACTIONS: Beautiful **Kahurangi National Park**, to the east, is an area of great ecological significance; short walks into the park include the 40-minute **Nikau Walk**, through groves of nikau palms, and a 45-minute walk through lush forest to **Scotts Beach**. There are dramatic limestone formations in the **Oparara Basin**, including the spectacular **Oparara Arch**, a 37m-high, 200m-long arch over a river; the **Honeycomb Hill Caves and Arch** can only be visited on a tour. The 82km Heaphy Track, one of New Zealand's 'Great Walks', leads through varied landscapes to the **Aorere Valley** in **Golden Bay**; the three- to five-day **Wangapeka Track** is a historic gold diggers' route. The road south from Karamea to **Westport** offers dramatic scenery, particularly from dramatic **Karamea Bluff**.

VISITOR INFORMATION: Bridge St, Ph: (03) 782 6652, www.karameainfo.co.nz

KAIKOURA

Whale watching near Kaikoura

The rugged seaside town of Kaikoura, beautifully situated at the base of the **Seaward Kaikoura Range** and bordered by the **Pacific Ocean**, is famous for its scenery and marine life. The submarine trenches off the coast of Kaikoura are thousands of metres deep, providing an ideal environment for whales, dolphins and seals. A whaling centre from

1843 until 1922, Kaikoura now draws thousands of international visitors for whale watching and other marine life encounters.

The area's food sources attracted significant Maori settlement in the area (Kaikoura is Maori for 'eat crayfish') — at least 14 pa (Maori fortified village) sites have been identified. Maori artefacts from the area can be seen at the **Kaikoura Museum**.

Stunning coastal alpine scenery and world-renowned eco-tourism have put this once sleepy little fishing village firmly on the map.

> *i* **Visitor information**
>
> **Kaikoura i-SITE Visitor Centre**
> West End, Kaikoura
> Ph: (03) 319 5641
> www.kaikoura.co.nz

Fur seal, Kaikoura

main attractions

- Dolphin and seal swimming
- Fyffe House
- Kaikoura Art Trail
- Kaikoura Museum
- Kaikoura Wilderness Walkway
- Kaikoura Wine Company
- Maori Leap Cave
- Reef diving
- Seaward Kaikoura Range
- Whale watching

■ Lake Tekapo   POP 305
Map 294, D6

Lake Tekapo township sits at the southern end of beautiful **Lake Tekapo**. Set in Canterbury's **Mackenzie Country**, the soaring peaks of the **Southern Alps** serve as a dramatic backdrop to this remote town. Lake Tekapo is often the first stop on a tour of the Southern Alps.
MAIN ATTRACTIONS: The stunning turquoise blue colour of Lake Tekapo and other lakes in the area is caused by 'rock flour', finely ground particles of rock held in suspension in the glacial water, which reflect the light. Beside the lake is the tiny, picturesque 1935 **Church of the Good Shepherd**, built from stone and oak. Close to the church is a bronze statue of a collie dog, a tribute to the

common sheepdog vital for every farmer's livelihood. **Kiwi Treasures** is a souvenir shop and visitors' centre. Local adventure, alpine and trekking companies organise transport and tours; Lake Tekapo also has an outdoor ice skating rink, open in winter.
NEARBY ATTRACTIONS: Lake Tekapo is a popular base for skiing. During the winter months it services the popular ski fields of **Roundhill** and **Mt Dobson**. **Lake Pukaki** is 45km south-west; from the lookout, it's possible on a clear day to see a perfect view of **Aoraki/Mount Cook** and its surrounding peaks, with the astonishing blue of the lake in the foreground. **Aoraki/Mount Cook National Park**, about 100km west, has snow-clad glacier valleys and mountainous peaks.

VISITOR INFORMATION: SH8, Ph: (03) 680 6686, www.laketekapountouched.co.nz

■ Lawrence   POP 475
Map 313, H1

Lawrence, 93km south-west of Dunedin, has had a central role in **Otago**'s history, as one of the region's first major gold finds was made at nearby **Gabriel's Gully** in May 1861. Hopeful miners rushed to the area, and by the following year, Lawrence had a population of almost 11 500, more than twice that of Dunedin, Otago's capital. There were a number of other finds nearby, including at **Monro's Gully**, the only major New Zealand gold field discovered by a woman.
MAIN ATTRACTIONS: Lawrence has many historic buildings; the **Lawrence**

South Island

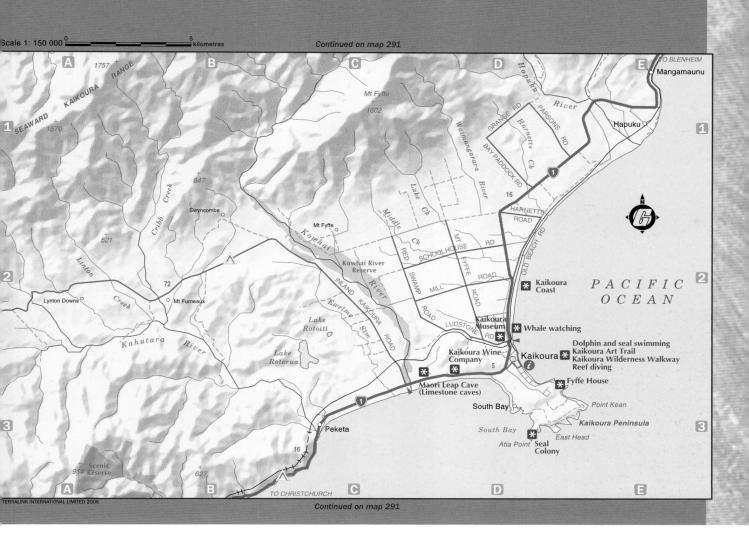

Continued on map 291

Scale 1: 150 000

TERRALINK INTERNATIONAL LIMITED 2006

Continued on map 291

Lake Pukaki

Information Centre/Museum has displays on the area's gold mining history. **Lawrence Chinese Camp**, 1km west, was a major village of up to 500 Chinese miners, and was a gateway to the gold fields from 1867. Archaeological work is being done on the camp, and there are plans to reconstruct the village. NEARBY ATTRACTIONS: Interesting walks can be done in the historic gold mining areas of **Gabriel's Gully**, 5km north, and nearby **Wetherstons**. The ruins of the **Black Horse Brewery** can be seen at Wetherstons, and it's still possible to pan for — and find — small amounts of gold. The **Tuapeka River**, south-west of Lawrence, offers good fishing. A historic river punt takes vehicles across the mighty **Clutha River/Mata-Au** at

Tuapeka Mouth, 27km south-west. Established in 1896, and propelled only by the river current using rudders and pulleys, the ferry is the only one of its kind in use in the southern hemisphere.
VISITOR INFORMATION: **17 Ross Pl,** Ph: (03) 485 9222, www.cluthadc.govt.nz

■ **Manapouri**   POP 245
Map 305, F5
The small **Fiordland** town of Manapouri is spectacularly located on the shores of **Lake Manapouri**, 19km south of Te Anau. The **Kepler Mountains** are a beautiful backdrop to the lake, which was the site of a conservation battle in the late 1960s when there were plans to raise it 30m to produce hydro-electricity. In the end a massive underground power station was built without

(CONTINUED P.255)

KAHURANGI NATIONAL PARK

Ecologically important Kahurangi National Park, created in 1996, has rugged mountains, glacier-carved valleys, remote rivers, untouched native forests and long stretches of pristine coastline in its 452 002ha. It's home to 50 % of all New Zealand plant species and 80 % of alpine plants; the rich wildlife includes more than 100 bird species, as well as carnivorous land snails and long-tailed bats.

The park features the southern hemisphere's largest known cave system, but the caves are suitable only for experienced cavers; there are beautiful limestone formations in the **Oparara Basin**. A number of *The Lord of the Rings* scenes were filmed in the park.

There are more than 570km of tracks to explore. The best known is the **Heaphy Track**, a four- to five-day 'Great Walk' leading from the **Aorere Valley** in **Golden Bay** to **Karamea** on the **West Coast**. Shorter walks are also possible from most road ends.

main attractions

◈ Aorere Goldfields Walk
◈ Heaphy Track
◈ Honeycomb Hill Caves & Arch
◈ Karamea River
◈ Kayaking and rafting
◈ Mount Arthur
◈ Oparara Arch
◈ Tasman Wilderness Area
◈ Wangapeka Track

ℹ Visitor information

Karamea Information & Resource Centre
Bridge St, Karamea
Ph: (03) 782 6652
www.karameainfo.co.nz

DOC Nelson Regional Visitor Centre
79 Trafalgar St, Nelson
Ph: (03) 546 9339
www.doc.govt.nz

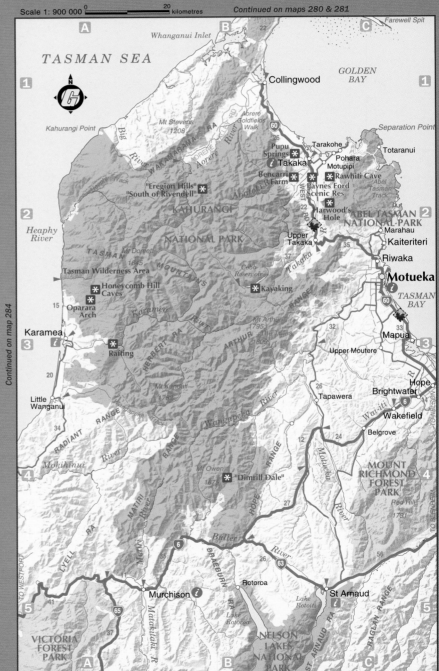

Continued on maps 280 & 281

Continued on map 284

Continued on maps 282 & 286

© TERRALINK INTERNATIONAL LIMITED 2006

Continued on maps 284, 285 & 286

Hiker and nikau palms, Scotts Beach, Heaphy Track

South Island

raising the lake, and the lake waters are channelled past turbines to produce electricity.

MAIN ATTRACTIONS: Lake Manapouri is New Zealand's second deepest lake; it has a bush-clad shoreline and many wooded islands, and offers good boating and trout fishing. Nearby walks include the three-hour **Circle Track** and a short walk along the river to **Frasers Beach**. One section of the **Kepler Track** skirts Lake Manapouri, and part of the track can be done as a day walk from the town.

NEARBY ATTRACTIONS: The **Manapouri Power Station**, on Lake Manapouri's **West Arm**, can be visited via an impressive 2km tunnel bored through solid rock. Spectacular **Doubtful Sound**, about 45km west, can be accessed by boat across the lake, then a bus over **Wilmot Pass**. Named in 1770 by the British explorer Captain James Cook, who sailed past the entrance and noted that it was doubtful the ship would get back out if it entered, the sound has towering peaks, beautiful waterfalls, rich forest and much wildlife. Like **Milford Sound**, it features deep-sea marine life close to the surface, and can be explored by diving, kayaking and cruising.

VISITOR INFORMATION: Lakefront Drive, Te Anau, Ph: (03) 249 8900, www.fiordlandnz.com

■ **Methven**   POP 1135

Map 296, B4

Methven, in central **Canterbury,** is a good base for exploring the **Canterbury Plains** or nearby mountains. One hour's drive west of Christchurch, Methven is transformed over winter with an influx of skiers and snowboarders.

MAIN ATTRACTIONS: Methven is regarded as the best area in New Zealand for hot air ballooning; it also offers good golfing and fishing.

NEARBY ATTRACTIONS: **Mt Hutt Village,** 13km north, is at the heart of

seven ski areas, with over 1000 square kilometres of the best heli-skiing terrain in New Zealand. **Mt Hutt Ski Area**, 25km north-west of Methven, boasts the longest ski season in the country, with five months of skiing from June to October. The area receives some of the deepest, lightest and driest powder in Australasia. Thrill seekers can test their nerve on the **Mt Hutt Bungy**, New Zealand's only on-field bungy. For *The Lord of the Rings* enthusiasts, there are daily tours from Methven to the filming site of '**Edoras**', the fortress city on **Mt Potts** high country station in the breathtaking **Rangitata Valley,** 77km south-west. Visitors can take a walk along the impressive **Rakaia Gorge walkway**, or see it much more quickly on a jet boat. **Mt Hutt Forest**, 14km west, is predominantly mountain beech. Adjoining this are the **Awa Awa Rata Reserve** and the **Pudding Hill Scenic Reserve** with their many scenic walking tracks. Beautiful **Lake Coleridge**, 25km north, has many beautiful walks.

VISITOR INFORMATION: Main St, Ph: (03) 302 8955, www.mthuttvillage.co.nz

■ **Middlemarch**   POP 200

Map 308, E4

The small historic town of Middlemarch, 82km north-west of Dunedin on the **Strath Taieri Plain,** has the impressive backdrop of the **Rock and Pillar Range**.

MAIN ATTRACTIONS: Middlemarch is a start or finish point for the **Otago Central Rail Trail**, the old Central Otago railway line to **Clyde**, now re-developed as a track for walkers, cyclists and horse riders. The **Strath Taieri Historical Museum** features the submarine 'Platypus', built in 1873 for the purpose of dredging gold using pumps and suction gear. The submarine was unsuccessful, and the company that built it was liquidated. Middlemarch is known

Historic stone building, Middlemarch

for its yearly **Singles Dance**, which sees an influx of hundreds of hopefuls looking for love, many of them on the specially-scheduled 'Love Train' from Dunedin.

NEARBY ATTRACTIONS: The historic and spectacular **Taieri Gorge Railway** journey makes a stop at Middlemarch in the summer months. **Sutton Lake**, about 10km south, is New Zealand's only inland salt lake, and has a pleasant walkway; the lake sometimes evaporates in warm weather. The Rock and Pillar Range has magnificent tors along the ridge, and offers hiking and ski touring for experienced hikers.

VISITOR INFORMATION: 48 The Octagon, Dunedin, Ph: (03) 474 3300, www.middlemarch.co.nz

■ **Milford Sound**   POP 95

Map 298, D5

This beautiful fiord, in **Fiordland National Park** 116km north-west of **Te Anau**, is one of New Zealand's most visited tourist attractions, and hosts tens of thousands of visitors every year.

MAIN ATTRACTIONS: Milford Sound is dominated by the steep cliffs and mountains that surround it, particularly majestic 1683m **Mitre Peak**. **Milford Road** from Te Anau to the sound is a stunning 119km alpine road through the World Heritage Area. The road passes some of the area's most striking features, including the **Mirror**

Lakes and waterfalls, and goes through the dark, narrow 1.2km **Homer Tunnel**, but alpine driving conditions can be challenging. Cruises on Milford Sound offer views of **Bowen Falls**, Mitre Peak, **Anita Bay** and **Stirling Falls**; wildlife includes seals, dolphins and the rare yellow-eyed penguin. Some operators offer overnight cruises. Sea kayaking and diving are also possibilities, with the phenomenon of deep water emergence creating an environment similar to the ocean depths at unusually shallow levels. One area of the sound has been designated as the **Piopiotahi Marine Reserve**; the **Milford Deep underwater observatory** allows visitors to view a completely natural marine community, including rare red and black coral, butterfly perch, anemones and sponges, scarlet wrasse and snake stars. Scenic flights are also available over the sound. The 54km **Milford Track** is reputed to be the finest walk in the world; it can be walked independently or with a guide. The number of walkers each year is limited.
VISITOR INFORMATION: Lakefront Drive, Te Anau, Ph: (03) 249 8900, www.fiordlandnz.com

■ Moeraki   POP 80
Map 309, J3
The small fishing village of Moeraki, 78km north of Dunedin on the scenic **Otago** coast, has a long history of Maori occupation; in its early days of European settlement, it was a whaling station.
MAIN ATTRACTIONS: The **Moeraki Boulders/Kaihinaki** are ancient spherical boulders up to four metres in circumference, which lie scattered along Moeraki's beach. More boulders continue to emerge from the cliffs, some of them splitting open. According to scientists, they were formed around 65 million years ago by a process

similar to an oyster forming a pearl; in Maori lore they are seen as food baskets washed out of the great voyaging canoe Arai-te-uru when it was wrecked on landing in New Zealand centuries ago. A walk through native bush leads to a viewing platform overlooking the boulders, and visitors can walk on the beach among them. The **Kotahitanga Church**, built in 1862, features stained glass windows made in Rome which depict the elderly local chief Matiaha Tiramorehu along with Christ and a Madonna and Child.
NEARBY ATTRACTIONS: **Katiki Beach**, 6km south, offers good swimming. **Shag Point**, 13km south, has a colony of rare yellow-eyed penguins, a seal colony and a lighthouse built in 1877.
VISITOR INFORMATION: 1 Thames St, Oamaru, Ph: (03) 434 1656, www.tourismwaitaki.co.nz

■ Motueka   POP 6890
Map 281, F5
The sunny coastal town of Motueka is located on **Tasman Bay** 47km north-west of Nelson, in the heart of the Tasman fruit-growing area.

MAIN ATTRACTIONS: Motueka has interesting galleries, good cafés and a Sunday market selling craftworks. **Motueka District Museum** offers displays about the area's colonial past, and there are historic salt water swimming baths on the waterfront. The **Motueka Walkway** leads around the town's waterfront and attractions. Craft and wine trail maps are available from the visitor centre.
NEARBY ATTRACTIONS: The surrounding countryside produces apples, berries, hops and olives; there's plenty of fresh fruit for sale directly from the producers. To the south, the **Moutere** hills, once a tobacco-growing area, are home to many wineries. The historic village of **Upper Moutere**, 18km south, started life as a German settlement called Sarau; its old Lutheran church is worth visiting. A 20-minute walk through native bush at the base of **Takaka Hill** leads to the **Riwaka Resurgence**. This source of the **Riwaka River**, where the river forms deep clear pools in an underground cavern, is sacred to Maori. The picturesque **Motueka Valley** has excellent trout fishing in

Milford Sound

South Island

the **Motueka River**, and also offers access to ecologically important **Kahurangi National Park**. The Riwaka River has good fishing, and there is white water rafting on the **Buller**, **Motueka** and **Gowan Rivers**. Motueka is also a base for visits to gorgeous **Abel Tasman National Park**, about 20km north.

VISITOR INFORMATION: Wallace St, Ph: (03) 528 6543, www.abeltasmangreenrush.co.nz

Mt Somers   POP 155
Map 296, A4

Located 40km north-west of Ashburton, about an hour and a half's drive south-west of Christchurch, the small settlement of Mt Somers is the gateway to the beautiful **Rangitata Valley**, one of **Canterbury**'s top ecotourism locations.

MAIN ATTRACTIONS: The 17km **Mt Somers Track** offers a contrasting spectrum of nature, including expanses of wild grasses, towering mountains, a deep river canyon and vast open plains. The walk passes old coal mines and impressive volcanic formations; there are two huts. Trampers should be aware the weather can change dramatically in this area. There are day tracks from the popular picnic spots of **Woolshed Creek** and **Sharplin Falls** at **Staveley**. The many outdoor activities include fishing, rafting, 4WD tours, horse treks, mountain biking, helicopter flights and ice skating. The area is rich in minerals, including coal, limestone and silica sand; these resources were the inspiration for the town's biennial **Minerals to Art Festival**.

NEARBY ATTRACTIONS: **Mount Hutt Ski Area**, 28km north, is considered to have the longest ski season in Australasia, but even off-season visitors to the mountain can do many beautiful walks. **Lake Clearwater**, just one of

many nearby lakes, is excellent for windsurfing. **Mt Potts Station** was the location for '**Edoras**' in *The Lord of the Rings*.

VISITOR INFORMATION: Main St, Methven, Ph: (03) 302 8955, www.ashburtontourism.co.nz

Murchison   POP 555
Map 285, F3

Murchison, on SH6 125km south-west of Nelson, was once a gold mining town. Almost completely destroyed by an earthquake in 1929, today it's a service centre for the surrounding area. Situated beside the **Buller River**, Murchison is a centre for outdoor activities, and is the southern gateway to **Kahurangi National Park**.

MAIN ATTRACTIONS: **Murchison District Museum** features artefacts from the town's history, including from the 1929 earthquake. Adventure activities in the area include kayaking, boating, fishing, rafting and mountain biking. Great trout fishing is also available on the local rivers.

NEARBY ATTRACTIONS: State Highway Six, leading west to the **West Coast**, is very scenic, and passes through the dramatic **Buller Gorge**. The 110m **Buller Gorge Swingbridge**, 14km from Murchison, is New Zealand's longest swingbridge, and leads to some interesting walks, including to the epicentre of the Murchison earthquake. Adrenalin aficionados may want to ride on the flying fox across the gorge, or go jet boating on the river. Gold panning is available on the Buller River, and at **Lyell Creek** and **Howard Valley**. The 1.5-hour **Lyell Walkway**, about 25km west, explores beech forest and some historic sites. **Maruia Falls**, 22km south-west, were created by the earthquake. **Nelson Lakes National Park**, about 50km east, has pristine beech forest and beautiful lakes. North-east of

Curling, Naseby

Murchison in Kahurangi National Park, 1875m **Mount Owen** was a filming location for *The Lord of the Rings*, for which it became '**Dimrill Dale**'. There are many walking tracks in this ecologically important park, including the track up **Matiri Valley** to **Lake Matiri**.

VISITOR INFORMATION: Waller St, Ph: (03) 523 9350, www.murchisonnz.com

Naseby   POP 100
Map 308, E1

The small settlement of Naseby, in the **Maniototo** 14km north of Ranfurly, was once a thriving gold rush town with over 20 hotels. It was the area's commercial and local government centre until Ranfurly took over these functions.

MAIN ATTRACTIONS: Naseby today is popular with visitors for its lovely heritage architecture, historic mud-brick buildings and outdoor activities. In winter it's a centre for ice skating, curling and ice hockey. The hills around the town, scarred by mining, are now softened by wilding trees, and offer good walking and mountain biking.

NEARBY ATTRACTIONS: **Kyeburn Diggings**, 15km north-east, and **Danseys Pass**, 25km north-east,

(CONTINUED P.259)

ABEL TASMAN NATIONAL PARK

Beautiful 22 530ha Abel Tasman National Park, New Zealand's smallest national park, has golden beaches, turquoise water, interesting rocky outcrops, plentiful wildlife and native forests.

The 51km **Abel Tasman Coastal Track**, classed as one of New Zealand's 'Great Walks', is a three- to five-day walk through native bush overlooking lovely golden-sand beaches; it can be done independently or as a guided walk. Sea kayaking is a popular way of exploring the coastline; many visitors choose to combine walking, kayaking and boat transport. The **Inland Track** is a more difficult walk through the park's hilly centre.

The **Tonga Island Marine Reserve** has a seal colony and is often visited by dolphins. Shags and little blue penguins also inhabit the coast, and there are tuis and bellbirds in the forest. The small township of **Marahau** is the main gateway to the park, and is a base for booking boats and kayaks.

attractions

◈ Abel Tasman Coastal Track
◈ Abel Tasman Inland Track
◈ Awaroa Lodge
◈ Cleopatra's Pool
◈ Falls River
◈ Separation Point
◈ Te Pukatea Bay
◈ Tonga Island Marine Reserve
◈ Totaranui

ℹ Visitor information

DOC Nelson Regional Visitor Centre
79 Trafalgar St, Nelson
Ph: (03) 546 9339

Kayaking in Abel Tasman National Park

South Island

are old gold mining areas; the historic **Danseys Pass Coach Inn**, 15km from Naseby, is still open for business. The inn was built in 1863, by a stonemason known as Happy Bill whose cheer was due to being paid in beer for his work — apparently a pint for each boulder he shaped and added to the walls. High in the **Rough Ridge Range** in the **Ida Valley**, 45km south-west, the remote **Poolburn Reservoir** area was used as a filming site for *The Lord of the Rings* trilogy, and featured in the films as the **'Plains of Rohan'**.

VISITOR INFORMATION: Charlemont St East, Ranfurly, Ph: (03) 444 1005, www.maniototo.co.nz

■ Nelson   POP 53 700

Map 321, C3

The main city in the Nelson region, Nelson is located on **Tasman Bay**, 134km west of Picton. New Zealand's second oldest city, settled in 1841, Nelson is known for its beaches and fruit-growing, and is home to many artists and craftspeople, breweries and wineries.

MAIN ATTRACTIONS: The art deco **Christ Church Cathedral** is the city's traditional symbol, and the stretch of restored 1860s workers' cottages in **South Street** is said to be the oldest preserved street in New Zealand. The exact geographical centre of New Zealand is in Nelson's **Botanic Gardens**; there are also lovely walks at **Isel Park gardens** and **Gardens of the World**. Tours are available through **Mac's Brewery** and **Founders Brewery**. Creatively designed wearable artworks are on display along with classic cars at the **World of WearableArt & Collectable Cars Museum; The Suter Te Aratoi o Whakatu** is the regional art gallery. Nelson is home to many talented artists, with studios and galleries open to visitors; every Saturday

the **Nelson Market** has fresh produce and arts and crafts for sale. **Tahunanui Beach** is a golden beach with excellent swimming, and other outdoor activities include paragliding, skydiving, rock climbing, sailing and horse treks. The 12km **Boulder Bank** is the world's longest natural breakwater, and features a historic lighthouse.

NEARBY ATTRACTIONS: In **Richmond**, 14km south-west, glass blowers demonstrate their art at **Höglund Art Glass**. **Rabbit Island**, 15km from Richmond and accessible by bridge, has an unspoilt beach backed by plantation forest. Visitors are welcome at the wineries on the **Waimea Plains**, 18km south-west, and around **Upper Moutere**, about 35km west. **Mapua**, 31km west of Nelson, is a seaside settlement with a historic wharf, cafés, galleries and a smokehouse producing smoked seafood. To the south, forested **Mount Richmond Forest Park** stretches 100km along an alpine fault line; it's popular for walking, fishing, hunting and mountain biking.

VISITOR INFORMATION: 77 Trafalgar St, Ph: (03) 548 2304, www.nelsonnz.com

■ Oamaru   POP 12 700

Map 322, D4

The interesting coastal town of Oamaru, 115km north of Dunedin in the **Waitaki** district, has a long history as an important port. Oamaru's first European dwelling was built from clay and cabbage tree leaves in 1853, and within 25 years, the town was New Zealand's ninth largest. An early trade in shipping frozen meat to the United Kingdom made Oamaru prosperous; today it draws visitors with its intriguing mix of elegant buildings, artists and penguins.

MAIN ATTRACTIONS: Oamaru's harbour area was developed first, and many imposing buildings in what is now the **Historic Precinct** were

Canola field, Oamaru

built from local cream-coloured limestone. The stone was soft enough to carve easily and lent itself to a range of building styles, from classical to Italianate to Venetian renaissance. The town is still dotted with elegant commercial buildings, some of them now home to cafés, shops and galleries. A vintage train runs from the harbour to the Historic Precinct on Sundays. **Whitestone Cheese Factory** produces organic cheeses; the **North Otago Museum** features the area's history, and the **Forrester Gallery** has regionally significant artworks. Oamaru is also notable for its penguin colonies. Blue penguins nest around the harbour, and can be seen just after dark each evening; there is a visitors' centre and viewing grandstand. Yellow-eyed penguins are now among the world's rarest, due to the loss of their coastal breeding grounds. A hide at **Bushy Beach** allows visitors to view these beautiful, shy birds, which come ashore several hours before sunset. Internationally renowned New Zealand writer Janet Frame (1924–2004) spent her school years in Oamaru, and a **Janet Frame Trail** leads visitors around sites from her books.

(CONTINUED P.261)

Nelson/Marlborough Wineries

Highfield Estate Vineyard, Renwick

Nelson and **Marlborough** are home to many boutique wineries in picturesque areas, and visitors can explore independently, or on organised tours.

Marlborough is known for its iconic sauvignon blanc, which took the international wine scene by storm in the early 1980s. More than 45% of New Zealand's vineyards are in Marlborough, and the area now also produces excellent chardonnay, pinot noir, riesling and sparkling wines. Vineyards are clustered west of **Blenheim** in the one-time farming area of the **Wairau Valley**, beautifully framed by mountains, and easily explored by cycling; the **Awatere Valley** is also a burgeoning wine area. The **Wine Marlborough Festival** is a popular annual event.

The Nelson region first had a brief foray into winemaking in the mid-19th century, but the latest crop of winemakers got started in the 1970s, taking advantage of the area's high sunshine hours. Located largely on the **Waimea Plains** and **Upper Moutere**, Nelson's wineries produce pinot noir, chardonnay, sauvignon blanc and riesling.

i Visitor information

Blenheim i-SITE Visitor Centre
Railway Station, Sinclair St, SH1, Blenheim
Ph: (03) 577 8080
www.destinationmarlborough.com

Nelson i-SITE Visitor Centre
Cnr Trafalgar and Halifax Sts, Nelson
Ph: (03) 548 2304
www.nelsonnz.com

Scale 1: 150 000

Continued on map 281

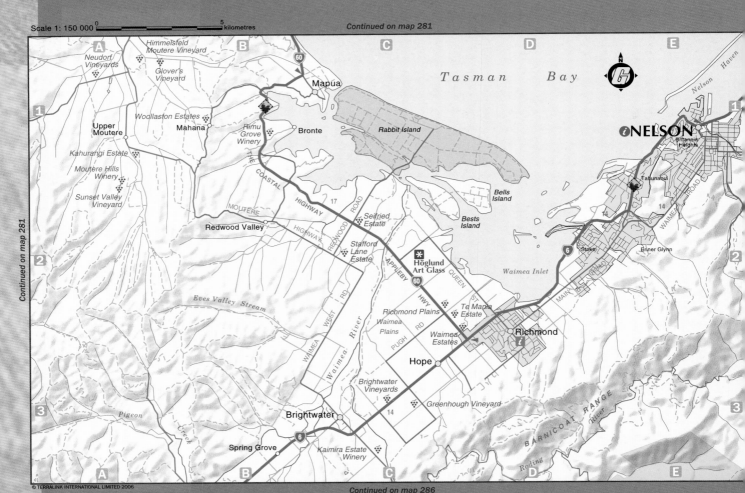

Continued on map 281

Continued on map 286

© TERRALINK INTERNATIONAL LIMITED 2006

South Island

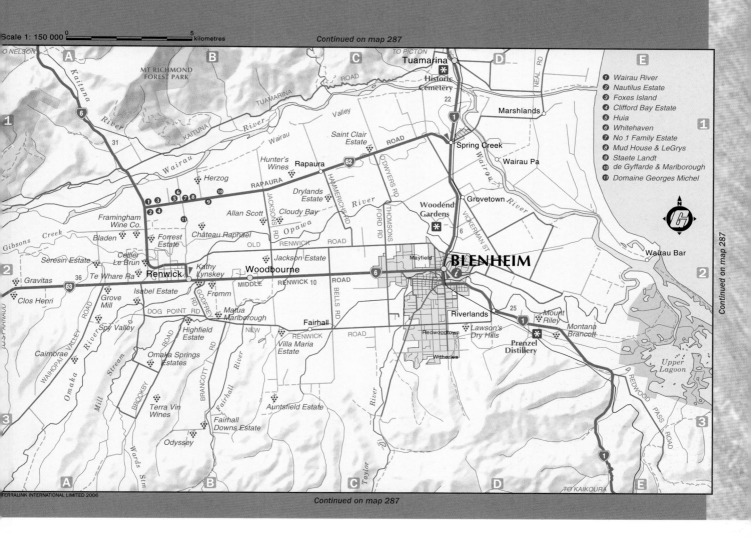

Continued on map 287

Scale 1: 150 000

Continued on map 287

① Wairau River
② Nautilus Estate
③ Foxes Island
④ Clifford Bay Estate
⑤ Huia
⑥ Whitehaven
⑦ No.1 Family Estate
⑧ Mud House & LeGrys
⑨ Staete Landt
⑩ de Gyffarde & Marlborough
⑪ Domaine Georges Michel

Continued on map 287

TERRALINK INTERNATIONAL LIMITED 2006

NEARBY ATTRACTIONS: **Totara Estate**, 8km south, was the site for the first shipment of frozen meat to the UK in 1882, thus establishing a vital trade which was to sustain New Zealand for the next century. There are park-like grounds, restored buildings and displays about the meat industry. At **Maheno**, about 12km south of Oamaru, **Clark's Mill** is a four-storeyed limestone flour mill, built in 1866.

VISITOR INFORMATION: 1 Thames St, Ph: (03) 434 1656, www.tourismwaitaki.co.nz

■ **Okarito**   POP 27
Map 293, J1

The tiny, isolated settlement of Okarito, on the southern **West Coast**, is a base for nature tours, walks and outdoor activities. The only New Zealand novel to win the Booker Prize, *the bone people* by Maori author Keri Hulme, is largely set in the area around Okarito.

MAIN ATTRACTIONS: **Okarito Lagoon** is New Zealand's largest unmodified wetland; a beautiful, peaceful place, it's a feeding ground for many birds, including the famed kotuku (white heron), and is a lovely spot for kayaking. There are many walks, including to a lookout with wonderful sea views at **Okarito Trig**, and a longer walk to **Three Mile Lagoon**.

NEARBY ATTRACTIONS: **Whataroa**, 20km east, is a base for tours to the kotuku breeding colony in the **Waitangi Roto Nature Reserve**; the reserve also has beautiful rainforest.

VISITOR INFORMATION: 7 Tancred St, Hokitika, Ph: (03) 755 6166, www.west-coast.co.nz

■ **Omakau**   POP 225
Map 307, J2

The small town of Omakau is located 27km north-east of Alexandra, in the old gold mining country of **Central Otago**.

MAIN ATTRACTIONS: Omakau is a stopping point for travellers on the **Otago Central Rail Trail**, a unique 150km trail for walkers, cyclists and horse riders on the redeveloped historic railway line from **Middlemarch** to **Clyde**.

NEARBY ATTRACTIONS: Once a bustling gold-rush centre, the quiet town of **Ophir**, 2km south, has a lovely collection of historic stone buildings, including the restored 1886 **Post and Telegraph Office**, which is still in operation. A historic swing bridge spans the nearby **Manuherikia River**.

CATLINS

This beautiful, isolated region has waterfalls, forests, remote beaches, rugged coastline, tranquil estuaries, historic relics and a plethora of wildlife. Maori have a long association with the area; later came European whalers, timber millers and farmers. The settlement of **Owaka** is a base for touring the area.

Nugget Point has cliffs, sea views and an 1869 lighthouse; wildlife includes rare Hector's dolphins, shags, three penguin species, a gannet colony, fur seals, sea lions and elephant seals.

Purakaunui Falls is a spectacular three-tiered waterfall; the five-hour **Catlins River Walk** leads through beech forest with many native birds. The 55m-deep **Jack's Blowhole** is connected to the sea, 200m away, by an underground cavern; it's dramatic in stormy weather. **Cathedral Caves** have a soaring 30m ceiling; at **Curio Bay**, a 160-million-year-old petrified forest is visible at low tide. **Slope Point** is the South Island's southernmost point.

Purakaunui Falls, Catlins

main attractions

- Cannibal Bay
- Cathedral Caves
- Catlins River Walk
- Curio Bay
- Jack's Blowhole
- Nugget Point
- Papatowai Beach
- Purakaunui Falls
- Slope Point
- Tautuku Bay

(i) Visitor information

Catlins Visitor Centre
20 Riley St, Owaka
Ph: (03) 415 8371
www.catlins-nz.com
www.catlins.org.nz

The Clay Cliffs, Omarama

Remote **Poolburn Reservoir**, 22km south-east, was a filming location for *The Lord of the Rings*, and featured as the **'Plains of Rohan'**.
VISITOR INFORMATION: Centennial Ave, Alexandra, Ph: (03) 448 9515, www.centralotagonz.com

■ **Omarama**   POP 280
Map 301, H3
This small town is located in majestic high country at the head of the **Waitaki Valley**, 119km north-west of Oamaru, at the junction of SH83 and SH8. Omarama is in a scenic area of many man-made lakes associated with the production of hydro-electric power.
MAIN ATTRACTIONS: The **Clay Cliffs Estate Winery** produces pinot gris, pinot noir, riesling and chardonnay; it offers tastings, and has a restaurant. The **Ahuriri River** offers great trout fishing and rich bird life; Omarama is also popular for gliding, due to the area's excellent north-west thermals which rise up to 15000m.
NEARBY ATTRACTIONS: The **Clay Cliffs** are a spectacular eroded landform on farmland 10km west. Man-made **Lake Benmore**, five minutes' drive south-east, is popular for boating, picnicking and camping. **Ohau Snow Fields** has 125ha of skiable area and beautiful views over **Lake Ohau**.
VISITOR INFORMATION: 6 Chain Hills Hwy, Ph: (03) 438 9816, www.tourismwaitaki.co.nz

■ **Otematata**   POP 250
Map 302, C4
This small township in the **Waitaki Valley**, 96km north-west of Oamaru, was established in 1958 as a construction village for the **Aviemore** and **Benmore** hydro-electric developments; today, it's around half the size it was when the dams were being constructed. Merino sheep are farmed on the

South Island

Continued on maps 312 & 313

Scale 1: 300 000

PACIFIC OCEAN

Continued on maps 312 & 313

surrounding high country stations.

MAIN ATTRACTIONS: Walking, boating, fishing and cycling are all popular around the town. There are many tracks through a **Wildlife Reserve**, and a lakeside walk.

NEARBY ATTRACTIONS: Guided tours are available at hydro-electric **Benmore Power Station**, 12km north, which features New Zealand's largest earth dam and largest man-made lake. The route across the dam and along **Lake Aviemore**'s northern shore is scenic; both Lake Aviemore and **Lake Benmore** are popular spots for watersports, and lookouts overlook the lakes. The early **Takiroa Maori rock drawings**, near historic **Duntroon**, 52km south-east, are drawn in charcoal and red ochre under a limestone bluff. Duntroon is also home to the **Vanished World**

Centre, which has exhibits on the area's fossil heritage; the **Vanished World Trail** leads around fascinating fossil and geological sites.

VISITOR INFORMATION: 6 Chain Hills Hwy, Omarama, Ph: (03) 438 9816, www.tourismwaitaki.co.nz

■ Owaka   POP 365

Map 313, H5

Picturesque Owaka, 115km south of Dunedin, is the service centre for the beautiful, remote **Catlins** area, and is a good base for visitors exploring the region.

NEARBY ATTRACTIONS: Historic pioneer houses can be seen in the **Owaka Valley**, to the west. Wildlife at **Nugget Point**, a 30-minute drive east, includes gannets, fur seals, elephant seals and the rare yellow-eyed penguin. Many wading

birds can be seen at the tidal **Catlins Lake**. Hooker's sea lions breed at **Cannibal Bay**, and **Surat Bay** was the site of a shipwreck in 1874. **Kaka Point**, 16km north-east, is a picturesque coastal village with swimming beaches, and is popular with holidaymakers. **Jack's Blowhole**, a 55m deep sinkhole

Lake Benmore, near Otematata

200m from the sea, is named after the Ngai Tahu Maori chief Hone (Jack) Tuhawaiki. The blowhole is best viewed at high tide when waves come rushing in through an underground cavern. The small settlement of **Papatowai**, 26km south-west, is the area's other service town.

VISITOR INFORMATION: 20 Ryley St, Ph: (03) 415 8371, www.catlins-nz.com, www.catlins.org.nz

Oxford   POP 1580
Map 296, E1

Oxford is a small rural town at the northern edge of the vast **Canterbury Plains**, 55km north-west of Christchurch in the **Waimakariri** district. Nestled in the foothills of the **Southern Alps**, Oxford is the centre of a prosperous farming community, and has many scenic areas and bush walks.

MAIN ATTRACTIONS: **The Colour Purple Lavender Farm** has approximately 900 lavender plants, creating a fragrant swathe of purple with the Southern Alps as a backdrop. Tours and visits to the lavender farm can be arranged. On the first Sunday of each month a **Craft Market** is held in the **Oxford Town Hall** with a selection of crafts made by local artists and craftspeople. A **Historical Walk** leads around town; the **Oxford Museum** has exhibits and information about the local area.

NEARBY ATTRACTIONS: **Ashley Gorge**, 8km north of Oxford, is a

Picton Harbour

popular picnic spot with good swimming, fishing and camping. The **Ashley River** is a prime spawning habitat for whitebait. To the south, the **Waimakariri River** offers excellent salmon and trout fishing; the **Waimakariri Gorge** has spectacular scenery.

VISITOR INFORMATION: **Old Chief Post Office, Cathedral Sq West, Christchurch,** Ph: (03) 379 9629, www.waimakariri.co.nz

Palmerston   POP 805
Map 309, H4

The small town of Palmerston, 56km north of Dunedin near the **Otago** coast, has a long history of gold mining, and has been revitalised by the reopened gold mine at **Macraes Flat**.

MAIN ATTRACTIONS: Visitors can walk among butterflies at the **Palmerston Butterfly and Bird Haven**. **Puketapu** — literally, the sacred hill — is the town's landmark, and features a monument to the early politician John McKenzie. Palmerston is a starting point for the **Otago Goldfields Heritage Trail**, which leads around historic gold mining sites.

NEARBY ATTRACTIONS: At **Tavora Reserve**, 7km south-east, the coastal habitat for rare yellow-eyed penguins is being restored. Seals, penguins, shags and occasionally whales can be seen at **Shag Point**; there's also an 1877 lighthouse. Some 35km inland, near the small town of Macraes Flat, is the **Golden Point Historic Reserve**. The Golden Point mine was opened in 1889 and closed in 1930; its small battery, in the original building, is still in working order, and the miners' sod cottages can also be seen in the reserve. A mine reopened at Macraes Flat in 1988, and is now New Zealand's largest working gold mine; guided tours are available.

VISITOR INFORMATION: 117 Ronaldsay St, Ph: (03) 465 1950, www.tourismwaitaki.co.nz

Picton   POP 3990
Map 323, B5

This port town in the **Marlborough Sounds** at the head of **Queen Charlotte Sound** sees many visitors arrive on the inter-island ferry from Wellington. Originally known as Waitohi, and the site of a Maori pa of the Te Ati Awa tribe, Picton was first settled by Europeans in the 1840s, and many colonial buildings remain on the waterfront.

MAIN ATTRACTIONS: **Picton Museum** explores the town's history as a whaling port and Maori trading settlement; **Seahorse World Aquarium** features interesting marine life. The *Edwin Fox,* berthed on Picton's waterfront, was the last surviving ship to carry convicts to Australia. **Karaka Point**, 8km east, has the remains of an early Maori pa, whose inhabitants were the victims of attacks by other tribes. Walks in Picton include the 1km walk to **Bob's Bay**, and the **Tirohanga Walkway**, which has wonderful views of the Sounds. 'Myths and legends' cruises of the Sounds are offered by a local Maori family.

NEARBY ATTRACTIONS: **Long Island–Kokomohua Marine Reserve**, about 30km north-east, has rich marine life and offers wonderful diving, as does the wreck of the *Mikhail Lermontov.* **Motuara Island**, now a bird sanctuary with rare saddlebacks and South Island robins, is where Captain James Cook proclaimed British sovereignty over the South Island, and can be visited by boat. The **Queen Charlotte Track** is a popular three- to four-day walk between **Anakiwa**, 22km west of Picton, and Cook's 18th-century base **Ship Cove**. The track leads through lush coastal forest and beautiful coves; at Ship Cove is a monument to the great explorer. **Tuamarina**, 19km south of Picton, is the site of the infamous 1843

Skiers on Coronet Peak, Queenstown

Wairau Massacre, the South Island's only incident of armed conflict between Maori and European settlers; a memorial in the cemetery commemorates the massacre.
VISITOR INFORMATION: The Foreshore, Ph: (03) 520 3113, www.destinationmarlborough.com

■ Punakaiki   POP 110
Map 284, A5
The small settlement of Punakaiki, 56km south of Westport on the **West Coast**, is a gateway to **Paparoa National Park**.
MAIN ATTRACTIONS: Punakaiki is most famous for its **Pancake Rocks and Blowholes**. These intriguing layered limestone formations spout water in a dramatic geyser-like display when sea and weather conditions are right. A 15-minute walk leads around the rocks and blowholes.
NEARBY ATTRACTIONS: **Paparoa National Park**, to the east, features lush forests, limestone cliffs, caves and beautiful coastline in its 30 000ha. Walks include the **Truman Track**, which leads through forest to clifftops, the 27km **Inland Pack Track**, and the **Pororari River Track**, which follows a dramatic limestone gorge. South of the **Punakaiki River** is the world's only known breeding colony for the Westland petrel/titi; the park is also home to the nocturnal and secretive great spotted kiwi,

more often heard than seen. The **Punakaiki Cavern** and **Fox River Tourist Cave** provide easy caving for beginners. **Barrytown**, 16km south, has a historic hotel. The **Coast Road** offers spectacular sea views over the wild coastline. Isolated today, this old gold mining area was once home to bustling towns; tiny **Charleston**, 31km north, had 40 000 residents and 80 hotels at one time. **Mitchell's Gully Gold Mine**, 7km further north, is a historic gold mining site with a working stamper battery.
VISITOR INFORMATION: 1 Brougham St, Westport, Ph: (03) 789 6658, www.westport.org.nz

■ Queenstown   POP 8540
Map 324, D3
This important holiday destination is gorgeously positioned on the shores of **Lake Wakatipu**, surrounded by the fine mountain scenery of the **Remarkables** and **Eyre Mountains**. Queenstown started life in the 1860s, first as a sheep drovers' settlement known as 'The Camp', and then a rough gold mining town. The town today is a far cry from its humble origins, and offers magnificent scenery, adventure opportunities and a luxurious lifestyle.
MAIN ATTRACTIONS: The gondola up **Bob's Peak** gives visitors impressive views over the town and beyond, as does the easy climb up **Queenstown Hill** and the more difficult ascent of **Ben Lomond**. A huge array of adventure activities is on offer, and visitors can skydive, paraglide, bungy jump, canyon swing, or hurtle along the **Shotover** or **Kawarau Rivers** in a jet boat. Other river-based activities are river surfing and white water sledging. Canyoning trips include waterslides, rock jumps and abseiling. For the less adventure-inclined, there are fine dining and boutique shopping, walks along the waterfront,

lake cruises on the century-old steamer *TSS Earnslaw*, scenic flights and hot-air balloon trips. The **Kiwi and Birdlife Park** has two kiwi houses and a nursery raising endangered birds.
NEARBY ATTRACTIONS: Skiing in the area is excellent, including at **Coronet Peak**, the Remarkables, **Cardrona**, **Waiorau Snow Farm** and **Treble Cone**. At **Kingston**, 45km south, the heritage steam train **Kingston Flyer** offers rides. **Arrowtown**, 20km north-east, is a historic gold mining town with pretty wooden buildings and a restored Chinese miners' settlement. The striking **Gibbston Valley**, about 20km east, is Queenstown's main wine-producing area, and has wineries in beautiful settings, including **Gibbston Valley Wines**, New Zealand's most visited winery, and the amazingly sited **Chard Farm**, a vertiginous drive up a narrow cliffside road. Nearby, thrill-seekers can bungy jump from a historic 1880 suspension bridge over the Kawarau River. The old gold mining area of **Skippers Canyon**, about 12km north, offers adventure activities; there are spectacular views from **Skippers Road**, hand-carved out of solid rock. To the north, there are historic sites in the scenic **Cardrona Valley**; the road over the **Crown Range** between Queenstown and **Wanaka** is New Zealand's highest main road at 1121m, and the views are extraordinary.
VISITOR INFORMATION: Clocktower Bldg, Ph: (03) 442 4100, 0800 668 888, www.queenstown-vacation.com

■ Ranfurly   POP 730
Map 308, E2
The main town on the beautiful **Maniototo Plain**, Ranfurly developed rapidly in the 1930s, and was also subject to arson attacks which destroyed some buildings; as a result it features an impressive array of art deco buildings, and has

The beautiful Marlborough Sounds are a collection of drowned river valleys, formed after the ice ages. In Maori legend, the sounds were created during a battle between the famed early explorer Kupe and a giant octopus.

The three sounds — **Queen Charlotte**, **Kenepuru** and **Pelorus Sounds** — are bordered by forested hills which rise almost vertically from the water's edge, and there are many lovely bays, coves and islands. Marine and bird life, including dolphins, seals and penguins, is plentiful in the area. Visitors can explore by kayak, yacht or on a cruise.

There are lovely walks, including the three- to four-day **Queen Charlotte Track**; the area around remote **Te Aumiti (French Pass)** is particularly rich in wildlife. **Picton** and **Havelock** are bases for exploring the area. Getting around is often easiest by boat, with some places accessible only by water.

Swimmers at Pelorus River, Marlborough

main attractions

◆ Long Island–Kokomohua Marine Reserve
◆ Motuara Island
◆ Nydia Track
◆ Kenepuru Sound
◆ Pelorus Sound
◆ Queen Charlotte Sound (Totaranui)
◆ Queen Charlotte Track
◆ Rangitoto ke te tonga (D'Urville Island)
◆ Ship Cove (Meretoto)
◆ Te Aumiti (French Pass)

ⓘ Visitor information

Picton i-SITE Visitor Centre
The Foreshore, Picton
Ph: (03) 520 3113
www.destinationmarlborough.com

---

recently reinvented itself as a rural art deco capital.

MAIN ATTRACTIONS: The refurbished **Centennial Milk Bar** exhibits art deco pieces, and every February the town hosts the **Ranfurly Rural Art Deco Weekend**. The erstwhile train station is now a **Visitors' Centre** with displays about the town

and the railway. The old railway line has been redeveloped as the **Otago Central Rail Trail**, a 150km track for walkers, mountain bikers and horse riders through remote, beautiful areas of central Otago.

NEARBY ATTRACTIONS: The well-preserved historic **Hayes Engineering Works**, built from mud-brick and corrugated iron, can be seen south of **Oturehua**, about 25km north-west; the internationally famous Hayes Wire Strainer was invented here. The nearby **Idaburn Dam** is the site for the popular mid-winter **Brass Monkey Motorcycle Rally**. The **Taieri River**, to the south, has some of New Zealand's best trout fishing. Close to the small township of **Patearoa**, 18km south, the remains of a small

Chinese miners' settlement can be reached from the **Sowburn Walkway**. At **Paerau**, 4km further south, is the historic **Styx Jail**, a lock-up where gold bullion was protected during overnight stops; the rings to which the gold chest was padlocked can still be seen.

VISITOR INFORMATION: Charlemont St East, Ph: (03) 444 1005, www.maniototo.co.nz

■ Reefton   POP 985

Map 284, D5

The **West Coast**'s only inland town of any size, Reefton is in the **Inangahua River Valley** 78km north-east of Greymouth. The town developed during the West Coast's 1860s gold rush; in August 1888 it was the first settlement in the southern hemisphere to have a public supply of electricity — at a

(CONTINUED P.268)

Hayes Engineering Works stables, Oturehua

South Island

Scale 1 : 300 000

0 10
ilometres

A B C D E

COOK STRAIT

Cape Koamaru
Arapawa Island
Arapawa Island Scenic Reserve
Perano Head
Ferries to Wellington
East Head
West Head
Raukawa Rock
Lucky Point
Bushy Point
Glasgow Bay
Rununder Point
Fighting Bay (Oraumoa)
Karaka Bay
Robertson Point
Port Underwood
RD

Cape Jackson
Walhi Point
Kempe Point
Anakakata Bay
Cannibal Cove Scenic Res
Cannibal Cove
Motuara Island
LONG ISLAND-KOKOMOHUA MARINE RESERVE
Long Island
Clark Pt
Pickersgill I
Wharehunga Bay Rec Res
Katbal Pt Scenic Res

Cape Lambert
Port Gore
Pig Bay
Waitui Bay
Mikhail Lermontov wreck
Melville Cove
Scenic Res
Captain Cook's Monument
Ship Cove (Meretoto)
Ship Cove Historic Res
Resolution Bay
Scott Pt
Blumine Island (Oruawairua)
Liap Bay Scenic Res
Bay of Many Coves
Ngaruru Scenic Res
Perano Pass
Tory Channel (Kura Te Au)

Alligator Head
Guards Bay
Tahuahua Scenic Res
Grants Lookout Scenic Res
Endeavour Inlet
Endeavour Inlet
Big Bay Scenic Res
Pukekoikoi
Kenepuru Head
Karaka Pt
Curious Cove
Ruaomoko Pt Scenic Res

Sentinel Rock
Chetwode Islands
Te Kakaho Island
The Haystack (Moturaka)
Nukuwaiata Island
Ninepin Rock
Culdaff Point
Lord Ashley Bay
Orchard Bay
Annie Bay
Forsyth Island (Te Paruparu)
Titi Island
Titirangi Bay
Anakoha Bay
Mt Stokes 1203
Mount Stokes Scenic Reserve
Mt McMahon 1067
Waitaria Bay
Portage
Torea Bay
Wedge Pt
Waikawa
Picton
Mt Pleasant
Koromiko
22

Clay Point
Te Akaroa (West Entry Pt)
Kaitira (East Entry Pt)
Bird I
Forsyth Allen Bay
Beatrix Bay
Waimaru Rec & Scenic Res
Clova Bay
Manaroa
Crail Bay
Crail Bay
Nopera
Te Mahia
Double Bay
Kenepuru Sound
Allports Island
Grove Arm
Mt McCormick 953
Mt Robertson 1036
Robertson Range Scenic Reserve

D'Urville Peninsula
Stewart Island (Te kuru kuru)
Anatakupu Island
French Pass (Anaru)
Port Ligar
Ketu Bay
Reef Pt (Kaiaua)
Richmond Bay
Kenny Isle Scenic Res
Maud Island (Te Hoiere)
Tawero Pt
Opani-aputa Point
Pelorus Sound
North West Bay
Nydia Bay
Kaiuma Bay
Mahakipawa Arm
Mt Cullen 1055
Whenuora Scenic Res
Anakiwa
Linkwater
The Grove
35
Cullen Ck
QUEEN CHARLOTTE

Rangitoto ke te tonga (D'Urville Island)
Tasman Bay
Catherine Cove
Attempt Hill 729
Te Aumiti (French Pass)
Current Basin
Hamilton Bay
McShewe's E Deep Bay
Waitata Bay
Channel
Waitata Reach
Okuri Point
Okuri Bay
Fitzroy Bay
Elaine Bay
Tawhitinui I
Tawhitinui Reach
Tennyson Inlet
Tennyson Inlet Scenic Reserve
Mt Stanley
Duncan Bay
Fairy Bay
Penguin Bay
Hikapu Reach
Pinohia
Whatanihi
Mohau Sound
Moenui
Havelock
10
Canvastown
Mahau Sound

Cape Soucis (Raetihi)
Pukerau Point
Motuanauri Island
Otuhaereroa Island
Croisilles Harbour
Squally Cove
Game & Scott Bays Scenic Res
Papawai Bay
Taipare Bay
CROISILLES RD
Okiwi Bay
Okiwi Bay
BULL RANGE
OPOURI ROAD
Tunakino River
Opouri River
Ronga River
RONGA ROAD
Carluke
22
Rai Valley
6
Pelorus Bridge
Pelorus Bridge Scenic Reserve
Pelorus Bridge Rec Reserve
Wakamarina River
Canvastown
Kaituna River
TO BLENHEIM
TO NELSON
Rai River
Whangamoa River
Barbown

Continued on maps 282 & 283

Continued on map 282

© TERRALINK INTERNATIONAL LIMITED 2006

CENTRAL OTAGO WINERIES

Rippon Vineyard, Lake Wanaka

New Zealand's fastest growing wine region, Central Otago is the world's southernmost wine production area, with many of its vineyards in gorgeous, dramatic settings.

Wine was first produced there in the 19th century for sale to gold miners, but it was another 100 years till the industry took off. There's a huge emphasis on pinot noir, as the hot summers and cold winters are ideal for the variety; good pinot gris is also produced.

The region's wineries fall into four main areas: the spectacular **Gibbston Valley**, east of **Queenstown**; **Lake Wanaka**; the **Cromwell Basin**, including the old gold mining area of **Bannockburn**; and around **Alexandra**.

Bannockburn's **Felton Road** has an international reputation for its pinot noir. **Gibbston Valley Wines**

is New Zealand's most visited winery; **Chard Farm Winery**, set high above the **Kawarau River**, and **Rippon Vineyard** on the shores of Lake Wanaka, both have extraordinarily beautiful locations.

 Visitor information

Alexandra i-SITE Visitor Centre
Centennial Ave, Alexandra
Ph: (03) 448 9515

Cromwell and Districts i-SITE Visitor Centre
47 The Mall, Cromwell
Ph: (03) 445 0212

Lake Wanaka i-SITE Visitor Centre
100 Ardmore St, Wanaka
Ph: (03) 443 1233

Queenstown i-SITE Visitor Centre
Clocktower Bldg, Queenstown
Ph: (03) 442 4100
www.otagowine.com

time when even suburbs of London and New York lacked such niceties! Today it's a quiet town in a coal mining and dairy farming area.
MAIN ATTRACTIONS: Reefton has many historic buildings from the gold rush days; these can be explored on a heritage walk, and a historic locomotive is on display. The replica **Miners Hut** is staffed by replica bearded old-time miners; **Reefton School of Mines** opened in 1886 to teach miners their trade.
NEARBY ATTRACTIONS: Surrounding **Victoria Forest Park** has beech forests, wonderful bird life, and historic relics from the early mining days; the park offers good walking, hunting and fishing. **Blacks Point Museum**, 2km east at **Blacks Point**, has gold prospecting relics; next door is a historic **Gold Stamper**

Battery, which still operates. **Waiuta**, on a side road off SH7 38km south-west, and **Big River**, 25km south, are early gold mining townships with many historic sites. **Maruia Springs**, about 60km south-east, has natural thermal springs and a Japanese bath house on the banks of the **Maruia River**.
VISITOR INFORMATION: 67–69 Broadway, Ph: (03) 732 8391, www.reefton.co.nz

■ Riverton/Aparima   POP 1655
Map 311, J5
This seaside resort on the western **Southland** coast, 38km west of Invercargill, is one of New Zealand's oldest European settlements. The area was an important point of contact between early Europeans and southern Maori, for whom

it provided rich food resources. European sealers first visited in the late 18th century, and a whaling station was established in 1836.
MAIN ATTRACTIONS: Sometimes optimistically called Southland's Riviera, Riverton has safe, beautiful beaches which offer good swimming, surfing and kayaking;

(CONTINUED P.270)

Family enjoying Maruia Springs

South Island

0   kilometres   5

Continued on maps 306 & 307

Map a

A   B   C   D   E

1   2   3

Arrowtown
Lakes District Museum
MALAGHANS ROAD 7
LOWER SHOTOVER ROAD
SPEARGRASS FLAT RD
Taramea Winemakers Centre
Lake Hayes
ARROWTOWN-LAKE HAYES RD
CENTENNIAL AVE
Arrow Junction
Amisfield
Crown Terrace
CROWN RANGE
+1731
26
CROWN RANGE RD
6   10
Kawarau River
Kawarau Gorge Suspension Bridge
van Asch Wines
Chard Farm
"Pillars of the Kings" "River Anduin"
Gibbston Valley
Peregrine
Gibbston
Waitiri Creek
Mount Edward
GIBBSTON
Mt Rosa
GIBBSTON HIGHWAY
Kawarau River
6
Waitiri
31
Lower Shotover
Rastus
6
Frankton
Kawarau Falls
"Middle Earth"
THE REMARKABLES
41
6
Remarkables Ski Field
"Dimrill Dale"
Lake Alta
2319
Rastus Burn
Right Branch
Doolans Creek
Nevis River
Branch
D Branch
CARRICK RANGE
+1312
TO KINGSTON
TO CROMWELL
TO QUEENSTOWN
Continued on map 307

Continued on maps 306 & 307

Continued on map 307

Map b

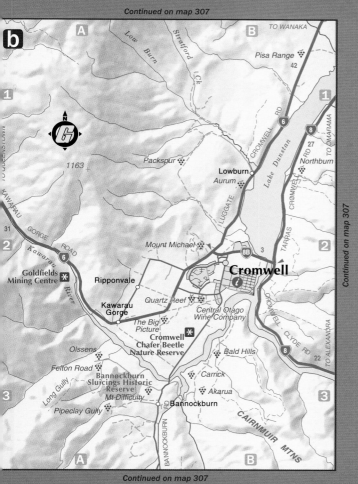

A   B

1   2   3

TO WANAKA
Low Burn
Stratford Ck
Pisa Range
42
CROMWELL RD
6
8
27
Northburn
Packspur
Lake Dunstan
Lowburn
Aurum
ILLUGGATE
TARRAS - CROMWELL RD
1163
KAWARAU GORGE ROAD
31
6
Kawarau Gorge
Goldfields Mining Centre
Ripponvale
Mount Michael
8B   3
Cromwell
Quartz Reef
The Big Picture
Central Otago Wine Company
Cromwell Chafer Beetle Nature Reserve
Kawarau River
Olssens
Felton Road
Bannockburn Sluicings Historic Reserve
Long Gully
Mt Difficulty
Pipeclay Gully
Bannockburn
Bald Hills
Carrick
Akarua
CAIRNMUIR MTNS
CROMWELL CLYDE RD
22
6
TO ALEXANDRA
BANNOCKBURN RD

Continued on map 307

Map c

A   B

1   2   3

TO CROMWELL
Lake Dunstan
22
Clyde Dam
Clyde
8
Muttontown
SPRINGVALE ROAD
Springvale
85
Springvale
TOOMAKAU River
Galloway
Two Paddocks
Earnscleugh or Fraser River
EARNSCLEUGH RD
LETTS GULLY
Hawkdun Rise
William Hill
Leaning Rock
Manuherikia River
27
DUNSTAN RD
11
Earnscleugh
Earnscleugh Flat Tailings
Judge Rock
MANUHERIKIA RD
Central Otago Rail Trail
Curling & Ice Skating
Lower Manorburn Dam
Blackmans
Kenley
Dry Gully
Alexandra
Black Ridge
Fraser River
Rock'n Pillar
Bridge Hill
CONROYS RD
CHAPMAN RD
8
Conroys Gully
Conroys Dam
32
FRUITLANDS ROAD
Lake Roxburgh
Butchers Gully
ALEXANDRA
Butchers Dam
Lake Roxburgh
TO ROXBURGH

Continued on map 307

Vulcan Hotel, built in 1882, St Bathans

these include **Riverton Rocks** and **Taramea Bay**. There's plenty of bird life, and seals and dolphins can often be seen. The **Riverton Museum**, in the town's 1883 courthouse, has displays about Maori, pioneer and Chinese mining history. **Southern Paua** is a factory producing jewellery and souvenirs from paua shell. Riverton also has a **Heritage Trail** and a **Crafts Trail** around local artists' studios.

NEARBY ATTRACTIONS: The **Templeton Flaxmill**, 4.5km east at **Otaitai Bush**, has been restored to working order; it can be visited by arrangement. The surf beach of **Colac Bay/Oraka**, 14km west, was originally home to a Maori settlement; **Round Hill** was the site of a gold find in 1868. At the historic gold mining town of **Orepuki**, 29km west of Riverton, gemstones can be found on the beach. The dramatic **Takitimu Mountains**, a considerable drive north, offer good hiking, hunting and fishing; the walking tracks' entrance is about 75km from Riverton, off the road to **Mossburn**.

The mountains were named after the ancestral Maori canoe Takitimu.
VISITOR INFORMATION: 172 Palmerston St, Ph: (03) 234 9991,
www.riverton-aparima.co.nz

■ **Roxburgh** POP 620
Map 307, G5
Roxburgh is in the heart of **Central Otago**'s productive fruit growing area, 40km south of Alexandra, surrounded by hills, rivers and lakes in the **Teviot Valley**.

MAIN ATTRACTIONS: Roxburgh has some appealing historic buildings made from mud-brick and stone. Stone fruit, strawberries, apples, raspberries and pears are all grown around the town, and can be bought from roadside stalls.

NEARBY ATTRACTIONS: Salmon and trout fishing are good in the **Clutha River** and **Lake Roxburgh**, north of the town; there are many walks in the hills, offering beautiful views. The **Roxburgh Dam**, 8km north, was built in 1962; its lookout has views over Lake Roxburgh. **Gorge Creek**, 15km further north, has a monument to gold miners

who died in the 1863 snows on **Old Man Range**. The remains of early Maori excursions through the area in search of greenstone can be seen around **Millers Flat**, 15km south. The **Lonely Graves Historic Reserve**, 20km south, has the graves of an unknown miner, 'Somebody's Darling', and the man who found and buried him.
VISITOR INFORMATION: 120 Scotland St, Ph: (03) 446 8920, www.centralotagonz.com

■ **St Arnaud** POP 95
Map 285, J3
This picturesque alpine village in the **Nelson** region, on the shores of **Lake Rotoiti** 92km west of Blenheim, is the gateway to **Nelson Lakes National Park**.

NEARBY ATTRACTIONS: Pristine 102 000ha Nelson Lakes National Park has beech forest, craggy mountains, clear streams and large and small lakes. The two largest lakes are Lake Rotoiti and **Lake Rotoroa**, both formed by the movement of glaciers gouging the land. The park's alpine areas are thick with flowers in spring, and from January to April the beech trees are coated with honeydew, a food source for native wildlife. The forests are full of birds, including New Zealand's smallest bird, the rifleman, and the South Island kaka. The **Rotoiti Nature Recovery Project** is an initiative to create an 825ha pest-free refuge or 'mainland island' in the forests by Lake Rotoiti, so native species can be reintroduced and established. The park has an excellent network of tracks for both day walkers and more experienced hikers and climbers, including a three-day track to beautiful alpine **Lake Angelus**, and some easy lakeside walks by Lake Rotoiti. There are many huts in the park, and a 1920s fishing lodge at Lake Rotoroa.
VISITOR INFORMATION: View Rd, Ph: (03) 521 1806, www.nelsonnz.com, www.doc.govt.nz

South Island

■ St Bathans   POP 9
Map 301, G6

The tiny, picturesque village of St Bathans is located 45km north-west of Ranfurly, beneath the **Hawkdun Range** and the **Dunstan Mountains**, and was once a thriving gold rush town occupied by 2000 miners. MAIN ATTRACTIONS: The town had an amazing 13 hotels at one point; today, only the mud-brick **Vulcan Hotel**, built in 1882, is still open for business. St Bathans has many pretty mud-brick cottages, and visitors can see the ruins of the old school, which was damaged in an earthquake. The two-storey **Post Office**, built from kauri in 1909, is still operating. The nearby **Blue Lake** is a flooded mining pit, which was once the deepest hydraulic mining lift in the world; it started out as a 120m-high hill, was dug to a depth of 69m, and then was flooded in 1935 when mining was abandoned. The lake's intense blue colour is due to minerals in the surrounding cliffs. VISITOR INFORMATION: Centennial Ave, Alexandra, Ph: (03) 448 9515, www.maniototo.co.nz

■ Takaka   POP 1190
Map 280, E3

The main town in **Golden Bay**, relaxed Takaka is 103km north-west of Nelson. Busy in summer, it has a lively arts and café scene. MAIN ATTRACTIONS: A cooperative **Artisans' Shop** exhibits work from local potters, painters, jewellery and clothes designers, and a craft trail pamphlet has details of galleries and workshops. The **Golden Bay Museum and Gallery** has displays of historical material. **Bencarri Farm**, 2km south-west, features tame **Anatoki River** eels; the tradition of hand-feeding them goes back to 1914. NEARBY ATTRACTIONS: **Pupu Springs**, 7km west, are the southern hemisphere's largest fresh water spring, throwing up around 14 000 litres of water a second, including from one spring with dancing sands. The tiny beach resort town of **Pohara** is 10km east. The road from Pohara to the northern end of the **Abel Tasman Coastal Track**, in beautiful **Abel Tasman National Park**, is very scenic. En route, **Ligar Bay** features a memorial to the Dutch navigator Abel Tasman, the first European to visit Golden Bay. **Rawhiti Cave**, 7km east of Takaka, has the largest entrance of any cave in New Zealand. **Takaka Hill**, south of Takaka, is known as the marble mountain, and offers spectacular views and karst formations. Scenes for *The Lord of the Rings* film trilogy were shot here, with the hill featuring as **'Chetwood Forest'**. Near the summit, the **Ngarua Caves** can be visited on a guided tour, and contain bones from the extinct moa (a giant flightless bird). Also on the hill, **Harwood's Hole** is the deepest vertical shaft in the southern hemisphere. VISITOR INFORMATION: Willow St, Ph: (03) 525 9136, www.nelsonnz.com/golden

■ Te Anau   POP 1855
Map 305, G4

Fiordland's largest town, Te Anau is beautifully located on the shores of **Lake Te Anau** and looks out over the water to **Mount Luxmore** and the **Murchison Mountains**. Te Anau is a gateway to **Fiordland National Park**, and a base for trips to **Milford Sound**. MAIN ATTRACTIONS: Cruises are available on Lake Te Anau, which is the South Island's largest and New Zealand's second largest, and is 417m deep at its deepest point. Kayaking and jetboating trips explore the Fiordland waterways, and scenic flights are available. The **Te Ana-au Caves** on the lake's western shores can only be reached by boat. Visitors can then explore the huge, geologically-active limestone caverns by foot and punt to see underground waterfalls, whirlpools and a glow-worm grotto. **Te Anau Wildlife Centre**, on the road to **Manapouri**, has many native birds, including the rare flightless takahe. The Department of Conservation's **Fiordland National Park Visitors Centre** has displays of pioneer relics, and takes bookings for the **Milford**, **Routeburn** and **Kepler Tracks**. The 60km Kepler Track, one of New Zealand's 'Great Walks', starts just outside Te Anau and heads west into the **Kepler Mountains**, taking in lake edges, beech forests, alpine areas and a glacial valley. NEARBY ATTRACTIONS: The drive from Te Anau to Milford Sound through the World Heritage Area is known as one of the world's best alpine drives, passing through some spectacular scenery and the 1.2km **Homer Tunnel**. Boat transfers to the start of the famous 54km **Milford Track** leave from **Te Anau Downs**. VISITOR INFORMATION: Lakefront Drive, Ph: (03) 249 8900, www.fiordlandnz.com

■ Temuka   POP 4000
Map 303, H2

In southern **Canterbury**, 145km south of Christchurch and 18km north of Timaru, the historic town of Temuka is home to an eponymous, iconic pottery factory, in business since the 1920s. MAIN ATTRACTIONS: A visit to

(CONTINUED P.274)

Harwood's Hole, Takaka

FIORDLAND NATIONAL PARK

Part of Te Wahipounamu South-west New Zealand World Heritage Area, spectacular 1.2 million ha Fiordland National Park is one of the southern hemisphere's great wilderness areas.

Once traversed by Maori gathering greenstone, and later by European sealers and whalers, this remote area features snow-topped mountains, peaceful lakes, dense forests and tussock grasslands. Fourteen deep fiords, carved by glaciers in successive ice ages, cut through the area, with waterfalls cascading into them. The rest of the park is covered in virgin beech and podocarp forest, including 800-year-old trees. Some of New Zealand's best examples of flora and fauna from the ancient super-continent of Gondwana are found here.

A network of 500km of walking trails allows visitors to explore this pristine area. The park has three of New Zealand's 'Great Walks' — the **Milford**, **Kepler** and **Routeburn Tracks** — and there are many other spectacular hikes,

including the **Hollyford Track**. The Milford, Routeburn and Hollyford Tracks can be done as guided walks. The Department of Conservation provides more than 50 huts for walkers, and huts on the three Great Walks offer a higher level of comfort.

Mount Cook lilies, Hollyford Valley

 Visitor information

DOC Fiordland National Park Visitors Centre
Lakefront Dr, Te Anau
Ph: (03) 249 8514
www.doc.govt.nz

Milford Track

This famous 54km track, renowned for its glacially carved valleys, rainforest, mountain views, alpine flowers and waterfalls, has been described as the finest walk in the world, and can be done independently or as a guided walk. The number of walkers each year is limited; book well ahead to get a place.

main attractions

◈ **Doubtful Sound**
Fiordland's deepest sound has towering mountains, waterfalls and rich wildlife.

◈ **Hollyford Track**
Spectacular scenery of mountains, lakes, the Hollyford River and St Martins Bay make this four-day walk popular.

◈ **Kepler Track**
Bookings are required in the high season for this 60km track which passes lakes, forest, alpine areas and a glacial valley.

◈ **Lake Manapouri**
This beautiful lake offers good fishing and boating.

◈ **Marine reserves**
Te Awaatu Channel Marine Reserve in Doubtful Sound and Piopiotahi Marine Reserve in Milford Sound offer fantastic diving among rich marine life.

◈ **Milford Road**
The 116km Milford Road is a hugely scenic alpine road passing waterfalls and the Mirror Lakes.

◈ **Milford Sound**
This beautiful forested sound is a huge tourist drawcard, and offers wonderful diving.

◈ **Routeburn Track**
This 32km track leads through Fiordland and Mt Aspiring National Parks, and takes in waterfalls, forested valleys, bird life, lakes and mountain scenery.

Giant Gate Falls, Milford Track

South Island

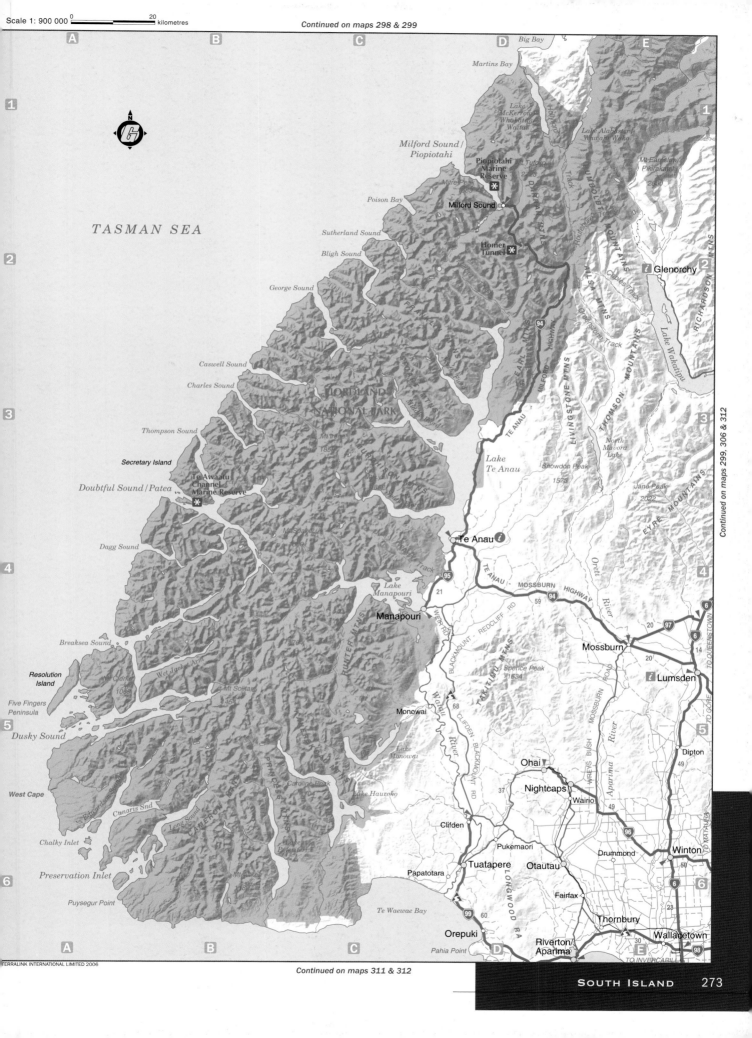

0   20 kilometres

Continued on maps 298 & 299

TASMAN SEA

Big Bay

Martins Bay

Lake McKerrow/
Whakatipu
Waitai

*Milford Sound /
Piopiotahi*

Lake Alabaster/
Wawahi Waka

Mt Earnslaw
Pikirakatahi
2830

Mt Tutoko
2723

Piopiotahi
Marine
Reserve ✳

Poison Bay

Milford Sound

Mitre Peak
1683

Glenorchy

Homer
Tunnel ✳

Sutherland Sound

Bligh Sound

George Sound

94

Caswell Sound

FIORDLAND
NATIONAL PARK

Charles Sound

Thompson Sound

94

Mitre
1850

Snowdon Peak
1573

Lake
Te Anau

North
Mavora
Lake

Secretary Island

Doubtful Sound / Patea

Te Awaatu
Channel
Marine Reserve ✳

Jane Peak
2022

Dagg Sound

Lake
Manapouri

Te Anau ℹ

95

21

59

94

Manapouri

Breaksea Sound

Resolution
Island

Spence Peak
1634

Mossburn

Lumsden ℹ

Five Fingers
Peninsula

20

97

6

6

14

Mt Clerke
1088

Mt Solitary
1465

20

Dusky Sound

Monowai

68

Dipton

49

West Cape

Lake
Monowai

Ohai

Caroline Peak

37

Nightcaps

Cunaris Snd

Lake Hauroko

Wairio

49

Chalky Inlet

Lake
Poteriteri

Clifden

Pukemaori

Drummond

Winton

96

50

Preservation Inlet

Fairfax

23

Puysegur Point

Tuatapere

Papatotara

Otautau

Thornbury

Wallacetown

Te Waewae Bay

99

60

Orepuki

Riverton/
Aparima

98

Pahia Point

TO INVERCARGILL

Continued on maps 311 & 312

Continued on maps 299, 306 & 312

SOUTH ISLAND   273

OTAGO PENINSULA

Peaceful Otago Peninsula, stretching along the south-east side of **Otago Harbour**, is rich in wildlife, historic places and natural beauty. **Taiaroa Head** is home to the **Royal Albatross Colony**, the world's only mainland breeding colony of royal albatross; the peninsula's impressive range of wildlife also includes blue penguins, fur seals, Hooker's sea lions and the rare yellow-eyed penguin. Sea kayaking, cycling and diving trips are all available, and visitors can see the marine and bird life on tours and cruises.

Architecturally extravagant **Larnach Castle**, built in the 1870s by Dunedin banker and financier William Larnach, is New Zealand's only castle, and is open to visitors. Historic military fortifications at Taiaroa Head include tunnels and the **Armstrong Disappearing Gun**, installed in 1880 to protect against the supposed threat of Russian invasion.

There are also many beautiful walks around the peninsula.

main attractions

- ❖ Armstrong Disappearing Gun
- ❖ Glenfalloch Woodland Garden
- ❖ Larnach Castle
- ❖ Penguin Place
- ❖ Royal Albatross Centre
- ❖ Sandfly Bay
- ❖ Taiaroa Head
- ❖ Wildlife cruises

ⓘ Visitor information

Dunedin i-SITE Visitor Centre
48 The Octagon, Dunedin
Ph: (03) 474 3300
www.otago-peninsula.co.nz

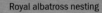

Royal albatross nesting

Temuka Homeware is a must; most New Zealanders have at least one piece of Temuka pottery in their home. The **Temuka Museum** explores the town's history. Pioneer aviator Richard Pearse is Temuka's most famous son. While there's debate over whether Pearse achieved powered flight just before or just after the Wright Brothers in the first years of the 20th century, his achievement was certainly remarkable. There's a **Richard Pearse Monument** at the site of his first attempted flight, 13.5km west.

NEARBY ATTRACTIONS: From Temuka it's an easy drive west to the spectacular scenery and lakes of the **Mackenzie Country**. At **Pleasant Point**, 15km west, the **Pleasant Point Museum and**

Railway draws railway enthusiasts from around the globe with its beautifully restored steam locomotives and the world's only Ford Model T railcar. Anglers from all over the world have long been drawn to Temuka by its reputation for fine fishing rivers — especially where the **Rangitata** and **Opihi** meet the **Pacific Ocean**.
VISITOR INFORMATION: 72–74 King St, Ph: (03) 615 9537, www.southisland.org.nz

■ Timaru   POP 26 750
Map 325, D4
Located 163km south of Christchurch, **Canterbury**'s only other city, Timaru, is a significant port for the local agricultural region. Timaru is set between the **Pacific Ocean** and the **Southern Alps**,

surrounded by rolling farmland; at one time a whaling station, it has impressive Victorian and Edwardian architecture.

Richard Pearse Monument, west of Temuka

South Island

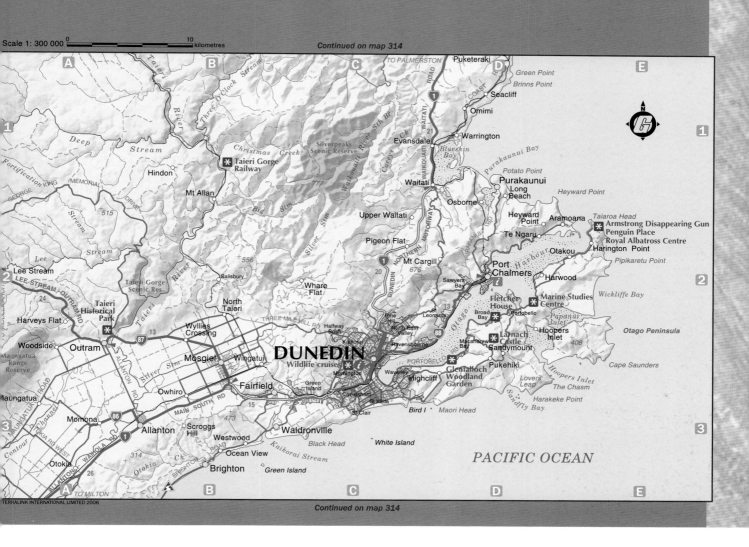

Continued on map 314

Continued on map 314

TERRALINK INTERNATIONAL LIMITED 2006

MAIN ATTRACTIONS: The **Aigantighe Art Gallery** boasts an excellent collection of New Zealand art and an outdoor sculpture garden. The gallery's Gaelic moniker means 'at home'. The **South Canterbury Museum** houses many local treasures. Roses grow superbly in the central South Island; a great display can be seen in the **Trevor Griffith Rose Garden** on **Caroline Bay**, which also has arbours, pools and a fountain. A **Blacksmithing Show** is on offer at the port, with art made in a traditionally fuelled coal forge for sale at the retail outlet in Stafford Street. Visitors can swim or relax over a meal at pretty Caroline Bay, or get out on the water for a cruise to check out the wide variety of marine life.

NEARBY ATTRACTIONS: There are several ski areas within two hours' drive of Timaru, including **Mt Dobson**, **Fox Peak**, **Mt Hutt**, **Ohau** and **Roundhill**. Timaru and the nearby **Waimate** district share some 500 sites of Maori rock art dating from the 16th century. **Pleasant Point**, 19km north, is home to the **Pleasant Point Museum and Railway**, the award-winning **Opihi vineyard**, **Denheath House** and a working blacksmith.

VISITOR INFORMATION: 2 George St, Ph: (03) 688 6163, www.southisland.org.nz

■ **Tuatapere**   POP 680
Map 311, G4

This small farming town in western **Southland**, 85km west of Invercargill on the **Waiau River**, is a gateway to the beautiful south coast and southern **Fiordland**'s remote lakes.

MAIN ATTRACTIONS: The **Tuatapere Domain** has a remnant of podocarp forest; the town also has a **Bushman's Museum**.

NEARBY ATTRACTIONS: Rare Hector's dolphins and southern right whales sometimes visit **Te Waewae Bay**, to the south. Picturesque **Cosy Nook**, once a settlement of the Ngai Tahu tribe, has a collection of classic Kiwi baches (small holiday homes). **Orepuki**, 18km south, is an old gold mining town; gemstones can be found on its beach. West of Tuatapere, the spectacular 53km **Tuatapere Hump Ridge Track** leads from the sea to the mountains, through forest and over historic viaducts. These include the world's largest remaining

(CONTINUED P.277)

The South Island has the southernmost vineyards in the world, and Canterbury's wineries are a vital part of their growing international reputation.

A research project at Lincoln University in 1973 led to the first trials of vineyards and winemaking in Canterbury. Today the fertile lowlands of Canterbury boast many excellent vineyards. The **Southern Alps** to the west shelter the plains from westerly rain, and long, dry autumns enable the fruit to ripen slowly with good levels of acidity.

The **Waipara Valley** is Canterbury's premier wine growing region. Approximately 45 minutes north of Christchurch, it is regarded as one of the fastest growing wine regions in New Zealand. Pinot noir, riesling, chardonnay and sauvignon blanc dominate local plantings in this cool climate grape growing area.

Many wineries welcome visitors and offer tastings; tours are available to wineries such as **Pegasus Bay** and **Canterbury House** in the Waipara Valley, and **Giesen Wine Estate** and **Morworth Estate** just south-west of Christchurch.

<table>
<tr><td>ℹ️ Visitor information</td></tr>
<tr><td>Christchurch i-SITE Visitor Centre
Old Chief Post Office, Cathedral Sq West, Christchurch
Ph: (03) 379 9629
www.christchurchnz.net</td></tr>
</table>

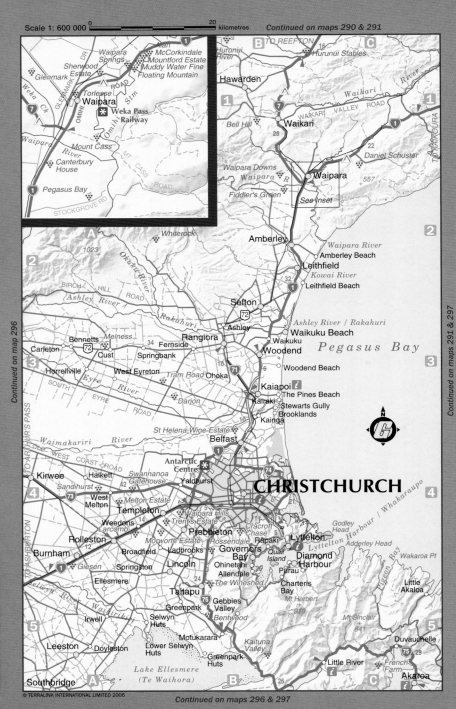

Canterbury House Vineyard, Waipara Valley

Continued on maps 290 & 291

Continued on map 296

Continued on maps 291 & 297

Continued on maps 296 & 297

Scale 1: 600 000

© TERRALINK INTERNATIONAL LIMITED 2006

South Island

Sunset at Te Waewae Bay, Southland

wooden viaduct, the **Percy Burn Viaduct**, 125m long and 36m above the creek bed. Walkers need to book for the track, which starts at **Bluecliffs Bay**. The **South Coast Track** leads west around the coast, taking four days to **Big River**. It's possible to walk over the elegant **Clifden Suspension Bridge**, built in 1899 over the **Waiau River**, about 13km north of Tuatapere; 23km from **Clifden**, **Dean Forest** is a reserve with 1000-year-old totara trees. Beautiful, secluded **Lake Hauroko**, 30km west of Clifden, is New Zealand's deepest lake; from here, jet boats head down the **Wairaurahiri River**. There's also a boat service to the **Dusky Track**, a difficult 84km hike to **Lake Manapouri**.
VISITOR INFORMATION: Orama Rd, Ph: (03) 226 6399, www.atoz-nz.com/tuatapere.asp

■ **Twizel** POP 1010
Map 301, H2
The town of Twizel was built in 1968 for construction of the nearby hydro-electric power scheme, the largest hydro power project ever undertaken in New Zealand. Located 284km west of Christchurch and just south of the astonishing turquoise blue **Lake Pukaki**, Twizel has all the beauty of the **Mackenzie Country** at its doorstep.
MAIN ATTRACTIONS: The **Mackenzie Basin** is home to the kaki/black stilt, the world's rarest wader species. The

Kaki Visitor Hide, located by the Department of Conservation-run captive breeding centre, has tours to view the rare bird. Helicopter flights offer great views over **Aoraki/Mount Cook National Park**; good fishing is available in local rivers and canals. Adrenaline junkies can take a helicopter up a mountain and make their way down by mountain bike.
NEARBY ATTRACTIONS: At **Lake Pukaki**, 9km north, lookouts offer wonderful views over the turquoise waters. To the west, the **Ben Ohau Station**, a high country sheep station, was the location for filming the final battle scenes in the third *The Lord Of The Rings* movie, *The Return Of The King*. With Aoraki/Mount Cook National Park a 45-minute drive away, Twizel is a popular base for skiers, climbers and hikers; it's also the closest town to popular **Ohau Snow Fields**, 50km south-west, which has 125ha of skiable area and views over **Lake Ohau**.
VISITOR INFORMATION: Market Place, Ph: (03) 435 3124, www.twizel.com

■ **Waikouaiti** POP 1100
Map 309, H5
This picturesque small seaside town, 42km north of Dunedin on the **Otago** coast, was settled by Europeans in the 1830s, and was once a centre for whaling. Waikouaiti was originally intended as Otago's main settlement, but was displaced from that position by Dunedin.
MAIN ATTRACTIONS: Waikouaiti's beach offers boating, fishing, surfing and swimming. **Waikouaiti District Museum**, in the old Bank of New Zealand stone building, has artefacts and memorabilia from the whaling days.
NEARBY ATTRACTIONS: **Karitane**, 5km south and now a popular seaside resort town, has a long history of Maori settlement. The lookout

above Karitane has impressive views over Waikouaiti and Karitane bays. New Zealand's oldest surviving farm buildings, dating from the early 1840s, can be seen at nearby **Matanaka**, 4km east. Built in the early 1840s by Johnny Jones, an ex-convict turned whaler, farmer, businessman and settler, the complex includes stables, a granary, store, schoolroom and unique three-hole privy.
VISITOR INFORMATION: 48 The Octagon, Dunedin, Ph: (03) 474 3300, www.dunedinnz.com

■ **Waimate** POP 2755
Map 303, G5
The small town of Waimate, in inland southern **Canterbury**, is known as 'The Centre of the South' due to its location about two hours' drive from Christchurch, Dunedin and Queenstown. Waimate is in a forestry, farming and berryfruit growing area.
MAIN ATTRACTIONS: Waimate is famous for its strawberries, and each December it holds the **Waimate Strawberry Fare**. It's possible to visit **The Cuddy**, built in 1854, the original home of the first European settlers; Waimate also has many lovely Edwardian buildings. There are a variety of native bush walks close to town. Most popular is the **Waimate Walkway** to the '**Whitehorse**', a huge white concrete horse set into the hillside; it was created as a tribute to the Clydesdale horses that were used to break the surrounding land into grass. **St Augustine's Church** was designed in 1872 by notable architect Benjamin Mountford.
NEARBY ATTRACTIONS: The major river of the **Mackenzie Basin** is the **Waitaki River**, about 25km south. One of the classic South Island braided rivers, it marks the boundary between the Canterbury and Otago regions, and has the man-made **Lake Benmore**,

Lake Aviemore and **Lake Waitaki** at its headwaters. The meandering river offers great salmon and trout fishing, guided fishing trips and jet boat tours.

Visitor Information: 2 George St, Timaru, Ph: (03) 688 6163, www.waimate.org.nz

■ **Waipara**   POP 275

Map 290, E6

Waipara, 59km north of Christchurch, is the southernmost destination point on the **Alpine Pacific Triangle Touring Route**, and is set in an important wine production area.

Main Attractions: The lovely **Waipara Valley** boasts many award-winning wineries. An original and relaxing way to tour the wineries is on a wagon pulled by Clydesdale horses; this lets visitors sample the wine and still get home safely. In Waipara township, the **Athena Olive Grove** offers informative tours and tastings of the traditionally pressed oils.

Nearby Attractions: Visitors can explore beautiful **Weka Pass**, 14km west, on a vintage steam or diesel-electric locomotive with the **Weka Pass Railway**. The railway was carved into limestone by hand during the 1880s. **Motunau Beach**, a 38km drive north-east of Waipara, is a beautiful coastal village offering marine and sightseeing tours and a selection of restaurants and cafés.

Visitor Information: Cathedral Sq West, Christchurch, Ph: (03) 379 9629, www.hurunui.com

Lake Wanaka

■ **Wanaka**   POP 3330

Map 326, D5

The relaxed town of Wanaka, on the shores of **Lake Wanaka**, is a popular resort in both winter and summer, and is a gateway to **Mount Aspiring National Park**.

Main Attractions: Scenic flights are available from **Wanaka Airport**, and the **Warbirds Museum** has a collection of fighter aircraft from World War II. **Warbirds over Wanaka** is a huge air show held every second Easter, featuring historic aircraft and aerobatics. **Puzzling World** has a maze, holograms and 'illusion rooms'.

Nearby Attractions: **Rippon Vineyard**, 4km west, is picturesquely sited on Lake Wanaka's shores. In winter Wanaka is a base for skiing on the classic ski fields of **Cardrona** and **Treble Cone**, heli skiing in the **Harris Mountains** and Nordic skiing at **Waiorau Snow Farm**. Other activities include horse trekking, mountain biking, rock climbing and paragliding. Lake Wanaka and the mighty **Clutha River** are the place for lake cruises, jet boat trips, kayaking and white-water rafting and sledging; there's excellent trout fishing on Lake Wanaka and **Lake Hawea**, 15km east. Several operators offer beginner courses in mountaineering, ski-mountaineering tours in the **Southern Alps** and guided ascents of **Mounts Aspiring/Tititea**, **Tasman** and **Tutoko**. The easy walk up **Mount Iron** allows excellent views over the area; **Roys Peak** is a more demanding full-day walk with sweeping views from its summit. There are short and long walks in the **Matukituki Valley**, an hour's drive north-west in Mount Aspiring National Park; the **Rob Roy Track** (three to four hours return) offers alpine scenery and views of the **Rob Roy Glacier**. **Makarora**, 64km north at the northern tip of Lake Wanaka, is the base for the **Siberia**

Experience, a six-hour outdoor adventure which involves a scenic flight, bushwalking in a remote valley and a jet boat trip. **Cardrona**, 25km south, has a historic 1863 hotel and old gold mining sites in a picturesque valley.

Visitor Information: 100 Ardmore St, Ph: (03) 443 1233, www.lakewanaka.co.nz

■ **Westport**   POP 3785

Map 327, C4

The main town on the northern **West Coast**, 100km north of Greymouth at the mouth of the mighty **Buller River**, Westport is a coal mining centre and port; the late 19th century also saw a gold rush in the area.

Main Attractions: **Coaltown Museum** has historical exhibitions focusing on coal mining, including a simulated mine, and a section about the dredging of Westport's harbour.

Nearby Attractions: Fur seals are present year-round at the **Tauranga Bay** seal breeding colony, at **Cape Foulwind**, 15km west; there are viewing platforms and a walkway. Cape Foulwind was named in 1770 by the British explorer Captain James Cook, who arrived there in a nasty storm. **Denniston**, about 25km north-east, was once New Zealand's biggest producer of coal, which was trucked out via the startlingly steep **Denniston Incline**; there's a walkway with good views. From **Granity**, 32km north-east, a turn-off leads to the semi-ghost towns of **Millerton** and **Stockton**. The **Charming Creek Walkway** is an interesting five-hour walk through rich rainforest and the **Ngakawau Gorge**. Remote **Gentle Annie Beach**, about 45km north, offers swimming, surfing and fishing. **Charleston**, 19km south, was home to 40 000 residents and 80 hotels in the glory days of gold mining.

Visitor Information: 1 Brougham St, Ph: (03) 789 6658, www.westport.org.nz

South Island

SOUTH ISLAND KEY MAP

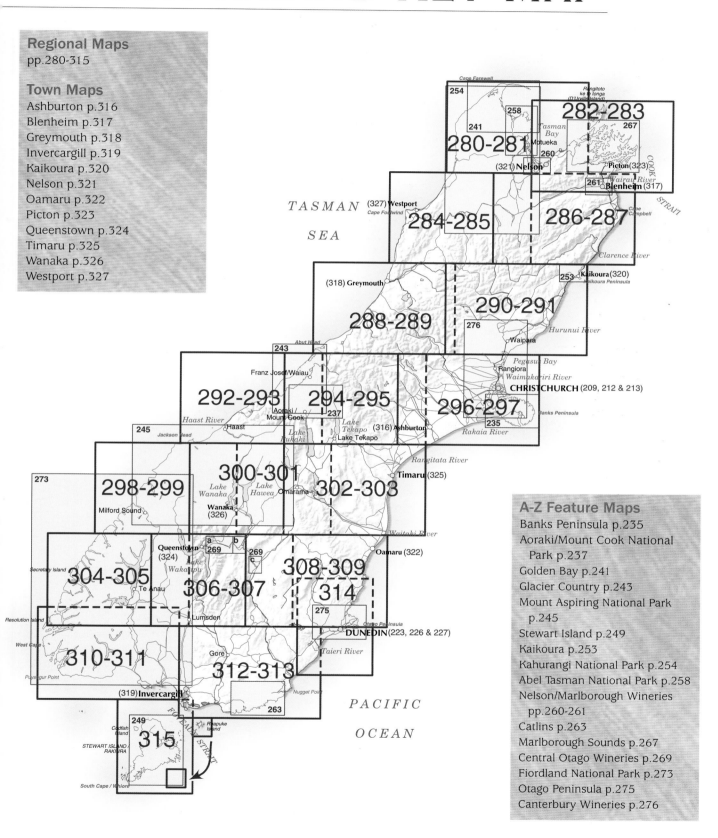

TASMAN

SEA

Cape Farewell

254

258

241

282-283

267

Rangitoto ke te tonga (D'Urville Island)

Tasman Bay

280-281

Motueka

260

(321) Nelson

Picton (323)

COOK

261

Wairau River

Blenheim (317)

STRAIT

(327) Westport

Cape Foulwind

284-285

286-287

Cape Campbell

Clarence River

253

Kaikoura (320)

Kaikoura Peninsula

(318) Greymouth

290-291

288-289

276

Hurunui River

Waipara

Abut Head

243

Pegasus Bay

Rangiora

Franz Josef/Waiau

Waimakariri River

292-293

294-295

CHRISTCHURCH (209, 212 & 213)

Aoraki / Mount Cook

237

296-297

Banks Peninsula

Haast River

Haast

Lake Tekapo

(316) Ashburton

235

245

Jackson Head

Lake Pukaki

Lake Tekapo

Rakaia River

Rangitata River

273

298-299

300-301

Lake Hawea

302-303

Timaru (325)

Lake Wanaka

Wanaka (326)

Omarama

Milford Sound

Waitaki River

Oamaru (322)

Secretary Island

Queenstown (324)

a 269 b

269 c

308-309

304-305

Lake Wakatipu

306-307

314

Te Anau

275

Resolution Island

Lumsden

Otago Peninsula

West Cape

DUNEDIN (223, 226 & 227)

310-311

Gore

312-313

Taieri River

Puysegur Point

(319) Invercargill

263

Nugget Point

PACIFIC

249

FOVEAUX STRAIT

Ruapuke Island

OCEAN

Codfish Island

315

STEWART ISLAND / RAKIURA

South Cape / Whiore

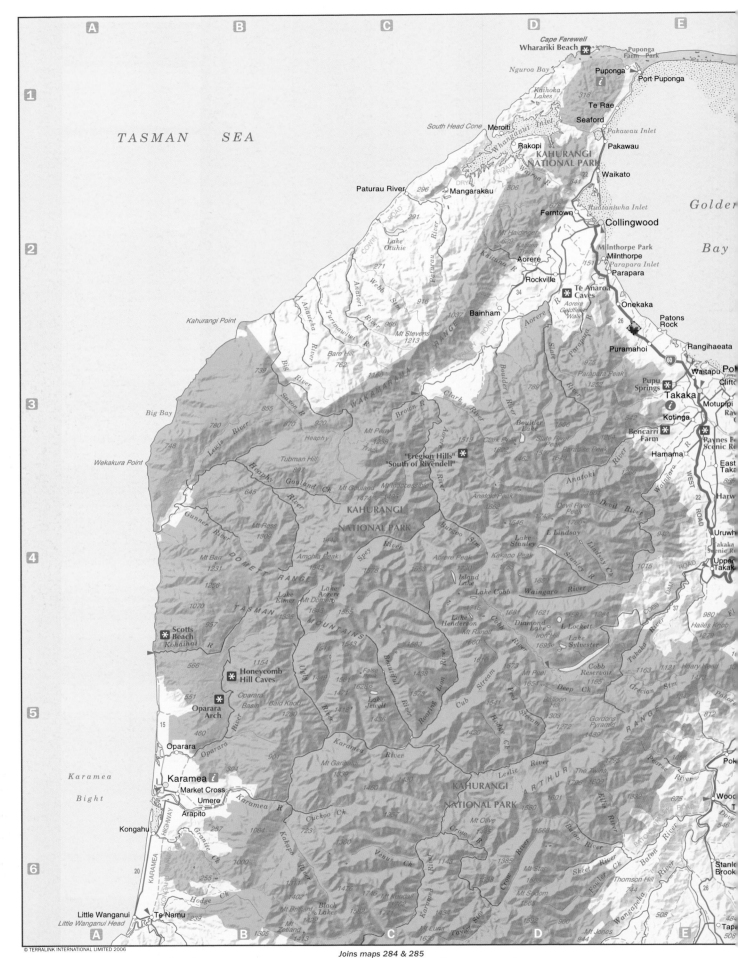

TASMAN SEA

Golden

Bay

Cape Farewell
Whariwharariki Beach
Wharariki Beach
Nguroa Bay
Puponga
Farm Park
Puponga
Port Puponga
Kaihoka
Lakes
318
Te Rae
South Head Cone
Meroiti
Seaford
Pakawau Inlet
Whanganui Inlet
Rakopi
Pakawau
KAHURANGI
NATIONAL PARK
Waikato
Paturau River
296
Mangarakau
506
Ruataniwha Inlet
341
291
Ferntown
Collingwood
COWIN
ROAD
Lake
Otuhie
271
Mt Haidinger
629
Kaituna
Track
Milnthorpe Park
Milnthorpe
Aorere
151
Parapara Inlet
Parapara
Rockville
34
Te Anaroa
Caves
Onekaka
Webb
Stm
916
Bainham
1037
Aorere
Goldfields
Walk
Patons
Rock
26
Kahurangi Point
1150
Slate
Parapara Peak
1252
Puramahoi
Rangihaeata
Pupu
Springs
60
Waitapu
Po
748
Big Bay
855
870
920
Brown R
Clark River
789
Takaka
Clifton
Motupipi
Kotinga
Bencarri
Farm
Raynes
Scenic Re
Hamama
East
Taka
Big
River
739
780
Heaphy
Mt Perry
1238
"Freglon Hills"
"South of Rivendell"
1519
Boulder
Lake
1506
Clark Peak
462
Slate River
Peak
1618
Wekakura Point
Saxon R
Tubman Hill
897
Mt Gouland
1474
Mt Inaccessible
1495
Anatoki
Peak
1662
Anatoki
1601
Devil River
Peak
1743
1780
Devil River
942
Harw
22
Uruwh
Gunner
River
Goulund
Ck
645
KAHURANGI
NATIONAL PARK
1546
L. Lindsay
Lindsay Ck
1015
Mt Ross
1309
1643
Amphoa Peak
1542
Burgoo Stm
Lake
Stanley
Kakapo Peak
Stanley
R
Upper
Takak
1256
Mt Barr
1231
Spey
River
1678
Aorere Peak
790
Island
Lake
1850
Waingaro
River
1070
Lake
Aorere
1565
1653
Lake Cobb
1294
37
980
Hailes Knob
1279
957
1325
Lake
Elmer
Mt Domett
1649
Lake
Henderson
716
1681
1621
Diamond
Lake
560
Iron Hill
1695
Lake
Sylvester
Cobb
River
Cobb
Reservoir
1165
1163
1121
Hoary Head
1470
Scotts
Beach
566
1154
1618
1543
1583
Beautiful
River
1438
1573
Avon
River
1610
1673
Mt Peel
1654
Deep
Ck
Balloon
Hill
303
1272
Grecian
Stm
812
Kohaihai
R
Honeycomb
Hill Caves
False
Peak
1561
1629
1474
1818
Lake
Jewell
1436
Roaring
Cub
1511
1420
Hodge Ck
Peel
Stream
Gordons
Pyramid
1489
551
460
Oparara
Arch
Oparara
Basin
Bald Knob
1280
Karamea
River
Mt Garibaldi
1538
1430
1460
Leslie
River
1601
1795
The Twins
1788
1609
1832
Pok
15
Oparara
901
KAHURANGI
304
Venus Ck
1357
NATIONAL PARK
1580
ARTHUR
1385
675
Wood
T
Karamea
Bight
Karamea
Market Cross
Umere
Arapito
Karamea
R
Cuckoo Ck
723
1360
Mt Olive
1348
Crow
R
1563
Eills
River
Baton
River
Baton
River
546
Kongahu
257
1084
Kahapa
River
1000
1402
1475
1748
Mt Kendall
1494
Kanawa
River
1142
1398
Crow
R
1385
Mt Snow
566
Skeet
River
Fowler Ck
Wangapeka
River
508
Stanle
Brook
20
255
Hodge
Ck
255
1305
1413
Mt Brilliant
1422
Mt Zetland
239
Black
Lakes
1582
Mt Luna
1630
Mt Kendall
Taylor
Stm
1494
1503
980
508
Mt Jones
944
Tapu
Pok
Little Wanganui
Little Wanganui Head
Te Namu
Kongahu
KARAMEA
HIGHWAY
Granite
Ck

26

0   15 kilometres

rewell Spit Nature Reserve

Farewell

Spit

1

2

/ Tasman
Point

Separation Point
Mutton Cove
Anapai Bay

Gibbs Hill
805

Wainui
Inlet

arakohe

27

Totaranui

Rangitoto ki te tonga
(D'Urville Island)

Greville Harbour

Ragged Pt.

3

Abel Head

ay Peak   946
750   608

1156

Awaroa R.

Anatoki R.

Tonga Roadstead

Bark Bay

544

Tonga Roadstead

632

574

Manuhakapakapa

130

466

Current Basin

ABEL TASMAN

NATIONAL PARK

740

Torrent Bay

800

680

"Chetwood
orest"

evans

682

Bata Hill

692

Astrolabe Roadstead

Adele I

Papawai Bay

Taipare Bay

Okuri Peak

529

Bobs Peak

Joins map 282

3 Ngarua
Caves

Marahau R.

Marahau

Sandy Bay

Otuwhero Inlet

Otuhaereroa I
Motuanauru I

Askews Hill
520

608

Garne
Bays Scenic Res

4

Riwaka
Resurgence

35

Waimea River

Kaiteriteri

312

Tasman Bay

Cape Soucis (Raetihi)

Croisilles Harbour

282

Squally Cove

Symonds Hill

366

Elaine
Bay

Tennyson Inlet

Riwaka

803

Brooklyn

Motueka River

Whangamoa Head

Croisilles Hill
694

Whangamoa River

Okiwi Bay

CROISILLES RD

CROISI

Tennyson Inlet
Scenic Reserve

Mt Stanley

Ratawhenua River

Motueka ⓘ

Mariri

Port Motueka

Jackett Island

32

Lower
Moutere

Moutere Inlet

16

Pepin Island

Cable Bay

401

Delaware
Bay

Mt Duppa
1133

South Castor
Peak
888

Elliot Peak
861

1040

850

Okiwi Bay

22

Lookout Peak
990

Nydia Bay
Scenic Res
Opouri Peak
920

639

Nydia Bay

Paradise Bay
Scenic Reserve

976

5

ngatotara

Kina

Glenduan
657

Blue Hill
609

930

Rai River

Ronga River

Tunakino R.

Opouri River

OPOURI ROAD

TONGA ROAD

907

atimoti

Braeburn

Tasman

60

*Moutere
Bluff*

Ruby Bay

Wakapuaka

48

Hira

Marybank

Atawhai

596

Mt Duppa
1133

Scenic
Res

Rai Valley

680

Carluke

1006

Scenic Reserve

Moenui

oco

Harakeke

Mapua

*Rabbit
Island*

Brooklands

1066

Saddle Hill
1215

NELSON ⓘ

Britannia
Heights

Nelson Haven

821

Pelorus Bridge
Scenic Reserve

Benbown

Havelock

6

215

NEUDORF RD

116

**Upper
Moutere**

Mahana

Bronte

Tahunanui

Pelorus Bridge
Rec Reserve

Pelorus
Bridge

17

Canvastown

856

6

1055

ovedale

Redwood Valley

MOUTERE HWY

WAIMEA WEST RD

*Waimea
Inlet*

Hoglund
Art Glass

*Waimea
Plains*

Stoke

Enner Glynn

776

1111

1129

1143

Little Twin

1060
1043

**MOUNT RICHMOND
FOREST PARK**

782

995

Wairoa River

Wakamarina River

WAKAMARINA

635

1038

29

356

Richmond ⓘ

541

Roding River

Mt Malita
999

Johnson Ck

935

Kaituna River

31

844

Pigeon Ck

259

Hope

5

395

369

14

Brightwater

6

Spring Grove

Pelorus River

956

1330

Johnson Ck

1168

Joins maps 286 & 287

Joins map 281

Joins maps 286 & 287

South Island

0   15   kilometres

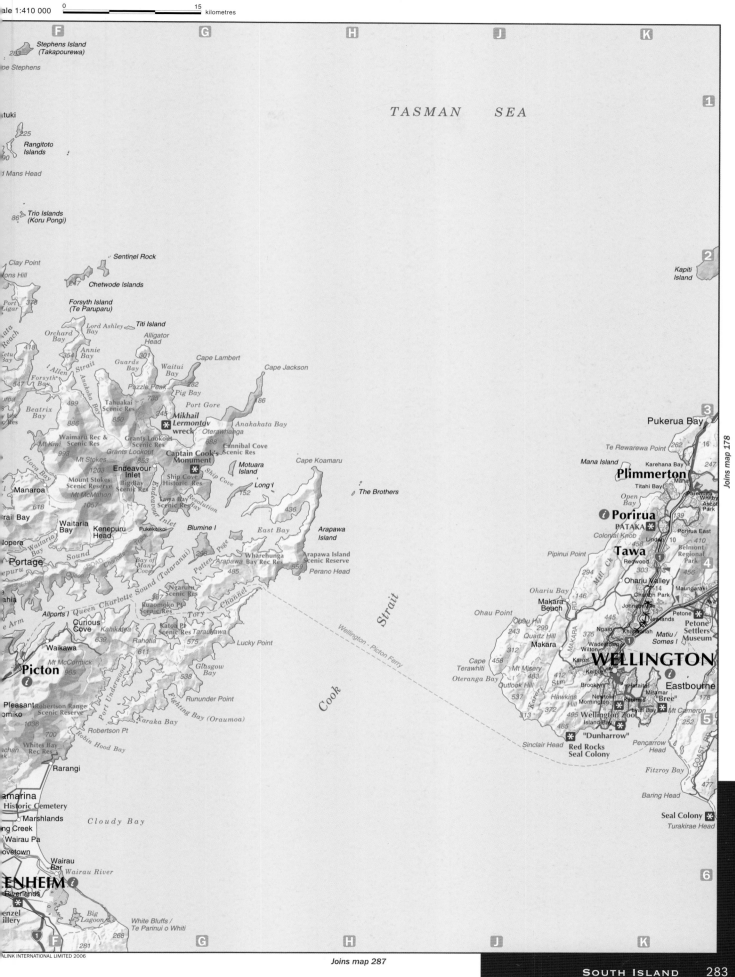

TASMAN SEA

Stephens Island
(Takapourewa)
283
be Stephens

tuki

225

Rangitoto
Islands

90

d Mans Head

Trio Islands
(Koru Pongi)

86

Sentinel Rock

Clay Point
ons Hill
247   Chetwode Islands

Port   378
Ligar
Forsyth Island
(Te Paruparu)

Titi Island

Lord Ashley
Bay
Orchard   354
Bay   Guards   301   Waitui
Annie   Bay   Bay
Reach   Bay
Ketu   au   547   Alligator
Forsyth   Bay   Head
Bay   Puzzle Peak   282   Cape Lambert
uroa   499   Pig Bay   Cape Jackson
Tahuakai   735
Beatrix   Scenic Res   345   Port Gore   186
Bay   850
886   Mikhail
Isle   Lermontov   688   Anakakata Bay
Res   Grants Lookout   wreck   Oterawhanga
Waimaru Rec &   Scenic Res   Captain Cook's
Mt Kiwi   Scenic Res   Monument   Cannibal Cove
993   Grants Lookout   Scenic Res   Cape Koamaru
Mt Stokes   853   Motuara
1203   Endeavour   Island
Manaroa   Mount Stokes   Inlet   Ship Cove   Cape Koamaru
Scenic Reserve   Big Bay   Historic Res
618   Mt McMahon   Scenic Res   The Brothers
1057   Tawa Bay
Waitaria   Kenepuru   Scenic Res   152   Long I
Bay   Head   Pukekoikoi   436
Iopera   Blumine I   East Bay   Arapawa
Portage   Bay of   Island
puru   Many   Patten   Arapawa Island
Coves   Scenic Reserve
hia   Wharehunga   Perano Head
e Arm   587   Ngaruru   Arapawa Bay Rec Res   559
Curious   Scenic Res   485
Cove   Ruamoko Pt   Tory
639   Scenic Res
Kahikatea   Katoa Pt   Channel
Waikawa   Rahotia   Scenic Res Taraukawa   Lucky Point
611   575
Mt McCormick
Picton   965   Glasgow
538   Bay
Rununder Point
Pleasant   Robertson Range
omiko   Scenic Reserve   Fighting Bay (Oraumoa)
1036
700   Karaka Bay
Whites Bay   Robertson Pt
chan   Rec Res   Robin Hood Bay
k
Rarangi

amarina
Historic Cemetery
Marshlands
g Creek   *Cloudy Bay*
Wairau Pa
ovetown
Wairau
ENHEIM   Bar   *Wairau River*
Riverlands
enzel   Big
illery   Lagoon   White Bluffs /
268   Te Parinui o Whiti
281

Pukerua Bay

Te Rewarewa Point   262   16

Mana Island   Karehana Bay   247
Plimmerton   *Mana*
Titahi Bay   *Paromata*
Open   *Whitby*
Bay   *Ascot*
i Porirua   139   *Park*
PATAKA   Porirua East
Colonial Knob   458   10
Pipinui Point   Lindan   410
Tawa   Belmont
Oharíu Bay   146   303   Regional
294   Redwood   Park
Ohariu Valley   456
*Makara   445   Church Park   14
Beach*   Johnsonville   *Newlands*   Maungaraki
Ohau Point   Ngaio   Petone
Ohau Hill   Khandallah   Petone
243   299   375   Wilton   Settlers
Makara   Wadestown   Matiu /   Museum
312   Karori   Somes I
Cape   458   Mt Misery   412   Kelburn
Terawhiti   483   Sim   WELLINGTON
Oteranga Bay   Outlook Hill   Brooklyn   *i*
537   Hataitai   Eastbourne
Hawkins   Newtown   Miramar   "Bree"
513   Hill   372   495   Lyall Bay   Mt Cameron
Wellington Zoo   178
485   Island Bay   252
"Dunharrow"   Pencarrow
Sinclair Head   Red Rocks   Head
Seal Colony   Baring Head

Fitzroy Bay
477

Seal Colony
Turakirae Head

Wellington - Picton Ferry

Cook   Strait

1   2   3   4   5   6

F   G   H   J   K

Joins map 178

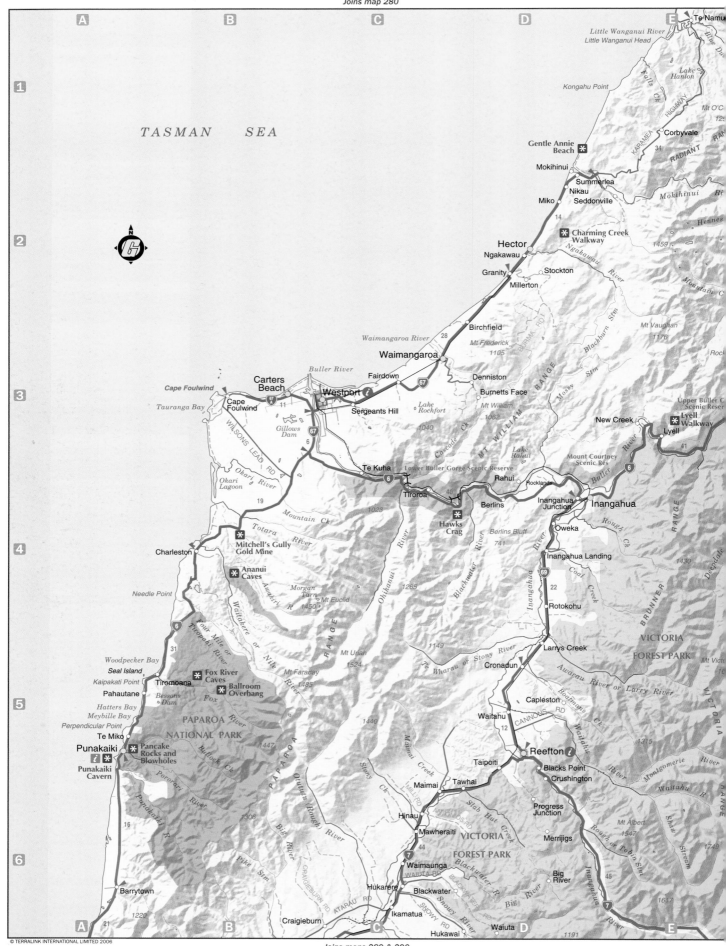

South Island

© TERRALINK INTERNATIONAL LIMITED 2006

Scale 1:410 000

0   15 kilometres

Brightwater

Spring Grove

Wakefield

Tapawera

Rakau

Matariki

Tadmor

Mararewa

Wai-iti

Foxhill

Belgrove

Motupiko

Kohatu

Hiwipango

Korere

Golden Downs

Kaka

Tui

MOUNT RICHMOND FOREST PARK

KAHURANGI NATIONAL PARK

"Dimrill Dale"

Kaka Scenic Res

Atapo

Ben Nevis 1619

Red Hill 1791

Glenhope

Kikiwa

Owen River

Owen Junction

Kawatiri

Howard Junction

Beebys Knob 1442

Six Mile Scenic Res

Gowanbridge

Mt Murchison 1469

Glenhope Scenic Res

Howard

Tophouse

Buller Gorge Swingbridge

Longford

Murchison

Rotoroa

Speargrass

St Arnaud

Lake Rotoiti

Ariki

Mangles Valley

Tutaki

Lake Rotoroa

Glengarry

Maruia Falls

Shenandoah

Six Mile

Rainbow Skifield

Scotts Knob 2160

Matakitaki

Lake Angelus

Angelus Peak 2075

Matakitaki Station

NELSON LAKES NATIONAL PARK

Mt Travers 2338

Burnbrae

Upper Matakitaki

Blue Lake

Mt Franklin 2340

Lake Constance

Lake Thompson

Mt Weld 2114

Fish Lake

Bowscale Tarn

Lake Sedgemere

Island Lake

Warwick Junction

Lake Tennyson

Tarndale

Princess Bath

Maruia

Mt Una 2300

Crimea Creek

Mt Sebastopol 2019

Lake Daniells

Lake Guyon

WESTBANK

SPENCER MOUNTAINS

BODDINGTON RANGE

CRIMEA RANGE

INK INTERNATIONAL LIMITED 2006

Joins maps 280 & 281

Joins map 285

A
B
C
D
E
1
2
3
4
5
6
Mt Gomorrah
1592
960
Wangapeka
River
Devils Thumb
1206
Granity Ck
Dart River
1358
HOPE RANGE
Mt Owen
1875
"Dimrill Dale"
1577
KAHURANGI
NATIONAL PARK
Brewery Ck
Glenhope
1264
Hope River
Kawatiri
Howard
Junction
35
Gowanbridge
1141
Glenhope
Scenic Res
GOWAN VALLEY RD
Gowan River
BRAEBURN
Rotoroa
BRAEBURN RD
Mt Cotton
1256
RANGE
Lake Rotoroa
Mt Hutton
1400
ELLA RANGE
Mt Watson
1871
D'Urville River
MAHANGA RANGE
Sabine R
Mt Ella
2263
Blue Lake
Lake Constance
2196
Lake Thompson
Mt Franklin
2340
Mt Travers
2338
NELSON
NATIONAL PARK
LAKES
TRAVERS
RANGE
2278
Travers River
Lake Angelus
Angelus Peak
2075
MOUNTAINS
SPENCER
Mt Una
2300
2126
Princess Bath
Lake Tennyson
Ada River
Lake Guyon
26
Tapawera
Rakau
Matariki
Tadmor
TADMOR VALLEY RD
Sherry River
Tadmor R
Mararewa
Motupiko
Kohatu
12
Motupiko R
VALLEY ROAD
Korere
Golden Downs
Kaka
Tui
Donald Ck
GLENHOPE RD
TADMOR
Kaka
Scenic Res
6
DRIVE
BUSH
BIG
27
Atapo
Clark River
730
RAINY RIVER RD
KORERE
TOPHOUSE
ROAD
Rainy River
KERR HILL RD
Motueka River
Kikiwa
Cow Ck
Station Ck
Buller River
926
Rainy R
Prospector Ck
26
Howard
Howard R
Maud Creek
Maggie Creek
Speargrass
1030
St Arnaud
Tophouse
63
Lake Rotoiti
Rainbow Skifield
1916
ROAD
ST ARNAUD RANGE
Arnst R
HANMER SPRINGS
WAIRAU
Beebys Knob
1442
Six Mile
Scenic Res
Brightwater
Spring Grove
14
River
Wai-iti
Wakefield
Wai-iti
190
Foxhill
Belgrove
24
Wai-iti R
WAI-ITI VALLEY RD
EIGHTY EIGHT VALLEY RD
Hiwipango
ROAD
STOCK
Wairoa River
676
Wairoa River Right Br
Wairoa River Left Branch
Ben Nevis
1619
1104
1100
1685
Red Hill
1791
Porter Creek
Mt Malita
959
956
Goat Hill
549
516
Mackett Ck
Serpentine R
Mt Stewart
1278
Pelorus R
Fishtail Stm
Hackett Peaks
1438
Mates Ck
1496
RANGE
1528
Lee River
1114
1495
Mt Richmond
1756
MOUNT RICHMOND
FOREST PARK
1538
RICHMOND
Armchair Stm
1309
Mt Rintoul
1731
1643
1514
Top Valley Stm
1086
Te R
1522
Lake Chalice
1225
724
1460
Goulter River
1257
1293
1388
Wairau River
Mt Patriarch
1656
Patriarch
Hille
Birch Hill
Manuka Island
Ngaruru
LEATHAM RD
56
Boundary Ck
Wye River
Mt Phillips
1542
Wye River Reserve
Te Arowhenua
Scenic Res
Leatham
RAGLAN RANGE
Silverstream
Scotts Knob
2160
Branch River
Wairau River
1815
Boulder Stm
Pinnacle
2120
Waihopai River
Spray River
Misery Stm
2059
Blue Mountain
2051
Lees Creek
2189
2205
Rainbow River
Beeby Ck
Judges Ck
Severn R
Severn
2027
Saxton River
Shingle Peak
2089
Castle R
Langridge
Mid
Kennet R
ROAD
Yarra River
2131
AWATERE
VALLEY
Muller
Molesworth
Awatere River
Tone River
2300
Paske Ck
Mt Weld
2114
Fish Lake
Bowscale Tarn
Lake Sedgemere
1617
Island Lake
Wairau River
2167
1789
Cat Ck
Tarndale
Alma River
1928
Turks Head
1958
Lake McRae
Elliott Stm
CRIMEA RANGE
Crimea Creek
Mt Sebastopol
2013
BODDINGTON RANGE
Yarra River
Guide River
Dillon R
Dillon Cone
2173
Clarence River
Tweed R
Gore Stream

Joins maps 290 & 291

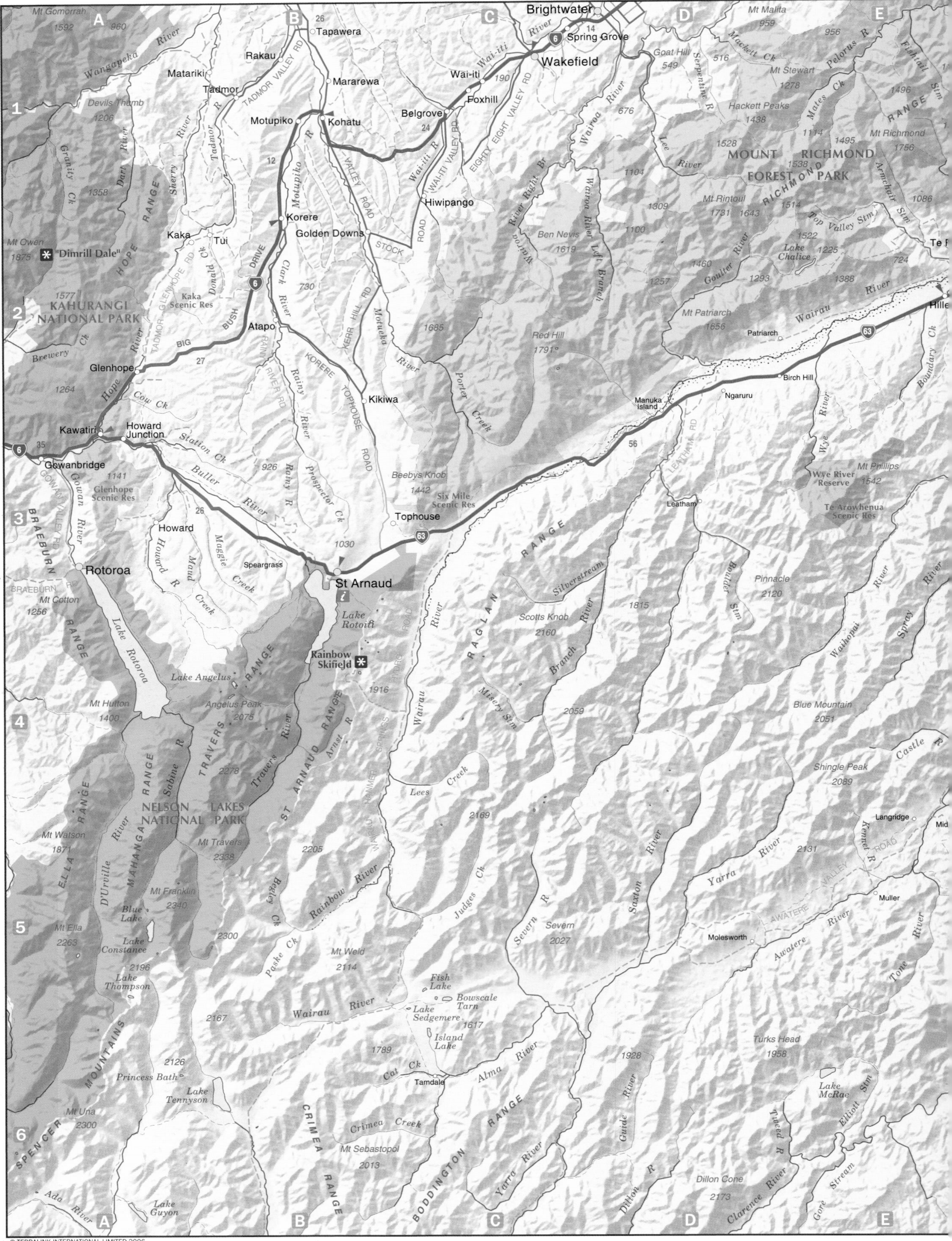

Scale 1:410 000

0   15
kilometres

F **G** **H** **J** **K**

1

Para
Whites Bay
Rec Res
Strachan
Peak
Rarangi
611
22
Cloudy Bay
Tuamarina
✳ Historic Cemetery
Marshlands
Spring Creek
Wairau Pa
Grovetown
Wairau
Bar
Wairau River
Okaramio
31
894
702
685
600
543
436
Rapaura
Woodend
Gardens
BLENHEIM
✳
Mayfield
Riverlands
White Bluffs /
Te Parinui o Whiti
Big
Lagoon
268
281
Renwick
Woodbourne
Fairhall
Redwoodtown
Withenga
✳
Prenzel
Distillery
422
Wairau Valley
63
36
199
173
25
Awatere River
1

2

Craiglochart
The Tummil
Avondale
954
909
645
Lake Jasper
Blairich
River
AWATERE VALLEY RD
Seddon
Blind River
Clifford
Bay

3

Black Birch
Scenic Reserve
Lake
Alexander
1696
1307
Malvern Hills
1670
Altimarlock
Richmond
Brook
Marathon
Downs
Upton
Downs
The Haldons
The Waterfall
Awatere
Valley ✳
MARAMA
Richmond
Lake Grassmere
✳ Saltworks
Lake
Grassmere
Kapara Te Hau
Marfells
Beach ✳
Hauwai
Flaxbourne
Blainch
828
Welds
Hill
Flaxbourne
River
Taimate
20
Lake
Elterwater
Long Point

4

Barometer
1780
Jordan
Camden
Glenlee
Upcot
Grey
River
2011
Blue Mountain
1243
Peggioh
Mirza
368
Ward
Te Rapa
Needles Point
Waima
River
Ben More
1244
Woodside Ck
23
Wharanui
GULCH RD
RUDDS RD

5

2371
Tapuae-o-Uenuku
Tapuaenuku
Scenic Reserve
2885
Clarence Bend
Scenic Res
Peninsula
1247
Ngaio Downs
Parikawa
19
1
Kekerengu
2295

6

SEAWARD
Manakau
2608
Mount Manakau
Scenic Reserve
Mount Uwerau
Nature Res
1502
KAIKOURA RANGE
Clarence
River
1195
Clarence
Clarence River
Waipapa Bay
Okiwi Bay
24
Half Moon Bay
Rakautara
Mangamaunu

PACIFIC

OCEAN

NK INTERNATIONAL LIMITED 2006

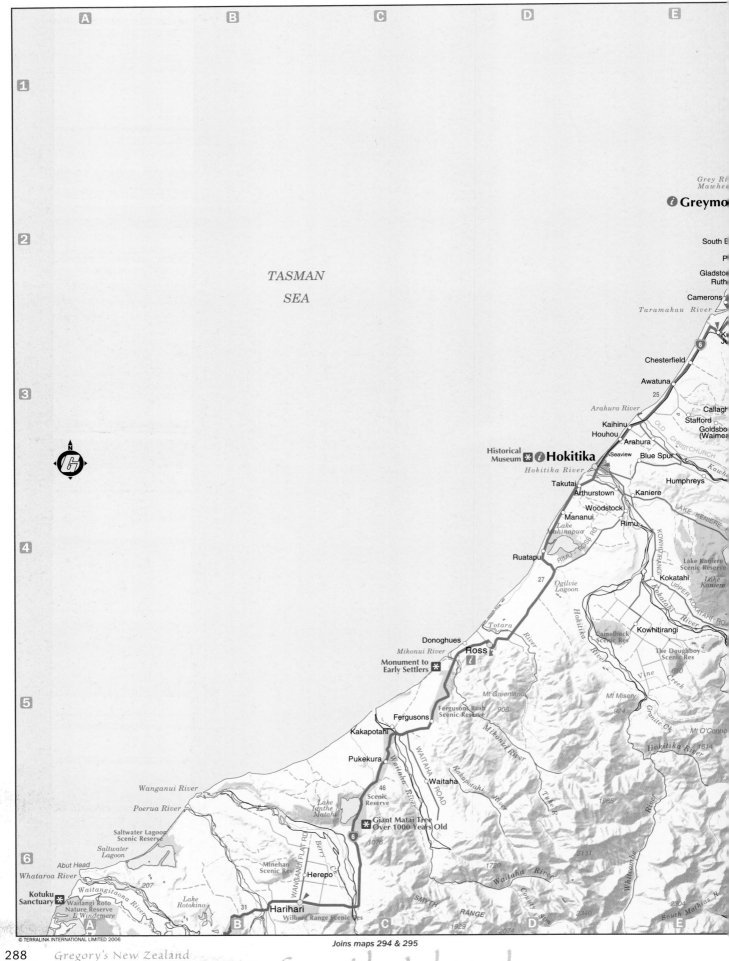

TASMAN

SEA

Grey Ri
Mawhe

ⓘ **Greymo**

South E

Gladsto
Ruth

Camerons

Taramakau River

K
J

Chesterfield

Awatuna

25

Arahura River

Callagh

Kaihinu

Stafford

Houhou

Goldsbo
(Waimea

Arahura

Historical 🎔ⓘ **Hokitika**
Museum

Seaview

Blue Spur

Hokitika River

Takutai

Humphreys

Arthurstown

Kaniere

Woodstock

Mananui

Lake
Mahinapua

Rimu

Ruatapu

Kokatahi

27

Ogilvie
Lagoon

Lake Kaniere
Scenic Reserve

Lake
Kaniere

Kowhitirangi

Camelback
Scenic Res

Totara

The Doughboy
Scenic Res

610

Donoghues

Mikonui River

Ross
ⓘ

Monument to 🎔
Early Settlers

Mt Greenland
905

Mt Misery
924

Mt O'Conno

Fergusons

Fergusons Bush
Scenic Reserve

Mikonui River

Kakapotahi

Hokitika River
1814

Pukekura

Waitaha

Waitaha River

1985

Wanganui River

46
Scenic
Reserve

Giant Matai Tree 🎔
Over 1000 Years Old
6

Kakapotahi River

Tuke R

Poerua River

Lake Ianthe
Matahi

Waitaha River

2340

Saltwater Lagoon
Scenic Reserve

1076

Abut Head

Saltwater
Lagoon

Minehan
Scenic Res

1720

2131

Whataroa River

Herepo

SMYTH

County Str

2504

Waitangitaona River

207

Kotuku 🎔
Sanctuary

Waitangi Roto
Nature Reserve
L Windemere

Lake
Rotokino

31

Harihari

Wilberg Range Scenic Res

RANGE

1929

2074

South Mathias R

© TERRALINK INTERNATIONAL LIMITED 2006

Joins maps 294 & 295

288 *Gregory's New Zealand*

South Island

le 1:410 000
0   15
kilometres

F   G   H   J   VICTORIA   K

1220

Greigs
21
Roa
Blackball
Rapahoe
Rewanui
Dunolile
Brunner Mine
Industrial Site
Brunner
Taylorville
Dobson
Kaiata
Omoto
Boddytown
Kokiri
Kamaka
Notown
Kaimata
Kotuku
Dunganville
Aratika
Moana
Ruru
Te Kinga
Mitchells
Molloy Bay
Carew Bay
Uncle Bay
Inchbonnie
Jacksons
Aickens
Poerua
Rotomanu
Bell Hill

Craigieburn
Slaty Creek
Raupo
Totara Flat
Ikamatua
Hukawai
Waipuna
Nobles

44

Waiuta
FOREST PARK
1191

Inangahua River
7
Mt Kemp
1637

1

LAKE SUMNER
FOREST PARK

1602

1374

1462

1497

2

Mt Hochstetter
1575

582
Lake
Ahaura
839

Kopara
Haupiri
Mt Ajax
1834

1474

Mt Tuke
1723

3

LAKE SUMNER
1729

FOREST PARK

Harper Pass
Track

1815

Otira
1776
30

Temple Basin
Ski Field
Dobson
Monument
Arthur's Pass

ARTHUR'S   PASS   NATIONAL   PARK

Mt Franklin
2146
Lake Sally
Mt Valiant
1847
Lake Mavis

1740

Mt Turnbull
2024

4

Harman
Pass Track
Bealey
Cora Lynn
73
51
1911

Cass

CRAIGIEBURN
FOREST
PARK

Grasmere

Craigieburn
Ski Field
Broken River
Ski Field
Cheeseman
Ski Field
Mount
Olympus
Ski Field

Flock Hill

Cave Stream
Scenic Reserve

Avoca

Craigieburn
1936

Chest Peak

Whistler R

1254

6

NK INTERNATIONAL LIMITED 2006

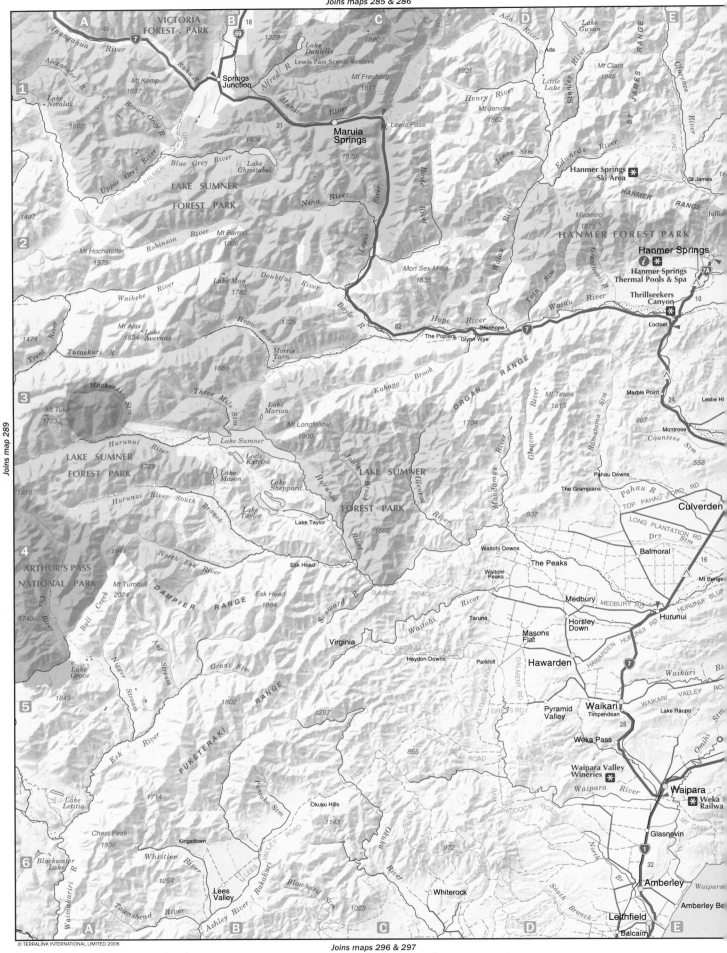

South Island

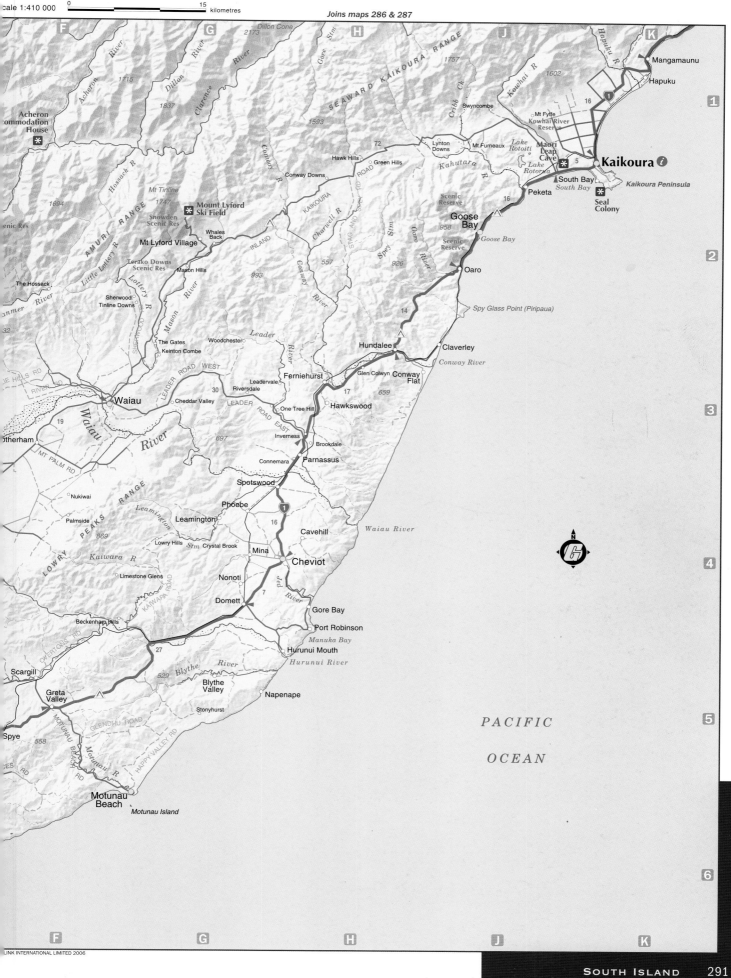

Scale 1:410 000

0   15
kilometres

PACIFIC

OCEAN

LINK INTERNATIONAL LIMITED 2006

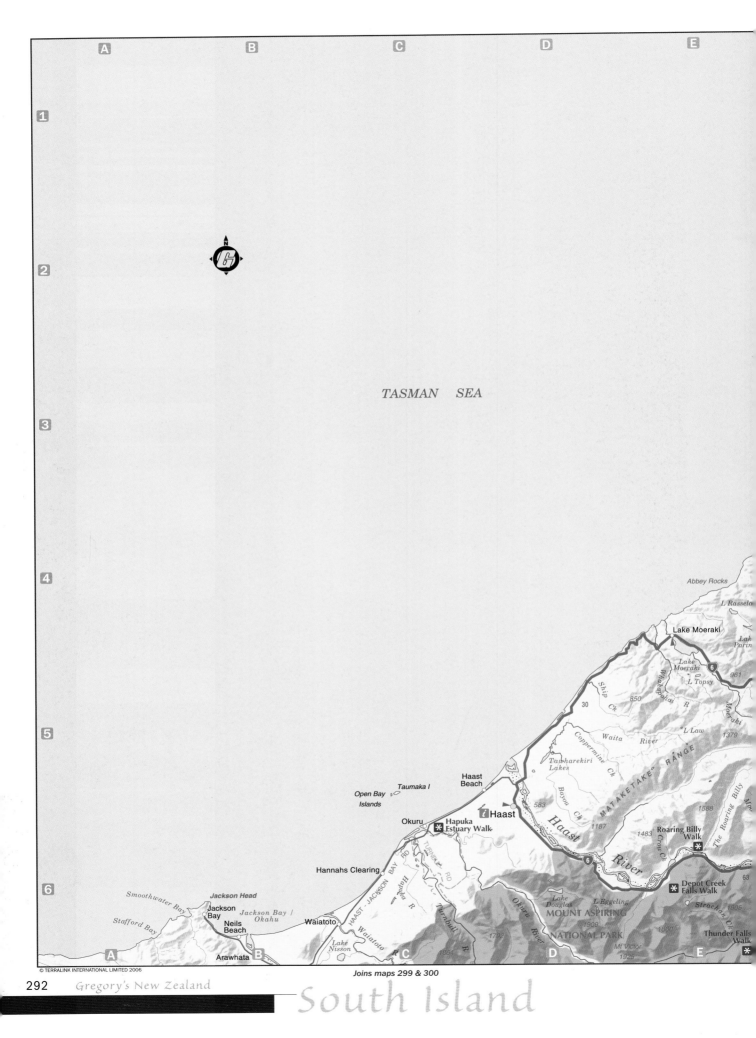

1

2

TASMAN   SEA

3

4

Abbey Rocks

L Rasselas

Lake Moeraki

*Lak
Parin*

*Lake
Moeraki*   6

L Topsy   961

30   850

Ship Ck

5   *Coppermine Ck*

Waita   River   *L Law*

*Tawharekiri
Lakes*   1379

MATAKETAKE RANGE

Haast
Beach

Taumaka I   583   *Bayou Ck*   1588

*Open Bay
Islands*   *Haast*   1483   Roaring Billy
Walk   *The Roaring Billy*

Okuru   Hapuka   1187   ✱

Estuary Walk   *Haast*

6   *River*   63

Hannahs Clearing   6   Depot Creek
Falls Walk   1805

Smoothwater Bay   Jackson Head   ✱   *Strachan Ck*

Jackson   *Jackson Bay /
Okahu*   *Lake
Douglas*   *L Eggeling*

Bay   Neils   Waiatoto   *Okuru*   1800

Stafford Bay   Beach   MOUNT ASPIRING   Thunder Falls

Waiatoto   1909   Walk

Lake   NATIONAL PARK

Nisson   *Turnbull R*   1792

Arawhata   *Mt Victor
1928*   ✱

Joins maps 299 & 300

South Island

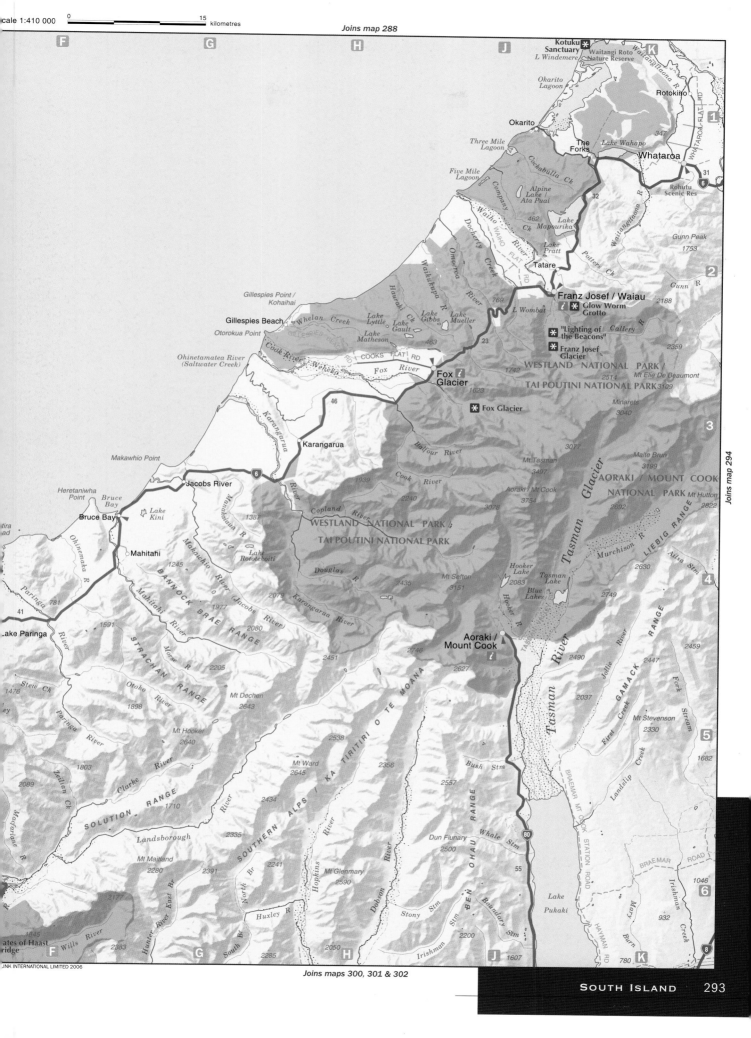

scale 1:410 000

0   15   kilometres

Kotuku
Sanctuary *
L Windemere   Waitangi Roto   Waitangitaona R   K

Okarito
Lagoon   Rotokino   347   1

Okarito   The
Forks   Lake Wahapo   Whataroa

Three Mile
Lagoon   Cockabulla Ck   Whataroa   31

Five Mile
Lagoon   Company   Alpine
Lake
Ata Puai   Lake
Mapourika   32   Rohutu
Scenic Res   6

462
Ck   Waitangitaona R   Gunn Peak
1753

Waiho   Lake
Pratt   Dochery
Creek   WAIHO   L Wombat   Gunn R   2

Gillespies Point /
Kohaihai   Omaroa
River   RD   769   Tatare   Potters Ck   2188

Gillespies Beach   Whelan Creek   Waikukupa R   Lake
Lyttle   Hauraki Ck   Lake
Gibbs   Lake
Mueller   Franz Josef / Waiau   i *   Glow Worm
Grotto

Otorokua Point   GILLESPIES BEACH RD   Lake
Matheson   Lake
Gault   463   23   Callery R   * "Lighting of
the Beacons"

Ohinetamatea River
(Saltwater Creek)   Cook River   Wahela   COOKS   FLAT   RD   1742   * Franz Josef
Glacier   2359

Fox   River   Fox
Glacier   i   1623   WESTLAND NATIONAL PARK /
TAI POUTINI NATIONAL PARK   Mt Elie De Beaumont   2514   3109

46   * Fox Glacier   Balfour River   3077   Minarets
3040

Karangarua   Karangarua   Mt Tasman
3497   Malte Brun
3199   3

Makawhio Point   Cook   River   Aoraki / Mt Cook   AORAKI / MOUNT COOK
NATIONAL PARK   Mt Hutton

Heretaniwha
Point   Bruce
Bay   Lake
Kini   Monakikaua R   1387   1939   River   3754   2692   2822

Bruce Bay   Jacobs River   Copland   River   3078   Murchison R   LIEBIG RANGE   Ailsa Stm

Ohinemaka R   6   Makawhio River (Jacobs River)   Lake
Rototehoiti   2240   2630   2749   4

Mahitahi   1245   Douglas   R   Mt Sefton
3151   Hooker
Lake
2083   Tasman
Lake   GAMACK RANGE

Paringa   781   41   Mahitahi River   2079   Karangarua River   2435   Blue Lakes   Hooker R   2490   2459

Lake Paringa   River   1591   1977   Morse R   2080   Aoraki /
Mount Cook   i   TASMAN   2037   First Creek   Mt Stevenson
2330   1682

Stew Ck   1476   STRACHAN RANGE   Otoko River   1898   Mt Dechen
2643   2451   2746   Tasman River   Mt Hutton   5

2089   Paringa River   1803   Clarke   River   SOLUTION RANGE   1710   Mt Hooker
2640   2627   BRAEMAR MT COOK STATION ROAD   1046

Zellian Ck   Landsborough   2335   Mt Ward
2645   SOUTHERN ALPS / KA TIRITIRI O TE MOANA   2538   2356   BEN OHAU RANGE   80   Landslip Creek   HAYMAN RD   932   6

Macfarlane R   2177   Mt Maitland
2280   2391   North Br   2241   Hopkins   River   Mt Glenmary
2590   2557   Dun Fiunary
2500   Whale Stm   Lake
Pukaki   BRAEMAR ROAD   Irishman
Creek   8

Gates of Haast
bridge   1845   Wills River   2383   South Br   2285   Huxley R   2050   Dobson   River   Stony Stm   2200   Bush Stm   Boundary Stm   55   Irishman Stm   780   1607

LINK INTERNATIONAL LIMITED 2006

Joins map 294

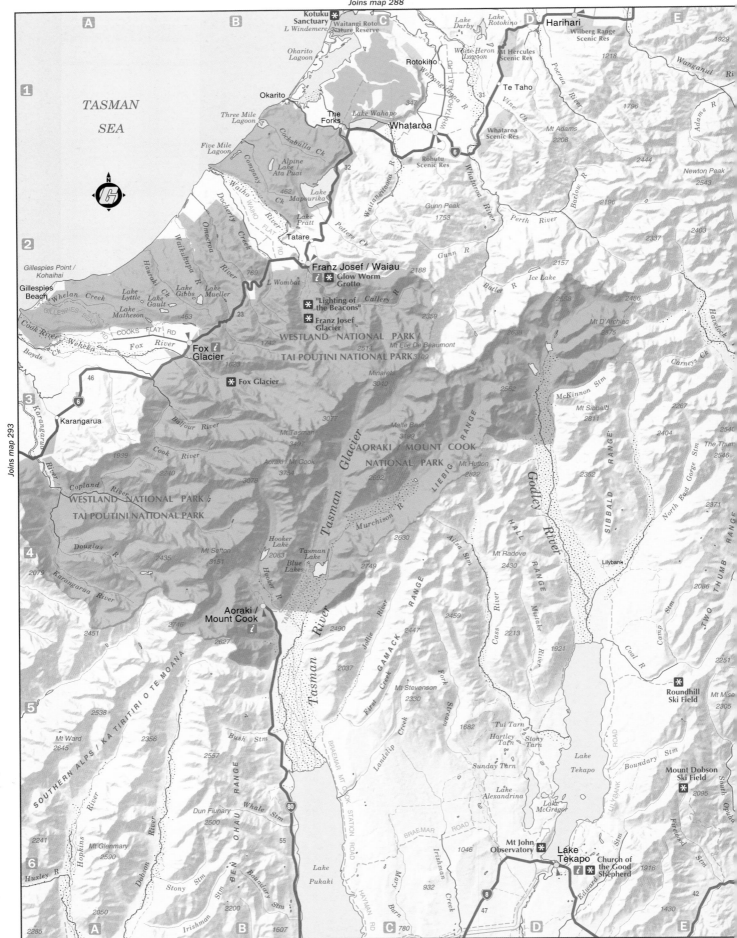

TASMAN
SEA

A · B · C · D · E

1

South Island

© TERRALINK INTERNATIONAL LIMITED 2006

ale 1:410 000

0   15
kilometres

F   G   H   J   K

Mount Olympus Ski Field

Lake Lilian

Harper River

Cave Stream Scenic Reserve *

Mt Ida 1695

Lake Henrietta

Lake Catherine

Lake Ida

Castle Hill Village

Castle Hill Scenic Reserve *

51

County Stm

2340

2304

South Mathias R

Mistake Creek Stm

2209

1633

Mount Algidus

1

2074

Mt Whitcombe 2650

2485

2155

Mathias River

Wilberforce R

Lake Selfe

Lake Evelyn

CRAIGIEBURN

2194

Ryton R

Porter River

Porter Heights Ski Field *

Porters Pass *

2335

R

Rakaia River

DOUBLE HILL RUN ROAD

Lake Coleridge

Lake Georgina

Lake Lyndon

1655

2512

The Warrior 2580

2421

Lake Stream

2087

2114

Lake Coleridge

Acheron R

2

Sinclair R

Lawrence River

2410

Cameron River

Smite River

2085

Ashburton River / Hakatere North Branch

COLERIDGE RD

HIGH PEAK RD

Clyde River

2419

Ashburton R / Hakatere South Br

1598

Lake Heron

Swin R

Mt Hutt 2185

Mount Hutt Ski Area & Bungy *

Windwhistle

77

72

LEACHES ROAD

19

Mount Potts Ski Field *

2184

Boundary Ck

Powerhouse Stm

Mystery Lake

Seagull Lake

Mt Taylor 2533

Manuka Lake

Pudding Hill Scenic Reserve

Awa Awa Rata Reserve *

Mount Hutt

7

BLACKFORD RD

3

"Edoras" *

Erewhon Park

Potts River

HAKATERE

Maori Lakes

Lake Emily

Taylor's Stm

13

9

lack Birch Ck

Lake Clearwater

Spider Lakes

Paddle Hill Ck

HERON ROAD

1700

Bowyers Stm

Sharplin Falls Scenic Res

Alford Forest

RAKAIA GORGE RD

Highbank

Lake Clearwater

Lake Camp

Mt Harper / Mahaanui 1829

Lake Emma

Lake Denny

Blondin Stm

ASHBURTON

1364

Woolshed Ck

Bushside

Staveley

46

Springburn

FORKS ROAD

Methven

BACK METHVEN CHERTSEY RD

Mesopotamia

RANGITATA GORGE

Hewson River

1593

1617

Hinds River (North Branch)

GORGE ROAD

72

Mt Somers

Cavendish

TRAMWAY RD

Buccleuch

Ashburton Forks

Cairnbrae

Lyndhurst

POLE RD

Urrall

4

Rangitata River

ROAD

BEN McLEOD RANGE 1950

1674

Mount Peel Ck

Mt Peel 1743

HINDS GORGE RD

Limestone Ck

Anama

Montalto

Valetta

Punawai

Hackthorne

Westerfield

VALETTA RD

ASHBURTON STAVELEY RD

34

Greenstreet

Winchmore

5

Forest Creek

2001

North Opuha R

Mowbray RD

Orari River

Peel Forest Park

Blandswood

Peel Forest

MOORHOUSE RD

EALING MONTALTO RD

Ruapuna

Mayfield

RD

Lismore

LISMORE MAYFIELD RD

TIMARU TRACK

Lagmhor

FRASERS RD

Ashburton

Plains Historic Railway *

Tinwald

eak ield *

LOCHABER ROAD

Clayton

1653

Orari River

72

CRACROFT

28

MARONAN RD

Maronan

Winslow

MARONAN ROAD

18

Sherwood Downs

MIDDLE RD

Opuha Lake

1587

Tripp Settlement

PEEL FOREST RD

Carew

TREVORS RD

EALING RD

Hinds

Windermere

BOUNDARY RD

Willowby

Huntingdon

Flemington

Eiffelton

6

Ashwick Flat

1169

Griffiths Stm

Waihi River

WOODBURY RD

Four Peaks

Woodbury

Coopers Creek

Arundel

ARUNDEL RD

Ealing

18

1

SURVEYORS RD

LONGBEACH RD

POPULAR ROAD

Waterton

Trentham

79

Cattle Valley

858

Te Moana

Orari Bridge

79

15

Rangitata

Rangitata R

ISLEWORTH RD

Allandale

Pleasant Valley

Geraldine Downs

Geraldine

Joins map 303

F   G   H   J   K

NK INTERNATIONAL LIMITED 2006

Joins map 296

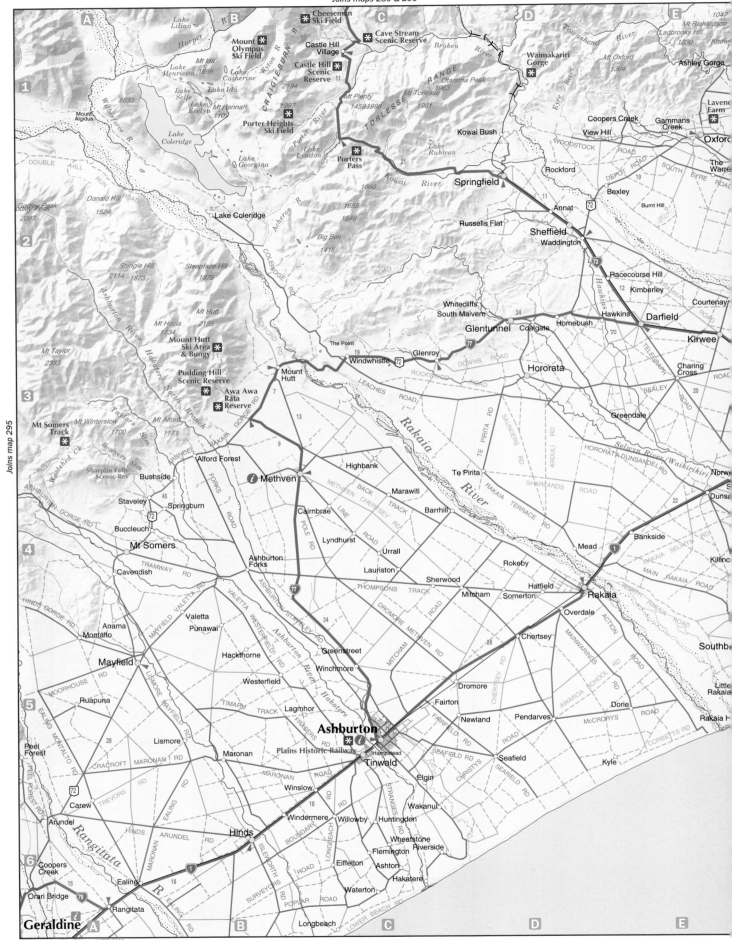

South Island

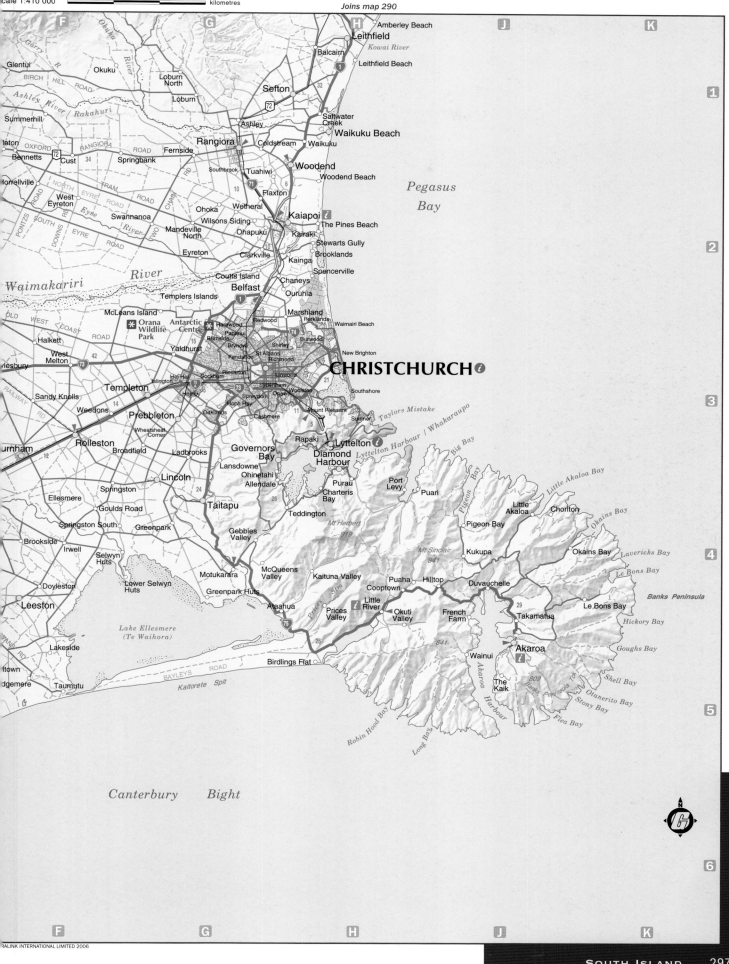

0   15   kilometres

F   **G**   **H**   **J**   **K**

Amberley Beach
Leithfield
Balcairn
Kowai River
Leithfield Beach

Glentui
Okuku
Loburn North
Loburn
Sefton

BIRCH HILL ROAD
Summerhill
Ashley River / Rakahuri

Saltwater Creek
Waikuku Beach

...ton OXFORD ROAD
Bennetts
Cust
Springbank
Fernside
Rangiora
Coldstream
Waikuku

RANGIORA ROAD

Woodend
Woodend Beach

Pegasus Bay

Morrellville
West Eyreton
Southbrook
Tuahiwi
Flaxton

Eyre River
Swannanoa
Mandeville North
Ohoka
Wetheral
Wilsons Siding
Ohapuku

Kaiapoi
The Pines Beach
Kairaki
Stewarts Gully

Eyreton
Clarkville
Kainga
Brooklands

Waimakariri
River
Coutts Island
Chaneys
Spencerville

Belfast
Ouruhia

Templers Islands
Marshland
Waimairi Beach

McLeans Island
Orana Wildlife Park
Antarctic Centre
Harewood
Redwood
Parklands

Halkett
Yaldhurst
Papanui
Bromley
Burwood

West Melton
Fendalton
St Albans
Shirley
Richmond
New Brighton

Templeton
Islington
Sockburn
Riccarton
Linwood

CHRISTCHURCH

Sandy Knolls
Hornby
Sydenham
Opawa
Woolston
Southshore

Weedons
Hei Hei
Spreydon

Prebbleton
Oaklands
Cashmere
Mount Pleasant
Sumner
Taylors Mistake

Rolleston
Wheatsheaf Corner
Rapaki
Lyttelton

Broadfield
Ladbrooks
Governors Bay
Diamond Harbour
Lyttelton Harbour / Whakaraupo
Big Bay

...rnham
Lincoln
Lansdowne
Ohinetahi
Allendale
Purau
Port Levy
Puari
Pigeon Bay
Little Akaloa Bay

Springston
Taitapu
Teddington
Charteris Bay
Little Akaloa
Chorlton
Okains Bay

Ellesmere
Goulds Road
Greenpark
Mt Herbert
919
Pigeon Bay
Okains Bay
Lavericks Bay

Springston South
Mt Sinclair
841
Kukupa
Le Bons Bay

Brookside
Irwell
Selwyn Huts
Motukarara
McQueens Valley
Kaituna Valley
Puaha
Hilltop
Duvauchelle
Le Bons Bay
Banks Peninsula

Doyleston
Lower Selwyn Huts
Greenpark Huts
Cooptown
Little River
French Farm
Hickory Bay

Leeston
Ataahua
Prices Valley
Okuti Valley
Takamatua
Le Bons Bay

Lake Ellesmere (Te Waihora)
Wainui
Akaroa
Goughs Bay

Lakeside
841
The Kaik
809
Shell Bay

...town
...dgemere
Taumutu
Birdlings Flat
Banks Peninsula Tra
Otanerito Bay
Stony Bay
Flea Bay

BAYLEYS ROAD
Kaitorete Spit

Robin Hood Bay
Long Bay

Canterbury   *Bight*

1
2
3
4
5
6

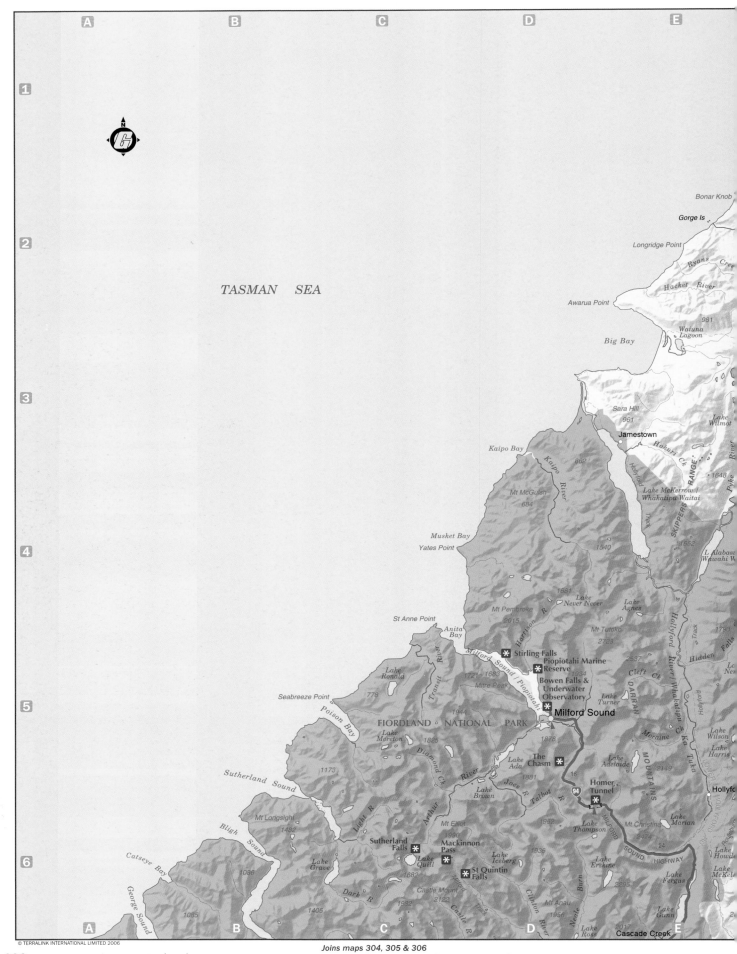

TASMAN SEA

Bonar Knob

Gorge Is

Longridge Point

Ryans Creek

Awarua Point

Hacket River

981

Big Bay

Waiuna Lagoon

Sara Hill
961

Jamestown

Lake Wilmot

Kaipo Bay

Kaipo River

862

Hokuri Ck

Lake McKerrow / Whakatipu Waitai

SKIPPERS RANGE

1648

Mt McGulsh
684

1540

1552

L Alabast Wawahi W

Pyke River

Musket Bay

Yates Point

1661

Lake Never Never

Lake Agnes

Mt Pembroke
2015

Harrison R

Mt Tutoko
2703

1793

St Anne Point

Anita Bay

Milford Sound / Piopiotahi

Stirling Falls

Piopiotahi Marine Reserve

Hidden

Lo Ne

Lake Ronald

Transit River

1934

Cleft Ck

2537

DARRAN

Hollyford River / Whakatipu Ka Tuka

Bowen Falls & Underwater Observatory

Lake Turner

Seabreeze Point

Poison Bay

779

1721 1683

Mitre Peak

Milford Sound

1944

1878

Moraine Ck

MOUNTAINS

2149

Lake Wilson

Lake Harris

FIORDLAND   NATIONAL   PARK

Lake Moreton

1825

Diamond Ck

Lake Ada

1881

The Chasm

Lake Adelaide

Sutherland Sound

1173

River

Joes R

16

Homer Tunnel

Lake Brown

Talbot R

94

Mt Longsight
1482

Light R

Arthur R

Mt Elliot
1990

1962

Lake Thompson

Mt Christina
2474

Lake Marian

Bligh Sound

Sutherland Falls

Lake Quill

Mackinnon Pass

Lake Iceberg

1936

Lake Erskine

MILFORD SOUND

24

HIGHWAY

Hollyfo

Catseye Bay

1086

Lake Grave

1682

St Quintin Falls

Lake Fergus

Lake Howde

Lake McKel

George Sound

Dark R

Castle Mount
3122

Castle R

Clinton River

Mt Anau
1956

2295

Lake Gunn

1085

1405

1933

Neale Burn

Lake Ross

201

Lake

Cascade Creek

0   15

kilometres

Neils Beach

Arawhata

Cascade Point

Lake Jumbuck

Duncan Creek

Stafford River

L Mary

L Greaney

Lake Ellery

Lake Nisson

Mt Victor 1925

Mt Victor

Okaru

River

Mueller

Selborne Range

Disappearing Lake

993

Jackson River

1189

Lake Clarke

L Leeb

L Dan

L Bux

1476

1753

1708

Te Naihi River

1864

1862

Ngatau River

North Branch

2192

South Branch

1934

1946

Young River

Smiths Ponds

852

Delta Tarn

719

1148

Theta Tarn

1271

Joe Peak 1927

Arcade Ck

Retreat Ck

1951

1605

1918

McArthur Ck

Arawhata River

Thomson Ck

1683

Waipara

1374

River

Fingals Head 1986

Cloudmaker Lake

2352

Waiatoto River

Drake River

MOUNT ASPIRING NATIONAL PARK

Mt Alba 2360

Mt Pollux 2596

Lucidus Lake

L Castalia

Newland Stm

Siberia Stm

2093

2035

2150

2127

Wilkin River

Mt Jumbo 1945

1914

Craigie Burn

2064

Albert Burn

MAKARORA

i Makarora

15

6

3

OLIVINE RANGE

Eros Ck

2266

Mt Aspiring / Tititea 3033

2165

2193

1972

Estuary Burn

46

Lake Wanaka

Ark 2291

Jow River

2448

Mt Edward 2620

2252

2644

Rob Roy Glacier

*

Rob Roy Track *

Rob Roy Stm

Matukituki River East Branch

Minaret Burn

2193

Mt Alta 2339

1653

4

2004

MOUNT ASPIRING NATIONAL PARK

BARRIER RANGE

2353

McBride Burn

Te Awa Whakatipu

Dart River

Rees - Dart Track

Matukituki River West Branch

Mount Aspiring

2240

Black Peak 2289

2100

2058

Treble Cone

* Treble Cone Ski Field

"South of Rivendell" *

West Wanaka

Bishops Bay

12

6

Albert Town

3

84

6

5

Beans Burn

2252

Hunter Ck

Mt Earnslaw / Pikirakatahi 2630

2510

Snowy Ck

Lochnagar

Shotover River

2202

Shiel Burn

Polnoon Burn

Harris Creek

Blue Mountains

Mt Motatapu 2030

Motatapu River

Roys Burn

21

Glendhu Bay

Rippon Vineyard *

Wanaka

i

Puzzling World *

Spotts Ck

Quartz Ck

Lake Unknown

1940

Lake Sylvan

"Lothlorien" "Amon Hen" *

1875

Earnslaw Burn

Rees River

Invincible Ck

Robertson Ck

2525

Centaur Peaks

Flood Burn

2055

Arrow River

Mt Cardrona 1936

Fern Burn

1837

Branch Burn

Cardrona River

Luggate Creek

1408

Rock Burn

"Isengard" *

Paradise

Diamond Lake 1375

Mt Aurum 2245

Mount Aurum Reserve

"Ford of Bruinen" *

Skippers

Bridal Veil Falls *

Macetown

Old Mining Town of Macetown *

1752

Cardrona Skifield *

Cardrona Valley *

25

CARDRONA VALLEY

Mt Bonpland 2348

Kinloch

Twelve Mile Ck or Ox Burn

2066

Skippers Ck

Stony Creek

Skippers Canyon *

Deep Creek

1809

"Ford of Bruinen" *

"Gladden Fields" *

Cardrona

CROWN RANGE RD

Roaring Meg

Kirtle Burn

PISA RANGE

1691

HUMBOLDT MOUNTAINS

Lake Wakatipu

45

Glenorchy *i*

Mt Larkins 2300

1787

RICHARDSON MOUNTAINS

Shotover River

Skippers Rd

Pigeon I

Caples River

Caples Track

F   G   H   J   K

1   2   3   4   5   6

Joins map 299

MOUNT ASPIRING
NATIONAL PARK

MOUNT ASPIRING
NATIONAL PARK

Rob Roy
Glacier

Rob Roy
Track

Mount
Aspiring

Treble Cone
Ski Field

"South of
Riverdell"

West
Wanaka

Bishops
Bay

Makarora

Boundary Creek
Scenic Res

Lake
Wanaka

Lake
Hawea

Gates of Haast
Bridge

Thunder Falls
Walk

Fantail Falls
Walk

Gladstone

Lake Hawea

Hawea Flat

Maungawera

Lagoon Valley

Rippon
Vineyard

Albert
Town

Glendhu
Bay

Wanaka

Puzzling
World

Warbirds
Museum

Luggate

Tarras

Queensberry

Waiorau
Snow Farm

Lake McKay

Locharburn
Scenic Res

"Flight to the Fo
"Great East Roa

Ardgour

"Ford of
Bruinen"

Skippers

Bridal
Veil Falls

Macetown
Old Mining
Town of
Macetown

Cardrona
Ski Field

Cardrona
Valley

Cardrona

Mount Pisa

Lindis
Crossing

Abandoned
Gold Towns

Bendigo

Crippletown

Bendigo
Scenic Res

Bendigo
Historic Res

Skippers
Canyon

Mt Larkins
2300

"Ford of
Bruinen"

"Gladden
Fields"

South Island

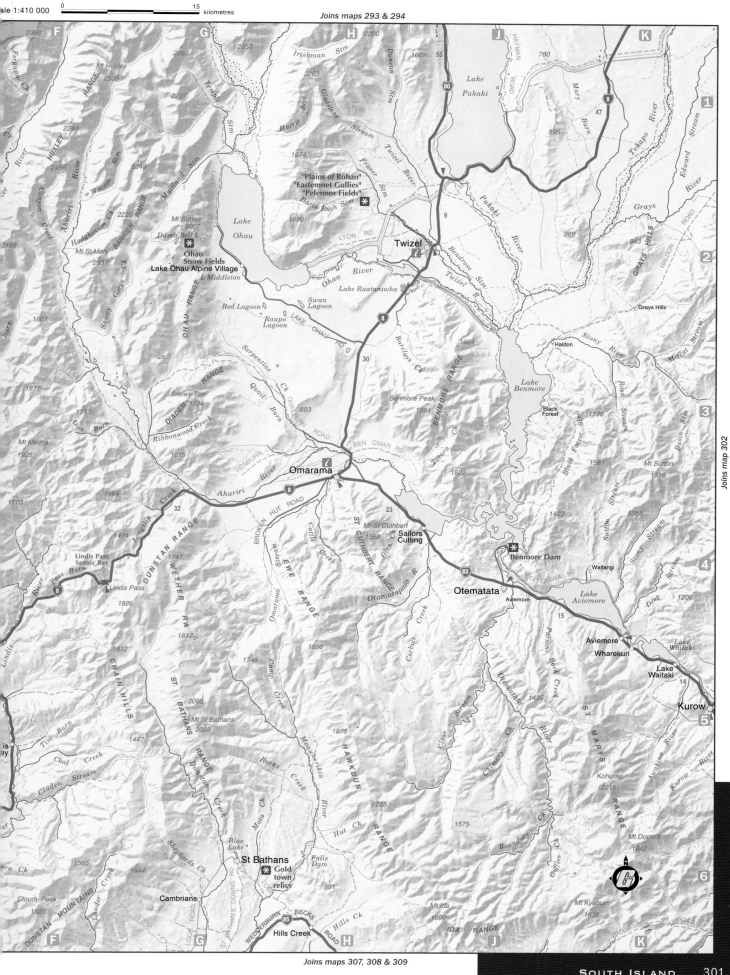

ale 1:410 000

0   15 kilometres

F   G   H   J   K

"Plains of Rohan"
"Eastemnet Gullies"
"Pelennor Fields" *

Twizel i

Mt Sutton
2007
Dumb-Bell L
Ohau
Snow Fields
Lake Ohau Alpine Village

Lake
Ohau

Lindis Pass
Scenic Res

Lindis Pass

Omarama i

Benmore Dam *

Otematata

Aviemore
Wharekuri

Kurow

St Bathans *
Gold
town
relics

Cambrians

Hills Creek

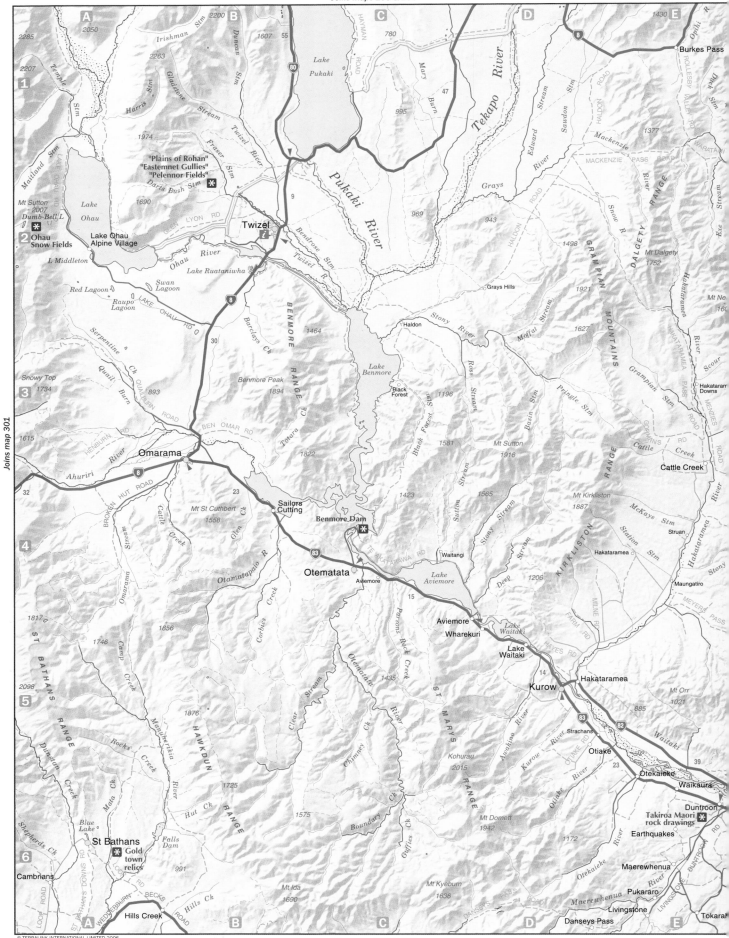

Joins map 301

© TERRALINK INTERNATIONAL LIMITED 2006

302   *Gregory's New Zealand*

South Island

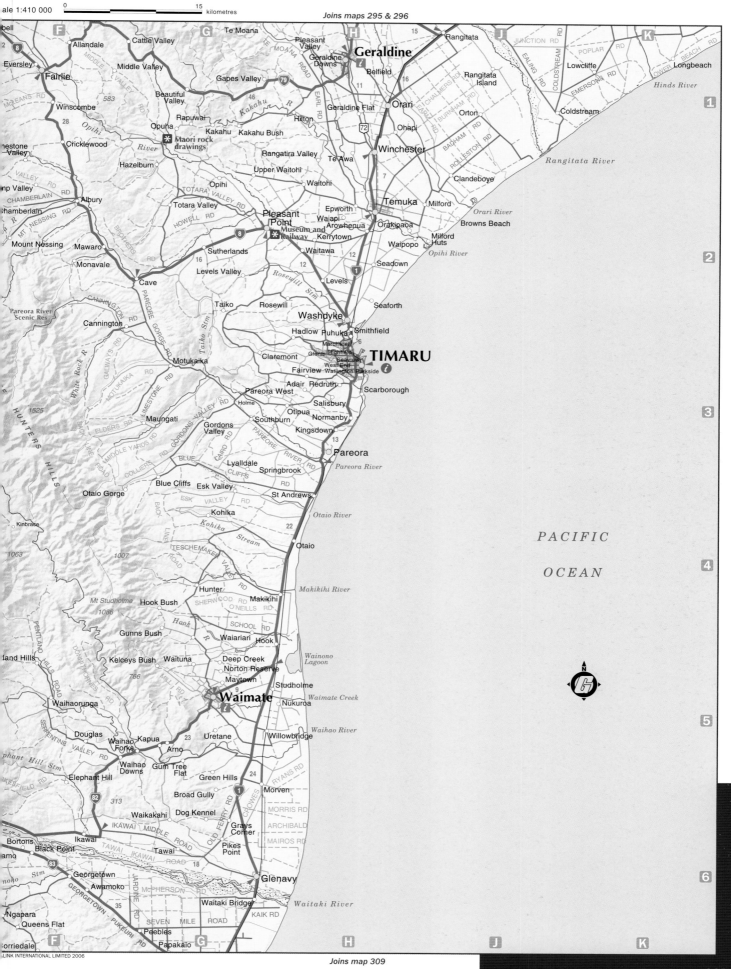

ale 1:410 000

0   15

kilometres

F   **G**   **H**   **J**   **K**

15

Rangitata

Te Moana

Pleasant Valley

Geraldine

Geraldine Downs

Belfield

Rangitata Island

JUNCTION RD

Lowcliffe

Longbeach

POPLAR RD

LOWER BEACH RD

COLDSTREAM RD

EALING RD

Hinds River

Allandale

Cattle Valley

Middle Valley

Gapes Valley

79

46

Fairlie

Winscombe

583

Beautiful Valley

Rapuwai

Kakahu R

Hilton

Geraldine Flat

11

16

Orari

72

Orton

BURNHAM RD

Coldstream

Rangitata

BADHAM RD

28

Opuha

Kakahu

Kakahu Bush

Ohapi

Rangitata River

1

Cricklewood

Opihi River

Maori rock drawings

Winchester

ROLLESTON RD

Hazelburn

Rangatira Valley

Te Awa

7

Clandeboye

CHAMBERLAIN RD

Upper Waitohi

Waitohi

Totara Valley

Opihi

Temuka

Milford

Orari River

Albury

Totara Valley

Epworth

Arowhenua

Browns Beach

TOTARA VALLEY RD

Pleasant Point

Waiapi

Orakipaoa

Mount Nessing

HOWELL RD

Museum and Railway

Kerrytown

Milford Huts

MT NESSING RD

Mawaro

16

Sutherlands

Waitawa

Waipopo

Monavale

Levels Valley

12

Opihi River

2

BROTHERS RD

Cave

12

Levels

Seadown

PAREORA GORGE RD

Rosewill Stm

8

Taiko

Rosewill

Seaforth

Pareora River Scenic Res

CANNINGTON RD

Cannington

Washdyke

Smithfield

Taiko Stm

Hadlow

Puhuka

Claremont

Marchwiel

TIMARU

Glandi Highfield

Motukaika

Seaview

LIMESTONE RD

Fairview

West End

Watlington

Parkside

1525

HUNTERS HILLS

GALWAYS RD

Sutherlands

Pareora West

Holme

Adair

Redruth

Scarborough

MOTUKAIKA RD

Gordons Valley

Southburn

Otipua

Salisbury

3

ELDERS RD

MIDDLE YARDS RD

COLLIERS RD

Maungati

Normanby

CARD RD

Kingsdown

13

BLUE CLIFFS

Lyalldale

Springbrook

PAREORA RIVER RD

Pareora

Blue Cliffs

Esk Valley

Pareora River

Otaio Gorge

ESK VALLEY RD

St Andrews

BACK LINE ROAD

Kohika

Kohika Stream

22

Otaio River

PACIFIC

1063

1007

TESCHEMAKERS ROAD

Otaio

OCEAN

4

Kinbrace

Makikihi River

Hunter

SHERWOOD RD

Makikihi

Mt Studholme

Hook Bush

O'NEILLS RD

1086

Hook R

SCHOOL RD

Hook

Gunns Bush

Waiariari

Wainono Lagoon

Kelceys Bush

Waituna

Deep Creek

PENTLAND HILLS ROAD

766

Norton Reserve

land Hills

Maytown

N

Waihaorunga

9

Studholme

Waimate Creek

Waimate

Nukuroa

5

DONKEY RD

Douglas

Kapua

23

Uretane

Waihao River

MILL RD

Waihao Forks

Arno

Willowbridge

SERPENTINE VALLEY RD

Waihao Downs

Gum Tree Flat

Green Hills

24

RYANS RD

phant Hill Stm

Elephant Hill

1

Morven

82

313

Broad Gully

MORRIS RD

kesfield RD

Waikakahi

Dog Kennel

Grays Corner

ARCHIBALD RD

OLD FERRY RD

MAIROS RD

CROMES RD

Bortons

Ikawai

Tawai

Pikes Point

Black Point

83

IKAWAI MIDDLE ROAD

18

arno

Georgetown

Stm

Awamoko

Glenavy

6

noho

35

SEVEN MILE ROAD

Waitaki Bridge

JARDINE RD

McPHERSON RD

Ngapara

Queens Flat

Peebles

Papakaio

KAIK RD

Waitaki River

GEORGETOWN - PUKEURI RD

orriedale

F   **G**   **H**   **J**   **K**

LINK INTERNATIONAL LIMITED 2006

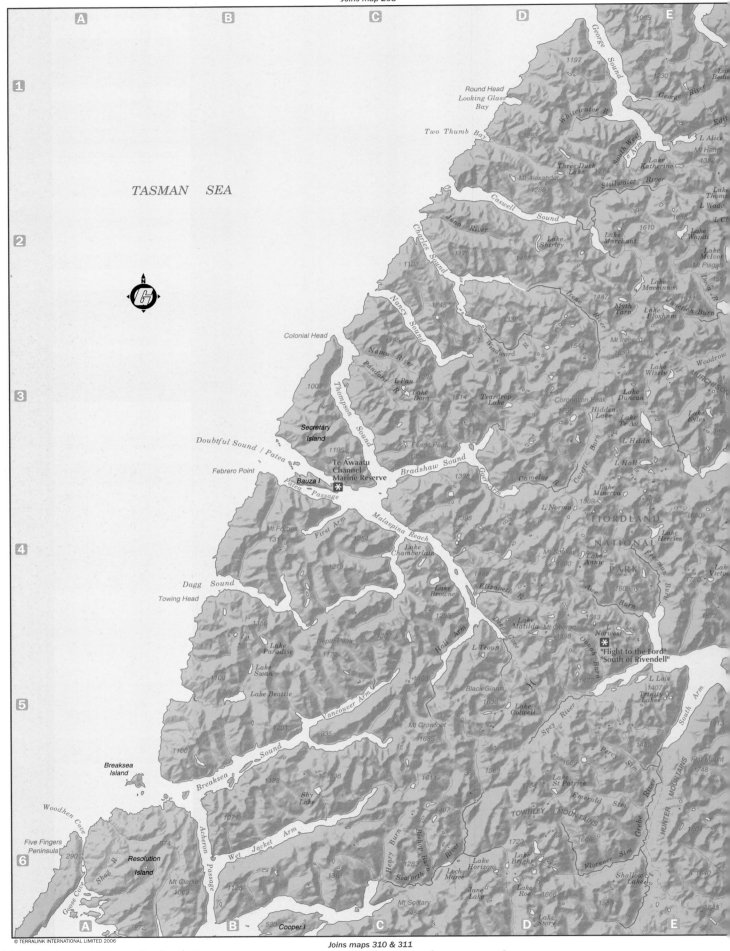

TASMAN SEA

© TERRALINK INTERNATIONAL LIMITED 2006

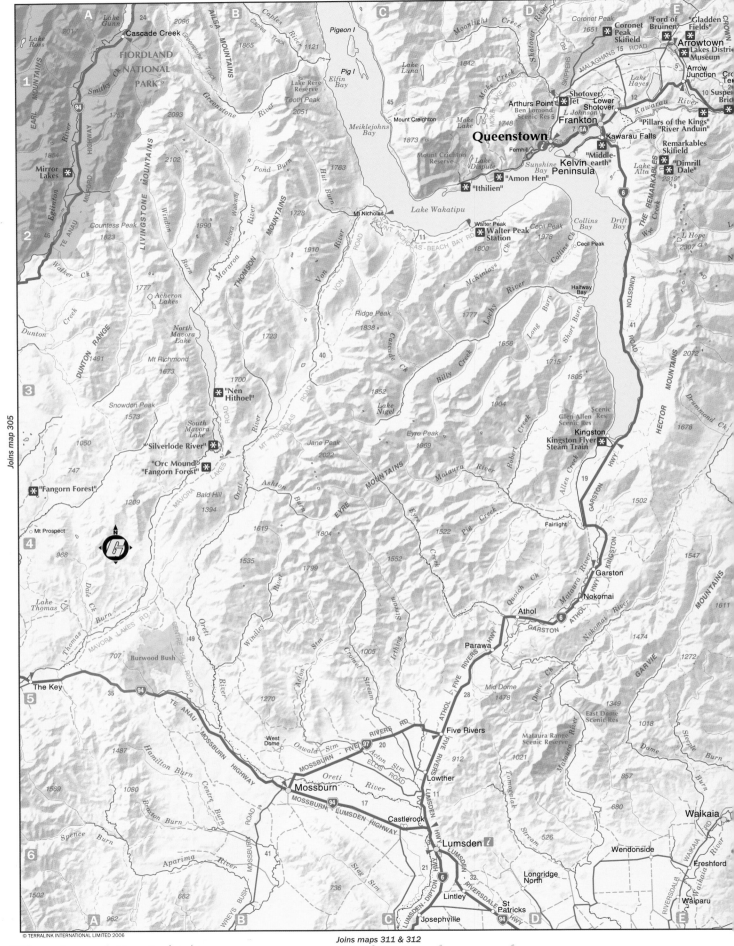

South Island

Joins map 305

Scale 1:410 000

0   15 kilometres

F G H J K

Mount Pisa

42

LUGGATE - CROMWELL RD

Bendigo
Crippletown
Bendigo
Historic Res
Bendigo
Scenic Res

Abandoned Gold Towns

Lowburn

1691

Roaring Meg or Kirtle Burn

Cardrona River

Devils Creek

1163

DUNSTAN MOUNTAINS

GORGE ROAD

Thomsons Ck

Beggs Ck

Lauder RD

Hills Creek

BECKS

40

WEDDERBURN

Becks

Drybread

Matakanui

GLASSFORD RD

Oturehua

85

'Brass Monkey' Motorbike Rally Site

LOOP RD

Goldfields Mining Centre

Gibbston

6

Waitiri 1285

Kawarau Gorge

Cromwell Chafer Beetle Nature Reserve

Ripponvale

6

8B

Cromwell i

Quartz Reef Ck

Dunstan 1668

Neds Creek

RACECOURSE RD

MUDDY CREEK RD

BECKS LAUDER RD

Ida Valley

Auripo

Idaburn Dam

971

Lauder

1

Kawarau R.

Nevis River

1312

Carricktown

Bannockburn

Waenga

CROMWELL

22

CLYDE

Lake Dunstan

1130

Waikerikeri

CHATTO CREEK - SPRINGVALE RD

Chatto Ck

Omakau

Ophir

85

Poolburn

RAGGEDY RANGE

39

1060

2

Nevis Crossing

Abandoned Gold Fields

Lower Nevis

1607

Coal Ck

1749

OLD WOMAN RANGE

Omeo Ck

Campbell Ck

ROAD

Fraser Dam

Earnscleugh or Fraser R.

Clyde Dam

Clyde

11

Muttontown

Earnscleugh

Earnscleugh Flat Tailings

Blackmans

Conroys Gully

Conroys Dam

Alexandra i

Bridge Hill

Springvale

Galloway

CRAWFORD HILLS ROAD

Curling & Ice Skating

661

Manor Creek

779

Dip Ck

Manuherikia R.

27

POOLBURN - MOA CREEK RD

UPPER MANORBURN RD

Moa Creek

Dovedale Creek

Maori Creek

1024

'Plains of Rohan' 'Rohirrim Village'

ROUGH RIDGE

PUKETOI RUNS

Stony Ck

Totara

1176

3

Obelisk 1695

Butchers Ck

Butchers Gully

Little Valley

32

ALEXANDRA - FRUITLANDS RD

Fruitlands

Shanty Ck

Lake Roxburgh

Gorge Creek

Miners Monument

Tawhiti

Coal Ck

1673

938

KNOBBY RANGE

1004

Little Valley Creek

Hopes Creek

Bickerstaffe Creek

822

Manorburn Reservoir

Greenland Reservoir

Deep Ck

1081

Serpentine Reserve

Serpentine Ck

Linn Burn

Waimonga Ck

Loganbrae 1013

4

1869

Waikaia River

West Branch

Rocky Mount 1885

Garvie Creek

East Branch

Potters

1366

FRUITLANDS - ROXBURGH RD

Shingle Creek

Washpool Ck

1440

Lake Roxburgh

Roxburgh Dam

Coal Creek Flat

8

Pinelheugh 1124

1127

1015

5

1254

Waikaia River

Whitcoomb 1455

UMBRELLA MOUNTAINS

Leithen Burn

ROAD

Bullock Ck

Roxburgh i

8

Dumbarton

12

Teviot

Roxburgh East

Teviot River

595

Tima Burn

977

Lake Onslow

Boundary Ck

Fortification Ck

LAMMERLAW RANGE

1210

1132

Te Papanui Conservation Park

1159

Deep Ck

750

5

1156

Sandy Ck

731

MOA FLAT ROAD

Benger Burn

Benger Burn Sth Br

Ettrick

Millers Flat

Clutha Mata-Au River

21

Gibbons Ck

726

Talla Burn

Rigney

Lonely Graves Historic Reserve

Beaumont Station

Craig Flat

Beaumont River

590

979

Lammerlaw Stm

Lake Mahinerangi

Waipori

6

751

845

Arais Burn

Pomahaka River

Tuapeka River

1107

Leithen Bush Scenic Res

1254

Thomsons Ck

WILDEN RUNS RD

Wilden

Spylaw Burn

596

Spylaw Burn

Dunrobin

SWITZERS ROAD

Park Hill

612

Heriot

Mathesons Corner

Edievale

29

Anguilla Burn

675

Mata-Au River

Raes Junction

90

BEAUMONT HIGHWAY

Beaumont

8

26

Craigellachie

Waipori River

687

Pioneer Stream Historic Res

Waipori

F G H J K

NK INTERNATIONAL LIMITED 2006

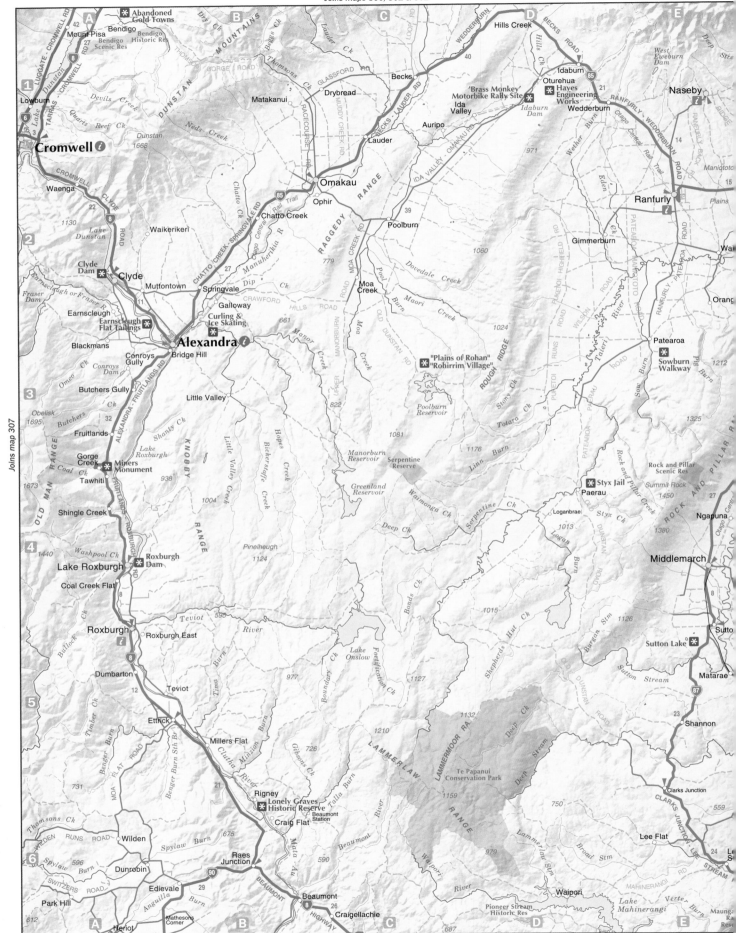

South Island

© TERRALINK INTERNATIONAL LIMITED 2006

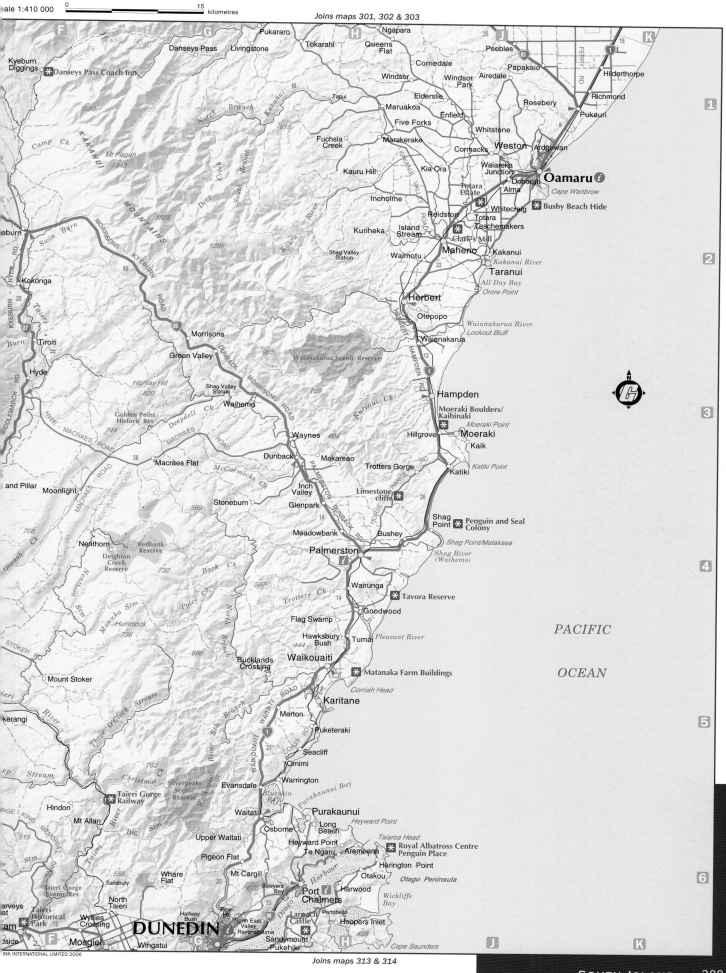

Scale 1:410 000

0   15
kilometres

F   G   H   J   K

1

Kyeburn
Diggings
* Danseys Pass Coach Inn

Danseys Pass   Livingstone   Pukararo

Tokarahi

Ngapara

Queens
Flat

Peebles

Papakaio

Hilderthorpe

Corriedale

Windsor

Windsor
Park

Airedale

Roseberry

Richmond

Pukeuri

Tapui

Elderslie

Maruakoa

Enfield

Whitstone

Mt Pisgah
1643

Fuchsia
Creek

Marakerake

Cormacks

Weston   Ardgowan

Kauru Hill

Kia Ora

Waiareka
Junction

Oamaru ⓘ

Cape Wanbrow

Kyeburn

Camp Ck

Kokonga

Incholme

Totara
Estate

Deborah
Alma

* Bushy Beach Hide

Kuriheka

Island
Stream

Reidston

Whitecraig

Totara
Teschemakers

2

Swin Burn

Shag Valley
Station

Waimotu

Clark's Mill

Maheno   Kakanui

Kakanui River

1528

1286

616

Taranui

All Day Bay
Orore Point

23

Tiroiti

Morrisons

65

Herbert

Otepopo

Waianakarua River
Lookout Bluff

Hyde

Green Valley

965

Waianakarua Scenic Reserve

Waianakarua

12

Highlay Hill
820

Shag Valley
Station

Waihemo

789

Hampden

Moeraki Boulders/
Kaihinaki
* Moeraki Point

3

Golden Point
Historic Res

744

Waynes

604

Hillgrove

Moeraki

Kaik

and Pillar

Macraes Flat

38

Dunback

Makareao

Trotters Gorge

Katiki

Katiki Point

Moonlight

Inch
Valley

Glenpark

599

Limestone
cliffs *

26

Nenthorn

Stoneburn

Meadowbank

Bushey

Shag
Point

* Penguin and Seal
Colony

4

708
Ck

Redbank
Reserve

Deighton
Creek
Reserve

732

Palmerston ⓘ

Shag Point/Matakaea

Shag River
(Waihemo)

587

Wairunga

Tavora Reserve *

Flag Swamp

14

Goodwood

PACIFIC

666

Hawksbury
Bush

Tumai

Pleasant River

OCEAN

444

Bucklands
Crossing

Waikouaiti

Mount Stoker

736

Cornish Head

* Matanaka Farm Buildings

5

kerangi

Merton

Karitane

Puketeraki

763

Seacliff

Omimi

Christmas

Silverpeaks
Scenic
Reserve

Warrington

Evansdale

Blueskin
Bay

Purakaunui Bay

Heyward Point

Taiaroa Head

* Royal Albatross Centre
Penguin Place

* Taieri Gorge
Railway

Hindon

Mt Allan

515

77

Waitati

Purakaunui

Long
Beach

Osborne

Upper Waitati

Heyward Point
Te Ngaru

Aramoana

Harington Point

Otakou

Otago Peninsula

6

Pigeon Flat

556

Mt Cargill

20

Salisbury

Whare
Flat

676

Sawyers
Bay

Harwood

Wickliffe
Bay

North
Taieri

Taieri
Gorge
Scenic Res

Halfway
Bush

Pine
Hill

Port
Chalmers ⓘ

Harbour

Hoopers Inlet

Taieri
Historical
Park

*

Wyllies
Crossing

DUNEDIN

North East
Valley
Ravensbourne

Larnach
Castle

Portobello

408

Hoopers Inlet

Mosgiel

Wingatui

Sandymount
Pukehiki

Cape Saunders

INK INTERNATIONAL LIMITED 2006

A B C D E

1

Breaksea
Island

Mt Crowfoot
1685

Spey R

Percy R

1605

Lake
St Patrick

1100

1336

935

1100

Breaksea Sound

1125

Shy
Lake

1611

1407

1283

1569

1784

TOWNLEY MOUNTAINS

Emerald
Stm

Woodhen Cove

1071

Acheron Passage

Wet Jacket Arm

Henry Burn

Bishop Burn

Seaforth River

1723

Lake
Bright

1606

290

974

Resolution
Island

1128

1361

1433

Loch
Maree

Lake
Horizon

Florence
Stm

Shall
La

Shag

Mt Clerke
1089

Jane
Lake

Lake Roe

1666

1558

2

Five Fingers
Peninsula

872

523

Cooper I

Mt Solitary
1454

Lake
Story

Gardner Burn

1406

Hauroko Burn

KAHEREKOAU MT

Grove Cove

417

Bowen Channel

620

Long Island

Cook Channel

1270

Lake
Mike

1290

Lake
Hay

Hay R

Sphinx
Lake

Lake
Jaquiery

Jaquiery Str

1556

Five Fingers Point

Anchor Island

Dusky
Sound

Fannin
Bay

483

1141

Lumaluma Ck

Oho Ck

1359

False
Lake

Long Burn

Cone Peak
1464

1325

1574

Lake
Purser

1246

Princess Burn

Barnett R

Bight

West
Cape

Newton R

Lake
Fraser

Lake Macarthur

889

Edwardson Sound

Lake
Cadman

Carrick R

Lake
Carrick

1045

Lake
Widgeon

Lake
Victor

1176

DARK CLOUD RANGE

Richard Burn

1340

1428

Lake
Kakapo

Caroline Peak
1704

Lake
Hauroko

3

1130

745

Lake
Rimmer

Cunaris Sound

Long Sound

1310

CAMERON MOUNTAINS

Tower Peak
1406

PRINCESS MOUNTAINS

Caroline Burn

1466

Rata Burn

1380

Lake
Hector

Lake
Thomas

165

Passage

Great
Island

Kohe Ck

1043

Blacklock Stm

1123

Lake
Monk

Lake
Mouat

4

Cape
Providence

Landing
Bay

Western Psge

Eastern

151

Dawson Burn

Gray R

FIORDLAND
NATIONAL
PARK

1153

1203

1133

Lake Poteriteri

652

Chalky
Inlet

Chalky
Island

Gulches Head

251

Otago Retreat

378

663

1129

Cavendish River

Mt Aitken
1189

Aan R

Grant Burn

424

313

Crombie Stm

Angus Burn

Waitutu River

Preservation Inlet

Coal
Island

389

Lake
Kiwi

Kiwi Burn

Fred Burn

Lake
Hakapoua

Lake
Marshall

Waitutu R

Wairaurahiki River

TASMAN

SEA

Puysegur
Point

Wilson River

Gold Burn

Grace Burn

615

Lake
Innes

South

Coast

313

Coast Track

5

Long Point

6

N

310 Gregory's New Zealand

South Island

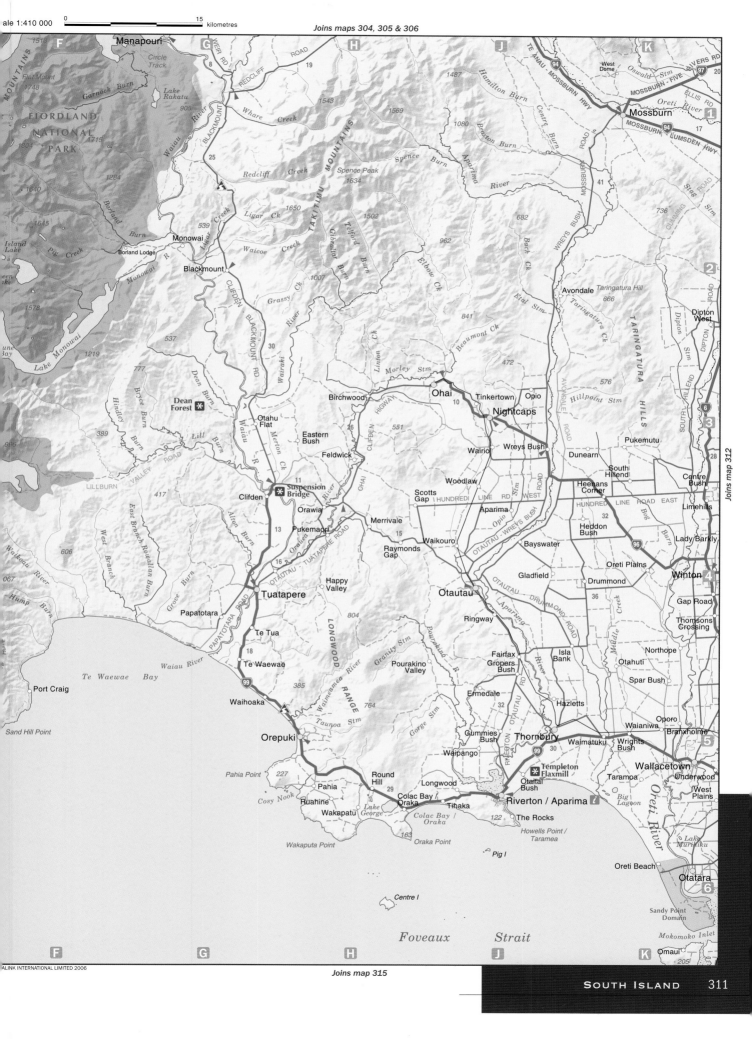

ale 1:410 000

0   15

kilometres

F   **G**   **H**   **J**   **K**

Manapouri

MOUNTAINS

1515
Flat Mount
1748

FIORDLAND
NATIONAL
PARK

1004

1715

1284

1640

1645

1219

1578

Island
Lake

une
Bay

Lake Monowai

777

606

067

Hump Burn

Port Craig

Sand Hill Point

Circle Track

WEIR RD

REDCLIFF

Lake Rakatu

905

Whare   Creek

19

1543

1569

1487

Hamilton Burn

TE ANAU - MOSSBURN HWY

94

West Dome

Oswald Stm

MOSSBURN - FIVE RIVERS RD

07

20

MOSSBURN

94

LUMSDEN HWY

Oreti River

17

1

BLACKMOUNT

Waiau River

25

Redcliff Creek

1650

Ligar Ck

539

1502

Telford Burn

1634

Spence Peak

Spence Burn

Aparima River

1080

Braxton Burn

Centre Burn

WREYS BUSH

682

736

41

Dipton West

Monowai

Borland Lodge

Monowai R

Blackmount

CLIFDEN BLACKMOUNT RD

1007

Gibraltar Burn

962

Elbow Ck

841

Beaumont Ck

Flat Stm

AVONDALE ROAD

Avondale

Taringatura Hill
666

Taringatura Ck

TARINGATURA HILLS

Dipton

CUMMING ROAD

576

SOUTH HILLEND ROAD

DIPTON WEST ROAD

2

6

3

537

Grassy Ck

30

Wairaurahiri River

Dean Burn

Waiau R

Merton Ck

26

Linton Ck

551

Morley Stm

472

Linton Stm

Centre
Bush

28

LILLBURN   VALLEY   ROAD

389

Dean
Forest

417

Otahu
Flat

Eastern
Bush

Feldwick

11

OHAI RIVER

Ohai

10

Tinkertown

Opio

Nightcaps

7

Wairio

Hillpoint Stm

Dunearn

Pukemutu

South
Hillend

Heenans
Corner

HUNDRED LINE ROAD EAST

Limehills

Lady Barkly

32

Bryce Burn

Hindley Burn

East Branch Rowallan Burn

West Branch

Grove Burn

Alton Burn

Oraiti

Clifden

Suspension
Bridge

Orawia

Pukemaori

13

16

Waikoau River

Happy
Valley

804

Tuatapere

Papatotara

Te Tua

OTAUTAU - TUATAPERE ROAD

Merrivale

15

Raymonds
Gap

CLIFDEN HIGHWAY

HUNDRED   LINE   RD   WEST

Scotts
Gap

Waikouro

Woodlaw

Aparima

OTAUTAU - WREYS BUSH

Opio

Bayswater

Heddon
Bush

Oreti Plains

Winton

4

96

Gladfield

Drummond

36

Gap Road

Thomsons
Crossing

LONGWOOD   RANGE

Waimeamea River

Granity Stm

Pourakino R

Otautau

Ringway

Aparima River

OTAUTAU DRUMMOND ROAD

Northope

Otahuti

Spar Bush

18

Te Waewae

385

99

Waihoaka

Gorge Stm

Taunoa Stm

764

Pourakino
Valley

Ermedale

Fairfax
Gropers
Bush

Isla
Bank

32

Hazletts

Middle   Creek

Oporo

Waianiwa

Branxholme

5

Orepuki

Pahia Point

227

Pahia

Round
Hill

Longwood

Gummies
Bush

Waipango

Thornbury

RIVERTON OTAUTAU RD

99

30

Waimatuku

Wrights
Bush

Wallacetown

Taramoa

Underwood

West
Plains

Cosy Nook

Ruahine

Wakapatu

Lake
George

29

Colac Bay /
Oraka

Tihaka

Colac Bay /
Oraka

163

Oraka Point

Templeton
Flaxmill

Otaitai
Bush

Riverton / Aparima

122

The Rocks

Big
Lagoon

Oreti River

Lake
Murihiku

Wakaputa Point

Howells Point /
Taramea

Pig I

Oreti Beach

Otatara

6

Centre I

Sandy Point
Domain

Te Waewae Bay

Waiau River

Foveaux   *Strait*

Mokomoko Inlet

Omaui

205

F   **G**   **H**   **J**   **K**

Joins map 315

Joins map 312

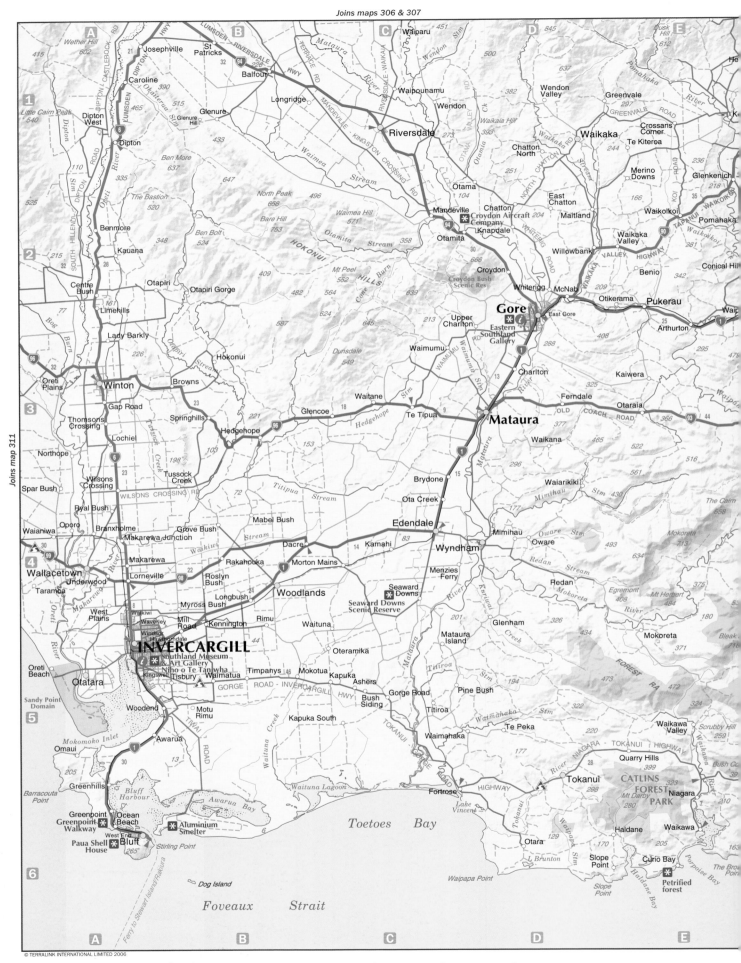

South Island

Scale 1:410 000
0　　　　　15 kilometres

Mathesons Corner
Crookston
Tapanui Hill
BLUE MTNS
John O'Groats Hill
Beaumont
Craigellachie
BEAUMONT HWY
RONGAHERE ROAD
Bowlers Creek
Evans Flat
Chinese Camp
Lawrence
WEST ROAD
Gabriels Gully
Wetherstons
Bungtown
Waipori
L Mahinerangi
Verter Burn
Maungatua Range Reserve
Harveys Flat
Woodside
Taieri Historical Park
Outram
Momona
Allanton
Maungatua
Waipori Falls
Mill Creek Scenic Res
Meggat Burn
Berwick
Otokia
Otokia Hill
Black Gully
Tuapeka West
Kononi
Tuapeka Flat
Forsyth
German Stm
Lake Waipori
Sinclair Wetlands
Henley
Kuri Bush
Rongahere
Tuapeka Mouth
Waitahuna West
Waitahuna
Waitahuna Gully
Johnston
Table Hill
Waitahuna R West
Fort Hill
Lake Waihola
Waihola
Taieri River
Rankleburn
Puketi
Round Hill
MANUKA GORGE HIGHWAY
Tokomairiro R East Br
Milburn
Clarendon
Kapiti
Taieri Mouth
Taieri Beach
Wharetoa
Greenfield
Manuka Creek
Manuka Gorge Rail Tunnel
Pukekoma
Mount Stuart
Glenore
Adams Flat
Clydevale
Awamangu
Hillend
Crichton
Milton
Clarksville
Tokoiti
Akatore Creek
Popotunoa
Taumata
Pukeawa
Pukepito
Old Sod Cottage
Lovells Flat
Moneymore
Glenledi
Quoin Point
Ashley Downs
Clifton
Stony Creek
Benhar
Poverty Hill
Toko Mouth
Clinton
Kuriwao
Waiwera South
Kaihiku
Te Houka
Balclutha
Stirling
L Tuakitoto
Kakapuaka
Finegand
Kaitangata
Wangaloa
Warepa
Waitepeka
Otanomomo
Matau
Summer Hill
Matau Branch
Clutha River
Koau Branch
Brown Dome
Lochindorb
Puerua
Paretai
Romahapa
Port Molyneux
Molyneux Bay
Purekireki
Glenomaru Valley Scenic Res
Glenomaru
Ahuriri Flat
Kaka Point
Willsher Bay
Catlins Cone
Wisp Hill
Tahatika
Otekura
Hays Gap
Tirohanga
Mt Pye
Mt Tautuku
Owaka Valley
Owaka
Pounawea
New Haven
Cannibal Bay
Nugget Point
Sandy Bay
Ajax Hill
CATLINS FOREST PARK
Catlins River Walk
Tawanui
Puketiro
Houipapa
Hinahina
Makura
Jack's Blowhole
Surat Bay
Kenneths Peak
Table Hill Scenic Res
Caberfeidh
Purakaunui
Ratanui
Hinahina Hill
Penguin Bay
White Head
Tahakopa
Kahuika
Maclennan
Tarara
Purakaunui Falls
Purakauiti
Purakaunui Bay Scenic Reserve
Hinahina Cove
Stuarts
Papatowai
McArthurs Hill
Purakaunui River
Veil or Aurora Falls
William King Scenic Res
Tautuku
Cathedral Caves
Tahakopa Bay
Irihuka (Long Point)
Chaslands
Tautuku Bay Scenic Res
Tautuku Peninsula
Makati (Chaslands Mistake)

PACIFIC

OCEAN

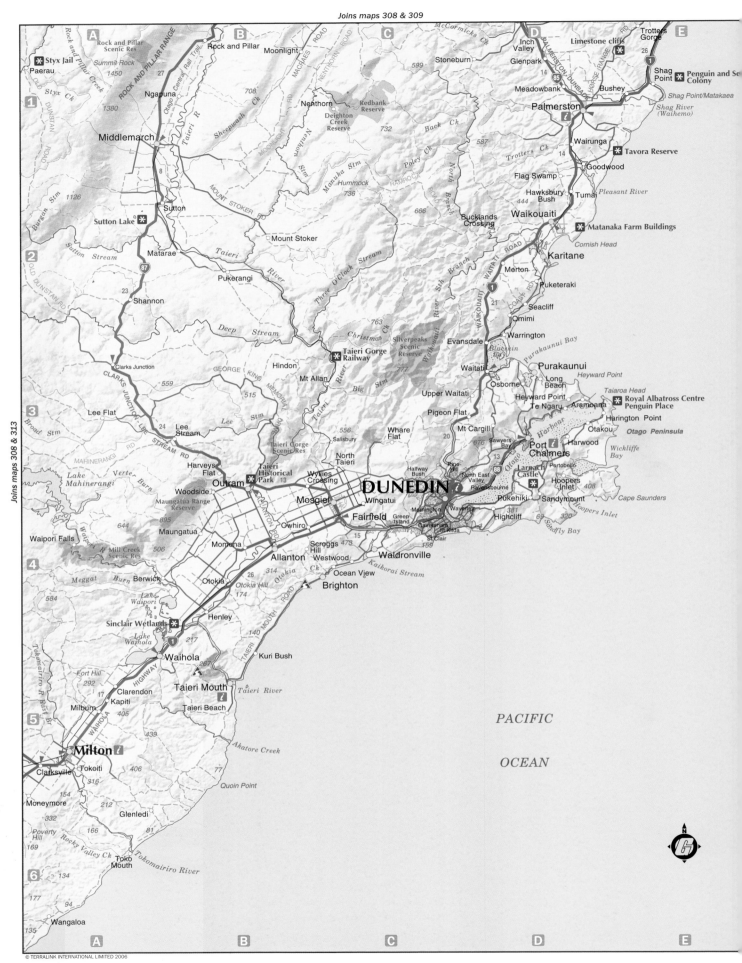

South Island

ale 1:410 000

0   15 kilometres

F G H J K

Mokomoko Inlet
Awarua
Omaui
1
30
205
Greenhills
Barracouta Point
Bluff Harbour
Greenpoint
Greenpoint Walkway
Ocean Beach
West End
Paua Shell House
Bluff
265
Aluminium Smelter
Stirling Point

Foveaux

Dog Island

See Ruapuke Island Inset

Strait

Bishops and Clerks Islands
Black Rock Point
44
Rugged Islands
159
360
530
750
Saddle Point
Mt Anglem/ Hananui
888
980
Little Mt Anglem
738
Garden Point
North West Bay
Sealers Bay
Codfish Island (Whenuahou)
27
Red Head Peak
510
Waituna Bay
Big Bight
250
385
607
Freshwater
382
565
606 The Paps
610
Lake Sheila
399
430
302
Port William / Potirepo
Titi / Muttonbird Islands
River
219
Rocky Mount
511
549
305
43
Horseshoe Bay
Halfmoon Bay
STEWART ISLAND/ RAKIURA
315
267
Scott Burn
223
193
Halfmoon Bay (Oban)
Halfmoon Bay
Abbott Passage
Lower Island Hill
258
Tolson
R
Prices Inlet
Mason Bay
137
345
Paterson Inlet / Whaka a Te Wera
Carter Passage
Big Sandhill
156
Mt Rakeahua
681
292
352
Ulva I
547
Walkers Hill
487
329
Bench Island
63
Ernest Islands
146
Traills Hill
457
Rakeahua
River
Bald Hill
514
344
Big Glory Bay
165
95
Chew Tobacco Bay
Southern
511
222
224
East Cape (Koromere)
RAKIURA
Doughboy Hill
411
NATIONAL PARK
239
Adventure Hill
266
Heron R
136
Pikaroro Bay
Circuit
Doughboy Bay
Table Hill
716
301
Port Adventure Scenic Reserve
Sinbads Mistake
389
DECEIT PEAKS
563
Blaikies Hill
703
270
Pegasus Nature Reserve
150
Port Adventure
Breaksea Islands
Titi / Muttonbird Islands
South Red Head Point
356
472
Granite Knob
637
Mt Allen
750
Lees Knob
590
Kirklands Hill
282
473
Gorge Ck
Toitoi R
118
91
135
Horomamae / Owen Island
Boat Group
269
180
503
TIN RANGE
386
Newton Ck
Kopeka R
372
Tutaepawhati Bay
Big Kuri Bay
Mokinui / Big Moggy Island
55
Easy Harbour
Pegasus Ck
119
Robertson R
304
Titi / Muttonbird Islands
185
Magog
Gog 282
407
Pearl Island
144
Port Pegasus / Pikihatiti
Putauhina Island
69
Bald Cone
230
154
245
387
Smiths Lookout
474
170
Broad Bay
235
470
493
271
110
Wilsons Point
ihepa / South Island
206
South West Cape / Puhiwaero
South Cape / Whiore

PACIFIC

OCEAN

INSET
North Head
Ruapuke Island
Lagoon Bay
Green Island
Bird Island
Henrietta Bay
South Point
Hazelburgh Group

F G H J K

1
2
3
4
5
6

SOUTH ISLAND 315

Scale 1:20 000

0   750 metres

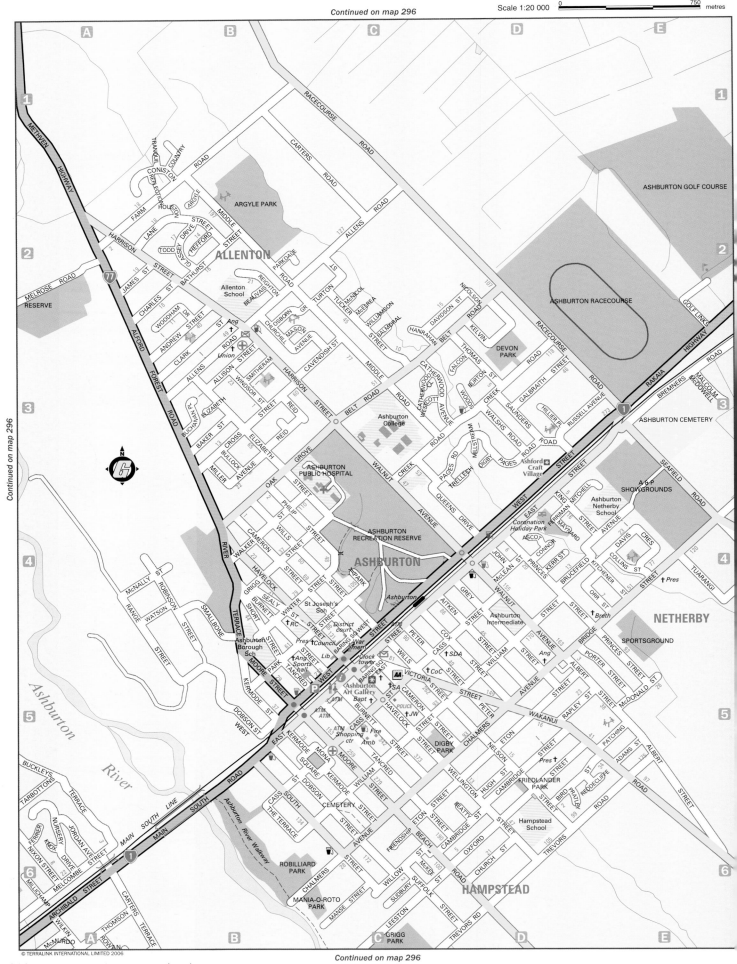

ASHBURTON GOLF COURSE

RACECOURSE ROAD

CARTERS ROAD

ARGYLE PARK

ALLENTON

MELROSE ROAD RESERVE

Allenton School

ASHBURTON RACECOURSE

DEVON PARK

ASHBURTON CEMETERY

Ashburton College

A & P SHOWGROUNDS

Ashburton Public Hospital

Ashford Craft Village

Ashburton Netherby School

Coronation Holiday Park

ASHBURTON RECREATION RESERVE

ASHBURTON

NETHERBY

Ashburton Intermediate

SPORTSGROUND

St Joseph's Sch

District court

Ashburton Borough Sch

War mem

Clock tower

Ashburton Art Gallery

POLICE

Digby Park

Fire Amb

Shopping ctr

ATM

Friedlander Park

Hampstead School

MONA SQUARE

Robilliard Park

HAMPSTEAD

Mania-o-Roto Park

GRIGG PARK

Ashburton

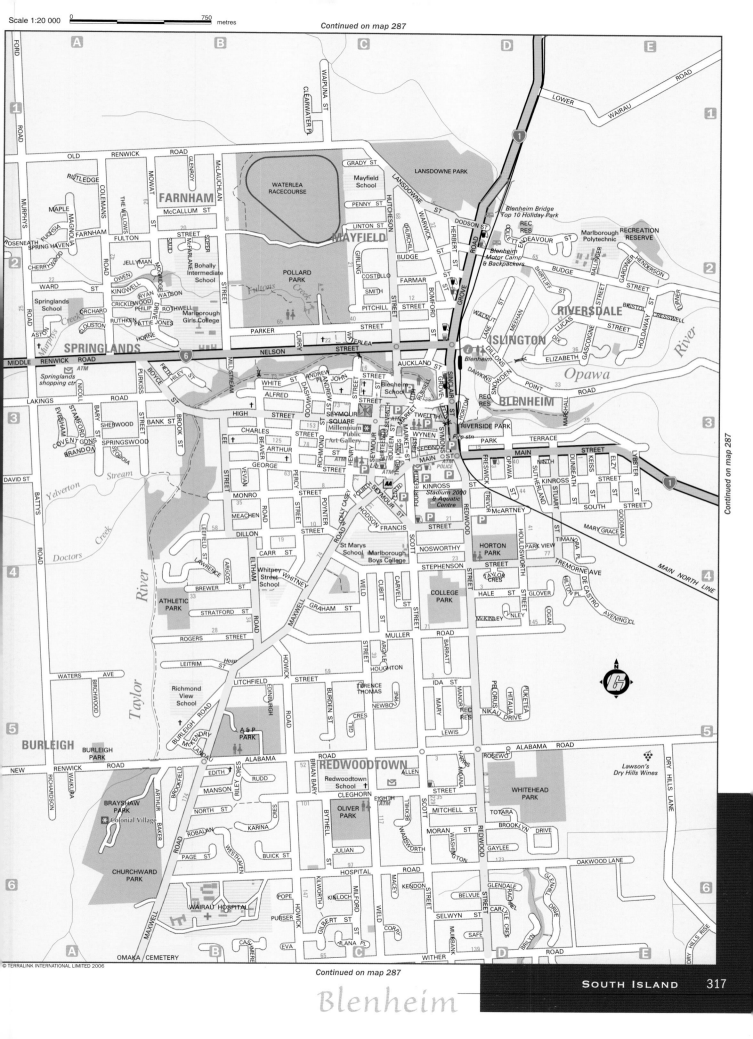

Continued on map 287

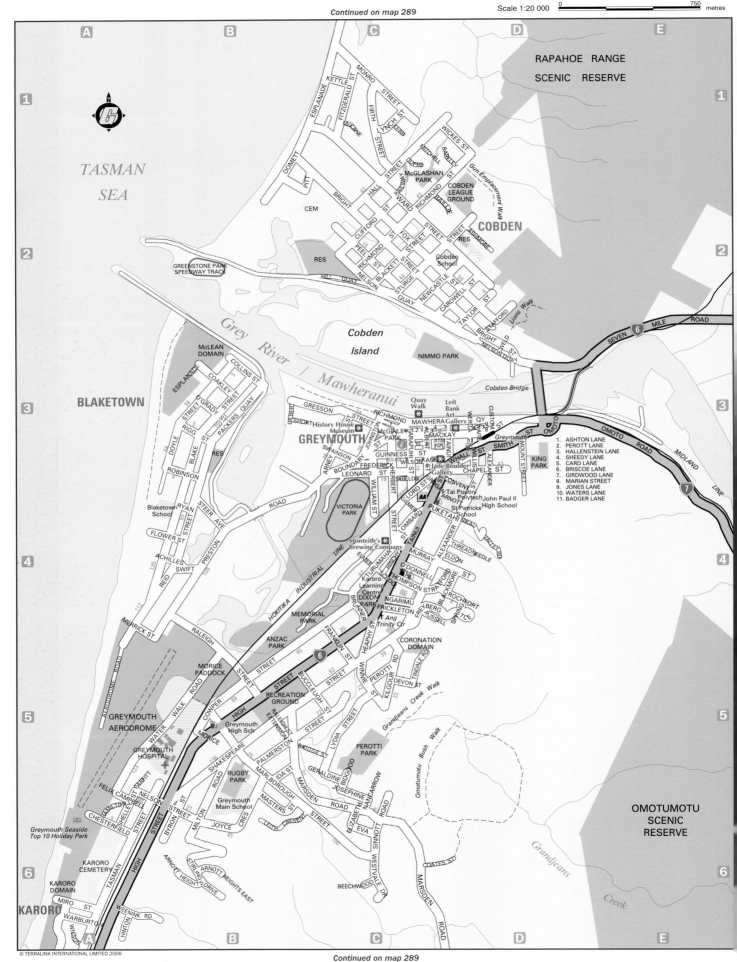

Scale 1:20 000

0   750 metres

RAPAHOE RANGE
SCENIC RESERVE

TASMAN
SEA

GREENSTONE PARK
SPEEDWAY TRACK

CEM

COBDEN LEAGUE GROUND

COBDEN

McGLASHAN PARK

RES

Cobden
School

Grey River / Mawheranui

Cobden
Island

NIMMO PARK

Cobden Bridge

SEVEN MILE ROAD

Lions Walk

Gun Emplacement Walk

BLAKETOWN

McLEAN DOMAIN

Quay
Walk

Left
Bank
Art
Gallery

Mawhera

GREYMOUTH

History House
Museum

McGINLEY PARK

Monteith's
Brewing Company

VICTORIA
PARK

Blaketown
School

Karoro
Learning
Centre

DIXON
PARK

Ang
Trinity Ctr

Jade Boulder
Gallery

Tai Poutini
Polytech

St Patricks
School

John Paul II
High School

KING
PARK

1. ASHTON LANE
2. PEROTT LANE
3. HALLENSTEIN LANE
4. SHEEDY LANE
5. CARD LANE
6. BRISCOE LANE
7. GIRDWOOD LANE
8. MARIAN STREET
9. JONES LANE
10. WATERS LANE
11. BADGER LANE

OMOTO ROAD

MIDLAND LINE

MEMORIAL
PARK

ANZAC
PARK

CORONATION
DOMAIN

Grandjeans Creek Walk

Omotumotu Bush Walk

MORICE
PADDOCK

RECREATION
GROUND

PEROTTI
PARK

GREYMOUTH
AERODROME

Greymouth
High Sch

OMOTUMOTU
SCENIC
RESERVE

GREYMOUTH
HOSPITAL

Grandjeans

Greymouth Seaside
Top 10 Holiday Park

Rugby
Park

Greymouth
Main School

Creek

KARORO
CEMETERY

KARORO
DOMAIN

KARORO

Scale 1:20 000

750 metres

Invercargill

© TERRALINK INTERNATIONAL LIMITED 2006

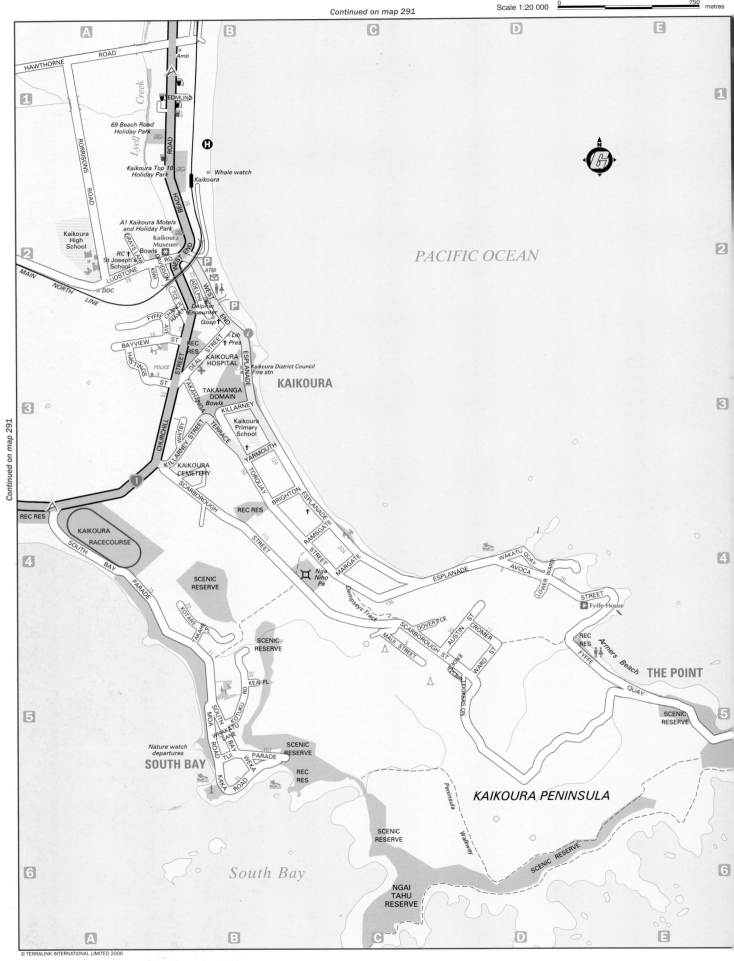

Scale 1:20 000

0   750 metres

PACIFIC OCEAN

KAIKOURA

Kaikoura High School

69 Beach Road Holiday Park

Kaikoura Top 10 Holiday Park

Whale watch Kaikoura

A1 Kaikoura Motels and Holiday Park

Kaikoura Museum

RC † St Joseph's School

Bowls

DOC

Dolphin Encounter

Gosp †

Lib † Pres

Kaikoura Hospital

POLICE

Kaikoura District Council Fire stn

TAKAHANGA DOMAIN
Bowls

Kaikoura Primary School †

Kaikoura Cemetery

REC RES

Nga Niho Pa

KAIKOURA RACECOURSE

SCENIC RESERVE

SCENIC RESERVE

Nature watch departures

SOUTH BAY

SCENIC RESERVE

REC RES

South Bay

Fyffe House

THE POINT

Armers Beach

SCENIC RESERVE

KAIKOURA PENINSULA

Peninsula Walkway

SCENIC RESERVE

NGAI TAHU RESERVE

SCENIC RESERVE

HAWTHORNE ROAD

RORRISONS ROAD

MAIN NORTH LINE

BEACH ROAD

Lyell Creek

WEST END

CHURCHILL STREET

ESPLANADE

SOUTH BAY PARADE

WEKA ROAD

KAKA ROAD

TUI

MOA

KEA PL

KOTARE PL

TAKAHE PL

WHAKATU KOTUKU BAY

SCARBOROUGH STREET

TORQUAY

YARMOUTH

BRIGHTON

RAMSGATE

MARGATE

ESPLANADE

AVOCA

WAKATU QUAY

LOWER WARD

FYFFE QUAY

Dempsey's Track

SCARBOROUGH ST

MAUI STREET

DOVER TCE

AUSTIN ST

CROMER ST

WARD ST

COOKERS LN

Kaikoura

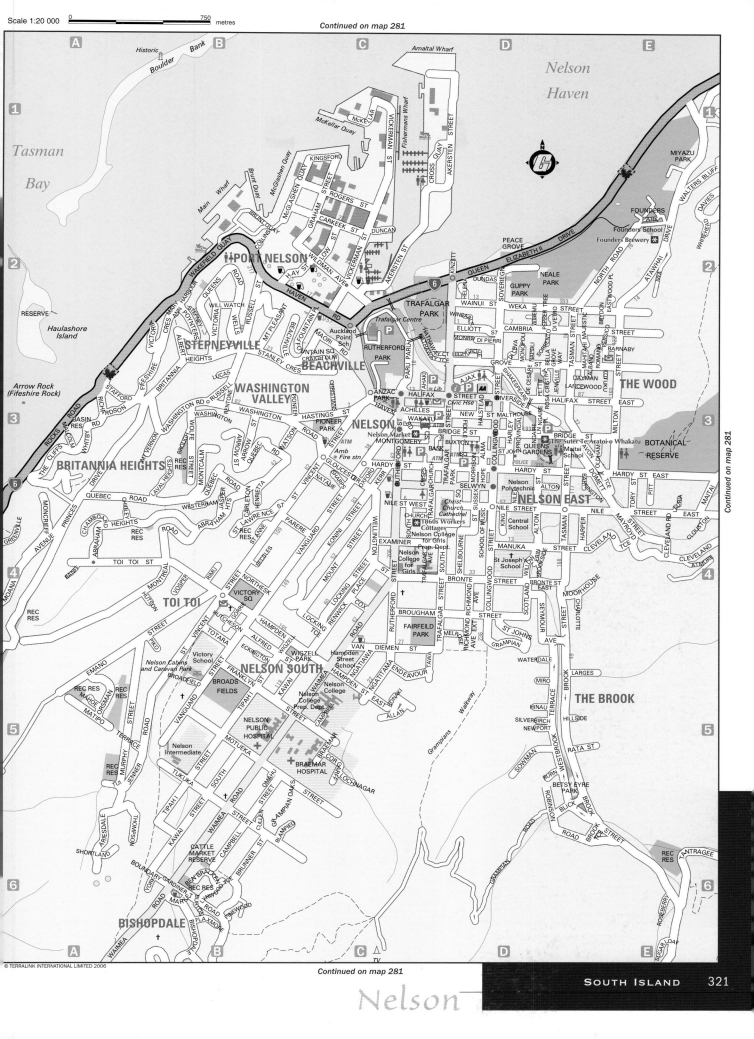

Scale 1:20 000

750 metres

A **B** **C** **D** **E**

Nelson

Haven

Tasman

Bay

RESERVE

Haulashore Island

*Arrow Rock
(Fifeshire Rock)*

THE CLIFFS

PORT NELSON

STEPNEYVILLE

BEACHVILLE

WASHINGTON
VALLEY

NELSON

BRITANNIA HEIGHTS

TOI TOI

NELSON SOUTH

BISHOPDALE

THE WOOD

NELSON EAST

BOTANICAL
RESERVE

THE BROOK

MIYAZU
PARK

FOUNDERS
PARK

TRAFALGAR
PARK

Continued on map 281

Nelson

© TERRALINK INTERNATIONAL LIMITED 2006

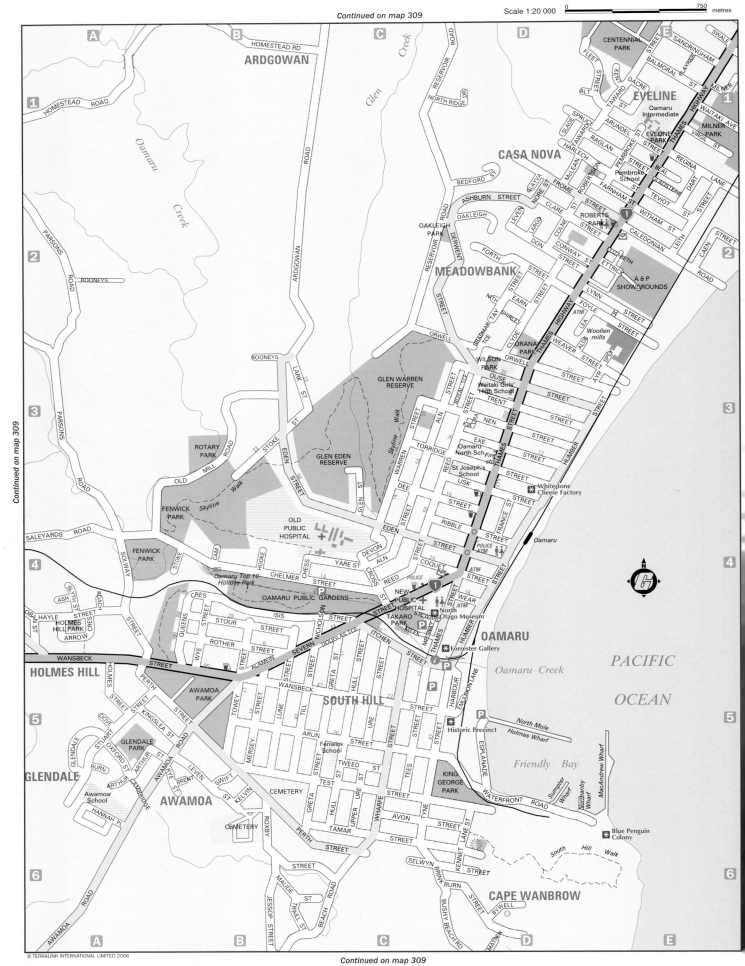

Scale 1:20 000

0   750 metres

Continued on map 309

ARDGOWAN

EVELINE

CASA NOVA

MEADOWBANK

GLEN WARREN
RESERVE

GLEN EDEN
RESERVE

ROTARY
PARK

OLD
PUBLIC
HOSPITAL

FENWICK
PARK

FENWICK
PARK

OAMARU PUBLIC GARDENS

HOLMES HILL

GLENDALE

AWAMOA

SOUTH HILL

OAMARU

PACIFIC

OCEAN

Friendly Bay

CAPE WANBROW

Continued on map 309

Oamaru

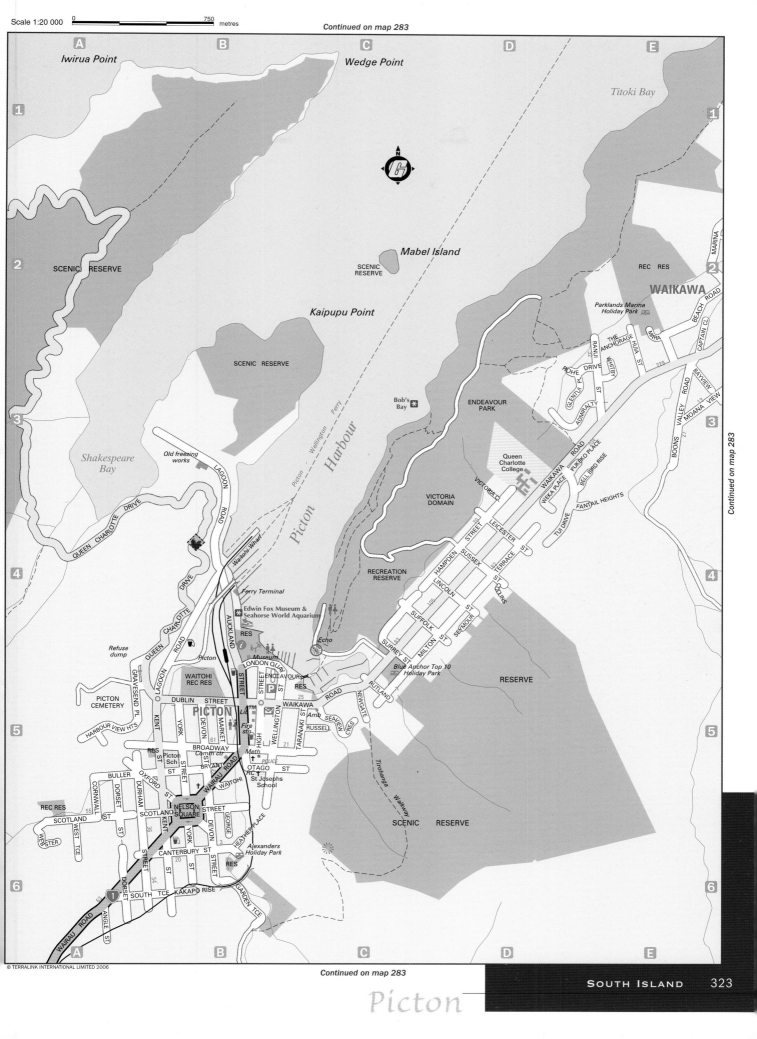

Scale 1:20 000

0   750   metres

Iwirua Point

Wedge Point

Titoki Bay

A   **B**   **C**   **D**   **E**

SCENIC RESERVE

Mabel Island

SCENIC RESERVE

WAIKAWA

Kaipupu Point

SCENIC RESERVE

REC RES

Parklands Marina Holiday Park

THE ANCHORAGE

ROHE DRIVE

RANUI

WHITBY ST

HUIA ST

MARA

ADMIRALTY

GLENTUI PL

279

BEACH ROAD

CAPTAIN CL

BAYVIEW

MOANA VIEW

Bob's Bay

ENDEAVOUR PARK

BOONS VALLEY ROAD

Shakespeare Bay

Old freezing works

LAGOON ROAD

QUEEN CHARLOTTE DRIVE

Picton — Wellington Ferry

Picton Harbour

Queen Charlotte College

VICTORIA CL

WAIKAWA ROAD

PUKEKO PLACE

BELL BIRD RISE

FANTAIL HEIGHTS

WEKA PLACE

TUI DRIVE

Refuse dump

Waitohi Wharf

Ferry Terminal

Edwin Fox Museum & Seahorse World Aquarium

RES

Echo

VICTORIA DOMAIN

VICTORIA STREET

LEICESTER ST

TERRACE

COLLINS

Picton

Museum

ENDEAVOUR ST

RES

25

RECREATION RESERVE

HAMPDEN ST

SUSSEX ST

SEYMOUR

SUFFOLK

LINCOLN ST

MILTON ST

LONDON QUAY

WAIKAWA

Blue Anchor Top 10 Holiday Park

SURREY ST

RUTLAND

NEWGATE

RESERVE

Picton Cemetery

GRAVESEND PL

LAGOON ST

QUEEN CHARLOTTE ROAD

AUCKLAND STREET

DUBLIN STREET

MARKET

HIGH

WELLINGTON ST

TARANAKI ST

RUSSEL

SEAVIEW CRES

HARBOUR VIEW HTS

PICTON

ATM

Fire stn

Amb

WAITOHI REC RES

KENT

YORK

DEVON

Comm ctr

BROADWAY

RES

Picton Sch

BRYANT

Meth

OTAGO ST

St Josephs School

RC

P LICE

BULLER

CORNWALL ST

DORSET ST

DURHAM

OXFORD

KENT

SCOTLAND

NELSON SQUARE

DEVON

GEORGE

HEATHERPLACE

REC RES

SCOTLAND

WEST TCE

WEBSTER

55

36

YORK ST

CANTERBURY ST

DEVON STREET

Alexanders Holiday Park

RES

20

Tirohanga Walkway

SCENIC RESERVE

1

DORSET STREET

ANGLE ST

SOUTH TCE

KAKAPO RISE

GARDEN TCE

54

WAIRAU ROAD

SCENIC RESERVE

Picton

© TERRALINK INTERNATIONAL LIMITED 2006

Scale 1:20 000

0   750 metres

Continued on map 306

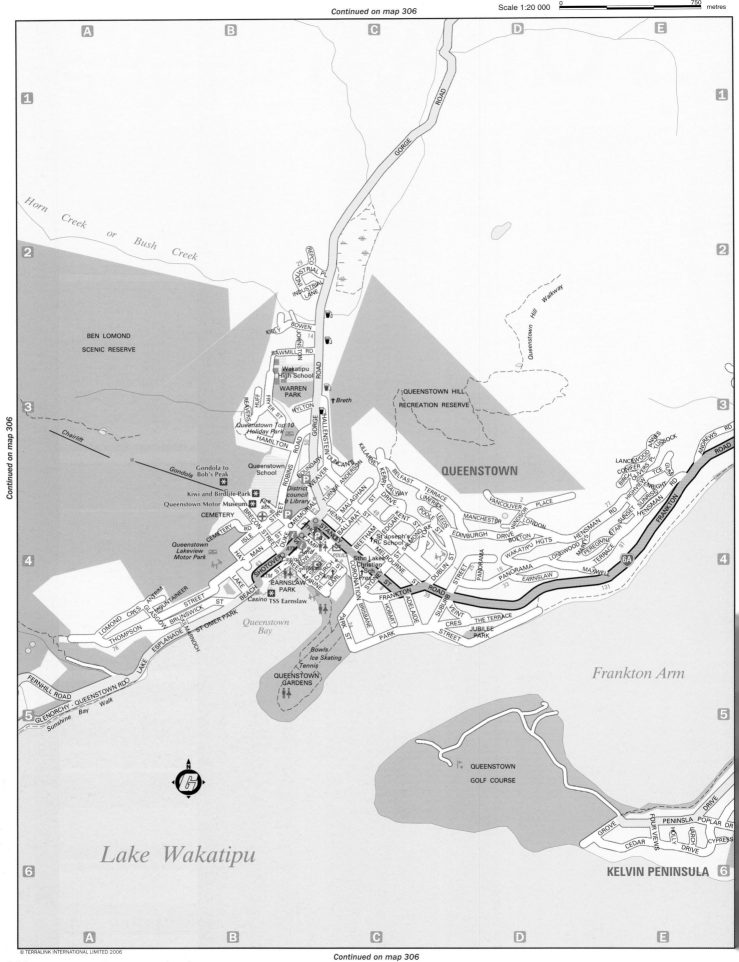

Horn Creek or Bush Creek

BEN LOMOND
SCENIC RESERVE

Chairlift

Gondola

Gondola to
Bob's Peak

Kiwi and Birdlife Park

Queenstown Motor Museum

CEMETERY

Queenstown
Lakeview
Motor Park

LOMOND CRES
THOMPSON
GLASGOW
ANTRIM
MOUNTAINEER
BRUNSWICK
ELMARNOCH
ST OMER PARK
LAKE ESPLANADE
GLENORCHY - QUEENSTOWN RD
Fernhill Road
Sunshine Bay Walk

Queenstown
Bay

Lake Wakatipu

REPCO PL
INDUSTRIAL PL
INDUSTRIAL LANE
29

KIELY
BOWEN
JOHNSTON
SAWMILL RD
GORGE ROAD
14

Wakatipu
High School
WARREN
PARK
REAVERS
HUFF
FRYER ST
HYLTON
HAMILTON
† Breth

Queenstown Top 10
Holiday Park

Queenstown School
ROBINS STREET
BRECON STREET
CEMETERY RD
ISLE
MAN ST
HAY
LAKE
BEACH
SHOTOVER
ST
Casino
EARNSLAW
PARK
TSS Earnslaw
Casino
MARINE
DUKE STREET
MEMORIAL
STANLEY
CAMP
BALLARAT ST
EARL
CORONATION
PARK ST
BOUNDARY
HALLENSTEIN
DUNCANS
WEAVER
TURNER
HENRY
BEETHAM
MELBOURNE
SYDNEY
FRANKTON
ANDERSON
MALAGHAN
KILLARNEY
KERRY
BELFAST
GALWAY
KENT ST
POOLE
YORK ST
EDINBURGH DRIVE
BOLTON
DUBLIN ST
ADELAIDE
HOBART
BRISBANE
PARK
VEINT
SUBURB ROAD
JUBILEE PARK
CRES
THE TERRACE
STREET

District
Council
& Library
Fire
Stn
St Joseph's
RC School
Sthn Lakes
Christian Sch
Prec Sch
POLICE
CHURCH

QUEENSTOWN HILL
RECREATION RESERVE

Queenstown Hill Walkway

QUEENSTOWN

LANCEWOOD
CONIFER
BIRCH
OLIVERS PL
HIGHVIEW
ANNES
TUSSOCK
GUM
WAINWRIGHT
HENSMAN
RD
ANDREWS RD
FRANKTON ROAD
VANCOUVER
PLACE
2
MANCHESTER
WINDSOR
LONDON
WAKATIPU HGTS
LONGWOOD
MATTS ST
PEREGRINE
PANORAMA
EARNSLAW
MAXWELL
PANORAMA
TERRACE
STAR
SUNSET
SUNRISE
6A
77
81
131
18
33

Bowls/
Ice Skating
Tennis
QUEENSTOWN
GARDENS

Frankton Arm

QUEENSTOWN
GOLF COURSE

KELVIN PENINSULA
GROVE
CEDAR
FOUR VIEWS
HOLLY
LARCH
PENINSLA
DRIVE
POPLAR DR
CYPRESS

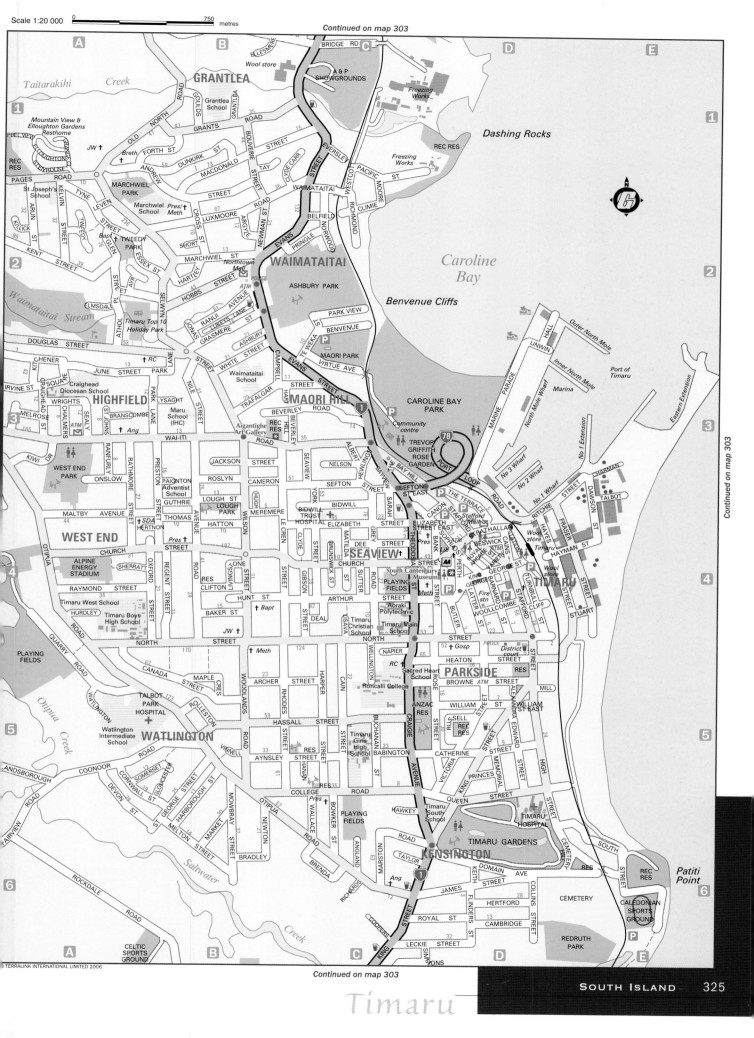

Scale 1:20 000

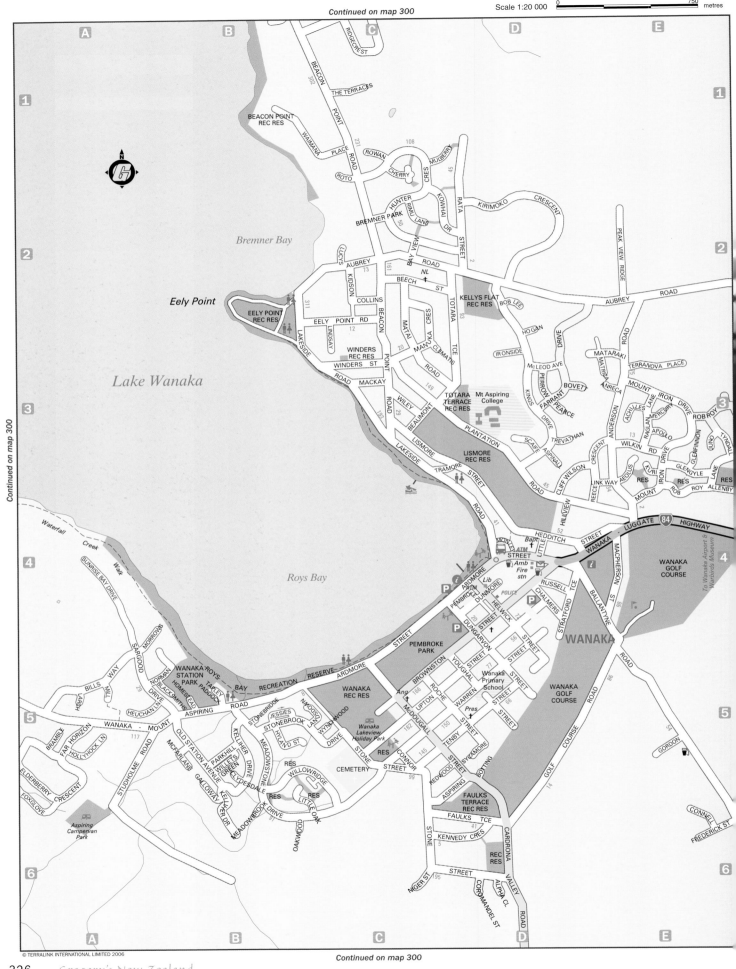

Continued on map 300

Bremner Bay

Eely Point

Lake Wanaka

Roys Bay

WANAKA

Wanaka

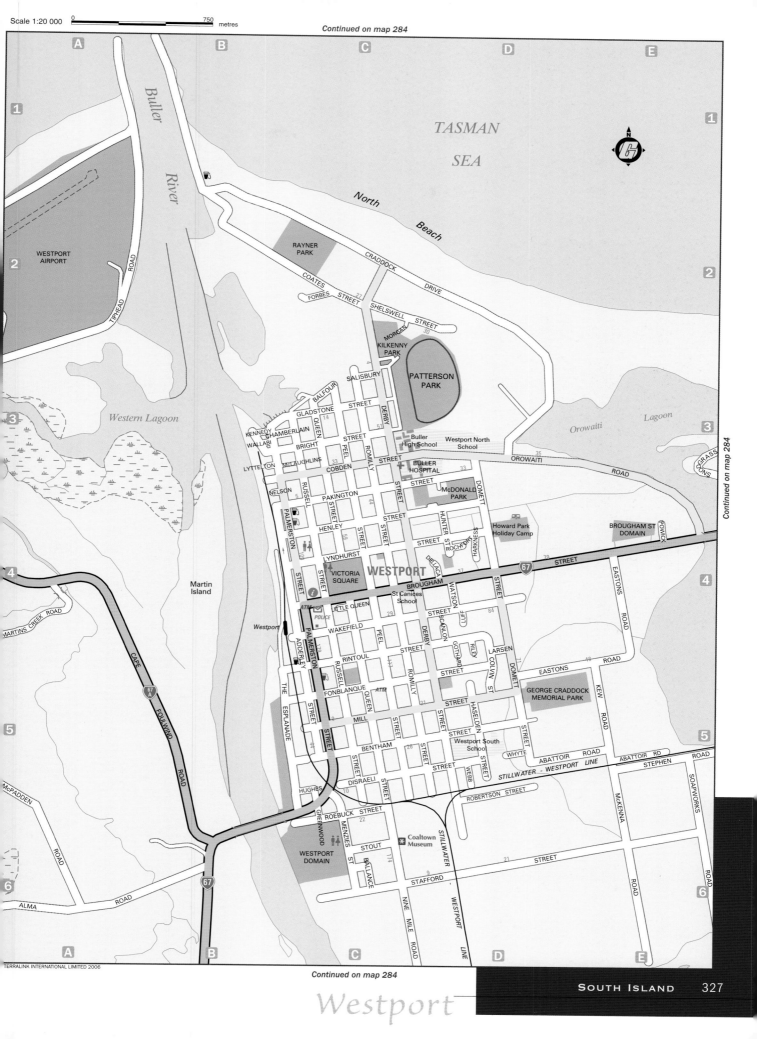

TASMAN

SEA

Buller River

Western Lagoon

WESTPORT
AIRPORT

North

Beach

Orowaiti Lagoon

RAYNER
PARK

Martin
Island

Westport

WESTPORT

PATTERSON
PARK

Buller
High School

Westport North
School

Buller
Hospital

McDONALD
PARK

Howard Park
Holiday Camp

BROUGHAM ST
DOMAIN

St Canices
School

George Craddock
Memorial Park

Victoria
Square

Westport South
School

Westport
Domain

Coaltown
Museum

STILLWATER - WESTPORT LINE

Continued on map 284

Continued on map 284

INDEX

This alphabetical index covers the cities, suburbs, towns, localities and homesteads shown in this publication, as well as national parks, selected topographical features and selected places of interest.

The indexed entries are followed by the island to which they belong, the page number in the case of text references, and the page number and grid reference in the case of maps. All page references are in numerical order, eg. Cleopatra's Pool, SI, 241 E5, 258, 258 B3

Entries under one word are grouped together. Where entries consist of two or more words, the alphabetical sequence is governed by the first, then the second word, eg. Lake Waitaki, Lake Wakatipu, Lake Wanaka, Lakes District Museum, Lakeside

If there are two or more features of the same name within the same island, the name of the regional tourism organisation in which the feature is located, is shown in brackets after the name. If one of these features is a suburb, then the town to which it belongs is shown in brackets after the name, eg. Horahora (Northland), Horahora (Waikato), Horahora (Whangarei).

References in bold type indicate locations to be found on the North or South Island regional maps eg. Adair, SI, **303 H3**

Entries in italic type indicate homesteads, eg. *Ada*, SI, **290 D1**

Entries beginning with Mt are indexed as Mount and those beginning with St are indexed as Saint.

The following abbreviations are used to designate the island to which the entry belongs; NI - North Island; SI - South Island.

Other abbreviations used in the index are; NP - National Park; FP - Forest Park.

Note: this index does not purport to include every city, suburb, town, locality or homestead in New Zealand

Port Nelson, SI **321 B2**
Port Ohope, NI **164 B4**
Port Puponga, SI 241 A4, **280 E1**
Port Robinson, SI **291 H4**
Port Waikato, NI 122, **160 A1**
Port Whangarei, NI **155 G4**
Portage, SI 267 D4, **283 F4**
Porter Heights Ski Field, SI **296 B1**
Porters Pass, SI **296 C2**
Portland, NI **155 G5**
Portobello, SI 227 H4, 275 D2, **314 D3**
Potaka, NI **165 H1**
Potters, SI **307 G4**
Pouakai Circuit, NI 112
Pouawa, NI 93 D2, **171 J2**
Poukawa, NI **175 H3**
Poukiore, NI 147 D5, **174 B4**
Pounawea, SI 263 E1, **313 H5**
Pourakino Valley, SI **311 J5**
Pourerere, NI **175 J5**
Pouto Point, NI **156 C4**
Pouwhakaura, NI 147 E5, **174 C4**
Poverty Bay, NI 38
Prebbleton, SI 212 D5, 276 B4, **297 G3**
Prenzel Distillery, SI 261 D3, **287 H2**
Prices Valley, SI 235 B2, **297 H4**
Progress Junction, SI **284 D6**
Puaha, SI 235 C2, **297 H4**
Puahue, NI **160 E5**
Puao, NI 147 A5, **173 G6**
Puari, SI 235 C1, **297 H4**
Pudding Hill Scenic Reserve, SI **296 B3**
Puerua, SI **313 H4**
Puha, NI 93 B1, **171 G1**
Puhata, NI **154 A1**
Puhinui, NI 53 G5
Puhipuhi, NI **155 G3**
Puhoi, NI 121 A3, **158 B1**
Puhuka, SI **303 H3**
Pukaha Mount Bruce National Wildlife
    Centre, NI 40, 72, **179 F1**
Pukahu, NI 109 C6, **175 H3**
Pukapuka, NI 121 A3, **158 B1**
Pukararo, SI **302 E6**
Pukawa Bay, NI 115 D1, 133 B5, 147 E1,
    168 C3
Puke Ariki, NI 70, **184 B2**
Pukearuhe, NI **166 D5**
Pukeatua, NI **161 F5**
Pukeawa, SI **313 G3**
Pukehamoamoa, NI 109 A3, **175 H2**
Pukehiki, SI 227 H5, 275 D3, **314 D4**
Pukehina, NI **163 H2**
Pukehou, NI **175 G4**
Pukehuia, NI **155 F5**
Pukeinoi, NI 137 A2, **160 B6**
Pukeiti Rhododendron Trust, NI 113 C1,
    172 C2
Pukekapia, NI **160 D2**
Pukekaroro, NI 121 A1, **156 D2**
Pukekawa, NI **160 C1**
Pukekohe, NI 123, 97 E4, 121 B6, **158 D6**
Pukekohe East, NI 97 E4, 121 C6, **158 D6**
Pukekoikoi, NI **283 G4**
Pukekoma, SI **313 H2**
Pukekura, NI **160 E5**
Pukekura, SI **288 C5**
Pukemaori, SI 273 D6, **311 H4**
Pukemiro (Northland), NI **152 E6**
Pukemiro (Waikato), NI **160 C3**
Pukemoremore, NI **160 E4**
Pukemutu, SI **311 K3**
Pukengahu, NI **172 E3**
Pukenui, NI **152 D4**
Pukeokahu, NI **174 D2**
Pukeoware, NI 121 B6, **158 C6**
Pukepito, SI **313 H3**
Pukepoto, NI **152 D6**
Pukerangi, SI **309 F5**
Pukerau, SI **312 E2**
Pukerimu, NI **160 E4**
Pukeroro, NI **160 E4**
Pukerua Bay, NI **178 B2**
Puketaha, NI **160 E3**
Puketapu, NI 109 B3, **175 H2**
Puketeraki, SI 275 D1, **309 H5**
Puketi, NI **154 D1**
Puketi, SI **313 G2**
Puketiro, SI 263 D1, **313 G5**
Puketitiri, NI **169 G6**
Puketoi, NI **177 G5**
Puketona, NI 129 B2, **154 E1**

Puketotara, NI 137 D1, **160 D5**
Puketui, NI 88 B4, **159 H5**
Puketurua, NI **161 F6**
Puketutu, NI **167 H2**
Pukeuri, SI **309 K1**
Pukio, NI 106 A5, **178 E4**
Punakaiki, SI 265, **284 A5**
Punakaiki Cavern, SI **284 A5**
Punakaiki Pancake Rocks, SI 204
Punakitere, NI **154 D3**
Punakitere Valley, NI **154 E3**
Punaromia, NI 127 D3, **163 G5**
Punaruku, NI 129 D3, **155 G2**
Punawai, SI **296 B5**
Punehu, NI **154 B2**
Pungaere, NI 129 A1, **153 H6**
Pungapunga, NI 115 A1, 147 D1, **167 H5**
Pungarehu (Manawatu), NI 147 C5, **173 J6**
Pungarehu (Taranaki), NI 113 A2, **172 A3**
Pungataua, NI 147 E4, **174 D2**
Puni NI 121 B6, **158 C6**
Puniho, NI 113 A1, **172 B2**
Puninga, NI **171 G4**
Puniwhakau, NI 147 A3, **173 F3**
Puponga, SI 241 A4, **280 E1**
Pupu Springs, SI 200, 240, 241 D4,
    254 B2, 258 A2, **280 E3**
Pupuke, NI **153 G5**
Purakauiti, SI 263 D2, **313 G5**
Purakaunui (Dunedin), SI 227 H2, 275 D1,
    314 D3
Purakaunui (Southland), SI 263 D2, **313 G5**
Purakaunui Falls, SI 262, 263 E2, **313 G5**
Puramahoi, SI 241 D4, 258 A1, **280 D3**
Purangi (Coromandel), NI 88 C3, **159 H4**
Purangi (Taranaki), NI **173 F2**
Purau, SI 235 B1, 276 B5, **297 H4**
Purekireki, SI **313 G4**
Pureora, NI **167 J3**
Pureora FP, NI 40, 56, 66, 115 C1, 133 A3,
    147 D1, **167 J4**
Purerua, NI 129 B1, **153 J6**
Puriri, NI 88 B5, 121 E6, **159 H6**
Purua, NI **155 F4**
Pururu, NI 137 E3, **167 H1**
Putangirua Pinnacles, NI 74, **178 D5**
Putara, NI **176 D6**
Putaruru, NI 123, **161 G5**
Putiki, NI **189 D5**
Putiki Church, NI **189 D6**
Putorino (Hawke's Bay), NI **170 B5**
Putorino (Manawatu), NI 147 D6, **174 B5**
Puwera, NI **155 G5**
Puzzling World, SI 245 D3, **300 D5**
Pyes Pa, NI **161 J4**
Pyramid Valley, SI **290 D5**

Q
Quail Island, SI 234
Quarry Hills, SI **312 E5**
Quay Walk, SI 318 C3
Queen Charlotte Drive, SI 202
Queen Charlotte Sound (Totaranui), SI
    202, 266
Queen Charlotte Track, SI 202, 266
Queen Street, NI 48, 49 C4
Queens Flat, SI 303 F6
Queensberry, SI **300 E6**
Queenstown, SI 193, 216, 265, **306 D1**,
    324 D3
Queenstown Motor Museum, SI 324 B4

R
Racecourse Hill, SI **296 E2**
Raes Junction, SI **307 H6**
Raetihi, NI 66, 123, 115 A6, 147 C3,
    173 K4
Raglan, NI 56, 124, **160 B4**
Rahanui, NI **160 B5**
Rahiri, NI **154 D1**
Rahotu, NI 113 A2, **172 B3**
Rahui, SI **284 D4**
Rahui Island, NI 142
Rai Valley, SI 267 D1, **282 D4**
Rainbow Mountain, NI 127 D4, **163 G6**
Rainbow Point, NI 133 D4, **168 E2**
Rainbow Skifield, SI **285 J4**
Rainbow Springs, NI 127 B2, **163 F4**
Rainbow Warrior wreck, NI **153 J4**
Rainbow's End Adventure Park, NI 53 H6,
    97 C4, **158 D4**
Raio, NI **152 D4**

Rakahouka, SI **312 B4**
Rakaia, SI **296 D4**
Rakaia Huts, SI **296 E5**
Rakau, SI **285 J1**
Rakaunui (Manawatu), NI **177 G6**
Rakaunui (Waikato), NI 137 B1, **160 B6**
Rakauroa, NI **164 D6**
Rakautao, NI **154 E2**
Rakautara, NI **287 G6**
Rakautahi, NI **177 H2**
Raketapauma Pa, NI 147 E4, **174 B2**
Rakiura Museum, SI 248, 249 D3
Rakiura NP, SI 197, 230, 248, 249 C4,
    315 H4
Rakiura Track, SI 248
Rakopi, SI 241 B3, **280 D1**
Ramanui, NI 147 B3, **173 H3**
Ramarama, NI 97 E4, 121 C6, **158 D5**
Ranana, NI 147 B4, **173 J5**
Randwick Park, NI 53 H6
Ranfurly, SI 218, 265, **308 E2**
Rangataua, NI 115 B6, 147 D4, **174 A1**
Rangatira Valley, SI **303 H1**
Rangi Point, NI **154 B2**
Rangiahua, NI **154 D2**
Rangiaowhia, NI 137 E1, **160 E5**
Rangiatea, NI 137 E2, **160 E6**
Rangihaeata, SI 241 D4, 258 A1, **280 E3**
Rangiora, NI **154 C2**
Rangiora, SI 276 B3, **297 G1**
Rangiotu, NI **176 C4**
Rangipo, NI 115 E3, 147 E2, **168 C5**
Rangiputa, NI **152 D4**
Rangiriri, NI 56, **160 D1**
Rangiriri West, NI **160 C1**
Rangitaiki, NI **169 F3**
Rangitata, SI **303 J1**
Rangitata Island, SI **303 J1**
Rangitatau, NI 147 A5, **173 G6**
Rangitihi, NI **152 E5**
Rangitikei River, NI 72
Rangitito Island, NI 120
Rangitoto, NI **167 H2**
Rangitoto ke te tonga (D'Urville Island), SI
    202, 266, 267 A2, **282 D1**
Rangitukia, NI **165 J3**
Rangitumau, NI **179 G1**
Rangiuru, NI **163 G2**
Rangiwaea Junction, NI 147 D4, **174 B2**
Rangiwahia, NI 147 E6, **174 D4**
Rangoon Heights, NI **82 D4**
Rankleburn, SI **303 J1**
Ranui (Auckland), NI 52 B3, **158 B4**
Ranui (Waikato), NI **160 C4**
Ranui Heights, NI **82 E2**
Rapahoe, SI **289 F1**
Rapaki, SI 213 G6, 235 B1, 276 B4, **297 H3**
Rapanui, NI 147 B5, **176 A1**
Rapaura, SI 261 C1, **282 E6**
Rapuwai, SI **303 G1**
Rarangi, SI **287 H1**
Rarawa Beach, NI **152 D3**
Raroa, NI **82 D4**
Raroa Pa, NI **164 A5**
Rata, NI 147 D6, **174 A5**
Rataiti, NI 147 D6, **174 A4**
Ratana, NI 147 C6, **176 B2**
Ratanui, SI 263 E2, **313 H5**
Ratapiko, NI 113 E1, **172 E2**
Raukawa, NI **175 G3**
Raukokore, NI **165 F2**
Raukumara FP, NI **165 F3**
Raumai, NI **176 E3**
Raumanga, NI **191 A6**
Raumati, NI **177 G3**
Raumati Beach, NI **178 C2**
Raumati South, NI **178 C2**
Raupo, NI **156 B2**
Raupo, SI **289 H1**
Raupunga, NI **170 C5**
Raureka, NI 109 C5, 175 J3, **182 A3**
Raurimu, NI 115 B3, 147 D2, **168 A5**
Raurimu Spiral, NI 66, 115 B3, 147 D2,
    168 A5
Ravensbourne, SI 227 G5, 275 C2, **314 D4**
Rawene, NI 124, **154 C2**
Rawhia, NI **154 C2**
Rawhiti, NI 129 D2, **155 G1**
Rawhiti Cave, SI 240, 241 E5, 254 C2,
    258 B2, **280 E3**
Rawhitiroa, NI 113 E3, **172 E4**
Raymonds Gap, SI **311 H4**

Red Barn, NI **164 A3**
Red Beach, NI **158 C2**
Red Crater, NI **115 D3**
Red Hill, NI **158 D5**
Red Jacks, SI **289 G2**
Red Rocks, NI 76
Red Rocks Seal Colony, NI **178 A5**
Redan, SI **312 D4**
Redcliffs, SI **213 H5**
Redhill, NI **156 A2**
Redruth, SI **303 H3**
Redvale, NI 121 A4, **158 C2**
Redwood, NI 82 D2, **178 B3**
Redwood, SI 213 F3, **297 G2**
Redwood Valley, SI 260 B2, **281 F6**
Redwoodtown, SI 261 D2, 287 H2, **317 C5**
Reefton, SI 266, **284 D5**
Reena, NI **154 B2**
Rees-Dart Track, SI 244
Rehia, NI **156 B2**
Rehutai, NI **154 D6**
Reidston, SI **309 J2**
Reikorangi, NI **178 C2**
Remarkables, SI 216
Remarkables Ski Field, SI 269a B3, **306 E1**
Remuera, NI 53 F3, **158 C4**
Remuera Settlement, NI 129 A3, **154 E2**
Renown, NI **160 C2**
Renwick, SI 261 B2, **287 G1**
Reotahi Bay, NI **155 H5**
Repia, NI **156 A2**
Reporoa, NI 127 C5, **163 G6**
Reporua, NI **165 J3**
Rere, NI **171 F1**
Rere Falls, NI **171 F2**
Rerewhakaaitu, NI 127 E4, **163 H6**
Retaruke, NI 147 C2, **173 J2**
Retaruke Upper, NI 115 A3, 147 C2, **173 K2**
Rewa, NI 147 D6, **174 B5**
Rewanui, SI **289 F1**
Rewarewa, NI 137 E3, **162 A5**
Rewiti, NI 97 A1, 121 A4, **158 A3**
Riamaki (Upper Ruatiti), NI 147 C3, **173 J2**
Riccarton, SI 212 E4, **297 G3**
Riccarton House and Bush, SI 212 E4
Richmond (Christchurch), SI 209 E1,
    213 G4, **297 H3**
Richmond (Dunedin), SI **309 K1**
Richmond (Invercargill), SI **319 E2**
Richmond (Nelson), SI 260 D2, **281 G6**
Richmond Brook, SI **287 H3**
Richmond Cottage, NI **184 B2**
Richmond Downs, NI **161 F4**
Richmond Heights, NI **187 E6**
Richmond Hill, SI **213 H5**
Rigney, SI **307 H6**
Rimu (Southland), SI **312 B4**
Rimu (West Coast), SI **288 E4**
Rimu Track, NI 115 B5, **168 A6**
Rimutaka FP, NI 83 G6, **178 C4**
Rimutaka Incline Walk, NI **178 D3**
Ringway, SI **311 J4**
Riponui, NI **155 F3**
Rippon Vineyard, SI 214, **300 D5**
Ripponvale, SI 269b A2, **307 G1**
Rissington, NI 109 A1, **175 H1**
Riverdale, NI **180 A1**
Riverhead, NI 97 A2, 121 A4, **158 B3**
Riverlands, SI 261 D2, **287 H2**
Riverlea, NI 113 C3, **172 C4**
Riversdale (Blenheim), SI **317 E2**
Riversdale (Canterbury), SI **291 G4**
Riversdale (Southland), SI **312 C1**
Riversdale Beach, NI **179 J3**
Riverside, NI **191 E4**
Riverside, SI **296 C6**
Riverstone Terraces, NI **83 H1**
Riverton / Aparima, SI 230, 268, 273 D6,
    311 J5
Riwaka, SI 254 C2, 258 B4, **281 F4**
Riwaka Resurgence, SI 258 B4, **281 F4**
RNZAF Museum, NI **176 C3**
Roa, SI **289 G1**
Roaring Billy Walk, SI **292 E6**
Rob Roy Glacier, SI 244, 245 C2, **300 B3**
Rob Roy Track, SI 214, **300 B4**
Rock and Pillar, SI **309 F4**
Rockford, SI **296 D2**
Rocklands, SI **284 D4**
Rockville, SI 241 C3, **280 D2**
Rokeby, SI **296 D4**
Rolleston, SI 212 B6, 276 A4, **297 F3**

Tahunga, NI **170 E2**
Tahuroa, NI **161 F3**
Taiaroa Head, SI **274**
Taieri Beach, SI **313 K2**
Taieri Gorge Railway, SI 220, 275 B1, **314 C3**
Taieri Historical Park, SI 275 A2, **314 B3**
Taieri Mouth, SI **313 K2**
Taihape, NI 72, 129, 147 E5, **174 C3**
Taiharuru, NI **155 J4**
Taihoa, NI **161 G4**
Taikirau, NI **155 F3**
Taiko, SI **303 G2**
Taikorea, NI **176 C4**
Taimate, SI **287 J3**
Taingaehe, NI **156 B3**
Tainui, SI **227 F5**
Taipa, NI **153 F5**
Taipoiti, SI **284 D5**
Taipuha, NI **155 G6**
Tairawhiti Museum, NI 64, **180 C4**
Tairua, NI 88 C3, 130, **159 J4**
Taita, NI 83 G3, **178 C3**
Taitville, NI 79 A4, **82 C5**
Takahiwai, NI **155 H5**
Takahue, NI **152 E6**
Takaka, SI 240, 241 D4, 254 B2, 258 A2, 271, **280 E3**
Takamatua, SI 235 D2, **297 J4**
Takamore, NI **165 H3**
Takanini, NI **158 D5**
Takapau (Eastland), NI **165 H4**
Takapau (Eastland), NI **165 H6**
Takapau (Hawke's Bay), NI **177 H2**
Takapu Valley, NI **82 E2**
Takapuna, NI 52 E1, **158 C3**
Takaputahi, NI **164 D4**
Takapuwahia, NI **82 D1**
Takaro, NI 176 D4, **185 A3**
Takatu, NI 97 E1, 121 B2, **157 F4**
Takiroa Maori rock drawings, SI **302 E6**
Takou, NI 147 A3, **173 F4**
Takou Bay, NI **153 J5**
Takutai, SI **288 D4**
Tamahere, NI **160 E4**
Tamaki, NI 53 G3, **158 C4**
Tamaki Maori Village, NI 60, 127 C3, **163 G5**
Tamarau, NI **171 H3**
Tamatea, NI 109 D3, **175 J2**
Tamaterau, NI **155 H5**
Tamihana, NI **161 G3**
Tanatana, NI **164 B5**
Tane, NI **177 F5**
Tane Mahuta (Giant Kauri), NI **154 C3**
Taneatua, NI **164 A4**
Tanehopuwai, NI **167 G2**
Tanekaha, NI **155 G3**
Tangahoe, NI 147 B3, **173 H3**
Tangarakau, NI 147 B2, **173 G1**
Tangihanga, NI 93 B2, **171 G2**
Tangihua, NI **155 F5**
Tangimoana, NI **176 B4**
Tangiteroria, NI **155 F5**
Tangitu, NI **167 H3**
Tangiwai, NI 115 C6, 147 D4, **174 B1**
Tangoake, NI **152 C2**
Tangoio, NI **170 B6**
Tangoio Falls Scenic Reserve, NI **170 A6**
Tangowahine, NI **154 E5**
Taniwha, NI 88 A5, **160 D1**
Tanoa, NI **156 D3**
Tanupara, NI 147 C4, **173 J4**
Taonui, NI **176 D3**
Taoroa Junction, NI **174 D3**
Taotaoroa, NI **161 F5**
Tapanui, SI **313 F1**
Tapapa, NI **161 G5**
Tapapakanga Regional Park, NI **158 E4**
Tapatu, NI **165 H2**
Tapawera, SI 254 C3, **285 J1**
Tapora, NI **156 C4**
Tapu, NI 88 A3, 121 E5, **159 G4**
Tapuae-o-Uenuku, SI **287 F4**
Tapuhi, NI **155 G3**
Tapui, SI **309 H1**
Tapuwae, NI **154 B2**
Tara, NI 121 A1, **156 E2**
Taradale, NI 109 C3, **175 J2**
Tarakohe, SI 241 D5, 254 C1, 258 B2, **281 F3**

Taramakau, SI **289 F3**
Taramoa, SI **312 A4**
Taranaki, NI **70**
Taranui, SI **309 J2**
Tarara, SI 263 D2, **313 G5**
Tararu, NI 88 A4, 121 E6, **159 G5**
Tararua FP, NI 74, 76, 106 A2, **178 E1**
Tararua Range, NI **74**
Tararua Wind Farm, NI **176 E4**
Tarata, NI 113 E1, **172 E2**
Taraunui, NI **155 H4**
Tarawera, NI **169 G4**
Tarawera Falls, NI 127 E2, **163 H5**
Tariki, NI 113 D2, **172 D2**
Taringamotu, NI 147 C1, **167 H5**
Taringamotu Valley, NI 147 D1, **167 H5**
Tarndale, NI **164 E5**
Tarndale, SI **286 C6**
Taronui Bay, NI 129 B1, **153 J6**
Tarras, SI 245 D3, **300 E6**
Tarukenga, NI 127 B1, **163 F4**
Taruna, SI **290 D4**
Tarurutangi, NI **172 D1**
Tasman, SI 258 C5, **281 F5**
Tasman Bay, SI 200, 241 E6, 254 C3, 258 C4, 260 C1, 267 A1, **281 G4**, **321 A1**
Tasman Glacier, SI **236**
Tasman Sea, SI **204**
Tasman Wilderness Area, SI **254**
Tataiahapi Pa, NI **164 B5**
Tatapouri, NI 93 D2, **171 J2**
Tataraimaka, NI 113 B1, **172 B2**
Tataramoa, NI **177 G3**
Tatarariki, NI **156 A2**
Tatare, SI 243 D3, **293 J2**
Tatu, NI 147 B1, **167 F5**
Tatuanui, NI **161 F3**
Tauakira, NI **173 J6**
Tauhara, NI **187 E3**
Tauhei, NI **160 E3**
Tauherenikau, NI 106 A4, **178 E3**
Tauhoa, NI 121 A2, **156 D4**
Taumarere, NI 129 B3, **155 F2**
Taumaruiti, NI 115 A1, 147 C1, **167 H5**
Taumarunui, NI 66, 130, 115 A1, 147 C1, **167 G5**
Taumata, SI **313 G3**
Taumatatahi, NI 147 A4, **173 G5**
Taumutu, SI **297 F5**
Taunoko, NI 147 B4, **173 H4**
Taupaki, NI 52 A2, 97 B2, 121 A4, **158 B3**
Taupiri, NI **160 D3**
Taupiri Mountain, NI **160 D2**
Taupo, NI 62, 131, 132, 133 D4, **168 E2**, **187 B3**
Taupo Bay, NI **153 G5**
Taupo Hot Springs Spa, NI 133 D4, **168 E2**, **187 E5**
Tauranga, NI 58, 131, **161 J3**, **188 E3**
Tauranga Bay, NI **153 H5**
Tauranga South, NI 161 J3, **188 C6**
Tauranga Valley, NI **153 H5**
Tauranganui, NI **158 C6**
Taurangaruru, NI 121 A6, **158 B6**
Tauraroa (Northland), NI **155 G5**
Tauraroa (Waikato), NI **162 B5**
Taurewa, NI 115 C2, 147 D2, **168 B4**
Tauriko, NI **161 J3**
Taurikura, NI **155 J5**
Tautoro, NI **154 E3**
Tautuku, SI 263 D2, **313 F5**
Tautuku Bay, SI **262**
Tauweru, NI **179 G2**
Tauwhare (Bay of Plenty), NI **164 B6**
Tauwhare (Waikato), NI **160 E4**
Tauwhare Pa (Bay of Plenty), NI **164 B4**
Tauwhare Pa (Waikato), NI **160 E4**
Tauwharemanuka, NI **164 B6**
Tauwhareparae, NI **165 G5**
Tauwhareparae, NI **165 G6**
Tavora Reserve, SI **309 H4**
Tawa, NI 82 D2, **178 B3**
Tawai, NI **303 G6**
Tawanui, SI 263 D1, **313 G5**
Tawataia, NI **176 E6**
Tawhai, SI **284 D5**
Tawhana, NI **164 B6**
Tawharanui, NI 121 B2, **157 F4**
Tawhata, NI 147 B2, **167 F6**
Tawhiti, SI **307 G4**
Tawhiti Museum, NI **172 E5**

Tawhiwhi, NI 147 A4, **173 G5**
Taylors Mistake, SI **213 H5**
Taylorville, SI **289 F2**
Te Ahuahu, NI 129 A3, **154 E2**
Te Akatea, NI **160 C3**
Te Akau, NI **160 B3**
Te Akau South, NI **160 B3**
Te Ana-au Glow-worm Caves, SI 228, **305 F3**
Te Anaroa Caves, SI 241 C3, **280 D2**
Te Anau, SI 228, 271, 273 D4, **305 G4**
Te Anau Downs (Fiordland), SI **305 G3**
Te Anau Downs (Fiordland), SI **305 G3**
Te Anga, NI 137 A3, **167 F1**
Te Apiti Wind Farm, NI **176 E4**
Te Aputa, NI 133 A4, 147 D1, **168 B3**
Te Arai, NI 121 A2, **156 E3**
Te Arai Point, NI 121 A1, **156 E2**
Te Arakura, NI **176 D4**
Te Araroa, NI 132, **165 J2**
Te Ariuru, NI **165 H5**
Te Aro, NI 79 C4, **82 C5**
Te Aroha, NI 56, 134, **161 G2**
Te Aroha Domain, NI **161 G2**
Te Aroha West, NI **161 G2**
Te Atatu Peninsula, NI 52 C2, **158 B3**
Te Atatu South, NI 52 C3, **158 B4**
Te Aumiti (French Pass), SI 202, **266**
Te Aute, NI **175 H3**
Te Awa, NI 109 D3, 175 J2, **183 D6**
Te Awa, SI **303 H1**
Te Awaatu Channel Marine Reserve, SI 273 B3, **304 C3**
Te Awamutu, NI 134, 137 E1, **160 E5**
Te Awanga, NI 109 E5, **175 J2**
Te Edge Entertainment Precinct, NI **48**
Te Hana, NI 121 A2, **156 E3**
Te Hapara, NI **171 H2**
Te Hapua, NI **152 C2**
Te Haroto, NI **169 G5**
Te Hauke, NI **175 H3**
Te Henga (Bethells Beach), NI 97 B1, 121 A5, **158 A4**
Te Henui, NI 113 C1, **172 C2**
Te Hihi, NI 97 D3, 121 B6, **158 C5**
Te Hoe (Eastland), NI **170 A4**
Te Hoe (Waikato), NI **160 E2**
Te Horo, NI **178 D1**
Te Horo Beach, NI **178 C1**
Te Horoa, NI 147 D4, **174 B2**
Te Houka, SI **313 G3**
Te Huahua, NI **154 C2**
Te Hue, NI **165 J2**
Te Huia, NI **153 H5**
Te Hutewai, NI **160 B4**
Te Ika A Maui, NI **38**
Te Iringa, NI **154 D2**
Te Kaha, NI 134, **164 E2**
Te Kainga, NI **82 C4**
Te Kao, NI **152 C3**
Te Karae, NI **154 C1**
Te Karaka (Eastlland), NI 93 B1, **171 G1**
Te Karaka (Northland), NI **154 B2**
Te Kauri, NI **160 D2**
Te Kauwhata, NI 135, **160 D1**
Te Kauwhata Wineries, NI **160 C1**
Te Kawa, NI 137 E1, **160 D6**
Te Kawa West, NI 137 D1, **160 D6**
Te Kinga, SI **289 G3**
Te Kiri, NI 113 B3, **172 B4**
Te Kiteroa, SI **312 E1**
Te Kohanga, NI 121 B6, **158 C6**
Te Kopua, NI 137 D1, **160 D5**
Te Kopuru, NI **154 E6**
Te Koraha, NI 137 B2, **160 C6**
Te Kouma, NI 88 A2, 121 E4, **159 G3**
Te Koura, NI 147 C1, **167 H4**
Te Kowhai (Northland), NI **156 B2**
Te Kowhai (Waikato), NI **160 C3**
Te Kuha, SI **284 C3**
Te Kuiti, NI 135, 137 D3, **167 G1**
Te Kumi (Eastland), NI **165 G2**
Te Kumi (Waikato), NI 137 D3, **167 G1**
Te Mahia, SI 267 D4, **283 F4**
Te Mahoe, NI **163 K4**
Te Maika, NI 137 A1, **160 A6**
Te Maire, NI 147 C1, **167 G5**
Te Manawa, NI **185 B3**
Te Mapara, NI **167 G2**
Te Marua, NI 83 K1, **178 D3**
Te Mata (Coromandel), NI 88 A3, 121 E5, **159 G4**

Te Mata (Waikato), NI **160 B4**
Te Mata Peak, NI 68, 109 D6, **175 J3**
Te Matai, NI **163 G2**
Te Maunga, NI **161 K3**
Te Mawhai, NI 137 E1, **160 D5**
Te Miko, SI **284 A5**
Te Miro, NI **161 F4**
Te Moana, SI **303 G1**
Te Moana Maritime Museum, NI **180 C4**
Te Moananui, NI **161 F1**
Te Moe, NI **171 G5**
Te Moehau Junction, NI 147 E4, **174 C2**
Te Namu, SI **280 A6**
Te Ngae, NI 127 C2, **163 G4**
Te Ngaere, NI **153 H5**
Te Ngaru, SI 227 J3, 275 D2, **314 D3**
Te Ohaki Pa, NI **161 H4**
Te Ore Ore, NI 106 C2, **179 F2**
Te Pahu, NI **160 C4**
Te Papa, NI 37, 76, 78, 79 **D4**
Te Papapa, NI **53 F4**
Te Papatapu, NI **160 B5**
Te Peka, SI **312 D5**
Te Pirita, SI **296 C4**
Te Pohue, NI **169 H6**
Te Poi, NI **161 G4**
Te Popo, NI 113 E2, **172 E3**
Te Pouwhakatutu, NI 127 A6, 133 D2, **168 D1**
Te Pu, NI 127 B1, **163 F3**
Te Pua, NI 121 A4, **158 A2**
Te Puhi, NI **153 F6**
Te Puia, NI **60**
Te Puia Springs (Eastland), NI **165 J4**
Te Puia Springs (Waikato), NI 137 A1, **160 A5**
Te Puka, NI **165 H5**
Te Pukatea Bay, SI **258**
Te Puke, NI 135, **163 G2**
Te Puna, NI **161 J3**
Te Puninga, NI **161 F2**
Te Puru, NI 88 A4, 121 E5, **159 G5**
Te Rae, SI 241 A4, **280 D1**
Te Rahu, NI **160 E5**
Te Raina, NI 133 A5, 147 E1, **168 B3**
Te Ranga (Bay of Plenty), NI **163 G3**
Te Ranga (Tauranga), NI **161 J4**
Te Rangiita, NI 133 B5, **168 C3**
Te Rapa, NI **160 D3**
Te Rapa, SI **287 J4**
Te Rauamoa, NI 137 C1, **160 C6**
Te Raumauku, NI 137 D2, **160 D6**
Te Raupo, NI **152 D3**
Te Reinga, NI **170 E3**
Te Reinga Falls, NI **170 E3**
Te Rere Marae, NI **164 C4**
Te Rerenga, NI 88 B2, 121 E4, **159 G3**
Te Rore (Northland), NI **152 E6**
Te Rore (Waikato), NI **160 D5**
Te Roti, NI **172 D4**
Te Rou, SI **282 C6**
Te Tahi, NI 137 C1, **160 C5**
Te Taho, SI **294 D1**
Te Tapuwae O Rongokako Marine Reserve, NI 93 E2, **171 J2**
Te Teko, NI **163 J4**
Te Tii, NI 129 B1, **153 J6**
Te Tipua, SI **312 C3**
Te Toro, NI 97 E2, 121 A6, **158 B5**
Te Tua, SI **311 H4**
Te Tuhi Junction, NI 147 B4, **173 H5**
Te Tumu, NI **163 G2**
Te Uku, NI **160 C4**
Te Uku Landing, NI **160 C4**
Te Upoko o Te Ika, NI **76**
Te Urewera NP, NI 37, 40, 64, 142, 143 C2, **170 B3**
Te Uri, NI **177 H3**
Te Waewae, SI **311 G5**
Te Waha-o-Rerekohu (Largest Pohutukawa Tree), NI **165 J2**
Te Wahipounamu, SI **194**
Te Waihou Walkway, NI **161 G5**
Te Waiiti, NI 143 D1, **169 K2**
Te Wairoa, NI 127 C3, **163 G5**
Te Waitere, NI 137 A2, **160 B6**
Te Waka a Maui, SI **194**
Te Wera, NI **170 E1**
Te Wera, NI **173 F3**
Te Whaiti, NI 143 B1, **169 H2**
Te Whakarae, NI 147 C1, **167 G5**

ACKNOWLEDGEMENTS

This atlas was produced with the help of regional and local tourist offices and other agencies throughout New Zealand, whose kind assistance is gratefully acknowledged.

The publisher would like to thank the following individuals and organisations for their assistance:
Department of Conservation; Hinemoana Baker; Alastair Bull; Lynn Davidson; Jessica Ebrey; Land Transport New Zealand; Malcolm McKinnon; New Zealand Automobile Association; Regional Tourism Organisations; Road Safety Trust; Sport and Recreation New Zealand; St John; Te Ara the Encyclopedia of New Zealand, www.teara.govt.nz; Water Safety New Zealand; Jenny Whyte

The publisher would also like to thank the following individuals and organisations for their generosity in supplying photographs and images, and for their permission to reproduce photographic material used in this atlas:

allblacks.com: p.22 (B)
Geoff Best: p.81, 208, 210 (B), 211 (B)
Theresa Braniff: p.14, 18 (T), 228 (T), 236 (TR, ML)
Kate Bridge: p.91
Christchurch City Council, www.christchurch.org.nz: p.211 (T)
Graham Dow: p.38 (B), 70 (T, B), 110
Focus New Zealand: p.12 (B), 13 (T), 15 (TL, MR, BL, BR), 16 (T), 17 (TR, BL, BR), 18 (B), 19 (T, B), 20, 21, 22 (T), 23, 24 (T), 25 (T, B), 30 (T, B), 32, 33 (T), 34, 35, 41, 42, 43, 51 (T), 56 (B), 58 (B), 64 (T, B), 66 (T), 68 (T, B), 84, 85, 89, 92, 94, 95, 96 (TL, MR, BL), 98, 99, 101, 102, 104, 105, 106, 107, 108 (TR, ML, BL), 111, 112, 113, 114 (T), 116, 118, 119, 120 (T), 122 (M), 123, 124, 130, 131, 134, 135, 136 (MR), 138, 139, 140, 143, 145, 146 (ML), 149, 198, 199, 202 (T), 218, 222, 224, 225 (B), 230, 234 (M), 238, 244 (B), 247, 248, 252 (TL, TR), 254, 255, 257, 258, 260, 262 (ML), 266 (M, B), 268 (T, B), 272 (T, B), 274 (M, B), 276, 277
Frank Froelicher: p.5 (B), 6 (M), 11, 29, 78, 86, 125, 141, 210 (T), 228 (B), 242 (T), 256, 262 (ML), 270
Jono Haimes: p.3
Russell Hooper: p.66 (B)
Fanny Lariviere: p. 194 (B), 200 (T)
Jacques Lariviere: p.54 (T)
Matt Middleditch: p.12 (T)
Gary Milbanke: p.6 (B), 39, 40, 90, 126, 200 (B), 250, 271
Evan Perry: p.58 (T)
SeeninDunedin, www.seenindunedin.co.nz: p.225 (T)
Megan Smith: p.13 (B), 38 (T), 72, 144
Spectec: p.4-5 (T), 6 (T), 10 (T), 16 (B), 27 (T), 28, 33 (B), 36-37, 44, 46, 48, 50 (T, B), 51 (B), 54 (B), 56 (T), 60 (B), 62, 74, 87, 88, 103, 114 (B), 120 (B), 122 (B), 128 (M, B), 132 (TR), 137, 142, 150, 192-193, 194 (T), 197, 202 (B), 204 (T, B), 206, 214, 216, 220, 232, 235, 237, 240 (T, B), 244 (T), 246, 251, 259, 264, 278, 345
Mark Strang: p.76, 80
Karl Strode-Penny: p.265
Louise Taylor: p.148, 195, 239
Ning Teahan: p.10 (B), 24 (B), 60 (T), 117, 132 (ML), 136 (TL), 146 (T, R), 196, 233, 242 (B), 253, 263
Leon Toorenburg: p.100
Universal Publishers Pty Ltd: p.26 (T, B), 27 (B)
Caren Wilton: p. 234 (B)

Note: Population figures for towns in the A to Z sections are the 'usually resident population' figures from the 2001 census, New Zealand's last census count at the time of writing. Population totals for the North Island, South Island and New Zealand overall are based on Statistics New Zealand's population projections for 2004. All figures have been rounded for convenience (to the nearest 5 for small centres and to the nearest 1000 for the largest cities), except where a town had less than 50 residents!

Motu Gorge, Matawai

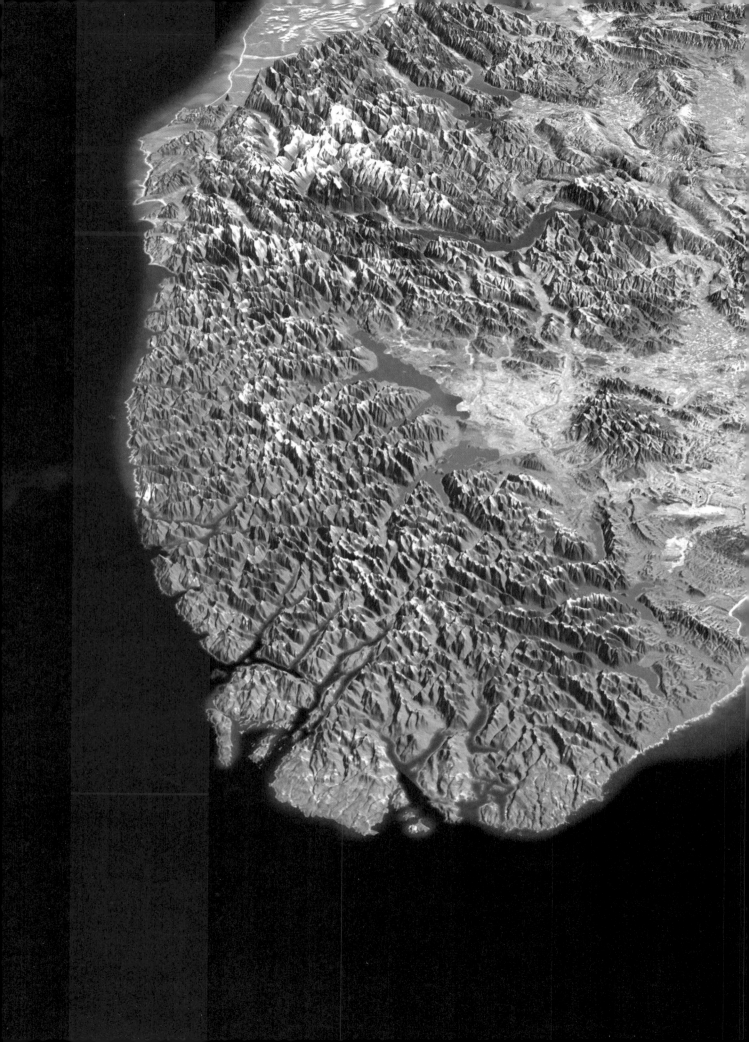